Henry Whittemore

History of Montclair Township State of New Jersey

Including the History of the Families who Have Been Identified with....

Henry Whittemore

History of Montclair Township State of New Jersey
Including the History of the Families who Have Been Identified with....

ISBN/EAN: 9783337143824

Printed in Europe, USA, Canada, Australia, Japan

Cover: Foto ©ninafisch / pixelio.de

More available books at **www.hansebooks.com**

HISTORY

OF

MONTCLAIR
TOWNSHIP

STATE OF NEW JERSEY

INCLUDING THE

HISTORY OF THE FAMILIES WHO HAVE BEEN IDENTIFIED WITH
ITS GROWTH AND PROSPERITY

ILLUSTRATED

Our transplant, sustine.

BY

HENRY WHITTEMORE

AUTHOR OF THE REVOLUTIONARY HISTORY OF ROCKLAND COUNTY, N. Y.
HISTORY OF MIDDLESEX COUNTY, CONN. HISTORY OF SEVENTY-FIRST
REGIMENT, N G S N Y. HISTORY OF FREEMASONRY IN NORTH
AMERICA. HISTORY OF STEAM NAVIGATION. ILLUSTRATED
HISTORY OF PROSPECT PARK, BROOKLYN, ETC.

New York:
THE SUBURBAN PUBLISHING COMPANY
1894

CHAPTER I.

CHAPTER II.

CHAPTER III.

CHAPTER IV.

CHAPTER V.

CHAPTER VI.

CHAPTER VII.

CHAPTER VIII.

CHAPTER IX.

CHAPTER X.

CONTENTS

CHAPTER XI.

CHAPTER XII.

CHAPTER XIII.

CONTENTS.

PREFACE

MONTCLAIR, in its natural prosperity, in its elevated, moral and religious life, and in the social and intellectual culture of its people, stands pre-eminent among the suburbs of our great metropolis. These characteristics of a high civilization are not the result of accident, but are due largely to the influence of a few energetic, enterprising and progressive individuals, who from the beginning have directed its affairs, and have contributed to its physical, social and moral development.

The early Connecticut settlers of this locality adopted as their motto that inscribed on the arms of their native State, viz.: *"Qui transtulit, sustinet,"* and the thousands of settlers from various parts of the country, who have beautified and developed this Paradise of Nature, have shown by their acts that they too have implicit faith in an overruling Providence to sustain them in their *new work*. [The original Connecticut settlers named their "Towne on the Pesayick" "*New Worke*" (Newark), indicating their new enterprise.]

To show the result of their efforts has been the aim of the compiler of this work. If he has failed to give credit to any individual who, during the early settlement of the new township, or its later development, has contributed to its greatness and prosperity, it is because of his inability to obtain the requisite information. To enumerate all who have aided him in this undertaking would require more space than is usually allotted to a Preface or Introduction.

His acknowledgments are due first of all to Mr. Julius H. Pratt, one of the pioneers in the new settlement who, from the inception of the enterprise, has done everything in his power to make the "HISTORY OF MONTCLAIR" a success, and has contributed much valuable data, attainable from no other source.

To Dr. J. J. H. Love, who is recognized as the chief founder and promoter of the splendid system of public school education for which Montclair is famous, the writer is greatly indebted—not only for information concerning its educational affairs, but other matters of historic interest.

Joseph Dorenus, the recognized authority on all matters connected with the history of this locality and its early settlers, has rendered invaluable aid.

The assistance of Colonel Frederick H. Harris in supplying data of early railroads, early settlers, etc., is gratefully acknowledged.

Many of the beautiful landscapes and other illustrations with which this work is embellished are reproductions of photographic views taken by Mr. Randall Spaulding, Superintendent of the Public Schools, who has also supplied additional matter to that of Dr. Love on Educational Development in Montclair.

Mr. W. I. Lincoln Adams has also assisted the author in the illustration of this work, both by supplying original photographs of his own and in giving the benefit of his knowledge in photographic reproduction processes.

The article "Cranetown in the Revolution," by the Rev. Oliver Crane, D.D., forms an interesting contribution to the work.

Acknowledgments are also due to the Rev. Amory H. Bradford, D.D., for many valuable suggestions and other assistance rendered; to Mr. John B. Howard, Mr. Paul Wilcox and Mr. A. H. Siegfried, for information of "Montclair," "Outlook," and other Clubs, Young Men's Christian Association, and social organizations; to Mrs. Jasper R. Rand, one of the founders and most active promoters of the Children's Home, for the facts concerning the history of that institution; to Mr. John H. Wilson and Mr. A. C. Studor for many favors; to Dr. Albert J. Wright for information concerning the Fire Department; to Mr. James Owen for the article on Montclair Water Works; to Mr. Yost and other township officers for information on township affairs.

The writer is also indebted to the editor of the *Montclair Times* for valuable extracts taken from its files, and for other courtesies extended; also to the proprietor and editor of the *Montclair Herald* for similar favors.

Chapter I.

N 1524, John de Verazzano, a Florentine navigator in the service of Francis I. of France,
made a voyage to the North American coast, and, as is believed from the account which
he gave, entered the harbor of New York. No colonies were planted and no results
followed.

Though discoveries were made by the French north from this point, and colonies
planted by the English farther to the south, it is not known that New York was again
visited by Europeans till 1609, when the Dutch East India Company sent Hendrick
Hudson, an Englishman by birth, on a voyage of discovery in a vessel called the "Half
Moon." He reached the coast of Maine, sailed thence to Cape Cod, thence southwesterly
to the mouth of Chesapeake Bay; then, coasting northward, he entered Delaware Bay
on the 28th of August. From thence he proceeded northward, and on the 3d of September,
1609, anchored in New York Bay. On the 12th he entered the river that bears his name, and proceeded
slowly up to a point just above the present site of the City of Hudson; thence he sent a boat's crew to
explore farther up, and they passed above Albany. September 23d he set sail down the river and
immediately returned to Europe.

In 1607, Samuel Champlain, a French navigator, sailed up the St. Lawrence, explored its tributaries, and on the 4th of July in that year discovered the lake which bears his name.

At the time of the discovery of New York by the whites, the southern and eastern portions were
inhabited by the Mohican or Mohegan Indians; while that portion west from the Hudson River was
occupied by five confederate tribes, afterward named by the English the Five Nations, and by the
French, the Iroquois, and by themselves called Hodenosaunee—people of the Long House. The long
house formed by this confederacy extended east and west through the State, having at its eastern portal
the Mohawks, and at its western the Senecas; while between them dwelt the Oneidas, Onondagas, and
Cayugas; and, after 1714, a sixth nation, the Tuscaroras, southeast from Oneida Lake. Of these Indians,
Parkman says that at the commencement of the seventeenth century, "in the region now forming the
State of New York, a power was rising to a ferocious vitality, which, but for the presence of Europeans,
would probably have subjected, absorbed, or exterminated every other Indian community east of the
Mississippi and north of the Ohio.

"The Iroquois was the Indian of Indians. A thorough savage, yet a finished and developed
savage, he is, perhaps, an example of the highest elevation which man can reach without emerging from
his primitive condition of the hunter. A geographical position commanding on the one hand the portal
of the great lakes, and on the other the sources of the streams flowing both to the Atlantic and the
Mississippi, gave the ambitious and aggressive confederates advantages which they perfectly understood
and by which they profited to the utmost. Patient and politic as they were ferocious, they were not
only the conquerors of their own race, but the powerful allies and the dreaded foes of the French and

English colonies, flattered and caressed by both, yet too sagacious to give themselves without reserve to either. Their organization and their history evince their intrinsic superiority. Even their traditionary love, amid its wild puerilities, shows at times the stamp of an energy and force in striking contrast with the flimsy creations of the Algonquin fancy. That the Iroquois, left under their own institutions, would have ever developed a civilization of their own, I do not believe."

These institutions were not only characteristic and curious, but almost unique. Without sharing Morgan's almost fanatical admiration for them, or echoing the praises which Parkman lavishes on them, it may be truly said that their wonderful and cohesive confederation furnished a model worthy to be copied by many civilized nations, while, so long as they were uncontaminated by the vices of civilization, they possessed, with all their savagery, many noble traits of character, which would adorn any people in their public, social, or domestic relations.

They made themselves the dreaded masters of all their neighbors east of the Mississippi and carried their victorious arms far to the north, the south and the east. Their dominance is eloquently pictured in Street's " Frontenac " :

> " The fierce Adirondacs had fled from their wrath.
> The Hurons been swept from their merciless path.
> Around, the Ottawas, like leaves, had been strewn
> And the lake of the Eries struck silent and low ;
> The Lenapé, lords once of valley and hill
> Made women, bent low at their conqueror's will :
> By the far Mississippi the Illini shrank
> When the trail of the TORTOISE was seen on the bank :
> On the hills of New England the Pequod turned pale
> When the howl of the WOLF swelled at night on the gale :
> And the Cherokee shook in his green, smiling bowers
> When the foot of the BEAR stamped his carpet of flowers."

Hudson's journal indicates that the Indians on the east side of the Hudson River held no intercourse with those on the west side, and that the former were a much more fierce and implacable people than the latter. This probably arose from the fact that those east of the Hudson and along the upper banks were allies of the Iroquois.

On the point where New York is now built Hudson found the Indians a very hostile people, but those living on the western side from the Kills upward, " came daily on board the vessel while she lay at anchor in the river, bringing with them to barter furs, the largest and finest oysters, Indian corn, beans, pumpkins, squashes, grapes, and some apples, all of which they exchanged for trifles."

Most writers on Indian antiquities have considered the tribes of the lower Hudson, and of East New Jersey, as branches of the general Delaware nation, or Lenni Lenapé, which means *original people*. This was a title which they had adopted under the claim that they were descended from the most ancient of all Indian ancestors. This claim was admitted by the Wyandots, Miamis, and more than twenty other aboriginal nations, who accorded to the Lenapé the title of *grandfathers*, or a people whose ancestors ante-dated their own. The Rev. John Heckewelder, in his " History of the Manners and Customs of the Indian Nations," says of the Delaware nation :

" They will not admit that the whites are superior beings. They say that the hair of their heads, their features, and the various colors of their eyes, evince that they are not, like themselves, Lenni Lenapé, an *original people*—a race of men that has existed unchanged from the beginning of time, but that they are a mixed race, and therefore a troublesome one. Whoever they may be, the Great Spirit, knowing the wickedness of their disposition, found it necessary to give them a Great Book, and taught them how to read it, that they might know and observe what He wished them to do, and what to abstain from. But they—the Indians—have no need of any such book to let them know the will of their Maker; they find it engraved on their own hearts ; they have had a sufficient discernment given to them to distinguish good from evil, and by following that they are sure not to err."

The Delawares, or Lenni Lenapé, occupied a domain extending along the seashore from the Chesapeake to the country bordering Long Island Sound. But from the coast it reached the Susquehanna Valley to the foot of the Alleghany Mountains, and on the north joined the southern frontier of their domineering neighbors—the hated and dreaded Iroquois. This domain included not only the counties of Bergen, Passaic, Hudson and Essex, but all of the State of New Jersey.

In the organization of the savage communities of the continent, one feature, more or less conspicuous, continually appears. Each nation or tribe—to adopt the names by which these communities are usually known— is subdivided into several clans. These clans are not locally separate, but are mingled throughout the nation. All the members of each clan are, or are assumed to be, intimately joined in consanguinity. Hence it is held an abomination for two persons of the same clan to intermarry; and hence, again, it follows that every family must contain members of at least two clans. Each clan has its name, as the clan of the Hawk, of the Wolf, or of the Tortoise; and each has for its emblem the figure of the beast, bird, reptile, plant, or other object, from which its name is derived. This emblem, called totem, is often tattooed on the clansman's body, or rudely painted over the entrance of his lodge. The child belongs to the clan, not of the father, but of the mother. In other words, descent, not of the totem alone, but of all rank, titles and possessions, is through the female. The son of a chief can never be a chief by hereditary title, though he may become so by force of personal influence or achievement. Neither can he inherit from his father so much as a tobacco-pipe. All possessions pass of right to the brothers of the chief, or to the sons of his sisters, since these are all sprung from a common mother.

The principal tribes composing the Lenni Lenapé or Delaware nation were those of the Unamis or Turtle, the Unalachtgo or Turkey, and the Minsi or Wolf. The tribes who occupied and roamed over the counties of Bergen, Passaic, Hudson and Essex, were those of the Turkey and Wolf branches of the Lenni Lenapé nation, but the possessions and boundaries of each cannot be clearly defined. There was probably a tribe for every ten or twenty miles, each taking their names from the streams near which they severally located.

In 1648 they were governed by about twenty kings, which might seem to warrant the belief that their numbers were great; but the insignificance of this regal sway is seen from the fact that in one case twelve hundred were under two kings, and some kings had only forty subjects, so that these rulers might with greater correctness be called chiefs.

The Wolf, commonly called the Minsi (corruptly called Minsey) had chosen to live back of the other two tribes, and formed a kind of bulwark for their protection, watching the nations of the Mungwe, and being at hand to afford aid in case of rupture with them. The Minsi were considered the most warlike and active branch of the Lenapé.

Those most intimately connected with this region were the Minisies and Mohicans—the former being the inhabitants of the range of country from Minisink to Staten Island, and from the Hudson to the Raritan Valley. The latter inhabited the east side of the lower Hudson to its mouth. The Dutch called them respectively Swannekins and the Manhicans. According to Brodhead the former were called Wabingi or Wappinges, the latter name, as Heckewelder claims, being derived from the Delaware word waping, signifying opossum. These were divided into numerous tribes, and the latter again into clans. In this section of New Jersey they were called Raritans, Hackensacks (or Ackinkes-hacky), Pomptons, and Tappaens. On Manhattan Island dwelt the fierce Manhattans, whom De Laet calls "a wicked nation," and "enemies of the Dutch."

These names, together with their chiefs, appear in the treaty between the Dutch and the Indians soon after the war in 1644 (brought on through the harsh and unjust treatment of the latter by Kieft), as follows:

"This day, being the 30th of August, 1645, appeared in Fort Amsterdam, before the Director and Council, in the presence of the whole Commonality, the Sachems of the savages as well in their own behalf, as being authorized by the neighboring savages, namely: ORATANEY, Chief of Ackinkes-hacky (meaning low lands), SESSEKENICK and WILLIAM, Chiefs of Tappaen and Reckgawawanck, PACHAM and

Pennewink (who were here yesterday and gave their power of attorney to the former, and also took upon themselves to answer for those of *Onaney* and the vicinity of *Majanacetinnemin*, of *Marchawick*, of Nyack and its neighborhood) and Aepmen, who personally appeared, speaking in behalf of *Wappins*, *Wiquaeskeeks*, *Sintsincks* and *Kichtawrons*."

Whitehead, in his "East New Jersey under the Proprietary Governments," concludes that there were not more than two thousand Indians within the province while it was under the domination of the Dutch. Fifty years later it was stated that they—the Indians—are greatly decreased in numbers. And the Indians themselves say that "two of them die to every one Christian that comes here."

Before the European explorers had penetrated the territories of the Lenape, the power and prowess of the Iroquois had reduced the former nation to the condition of vassals, and when in 1742 they were commanded by the old Iroquois chief, Connosseitigo, at the treaty of council in Philadelphia, instantly to leave the court house, and to prepare to vacate their hunting grounds on the Delaware and its tributaries, the outraged and insulted red men were completely crestfallen and crushed; but they had no alternative, and must obey. They at once left the presence of the Iroquois, returned to their homes, which were now to be their homes no longer, and soon afterward migrated to the country bordering the Susquehanna, and beyond that river.

The Indians of this locality were quiet, peaceable and domestic in their habits, and there existed among them a code of honor—engraven on their hearts by the Great Spirit—which would put to shame their white neighbors, who were kept in restraint only by wholesome laws vigorously enforced, and all attempts by the Dutch to corrupt and demoralize their savage (?) neighbors by the introduction of "fire water" met with a manly resistance on the part of the Indian Chiefs, as appears by the following:

"Warrant empowering Oratam, Chief of Hackingkeshacky, and Mattano, another Chief, to seize any brandy found in their country, and take it, with the persons selling it, to New Amsterdam.

"Whereas, Oratam, Chief of Hackingkeshacky, and other savages, have complained several times, that many selfish people dare not only to sell brandy to the savages in this city, but also to carry whole ankers of it into their country, and peddle it out there, from which, if it is not prevented in time, many troubles will arise, therefore the Director-General and Council of New Netherland, not knowing for the present a better way to stop it, authorize the said chief, together with the Sachem Mattenonck, to seize the brandy brought into their country for sale, and those offering to sell it, and bring them here, that they may be punished as an example to others."

Local Indian names, and other evidences, clearly indicate that the territory comprised within the present township of Montclair was at one time the habitation of one or more of the several clans of Indians. Early surveys show that Indian paths led through this region of country, and that the route of the various tribes in passing from the seashore to the interior led along this line. On one of the early maps is shown the Indian path which led to the Minisink. From the Shrewsbury north-west it crossed the Raritan west of Amboy, and thence northerly to Minisink Island in the Delaware. This was the great path from the sea to the Minisink, the Indian council seat. The most direct route from the Hudson to Minisink Island was through the great notch on the first mountain, four miles north of Montclair, which struck the main path near Little Falls. There were also intersecting paths through the same territory. The several routes led to the Minisink, about seven miles west of Watchschunk Mountain, through the notch at Eagle Rock and other openings through the mountain.

LOCAL NAMES.

Nearly, if not quite all the Indian names in this locality indicate their origin from the language of the Delaware Indians, most of them being mispelt as well as misinterpreted. *Wachung*, referring to the First Mountain, is evidently a corruption of Wachtschunk, meaning "on the hill." The name of

" Watsessing" or " Wardsesson " as early applied to Bloomfield, is doubtless from the word Waktschiechen, meaning crooked. Mr. D. G. Brinton, author of " ABORIGINAL AMERICAN AUTHORS AND THEIR PRODUCTIONS," writes: " I would say that you are quite right in supposing Wachung—Wachtschunk—on the hill, or, at the mountain, or, the hilly spot. The name Watsessing I take to be a form of Waktschiechen, *it is crooked* (*i.e.*, a road, a stream, etc.). In this case the traditional rendering you give seems to me well founded."

Pachseyink—*in the valley*—is doubtless the original of " Passaic," or " Pesayie," as spelled in the early records. Hachkihacanink—in the field ; Sepunk—to or on the river ; Hatink—in or near the earth ; Mecehekachink—at the big rock ; Tekenink —in the woods ; Tapewi—on the river bank.

HABITS AND GOVERNMENT OF THE DELAWARES.

The ordinary form of salutation of the Delawares was : " I thank the Great Spirit that he has preserved our lives to this time of our happy meeting again. I am indeed very glad to see you."

"They do not fight with each other ; they say that fighting is only for dogs and beasts ; they are, however, fond of play and passing a joke, *yet are very careful that they do not offend*."

" They have great respect for the aged ; they have a strong innate sense of justice."

A well-known writer says : " The Delawares were eminent for valor and wisdom, and held a prominent place in Indian history, but on the rise of the Iroquois power, they lost their independence and fell under suspicion because many of them applied themseves to agriculture.

" It may justly be a subject of wonder, how a nation without a written code of laws, or a system of jurisprudence without any form or constitution of government, and without even a single elective or hereditary magistrate, can subsist together in peace and happiness, and in the exercise of the highest virtues—how a people can be well and efficiently governed without any external authority. The secret of it is found in the early education of their children. The first step that parents take toward the education of their children is to prepare them for future happiness by impressing upon their tender minds that they are indebted for their existence to a great, good and benevolent Spirit, who has not only given them life, but has ordained them for certain great purposes. That he has given them a fertile, extensive country, well stocked with game of every kind for their subsistence, and that by use of his inferior spirits he has also sent down to them from above coon, pumpkins, squashes, beans, and other vegetables, for their nourishment. That this great Spirit looks down upon the Indians to see whether they are grateful to him, and make him a due return for the many benefits he has bestowed ; and, therefore, that it is their duty to show their thankfulness by worshiping and doing that which is pleasing in his sight. They are taught in everything to please the Great Spirit. When the child does a commendable act the father will say : ' May the Great Spirit who looks upon him grant this child a long life ' "

TREATMENT OF THE WOMEN. An Indian loves to see his wife well clothed, which is a proof that he is fond of her. In bartering the skins and pelfry with the trader, when the wife finds an article which she thinks will suit or please her husband she never fails to purchase it for him ; she tells him that it is *her* choice, and he is never dissatisfied. The more a man does for his wife the more he is esteemed in the community.

Chapter II.

N the 12th of March, 1664, Charles II., of England, granted to his brother James, Duke of York, *inter alias*, all that part of New Netherland lying east of Delaware Bay, and sent a force under Sir Robert Carr and Col. Richard Nicoll to dispossess the Dutch of their territory in the New World. General Stuyvesant, of New Amsterdam, was, by reason of his defenseless condition, compelled to surrender without resistance, and the conquest of the colony on the Delaware was accomplished by Sir Robert Carr "with the expenditure of two barrels of powder and twenty shot."

The Duke's squadron was yet on the Atlantic, and the country yet in possession of the Dutch, when he, by deeds of lease and release, dated the 24th of June, conveyed to John, Lord Berkeley, a brother of the Governor of Virginia, and Sir George Carteret, the tract of land lying between the Hudson and the Delaware Rivers, "which said tract of land is hereafter to be called by the name or names of *New Cæsarea* or New Jersey. [The name was given in compliment to Sir George Carteret, who had defended the island of Jersey against the long Parliament in the civil war, but the powers of government which had been expressly granted by the Duke were not in terms conveyed, though it would seem that both parties deemed them to have passed by the grant.]

The proprietors formed a constitution, or, as it was termed, "concessions and agreements of the lords proprietors," which secured equal privileges and liberty of conscience to all; and it continued in force till the division of the province in 1676. In August, 1665, Philip Carteret, a brother of Sir George, was appointed governor, and he made Elizabethtown the seat of government. The constitution established a representative government, and made liberal provision for the settlers. In a few years domestic disputes arose, and in 1672 an insurrection occurred, compelling General Carteret to leave the province.

In 1673 England and Holland were at war, and a squadron was sent by the Dutch to repossess New Netherlands, which was surrendered without resistance by Captain Manning, in the absence of Governor Lovelace. On the conclusion of peace between England and Holland, New Netherlands was restored to the former. The Governor of New York, Major Edmund Andros, claimed jurisdiction over New Jersey, insisting that the Dutch conquest extinguished the proprietary title; but early in 1675 Governor Carteret returned and resumed the government of the eastern part of the province. He was kindly received by the people, who had become dissatisfied with the arbitrary rule of Governor Andros. A new set of concessions was published, and peaceable subordination was established in the colony. Governor Andros, however, continued his efforts to enforce his claims of jurisdiction, and issued a proclamation abrogating the Carteret government, and requiring "all persons to submit forthwith to the King's authority as embodied in himself." To this the people of Newark replied: "The town being met together, give their positive answer to the Governor of York's writ that they have taken the oath of allegiance to the King, and fidelity to the present government, and until we have sufficient order from his Majesty we will stand by the same." Subsequently Carteret himself wrote to Andros : " It was by his Majesty's commands that this government was established, and without the same commands shall never be resigned but with our lives and fortunes, the people resolving to live and die with the name of true subjects, and not traitors." The difficulty was finally settled by a reaffirmation from England of Carteret's authority, and a complete renunciation by the Duke of York of governmental right in New Jersey.

Sir George Carteret died in 1679. By his will he directed the sale of that part of the province for the payment of his debts, and it was accordingly sold to William Penn and eleven others, who were termed the twelve proprietors. A fresh impetus was given to the settlement of the country, especially by the people of Scotland. Each of the twelve proprietors took a partner, and they all came to be known as the twenty-four proprietors, and to them the Duke of York, on the 14th of March, 1682, made a fresh grant.

Under the new regime in New Jersey, Robert Barclay, one of the proprietors, was chosen Governor for life, with power to name his deputies. There were, in succession, Thomas Rudyard (1683), Gawen Lawrie, Lord Neil Campbell, and Alexander Hamilton.

In West New Jersey Samuel Jennings was commissioned deputy governor by Byllinge in 1680, and during the next year he convened an assembly which adopted a constitution and form of government. His successors were Thomas Olive, John S. Keene, William Welsh, Daniel Coxe and Andrew Hamilton.

In 1701 the condition of affairs in both provinces had arrived at that state when the benefits of good government were not attainable. Each had many proprietors, and their conflicting interests occasioned such discord that the people became quite willing to listen to overtures for a surrender of the proprietary government. "The proprietors, weary of contending with each other and with the people, drew up an instrument whereby they surrendered their right of government to the crown, which was accepted by Queen Anne, on the 17th of April, 1702. The Queen at once reunited the two provinces, and placed the government of New Jersey, as well as of New York, in the hands of her kinsman, Lord Cornbury."

Cornbury's rule was terminated by the revocation of his commission in 1708. He was succeeded by John, Lord Lovelace, who soon died, and the functions of government were discharged by Lieutenant-Governor Ingleshy till 1710, when Governor Hunter commenced his administration. He was followed in 1720 by William Burnet, who was removed to Boston in 1727. John Montgomerie then became Governor, and continued until his death in 1731. The government then devolved on John Anderson, President of the Council, who died in about two weeks, and was succeeded by John Hamilton (son of Andrew Hamilton, Governor under the proprietors, who served nearly two years. In 1738 Lewis Morris, Esq., was appointed Governor of New Jersey, "separate from New York." His successors were John Reading, Jonathan Belcher, John Boone, Josiah Hardy, and, in 1763, William Franklin, the last of the royal governors, and a son of Benjamin Franklin.

Chapter III.

GEOLOGICAL FORMATION OF ESSEX COUNTY.

(From Prof. George H. Cook's Geology of the State.)

HAT portion of New Jersey which is of the Triassic or Red Sandstone Age, is included in a belt of country which has the Highland range of mountains on its north-west side, and a line almost straight from Staten Island Sound, near Woodbridge, to Trenton, on its south-east. It has the northern boundary and the Hudson River on the north-east, and the Delaware on the south-west. The area within these bounds is entirely free from rocks of an earlier age, and also from any extensive formations of a later period. The strong and decided red color of the prevailing rock of this formation has given name to the whole, and while most of the names of the kind have been discarded by the geologists, this is so striking and suggestive that it receives the approval of all.

Prominent in the Triassic district are the two long and parallel ranges of trap-rock, known in Essex county as the First and Second Mountains. The easternmost or outer ridge we shall call, for convenience of description, the First Mountain, while the inner parallel range may be termed Second Mountain. The former, rising at Pluckamin, in Somerset county, has an east-southeast trend, for seven miles, to the gorge through which passes Middle Brook. The continuous ridge runs thence on an east and north-east course to Millburn, in Essex county, a distance of sixteen miles, where the gap between the two ends of the disconnected range is about one and a half miles. From Millburn to Paterson, a distance of fifteen miles, its course is a little east of north. The whole length of this mountain from its rise at Pluckamin to its terminus near Siccomac is forty-eight miles, and its general trend is north-northeast.

The prominent and characteristic feature of this mountain is the great difference between its inner and outer slopes. That toward the Second Mountain is gentle, while that toward the red sandstone country is steep, and in many places precipitous. The former corresponds to the dip of the shale or sandstone which forms the basis upon which the trap rests, and at nearly all points trap constitutes the rock of this declivity. The steep outer slope shows sandstone or shale at the base, and up to the precipitous bluffs of trap, covered, however, in places, by the débris from the rock above. The breadth of this range is quite uniform, from one to two miles. The height is also remarkably uniform, ranging from three hundred to six hundred and fifty feet above the level of the sea.

Everywhere the trap forms the crest and upper portion of this slope, under which is the sandstone, generally covered by trap débris. The top of the sandstone is from one hundred to one hundred and fifty feet below the top of the mountain. The located line marks the base of this steep face, and is at the same distance from the top of the mountain. It is plain on all roads crossing the ridge, e.g., on the old South Orange Turnpike, the mountain road, Mount Pleasant Turnpike, near the Llewellyn S. Haskell place, also in the Park, in West Orange Township.

The western boundary line of the trap of the First Mountain follows the general direction of the valley included between the First and Second Mountains. The drift here, also, renders the tracing of a geological line quite difficult. But from the known uniformity of the trap slope, and an examination of the surface configuration of the county, and a few points of outcrop, the line can be quite accurately fixed and described. Generally it follows the line of least elevation, or at the bottom of the valley, and this is in most cases at the foot of the first mountain slope. Beginning at the northern end of this range, the Oldham Creek is coincident with a line almost to the pond north of Haledon, thence running east of this village, and at the same side of the creek, it meets the Passaic River west of the mouth of Oldham Creek, and follows the river for a mile to the Morris and Essex Canal, which constitutes the west boundary of this range to the Little Falls and Notch Road. The trap appears at several points along the river from the mouth of the creek to the bend in the former, where the line leaves it. East of this the First Mountain is made up of several rocky ridges, separated by narrow valleys.

From the Notch Road southward the trap boundary follows the same general direction as the mountains; crosses the county line, the crest forming the boundary line between Caldwell and Montclair townships to the east of Verona Village to the watershed of the Verona Valley, near the upper side of Llewellyn Park, west of Eagle Rock; thence down the valley of the west branch of Rahway River as far as the old South Orange Road. Approaching the stream, it at length crosses it, and intersects the Morris and Essex branch of the D., L. & W. R.R., about three-quarters of a mile west of Millburn Village. Along the line just mentioned, drift knolls and beds rest upon the lower portions of the trap slope; near the crest of the main and subordinate ridges the rock is frequently seen. Near Millburn the slope is less obscured by drift, although west and south-west of the village it hides all rocks.

The features of the Second Mountain are similar to those of the First. The boundary line between them is of the same general course as that of the mountain itself, and also parallel throughout with the First Mountain. The prolongation of the range, at each extremity beyond the ends of the outer range, makes this mountain longer than the other by five miles. Throughout a portion of the range its structure is apparently complicated by one or more subordinate ridges, quite similar to the main or outer one. There can scarcely be a doubt that the whole mass is one unbroken body of trap-rock.

Chapter IV.

HAT is now the State of Connecticut originally consisted of two colonies—Connecticut
and New Haven. The settlement of the former began at the mouth of the Connecticut
River in 1631, under a patent granted to Lord Say and Seal and Lord Brook- the
location receiving the name of Saybrook. The free planters of Hartford, Windsor and
Wethersfield (emigrants from the Mass. Colony) resolved to form themselves into a distinct
commonwealth, and on the 14th of January, 1639, they convened at Hartford and adopted
a constitution. The preamble of this instrument set forth that it was to preserve " the
liberty and purity of the Gospell," as they understood it, "and the regulation of civil
affairs."

This was the first constitution adopted in the New World, and it recognized among
its fundamental principles the great bulwark of American freedom. It has been said of
it that it was "simple in its terms, comprehensive in its policy, methodical in its arrangement, and
beautiful in its adaptation of parts to a whole."

The same year—1639—Fairfield and Stratford were founded under the jurisdiction of Connecticut, and in 1644 the Colony of Connecticut purchased from Colonel Fenwick the jurisdiction right in
the Colony of Saybrook. This then embraced the territory of the Connecticut Colony.

On the 4th of June, 1639, the free planters of Quinnepeac, or New Haven, met and formed a
civil and religious organization. The constitution, if such it may be termed, of this colony, was original,
and in some of its provisions unique. It was widely different from that of Connecticut, and was in many
respects similar to the old Jewish theocracy.

In December, 1639, the planters of this colony purchased of the Indians a tract of land called
Totoket or Branford. Among the purchasers were Jasper Crane, Lawrence and George Ward and
Daniel Dod. The same year the towns of Milford and Guilford were added to the colony.

Conspicuous among the New Haven settlers, in civil affairs, were Robert Treat and Jasper Crane,
who afterward became leaders in the new enterprise or " New Worke."

Colonel Robert Treat, born in England, son of Richard, was with his father at Wethersfield in
1640; was at Milford, where he was Town Clerk; was an assistant in the New Haven Colony in 1659; was
also a Magistrate. For his " expense with the Indians about purchasing" on Pesayack River in 1666, he
had "given him two acres of land in the town plot, near the frog pond," and in the choice of lots had the
first. In 1672 he returned to New England, and in 1675 " Major Treat was dismissed from the Church
of Christ, at Newark, to the church at Milford. In Phillip's War he was Commander-in-Chief; in 1676

Deputy Governor; and, in 1683, Governor of Connecticut. He served in that place fifteen years, and retired from old age, and died 12th of July, 1710, aged 88

JASPER CRANE was one of the original settlers of the New Haven Colony, "the only remaining occupant of the east centre square; was presumably from London, as he was much connected with the London men in various ways. He first put his estate at one hundred and eighty pounds, and land was assigned him according in amount with that appraisal; but before the meadows and the outlands of the third division were allotted he was permitted to increase his appraisal to four hundred and eighty pounds, and receive thereafter corresponding allotments of land. He signed the first agreement 4th June, 1649, at general meeting of all the planters, in Mr. Newman's barn; took the oath of fidelity at the organization of the government, with Campfield, Pennington, Governor Eaton and others. In 1644 he was "freed from watching and trayning in his own person, because of his weakness, but to find one for his time." At East Haven he was interested in a bog furnace in 1651; he removed to Branford in 1652, and represented the town in the General Court of the Jurisdiction in 1653.

The restoration of the Stuarts in 1660 was not favorably received in New England, and when the time arrived for the next election in New Haven Jurisdiction it was difficult to find persons willing to accept office.

Mr. William Leite was chosen Governor. Mr. Matthew Gilbert, Deputy Governor, Mr. ROBERT TREAT and Mr. JASPER CRANE, Magistrates.

After the restoration of Charles II., Whalley and Goffe, the Regicide Judges, escaped to New England and were reported in the New Haven Colony. The pursuivants who were sent in pursuit of the fugitives applied to Deputy Governor Leite, and demanded military aid, and a power to search and apprehend. "The Court was called together and Magistrate CRANE, of Branford, had arrived in company with Liete."

"The Magistrates held a consultation of two or three hours, after which, being further pressed by the pursuivants to do their duty and loyalty to his Majesty or not, it was answered they would first know whether his Majesty would own them."

Magistrates Crane, Gilbert and Treat subsequently issued a warrant for the arrest of the fugitives, but as the most prominent men in the colony were in sympathy with, and aided in concealing them, the warrant was never executed. Rev. Mr. Davenport, their leader, covertly advised them so to do. He preached to his people from Isaiah xvi., 3 and 4: "Take counsel, execute judgment, make thy shadow as the night in the midst of the noonday; *hide the outcasts*, betray not him that wandereth. Let mine outcasts dwell with thee. Moab, be thou a covert to them from the face of the spoiler."

In this controversy between the Colonies of Connecticut and New Haven, growing out of the new charter granted to Connecticut by Charles II., in 1662, JASPER CRANE and ROBERT TREAT bore a prominent part in bringing about a peaceful settlement.

A communication from the Connecticut Colony was read at a meeting of the freemen of the New Haven Colony held at New Haven, November 4, 1662, setting forth the advantages of the patent, with the "earnest desire that there may be a happy and comfortable union between yourselves and us according to the terms of the charter."

The reply to this communication was signed by William Leite, Matthew Gilbert, Benjamin Fenn, JASPER CRANE, ROBERT TREAT, William Jones, John Davenport, Nicholas Street, Abrah. Pierson, and Roger Newton.

On the 19th of August a "committee was appointed to treat with our honored friends of New Haven, Milford, Branford and Guilford, about settling the union, and incorporate with the Colony of Connecticut."

Among the queries propounded by the New Haven Colony, and finally accepted by Connecticut, was one providing "That the Worshipful Mr. Leite, Mr. Gilbert, Mr. Jones, Mr. Fenn, Mr. Treat and Mr. CRANE be and remain in magisterial power within the county, and any three or more of them as they see cause to have power to keep a county court, they choosing out from amongst themselves a moderator *pro tempore*, in the president's absence, whom we hereby nominate to be Worshipful Mr. Leite for the county, and they to stand in force until an orderly election of officers at general election in May next," etc.

Notwithstanding these peaceful negotiations, the inhabitants of the New Haven Colony were greatly disturbed at the possible termination of affairs. Mr. Davenport and other ministers were strongly of the opinion that all government powers should be vested in the churches, and the churches were unanimously opposed to being united with Connecticut. In New Haven, only church members in *full communion* could be freemen. The adopted tenet of the Connecticut Colony was that all baptized persons, not convicted of scandalous actions, are so far church members that, upon acknowledging their baptismal covenant, and promising an *outward* conformity to it, though without any pretension to inward and spiritual religion, they may present their children for baptism. This was known as the "Half-Way Covenant," and continued in force in Connecticut for more than a hundred years.

The proposed union aroused deep feeling through all the New Haven Colony settlements. Branford people were especially disturbed. Rev. Mr. Pierson and others had left Southampton, L. I., because they found it was claimed by Connecticut. Now they were to be under Connecticut jurisdiction after all. This was the blighting of all their hopes. They did not believe there could be any good and safe government for Christian people unless the voting and office-holding were all in the hands of Christians. Having "spent so much of their means and so much of their labor on houses, fences, mills, lands, and done so much for living comfortably, it was a serious matter to break up, go into another wilderness, and begin again." Their labor of twenty-three years meant a great deal.

Excessively alarming and distasteful were these views to the supporters of the policy of the fathers. Without money, credit, or political affiliations of any importance, they yet clung to the hope of independence, believed the danger from England to be averted, and spurned "the Christless rule of Connecticut." Mr. Davenport was very bitter at the action of Leite. He wrote to Gov. Winthrop in 1663: "As for what Mr. Leite wrote to yourself, it was his private doing, without the consent or knowledge of any of us in the colony; it was not done by him according to his public trust as Governor, but contrary to it."

A serious division of sentiment had arisen in the colony which threatened its very existence. New Haven and Branford supported the cause of "Godly Government"; but Mr. Leite was continued in his office, and the nominal head of the elder faction, Matthew Gilbert, was, as usual, chosen to the subordinate office of Deputy Governor. Many now began openly to declare themselves citizens of Connecticut, and to ignore the New Haven officers and laws. Taxes could not be collected, and the colony, unable to pay the regular salaries of its officials, was plunging deeper and deeper into debt. Discouraged and almost disheartened at the inexorable logic of events, Mr. Davenport exclaimed, "The cause of Christ in New Haven is miserably lost."

Chapter V.

HE events narrated in the preceding chapter which seemed so dark and foreboding to the New Haven colonists proved to them a blessing in disguise. The "land of promise"—the New Canaan—was awaiting them, where they could not only "worship God under their own vine and fig tree," but where they could regulate their civil affairs in accordance with their own convictions of truth and right.

The possible overthrow of his plans had been foreseen by Mr. Davenport, and by the leaders of his party during the quarrel with the townsmen in 1658-60, and at that time they had secretly sent out "wise men of good report" in search of a New Canaan.

They turned naturally to the Delaware region with which they were already familiar, having previously invested large amounts in that locality. A Committee of Inspection was sent thither in 1661, and on the 5th of November, Matthew Gilbert, Deputy Governor of the Colony of New Haven, wrote from Milford to Governor Stuyvesant at New Amsterdam, informing him that "a Companie of Considerable that came into N. E. that they might serve God wth a pure conscience and enjoy such liberties and priveledges, both Civill and Ecclesiasticall, as might best advantage unto, and strengthen them in the end and worke aforesaid, wch also, through the mercy of God, they have enjoyed for more than twentie yeares together, and the Lord having blessed them wth posterities so that their numbers are increased and they being desirous to p'vide for their posterities so that their outward comfortable subsistence and their soules' welfare might in the use of suitable means through the blessing of the Almighty, be obtained,—that this company having been encouraged so to do by the courtesy extended by the Governor to persons appointed to visit 'some adjacent parts' on a previous occasion, had appointed a committee of four of their most prominent men, at the head of which was Robert Treat, to confer with him relative to the terms upon which they might 'begin to plant,' and thereafter secure additions to those who might wish to join them 'for the enlargement of the Kingdom of Christ in the Congregational way,' and secure all other means of comfort, and subordination thereunto." In behalf, therefore, of the Committee sundry propositions were submitted, for which, as they were from "true men and not spies," a careful consideration was solicited with a view to a return of a definite answer to each.

Five conditions of willingness to settle under Dutch rule were submitted to Stuyvesant, and he refused assent to all of them, desiring especially to retain control of the election of officers, and the right of appeal to the Dutch tribunals. These negotiations remained for a time in abeyance.

Stuyvesant, however, was exceedingly anxious to obtain such immigration, and in the winter of 1662-3, Robert Treat, Philip Groves and John Gregory again communicated with him, and found him disposed to make some concessions; he finally wrote home for instructions. In June, 1663, Mr. Treat wrote to Stuyvesant to inquire if the instructions had come, and complained of hindrances at home to the consummation of the scheme.

Stuyvesant's instructions, which finally arrived, bearing date March 23, 1663, urging him to secure the English for subjects by every means and every concession if necessary. Stuyvesant replied to Treat July 20, inviting him to come, and reserving only a formal confirmation of officers, and the right of appeal in important causes and in capital cases, unless the criminal party confessed. The rapid succession of events checked the transaction with the Dutch at this point. The high-handed discourtesy of the Connecticut Legislature united for a time all the New Haven factions in opposition to Winthrop's Charter, and led to important action on the part of the Colonists. In January, 1664, the General Court for the Jurisdiction voted that "The Committee shall treate with Captain Scott about getting a pattent for Delaware."

The summer of 1664 brought the unexpected surrender of the New Netherlands to the Duke of York, and on the 13th of December following, New Haven, Branford and Guilford voted to submit to Connecticut. One week after the surrender to Connecticut had been recorded, a letter was addressed by William Jones, magistrate of New Haven, to Colonel Nicolls, depicting the great "wrong and injury" of the Colony at Delaware Bay. "The Indians of whom we purchased the land there do owne our right and much desire the coming of the English." It was hoped that "A further search of our records may be further improved by your honor as your wisdom shall think fit."

Appeals to Colonel Nicolls were futile: in the meantime Governor Philip Carteret arrived and fixed his capital at Elizabethtown. In August, 1665, he sent letters to New England, offering to settlers every civil and religious privilege. A committee, consisting of Robert Treat and one or two other prominent men of Milford, was dispatched to New Jersey to satisfy the community that the picture presented of the great advantages to be derived was not overdrawn. Reference has been made to the fact that unsuccessful attempts had been made, at different times, to plant an offshoot of the New Haven Colony on the banks of the Delaware, and it seems that the Milford committee first turned their steps thither with a view of selecting a site near the present Burlington. But not being pleased with what they saw in West Jersey, they returned and visited Governor Carteret at Elizabeth, at whose suggestion they determined upon a location on the Passaic. It is said that a formal agreement, comprising fifteen articles, was entered into after a full discussion of the provisions of the "concessions," but the document is lost. There was probably a reference to it in the record of a Town Meeting at New Haven, December 4, 1665: "Mr. Jones tolde thee towne about Delaware. The Articles were read, and it was said that a Committee for the ordering of that affayre was appointed."

As the concessions required all land to be taken up under a warrant from the Governor, and as Treat and his companions were equally decided in requiring an extinguishment of the Indian title prior to settlement, these mutual requirements were considered satisfactorily met by Carteret's furnishing Treat with a letter to the Sachem having control of the desired tract, requesting him to give the immigrants possession, and promising to pay therefor, there having been some prior negotiations for the land. "On the subject of real estate in the New World," says Bancroft, "the Puritans differed from the lawyers widely: asserting that the heathen, as a part of the lineal descendants of Noah, had a rightful claim to their lands." Charged with this document, Treat and his friends returned to Connecticut to make arrangements for the removal, and early in the Spring of 1666 the first immigrants from Milford embarked for New Jersey. The record states that "At a meeting touching the intended design of many of the inhabitants of Branford the following was subscribed: Deut. 1, 13; Ex. 18, 2; Deut. 17, 15; Jere. 30, 21. ('Take you wise men and understanding, and known among your tribes, and I will make them rulers over you.' 'Moreover, thou shalt provide out of all the people able men, such as fear God, men of truth, hating covetousness; and place such over them to be rulers of thousands, of hundreds, rulers of fifteen, and rulers of tens,' etc.) 1. That none shall be admitted freemen, or free burgesses within our town, upon Passaic River in the province of New Jersey, but such planters as are members of some or other of the Congregational churches: nor shall any but such be chosen to magistracy: or to carry on civil judicature.

or as deputies or assistants to have power to vote in establishing laws, and making or repealing them, or to any chief military trust or office; nor shall any but such church members have any vote in such elections; though all others admitted to be planters have right in their proper inheritance, and do so and shall enjoy all other civil liberties and privileges according to all laws, orders, grants, which are, or shall hereafter be, made for this town. 2. We shall with care and dilligence, provide for maintenance of the purity of religion as professed in Congregational churches." Whereunto inscribed the inhabitants from Branford:

Jasper Crane, Abra Pierson, Sam'l Swaine, Lawrance Ward, Thomas Blatchly, Samuel Plum, Josiah Ward, Samuel Rose, Thomas Pierson, John Warde, John Catling, Richard Harrison, Ebenezer Canfield, John Ward Senior, Ed. Ball, John Harrison, John Crane, Thos. Huntington, Delivered Crane, Aaron Blatchly, John Johnson (his mark), Thomas L. Lyon (his mark).

Most of these signers moved with Mr. Pierson to Newark. They went by vessel down Long Island Sound. There is a tradition that Elizabeth Swaine, the daughter of Samuel, was the first to land on the shore of Newark, having been merrily handed up the bank by her gallant lover, Israel Ward, in his ambition to secure for her that mark of priority. She was then nineteen years of age.

The omission on the part of Treat to deliver promptly the letter to the Indians with which he was furnished by Carteret, and to complete the arrangements for the occupancy of the desired tract, was the cause of unexpected embarrassment and delay. On attempting to land their goods at some point on the river, they were warned off by Indians on the ground, who claimed to be the owners, and informed them that they had not yet parted with their right thereto. The goods were therefore reladen and a report of the circumstances made to the Governor.

In the interview that followed, these difficulties were probably removed. Samuel Edsall, a resident on Bergen Neck, to whom the neighboring chiefs had become known, through several negotiations with them that he had conducted, both on his own account and as interpreter for others, was authorized by Carteret to effect the purchase. Accompanied by Treat and some others of the new-comers, he proceeded up the Hackensack to confer with those who claimed to be the proprietors of the land west of the Passaic. In Treat's account of the negotiations he says: "One Perro laid claim to the said Passaic lands, which is now called Newark, and the result of our treaty was, that we obtained of a body of said Indians to give us a meeting at Passaic, and soon after they came, all the proprietors, viz.: Perro, and his kindred, with the Sagamores that were able to travel; Oraton being very old, but approved of Perro's acting, and then we acted by the advice, order and approbation of the said Governor (who was troubled for our sakes) and also of our interpreters, the said Governor approving of them (one John Capteen, a Dutchman, and Samuel Edsal), and was willing and approved that we should purchase a tract of land for a township."

A bill of sale was made out, arrangements made for taking possession, and soon the little party, relieved from their close quarters on board the vessels, were established on the site of the contemplated town.

While these preliminary measures were being consummated, an opportunity was afforded for the preparation and execution of written stipulations with certain agents from Guilford and Branford—who had either been fellow-passengers with the Milford people, or had arrived subsequently—that the settlers from those places should be permitted to join in forming one common township, provided definite intimations to that effect should be received prior to the ensuing 1st of November. The meeting at which this agreement was made was held, probably, on board of one of the vessels lying "near Elizabeth-town," on the 21st of May, and was verified by the signature of Robert Treat for the Milford people, and Samuel Swain for those of Guilford and Branford, on the 24th of the same month; it being, they say, their "desire to be of one heart, and consent, through God's blessing, with one hand they may endeavor the carrying on of spiritual concernments, as also civil and town affairs, according to God and a godly government."

The document signed by the people of Branford already referred to, was dispatched to Milford, and in the ensuing month, the inhabitants "declared their consent and readiness" to conform to its requirements. Subsequently, at a meeting on the 24th of June, 1667, shortly after the arrival of the Branford families, the Milford men also subscribed the document: the following is the list of names in their order:

Robert Treat, Obadiah Bruen, Matthew Camfield, Samuel Kitchell, Jeremiah Peeke, Michael Tompkins, Stephen Freeman, Henry Lyon, John Browne, John Rogers, Stephen Davis, Edward Rigs, Robert Kitchell, his mark; J. B. Brooks, his mark; Robert V. Lymens, his mark; Francis V. Linle, his mark; Daniel Tichenor, John Baldwin, Sen., John Baldwin, Jr., John Tompkins, Geo. Day, Thom. —Johnson, John Curtis, Ephraim Burwell, his X; Robert R. Dennison, his X; Nathaniel Wheeler, Zechariah Burwell, William Campe, Joseph Walters, Robert English, Hanns Albers, Thomas Morris, Hugh Roberts, Eph'm Pennington, Martin Tichenor, John Browne, Jr., Jona. Seargeant, Azariah Crane, Samuel Lyon, Joseph Riggs, Stephen Bond.—

The arrangement entered into with the Indians through the agency of Samuel Edsall, which preceded the settlement, was perfected by the execution of a more formal instrument at a conference with them held "at the head of the Cove of Bound Brook," July 11, 1667, which defines the boundaries as follows:

THAT WEE the said Wapamuck, the Sakamaker, and Wamesane, Peter, Captamin, Weeaprokikam, Napeam, Perawae, Sessom, Manustome, Cacanakrue, and Harish, doe, for ourselves and With Consent of the Indians, Bargain, sell and deliver, a Certain tract of Land, Upland and Meadow of all sorts; Wether Swamps, Rivers, Brooks, Springs, fishings, Trees of all sorts, Quaries and Mines, or Metals of what sort soever, With full liberty of hunting and fouling upon the same. Excepting Liberty of hunting for the above said proprietors that were uppon the upper commons, and of fishing in the above said Pesayak River; which tract of Land is bounded and Limited with the bay Eastward, and the great River Pesayak Northward, the great Creke or River in the meadow running to the head of the Cove, and from thence bareing a West Line for the South bounds, wh. said Great Creke is Commonly Called, and Known by the name of Weequachick on the West Line backwards in the Country to the foot of the great mountain called Watchung, being as is Judged, about seven or eight miles from Pesayak town; the said Mountaine as Wee are Informed, hath one branch of Elizabethtown River running near the above said foot of the mountaine; the bounds northerly, viz.: Pesayak River reaches to the Third River above the towne, ye River is called Yanntakah; and from thence upon a northwest line to the aforesaid mountaine; all of which before mentioned Lands for the several kinds of them, and all the singular benefits and Privileges belonging to them, with ye several bounds affixed and expressed herein, as also free liberty and range for Cattle, horses, hoggs, and that though they range beyond any of the bounds in this Deed expressed, to feed and pasture Without Molestion or of damage to the owners of cattle &c, above said. Wee, the above said Indians, Wapamuck &c doe sell, Alienate, make over, and Confirm all Right, Title and Interest of us, our heires and Successors, for ever Unto the said Lands, &c as above-mentioned to Mr. Obadiah Bruen, Mr. Samel Kitchell, Mr. Michael Tompkins, John Browne, and Robert Denison, townsmen and Agents for ye English Inhabitants of Pesayak, to them, their heires and associates for Ever; to have hold and dispose of, Without Claim, Let or Molestation from ourselves or any other Whatsoever. These Lands, &c are thus sold and delivered for and in consideration of fifty double hands of powder; one hundred bars of lead, twenty axes, twenty Coates, ten Guns, twenty Pistols, ten Kettles, ten Swords, four blankets, four barrells of beere, ten pair of breeches, fifty knives, twenty howes, eight hundred fathem of wampem, two Ankers of Lieqners, or something Equivalent, and three troopers' Coates; these things are received, only a small number engaged to them by bill," etc.

Eleven years later, on the 13th of March, 1678, the western limits of the tract were extended to the top of the mountain by a deed from two other Indians, the consideration for the extension being "two guns, three coats and thirteen cans of rum." The boundary line of the town on the south, separating it from Elizabethtown, as agreed upon on the 20th of May, 1668, ran from "the top of a little round hill named Divident hill; and from thence to run upon a northwest line into the country" until it reached the Watchung Mountain. The commissioners appointed for this work from Newark were Jasper Crane, Robert Treat, Matthew Camfield, Samuel Swaine, and Thomas Johnson; from Elizabethtown, John Ogden, Luke Watson, Robert Bond, and Jeffrey Jones.

It was proposed by the Milford settlers to call the new settlement after their own town in the New Haven Colony, and it was called Milford until the arrival of the Branford people. Then, upon a formal organization of the town government, the name was dropped and Newark substituted. The substitute appears to have been agreed upon in honor of Rev. Abraham Pierson, the first Pastoral Shepherd of the place, who came originally from Newark-on-Trent, and who, although second on the list of the Branford emigrants, was second to none in the esteem and reverence of the entire community. In the old "Town Book" which is still preserved, the name is written NEW-WORKE.

The territory thus acquired by *moral* right from the natives, and by a legal right from the proprietors, embraced the present townships of Newark, Orange, Bloomfield, Belleville, Clinton, and Montclair.

In the division of the lands, each settler received a "home lot" in the town laid out on the river, for which lots were drawn, the division being in strict conformity with Hebrew precedents—always the Puritanic model. There were, also, first, second, and third divisions of the "upland," with an equitable distribution of the "bogged meadow."

Chapter VI.

HE little band of expatriated New Haven Colonists, after nearly thirty years of wanderings, found at last their ideal "Canaan." Without counting the exodus from England to Lynn, Mass., there were then three removals within thirty years and each time in search of a "Government according to God." 1. From Lynn to Southampton, L. I. 2. Thence to Branford. 3. From Branford to New Jersey. It has been stated that Branford moved bodily to Newark; this, however, is an exaggeration. Mr. Pierson was a more bitter partisan than Mr. Davenport, and the history of his flock was indeed a "moving" one.

"Our Towne on Passaick" was fitly named by its founders "New-Worke." It was to be a work of love. Recognizing as they did the "Fatherhood of God" and the "Brotherhood of Man," they built accordingly. A government was established in the wilderness, the fundamental principles of which were drawn from the Mosaic Law. The history of this people for more than a quarter of a century was a repetition of God's chosen people under the rule and guidance of the judges and prophets. On entering the "land of Canaan," however, they did not attempt to "drive out the heathen," but lived at peace with their Indian neighbors. In the testimony of the Council of Proprietors at a later period it is stated that : "We are well assured that since the first settlement of New Jersey, there is not one instance can be assigned of any breach of peace with the Indians thereof (though very few of the other provinces can say so as to their Indians); nor that any proprietor ever presumed to dispossess one of them, or disturb him in his possession ; but have alway amicably paid them for their claims, from time to time, as they could agree with them."

There was nothing false, nothing Pharisaical about these Puritan settlers. They were brave and honest enough to say exactly what they meant and what they desired, and while they encouraged honest settlers to come among them, they embodied in their Fundamental Agreements the following article : " The planters agree to submit to such magistrates as shall be annually chosen by the Friends from among themselves, and to such laws as we had in the place whence we came." Another provision was as follows :

" Item, it is agreed upon that in case any shall come into us or rise up amongst us that shall willingly or willfully disturb us in our Peace and Settlements, and especially that would subvert us from the Religion and Worship of God, and cannot or will not keep their opinions to themselves, or be reclaimed after due time and means of conviction and reclaiming hath been used; it is unanimously agreed upon and consented unto. as a Fundamental Agreement and Order that all such persons so ill-disposed and affected. shall, after notice given them from the town, quietly depart the place seasonably, the Town allowing them valuable consideration for their Lands and Houses as indifferent men shall price them, or else leave them to make the best of them to any Man the Township shall approve of."

The capacity of this people for self-government was early tested. "Will you know," inquires Bancroft, "with how little government a community of husbandmen may be safe? For twelve years the whole province was not in a settled condition. From June, 1689, to August, 1692, East Jersey had no government whatever." The maintenance of order during this period rested wholly with the local authorities and with the people themselves. A town meeting was accordingly convened, March 25, 1689-90, to provide for the exigency. Hamilton, the Deputy Governor, having left for Europe the preceding August, it was "Voted, that there shall be a committee chosen to order all affairs, in as prudent a way as they can, for the safety and preservation of ourselves, wives, children and estates, according to the capacity we are in." The committee consisted of Mr. Ward, Mr. Johnson, Azariah Crane (son of Jasper Crane), William Camp. Edward Ball, and John Brown, "with those in military capacity." It was well for the little commonwealth, in those times of disorder, that they were qualified, not only for "the carrying on of spiritual concernments," but also for the regulation of "*civil and town affairs, according to God and a godly government.*" It was not simply that they were a *community of husbandmen,* as intimated by the historian, that made them safe without the protection of provincial laws; they had a higher law, a more imperative rule of action, *written upon the heart.*

Among the inducements held out to emigrants at an early period to settle in New Jersey was that it was "worthy the name of Paradise," because in addition to its natural advantages it had "no lawyers, physicians or parsons." At this period, however, lawyers were in great demand, and it was said that "no men grow rich here so fast as gentlemen of the bar." The "parsons" too exercised a potent influence on the local government.

Jasper Crane and Robert Treat, whose descendants (the latter through the marriage of Dea. Azariah Crane with Robert Treat's daughter) were the first settlers of Cranetown (later West Bloomfield and now Montclair Township), were leaders in the civil and religious affairs of Newark during the first quarter of a century after its settlement. Their influence in the community is shown by the various positions of honor to which they were elected. The following extracts relating to their public service are taken from the Town Records of Newark compiled by Mr. William A. Whitehead and Mr. Samuel H. Conger for the New Jersey Historical Society:

TOWN MEETING, Jan. 1668. Mr. Crane and Mr. Treatt are Chosen Magistrates for the Year Insueing for our Town of Newark.

Item, Mr. Crane and Mr. Treatt are Chosen deputies or Burgesses for the General Assembly, for the Year Insueing; and Lieut. Samuel Swaine is Chosen a Third man in Case of either the other Failing.

TOWN MEETING, the first of January 1669. Mr. Jasper Crane and Mr. Robert Treatt and Mr. Matthew Canfield are chosen Magistrates for our Town for the ensueing year. Item. The said Mr. Crane and Mr. Treatt are chosen Deputies for the General Assembly if there be any. Item Mr. Robert Treat is chosen Recorder in our Town for the Year ensueing, and the Salary is the same as it was last Year.

TOWN MEETING, 2nd *Jan'y,* 1670. Mr. Jasper Crane is chosen Magistrate in our Town for the Year Insueing. Mr. Crane and Mr. Treatt are Chosen deputies for the General Assembly and Lieut. Swain is the Third Man.

Town Meeting 28th *Dec'r* 1670. Mr. Jasper Crane Had Given Him a Little piece of Land Adjacent to His Home Lott upon the Acc't of His Second Division of Land.

TOWN MEETING 1st Jan'y, 1672. Mr. Jasper Crane is Magistrate for the Year Insueing. Item. Crane and Mr. Bond are chosen Deputies for the General Assembly, for the Year ensueing.

TOWN MEETING, Sep. 6, 1673.—It was thought fit and agreed upon, that a Petition should be sent to the Generals at Orange, that if it might be. We might have the Neck.

Item.—Mr. Crane and Mr. Johnson are chosen to carry this Petition, and treat with the Generals about the Neck.

Item. Mr. John Ogden, Mr. Jasper Crane, Mr. Jacob Molynes, Mr. Samul Hopkins, Mr. John Ward, Mr. Abrahm Pierson, Senior, and Stephen Freeman are chosen to take the Pattent in their Names in the Town's Behalf and to give Seenrity for the Payment of the Purchase.

Item—Captain Swain is chosen to be joined with Mr. Crane to sue for Easment in Respect of Payment for the Neck and what is else needful concerning that Matter.

TOWN MEETING June 29, 1674. It is voted that there shall be a Petition sent to the Governor (and Council) for the obtaining a Confirmation of our bought and paid for Lands, according to the General's promise.

Item. Mr. Crane and Mr. Pierson Jun'r is chosen to carry this Petition, and present it to the Governor and Council at N. Orange, in order to the obtaining a Confirmation as above said.

Jasper Crane continued to hold office down to 1674. He was a Deputy to the Provincial Assembly from 1669 to '73, Magistrate 1669 to '74, President of the Town Court 1671, Town's Men 1681, '87, '88, '93, '97.

Mr. Treat, or "Major Treat," as he was known, served the town in various capacities about six years, returning to Connecticut in 1672. The records show that "Major Treat was dismissed from the church of Christ at Newark," and recommended to the church at Milford. He found a wider field in Connecticut for the display of those remarkable traits of character that distinguished him through life. Besides taking a commanding military position in early colonial Indian warfare he served the Colony for thirty-two years, as Deputy Governor and Governor. During the exciting scenes in the Assembly Chamber at Hartford, when Sir Edmund Andros attempted to wrest from Connecticut her original charter, to prevent which the lights were suddenly extinguished and the charter seized by Captain Wadsworth and hid in the Charter Oak, Governor Treat was in the chair. He died July 12, 1710, in his 85th year. Trumbull, the Connecticut historian, says of him: "Few men have sustained a fairer character or rendered the public more important services. He was an excellent military officer; a man of singular courage and resolution, tempered with caution and prudence. His administration of government was with wisdom, firmness and integrity. He was esteemed courageous, wise and pious. He was exceedingly beloved and venerated by the people in general, and especially by his neighbors at Milford, where he resided."

Mary, the daughter of Governor Treat, became the wife of Deacon Azariah Crane (eldest son of Jasper Crane), who left his "silver bole," to be used by "the church in Newark forever."

The "First Church of Newark," of which Azariah Crane afterward became "Deacon," was actually established before Newark was settled, it having been organized in Branford in 1644. In October, 1666, the church, with its pastor, its deacons, its records, and the major portion of its congregation, was simply translated from Branford to Newark; so that its "church work" was really continued uninterruptedly. Dr. Stearns says of it: "The First Church in Newark appears to be the oldest fully organized church in the State of New Jersey. On Sep. 10 1668 steps were first taken to erect a place of worship. It was voted in the town meeting to 'build a meeting house as soon as may be.'" This was the central object of interest in every community of the Puritans. A joint letter sent in 1684 to the Proprietors in Scotland by David Barclay, Arthur Forbes, and Gawen Lawrie, says: "The people being mostly New England men, do mostly incline to their way; and in every town there is a *meeting-house*, where they worship publicly every week. They have no public laws in the country for maintaining public teachers, but the towns that have them make way within themselves to maintain them."

The whole town helped in the erection of the building. It was 36 feet in length, 26 feet in breadth, and 13 feet between the joists, "with a leuter to it all the length, which will make it 36 feet square." The site selected was on the highway leading to the mountain; it was said to be nearly opposite what is now Mechanic Street, or in the corner of what is known as the old town burying-ground. It stood then with its gable ends pointing to the north and south, and the broadside "nigh pointing on a square with the street," in the precise spot which Mr. Pierson, the elder, Deacon Ward and Mr. Treat had assigned for it. It was Newark's first church edifice, and first place of general business—the theatre of all important transactions, religious, civil, military, during the first half-century of its existence. There the townsmen, "after lecture," held their stated meetings, and there, on any alarm, the brave soldiers of the little community assembled with their arms at the beat of the drum to defend their homes and altars, their little ones, and their wives.

In the Newark Town Records, it is recorded January 1, 1666 7, "that John Baldwin Junior, Thomas Pierson Junior, Thomas Pierson Senior, John Catlin, William Camp, AZARIAH CRANE and George Day are chosen townsmen for the year ensuing. These townsmen are appointed to meet every lecture day in the afternoon."

Rev. Abraham Pierson, the "Moses" who led his people out of the wilderness to this New Canaan, was an old man when he came to Newark, and after twelve years' faithful service, he was "gathered unto his people." He was succeeded by his son, who was his assistant during nine years of his pastorate. Others followed the younger Pierson, and continued in the good old way. The sixth regular pastor of the First Church was Rev. Joseph Webb, a graduate of Yale, who was ordained by the Presbytery of Philadelphia, Oct. 22d, 1719. The Presbyterian ordination and settlement of Mr. Webb is the first indication which appears of the people turning aside from "the Congregational way." Though the leanings of the second Pierson were toward Presbyterianism, the form of worship in his time and during the time of his successors, until Mr. Webb's advent, was Congregational. There is no record of the precise time of the change. The difference between the two forms was comparatively so slight, that from the first, in New England and in New Jersey, persons of both persuasions lived in peace, harmony and good fellowship together, except when firebrand zealots appeared in their midst and sowed discord. About the year 1682, when half the twenty-four Proprietors were Scotch, great numbers of that race arrived and settled in New Jersey, and the historian Grahame remarks that "American society was enriched with a valuable accession of virtue that had been refined by adversity and piety, and invigorated by persecution."

As the population increased, the settlement on the Passaic River began to spread itself toward the mountain and in other directions. At what time the settlement of the mountain district began is not definitely known, but in the year 1684 the town ordered the laying out of the highway as far as the mountain. It is highly probable that some of the original settlers had taken up quarters in that direction. In 1715 Deacon Azariah Crane (who "in the overturn of the government by the Dutch," in 1673, was "betrusted with the concerns of his honorable father-in-law, Mr. Robert Treat") is spoken of by himself as having been "settled" for many years at the mountain. So, at the same time testified Edward Ball. At a town meeting held Jan. 1, 1697-8, it was "voted that Thomas Hayse, Joseph Harrison, Jasper Crane and Matthew Canfield shall view whether Azariah Crane may have land for a tan yard at the front of John Plum's home lot, out of the common, and in case the men above-mentioned agree that Azariah Crane shall have the land, then he, the said Azariah Crane, shall enjoy it so long as he doth follow the trade of tanning." As is shown by the Towne Book that he and Edward Ball had been settled near the mountain many years it is to be supposed that the decision of the examiners in the matter of the tan yard was against him.

Jasper Crane, Thomas Huntington, Samuel Kitchell, and Aaron Blatchley, are owners of land "at the head of Second River."

Samuel Swaine 40 acres at the foot of the mountain with John Baldwin Sen'r on the north.

"By warrant April 27, 1694, there was laid out by John Gardner a tract of land at the foot of the mountain, having Azariah Crane on the northeast and Jasper Crane on the southwest."

Cranetown and Watsessing, which were subsequently included in the township of Bloomfield, were simply outlying plantations of the "Towne on the River," taken up and occupied by a few of the original settlers of Newark. While it is evident that there were other settlers in this locality, the name of Cranetown was doubtless given in honor of Jasper Crane and Deacon Azariah, his son, both of whom were held in high esteem throughout the entire community. At just what period the name was given, and the exact boundaries included in the original purchase is not known. Rev. Charles E. Knox, in his History of Montclair Township, under the head of the EARLY OUTLANDS AND HOUSES, says: "Even before the second purchase from the Indians had fully established the right to the slope of the mountains the first land owners had made their way from the Passaic to the top of the mountain. In the proprietory records the first name on the list of surveys of these outlands is Jasper Craine, in 1675. Besides his ' home lot ' in the settlement, his lots on the ' Great Neck,' and his lot near the head of Mill Brook, he has land that year 'at the *head* of y⁰ Second River,' twenty acres, with Mr. Samuel Kitchell on the north, with Thomas Huntington on the east, and with common land south and west. Another adjoining land-owner is Aaron Blackley. This group of four land-owners, three with surveys in 1675 and one with a survey in 1679, is located, according to the descriptions, 'at the head of Second River,' 'lying in the branches of Second River,' 'by the first branch of the Second River,' with a highway running east and west along the side of one of the tracts. This location was, no doubt, in the heart of the present Montclair, somewhere between the old Fordham Crane mansion [on the Valley Road] and south end of the town, along the Second River. The east and west road *may* have been the present Church street or a road connecting eastward with Watseson as Bloomfield was then called.

" In addition to these owners of outlands in the centre of the present population, there were also extending along the mountain from the northern part of Orange to the northern part of Montclair a good number of others whose names can be traced. There were *near* the mountain, in 1675, John Ward (turner) and John Baldwin Sr. *At* the mountain, in 1675, Robert Leyman, Sergt. Richard Harrison and Samuel Swaine ; in 1684 Azariah Crane and John Gardner, and in 1686 Nathaniel Wheeler, John Johnson, Mr. Ward and the Widow Ogden. *Between* the mountain and Wigwam Brook, in 1685, Mathew Williams, Paul, George and Samuel Day, and Mary Day, 'now Mary Oliff.' *Upon* the mountain, Robert Leyman and John Baldwin. At the mountain, with land reaching to the *top* of the mountain, in 1675 John Catlin and John Baldwin, Sr., Hannah Freeman and Richard Harrison. At the *foot* of the mountain, in 1679, Samuel Harrison, Anthony Oliff (Olive) John Catlin and Thomas Johnson; in 1694, John Condner, AZARIAH CRANE, and John Baldwin Jr. *Along* the mountain, Edward Ball in 1694 ; [Dr. Wickes, in his History of the Oranges, places the residence of Azariah Crane, near the present Valley Road, a little south and west of Church street ; and that of Edward Ball, at or near the corner of Valley Road and Church street] between Third River and the mountain at the Acquackanonk line, at about the end of the century, John Cooper and Samuel Kitchell ; and between Toney's Brook and the mountain, in the new century, in 1724, Joseph Ogden, 'adjoining to the plantation of Vanneuklos, on which he now dwells.'

" These land-owners, who had penetrated beyond the land-owners at Watseson and Wigwam Brook, did not venture to build houses. We have hints of the woods and the swamps, of the wigwam and the ford, but no intimation as yet of a house. Although the Indians were friendly, the apprehension of 'a rising' on the part of the natives had been one cause to prevent immediate settlements in the out-lands. There had been Indian wars in Connecticut, and this colony was directly connected with those who were engaged in bloody battles against the native tribes there.

" The saw-mill which Thomas Davis had liberty to set up in 1695 is supposed to have been located near the Peter Davis land, the site being not far from the ruins of the Crane or Wilde woollen mill ; the saw-mill implies houses soon after. Anthony Olive had a house in Wigwam Brook, in Orange, in 1712 ; Joseph Jones a house in 1721, on the mountain road, (probably in East Orange) ; Daniel Dodd a house in the present Bloomfield, in 1719 ; Capt. John Morris, a grist mill, 'lately built,' in 1720, on the Morris plantation ; but no authentic date of a house appears here earlier than that of a dwelling of one Vanneuklos, near Toney's Brook, in 1724. Stone houses which were then antiquities were one hundred years ago all along the Orange and Paterson and Bloomfield roads. There were two stone houses on the Vincent property. There were the Charles Crane, the Phineas Crane, the Samuel Jedediah Ward, and the Joseph Baldwin houses along the old Orange Road in the same vicinity. There were the houses of the Cranes ; –

Benjamin, Stephen, Eliazer, Nathaniel, Aaron (so known afterwards) built some of them before the Revolution, and some of them, it can hardly be questioned, in the early part of that century. The William Crane house, called afterwards the Amos Crane house, or the Fordham Crane house [' Washington's headquarters'] appears in 1743, and Levi Vincent, John Low, Johannes Kiper and Thomas Cadmus are residents that year. The Egbert houses, the Joseph Baldwin house, the houses of the Van Giesons, of Jacob Kent, of the Seiglers and the Speers, along the Valley and the Falls roads northward, go back undoubtedly before the Revolution. The Parmenus Dodd house, on the site of the Presbyterian Church, facing the road southwards ; the Nathaniel Dodd house, half way down from the church to the depot, facing the old road northward ; the John Smith house and the Peter Davis house, farther east on the same road, were built probably between the middle of the century and the Revolution. The most of these houses, two rooms long and one story high, were built of field stone rudely dressed. The freestone first began to be quarried in 1721 but was not used for house-building.

"In the account of a hurricane which swept along the mountain, reported in a New York newspaper in July, 1756, orchards, fences, cornfields and woodlands, for a mile and a half along the mountain and Doddtown region are mentioned, with twenty-five houses and barns as being injured or destroyed. This shows a great advance in improvement and building."

OLD ROADS.

The first public statute passed by the General Assembly of the Province of East Jersey, made provision for the laying out and improvement of roads. This was in November, 1675. A resolution was adopted by the Town Meeting, at Newark, on December 12, 1681, "That there shall be Surveyors chosen to lay out a Highway as far as the Mountain, if need be."

Apparently no further action was taken at the time, and the planters at the mountain were obliged to follow the Indian paths in passing to and from the river, for some years.

On the 8th of October, 1705, the Commissioners for Newark, Andrew Hampton, Theopelus Pierson, and Jasper Crane, laid out the several highways, which are described as follows :

"First a Road from the Town to the foot of the Mountain, or Wheeler's as the Path now runs as streight as the Ground will allow.

"An other road from said Road, South, by a line of mark'd trees to Joseph Riggs' House.

"An other Road from the said Riggs' to Town to run by a path as streight as may be, and by a Line of mark'd Trees, from first mentioned Road North, at Foot of said Mountain.

"An other Road running by a line of marked Trees unto Anthony Olieve's (Olid) House.

"An other Road running from s'd Anthony's House to first mention'd Road, by a Line of mark'd Trees and path to the other Road running from s'd Anthony's Road to Caleb Ball's House, by path and mark'd Trees.

"An other Road, running N.E. from s'd Road to Town, by a path and Nuttman's line.

"An other High-way from the way at the foot of the Mountain, running up to the top of the Mountain, beginning on the North side of Amos Williams House ; thence in the line between Amos and John Johnson as near as may be to Rocks, North to the Notch."

The "mark'd trees" referred to indicate the Indian paths or the paths of the planters through the forests. The system of "marking" or "blazing" trees consisted in cutting with the hatchet, trees at intervals through the forests to mark the way so that a person might be able to return by the same route. The planters might have followed the Indian paths, or marked out new ones for themselves. When the surveyors first commenced laying out the road or roads to the mountain, instead of taking a direct line to the mountain, they evidently followed these beaten tracks or "paths," hence it is difficult at this late day to trace definitely the line of any of the old roads.

The *first* road described, viz., that "from Town to the Foot of the Mountain," was doubtless the one indicated on the early maps as the "Crane road." It began at the head of Market Street, near the present Court-House in Newark, and passed the residence of Jasper Crane at High Street, and ran through the present Warren Street to Roseville. The oldest maps of Essex County show a continuous road to the mountain connecting with the " Crane road." The continuation of this road is the Swinefield Road ; it was said to have been used by the aborigines in their journeys from the Hudson to the Delaware Rivers. Originally a " path," it branched from the present Main Street, Orange, at the Brick Church, and running through Tory Corner, crossed the mountain at Eagle Rock. From Tory Corner westward to the top of the mountain, it was laid out as a common highway in 1705, and afterward in 1733.

The *seventh* road seems to be the original Eagle Rock Road which was laid out anew in 1733. It was described in 1705 as " An other High-way from the way at the Foot of the Mountain, running up to the top of the Mountain."

The *fifth* road is referred to as " running from s'd Anthony's House to the first mention'd Road by a Line of mark'd Trees and path to the other Road running from s'd Anthony's Road to Caleb Ball's House, by path and mark'd Trees." It is shown by the records that in 1704, Edward Ball conveyed to his son Caleb a tract of land containing fifty acres, and lying north of the lot of Azariah Crane. This doubtless refers to Mr. Crane's property in Cranetown, and the road probably began at Anthony Oliff's house and ran thence in a northwardly direction to Caleb Ball's house in Cranetown.

What is now known in Montclair as Orange Road (but in Orange as North Park Street) begins at the Swinefield Road, near the house formerly owned by Samuel Condit, and, running northwardly, enters Montclair, near the town of Phineas Crane, now owned by Thomas Harrop, passes the house of Stephen W. Carey and Thomas Russell, and terminates at Bloomfield Avenue.

What for many years was known as the "Old Road," started from the centre of Newark and passed through that part of Bloomfield subsequently known as the turnpike; leaving the turnpike near Moffit's Mills, it ran from that point now known as Glen Ridge Avenue to Bloomfield Avenue, near Philip Doremus' store in Montclair ; thence across Bloomfield Avenue into what is now Church Street to the corner of Valley Road, thence along Valley Road to the Stephen Crane house, or "Washington's Headquarters," at the corner of what is now Clairmont Avenue, westerly along Clairmont Avenue, over the mountain to Horseneck, now Caldwell.

The present Valley Road was formerly known as the Speertown Road. It was laid out May 13, 1768, and began or terminated at the Stephen Crane house (Washington's Headquarters), running north to the road that leads from the house of Melville Seigler, over the mountain to Little Falls. That part of the Valley Road south of Stephen Crane's House, terminating at Church Street, was a part of the "Old Road," described as " running from the centre of Newark, through Bloomfield to Cranetown." Both Church Street and Glen Ridge Avenue then formed a part of the "Old Road."

There was another road laid out November 1, 1744, described as " Beginning at the highway that runs up to the Mountain, near the house of Amos Williams, bounded north upon his fence and a Chestnut Tree, thence running eastward over the brook on the land of Lewis Crane, by a line of marked trees, thence northeast across the land of Lewis Crane and David Crane to a maple bush, marked on four sides, in the line of Levi Vincent ; thence running eastward along the line, between David Crane and Levi Vincent to the highway that runs up to Nathaniel Crane's ; thence eastward on the South of the Brook on the land of David Crane to a burch bush ; thence turning over the brook and running by a line of marked trees, to the northeast corner of Johanes Cadmus, his land ; thence running down said Johanes, his land to *Toney's Brook* ; thence running over the brook by a line of marked trees to the road that runs by Jonathan Davis."

This road began at Eagle Rock Road at that point now known as Harrison Avenue, ran through Cedar Avenue, continuing through Cedar Avenue to the Orange Road, near the house of Calvin Taylor, thence across the Orange Road, from that point known as Washington Street, continuing in an easterly direction to Bloomfield Avenue in Bloomfield ; thence across Bloomfield Avenue, through what is now known as Green Street to the Old Road, now known as Franklin Street. The Baptist Church of Bloomfield stands at the junction of these two streets.

Chapter VII.

CRANESTOWN DURING THE REVOLUTIONARY WAR.

By Rev. Oliver Crane, D.D., LL.D.

O State of the Union was more continuously, or more annoyingly, subjected to the inci-
dental effects of the Revolutionary War than was the State of New Jersey; and no
portion of the State was more exposed to its alarms, and their attendant inconveniences,
than that portion lying between the Hudson River and the mountain ranges west of the
lower Passaic valley. In fact, the whole section from the New York line on the north,
to the Delaware, and extending back twenty or thirty miles into New Jersey, might be
equally included; for, although the main army of patriots, when not in active service,
was located to the west and north of this belt, still the suffering from deprivations by
incursions of the enemy, and from plunderings by a set of freebooters styled *refugees*
(consisting of what were called *cowboys* in the pay of the enemy), and *skinners* (who
were even more dreaded because of their irresponsible rapacity, though nominally classed
with patriots), was often exceedingly trying. This state of things existed almost from the outbreak to
the close of the war. From the time of the disastrous battles of Brooklyn (August 27, 1776), and of
White Plains (Sept. 15-16, 1776), and General Washington's consequent retreat into New Jersey, on to
the end of hostilities, that whole section was harassed by the attendants of war, and by not a few of its
actual devastations. The bloody struggle at Trenton (Dec. 26, 1776), followed by the equally severely
contested one at Princeton (Jan. 3, 1777), and the determined conflict of Monmouth (June 28, 1778),
and that of Springfield (June 23, 1780), attest the horrors of war endured on New Jersey soil, not to say
anything of the frequent minor skirmishes along the same line of territory intervening between the two
contending armies. But even where actual bloodshed did not occur, the feeling of insecurity was scarcely
less than where the battle-roar was heard. This was especially true of the section lying between the
Passaic (then called Second River) and the Watchung (then Newark) Mountain, and of course including
all the villages and towns between Paterson (or Totowa as then known) and the plains of Somerville,
Rahway and New Brunswick on the Raritan.

I have frequently, when a boy, heard my grandmother tell of the vexations alarms which were
experienced by her parents and neighbors residing in what was then termed Wardsesson, or Watsessing,
(Bloomfield), during the war times. She was at the time but a girl, still she well remembered how they
were suddenly called, sometimes by day yet often by night, to hurry all their easily movable household
goods into a farm wagon, and hasten away up over the mountains, leaving only a faithful old slave (for
slavery existed in New Jersey in those days) to guard the house and premises, they returning only after
all signs of danger were past. This, she stated, was no infrequent occurrence, especially after the British
were in possession of New York.

During the Revolutionary war, and for a long series of years previously, Montclair (a name of
scarcely 25 years' standing) was called Cranestown, shortened subsequently to *Cranetown*, and the pass

at Mount Prospect was called Crane's Gap, that being the main thoroughfare over the mountain north of Springfield, and consequently a very important point to be protected in such times. General Washington saw this and kept it, as well as every other avenue of ingress into the interior, well guarded by what were then styled *Minute men*, or militia ready for emergencies on call. Although General Washington's winter quarters (except when exigencies demanded, as at Valley Forge, Pa., 1777–8, and New Windsor, Ct., 1780–1) were divided between Newburgh on the Hudson, and Morristown, N.J.; yet his summer quarters were less permanent, and were frequently changed to meet the varying necessities of the war.

That General Washington had his headquarters for about three weeks at Cranestown, from near the middle of October on, is, as will be shown, a well-authenticated fact; and that he occupied the original Crane mansion, still standing at the junction of Valley Road and the present Clairmont Avenue, leading to, and through, Crane's Gap, is substantiated by very strong traditional testimony. But before citing proofs, let us succinctly state the historic connections, with such circumstances as can be gathered, which led to the occupancy. At no time during the war was the mind of Washington more harassed with perturbing anxieties than at the very time he was stopping, with his army, at Cranestown; but, as it proved, the darkness which brooded over the cause of freedom was the darkness just before the dawn; for exactly one year afterward (Oct. 19, 1781) the surrender of Lord Cornwallis occurred, and the Independence of the United States of America was achieved.

The preceding year (1779) General Lafayette, who had fought bravely by Washington's side in many a hot engagement, had returned to France for the purpose of enlisting the sympathies of the French government and people in the cause of freedom in America, and had so far succeeded as to secure a fleet of seven heavy ships of the line and thirty-two transports, with an armament of 6,000 well-equipped troops and as many more to follow, and funds and pledges of more, for a vigorous prosecution of the war. Lafayette reached Morristown on his return May 12, 1780, and Count Rochambeau, with the French fleet, arrived in Newport, R. I., July 11th succeeding. On the latter's arrival, Washington repaired at once to Newport to welcome and confer with Count Rochambeau, but did not remain long, his presence with his main army in New Jersey being important; but early in the following September the two— Washington and Rochambeau—held a more formal conference at Hartford, Ct., for the concentration of plans for future operations. In the meantime Major General Arnold, who had for eighteen months previously been in secret correspondence with Sir Henry Clinton, Commander-in-Chief of the British forces in New York, with a view of betraying the cause which he had hitherto been supposed to be honestly defending, had, in order to further his nefarious designs, at his own urgent request, been appointed Commander of the important stronghold of the Hudson, West Point. Washington, having completed his conference with the French Admiral at Hartford, was returning to his army, then stationed at Totowa (Paterson), N. J., and arrived at West Point on the very day, and even at the hour, when the treachery of Arnold was most opportunely discovered by the recent arrest of Major John André. Arnold escaping, almost under the eye of Washington, by precipitous flight to the British sloop of war, the "Vulture," then lying just below West Point. This occurred on the 25th of September (1780). Great was the consternation among the officers of the post and those accompanying General Washington on the discovery of the plot; and it is no wonder that Washington exclaimed to Generals Lafayette and Knox, with eyes suffused, "Arnold is a traitor and has fled to the British; whom can we trust now?" But, with his usual self-possession, he immediately issued orders for the thwarting of any attempt to carry out Arnold's treacherous designs. He at once appointed General Heath to the command of the post, and directed changes to be made in the fort so as to render it more secure against attack. On the 2d of October (Tuesday) Major André was hung as a spy at Tappan; and in the course of a few days General Washington proceeded to the army at Totowa, where it had been since its removal from winter quarters in Morristown the preceding spring.

In Gen. Washington's Revolutionary Orders issued during the years 1778–1782, and edited by Henry Whiting, Lt.-Col. U. S. A., New York, 1844, 1846, occurs the following order, viz.:

"HEADQUARTERS, TOTOWAY, October 23rd, 1780.

"The Corps of Light Infantry will remove from their present Encampment, and take post on the most convenient ground, to the Cranetown Gap and the Notch, for the more effectual security of our Right.—Gen. St. Clair will take care of the approaches on the Left. Col. Mayland's Regiment will furnish the necessary Patrols, and will take a new Position for that purpose. The Officers of the Army are to be furnished with two rations per day until further Orders."

This fixes the precise date of march from Totowa for the occupancy of what Gen. Lafayette calls "our Station at Crane'stown," but Gen. Washington "Cranetown Gap." The order, it will be noticed, is sufficiently definite for marching, but does not reveal the design of the movement; and for the obvious reason that it was not Gen. Washington's intention to do so, lest, by any unforeseen accident, the order he conveyed to the enemy, and so the secret aim—Gen. Lafayette's night attack on Staten Island—be known and thwarted. But it settles the point, that "the Post" occupied was "Cranetown Gap," or "Crane'stown Station," directly at the foot of Crane's Gap.

The forced inactivity of the army for six long months, made all the more unendurable by the recent treason of Arnold, whose report had pervaded the ranks prior to the return of the Commander-in-Chief, rendered both officers and soldiers exceedingly eager for a renewal of hostilities; especially was this true of General Lafayette, whose impetuous spirit could hardly brook delay, and be pained for an opportunity to avenge the treason which had seemed for the moment to stain the honor of the noble cause which he had so ardently espoused. He therefore entreating General Washington to be permitted to strike a blow, which, if successful, would be felt by the enemy.

It was known by scouts that Sir Henry Clinton had at this time a

THE OLD CRANE MANSION—WASHINGTON'S HEADQUARTERS

large amount of military stores on Staten Island, guarded mainly by Hessians. Lafayette proposed to secure these by a night attack; and such was his importunity that the Commander-in-Chief yielded; and in order to be in nearer proximity to aid, if needed, the endeavor, he gave orders for the main divisions of the army to move southward. This was done, and the station selected, in which to await the result of the movement under Lafayette, was at Cranestown. The position was well chosen, commanding as it did the pass across the mountain, and at the junction of the roads both from Newark and Orange to that point. Washington appropriated the largest house in the town, and one best located, *the old Crane mansion*, then owned by my great-grandfather, William Crane, himself at the time in the ranks. Washington took possession of the two lower rooms on the west side of the main hall, while members of his staff occupied the other side and all the second-story rooms. Just back of the rear and smaller room, was an old-fashioned *lean-to* which had been, and was then, the kitchen. I myself well remember that old lean-to, with its large open fire-place, but it has long since disappeared. On the evening of his Excellency's arrival, my great-grandmother, Mercy Crane, then in charge of the house, as she was having her slaves prepare supper for her distinguished guest, came to the General and apologetically explained to him her deep regret that she had no tea to serve to her guests. "Never mind, my good lady," replied his Excellency unperturbed. "please have a crust of bread toasted, and use it for tea. That is good enough tea for me." Her anxieties thus allayed, she hastened to furnish the best that her house afforded for the supper of her worthy guests. After supper another difficulty caused no slight solicitude in the mind of the patriotic hostess. Owing to the unusual demand for beds, none was left for Generals Washington and Lafayette in the lower back room, which had been chosen by them, but which had been hitherto used as a dining-room. This deficiency was made known to his Excellency by the hostess with even deeper regret than the fact of her having no tea. "But there is plenty of straw in the barn, is there not?" rejoined her courteous guest. "Abundance," was the quick response. Immediately Washington had several bundles ordered and spread in a corner of the room; and there on it, wrapped in their army blankets, that night slept two of the noblest Generals whose names are on the scroll of fame. Doubtless better accommodations were devised for their convenience while they remained in occupancy thereafter.

During the three weeks of Washington's remaining in headquarters at Cranestown, the troops were encamped directly to the south of the old mansion, their tents standing thick all along the meadows, then wholly unobstructed, from Valley Road to what is now Mountain Avenue, and guarding the intersection of the old Newark Road (now Church Street) with the road leading to Orange and thence to Elizabethtown and beyond. As Washington had brought his army there for a purpose, preparations were immediately set on foot to further the designs of the enthusiastic leader, Lafayette, in his plan of attack on Staten Island. Boats were ordered brought down the Passaic River to a point where the crossing of the Kill was to be effected; while others were hastily constructed on wagons to be conveyed overland to the required place of embarkation. All things seemed at length in readiness for the attempt which promised success. Lafayette, with his command, repaired to the designated spot with all secrecy on the evening of October 26th, not doubting but that the boats ordered would be there to convey his command over the narrow stream. All night long he and his splendidly equipped corps waited impatiently to hail the sight of the wished-for boats, but they came not. From some unaccountable cause they were delayed, until the dawn warned the disappointed watchers that their so much coveted opportunity was past, and that they had nothing now to do but to return to their quarters. But happily just at this point we are supplied with very important data respecting the fact of the occupancy of Cranestown by Washington at this juncture.

Soon after General Lafayette had fairly started on his return to headquarters, he dispatched a courier with a letter to the Commander-in-Chief, stating the unfortunate outcome of the attempt; and this letter we find in "The Memoirs of Lafayette," by his son, George Washington Lafayette, and published in English in New York, 1837. The letter is dated at Elizabethtown, October 27, 1780, and is found on pages 481-2 of the first volume. It reads as follows: "I have taken my position between Elizabethtown and Connecticut Farms. General Clinton has not the time of making any disposition against us. Tomorrow, at nine or ten, I will march to *our position of Crane'stown*, and the day after tomorrow to Totowa, unless I receive contrary orders. Newark Mountain (Orange) was rather too far to march it this night, and too near for tomorrow; because our men, being in want of blankets, will like better to join their tents again. If your Excellency approves of this arrangement, I beg you will order our baggage to wait for us on *our position of Crane'stown*; if you dislike the disposition, your orders may reach us on the road." This fixes exactly the date of the occupancy of Cranestown as temporary headquarters, and also supplies the specific object; while distinctly stating that the troops were there in tents.

Meanwhile, probably during the absence of General Lafayette on the abortive expedition referred to above, an alarm, as had often occurred before, but now of sufficient importance to awaken solicitude, came late one afternoon, that the British were about to make an attempt on the American lines in their somewhat insecure position at Cranestown. At all events Washington considered it of sufficient weight to cause him to be in readiness to meet it, if true; but in the emergency he did not deem it advisable to spare even a single man from the ranks to be sent to warn out the Minute men living beyond the so-called "first and second mountains." He called, therefore, for a volunteer out of the service. One of the sons of his hostess, who had been lame from his boyhood, and hence disabled from active military duty, and yet able to ride on horseback, and who knew every road and lane of the country to be visited, came forward and offered to undertake the somewhat hazardous and wearisome night journey ; for he was to go, if possible, to every hamlet and home where Minute men resided between the Second Mountain and the Passaic River, and this meant to Horseneck, Pine Brook, Swinefield, and all the intervening inhabited region. The offer was accepted, and Zadoc Crane, then but little, if any, rising twenty years of age, mounted his own spirited horse, and with a long, heavy cutlass as his only weapon, started, under the General's special orders, just after the sun had gone down behind the darkening mountains, on his journey. Nothing of note occurred until he reached the lonely space of woods then covering all the Second Mountain ; when, as he entered the shadows, he saw, or thought he saw, some *refugees* in the road ready to intercept his passage. Drawing his long cutlass he, with stentorian voice, cried out ; "Come on, men, we will take them if there are five thousand of them," and at once put spurs to his willing steed, and dashed through the dark and lonely pass, hearing, as I have often, as he rehearsed the adventure, heard him say, "a terrible crackling in the underbrush in the woods" as he speeded through. On he went, calling at every house, as far as in his power ; and just after daylight he drew up his squad of Minute men in line in front of the mansion doorstep, on which already General Washington stood in waiting to inspect them. No fence at that time, nor for many years afterward, obstructed the lawn in front of the house, and hence the parade of the squad was easy. "Well done, my man," was the salute of his Excellency, "now come in and take a *horn* of whisky, for you must need it." As it proved, the alarm was a false one. No British soldier had made their appearance during the night, but the heroic act was remembered, and often told as a reminiscence of the war in after times none the less.

Shortly afterward General Washington withdrew his troops from Cranestown to their strongly entrenched positions on the heights on the left bank of the Passaic at Totowa. Fortunately we have a very exact description of the location and appearance of each corps along the line of entrenchments here. The Marquis de Chastellux, a French officer under Count Rochambeau, was sent by the latter on a visit of observation at this very time through New Jersey and thence on into Virginia ; and he has given us a very clear statement of the disposition of the American forces at Totowa, as he found them November 23, 1780. It may be remarked, that General Lafayette (or the Marquis, as he was then usually styled) had, on the 7th of August previous, taken command of the corps of light infantry, consisting of six battalions, composed each of six companies of men chosen from the different lines of the army. These battalions were divided into two brigades, one commanded by General Hand, the other by General Poor. As the command of the Marquis was the pick of the army, it had assigned to it in position the post of honor as the vanguard. Both officers and soldiers were better clothed than the rest of the army, and made a handsomer appearance on parade. "Each soldier," says the Marquis de Chastellux, "wore a helmet made of hard leather, with a crest of horse hair. The officers were armed with espontoons, or rather half pikes, and the subalterns with fusils (muskets) ; but both were provided with short and light sabres brought from France, and made a present of to them by M. de la Fayette." "This corps was posted," says the Marquis de Chastellux, "in an excellent position. It occupied two heights separated by a small bottom, but with an easy communication between them. The river Totohaw, or Second River (Passaic), protects its right, and it is here that it makes a considerable elbow, and turning towards the south, falls into the bay of Newark. The principal front, and all the left flank to a great distance, are covered by a rivulet (saddle Creek), which comes from Paramus, and falls into the same river." Two miles beyond this position of the vanguard, keeping the river on the left, lay the main army, under the respective commands of Generals Wayne, Huntington, Glover, Knox (Commander of Artillery), and others. "The army," continues Marquis de Chastellux, "was encamped on two heights, and in one line, in an extended but very good position, having a wood in the rear, and in front the river, which is very difficult of passage everywhere except at Totohaw bridge. But the situation would be quite in favor of an army defending the left bank, the heights on that side everywhere commanding those of the right. Two miles beyond the bridge is a meeting-house of an hexagonal form, which is given to their places of worship by the Dutch Presbyterians, who are very numerous in the Jerseys." Not far from where the army lay, the same accurate observer tell- us, was "the great cataract called Totohaw (Passaic) Fall," which interested him much in passing. "At length, after passing thick woods on the right, I found myself in a small plain, where I saw a handsome farm; a small camp which seemed to cover it, a large tent extending to the court, and several waggons round it, convinced me that this was his Excellency's Quarter; for it is thus that Mr. Washington is called in the army, and throughout America."

Such, as far as we have been able, by throwing side-lights upon the screen to bring out more clearly the picture, were the circumstances attending General Washington's temporary occupancy of Cranestown with his army; and such the position of the several lines at Totowa, on his return thither in consequence of the abortive scheme of General Lafayette to attack Staten Island. For five long years had New Jersey been the scene of varying warfare; and for a full year no important aggressive movement had been made by the army; while signs of depression were becoming more and more evident in the minds of the patriots, and not a few even began to doubt the outcome of the already long continued struggle. The troops, at this time, were, and had for months been, poorly clad and scantily fed. The term of service of not a few was expiring, and they were anxious to return to their (in some instances, devastated) homes; Congress was well nigh powerless to aid by reason of the refusal of several of the States to recognize Congressional authority; the credit of the country was at discount, and money obtainable only on individual and responsible guarantees; treason had already shown itself, and might become unearthed elsewhere at any time—all these anxieties were pressing upon the mind of the Commander-in-Chief at once; and yet not a quiver of discouragement was apparent either in his countenance or his acts, but he proceeded to lay plans with the same imperturbability that had always characterized him. Just five days after the Marquis de Chastellux had left the entrenched army at Totowa (Nov. 28, 1780), General Washington assigned to the different divisions of the army (then reduced to only a little over 10,000 troops), their winter quarters, his own being established at New Windsor, Ct. The New Jersey line was to quarter at Pompton, N. J.; the Pennsylvania line at Morristown; the Maryland regiment of horse at Lancaster, Pa.; and Sheldon's horse at Colchester, Ct.; one New York regiment at Fort Schuyler, one at Saratoga, and the remainder of the line at Albany, Schenectady, and other exposed points. But a brighter dawn than any in the past was drawing nigh. As already stated, in less than a year from that very time (in October 17, 1781), came the surrender of Lord Cornwallis, and the recognition of American Independence by the European nations.

Doubtless Cranestown, in common with the adjacent towns, furnished its full quota of stalwart young men for the service during the war, but of these only a very few names have survived to identify them in it. The blood-stained trenches for the burial of the nameless, promiscuous dead found slain on battle-fields, and unknown graves in neglected church-yards, might tell of the patriot heroes of the war from its precincts within them, but they will not be known to the living on earth in time. Major Nathaniel Crane, of Cranestown, who survived the war many years and resided till his death therein, and whom I myself have often, when a boy, met, was in the ranks. William Crane, my great grandfather, the owner at the time of the "Head Quarters," was in Capt. Abraham Lyon's Company, Second Reg. Essex Co., and also served with the State troops, besides others whose names have been obliterated by time.

It only remains to add that the old Crane mansion, which General Washington and his staff occupied in the Autumn of 1780, still stands essentially the same that it was at that memorable period. The additions attached to the rear, and the stucco covering on the outside, were not there then. Some slight changes have been made in the interior but none materially modifying its original integrity as then seen.

Still stands lonely the mansion, a more than a century's relic,
Which, when men's souls trembled in watching the issues of warfare,
Opened its doors to the Chieftain, the father revered of his country,
Giving himself and his staff a hearty and generous welcome.
Still stands quaintly its gables to greet the return of the morning
Or to reflect from the hilltops fading the smile of the sunset.
Still stands sentry the mansion, but where are the tents that before it
Shone in the sheen of the sunlight and dazzled the eyes of beholders?
Where are the blasts of the bugle and tap of the martial drum-beats,
Echoing notes from the mountain, and giving the signals for rising?
Gone are the patriot heroes, who breasted the dangers of battle,
Prompted by love of their country and hope of entailing its freedom.
Still stands olden the mansion, guarding the memories sacred
Clustering hallowedly round it, and marking the spot for remembrance.
Where was encamping his army, and Washington's STATION AT CRANETOWN.

Additional data of this interesting period is given in "The Revolution and its Traditions," by Rev. Charles E. Knox. He says: "This part of the Newark colony touched the Revolutionary contest at several points. The fact that Nathaniel Crane, a private, after the Revolution well known as Major Nathaniel Crane,—was in the battle of Long Island on September 15, 1776, and one of the last to leave the field under a shower of bullets, indicates that citizens here early entered the military service. From 1777 the enlistments were common throughout the county. Among those known to have been from the Montclair region, were Capts. Abraham Speir, and Thomas Siegler, Second Lieut. Joseph Crane, Sergt Obadiah Crane, privates, Jonathan and Joseph Baldwin, Aaron, Matthias, Nathaniel, Joseph, Eleakine, Benjamin, Oliver, William and Phineas Crane, Peter Davis, Nathaniel and Parmenus Dodd, Amos Tompkins, Abraham and Francis Speer, John and Levi Vincent, John Smith and a Van Gieson.

"After the retreat of Washington from Acquackanonck, through the lower part of the town, to New Brunswick, universal consternation prevailed. The people fled to the mountains and over the mountains. The pastor of the Mountain Church was marked for capture. The scouting parties of the British carried devastation everywhere. But not till the reaction of the next year 1777, did the people venture back to their desolate lands and plundered houses.

"Nathaniel Crane—and we may infer that others were with him—was at the battle of Monmouth, in 1778, where was also Gen. Bloomfield.

"When Gen. Anthony Wayne—according to tradition—left his camp at Second River, just south of the ruins of the copper works, his troops took their march in the famous snow-storm of Jan'y, 1779 up the old road to Horseneck, posting a picket at Bloomfield, and abandoning their cannon embedded in the snow in Caldwell.

"The bold hill on the east side of the notch, was, it is said a favorite lookout of Washington. From that height he once detected a raiding party of British sallying from Elizabethtown to the mountains. He dispatched at once a troop of cavalry behind the hill to Springfield, who cut off the foragers, and reclaimed the fine lot of cattle they were driving off. The army here was in that deplorable condition which led, in 1781, to the mutiny of the Pennsylvania troops at Pompton. The detachment extended along the road and the mountain southward from the Crane homestead. Confiscated household furniture taken from the British, is still in possession of a family here, purchased with Continental currency earned by working for the soldiers." A part of this was destroyed by fire in the spring of 1890. The mahogany stand or writing table which was used by General Washington while at the Crane mansion is in the possession of Mrs. Harry C. Crane, daughter of Rev. Oliver Crane, D.D.

Chapter VIII.

OF the children of Deacon Azariah Crane only Nathaniel and Azariah, Jr., are mentioned in connection with the settlement at Cranetown. They acquired by purchase, as well as by inheritance, large tracts of land within the present boundaries of Newark, Orange and Montclair. Dr. Wickes, in his "History of the Oranges," states that: "Their lands were bounded south by the Swinefield Road, east by the Cranetown Road, now Park street, west by Wigwam Brook, which was the division line between the Crane lands and those of the Harrisons and Williams, and on the north by Antony's Brook at Montclair, the northern boundary of Second River. The family of Crane also held land on the south side of the Northfield Road to the summit of the Mountain. It afterwards came into the possession of Simeon Harrison (it being conveyed to him by the executors of Caleb Crane. There is a tradition that when the Lords Proprietors claimed the payments of the quit-rents for lands taken by Azariah and Nathaniel Crane, they brought in a bill for their services as surveyors in the employ of the Proprietors as an offset. Their bill was not accepted, and the controversy was finally settled in the Supreme Court in favor of the surveyors."

A RELIC OF SLAVERY.

KNOW ALL MEN BY THESE PRESENTS, that I, Enoch Williams, of the township of Newark, in the County of Essex, and State of New Jersey, for and in consideration of the sum of one hundred and eighty dollars paid, or secured to be paid by Phineas Crane of the Town, County and State aforesaid, unto the said Enoch Williams, for which payment I have given, granted, bargained and sold unto the said Phineas Crane, my Negro man named Tom; to have and to hold the said Negro man unto the said Phineas Crane, for himself, his heirs, executors, administrators and assigns; and doth warrant, secure, and forever defend the sale of said Negro man named Tom unto the said Phineas Crane, his heirs and assigns forever. IN WITNESS WHEREOF, I have hereunto set my hand and seal this twenty-ninth day of May, in the year of our Lord one thousand eight hundred and nine.

ENOCH WILLIAMS.

Sealed and delivered
in the presence of
    ELIZABETH CRANE.
    POLLY WILLIAMS.

After the erection of Bloomfield as a separate township Cranetown was embraced within its boundaries, and later became known as West Bloomfield. The latter remained as a part of the township of Bloomfield until the separation and erection of the new township in 1860, under the name of Montclair.

Bloomfield owes its name, as well as its existence as a township, to the organization of its first church society in 1796. Rev. Stephen Dodd, of East Haven, Conn., in his MS. History of Bloomfield, prepared in 1846, says:

"It had been the practice for many years to use the word Wardsesson, supposing that it was derived from some person or family by the name of Ward. But this was a palpable mistake. The real name was of Indian origin. *Watsessing, Watsesson*, written in both forms in the ancient records of Newark; but the first is doubtless the correct spelling. It was first used with reference to the School-house Hill and the adjacent Plains, as formerly named. Thus the ancient deeds of our ancestor, Daniel Dodd, and his brother, Samuel Dodd, the grandfather of the late Aaron Dodd, mention *Watsessing Hill, Watsessing Plains*, as also some other records. * * * The neighborhood north of the Meeting-house was once called Crab Orchard, from the crab-apple trees which were standing there in the time of the first settlers. The young men tried to introduce the name Hopewell, but did not succeed.

OLD HOMESTEAD OF DEACON JOSEPH CRANE.

"Crane Town was a name early given to that tract under the mountain settled by the *Crane* families from Newark. The two first were brothers, Azariah and Nathaniel. Azariah, the grandfather of Aaron, and my mother lived about where Elias B. Crane resided; the brother of Azariah, and father of William and Noah, lived where Major Crane died.

"Under these circumstances, our fathers thought it expedient to attempt to introduce some general name to apply to all the ground covered by the proposed Ecclesiastical Congregation. For this purpose they held several meetings for consultation, which resulted as follows:

"In the *Sentinel of Freedom*, of Dec. 7, 1796, I find the following notices:

"At a numerous meeting of the Congregation of Wardsesson, Oct. 13, 1796; Joseph Davis Esq. in the Chair:

"It appearing that agreeably to a resolution of a meeting held the 10th inst., advertisements have been set up in three of the most public places within the bounds of the Congregation, notifying the objects of the present meeting; the members proceeded to choose a name by which the society should be distinguished, when it appeared that the name of BLOOMFIELD had a large majority of votes.

"Extract from the minutes.   "ISAAC W. CRANE, Secretary."

"To the preceding I will add, from memory, in which I may be incorrect, that Isaac Watts Crane being acquainted with Gen Bloomfield, of Burlington, a man of wealth, and having no children thought it might be policy to take his name and engage his generosity towards this child of adoption. And, as it will appear in the sequel, the plan produced some good fruit. This plan was carried out by giving Gen. Bloomfield suitable notice of what had been done respecting the adoption of his name, accompanied with a barrel of cider, the produce of *Bloomfield*."

The *Sentinel* of July 12, 1797, contained the following:

"COMMUNICATION FROM BLOOMFIELD.—On Thursday, the 6th inst., Maj Gen. Bloomfield and his lady made a visit to the Society of Bloomfield. They were escorted from Orange by Lieut Baldwin's (Jesse?) division of cavalry, and other gentlemen, to the house of Joseph Davis Esq., where they were received by a numerous concourse of people belonging to the Society A procession was then formed in the following order :

" The farmers, headed by Col. Cadmus, and Mr Timothy Ward; the masons and laborers ; the trustees and managers ; the venerable clergy ; Gen. Bloomfield and suite ; the battalion officers ; Lieut Baldwin's division of horsemen ; forty young ladies uniformly dressed in *white*, their heads neatly ornamented with *turbans* and *coroni hedera*, crowned with ivy, besides two hundred young children belonging to the schools of Bloomfield ; and in the rear of the whole Capt. Crane's elegant company of infantry, giving the procession a dignified appearance. The procession being thus formed, proceeded to the new stone church and from thence to a large bower, prepared for the occasion, where a prayer was made by the Rev Mr White, adapted to the occasion ; and anthems were sung by forty young ladies, uniformly dressed in white. Gen Bloomfield, from an eminence, addressed the assembly, recommending the virtues of patriotism and of political and Christian union An answer was returned by Mr Watts Crane in behalf of the Society receiving the same sentiments"

A white marble tablet, with inscription, "Bloomfield, 1796," was set in the brown free-stone tower, to mark the beginning of a new township. The civil township was not erected until 1812, when it included the territory from the crest of the mountain to the Passaic River.

THE TOWN PATENT OR CHARTER of Newark, given in 1713, defines the west, north and east line of what became afterward Bloomfield :

" Purchased from ye Indians, now known by ye Name of Newarke, Bounded easterly by a great creek that runs from Hackingsack Bay, through ye Salt Meadow called by the Indians Wequahick, and now known by the Name of Bound Creek, and continuing from the head of ye Said Creek to the head of a Cove to a Markt Tree ; from thence it Extended Westerly upon a Straight Line, by Computation Seven Miles be the Same more or Less, to the End or foot of the Great Mountain, and to the Ridge thereof, called by the Indians Wachung, Near where Runs a branch of the Rahway River ; from thence extending on a Northerly Course along the Ridge of the Said Mountain to a heap of Stones Erected to Ascertain the Boundary between the s'd Town of Newark and the Town of Achquickatonnck ; from thence Running a South-east course by Achquickatonnck Bound Line to where the brook or Rivalet Called by the Indians Yantokah, but now known by the Name of the Third River, Emptieth itself into Pasayack River, and from thence Continuing Down along by the said Passaick River and Hackingsack Bay to the mouth of the said Bound Creek."

The southern line of Bloomfield was established in 1806, when the township of Newark was divided by its own authority into three wards—the Newark Ward, the Orange Ward and the Bloomfield Ward. The Orange Ward became that same year the township of Orange, and the Bloomfield Ward became the township of Bloomfield in 1812. The line between the Orange and the Bloomfield Wards was established, in 1806, as follows :

" Beginning at the Green Island in Passaik River and running thence to the Boiling Spring on land of Phineas Baldwin, dec'd and from thence to the Bridge at the Slough between the houses of Jonathan Baldwin and Elihu Pierson, and from thence to the bridge near Martin Richards', and from thence to Turkey Eagle Rock, on the top of the first Mountain ; which we agree shall be the line between the Bloomfield Ward and the wards of Newark and Orange."

The "inhabitants of Second River and the Body of Newark" acted separately "in all affairs relating to the Poor for fifty-three years." The line of division was in part the line which afterward divided Belleville from Bloomfield. The description given in 1743-44 is as follows:

"Beginning at Passaick River at the Gully near the house of Dr Pigot, thence northwest to Second River, thence up the same to the Saw Mill belonging to George Harrison, thence a direct line to the northeast corner of the Plantation of Stephen Morris, thence to the Notch in the mountain, leaving William Crane's house to the southward, thence on a direct line to Stephen Van Sile's Bars and Abraham Francisco's to the Northward of said line; and it was agreed that all on the Northward of said lines should be esteemed Inhabitants of Second River, and all on the southward of the Body of Newark."

The Notch referred to is probably the little opening in the mountain just north of the present Mountain House.

"Cranetown" by popular designation became after 1812 West Bloomfield, and so continued until 1868. Its *Surface Streams and Soil* are thus described by Rev. Mr. Knox in his History of Bloomfield

VIEW ON TONEY'S BROOK.

Township: "Between the natural boundary of the mountain crest on the west and the natural boundary of the Passaic River on the east lies an unusually diversified and beautiful expanse of country. Parallel waves or ridges of land run from north to south. The mountain slope descends into plain and valley, and rises again upon a wave nearly the length of the township known now as the Ridgewood line. This territory forms the beautiful region of what is now Montclair."

Two rivulets rise in the northern part of the present township which flow southward and eastward to form in Bloomfield the little stream anciently known as Second River. The first of these known as "Tony's Brook" named probably from Anthony Oliff, one of the early settlers at the mountain, though now an insignificant stream, was early utilized for manufacturing purposes, and furnished sufficient power to run two or three mills, which gave this part of the township its first impetus. As early as 1695, according to the "Towne Records of Newark," Thomas Davis had "liberty to set up a saw mill." It has been supposed that this was the saw mill on a site near the pond above the old dilapidated vacant building formerly known as Wheeler's paper mill. Israel Crane, who, in 1804, in connection with Charles Kinsey, leased a mill seat at Paterson, and erected the second cotton mill there, was the first to make use of Toney's Brook for manufacturing purposes. About 1812-15 a company was organized under the name of the West Bloomfield Manufacturing Company. The prime mover in the enterprise was Israel Crane. Associated with him were Daniel P. Beach, E. P. Stiles, Michael Cockfair, Peter Doremus and others. Two large buildings were erected near the present Wheeler mill, where the manufacture of cotton and woolen goods was carried on for some years. The property subsequently passed into the hands of Israel Crane, and the factories were closed for some time.

In 1827 these mills were leased to Henry Wilde and Sons, who came from Yorkshire, Eng. He had long been engaged in the manufacture of broadcloths and other woolen goods in the old country, as had also his father and grandfather. He began the manufacture of plaid shawls which, it is said, were

WHEELER'S MILL.

the first ever made in this country. He made many changes and improvements in the machinery, utilizing the water power for spinning and carding the wool; the manufacture of the goods was all done on hand looms. Mr. Wilde employed about 100 hands, most of whom were brought from England. The manufactured goods were disposed of in the New York market, and Mr. Wilde was awarded a number of prizes by the American Institute Fair for the superior quality of his goods. Owing to the partial failure of the water power, which proved insufficient for the manufacture of heavy goods, they gave up the manufacture of these for goods of lighter weight, and engaged in the manufacture of white flannels of a high grade, said to be the best in the market. The firm became embarrassed during the panic of 1837, and the elder Wilde withdrew from the business in 1839.

John Wilde, of the New York firm of Wilde, Faulkner & Co., soon after occupied the premises and began the manufacture of calico prints, and disposed of their goods through Dennis Brigham & Co., who were subsequently obliged to take the business, owing to the failure of Wilde, Faulkner & Co. Dennis Brigham subsequently withdrew from his own firm and continued to carry on the print works until 1855.

The buildings remained unoccupied for some years, and in the interim the lower mill was burned. The remaining one was leased in 1856 by Grant J. Wheeler for the manufacture of paper and oakum, which was then done by hand. Associated with him were Jason Crane and James, the son of Israel Crane, under the firm name of Crane, Wheeler & Co. The business did not prove successful, and in 1857 the firm was obliged to go into liquidation. In 1858 Mr. Wheeler organized a new firm in connection with James C. Beach, under the name of J. G. Wheeler & Co., for the purpose of carrying on the manufacture of straw board. These goods were previously made by hand and dried in the sun. The new firm invented a process for making a continuous sheet of straw board, and, by means of steam rollers, drying it at the same time. They were the original inventors of this process, by which they were enabled to produce the goods in quantities in excess of the home market, and they worked up a large export trade. Through the increase of production it was soon discovered that the goods could be profitably used for other purposes, and thus the demand was largely increased, and a better class of goods produced. Under the old process the goods brought but $40 a ton, while under the new—even with the increased supply—the price advanced to $140 a ton. The wonderful success that followed induced competition, and although the process of manufacture as well as the machinery was covered by letters patent, a failure to patent one simple machine, and the discovery that a similar process had been used in France many years previous, led to prolonged and expensive litigation; and the price of goods fell from $140 to $50 a ton. Both Mr. Wheeler and Mr. Beach were men of great inventive genius, and but for the unfortunate oversight would have accumulated immense wealth. They made the material and constructed by hand the first paper car-wheel ever made in this country.

At the time they purchased the plant the waterfall of Toney's Brook was sufficient to furnish from 50 to 75 horse power, but the streams and rivulets from which it was supplied were diverted in their course, and the water supply cut off, so that the firm was obliged to resort to steam power in addition. A successful business was carried on until 1887. In the meantime the State Legislature having passed an act to prevent the pollution of the streams in East New Jersey, the successors of the old firm were indicted by the Board of Health and compelled to close the mill and remove their plant some miles distant to Waverly, N. J.

Referring to this stream and also what was known as Third River, Gordon (in 1830) says: "These streams are the source of wealth to the township, and have converted it almost wholly into a manufacturing village."

A few years ago, while excavating for the foundation of a steam-engine underneath Wheeler's mill, there was found, ten feet below the surface, a number of Indian relics, showing that the same locality had been used by the Indians for the construction of arrow heads, cooking utensils, and articles of stone for grinding corn, etc. Some forty years ago a number of valuable pearls were found near the source of Third River—known as Notch Brook—one of which, it is said, was sold to Tiffany & Co., and by that firm to Empress Eugenie for $2,000.

CONSTRUCTION OF NEWARK AND POMPTON TURNPIKE.—BUSINESS DEVELOPMENT.

Previous to 1800 the whole region of country comprising what was afterward Bloomfield township, was wholly devoted to agricultural purposes, and little or no business was transacted in this locality, the farmers relying principally on Newark for their supplies. The construction of the Newark and Pompton Turnpike, of which Israel Crane was the projector, wrought in the course of a few years a great change, and West Bloomfield became the centre of traffic, and at one time drew a large amount of trade from Paterson and beyond, and bid fair to rival that town in importance.

The Newark and Pompton Turnpike Company was incorporated February 24, 1806. The incorporators were John N. Cumming, John Dodd, Israel Crane, Noah Sayre, Isaac Mead, Robert Gould, and

Nathaniel Douglass; the commissioners, Andrew Wilson, Nathaniel Camp and Richard Edsal. Israel Crane was President of the Company. A part of the capital stock—four thousand dollars a mile—was made payable in work. The road was to cross the Passaic River, near Little Falls, and to pass through "the more convenient gap in the mountain near Cranetown." Starting from North Broad Street (near Belleville Avenue, Newark), it ran northwesterly direct to Bloomfield and Cranetown, thence over the First Mountain to Caldwell and Parsippany, crossing at Pine Brook, with branch from the west side of the mountain to Syngack; there were four toll gates, six miles apart—one near the Morris Canal, another at the top of the mountain, another at Pine Brook, the last at Syngack (near the upper Passaic). The road cut diagonally through several farms, and thus aroused a strong opposition on the part of some of the farmers, which was finally allayed.

The road was not a paying investment, and became largely indebted to Mr. Crane for repairs, etc., and finally passed into his possession. After his death it was sold by his heirs to the Essex Public Road Board; the Company still has, however, a nominal existence. Within a few years the road has been widened and graded, and now forms a beautiful drive through Bloomfield and Montclair, to the top of the mountain, thence to Caldwell, and is known as Bloomfield Avenue.

When the road was originally constructed Mr. Crane cut "the little turnpike"—the street past the present depot (now known as Spring Street)—from the turnpike to his store, and his business became very large and widely extended. He had a large quarry in Newark, where he employed a number of hands who obtained their supplies from this store. He also had a large cider mill and distillery, which before the days of temperance agitation were liberally patronized by the best class of people. A large peach production at one time was manufactured into brandy at the distillery, and the Jersey "peach brandy," became as famous as Jersey "applejack." The far famed Harrison, Canfield and Baldwin apples, which originated in this section, were shipped to every part of the country, and the cider made from these apples was said to be the best in the market. The Baldwins and Harrisons also did a thriving business in the manufacture of cider, and there was at one time upward of six thousand barrels a year of Newark cider produced, a large portion of which came from this locality.

The tannery of Smith & Doremus (Matthias Smith, father of Charles and Melancthon Smith, and Peter, the father of Joseph and Philip Doremus), south of the Presbyterian Church, soon after 1807 brought its hides from New York, its bark from over the mountain, and sold its leather to the boot and shoe manufacturers of Bloomfield and Orange. Peter Doremus also did an extensive business in dry goods and groceries, and being located at a convenient point on the turnpike, near the present store of his son Philip, caught a great deal of the farmers' trade before it reached other localities.

Gordon's Cyclopedia, published in 1832, gives the entire population of Bloomfield township, which then embraced an entire area of 14,000 acres, and included the present township of Belleville at 4,309. "In 1832 the township contained 500 taxables and 206 householders whose ratable estate did not exceed $30; 82 single men, 17 merchants, 6 grist mills, 2 cotton manufactories, 5 saw mills, 4 rolling mills for copper, 3 paper mills, 1 paint factory, 2 calico printing and bleaching works, one very extensive 40 ton vats, 3 woollen factories, and several very extensive shoe factories; 387 horses and mules, 862 neat cattle, above three years old. The township paid state tax $754.50, county $287.37, poor tax $1,200, road tax $1,200. The annual value of manufactured products probably exceeded $2,500,000."

Reference is also made to the villages of Bloomfield and West Bloomfield (designated as one village). "The chief part of the town lies upon the old road, but part of it on the turnpike. It contains about 1,600 inhabitants, above 250 dwellings, 2 hotels, an academy, boarding school, 4 large common schools, 12 stores, 1 Presbyterian church, 2 Methodist churches, (one in Bloomfield and one in West Bloomfield); a very extensive trade is carried on here in tanning, currying and shoemaking, and the following manufactories are considered annexed to the town—two woollen factories, 1 mahogany saw mill, 1 cotton mill, 1 rolling mill, 1 calico print works, 2 saw mills for ordinary work, 1 paper mill, 1 grist mill."

A thriving business was done here in the manufacture of fur and other hats—all hand made—and it is said that John Jacob Astor, of whom the skins were purchased, made occasional trips here to look after his interests. One of the largest manufactories in this line was carried on by Capt. Joseph Munn and Nathaniel Baldwin, under the firm name of Munn & Baldwin.

The introduction of machinery and the establishment of large manufactories in the East, which supplied the trade throughout the country, wrought a material change in West Bloomfield; it ceased to be a manufacturing centre, and became noted for its excellent boarding schools, and other educational advantages. A few years later parties from New York, who had sent their children here to be educated, were impressed with the healthfulness of the locality and the beauty of its surroundings, and began to make this a place of summer resort. It was not, however, until the opening of railroad communication with New York City, that business men were enabled to avail themselves of its many advantages as a place of permanent residence.

The history of railroads in the counties of Essex and Hudson is contemporaneous with the history of the introduction of these great highways of travel into the United States and almost parallel with the success of railroading in England. As early as 1812 Colonel John Stevens, of Hoboken, published a pamphlet urging the government to make experiments in railways traversed by steam carriages, and, if feasible, proposed the construction of such a railway from Albany to Lake Erie; and long before George Stephenson, of England, who in 1829 "demonstrated that the locomotive was competent, not only to move itself, but also to drag a heavy load," Stevens had demonstrated its practicability by constructing a circular railroad track around the town hall in Hoboken, where he ran his locomotive for some weeks to the delight of thousands who witnessed the experiment.

The first railroad enterprise started in New Jersey was that of the Camden and Amboy Railroad and Transportation Company, which was incorporated by the State Legislature on the 4th of February, 1830. [The road ran from Camden to Amboy.] At the same time the Delaware and Raritan Canal Company was incorporated, and in 1831 the two companies were consolidated. The Paterson and Hudson River Railroad was chartered in 1831, and subsequently became a part of the Erie Railroad. The New Jersey Railroad and Transportation Company was chartered by the State Legislature in 1832, having passed the Assembly by a vote of 39 to 5, after a bitter fight on the part of its opponent, the Camden and Amboy Railroad and Transportation Company.

NEWARK AND BLOOMFIELD RAILROAD COMPANY.

The people of Bloomfield and West Bloomfield had witnessed the effect of improved railroad communication with other suburban towns in New Jersey for many years which followed the substitution of the means of rapid transit over the old slow stage coach.

It was not, however, until 1854 that any actual steps were taken to open railroad communication between these points and New York. A few enterprising gentlemen of Bloomfield and West Bloomfield, after considering the feasibility of such an enterprise, obtained a charter from the Legislature for the organization of a company known as the Newark and Bloomfield Railroad Company.

The West Bloomfield incorporators were Zenas S. Crane, Grant J. Wheeler and William S. Morris; those from Bloomfield were Joseph A. Davis, Ira Dodd (who afterward became the Superintendent), David Oakes, Robert L. Cook, David Congar and Warren S. Baldwin.

The Company elected as its first Board of Directors William H. Harris, Grant J. Wheeler and Jared D. Harrison, of West Bloomfield; Joseph A. Davis, Ira Dodd, Wright F. Congar and Jason Crane, of Bloomfield. The Board organized by the election of Joseph A. Davis as President of the Company.

The comparatively small population and limited means of the inhabitants of Bloomfield Township, and the difference of opinion among them as to the best route and termination, made it very difficult to get the necessary subscriptions to the capital stock. Some favored the route to the Morris neighborhood, while others insisted that it should terminate at West Bloomfield. After repeated and unsuccessful efforts to secure sufficient funds to build the road, the New Jersey Railroad and Transportation Company encouraged the belief that they would give financial aid to the enterprise so that the road might be built. Two of the representatives of that road, Dr. John S. Darcy and John P. Jackson—recognized as two of the leading railroad men in the State of New Jersey—were elected members of the Board of Directors of the Newark and Bloomfield Railroad Company.

The design of that Company (The New Jersey Railroad and Transportation Company) was to reap the benefit of a condition in the contract which had been made with the Morris and Essex Railroad Company at the time of building the bridge over the Passaic and the connection with that railroad. This condition was that the New Jersey Railroad should have the right of way for the Newark and Bloomfield Railroad alongside of the track of the Morris and Essex Company as far as Roseville or East Orange, without expense, which privilege the New Jersey Railroad estimated to be worth at least One Hundred Thousand Dollars.

Having secured this position with the Newark and Bloomfield Railroad Company, they were not disposed to push the enterprise to completion, but rather to pursue a Fabian policy of delay. They suggested the advisability of interesting parties in Boonton and Paterson and other places, without avail. Finally, when the Bloomfield Directors became impatient at the delays, a survey was made by the engineers of the New Jersey Company, who placed the cost of building the road at from $175,000 to $225,000, and the only proposition which they considered feasible was that the subscription to the capital stock should be increased to at least $75,000, when the New Jersey Road would endorse the bonds of the new company to say $150,000, and thus secure the means for building the road.

The Board of Directors of the Newark and Bloomfield Road held several meetings, but made little or no progress. Finally, however, at a meeting of this Board, the representatives of the New Jersey Railroad and Transportation Company proposed that the Bloomfield Directors should be appointed a committee with power to secure the means for the construction of the road, and call a meeting of the full Board when that was secured. They evidently thought it impossible for them to obtain outside assistance. Complications had arisen between the New Jersey Railroad Company and the Morris and Essex Railroad Company in reference to their bridge contract, and the latter company felt very much aggrieved at the conduct of the New Jersey Company, and desired to relieve themselves, as far as possible, from the valuable privilege for right of way which they had given for the Newark and Bloomfield Railroad Company along their track.

The suggestion was made by their representatives to this committee that they would like to enter into negotiations with them for building the road. Thereupon a corps of their civil engineers was placed on the route from Roseville to West Bloomfield, and estimated the cost at $105,000, or about one-half the cost estimated by the engineers of the New Jersey Company. A written contract was then entered into between the Morris and Essex Railroad Company and the Committee of the Newark and Bloomfield Railroad Company, which provided that the Morris and Essex Company would subscribe $55,000 to the capital stock of the road, on condition that the Committee of the Newark and Bloomfield Road should increase their outside subscriptions from $40,000 to $50,000, the total sum according to estimates made ($105,000) to build the road. This agreement was made in writing and signed by the respective parties. A meeting of the full Board of Directors of the Newark and Bloomfield Railroad Company was then called and the committee reported the arrangements which they had made with the Morris and Essex Company. The New Jersey representatives were greatly surprised at the results, and suggested more favorable terms. But the agreement having been definitely settled, according to the authority previously given to that committee, there was no opportunity for any change. The representatives of the New Jersey Railroad Company in the Board, finding that their "occupation was gone," immediately resigned. These vacancies were filled by Messrs. Bassenger and Faitoute, representing the Morris and Essex Railroad Company.

The work of grading and constructing the road was begun in 1855, and completed to its present terminus in 1856. The $105,000 which was raised proved to be not only sufficient for grading and building the road, but left a balance sufficient to purchase a locomotive which was named the "Bloomfield." The trains commenced running to Bloomfield in the early part of the year 1856; the first trains were run to Montclair during the month of June of that year. The equipments consisted of one locomotive, two passenger cars, and one baggage car, which ran regularly between West Bloomfield and Newark, connecting with the Morris and Essex Railroad for New York. These equipments at the time were amply sufficient to accommodate travel.

There was a deficit of $330 at the end of the first seven months. When first opened the same person sold the tickets at West Bloomfield station and acted as brakeman on the railroad.

Although at first there was a small deficit, yet the Company did a profitable business, and $7,000 tickets were sold during the first year; at the end of the second year a small dividend was declared by the Company to its stockholders. The Morris and Essex Railroad Company, having a majority of the stock,

THE OLD D., L. & W. R. R. STATION.

proceeded to elect a majority of the Board of Directors, and so manipulated the expenses of the road that it practially absorbed all the income, and proposed in exchange Morris and Essex stock for the stock of The Newark and Bloomfield Railroad Company, which the individual stockholders accepted, so that the road finally fell into the hands of the Morris and Essex Railroad Company. When the lease was made by that Company to the Delaware, Lackawanna and Western Company it included the Bloomfield branch, which has since been operated by that Company.

Continuous trains from Montclair to New York were not run for several years after the road was built, and not until the Montclair and Greenwood Lake Railroad Company was built. It is believed by persons who are familiar with railroad enterprises that no piece of road of the same cost in this country produces a larger net revenue than is received by the Delaware, Lackawanna and Western from the original Bloomfield branch.

THE NEW SETTLEMENT—"QUI TRANSTULET SUSTINET."

With the opening of railroad communication, the influx of New York and other business men began. Among the earliest settlers were William H. Harris, Grant J. Wheeler, Frederick H. Harris, Dr. J. J. H. Love, Julius H. Pratt, Henry A. Chittenden, Stephen Parkhurst, Henry Nason, William B. Bradbury, Robert Hening, N. O. Pillsbury, Joseph B. Beadle, Samuel Wilde, Dr. H. H. Lloyd, and others.

These men formed the nucleus of the new settlement. They bought their little farms at $150 to $300 an acre, hoping to enjoy the quiet repose of a delightful and healthy country village, little dreaming of the great developments that awaited them. Could they have foreseen the changes that a few years would bring—that their farm lands would be worth as much per running foot as they paid per acre, they would have mortgaged all their possessions if necessary, and doubled their purchases. They builded better than they knew, and soon their plowshares were beaten into (rail) road shares, their pruning hooks into silver hooks; the beautiful country villas took the place of the old farm houses; the familiar well sweep disappeared, and the song of the "Old oaken bucket which hung in the well" was heard no more; the apostles of temperance laid an embargo on Jersey cider and Jersey "applejack"; the mills were closed, the "grinders ceased because they were few," and the piercing shriek of the locomotive reminded the farmer that the husking bees as well as the honey bees must take their departure, for the "city folks" had come to stay.

The newcomers brought with them new ideas not at all in harmony with the old. For nearly half a century this locality had been known as West Bloomfield, and the old people held the name in the greatest veneration because it was associated with General Bloomfield, who gave the original township its name. The new settlers, however, found it very inconvenient. Their letters frequently miscarried, and either stopped at Bloomfield or went to West Bloomfield in New York State. Strangers visiting the village, thinking it a part of Bloomfield, would purchase their tickets and check their baggage thereto. A public meeting was held in 1860, and a change in the name decided upon. Several names were suggested, but among those which received most favor were Eagleton, Hillside, and Claremont. On referring to the map of the United States it was found there were several places of the name of Claremont; the difficulty was solved however by Mr. Julius H. Pratt, who suggested reversing the name and calling it Montclair. This suggestion was favorably received, but when the matter was put to vote it was found that Eagleton had 73, Montclair 57, and Hillside 7 votes. There was nothing legally binding in this vote and the majority of the property holders were in favor of adopting the name of Montclair. They first induced the railroad managers to change the name of their station. A petition signed by a large number of the property holders was put in circulation by Mr. Robert M. Hening, and through his personal influence with Mr. Casson, the Assistant Postmaster General, the change in name of the post-office was adopted in 1860, the name of West Bloomfield being dropped and that of Montclair substituted.

The name of Montclair is unique. At the time this name was selected it was nowhere to be found on the map of the United States, and it had even been obliterated from the map of Europe. During the Franco-Prussian war a correspondent of the *New York Herald* discovered on the banks of the Rhine, in Germany, the ruins of an old castle formerly known as Montclair, which was destroyed during the crusades by Theodore Baldwin, the founder of the Baldwin family. That his descendants should have been one of the founders of this locality which has perpetuated the name is a noteworthy fact.

Chapter IX.

MONTCLAIR IN THE WAR OF THE REBELLION.

THE infant village of 1860 having received its baptismal name, and cast off its swaddling clothes, was looking forward to a bright and glorious future; when suddenly the tocsin sounded the call "*to arms!*" and men were brought face to face with the stern realities of war. All thoughts of village improvements and the speedy accumulation of wealth were for a time forgotten;—the spirit of '76 was again aroused;—the fires of patriotism re-enkindled; and the descendants of the brave men of '76 rallied around the flag to preserve inviolate the Union established by their forefathers.

The first man in Montclair—if not the first man in the State of New Jersey—to respond to President Lincoln's call for 75,000 volunteers to put down the rebellion, was Edward Moran. On the 19th of April, 1861, when the famous New York Seventh Regiment passed through Newark on their way to Washington, Moran boarded the train, and, being acquainted with one of the officers, offered his services, which were accepted. He was soon after provided with a uniform and served through the first campaign. He afterward enlisted in the U. S. Navy, and served until the close of the war.

Public meetings were held in Montclair, and the people became fully aroused to the dangers which threatened the Union. There was no lack of volunteers, and this little village furnished its full quota of troops. Some of its most promising young men entered the ranks of the Union army, bade farewell to their friends, and, with the benediction of their beloved pastor, took their departure—some of whom never returned.

An invasion of the North was frequently threatened during the war, and local military organizations sprung up in almost every town and village throughout the country, many of which rendered efficient service in cases of emergency. A company of "Mounted Wide Awakes" was organized in Montclair, with Julius H. Pratt as Captain, S. E. Hayes, First Lieutenant, and William J. Harris, Second Lieutenant. The commander of this company had seen service among the "Forty-Niners" in California, in the days when men used a Bowie knife as a tooth pick, and a six shooter as a plaything, and had the "emergency" arisen there is little doubt but that the "Wide Awakes" would have given a good account of themselves.

The citizens of Montclair did their full share in providing means to carry on the war, and they responded heartily to every appeal in behalf of the sick and wounded on the battlefield.

On the evening of August 25, 1862, a few of the leading citizens met together to pay their respects to Captain Frederick H. Harris, who had organized a company of the 13th Regiment N. J. Vols., and was about to depart for the front. On behalf of his fellow citizens Mr. Julius H. Pratt presented Capt. Harris with an elegant sword, and, after alluding to the demands of our country upon its young men, complimented the recipient on the alacrity with which he had responded, and on the indomitable energy and perseverance with which he had enrolled his company.

Mr. Pratt "presented the sword—*pointed*, that it might pierce the heart of the rebellion— *sharp*, that it might cleave the traitor's brow—*polished*, that it might reflect the *light* of liberty shining in the constitution—the *fires* of patriotism burning in his own soul—the lightning of Heaven's retribution descending on poor misguided rebels. The sword once drawn, it should never return to its scabbard until victory had been won and a peace conquered."

Capt. Harris responded in a few appropriate remarks. His friends crowded around him to say farewell—to bid adieu; they sung the song of the "Star Spangled Banner," and then he and they received the parting benediction by Rev. A. Brundage.

Among those who enlisted for three years in Company B, 7th Regiment N. J. Vols., were John H. Jacobus, Stephen P. Williams, Albert Woodruff (died of disease), John Dickinson (killed), Henry B. Ball (killed).

For three years in the 13th Regiment N. J. Vols., Robert Madison, William J. Madison, John B. Munn, James Taylor, John Webster, James Kane, David McNamara.

The following persons enlisted in the Twenty-sixth Regiment for nine months' service: First Lieut., William R. Taylor; Corporals William Egberton, James H. Williams, John M. Corby, and Edwin F. Dodd; Privates: Peter Arnold, Alfred T. H. Church, John Collins, Henry A. Corby, William H. Corby, James B. Crane, Edwin Dodd, Horace Dodd, Henry Glan, Cornelius Delhagen, Monroe Harrison, John H. Harrison, Richard Jacobus, Charles Johnson, Charles Leist, Eliot W. Little, John D. Penn, Peter King, Joseph W. Penn, George W. Post, William A. Riker, Mortimer Whitehead, Thomas Somerville, John Speller, George Ungeman, John E. Van Gieson, John M. Wheeler, Albert E. Munn, John J. Reese, Joseph W. Nason.

Joseph W. Nason enlisted at the age of eighteen in the Twenty-sixth N. J. Volunteers, and after the expiration of his nine months' service, was promoted to the rank of First Lieutenant and was assigned to the Thirty-ninth Regt. N. J. Vols. At the time of his enlistment he gave his bounty of $100 to be divided among ten men, who had the same amount as himself; he found it difficult to make up the quota and offered this as an extra inducement. He was killed on April 2, while leading a "forlorn hope" during the last day's fight in front of Petersburg. He lived but a few hours after being shot, and was buried within the enemy's lines; was carefully wrapped in his two blankets, his name pinned on the inside one, also a bottle inside, enclosing his name; and a head-board was placed at his grave, with his initials cut upon it. His parents endeavored to ascertain the names of those who so tenderly cared for their son in his last hours, but without success.

Nicholas Beadle was killed at the battle of Williamsburg. James Taylor at the battle of Antietam; John M. Wheeler at the battle of Fredericksburg, and John B. Munn at the battle of Chancellorsville; Charles Little died from disease in front of Fredericksburg.

Frederick H. Harris entered the service as Captain of Company E. 13th Regt. N. J. Vols., Aug., 1862, promoted to the rank of Major, to that of Lieut. Col., March 26th, 1865, and returned home at the close of the war in 1865. He had command of a brigade during his service, and was twice brevetted by the President of the United States; once for "gallant and meritorious service in Georgia and the Carolinas," and once for gallant service in the battle of Bentonville, N. C.

Dr. John J. H. Love was appointed volunteer surgeon by Governor Olden, of New Jersey, in April, 1862. He was engaged in a thirty days' service after the battle of Williamsburg, on May 5th, in the transportation and care of the wounded, was commissioned surgeon in the Thirteenth Regiment, N. J. Vols., on July 19th, and in August was mustered into the United States service. He was made surgeon-in-chief of a brigade in March, 1863, and in August was made surgeon-in-chief of a division, Twelfth Army Corps, in the Army of the Potomac. He served with distinction in this position, and returned home with the rank of lieutenant-colonel.

Chapter X.

AN ACT CREATING THE TOWNSHIP OF MONTCLAIR.—An Act to set off from the Township of Bloomfield in the County of Essex, a new township to be called the

TOWNSHIP OF MONTCLAIR

BOUNDARIES. "That all that portion of the township of Bloomfield, known as the second election district of said township, and lying west of a line running through as follows: Beginning at a point in the centre of the stone arch bridge over the stream crossing the road west of and near to the residence of Henry Stucky, on the Orange line, thence from said starting point in a straight line about north thirty-one degrees five minutes east to a point in the Passaic County line, which point is five hundred feet west on said county line, from the centre of the road running in front of the residence of Cornelius Van Houten, shall be and hereby is set off from the township of Bloomfield, in the County of Essex, and made a separate township, to be known as the township of Montclair."

The Act provided "That Robert M. Hening, Grant J. Wheeler, and Philip Doremus shall be and hereby are appointed commissioners on the part of said township of Montclair, to meet with three other commissioners on the part of said township of Bloomfield, previous to the fourth Tuesday in April, eighteen hundred and sixty-eight; that said meeting of said commissioners shall take place at the post office in Bloomfield, in said township of Bloomfield, at ten o'clock in the forenoon of the fourth Tuesday in April, eighteen hundred and sixty-eight; that the said commissioners shall then and there proceed by writing, signed by a majority of those present, to allot and divide between the said townships all property and money on hand or due, in proportion to the taxable property and ratables as taxed by the assessor, at the last assessment, and to ascertain the just proportion of debts, if there should be, to be paid by the inhabitants of the township of Montclair; and the decision of those present shall be final and conclusive, and the said commissioners, or a majority of them, shall and may sell and execute a deed of the township almshouse farm, which deed shall be deemed and taken to convey a good and sufficient title thereto; and said township of Montclair shall pay its proportion of the existing debt of the township of Bloomfield, at the time or times when payment, either principal or interest thereon, shall become due and payable, provided that it shall and may be lawful to adjourn the said meeting to such time or times, and place or places as a majority of those assembled as aforesaid may think proper."

The township is four and one-sixth miles in length on the western mountain crest, four and a half miles on the eastern ridge of Bloomfield, and has an average breadth of one and one-sixth miles.

The township of Verona lies west of the mountain summit, Acquackanonck lies on the north, Bloomfield on the east and Orange on the south. The village of Upper Montclair formerly known as Speertown, is divided from Montclair by Wachung Avenue but is embraced in the township of Montclair.

All the present territory of Montclair was included within the colony or "town" of Newark for one hundred and forty-six years, until the erection of the township of Bloomfield in 1812. It included all the northern end of the colony, and comprised about two-fifths of its territory. For twenty-seven years Bloomfield extended from the ridge of the mountain to the Passaic, until Belleville was formed in 1839.

The erection of Montclair as a separate township was occasioned by the refusal of the citizens of Bloomfield proper to consent to the bonding of their portion of the township of Bloomfield (of which the village of Montclair formed a part) for the purpose of constructing the Montclair Railway.

The organization of the Montclair Railway Company was the result of the inadequate facilities

A VIEW OF MONTCLAIR FROM THE MOUNTAIN.

afforded by the Morris & Essex R.R. Company to the people—more especially to the commuters—of Montclair. They were often delayed from ten to fifteen minutes at Newark, while en route to New York City, owing to the failure of the trains on the branch to connect with the main line. Owing to this change at Newark, the running time between Montclair and New York was one hour and twenty minutes.

The building of a railway at a cost of $4,000,000, the chief object of which was to connect a country village of 2,000 inhabitants with the city of New York was, at the time, as it would be now, regarded as a pure chimera. The very absurdity of the scheme enabled its friends to obtain a charter with but little opposition from a Legislature which might and would have demanded thousands of dollars from the natural enemies of such a project, had they dreamed of the future forces that it would call into life.

The project originated with Julius H. Pratt in 1866, and was the result of a sudden impulse, while waiting in the depot at Newark the usual slow connection of the train for New York. He suggested to those who were with him—viz., Samuel Wilde, Joseph B. Beadle, and Albert Pearce, that they obtain a new railroad charter. It was hoped that the mere possession of such a charter would compel the Morris and Essex Railway Company to afford better accommodations to the people of Montclair who had been vainly demanding through trains to New York. Mr. Henry C. Spalding, a man of large experience in railroad and legislative affairs, was present at the time, and his advice and counsel were solicited. He informed these gentlemen that it would cost $500 to get it through the Legislature. Each of the above named gentlemen agreed to subscribe their pro rata of the amount, and were named as incorporators. Further demands, to the extent of $5,000, were made upon them and Messrs. Wilde, Beadle and Pearce, rather than incur further responsibility, dropped out, and Mr. Pratt paid back to them the money they had invested. Mr. Spalding continued his interest and was active in promoting the enterprise. The act of the Legislature granting the charter, authorized the bonding of the towns along the line of the road, by and with the consent of two-thirds of the property holders in each township through which the road was to pass. Mr. Pratt reorganized the Montclair Railway Company, and soon after the charter was obtained learned that the New York and Oswego Midland Railway Company were looking for a route through New Jersey, and at once opened negotiations with them. Under his agreement with them his company was to construct the road from Jersey City to the State line at Greenwood Lake. The officers of the New York and Oswego Midland Company agreed to build their road from Middletown, Orange County, N. Y., to connect with the Montclair road at the Sate Line. They also agreed to indorse and guarantee all the bonds that might be issued to construct the Montclair Railway. The Montclair Railway Company carried out its contract and commenced operating the road in January, 1873. Mr. Pratt became President of the Company at its organization and continued to hold that office until the railway was completed and leased to the New York and Oswego Midland Company, which Company from that date—January, 7, 1873—assumed possession and control.

The misfortunes of the Midland Company were shared by its New Jersey protégé, and both became insolvent during the financial blizzard of '73.

The bonding of the township of Montclair was brought about by the action of the property owners, represented by Robert M. Hening, Hiram B. Littell, and Jared E. Harrison, who were appointed by the Court as Commissioners under the bonding act.

In a statement made to the township authorities in 1883, by Mr. Julius H. Pratt, regarding the bonding of Montclair township, he says:

"Under the original administration the interest of the Township Bonds had been promptly provided for by the Montclair Railway Company, but the failure of the lessee of the railway deprived the township of the means with which to pay interest thereafter, except by regular taxation of township property, and it seems that no township committee had the courage to order such taxation. The first default occurred in May, 1873, and consequently the original issue—$200,000, and ten years' interest—makes the total debt at present about $350,000.

"Can the township afford to pay this claim, and is it equitable? To understand this question we must refer back to the condition of our township just prior to the building of the new railroad. An outraged feeling on account of the abuses to which we were subjected by the insolent tyranny of the M. & E. Railroad Company was universally prevalent, and when the question of lending the credit of the township in aid of a new line was presented, more than two-thirds in amount of the taxpayers signed their written consent, and acknowledged it before Commissioners with the same solemn formality that they would a mortgage deed. Allowing for non-resident owners, trustees and others legally incapable of signing, but in fact favorable to the movement, it may be fairly assumed that not one-fourth of the property owners made any opposition to the issue of the bonds, while a large majority were enthusiastically in favor of it. This consent was given with the full knowledge that, from the time of signing, the claim became a lien on their property by their voluntary act and deed. The railroad company, in accepting the bonds, became morally bound to use the proceeds in the construction of the road within the township, and manifested their good faith by spending their own money greatly in advance of any avails obtained from the bonds.

The carrying out of this bargain cost the railroad company more than $1,000,000, and probably caused its subsequent bankruptcy. This statement may seem to require explanation, and I give it briefly thus:

"The Company had acquired under its charter and supplements the option to build its road by way of Paterson instead of Montclair on substantially the route afterward adopted for the main line of the D. L. & W., a line which would have cost at least $1,000,000 less than the Montclair route. The Company had, in consequence of the want of financial support from Bloomfield and Montclair, bought considerable right of way at Rutherford Park, and had a deed of right of way given by the Paterson Society of Useful Manufactures through more than one-half the distance across the city of Paterson, and an arrangement with the city authorities for the use of an avenue through the remaining distance for a trifling cost, by which the freight traffic of all the great locomotive works within a few rods of the line would have been at once secured. Rutherford Park had given consent to the issue of $200,000 of bonds in aid of the road on that line.

"The Montclair route involved the Kearney cut, costing $500,000, the expensive right of way through Newark, Bloomfield and Montclair, and continuous deep excavations across the ridges from the Passaic river westerly, making a difference in cost between the two routes of not less than $1,000,000. The acceptance of proffered hospitality is often expensive, and in this case was disastrous to the railroad company; for the road could have been built on the Paterson route at least one year sooner, and would have been in operation, and its securities marketed, before the financial crisis of '73, and would have been self-supporting from the start.

"It is certain that the road would not have been built through Montclair except for the issue of the bonds. No one connected with the railroad company employed either influence or effort to secure the taxpayers' consent; it was obtained by Commissioners appointed by the Court at the solicitation of many respectable freeholders of the township, and the entire movement was carried through by the influence of representative men of wealth and high standing in the community.

"What benefits did the township secure in consequence of the construction of the railroad? This question may be concisely answered thus: The value of its real estate was immediately and permanently increased at least $2,500,000, and the annual saving to our citizens has been at least $100,000 every year since the road was built. I have a statement carefully prepared with the aid of our real estate dealers, showing the prices of fourteen pieces of property in Montclair (about 500 acres) sold just prior to the locating of the road, also the prices at which the same pieces of property were resold just after the road became a fixed fact. The former prices range from $150.00 to $1,000 per acre; the latter from $1,000 to $3,500; the average profit on the transactions being over $1,100 per acre; and the property was fairly distributed over the township.

"Taking these prices as a criterion, the entire 4,500 acres in the township were enhanced in value *about five millions of dollars*. This startling conclusion will be better understood by noticing the fact that without the railroad two-thirds of the land in the township would have continued to this day purely agricultural in character, with only one railroad station near the south end, while now we have five stations, some one of which is in proximity to every acre of land in the township.

"Let us be moderate in our estimate, allowing something for subsequent shrinkage, and discount fifty per cent., then we have $2,500,000 as the increase of value in consequence of the construction of the new railroad.

"What has been the *annual saving* to our people? I show it approximately thus:

300 commutations formerly $13 per month; now $6.50—total	$19,500
15,000 tons of coal, $1 per ton	15,000
Other freight, say	10,000
Time of trips reduced twenty-five minutes each way for 500 passengers whose time is worth $3 per day	37,500
Profit in local trade from increased population, estimated	20,000
Total	$102,000

"Add the fact that every rod of land for right of way was bought and paid for, and generally at prospective prices, and another fact that not more than two men in the township of Montclair had invested a dollar in the original construction of the railroad which has benefited this community so largely, while non-resident investors to the extent of $3,000,000 lost it all, and you have facts sufficient to decide the question of equity involved in the issue of the Montclair Bonds."

Subsequent events show that Mr. Pratt's estimate of the accrued benefit to the property holders were altogether too low; and a comparison of the value of property in 1883 with that of ten years later, will convince any reasonable man that the construction of the Montclair Railway, with all its "concomitant evils" has indeed proved a "blessing in disguise."

The bonds of $200,000 issued by the new township extended over a period of twenty years, bearing interest at seven per cent., the principal maturing in sums of $10,000 at stated periods, the first of these falling due five years from the date of issue. Suit was commenced by the holders of the defaulted bonds, which was contested by the township, the defence being that the act authorizing the issue was unconstitutional—that the township of Montclair did not comply with the requirements of the State Constitution which requires that the purpose of the act shall be distinctly stated in the title—this having been omitted in the act. The defendants also claimed that the new assessor was not legally qualified to give the certificate by virtue of which the bonds were issued.

The Courts in deciding the matter held that inasmuch as the township of Montclair had permitted the bonds to go out it was therefore legally responsible. The case was continued for a number of years, the best legal talent being employed on both sides, and appeal having been made to the Supreme Court, the latter rendered decision in favor of the bondholders March 5, 1883.

The property holders of Montclair were appalled at the condition of affairs which now confronted them, the debt being virtually a lien on every man's property. The question of electing town officers was already under consideration. Three members of the Township Committee were practically forced upon the ticket. Messrs. Thomas Russell, Chairman, Stephen W. Carey, Chairman of the Finance Committee, and George P. Farmer had repeatedly declined to accept the nomination, but realizing the importance of the matter, their own wishes were ignored, and they were duly elected.

How to secure control of the bonds ($200,000 of which had not yet matured, and would bear interest at the rate of seven per cent. per annum until maturity), and the funding of the indebtedness at a lower rate of interest, were the problems with which these men had to deal. They immediately consulted with a few experienced citizens and obtained promises of co-operation.

When it is understood that the holders of these bonds had held them during many years of litigation and consequent uncertainty as to their payment, and that they were now reinforced by a decision of the highest legal tribunal of the country, it was hardly to be expected that any considerable discount could be obtained. It is said that some parties had taken them in payment of debt, and during the period of uncertainty had offered to part with them at a considerable discount.

Among the obstacles to be overcome was the refusal of individual firms or corporations, within the State or out of it, to accept the bonds as collateral for any advances except as they were additionally secured by the personal guarantee of entirely responsible men. This made it necessary for public-spirited citizens to raise upon their individual guaranty the entire amount needed to take up the bonds as fast as they could be secured. This they did, and placed at the disposal of the town not only their time, but their private fortunes as well. Previous to any arrangement for funding the new bonds, and at a time when very little encouragement had been received in reply to the applications they had made for a new loan, the actual amount jointly assumed by Messrs. Russell and Carey was $195,796.95.

Of course they hoped to effect a negotiation, but at this time little headway had been made.

The bonds were purchased, with the exception, perhaps, of a dozen or twenty, from those who had held them for years, and it was difficult to locate them; it was finally ascertained that but four bonds of the two hundred were owned within the township. In negotiations for a portion of the bonds, efficient aid was rendered by Mr. David F. Merritt. The committee made no effort to seek out these bondholders, but waited patiently, and resorted to means to resist payment of the full value, that, as private individuals, they would hardly have felt justified in doing. This was no hardship to the majority of the bondholders, as many of them are said to have obtained the bonds at a large discount.

The committee were as industrious in getting the new loan funded at a low rate of interest as they were in purchasing the old bonds; and as a result of their efforts the Mutual Benefit Life Insurance Company of Newark took the entire new issue of $335,000, running through a period of thirty-five years, and divided in series of $5,000, $10,000, and $15,000, bearing interest at five per cent. per annum; the last one, of $15,000, maturing in 1918; thus the entire debt of $400,000 cost the town not exceeding $335,000. Only the actual outlay for small legal expenses were incurred by the committee. The following estimate shows the result of their efforts:

Amount saved on purchase of bonds.	$65,000 00
Difference between 5 per cent. on $335,000 and 6 per cent. on $400,000—$7,250 per annum for say twenty-two years, average time the new bonds are to run.	159,500 00
Saving of interest in addition to the above on $90,000 of old bonds not yet matured, which were entitled to interest at 7 per cent. until maturity.	4,500 00
	$229,000 00

Several attempts were made by the citizens of Montclair to give substantial evidence of their appreciation of the work of this Township Committee, but the gentlemen composing it have modestly declined the offer, and the above record, which time cannot efface, is the only recognition of the eminent services rendered by them to restore the impaired credit of the township, and avert the impending financial disaster which threatened many of its citizens, and in this connection favorable reference should be made to Messrs. A. Eben Van Gieson and Warren S. Taylor, the other members of the Committee, who, with Mr. William L. Ludlam, the Town Clerk, rendered efficient aid.

The gentlemen who carried this financial load for the town until negotiations and the new issue of bonds were completed were Thomas Russell, Stephen W. Carey, George P. Farmer, W. L. Bull, Abraham Bussing, and H. A. Dike; Mr. John R. Livermore also offered aid in the matter, if needed.

TOWN OFFICERS FROM 1868 to 1893.

Judges of Election. James Crane, 1868 to 1875 inclusive; Nehemiah O. Pillsbury, 1873 to 1878 inclusive; James G. Crane, 1879 to 1883 inclusive; 1884, James Crane and James Owen; 1885, the same; 1886, the same; 1887, James Crane and George R. Milligan; 1888. Edward M. Benham and Edward Madison; 1889, Edward Madison, William M. Taylor and W. R. Green ; 1890, Edward Madison, George T. Bunten and John Goman.

From 1890 the system of election by the people was abolished and Judges of Election appointed by the County Committee, under the new ballot law of 1890.

Inspectors of Election.—1877, Jarvis G. Crane, George W. Taylor, James Crane, A. P. Kerr; 1878, Jacob B. McChesney, Jarvis G. Crane, James Crane, Francis Marion ; 1879, Jacob B. McChesney, F. A. Wheeler, James Crane, Francis Marion; 1880-1881, J. B. McChesney, F. A. Wheeler, Edgar T. Gould, Francis A. Marion ; 1882-3, J. B. McChesney, F. A. Wheeler, James C. Crane, Francis A. Marion ; 1884, Frank A. Wheeler, Frederick Richter, James C. Crane, Francis A. Marion ; 1885, F. A. Wheeler, J. B. McChesney, James C. Crane, Richard Sheridan ; 1886, F. A. Wheeler, James T. Crane (two Democrats omitted from records); 1887, Cyrus C. Corby, John Kenney, James C. Crane, Richard Sheridan ; 1888, Cyrus C. Corby, John Kenney, James C. Crane, George Courter; 1889, Wm. L. Doremus, George Courter, James C. Crane, J. B. McChesney, Cyrus C. Corby, John Kenney ; 1890, Wm. L. Doremus, John N. Halsey, James C. Crane, John N. Finnerty, Cyrus C. Corby, Walter Courter.

Clerks of Election.—1877, Frank A. Wheeler, Edward Madison ; 1878, I. Seymour Crane, Chas. H. Corby ; 1879, I. Seymour Crane, Edward Madison ; 1880–2, John Goman, Edward Madison ; 1883, John Goman, R. E. Van Gieson ; 1884-5, John Goman, John Poole, Jr.; 1886, John Goman, R. E. Van Gieson ; 1887, Henry L. Yost, I. Seymour Crane ; 1888, Henry L. Yost, Abner Bartlett, Jr.; 1889, I. Newton Rudgers, Henry L. Yost, Aaron Shepard ; 1890, the same.

Under the new ballot law of 1890 the election of this office by the people was abolished.

Inspectors and Clerks of Election Under the New Law.—The Law of 1890 abolished the offices of Judge and Clerk of Election, and substituted instead four Inspectors and Clerks, two Republicans and two Democrats.

Inspectors, First District.—For 1890, William B. Jacobus, Edwin B. George, Philip Young, Vaughn Darress. For 1891-2, the same.

Clerks, First District.—For 1890, Frank W. Crane and Edwin B. Littell. For 1891-2, the name of Theodore Badgley was substituted for that of Frank W. Crane.

Inspectors, Second District.—For 1890, Wallis Louvirer, Thomas P. Meyer, William Sigler and Elijah Pierce. Same for 1891-2.

Clerks, Second District.—For 1890, C. Alexander Cook, Calvin Smith. For 1891-2, the name of Hiram Sigler was substituted for that of Alexander Cook.

Inspectors, Third District.—For 1890, William Jacobus, J. D. Huntington, J. C. Williams and J. W. Potter. For 1891-2, the appointments were the same with the exception of John Goman in place of J. D. Huntington, deceased.

Clerks, Third District.—For 1890, William N. Jacobus, John Goman. For 1891-2, the appointments are the same with the exception of John C. Kingsley in place of John Goman.

Assessor.—1868-9, Zenas S. Crane; 1870-3, A. E. Van Gieson; 1874-6, Wm. Jacobus; 1877, Edmund Williams; 1878, Wm. Jacobus; 1879, Andrus B. Howe; 1880-90, Robt. B. Harris; 1891, Charles C. Morris (elected for three years).

Collector.—1868-76, Edwin C. Fuller; 1877, Edwin J. Heustis; 1878-90, Edwin C. Fuller; 1891, Edwin C. Fuller (elected for three years).

Town Clerk.—1868-74, Charles P. Sandford; 1875, Geo. W. Poole; 1876, E. G. Heustis; 1877, Edward Madison; 1878-81, Geo. W. Pool; 1882, Edward Madison; 1883, Wm. L. Ludlam; 1884 and 1885, John Poole, Jr.; 1886, Ranford E. Van Gieson; 1887 to 1892, Henry L. Yost; 1893, Henry L. Yost (elected for three years).

Chosen Freeholders.—1868, Robt. M. Hening, Grant J. Wheeler; 1869, Amos Broadnax, Grant J. Wheeler; 1870, Wm. Sigler, Grant J. Wheeler; 1871-7, M. W. Smith, Grant J. Wheeler; 1878-83, M. W. Smith, Philip Doremus; 1884, Melancthon W. Smith, J. Wesley Van Gieson; 1885-6, J. Wesley Van Gieson, Jasper R. Rand; 1887 and 1888, J. Wesley Van Gieson, Melancthon W. Smith; 1889, J. Wesley Van Gieson (held for two years).

[By the law of 1890 *Chosen Freeholders* were elected at the annual election in the Assembly District for two years.] 1890, James Peck, elected for two years; owing to insufficient legislation he held over to the spring of 1893, when Thomas McGowan was elected from the XIth Assembly District.

Surveyors of Highways.—1868, Edgar T. Gould, Joseph H. Baldwin; 1869, Joseph H. Baldwin, Wm. A. Torrey; 1870-73, Edgar T. Gould, Chas. Smith; 1874-77, Aaron Sigler, Chas. Smith; 1878, Nathaniel Dodd, Aaron Sigler; 1879-83, Nathl. R. Dodd, Jos. H. Baldwin; 1884-88, William Tichnor, Aaron Sigler; 1889, William Tichnor, Aaron Garabrant; 1890-93, William Tichnor, Melvin Sigler.

Town Committee.—1868, Chas. B. Baldwin, Amos Broadnax, Jos. H. Baldwin, Jacob B. Brautigam, Robt. J. Dodge; 1869, Peter H. Van Riper, Amos Broadnax, Wm. B. Holmes, Wm. S. Morris, John J. H. Love; 1870, John J. H. Love, Thos. C. Van Riper, Nathan T. Porter, Daniel V. Harrison, Wm. Frame; 1871, Saml. Wilde, Jr., Thos. C. Van Riper, Nathan T. Porter, Daniel V. Harrison, Edmund Williams; 1872, John J. H. Love, Alfred Taylor, Aaron Sigler, Daniel V. Harrison, Edmund Williams; 1873, John H. Parsons, Alfred Taylor, Philip Doremus, Clark W. Mills, Edmund Williams; 1874, J. J. H. Love, Alfred Taylor, E. T. Gould, Wm. Tichnor, Thos. Levy; 1875, W. I. Adams, Jacob C. Brautigam, Edgar T. Gould, Thos. A. Levy, A. E. Van Gieson; 1876, John H. Parsons, Jos. Van Vleck, A. A. Sigler, F. W. Doremus, Edmund Williams; 1877, Jos. Van Vleck, A. A. Sigler, F. W. Doremus, John H. Parsons, Thos. H. Bouden; 1878, Jos. Van Vleck, A. A. Sigler, Reynier Van Gieson, Thos. Russell, Wm. H. Wilson; 1879, Jas. R. Thompson, Jas. B. Pierson, Thorndike Saunders, Thos.

H. Bouden, Warren S. Taylor; 1880-81, Thos. H. Bouden, Jasper R. Rand, Jas. B. Pierson, Warren S. Taylor, Henry Speer; 1881-2, Jas. B. Pierson, Geo. P. Farmer, Jasper R. Rand, Warren S. Taylor, A. Eben Van Gieson; 1883, S. W. Carey, Warren S. Taylor. Thos. Russell, A. Eben Van Gieson, Geo. P. Farmer; 1884 and 1885, Thomas Russell, Stephen W. Carey, Shepard Rowland, A. Eben Van Gieson, Warren S. Taylor; 1886, Thomas Russell, Stephen W. Carey, James Owen, A. Eben Van Gieson, Warren S. Taylor; 1887 and 1888, Stephen W. Carey, Thomas Russell, James Owen, A. Eben Van Gieson, Warren S. Taylor; 1889, John H. Wilson, George Inness, Jr., A. Eben Van Gieson, Isaac Denby, Warren S. Taylor; 1890, John H. Wilson, Isaac Denby, George Inness, Jr., Morgan W. Ayres, Warren S. Taylor; 1891, John H. Wilson, Wilson W. Underhill, Amzi A. Sigler, James B. Pier, Morgan W. Ayres; 1892, John H. Wilson, Wilson W. Underhill, I. Seymour Crane, James B. Pier, Morgan W. Ayres; 1893, John H. Wilson, I. Seymour Crane, Hugh Gallagher, Moses N. Baker, Decatur M. Sawyer.

Commissioners of Public Roads.—1872-73, Hiram B. Littell, Nathan T. Porter, Samuel Holmes, Thos. C. Van Riper, Jacob C. Brautigam; 1874, N. O. Pillsbury, Saml. Holmes, Jos. Van Vleck, A. A. Sigler; 1875, N. O. Pillsbury, J. Van Vleck, A. A. Sigler, Saml. Wilde, Abram Speer; 1876, A. E. Van Gieson, N. O. Pillsbury, Samuel Wilde, Samuel Holmes, Elmer G. Doolittle; 1877, A. E. Van Gieson, Saml. Wilde, E. G. Doolittle, Saml. Holmes, E. M. Harrison; 1878, A. E. Van Gieson, Saml. Wilde, E. G. Doolittle, E. M. Harrison, Wm. Tichenor; 1879-80, Saml. Wilde, Elmer G. Doolittle, Saml. Holmes, E. M. Harrison, A. E. Van Gieson; 1881, A. E. Van Gieson, Saml. Wilde, Geo. P. Farmer, Saml. Holmes, E. M. Harrison; 1882, Theron A. Doremus, Saml. Wilde, W. Irving Adams, Saml. Holmes, A. P. Haring; 1883-88, Theron A. Doremus, Saml. Wilde, Robt. M. Boyd, Saml. Holmes, E. M. Harrison; 1889, Theron A. Doremus, Edwin M. Harrison, George P. Farmer, Charles W. English, A. P. Haring (the latter could not serve, not being a freeholder), Amzi A. Sigler, appointed in place of A. P. Haring; 1890, George P. Fowler, Amzi A. Sigler, Samuel Holmes, Edwin M. Harrison, Charles W. English; 1891-2, Charles W. English, Edwin M. Harrison, William J. Soveral, William B. Holmes, Theron A. Doremus; 1893, Edward B. Crane, Edwin M. Harrison, William J. Soveral, William B. Holmes, Theron A. Doremus.

Commissioners of Appeal.—1868-69, Edward H. Merritt, Hiram B. Littell, Wm. S. Morris; 1870-71, Alfred T. Taylor, Nehemiah O. Pillsbury, Wm. S. Morris; 1872, Amzi A. Sigler, Nehemiah O. Pillsbury, Clark W. Mills; 1873, A. A. Sigler, N. O. Pillsbury, John J. H. Love; 1874, Peter H. Van Riper, Joseph Doremus, Samuel Wilde; 1875-93, Peter H. Van Riper, J. J. H. Love, Joseph Doremus.

Township Treasurer.—This office was created in 1892, and I. Seymour Crane was the first appointed Treasurer, and was reappointed in 1893.

Police Force.—Previous to 1889, the only township officer who exercised the functions of police was the regularly elected constable. Two regular policemen were appointed this year by the Township

ELM STREET.

Committee, viz.: William Dunlap and James McNarar. Others have since been added and there are now seven, including the Captain, William C. Niederhauser.

Overseer of the Poor.—1868-69, Nathaniel R. Dodd; 1870-73, W. Corby; 1874-88, Charles Smith; 1889, William R. Greene; 1890-91, Melancthon W. Smith; 1892, John Sanford; 1893, John Sanford (elected for three years); deceased September 18, 1893; vacancy was filled by the Township Committee appointing John Goman.

Justices of the Peace.—1868, Zenas S. Crane, William S. Morris, Amos Broadnax, Stephen R. Parkhurst; 1869, Nehemiah O. Pillsbury, Charles B. Morris; 1870, no choice; 1871, A. E. Van Gieson; 1872, Zenas S. Crane; 1873, Joseph Lux; 1874, J. Ogden Clark, A. E. Van Gieson; 1875, N. O. Pillsbury, Charles B. Morris; 1876, Zenas S. Crane, George Ennis; 1877, Alfred Taylor, A. E. Van Gieson, Z. S. Crane; 1878, A. E. Van Gieson; 1880, N. O. Pillsbury, Charles B. Morris, A. E. Van Gieson; 1881, Franklin W. Dorman; 1882, F. W. Dorman, James C. Crane, H. E. Clark; 1883, George R. Milligan, Abram Speer, Edward B. Crane; 1884, Abram Speer, Edward B. Crane; 1885, J. Ogden Clark, Henry E. Clark, N. O. Pillsbury, Charles B. Morris; 1886, incumbents held over; no election; 1888, George R. Milligan; 1889, incumbents held over; no election; 1890, Charles B. Morris, J. Ogden Clark, Henry E. Clark, Hugh Gallagher (the latter did not serve); 1891, Edward B. Crane, elected but did not serve; Thomas P. Meyer, Louis Lang; 1892, Aaron Garabrant, Thomas Harrop (the latter did not qualify); 1893, George R. Milligan, William Jones (the latter did not qualify).

Constables.—1868, Ira Crane, Geo. Speer, Edward H. Merritt, Abram Speer; 1869, W. Corby, Jared Van Gieson, George Bowman; 1870, W. Corby, John H. Hayden, James C. Crane; 1871, W. Corby, John H. Hayden, Edwin J. Bacron, Henry S. Rodman; 1872, W. Corby, Geo. Simonson, Edwin J. Bacron, Wm. Simonson; 1873, W. Corby, Geo. Ungemah, Edwin J. Bacron, James Kane; 1874, John M. Layland, Jos. Dunn, Geo. DeLong, Edwin J. Bacron; 1875, Edwin J. Bacron, Joseph Dunn, Stephen W. Tibbs, Oliver Levy; 1876, Edwin J. Bacron, Thos. Wiggins, Francis Concannon, Geo. Simonson; 1877, J. H. Jacobus, Geo. Ennis, E. C. Fuller, E. J. Bacron, Thos. Wiggins; 1878, Thos. J. Courter, Geo. Ennis, Geo. T. Banten, E. J. Bacron, Jas. E. Murphy; 1879, Geo. T. Banten, Geo. Ennis, E. J. Bacron, Geo. Dipley, J. C. Doremus, Jr.; 1880, Geo. T. Banten, Jas. T. Norman, J. C. Doremus, Wm. R. Green, Thos. Courter; 1881, Geo. T. Banten, J. C. Doremus, Isaac A. Dodd; 1882, Isaac A. Dodd; 1883, Geo. T. Banten; 1884, John P. Doremus; 1885, Thomas Wiggins, James Kane; 1886, George T. Banten, Wm. F. Allsworth, Jr.; 1887, John P. Doremus; 1888, James Kane, William Mulligan; 1889, Wm. F. Allsworth, Jr., John Bowman, Isaac Dodd; 1890, Isaac Dodd, George Green; 1891, James Kane, Charles J. Dickson; 1892, Wm. F. Allsworth, Jr., Peter Whiting, Henry Kane, Isaac A. Dodd, Cornelius Halstead; 1893, Isaac A. Dodd.

Township Engineer.—This office was created about 1884, and James Owen was appointed by the Township Committee, and has been reappointed every year, with the exception of 1890, when the office was held by F. W. Crane.

PRESENT TOWNSHIP GOVERNMENT.

Township Clerk, Henry L. Yost; *Assessor,* Charles B. Morris; *Collector of Taxes,* Edwin C. Fuller; *Township Counsel,* Alfred S. Badgley; *Civil Engineer,* James Owen; *Township Physician,* James S. Brown; *Overseer of the Poor,* John Sandford; *Health Inspector,* Dr. Richard P. Francis; *Commissioners of Appeals,* Peter H. Van Riper, John J. H. Love, Joseph Doremus; *Commissioners of Public Roads,* William J. Soverel, Theron A. Doremus, Edward B. Crane, Edward M. Harrison, William B. Holmes; *Justices of the Peace,* Charles B. Morris, Geo. R. Milligan, Lewis Lange, Thomas P. Meyer, Aaron Garrabrant; *Constables,* Isaac A. Dodd, James Kane, William Allsworth, Jr., Henry Kain, Cornelius Halstead; *Police Justice,* Thomas P. Meyer.

TOWNSHIP COMMITTEE.

Chairman, John H. Wilson; *Members,* Decatur M. Sawyer, Hugh Gallagher, Moses N. Baker, I. Seymour Crane; *Treasurer,* I. Seymour Crane; *Finance Committee,* Crane, Sawyer; *Law,* Sawyer,

Baker; *Roads*, Crane, Sawyer; *Poor*, Gallagher, Baker; *Sidewalks*, Gallagher, Sawyer; *Water*, Baker, Crane; *Fire Committee*, Crane, Gallagher; *Sewers*, Crane, Baker; *Auditing*, Sawyer.

BOARD OF HEALTH.

Composed of Township Committee, Health Physician, Inspector and Assessor. *Chairman*, John H. Wilson; *Secretary*, Chas. B. Morris. Meets first Monday evening of each month, at Township Committee rooms.

THE OLD TOWNSHIP FORM OF GOVERNMENT UNDER THE GENERAL LAWS SUPPLANTED BY THE NEW LAW OF 1888.

When the township of Montclair was set off from Bloomfield, in 1868, the form of government adopted was that provided by the general laws which had been in existence for many years, and while the population was small and the wants of the people were few, no objection was raised to it. As the population increased, however, and large amounts were being expended for public improvements, the old laws were found to be entirely inadequate to meet the growing demands. Complications arose which necessitated frequent litigation to determine the rights of individuals, and citizens of one part of the township enjoyed privileges of which others were denied.

At a meeting of representative citizens held in April, 1893, the subject of a change of government was introduced by Mr. John H. Wilson, Chairman of the Township Committee, and fully discussed, which resulted in the appointment of a non-partisan committee, consisting of the following-named gentlemen: John H. Parsons, Stephen W. Carey, John J. H. Love, John R. Livermore, Charles H. Johnson, Charles K. Wilmer and Andrus B. Howe, to consider the question and the advisability of a change. This committee held several conferences during the summer and fall of 1893, and as the result of their deliberations found the existing form of government inadequate, antiquated and unsatisfactory, and recommended the adoption of the law of 1888, known as the "Short Law."

The preliminary steps were taken to submit the matter to a vote of the people, and on February 24, 1894, an election was held, and by a vote of more than two to one the new charter was adopted, and, with the life of the present Township Committee the old form of government ends.

Among the advantages to be derived under the new charter are: First, in the matter of appropriations, which will henceforth be made by the governing body or council; Second, in the administration of public schools, all the school interests are consolidated and the management placed in the hands of a central Board of Education, thus giving every citizen in the township equal privileges in the matter of common and also of high school education, of which, under the old law, many were deprived through the division into school districts. The management of the affairs of the township will be lodged in a council made up of representatives from wards into which the town will be divided. It lodges in the council all the powers heretofore exercised by Commissioners elected or appointed by the Court for levying assessments, opening streets, improving and regulating thoroughfares, etc. It simplifies matters in the form of government. It is substantially a City Charter without the usual executive head.

One of the most important changes under the new law is that relating to excise. Under the old law the township had no voice in the granting of licenses to liquor dealers, that power being vested solely in the Court of Common Pleas, at Newark. A written application, signed by ten Freeholders, enabled the applicant to procure a license from the Court. Under the new law the power is vested in the Town Council to "regulate, license, or prohibit inns, taverns and restaurants," and the sale or transfer of spirituous liquors, and to fix and prescribe the terms and conditions upon which license shall be granted, and to provide for the annulling of licenses for violations of conditions.

POSTMASTERS AND POSTAL FACILITIES.

Previous to and for some time after the erection of Bloomfield as a separate township the residents of Cranetown were dependent on the Newark post office for their mail. When in later years a post office was established at Bloomfield, and in addition thereto a regular daily mail service between there and New York City, it was hailed with delight by the citizens throughout the township, as it brought them into more direct communication with each other and with the outside world. Gradually, however, as business increased in West Bloomfield, and it became an important manufacturing centre, the want of better postal facilities was felt, and in 1830 application was made for the establishment of an office at the west end of the township.

It was at this period, during the administration of President Jackson, that the cry was raised, "To the victor belongs the spoils"; but as the political sentiment of the people of Bloomfield, and more especially the locality of West Bloomfield, was overwhelmingly whig, an acceptable democrat could not be found to fill the position.

Nathaniel H. Baldwin, a well-known business man, although a whig in politics, received the first appointment as postmaster of West Bloomfield in 1830. He was a bachelor, and boarded at the tavern kept by Munn & Baldwin. The mail was so small at that time, that it required but little of his time, and the proprietors of the tavern were very willing to have the office kept in their place, as it would naturally increase their patronage. Mr. Baldwin proved a very acceptable postmaster, and held the position from 1830 to 1841, during the democratic administrations of Jackson, Martin Van Buren, and a part of the whig administration of President Harrison.

Calvin S. Baldwin (no relation of the former) was appointed in 1841, under the administration of Tyler, who succeeded Harrison, the latter having died in office. Mr. Baldwin transferred the office to his own building, on the north side of Bloomfield Avenue, west of what is now Fullerton Avenue. There being no democrat to dispute his title, he held the office until 1853, under the whig administration of John Tyler, the democratic administration of James K. Polk, the whig administrations of Taylor and Fillmore, including a part of the democratic administration of Franklin Pierce.

Amzi L. Ball, a democrat, succeeded Calvin S. Baldwin, but only held the position for a short time. He kept the office in Sandford's tailor's shop, which was then located on the south side of Old Road—now Church Street.

William Jacobus, a democrat, who had frequently assisted Ball in his work, was appointed in 1858, under the administration of James Buchanan, and two years later the name of the post office was changed from West Bloomfield to Montclair. The office was still a small one, and under the percentage system, which then prevailed, was worth only about $200 to $300 a year.

John C. Doremus, a republican, was the first one appointed under a republican administration, which began in 1861 with President Abraham Lincoln. He kept the office in his own store on the south side of Bloomfield Avenue, opposite the residence of Judge Zenas S. Crane. The business had increased to a considerable extent, and the office became for the first time a salaried one. He held the position longer than any of his predecessors—a period of sixteen years—1861 to 1878—and served under Presidents Lincoln, Johnson, and the two terms of General Grant.

Charles P. Sandford, republican, was appointed postmaster under the administration of President Rutherford B. Hayes in 1876, and held the position until 1878. The office was located at that time on the south side of Church Street, on the site now occupied by Dr. Love's office. The business continued to increase during his term, and the office was well managed.

William Jacobus received his second appointment as postmaster under the administration of President Cleveland, in the spring of 1886. There had been a large increase in the population, but the income of the office was only about $7,000 a year, and while the salary appeared to offer sufficient inducement for him to accept the position, he found that, after paying rent, clerk hire and other expenses, he had nothing left. He was handling at this time a large amount of mail matter, requiring a corresponding clerical force, and he observed several New York business men were in the habit of buying their stamps at the New York office, the latter receiving the benefit which should accrue to Montclair. He called attention to this fact, and finally induced most of these parties to purchase their stamps at the Montclair office. As a result the income soon increased to $10,000, and the next year to $13,000, and the last year of his administration the amount had reached $15,450. This large increase brought the office up to one of second class with a corresponding increase in the salary, while the running expenses were then borne by the government. It also entitled the township to a free delivery, and efforts were made to accomplish the desired end. The houses were all numbered, and the streets properly named, in accordance with the requirements specified by the government authorities, and on January 1, 1890, the system of free delivery was established.

George A. Van Gieson, republican, was appointed postmaster in 1890, under the administration of President Harrison. The office is now located in what is known as the Morris Building, on Bloomfield Avenue, near the junction of Glen Ridge Avenue. The office is fully equipped with everything necessary for a complete postal service, and is conducted in a thorough business-like manner, satisfactory to the people of Montclair. When he took the position the income of the office was $16,000, and it now amounts (1893) to $24,000, an increase of one-third in three years. This is due to a large extent to the increase in population, especially that of summer residents. With the increase of business there has been no increase in the clerical force, and the whole expenses of the office are about $12,000 per annum. Four footmen and two mounted men attend to all the deliveries.

Mr. Van Gieson is a descendant of one of the old Holland families, originally of Acquackanonk, who settled in the latter part of the present century in what was then known as Speertown, now Upper Montclair. He was born in Speertown, Aug. 30, 1851. He was educated in the public school, and was afterward clerk in the store of John C. Doremus, and was also a clerk with him in the post office. He was a clerk in the grocery business for five years, and then went to New York with the firm of Hines, Ketcham & Co., with whom he remained eleven years until his appointment as postmaster in 1890. He is courteous and obliging and well liked in the community.

FIRST PRESBYTERIAN CHURCH.

Chapter XI.

RELIGIOUS INTERESTS OF MONTCLAIR.

Congregationalism and Presbyterianism.—Erection of the Second Meeting-house, 1753, of the Mountain Society (Orange).—Organization of the Church at Wat-sessing, known as the "Third" Presbyterian Church in the Township of Newark; later as the First Presbyterian Church of Bloomfield. Laying of the Corner-stone, &c. Subscribers to the New Edifice.—Legacy of Nathaniel Crane for a Presbyterian Church at Cranetown or West Bloomfield.—The "First" Presbyterian Church of Montclair.—Organization of the Church, 1837. The First Place of Worship—the School Building.—List of Original Members.—List of Pastors.—Erection of Church Edifice.—Purchase of Organ.—Erection of Parsonage.—Statistics of Membership, &c.—Sketches of Rev. J. F. Halsey, Rev. J. A. Priest, Rev. Nelson Millard, D.D., Rev. J. Romeyn Berry, D.D., Rev. Wm. F. Junkin, D.D., LL.D.—Sunday School. Trinity Presbyterian Church.—Sunday School.—Rev. Orville Reed.—Grace Presbyterian Church. Sunday School. Methodist Episcopal Church.—Sunday School.—St. Luke's Episcopal Church.—The Church of the Immaculate Conception, R. C.—First Congregational Church of Christ.—Rev. Amory Howe Bradford, D.D.—Sunday School. Pilgrim Mission.—First Baptist Church. Rev. Wm. N. Hubbell.—Sunday School.—The Unitarian Society.—Young Men's Christian Association.—The Women's Christian Temperance Union. The Colored Population and Their Churches. Union Baptist Church, Colored. St. Mark's Methodist Episcopal Church, Colored.

HE old Presbyterian Church has for long years been a noted landmark in Montclair. Standing at the intersection of six streets, and looking, from its commanding position, down the principal avenue of the town, it arrests the attention of every visitor. The religious organization, of which its solid stone walls are a fitting symbol, represents today, as it always has done, the Pauline doctrines of grace and the Covenant Theology, which are the glory and strength of Presbyterianism.

The spiritual life of the Church was the earliest fountain of religious and moral influences in the community; and the healthful flow of its current is increasingly marked and strong. Bancroft, the historian, writing half a century ago, records, that "Scottish Presbyterians of virtue, education and courage, blending a love of popular liberty with religious enthusiasm, hurried to East New Jersey between the years 1682 and 1687 in such numbers as to give to the rising commonwealth a character which a century and a half have not effaced. Meeting on her soil with Puritans and Quakers, their combined faith, institutions and preferences have given life and color to the common mind." Divergence of views naturally marked the progress of religious movements among such sturdy adherents of varying polities.

Dr. Charles Hodge tells us; "that on the soil of New Jersey at large Presbyterianism has not invaded and supplanted Congregationalism. It was the earlier and predominant type of ecclesiastical order, and naturally absorbed and assimilated the Congregationalism that came in. This assimilation was not, however, without a struggle between the two systems, and, in a community like that of Newark, originally composed of Congregationalists only, the process of change was necessarily slow. When the second Pierson (son of Rev. Abraham Pierson) manifested some leanings toward the Presbyterian order, the displeasure of his people was excited, and troubles arose which resulted in his dismissal. Yet, on the 22d of October, 1719, Joseph Webb, in the line of his successors, was ordained and settled over the same flock by the Presbytery of Philadelphia, and the next year took a seat in the Synod with a ruling elder from his church."

The people of Newark at that time were substantially a unit in favor of Presbytery, and those of the Mountain were united in favor of the old Congregational basis:

Rev. Jedediah Buckingham, a native of Saybrook, Conn., was engaged as a supply for the Newark church during a part of 1716-17. The withdrawal of Mr. Buckingham from the Newark pulpit was nearly coincident with the fact that "in 1718 many of the inhabitants of the Mountain broke off and formed a new society." This was known for some years as the Mountain Society, and afterward as the Second Church in Newark—now the First Presbyterian Church in Orange.

The records of this church show that Cranetown was largely represented in its membership. The first on the list of those who were "rated" in the parish in 1759 to pay the minister's salary was Jedediah Crane.

An "a Compt of the money received on account of the pasanage house" shows the names of David Baldwin, Nathaniel Crane, Noah Crane and Azariah Crane.

Among the list of subscribers for the erection of the second Meeting-house, in 1753, the "tribes of Crane" included Nathaniel Senr., Nathaniel Jr., Caleb, William, Job, Garniel, Noah, Stephen, Lewis, Jedediah, Elihu, Ezekiel; their total subscriptions amounted to £56, 16, 6. The "tribes of Baldwin," twelve in number (same number of the Cranes), subscribed £43, 1, 1.

Among the "Members in Communion of the Mountain Society prior to 1756" were Stephen, William, Noah and Caleb Crane, and Lewis Crane and his wife.

In the record of baptisms from 1756 to 1762 are found the names of Nathaniel, son of Noah Crane, 1757, Charles, son of Lewis Crane, John, son of Eliakim Crane, Lois, daughter of Stephen Crane.

Of those who "Entered into Covenant" from 1776 to 1783 are the names of Abigail, wife of Job Crane, Rhoda, wife of Stephen Crane, Timothy, and Sarah his wife, Elizabeth Crane, Jonathan and Rachel Crane, Matthias and wife Elizabeth, Hannah, wife of Joseph Crane, and Joseph Crane.

In the record of baptisms from 1765 to 1784 are Mary, daughter of Elder (Noah) Crane, Lois, daughter of Stephen Crane, Amos, son of William, Josiah, son of Eliakim, Jeremiah, son of Stephen, Nehemiah, son of Elder Crane (Noah), Zenas, son of Samuel and Mary Crane, 1774, Abigail, daughter of Matthias and Elizabeth Crane, Lydia, dau. of Jonas, Stephen Bradford, son of Stephen Crane, 1779, Eleazer and Nathaniel, sons of Joseph Crane, Nancy, Thomas, Jeptha and Hannah, children of Aaron Crane.

There were representatives of the Baldwins, Williams, Munns, and other families connected with this church, who were residents of Cranetown, but as the same names appear among the Orange families it is difficult to locate them.

The incipient measures for the organization of a separate congregation and church in Bloomfield were taken early in the year 1794 by the members of the above-named churches resident in what was afterward the township of Bloomfield. The Presbytery of New York then extended over all Southern New York and East New Jersey, and the matter was carried up before that body, at their meeting in May of that year, for advice and action. The Presbytery favored the movement, and appointed a committee to confer with a committee from the churches of Newark and Orange in reference to the matter. The meeting of these joint committees was held on the 16th of June following, at the house of Mr. Joseph Davis, of Watsessing. A petition was signed by ninety-eight heads of families requesting to be formally organized into a distinct congregation and to take the name of the Third Presbyterian Church in the township of Newark. It was not, however, until four years after this that the church was regularly organized after the Presbyterian form of government, in June, 1798, by the Rev. Jedediah Chapman, then pastor of the First Church in Orange. Eighty-two members constituted it—fifty-nine of whom were from his own church and twenty-three from the First Church in Newark. The ruling Elders and Deacons chosen at the time of its organization were Simeon Baldwin, Ephraim Morris, Isaac Dodd, and Joseph Crane.

The *Sentinel of Freedom*, of December 7, 1796, contained the following notes:

"At a meeting of the Trustees of the Wardsesson Congregation, Oct. 26, 1796:

"Agreeably to a resolution of the Congregation, the Trustees, having met this day, do assume to themselves the name and title of *The Trustees of the Presbyterian Society of Bloomfield*.

"Extract from the minutes.

"ISAAC DODD, President."

The erection of a Meeting-house for this Congregation was begun in the spring of 1797. The corner-stone was laid with Masonic ceremonies May 8th, 1797, by Dr. McWhorter, a member of the Masonic Fraternity.

The *Sentinel* of June 14, 1797, contained the following:

"COMMUNICATION FROM BLOOMFIELD:—The head workmen, mechanics and laborers, employed at Bloomfield Meeting-house, take this public way of expressing their acknowledgments to Deacon Morris and Mrs. Morris for their polite and agreeable repast of cake and cider which they gratuitously afforded to them (who were 10 in number) at the laying of the *corner-stone* of the said building, and cannot refrain from expressing a hope that this new method of laying *corner stones* may be adopted on all similar occasions. The building goes on rapidly."

The Trustees of this church, in 1797, were Samuel Ward, Ephraim Morris, Oliver Crane and Joseph Davis. The Managers of the building were Simeon Baldwin, Nathaniel Crane and Joseph Davis.

The following names were subscribed to "a promise to pay unto the trustees of the Presbyterian Society of Bloomfield, for the purpose of hiring a minister to preach the gospel for six months," with the date appended, "Cranetown, April 13, 1797":

Oliver Crane, Stephen Fordham, William Crane, Simeon Crane, Widow Susanna Crane, Job Crane, Isaac Tompkins, Phineas Crane, Widow Dorcas Williams, David Riker, Samuel McChesney, Samuel Ward, John Vincent, Noah Crane, Jr., Noah Crane, Phebe Dod, James Gnbs, Jr., Joseph Crane, John Baldwin, Nathaniel Dod, Israel Crane, Caleb Martin, Aaron Crane, Reuben Dod, Lewis Baldwin, Nathaniel Crane, Isaac Mitchell, Benjamin Crane, Eliakim Crane, Elizabeth Rouge, Thomas Force, William Holmes, Daniel Oughtltree, Levi Vincent, Cornelius Vincent, John Smith, Henry Shoemaker, John Fry, Widow Jane Crane, Jadok Crane, Samul Tichenor, Peter Davis, Matthew Dod.

In the original parchment subscription for building the church in 1796, among the principal subscribers are Eleazer Crane for £10, Joseph Crane for £60, Joseph Crane for £20, Oliver Crane for £25, William Crane for £22, Stephen Fordham for £15, Aaron Crane for £90, Caleb Martin for £12, Gideon Crane for £11, and Nathaniel and Israel Crane, each £100. Many Cranetown names also appear on the additional subscription in 1798, "for the use of the meeting-house." Most of these were from the First Church of Orange. Among the elders and deacons at the organization of the church was Joseph Crane, who had been an elder from 1794 to 1798 in the Orange Church.

On Nov. 8, 1812, the following ruling elders were elected: Joseph Crane, Joseph Davis, Ichabod Baldwin and Israel Crane, already deacons, together with David Taylor, Nathaniel Crane, Moses Dodd, and Josiah Ward.

The church bell was presented by Major Nathaniel Crane, who was also one of the original members of the church. Gen. Bloomfield, from whom the Society was named, gave $140 toward the erection of the building, and Mrs. Bloomfield presented a pulpit Bible and psalm-book. The damask silk for the covering of the pulpit was obtained from "a certain ancient lady who had a gown of that description," and who was induced to part with it for the sum of $30. It "was found to contain enough cloth for two dresses for the pulpit."

The pastors of this church previous to the organization of the church at West Bloomfield were Rev. Abel Jackson, 1800-10; Rev. Cyrus Gildersleeve, 1812-18; Rev. Gideon N. Judd, 1820-34; Rev. Ebenezer Seymour, 1834-47.

Religious services were held occasionally in Cranetown for more than fifty years before the first distinct church organization was established. No place for religious worship was erected in the westerly section of the town until the year 1837, previous to which time it had been the custom of the people to meet at the public school building for prayer and conference. The inhabitants had generally attended service at the Presbyterian churches in Newark, at the First Church in Orange, and afterward a number of them went to Bloomfield, and others to Caldwell, as churches were being erected at these several places; the large majority of them, however, were identified with the Bloomfield Church from the date of its organization, and religious services were held in the school-house at Cranetown on Sunday afternoons and evenings by members of the Bloomfield Church, the pastor of that church usually officiating. The place of meeting was the room in the second story of the public school building on a site just in front of the present church.

Major Nathaniel Crane, an elder in the Bloomfield Church, left a bequest at his death, in 1833, designed to assist in establishing a new organization. He directed that the residue of his estate, valued at about ten thousand dollars, should be invested for the support of a church in West Bloomfield, whenever that portion of the parish should form a separate congregation and erect a church edifice.

FIRST PRESBYTERIAN CHURCH.

A meeting was held at West Bloomfield on the 17th of August, 1737, to consider the propriety of a separate organization, and on the 31st of the month the new parish was created, taking the name of "The West Bloomfield Presbyterian Society," and electing as its first Trustees, Zenas S. Crane, Cyrus Pierson, Jared E. Harrison, Reuben D. Baldwin, James Baldwin, James Crane and William Smith.

The district school building, of stone, stood about twenty-five feet in front of the present church edifice; it had, on the second floor, a room which had long been used for religious meetings. This building was purchased and enlarged; the upper story was removed and over this was erected the new building, the old school room forming the lecture room, with pastor's study at one side of the vestibule, and the main auditory was placed above. With columns before the open vestibule it is said to have been quite an imposing edifice; though often mistaken by travelers for a public house; the addition was a frame building, painted white. It was dedicated on the 9th of August, 1838, the sermon being preached by the Rev. Mr. Hoover, of Newark. The church was organized at the same time by the Rev. Dr. Hillyer, of Orange, and the Rev. Mr. Seymour, of Bloomfield—a committee of the Presbytery of Newark. There were seventy-one original members of the church; sixty-six from the Church in Bloomfield, two from the Caldwell Church, two from the Church at Succasunny Plains, and one from the First Church at Orange. These were:

Zenas, Betsey and Joseph H. Baldwin, and Lydia A. his wife; Jane Ball, Hannah Benjamin, Ann Campbell, Ira Campbell, Sophia Collins, Tabitha, widow of Aaron Crane. Elias B. Crane, and Nancy his wife; George A. and Zenas S. Crane, and Maria Crane, wife of the latter; Matilda, wife of T. A. Crane; Harriet Crane, wife of Robert Earl, Amos Crane, Susan, widow of Oliver Crane, Stephen F. Crane, Oliver Crane (Rev.), Joshua Crane, Elizabeth, widow of Jeremiah Crane, Ira Crane, and his wife Margaret; Sarah Day, Nathaniel R. Dodd, John C. Dorennus, and Mary K. his wife; Rhoda, wife of Peter Dorennus, Caroline, wife of Joseph Dorennus, Sarah Earl, John H. Hoger, Sally, wife of Moses Harrison, Catharine W., wife of Jared E. Harrison; Warren Holt, Elizabeth, wife of Thomas Jackson, Phebe Kelly, widow; Robert Laing, Lydia, widow of Elias Littell. Electa, wife of William Mann, Isaac S. Miller, William S. Morris, Harriet P., wife of W. S. Morris, John Mann, and Eunice, his wife; Rhoda Mann, widow of J. Collins; Rachel, wife of Eli Mann, Nancy, widow of Dr. Cyrus Pierson, Sarah, wife of Richard Romer, Matthias Smith, and Jemima, his wife, William Smith, Harriet G. Smith; Mary Ann Smith, 2d wife of R. Earl, Matthias Smith, Jr., John Smith, Jane Smith, widow, Ephraim P. Stiles, and Ann, his wife, Moses Stiles, and Elizabeth, his wife, Ann Maria Stiles. Phebe C. Stiles, Ann, wife of James Tucker, Caleb S. Ward, and Eunice, his wife, Isaac B. Wheeler, and Harriet, his wife; Abraham Zuk.

The Church made choice of Matthias Smith and Elias Crane as its ruling elders; they having held that office in the Church at Bloomfield. John Munn, Isaac B. Wheeler and Moses Stiles were chosen the same year. Mr. Crane continued in office for twelve years; Mr. Wheeler for nine years; Mr. Stiles ten years; William Crane and William S. Morris were elected in 1844; Stephen F. Crane, 1849; John C. Doremus, Ira Campbell and Philip Doremus in 1858.

The book containing the list of elders from 1858 to 1870 has been lost or mislaid. The following is the list since that date:

Hiram B. Littell, 1870, Dr. Vincent Harrison, John M. Doubleday, Theodore B. Carter (no date); Thomas Russell, 1876, William J. Hutchinson, 1879, Frederick H. Harris, 1885, Theron H. Sanford, John S. Foster, Malcolm H. Smith, 1887, John Jefferson, 1888, Paul Babcock, Wilson W. Smith, 1890, Murdock Howell, 1891, Edward Bailey, 1893.

The first pastor of the new church was Rev. Samuel W. Fisher, D.D., who continued from 1839 to 1843, and was afterward pastor at Albany, N. Y., Cincinnati, Ohio, President of Hamilton College, New York, and pastor at Utica, N. Y. He was succeeded by Rev. Nathaniel E. Johnson, 1843-44, Rev. Aaron C. Adams, 1845-51, Rev. Job F. Halsey, D.D., 1852-56, Rev. Silas Billings, a stated supply of the pulpit, 1856-58, Rev. Josiah A. Priest, D.D., 1858-61, Rev. Nelson Millard, D.D., 1862-67, Rev. J. Romeyn Berry, D.D., 1870-87, Rev. William F. Junkin, D.D., LL.D., 1888, the present pastor.

The completeness of Presbyterian organization was not realized in the Church until 1893. In March of that year a Board of Deacons was elected and installed. Their valuable services have added much to the efficiency of the Church's work. The members of the Board are Lewis L. S. Clearman, Chairman, Herbert S. Kellogg, William K. Hunt, Francis T. A. Junkin, Levi W. Case, M.D., I. Seymour Crane, John Murphy and James Watkins.

During the first twenty-two years of its existence down to 1860 the church received 354 members; 151 on profession of their faith, and 203 by certificate from other churches. It dismissed during that period, to unite with other churches, 111, and lost 47 by death. At the close of 1860 it had 196 communicants, and the parish at that time comprised about 85 families.

Under the pastorate of Rev. Dr. Halsey the present church edifice was erected, and dedicated in 1856, the sermon being preached by the Rev. Dr. Rowland, of Newark.

One of the Newark papers, referring to the important work in connection with the affairs of this church under date of Oct. 24, 1856, says:

"The Presbyterian Church and congregation of West Bloomfield, N. J., have succeeded in the erection of a most substantial house of worship, some 85 by 55 feet in dimensions, and out of a material furnished by the rich freestone quarries in the immediate vicinity of the church.

"This house has been erected at a cost of about $16,000, and upon the basis of a subscription, obtained almost entirely within the bounds of the worshipping congregation. Some individual subscriptions have reached the sum of $1,000; and the people generally have manifested a degree of liberality and zeal in getting up this temple of prayer, worthy of the high praises of Him to whom it is now devoted.

"It deserves also to be noticed in this connection, that the ladies of the congregation have shown great zeal and untiring perseverance in this undertaking, and have succeeded in raising more than a thousand dollars from the use of their needles, and otherwise, and have appropriated the same to the purchase of all the requisite furniture necessary to gratify the taste and minister to the comfort of those who shall hereafter resort to this house of prayer.

"Nor must we pass over in silence the very generous—nay, magnanimous—offering made by our highly respected friend, Miss Mary Crane (daughter of Israel Crane), of a very rich and mellow-toned bell, from the foundry of Messrs. Jones & Hitchcock, Troy, N. Y.

"Our beautiful and well proportioned edifice is now completed, looking as though its massive walls of solid masonry would outlive a thousand generations. A house of sufficient dimensions to accommodate the people living within its immediate vicinity, and room in reserve for those who shall hereafter, as it is hoped, be induced to locate themselves in this elevated and healthy region."

Further additions and improvements were made to the church edifice in 1866 during the pastorate of Rev. Nelson Millard. One of the local papers stated that : " The Presbyterian Church at Montclair was reopened yesterday with services of a dedicatory character. * * *

" During the intermission very great changes have been accomplished. The capacity of the house has been increased by the addition of fifty pews, and about two hundred sittings. The congregation had

FIRST PRESBYTERIAN CHURCH.

overrun the church, and before long it will probably require extension. It will now seat about seven hundred people. A beautiful light, open iron balcony presents itself in front of a new narrow gallery, and the effect is very pleasing. * * * The old pulpit has been replaced by a new one, severely plain, in exact keeping with the simplicity of the service of the church and modern notions of pulpit architecture. It now consists of a mere platform, with a small movable desk."

In 1870 the organ was placed in the church at a cost of about $6,000. The public school building located on ground adjoining the church lot was purchased in 1869, and converted into a lecture room, and in 1883 that building was removed and the present chapel erected.

The first parsonage, on Bloomfield Avenue, opposite Park Street, was built about the time of the original church building, and first occupied by the Rev. Samuel Fisher, D.D., and his family ; his son, Rev. Samuel Fisher, pastor of the church, boarded with his parents. The strip of land on which the parsonage was built extended from Bloomfield Avenue to Church Street, and was a legacy from Nathaniel B. Baldwin. The present handsome and commodious parsonage, located in Church Street, was built during the pastorate of Rev. J. R. Berry, D.D.

In 1870 a large Colony went out from the First Presbyterian Church, and uniting with others formed the First Congregational Church of Montclair, and the separation took place amid such farewell greetings and benedictions as are expressed by an affectionate but overgrown family when its younger members go out to an independent life.

Most of these had united with the Presbyterian Church, though of Congregational convictions and preferences, with the understanding that they should, when it should become expedient, withdraw in order to organize a Congregational Church. The departing Colony received therefore the cordial *Godspeed* of the old MOTHER CHURCH.

During the pastorate of the Rev. Dr. Berry, the *Trinity Presbyterian Church* (of which a sketch appears elsewhere in this work) was established. Its charter members were set off from the First Church by the Presbytery of Newark, to compose the new organization.

Francis L. Patton, D.D., LL.D., President of Princeton University, supplied the pulpit of Trinity Church for a year ; after which the present devoted and highly esteemed pastor, the Rev. Orville Reed, was settled over the Church.

Since the Rev. Dr. Junkin became pastor of the First Church, two church edifices have been built in Montclair, at a cost to the Mother Church of ten or twelve thousand dollars.

The first of these is known as *Grace Presbyterian Church.* It stands on a beautiful and extensive plot of ground,—the generous gift to the Trustees of the First Church, for the purposes of this building, of Mr. Alfred J. Crane,—at the corner of Forest and Chestnut Streets. Within two years after the establishment of a Sunday school, by the First Church, in this section of the town, so hopeful was the progress of the work, the building was erected and a church organized ; a history of which will be found on another page of this work. The Rev. F. N. Rutan was called and installed as its first pastor, and the church has grown steadily during his pastorate. He and his people are held in high regard by the pastor and members of the Mother Church. The colony which she sent out has become a prosperous and growing church, and the building and plot of ground, which were transferred to their Board of Trustees by the Trustees of the First Church in 1893, has become the centre of most promising Christian activities.

The *Cedar Street Chapel* is the name of the second forward movement made by the First Presbyterian Church during the last few years. The lot on which it stands, one of the most eligible and beautiful in the south section of Montclair, was given to the First Church, as a site for the chapel, by Messrs. Edwin and J. Caldwell Williams. It was a most generous donation, and greatly encouraged and helped the devoted workers, who have labored so zealously to establish and carry on the Sunday school, which with preaching services conducted there on Sunday night, gives hopeful promise of Presbyterian advance in the south end of the town.

The policy of the First Church is that of organizing new enterprises, new centres of fresh aggressive movement, rather than of retaining over-crowded membership in the Mother Church.

The old landmark, so dear to the hearts of many, and so pleasantly familiar to the eyes of all the people of Montclair, will, however, soon be a thing of the past, a fragrant memory, rich with sacred associations. Arrangements are now being made which will result in the removal of the old and the erection of a new, larger and handsomer edifice. The same commanding site and extensive grounds will be used, and the new structure will, it is believed, be a worthy tribute of the present to the noble and generous past of this honored church. The able and judicious Board of Trustees, under whose efficient management this forward movement is rapidly taking shape, led by its earnest and devoted President, is composed of the following gentlemen: Benjamin Carter, President; William Wallace, Secretary; Arthur Horton, Treasurer; J. Seymour Crane, Andrew P. Morrison and John Maxwell.

The aggregate expenditure for grounds and buildings has been about $85,000. Since its organization the church has received 1,357 persons into its membership— 741 by certificate and 616 on profession of faith. There are now 450 communicants.

The record of expenditures for the first thirty-two years is incomplete and no accurate statement is possible. During the last 23 years $328,700 has been expended. Of this amount $220,681 was raised for congregational purposes, and $108,019 for benevolent objects.

Of the eight pastors who have presided over this church and congregation, data referring to the work of five only has been found.

REV. JOB FOSTER HALSEY, D.D.

Dr. Halsey was a graduate of Union College and was a classmate of Hon. Wm. H. Seward; he studied theology at Princeton Seminary. His first pastorate was over a church in Monmouth County. From thence he removed to Allegheny, but his voice failing him, he obtained a professor's chair at a college in Missouri, but soon resigned to open a female seminary at Raritan Hall, Perth Amboy. He accepted the pastorate of the First Presbyterian Church at West Bloomfield in 1852, continuing until 1856. It was during his pastorate in 1856 that the new church edifice was erected. He left this church to go to Norristown, Pa., where he died at the advanced age of eighty-two.

While he was thoroughly orthodox as to his religious tenets and his church, his heart was big enough and his charity broad enough to embrace every member of the human family within their influence. Simple-hearted and gentle as a child in mere worldly matters, in the cause of the Master he was not only valiant, but an aggressive soldier, who would not abate one jot of his faith, his loyalty and his allegiance.

The following reference to the installation of REV. J. A. PRIEST was published in one of the local papers at the time:

"The Rev. J. A. Priest was installed as pastor of the Presbyterian Church in West Bloomfield, N. J., on Tuesday of last week by the Presbytery of Newark. Rev. I. N. Sprague, of Caldwell, presided; Rev. J. Pingry of Roseville, read the Scriptures and offered the introductory prayer. Rev. Asa

D. Smith, D.D., of the Fourteenth Street Presbyterian Church, New York City, preached the sermon; Rev. I. N. Sprague offered the installation prayer; Rev. J. Few Smith, D.D. of Newark, delivered the charge to the pastor; Rev. C. M. N. Nickols, of Newark, the charge to the people. The discourse of Dr. Smith was based on Psalms lxxxvii. 7; "All my springs are in thee.'"

Referring to his resignation three years later, the same paper says: "Rev. J. A. Priest, of West Bloomfield, N. J., has resigned the charge of the Presbyterian Church at that place, and intends sojourning in Europe for a couple of years for health and study. We trust he may be abundantly prospered and return to labor for many years in that sacred calling in which he has already been so worthily successful."

Rev. Nelson Millard, D.D.

The pastorate of Rev. Mr. Millard extended from 1862 to 1867, and during this period the church increased in numbers and influence. A friend of Dr. Millard, under date of March 24, 1867, writes:

"Mr. Millard did not venture into the region of the pathetic, but in plain, familiar language, often interrupted by emotion, he led us back over the scenes of the past five years of honest, faithful ministry. This was his earliest settlement, and he will probably never fail to review the scenes of his ministry here with peculiar pleasure. Never were a people more perfectly united in a pastor. It is the sundering of ties, such as are seldom formed—of associations full of endearment. He counseled his people to avoid divisions—to be willing to bear and forbear, and to seek the general good of the church even to the sacrifice of private judgment. The church now numbers about three hundred members, half of which have joined under Mr. Millard's ministry. Of these additions twenty-two were by profession and seventy by certificate. There have been seventy baptisms (of which forty-eight were children) and twenty marriages."

Dr. Millard left this church to go to the Olivet Street Presbyterian Church in Chicago, and was afterward for ten years pastor of the First Presbyterian Church in Syracuse, N. Y., and was said to be "one of the ablest clergymen of that denomination in the Empire State."

Rev. J. Romeyn Berry, D.D.

Dr. Berry was born in Hackensack, N. J., in 1826, and died at Asbury Park, N. J., June 12, 1891. He was a graduate of Rutgers College and the Theological Seminary of New Brunswick. While quite young he became the pastor of the Reformed Church at Lafayette, now a part of Jersey City. From there he went to Fishkill, N. Y., serving as the pastor of the Reformed Church there. In 1870 he accepted the unanimous call of the First Presbyterian Church at Montclair. One of the Newark papers referring to the call said: "Dr. Berry's experience of nineteen years in the ministry, his well-known abilities and his invariable success in the several fields where he has labored, are a sufficient guarantee of success in his new field. These characteristics, together with his genial manners, are sure to prepare a hearty welcome for him among his Presbyterian brethren with whom he now casts his lot."

An impromptu gathering took place at the close of his first year's pastorate, and he was presented with a purse of $300 in gold. The surprise was complete and the response touching. He said that the year past had been a happy one with him, and that in his ministry he had never experienced so much kindness, nor spent a year so full of pleasant memories.

Just previous to the coming of Dr. Berry, some eighty members had withdrawn to organize the First Congregational Church of Montclair, but notwithstanding this loss the church prospered and there was a steady growth from year to year. During his pastorate of seventeen years,—far exceeding that of any of his predecessors,—532 persons were admitted to the church, 276 of whom united upon profession of their faith in Christ, and there was a constant growth of spirituality among its members, an increase in the benevolent contributions, and an improved material and financial condition of the church. Nearly $50,000 of the debt was liquidated, and the handsome chapel on Church Street was built during his ministration. An average of over $14,000 per annum was raised for congregational and benevolent

Very truly yours,

W. S. Hamilton

purposes, and during the last two years of his pastorate, 62 united with the church on confession of faith and 36 by certificate.

Just previous to his departure from Montclair, a large number of his fellow-citizens signed the following request:

"DEAR SIR:—The undersigned citizens of Montclair, recognizing the value of your ministry in our community, and feel indebted to you in ways it ing that these sentiments the churches, and among gratified to have a public their love for you as a you as a minister, ask you when they may meet you ing, in some formal way, and esteem. We feel that leave the place where you so efficiently without carrying ances of appreciation as we time and place as shall be

Dr. Berry, in his reply, fectionate suggestion, but his intended departure tunity for such a reception. sum of $5,000 was raised ed to him in token of their appreciation of his labors, noble qualities, foremost in mankind; as a preacher he ing from the Great Truths the sole purpose to build and to save his fellow-men.

ing that the whole town is cannot repay; and believ are shared by many in all all classes, who would be opportunity of expressing man, and their love for to name some near day for the purpose of present their tribute of affection we cannot allow you to have labored so long and ing with you such assur desire to express at such most pleasing to you." thanked them for the af stated that the nearness of would preclude the oppor Before his departure the by his people and present love to him and of their Dr. Berry was a man of all that tended to benefit was fervent and unwaver which he expounded with up the Kingdom of God In politics he was a staunch

REV. J. ROMAN BERRY, D.D.

Republican. Personally Dr. Berry was a kindly disposed gentleman, of commanding and dignified presence, and the attachment between him and his people was deep and lasting.

REV. WILLIAM FINNEY JUNKIN, D.D., LL.D.

It was certainly a "new departure," and an indication of the progressive spirit of its membership, for the First Presbyterian Church of Montclair to call as pastor a man who from his youth had been identified with the people of the South, and was as much a Southern man in principle as though to the manor born. They made no mistake in their choice, however, as results have proven. Dr. Junkin's work had been in a different field under different environments, but he readily adapted himself to his new field of labor, and found the people in hearty sympathy with him and ready to aid him in his work. The sketch of his life will be read with interest by those who have learned to love him as a man and admire him as a preacher.

Rev. William F. Junkin was born in Philadelphia, Pa., May 1st, 1831. He came of a sturdy lineage. His father was Rev. George Junkin, D.D., LL.D., the famous leader of the Presbyterian Church of his day, whose father in turn was Col. Joseph Junkin, an officer in the *Pennsylvania line* during the Revolution. An old record says of Col. Junkin: "His Company on the 7th of July, 1776, was on parade when a courier rode up with the news, that the Declaration of Independence had been adopted and and bringing a copy of the instrument. It was unanimously and by acclamation ratified on the spot. The Company volunteered at once, and soon were ordered to Amboy, New Jersey, where they were employed in guarding the Court. He was severely wounded at the Battle of Brandywine. Having fainted from loss of blood, the enemy passed him by, taking him for dead. Night came on. A shower of rain revived him. He arose, and dreading to fall into the enemy's hands he made his way across woods and fields and rejoined his command. A horse was procured for him and with a rope for a bridle, a knapsack stuffed with hay for a saddle and wrapped in his bloody garments, he arrived at his home, ninety miles in three days."

Joseph Junkin's grandmother was present at the immortal seige of Derry. "She saw from the walls of glorious old Derry the smoke of the most important gun ever fired, the lee-gun of the *Mountjoy*, which righted the ship, broke the boom, relieved the starving garrison, forced the allies to raise the siege and retreat upon the Boyne, where the arms of William and of liberty triumphed and completed the blessed Revolution of 1688." Just a century later her great-grandson, George Junkin, was born at the family seat in Cumberland County, Pennsylvania. From a Memorial Volume of distinguished Pennsylvanians we quote: " He was a man of God, devout, humble, prayerful. A strong intellect, great powers of generalization and analysis, a keen and discriminating logic, a power of language always clear and vigorous, often rising to the height of poetry, a glowing heart full of deep affection, a disposition firm as a rock when contending for the right, but gentle as a woman's in all social elements, made George Junkin the great and good man that he was." While a student of theology, under the distinguished Dr. John M. Mason, in New York, he assisted in organizing the first Sunday school formed in that city.

He was a prominent leader in the progress and conflicts of the Presbyterian Church. A staunch *Old School* man in the trying times of 1835–37, he maintained then and always, with pen and voice and undaunted courage, the views of truth as he believed them. He was the author of many books and addresses and essays of the times. As the founder and father, and President, for many years, of Lafayette College, at Easton, Pennsylvania, his name will be held in that influential institution in everlasting remembrance. He was President of Miami University, in Ohio, and for many years also President of Washington College, now Washington and Lee University, in Virginia. His influence in these seats of learning was felt and acknowledged throughout many States of the Union. He left his delightful home in Lexington, Virginia, in 1861, because he "would not live under any other flag than the *Stars and Stripes*." Dr. George Junkin had five sons and three daughters. Among these, William Finney was the youngest son. The eldest was Margaret J. Preston, of Virginia, whose writings, prose and poetry, have given her a name as one of the most gifted women of the country. She is often called affectionately the *Southern Poetess*. Another daughter, Elinor, was the beloved first wife of Gen. T. J. (Stonewall) Jackson. And Mrs. J. M. Fishburne, of Philadelphia, is an honored and useful officer of the Woman's Foreign Missionary Board of the Presbyterian Church. John Junkin, M.D., the Rev. E. D. Junkin, D.D., an able Presbyterian clergyman, late of Texas, and George Junkin, Esq., for years a distinguished and honored member of the Philadelphia Bar, are brothers of the subject of this sketch.

William F. Junkin was graduated at Washington College, in 1851, and in theology at the Seminary of the Presbyterian Church in Princeton, in 1854. His first pastorate was in the Falling Spring Church, one of the oldest and largest in the Valley of Virginia. Here he remained for thirteen years. Four of these years were years of Civil War. He volunteered in the Confederate Army, in 1861, serving under Generals Henry A. Wise and Robert E. Lee, in Western Virginia, and subsequently in the Army of Northern Virginia, as a private soldier, an officer, and volunteer chaplain. He was for a time Lieut.-Colonel of the Reserves. The permanent results of his ministry in his charge of the old Falling Spring Church were a large increase in the membership and efficiency of the Church, the erection of a beautiful manse, and the building of a large and handsome church which adorns one of the most picturesque sites in the Virginia Valley. In 1868 he was called to the pastorate of the First Church of Danville, Kentucky, in connection with the Southern Branch of the Presbyterian Church. While in Kentucky his *Alma Mater*, Washington and Lee University, conferred upon him the degree of *Doctor of Divinity*.

As a preacher and churchman, Dr. Junkin's influence and eloquence gave him high position throughout the State. His inherited devotion to educational interests led him into large fields of effort. His labors at Danville started the movement and did much to lay firmly the foundations of the *Central University of Kentucky*, which by its rapid growth and rich endowments has asserted a vast power for good in the southwestern section of our country. In the position of Chancellor of the University for a short period, and as Moderator for the Synod, expression was given of the regard in which he was held, by those who controlled large influence in Church and State. From Kentucky he removed, in 1876, to Charleston, South Carolina., to take the pastoral charge of the Glebe Street Presbyterian Church, in that city, to which he had been called by the unanimous vote of its people. He had been preceded in this charge by the renowned pulpit orator, Dr. Benjamin M. Palmer, now, and for many years, of New Orleans, and by Dr. J. L. Girardeau, whose fervid zeal, eloquence and scholarship have placed him high in the public esteem, both in his own State and throughout the South.

During Dr. Junkin's pastorate in Charleston, the Glebe Street Church drew into connection with itself the Central Presbyterian Church of that city. The united body assumed the name of the Westminster Presbyterian Church, whose imposing church edifice adorns the historic old King Street in the City by the Sea. Dr. Junkin's influence extended throughout the city and State, reaching far beyond denominational lines. He was prominently and actively identified with educational and other movements of public concern, and when he left his loved Southern home in Charleston—compelled to do so by the shattered health of members of his family—the Church, High School, School Board, the civic authorities and the city press were loud and earnest in their declarations of regret, and their expressions of admiration and regard. After a rest of a few months in his old Virginia home, he was, in 1889, greatly to his own surprise, asked to become pastor of the First Presbyterian Church of Montclair. His force of character, faithful and able pulpit ministrations, his eloquence and zeal, have won him many friends, and assigned him a place of prominence and large influence in the community. The aggressive character of his church work has advanced the Presbyterian interest, adding a new and flourishing Church and a most promising Chapel work to that denomination. The degree of LL.D. was conferred on Dr. Junkin during his early ministry in Montclair. In 1855 Dr. Junkin was married to Anna Aylett Anderson, eldest daughter of Judge Francis Thomas Anderson, Justice of the Supreme Court of Appeals of Virginia, where the record of his opinions ranks him with his illustrious fellow statesman, John Marshall. She, like her husband, comes of honored Revolutionary lineage and churchly Presbyterian ancestry. She reaches back through distinguished family lines during the Colonial period of Virginia's history to illustrious antecedents of English blood. She is the granddaughter of Andrew Alexander, of Virginia, oldest brother of Dr. Archibald Alexander, of Princeton Theological Seminary. Her maternal grandfather, William Aylett, was Commissary-general in the Revolutionary war. Her paternal grandfather, William Anderson, was an active colonel in the war of 1812, and also a distinguished soldier during the Revolution. In both these wars he was a volunteer.

Of Dr. Junkin's seven children five are living, two sons and three daughters. His oldest son, Francis T. A. Junkin, is a lawyer in New York City, and the youngest, William Alexander Junkin, a student at the University of Virginia. All the daughters are married.

SUNDAY SCHOOL.

It has been stated that the first Sunday school in the State of New Jersey was established as early as 1814 in connection with the First Presbyterian Church at Newark, in the house of Rev. Dr. Richards, who was then pastor of that church, but the oldest inhabitants of this section state that in 1813 Michael Osborn, an apprentice of W. Crane, then associated with Israel Crane in the cotton-spinning mills on Tony's Brook, started a Sunday school in Bloomfield in which he was assisted by Gorline Doremus.

The movement extended to West Bloomfield as early as 1816, and for many years before the First

Presbyterian Church was organized in West Bloomfield Sunday-school services were held in the public school building, and teachers from the First Presbyterian Church of Bloomfield came regularly on Sunday afternoons to assist in the work. This was the nucleus of the church and Sunday school, which was regularly organized in 1837-8. The first superintendent of the new school was Mr. Warren Holt, who at that time was a teacher in the district school. He was succeeded by Elias B. Crane, John Munn and J. B. Wheeler. The old school room which formed the lecture room of the new church was used for the Sunday school. After the changes were made in the old building and a more suitable room was provided for the Sunday school, Mr. William S. Morris became superintendent. Mr. Philip Doremus, who was one of the original scholars of the school, returned to his native place in 1848, after an absence of several years, and entered the school as a teacher, and in 1853 became superintendent. He had long been connected with a prominent church and Sunday-school in Brooklyn, and was thoroughly imbued with the advanced ideas of that period, the most important of which was Sunday-school missionary work. He introduced this and many other improvements, which proved of great and lasting benefit to this school. During his administration Mr. Wm. B. Bradbury, the famous author of Sunday-school hymn books, and the manufacturer of the piano which bears his name, was a frequent visitor to this school, and assisted in drilling the children in singing the tunes from his own books, which had been adopted by the school.

An event of interest at this time connected with the failing health of Mr. Bradbury, and expressing the warm attachment to him by the school, is worthy of mention.

On a beautiful Sabbath in June, at nine o'clock in the morning, the school assembled at the church, and, after forming in line, headed by the superintendent, marched in procession to the Mountain House, where Mr. Bradbury was then boarding. He was seated in an invalid chair at one end of the large parlor. The school formed in a circle about him and sang several choice selections from his own collection of Sunday-school hymns. The children then passed him in single file as they left the room, each one presenting him with a bouquet with their best wishes. It was a touching scene, which left its impress on the hearts of the children, while this "sweet singer of Israel" shed tears of joy and gladness, and carried with him these delightful memories as he passed through the dark valley, and the refrain of the children's songs was doubtless heard on the "other side" as he entered the eternal abode.

Mr. Doremus was connected with the school for nearly forty years—fifteen of which was as superintendent. During his faithful labors as teacher and superintendent, hundreds were added to the church from the ranks of the Sabbath school, many of whom have since become teachers in this and other schools. He was succeeded by Dr. H. H. Lloyd, who conducted the school with marked intelligence, interest and success, up to the time of his decease. Mr. Samuel Wilde, who had efficiently served the school as President of the Sunday-school Missionary Society, was chosen to succeed Dr. Lloyd, and, in his new relations, evinced the same zeal and devotion that characterized his previous work. His individual resources and extensive acquaintance with prominent Christian workers in different parts of the country, enabled him to contribute much to the public exercises of the school at its anniversary meetings and Christmas entertainments.

He was succeeded by Thomas B. Graham, who for a number of years did excellent service for the school by the introduction of new methods which were prosecuted with prudence and energy.

Dr. George Hawes was the next superintendent and conducted the affairs of the school very satisfactorily to the church, particularly in the study of the shorter catechism, and a higher class of Sunday-school music. His death occurred while still holding this position, and his loss was severely felt both by the church and school.

Elder Thomas Russell was the unanimous choice of the school as his successor, and for many years discharged the duties with fidelity and devotion, and with marked success. The school largely increased in numbers during his administration, and a deeper interest in the study of the Word of God was developed, and the school was held in close relationship with the church. He continued in office until the autumn of 1890.

Charles H. Baker was elected superintendent in October, 1890, and held the position until May,

1893. He was thoroughly qualified for the office, having filled a similar position in the First Presbyterian Church in Brooklyn. He was also assistant superintendent of the chapel connected with this church.

Mr. Baker resigned his position as superintendent of this school in May, 1893, and Mr. Thomas Russell accepted the position temporarily.

The present officers of the school (1894) are: Thomas Russell, Superintendent; J. A. Sanford, Assistant Superintendent; Charles H. Baker, Secretary; Miss Grace Howell, Treasurer; John Murphy and William Peake, Assistant Librarians.

The school numbers at the present time 245, of which 140 are in the main school and 35 in the primary department.

TRINITY PRESBYTERIAN CHURCH.

The preliminary efforts that led to the organization of this church were begun in the summer of 1886. The first meeting was held on August 17th, at the residence of D. V. Harrison. There were present at this meeting: D. Vincent Harrison, Abraham Bussing, William L. Ludlam, Edward S. Smith, Robert G. Hutchinson, Dr. John J. H. Love, E. Augustus Smith, Charles B. Morris and Philip Doremus. A committee consisting of Messrs. Harrison and Doremus was appointed to prepare a petition to the Presbytery of Newark, for the organization and secure the necessary signatures.

At a meeting held at the house of Mr. Harrison, Saturday evening, Oct. 2d, 1886, reported the following petition, signed by fifty eight church members:

"To the Presbytery of Newark.— We, whose names are subscribed, residents of Montclair, respectfully beg leave to make the following presentation to your body. After long and careful deliberation, it has become our conviction that the time has come for the organization of another Presbyterian Church in Montclair. In forming this opinion and seeking to give it effect through your authority we believe we are prayerfully seeking the interest of Christ's Kingdom in our community. We believe the best interests of our denomination require that the action now contemplated and sought from you should be no longer delayed. We therefore petition that your honorable body will take such steps as are requisite for the organization of a new Presbyterian Church in Montclair at your earliest practical convenience.

"Montclair, New Jersey, Aug. 18, 1886."

The petition was granted by a unanimous vote of the Presbytery, and at a meeting held in the old Presbyterian church, on Thursday evening, Oct. 14th, it was duly organized by the Presbytery of Newark, with fifty-eight members, fifty-seven on certificates (mostly from the Presbyterian Church in Montclair, and one on profession of faith, under the name of "Trinity Presbyterian Church of Montclair."

The following certificates were placed in the hands of the commissioners:

John J. H. Love, Francis J. Love, Edith Love, Philip Doremus, Hester A. Doremus, Carrie S. Doremus, Adah N. Doremus, Annette C. Goodell, S. C. G. Watkins, Mary Y. Watkins, Caroline Doremus, Martha M. Doremus, Mary K. Doremus, Julia N. French, Albert French, Caroline French, H. C. Dabney, D. Heber Baldwin, Effie K. Baldwin, Eveline P. Munn, Abbey M. Munn, Josephine French, William L. Ludlam, Anna R. Ludlam, Frances W. Priest, Martha B. Priest, S. Maud W. Priest, Daniel V. Harrison, Frances P. Harrison, Benjamin V. Harrison, Peter A. Tronson, M. Hattie

Tronson, Samuel T. Stewart. Mary C. Stewart, Julia B. Douglass, Charlotte Isabel Bayles, Edward S. Smith, Arabella G. Smith, Charles B. Morris, Fannie L. Bacon, Carrie A. Williams, Eliza M. Morris. Mary C. Meade, Harriet M. Meade, Samuel C. Munn, Abraham Bussing, Emma F. Bussing, Alice C. Bussing.

From the First Congregational Church, Montclair: Robert G. Hutchinson, Almira Hutchinson, Robert G. Hutchinson.

From the Congregational Church in Wells River, Vt.: Clara B. Morris, wife of C. B. Morris above.

From the Caldwell Presbyterian Church, Caldwell, N. J.: Mrs. Sarah Montanye, Miss Alice Montanye.

From the Reformed Church, Little Falls, N. J.: Mrs. Ella Obrien Munn, wife of Joseph W. Munn.

From the Brooklyn Tabernacle Presbyterian Church, Brooklyn, N. Y.: Mrs. Elizabeth C. Mead.

From the Lafayette Avenue Presbyterian Church, Brooklyn, N. Y.: Miss Sarah W. Walker.

Miss Marie Marguerite Tronson united with the church on profession of faith.

An election for Elders at this time resulted in the election of D. V. Harrison for a term of three years, and Philip Doremus for two years, both of whom were duly installed.

By permission of Presbytery the church provided for its pulpit and Prof. Francis L. Patton, D.D., of Princeton, N. J., was engaged by the Society to preach for them until a pastor could be secured.

The first regular service was held in Montclair Hall, October 17th, the Sabbath following the day of organization.

The first baptism took place Sabbath morning, December 12, 1886, being that of Annie Yarrington Watkins, born January 28, 1883, daughter of Dr. S. S. G. Watkins, and granddaughter of Philip Doremus.

The Society very soon purchased property containing about one and a quarter acres on the corner of Valley Road and Church Street, at a cost of $7,500, on which a frame building 40 by 68 feet was erected, fronting on Church Street, with a seating capacity of 350 persons. The cost of building, including furniture, fixtures, etc., was $5,781. The entire cost was $13,281. Of this amount $8,306 was raised by subscription, leaving a balance of $4,975, which was secured by mortgage on the property.

The chapel was opened for public worship May 29, 1887. Dr. Patton supplied the pulpit at intervals until the summer of 1888, when a call was extended to Rev. Orville Reed, and he was duly installed as pastor on the evening of October 11, 1888.

The first auxiliary society organized was that of the " Ladies Church Home Society," in 1887, its object being " the social development and material interest of the church."

The total amount raised the first year for regular expenses and benevolent purposes was $3,263. The second year the total amount raised was $12,395.58, which included the subscriptions to the church building fund. The amount raised the third year was $4,517. In 1890, $5,350. In 1891 the total sum was $9,115.42, of which $1,732.28 was contributed to Home and Foreign Missions. An organ was also purchased for the church at a cost of about $3,000. In 1892 the amount raised was $7,347.55, of which $2,284.08 was for benevolent purposes. In 1893 the total sum was $7,678.64, of which $1,890.71 was for benevolent purposes.

In 1887 the additions to the membership were 6, making total of 64. In 1888, there were 2 on profession of faith and 19 on certificate. In 1889, there were 2 on profession of faith and 16 on certificate; 2 dismissed; baptism of infants, 2. In 1890, there were 6 on profession of faith and 15 on certificate; 6 dismissed. In 1891, there were 10 united on profession of faith and 4 on certificate. In 1892, there were 10 received on profession of faith and 12 on certificate; 3 dismissed. In 1893, there were added by letter 12, and 4 on confession; 3 dismissed and 2 deceased. The total membership at the close of 1893 was 158.

The present officers of the church are: Elders, Philip Doremus, Benjamin Strong, Daniel V. Harrison, Edwin Ferris, E. A. Smith; Clerk, Benjamin Strong; Treasurer, Edwin Ferris.

Trustees.—Dr. John J. H. Love, President. D. H. Baldwin, Secretary. William L. Ludlam, Treasurer, Edwin B. Goodell, William Y. Bogle, Dr. S. C. G. Watkins, Adrian O. Schoonmaker.

Auxiliary Societies.—Ladies' Church Home Society, Woman's Foreign Missionary Society, Woman's Home Missionary Society, Young People's Society of Christian Endeavor, Children's Mission Band, Boys' Club.

SUNDAY SCHOOL.

The Sunday school was organized immediately after the first Sabbath morning service with a membership of fifty, and Mr. William L. Ludlam was chosen Superintendent, who, with the exception of one year, has continued up to the present time.

The school has steadily increased in numbers and interest under his able management. The report of 1892 shows a total of 19 teachers, 139 scholars, and an average attendance of 72. Number added to the church from the school, 17. Number of volumes in the library, 250.

Present Officers—William L. Ludlam, Superintendent, William Whitney Ames, Secretary and Treasurer, W. Leslie Ludlam, Jr., Assistant, W. E. Strong, Librarian.

REV. ORVILLE REED.

Trinity Presbyterian Church was fortunate in its selection of Rev. Orville Reed as its first pastor, a man whose training and experience eminently fitted him for the work of building up a new interest in a field of labor where the denomination he represents has held sway for more than a hundred years. Mr. Reed comes of Puritan-Holland-Dutch ancestry. He is the youngest of four brothers, all of whom are ministers of the gospel. His paternal ancestor was probably John Reed, of Norwalk, Conn., who came from England in 1660. He had served in the army of the Commonwealth, and at the restoration of Charles II. he left England with many others. He entered the army at the age of sixteen, and had risen to office in which he gained distinction for some heroic service. In 1760 four of his grandchildren, James, Ezra, Elijah and Eliakim settled in Armenia, N. Y., and became the projectors of this branch of the family.

On his mother's side Rev. Mr. Reed is descended from the Allens of Connecticut, and Abram Jacob Lansing, the founder of Lansingburg. Mr. Reed was prepared for college by a private tutor, and entered the Sophomore Class of Yale in 1874 and was graduated in 1877. He afterward taught for a year in the High School at Troy, and then entered Union Theological Seminary, where he spent two years, and was then sent abroad as tutor in Robert College, Constantinople. This gave him the opportunity to travel and acquaint himself with the customs of the East. He remained abroad three years returning in the autumn of 1883, and was graduated in Auburn Seminary in 1884. His first pastoral work was at Springfield, Mass., where he had charge of two mission chapels connected with the Congregational Church of that place. Later, he became associate pastor of Hope Congregational Church. He continued his labors there until the summer of 1888, when he accepted a call from the Trinity Presbyterian Church, and was soon after installed as its pastor. He was cordially received by the pastors of other denominations and given a hearty welcome by the community. He is faithful and earnest as a preacher, and the church has had a steady and healthy growth under his pastorate. He has been in hearty sympathy with and labored earnestly for the several reform and benevolent movements that have been organized from time to time in the community.

Mr. Reed married in 1884 Caroline Margaret, daughter of Dr T. L. Byington, of Constantinople, missionary to the Bulgarians. She is a native of Adrianople and was a teacher in the American College for young ladies at Scutari, opposite Constantinople.

GRACE PRESBYTERIAN CHURCH.

The movement which led to the establishment of this church was begun in 1889, by the First Presbyterian Church, and was the outcome of a desire on the part of the Presbyterian churches to extend their work into the section of Montclair north of Walnut Street. They recognized the fact that all the churches were centred around Bloomfield Avenue, and that the newer section was without a church.

During 1889 a collection was taken up in the First Presbyterian Church every Sabbath evening; this collection formed a nucleus of a fund with which to start the new enterprise, and early in 1890 the work was pushed forward. A joint committee of the two churches, consisting of Dr. Junkin and Mr. Wilson W. Smith, of the First Church, Rev. Orville Reed and Mr. Philip Doremus, of Trinity Church, took steps to organize the work. Through the kindness of the officers of the Greenwood Lake Railroad, the waiting room of the Montclair depot was secured as a temporary place of meeting until such time as a suitable building could be secured.

The first meeting was held at the depot on Sabbath afternoon, June 22d, 1890, and the services were conducted by Rev. William F. Junkin, D.D., of the First Presbyterian, and Rev. Orville Reed, of the Trinity Presbyterian Church.

On the following Sabbath, June 29th, Mr. Henry A. Strohmeyer was elected Superintendent, and Mr. Raymond S. Pearce, Secretary. There were present forty-one scholars and eighteen teachers. The school continued to meet in the depot until Dec., 1890.

A choice building lot on the corner of Chestnut and Forest Streets was presented to the Society by Mr. Alfred J. Crane, and on this a chapel was erected, which was formally dedicated on Sunday, Jan. 19, 1891. Dr. Junkin preached the dedicatory sermon, and Rev. Orville Reed made the dedication prayer.

Architecturally the chapel is a thorough success, effective in its outlines, and symmetrical in its proportions; the interior presents an artistic appearance, and is well arranged with a view to comfort and convenience. The pulpit is of carved oak, and is an elegant piece of work; it is a memorial of Mr. Hiram Littell, who was for many years an honored ruling elder in the First Presbyterian Church.

The church has been financially self-sustaining since the autumn of 1891, and in October of that year, Rev. F. N. Rutan was engaged to preach. On Feb. 15, 1892, it became a separate and distinct organization, under the name of Grace Presbyterian Church, and Mr. Rutan was called to be its regular pastor, March 1, 1892. The total membership at this time was 67, and the following were the first officers elected: *Elders.*—H. F. Torrey, C. A. Cook, F. P. Zeiger, G. S. Jellerson. *Deacons.*—H. A. Strohmeyer, T. J. Selever, William Clubb. *Trustees.*—F. P. Zieger, N. D. Wyman, A. J. Crane, G. M. Johnstone. *Trustees.*—F. P. Zieger, N. D. Wyman, A. J. Crane, G. M. Johnstone, I. Campbell.

The present officers are: *Elders.*—H. T. Torrey, C. A. Cook, H. A. Strohmeyer, G. S. Jellison. *Deacons.*—T. J. Selever, William Clubb, N. H. Cook. *Trustees.*—N. D. Wyman, Alfred J. Crane, G. M. Johnstone, R. Smith, James H. Renshaw.

The total number enrolled in the Sabbath school is 250, of which there are officers, 4, teachers, 21, and scholars, 225.

METHODISM AND THE MONTCLAIR M. E. CHURCH.

Although the birth of Methodism in Bloomfield and West Bloomfield can only be traced back some eighty odd years, there is little doubt but that the "circuit rider,"—whose circuit often extended over a territory from fifty to one hundred miles,—held at different times meetings in this locality, and that the seed thus scattered by the wayside, in due course of time, bore fruit which formed the nucleus of the first Methodist church within the limits of the present township.

Most of the facts in connection with the history of this organization are embodied in an historical sketch delivered by Rev. J. I. Boswell, in 1879, before a large assemblage, "in the last service held in the old building." He says:

MONTCLAIR METHODISM.

"About 1804 this region formed a small part of Haverstraw circuit, and was under the charge of Rev. Barney Matthias. The circuit was of great extent, and the preacher rode from place to place, preaching in school-houses, in private houses, and frequently in barns. The population was small and scattered, and the preacher enjoyed hard work and small pay. It was the day when sacrifices were made, the precious fruits of which we are now reaping. At the quarterly meeting held at the barn of Martiny Hogencamp's, near the pond in Clarkstown, Rockland County, N. Y., on Saturday, the 1st of November, 1805, there is an account of moneys received from the different classes. The amount received was $35.24, and the faithful preacher received as his salary for a quarter of the year, $27.68, with which he mounted his horse and rode on his way rejoicing.

"In 1811 the circuit was divided and this region became a part of Bergen circuit, and was under the charge of two preachers, whose names alone survive. This circuit was wide in extent, and the two preachers were not in the least danger of dying for lack of something to do. It included such places as Orange, then called Orange Furnace (or factory), Haverstraw and Nyack, in Rockland County, N. Y., and Fort Lee, Paterson and Newark, N. J. The first mention which we have of Bloomfield is in the year 1817. In August of the preceding year—1816—Bergen circuit held a quarterly conference. Newark paid in at this conference for the support of the two preachers, $7.62; Paterson, $1; Haverstraw, $6.87¼; and Bloomfield now makes its first appearance with $4.16 in its hand. The entire amount raised was $92.51, of which nearly one-third was raised by public collection. Bergen circuit formed a part of the East Jersey District, which district included such places as Trenton, Stroudsburg, Paterson and Staten Island. It was attached to the Philadelphia conference, which in those days included New Jersey, Delaware, Maryland and a large part of Pennsylvania."

In the year 1813, a young man named Michael Osborn was apprenticed to W. Crane, a joint proprietor with Israel Crane and others in the cotton spinning mills located near the present site of the vacant Wheeler mill just off from Bloomfield Avenue, where the D., L. & W. R.R. crosses it. He became acquainted with another young man named Gorline Doremus; and, both anxious to do good, they resolved to organize a Sunday school. Several of the parents objected as they thought that the day school was sufficient. The school was, however, opened with eight scholars, and met in the school-house which stood where the Presbyterian Church of Bloomfield now stands. This antedates the Sunday school of the First Presbyterian Church of Newark, which claims to be the oldest Sunday school in New Jersey. The school grew rapidly. The school attached to the church which was then located in Wall Street, New York City, of which young Osborn was a member, made a donation of books and tracts. In a short time Osborn left the place to receive an education and finally entered the ministry. Doremus left the school and soon after this he withdrew from the Presbyterian Church and connected himself with the Methodist Society. "The Society, which was feeble, met in a small stone church which was erected about 1818, and stood on the Paterson Road near Bay Lane. It was torn down in 1853 and a portion of its materials used in building the present Bloomfield Church. Meetings were held not only here but in the upper part of Garrabrant's wagon manufactory, and in the old house at the corner of Old Road and Bay Lane. On one occasion a young man stood up to preach a sermon. He was timid, for it was his trial sermon, and by it he was to be judged whether he was a suitable person to enter the ministry. He preferred to stand in front of the the pulpit and not in it. He was of delicate form and his voice was weak; but he gave the message of God to the people and he was licensed to preach. A great mission was before him, for in 1844 he was elected a Bishop of the Church, and for thirty-three years Bishop Edmund S. Janes did grand and faithful work and, dying, left behind him the reputation of being the most effective Bishop which the Methodist Episcopal Church in America has ever had."

The Methodist Episcopal Church at Montclair was an outgrowth from that at Bloomfield, as the Bloomfield Church was from that of Belleville. The three churches were on one wide circuit, and churches at Belleville, Bloomfield, Montclair and Orange were organized in order. The early Bloomfield Church worshiped for some years in the house of Mrs. Naomi Cockfair, north of the Morris neighborhood, previous to the erection of the stone church above Bay Lane. Meetings were held in the western part of the town about 1817, at Joel Crane's house across the turnpike from where Leist's hotel now stands. "Wood meetings" were also held south of the Joel Crane house at about the same time. In 1827 James Wilde and family came from Saddleworth, Lancashire, England, and established a woolen factory in the Israel Crane mill. During the early years Rev. Isaac Winner, who supplied the circuit, organized a church in Orange, in which Henry Wilde, of West Bloomfield, was a trustee. The Wildes were originally Church of England people, but the second Mrs. Wilde had become a Wesleyan in England. The earlier portion of the Wilde family—especially John, who was a son of James by his first wife—gave assistance in the organization of St. Luke's Episcopal Church, but the latter portion supported the Methodist organization. The strength, therefore, in the town was transferred to the vicinity of the factories. The Washington School-house was erected in the immediate vicinity by James Wilde, the elder. The first sermon in it was preached by the Rev. John Kennedy. Few of the children could attend the school as they nearly all worked in the mills, so a Sunday school was organized with Mr. Radcliffe as Superintendent. Two sessions were held and the room was full of scholars. There was also preaching service every Sunday afternoon. Reading and writing were taught, as well as the Bible and catechism, and parents and children alike attended. When the day school was established secular instruction was omitted in the Sunday school. Here the school met until the erection of the present church building in 1836 (now occupied by the colored M. E. Church, on Bloomfield Avenue), when the school was transferred to the gallery of the church.

"On February 20th, 1828, at a meeting of the male members, the following persons were duly elected Trustees (the first Trustees of the congregation): John Moore, Gorline Doremus, Josiah W. Crane, Michael Cockefair and James Wilde. Gorline Doremus was probably the most useful member the church has ever had. For forty-three years he was closely identified with its interests, and his name constantly appears on the records of the church. For a portion of that long period he was Treasurer, class leader, and Sunday-school teacher, and his house was always open to a Methodist preacher. He died March 21st, 1873, at the age of 81 years, and on his tombstone are engraved these words: 'His record is on high.'

"In 1830 Bloomfield became the head of the circuit, which included Orange, Woodbridge, and several other places. The first quarterly conference was held at Fairfield, June 12. Among those present was the Presiding Elder, Rev. Charles Pitman, who afterward became Missionary Secretary of the Methodist Church. There was present also as a class-leader, Edwin L. Janes, twin brother of Bishop Janes, and who at this conference received license to preach; and Henry Wilde, a son of James Wilde, who acted as secretary for the quarterly conference from 1830 to 1833. (Still living 1894).

"In 1835 the quarterly conference was formed into a two weeks' circuit with one preacher, and a year later Rev. Mr. Swain was appointed to the Orange Society, and from that time Bloomfield was no longer a circuit, but rose to the dignity of a station.

"In the year 1831 lots were procured for a church and parsonage. The deed shows that the money was paid for these lots, but it is said that the ground was given by James Wilde, although the amount was not entered in the deed. In that same year a contract was made with Michael Cockefair to erect a parsonage at a cost of $1,000. It was not until five years later that the building was erected. It was finished in the autumn of 1836."

The pastor at this time was Rev. Waters Burrows, who was also one of the trustees; he died March 4, 1869, aged seventy-nine years.

The church had for many years a financial struggle. The members were few in number, and many of them able to give but little money.

In those years the salary of the ministers was small. In 1853 it was unanimously voted that the preacher should receive a salary of $350 a year. In 1864, when the price of everything was at the highest point, the estimate for the preacher was $600. From that time it advanced to $700, then $1,000, and then to $1,200, and has since been still further increased.

The church during its history has raised considerable money for benevolent purposes. The year 1866 was known as the Centenary year. Large collections were raised in all Methodist churches to what was called the Centenary Fund—to commemorate the one hundredth anniversary of the first sermon preached by a Methodist preacher in America. This church raised for that fund $862.

There have been a number of revivals in the church, but the greatest of these was under the pastorate of Rev. John Scarlet, in the winter of 1857-8, when a great revival spread over the whole country. Crowded meetings were held night after night for many weeks; the whole town was stirred, and 90 persons were added to the church, which then had but 86 members.

In 1851 the Methodists of Bloomfield began to solicit subscriptions for the purpose of building a church edifice; the building however was not completed until 1853, and the church did not have a separate preacher until the spring of 1858. The new organization as a separate body left the old in a weakened condition, and for a short time the later was known as the West Bloomfield Mission. The great revival referred to however, in 1857-8, added materially to its numbers, and it then became known as the

WEST BLOOMFIELD METHODIST EPISCOPAL CHURCH; AFTER 1860, MONTCLAIR M. E. CHURCH.

For several years the subject of changing the location of the church to a more central neighborhood was considered, but nothing definite was accomplished until 1879, when a lot was

M. E. CHURCH AND   SE.

purchased on the west side of Fullerton Avenue, north of Bloomfield Avenue, on which was erected a handsome wooden structure. An ample parsonage adjoining the church lot was completed and occupied in November, 1884. The total valuation of the present church property is about $30,000. The old church edifice was vacated after the last meeting, held on Sunday evening, December 7, 1879, and since 1883 has been occupied by the colored Methodists.

The new church edifice was formally dedicated December 14, 1879, with appropriate ceremonies.

Chaplain McCabe led the congregation in prayer, and Dr. Hunt read a portion of the "form prescribed for the dedication of a church," by the book of discipline. The morning sermon was preached by Rev. J. F. Hurst, D.D.

The statement was made by Chaplain McCabe that the cost of the church, and the land on which it stood, was about $40,000. There was at that time a balance due of about $5,000. The amount subscribed at the morning service was over $3,000.

Chaplain McCabe preached the evening sermon, at which time subscription lists were again opened, and the total sum raised at this and two previous sessions amounted to $5,234.

Rev. Dr. Berry of the Presbyterian, and Rev. A. H. Bradford, D.D., of the Congregational Church, took part in the ceremonies and spoke encouraging words for the movement.

The following is a list of those who have served since 1865: Rev. Jeremiah Cowins, 1865 to '67; Rev. Jesse Lyman Hurlburt, 1867 to '69; Rev. Thomson H. Landon, 1869 to '72; Rev. James L. Ayers, 1872 to '74; Rev. G. W. Smith, 1874 to '77; Rev. Jonathan K. Burr, March, 1877, to Nov., 1878; left on account of sickness; Rev. James I. Boswell, March, 1879, to March, 1880; Rev. John J. Reed, 1880 to 1881; Rev. John Crawford, April, 1881, to March, 1884; Rev. Morris D. Church, April, 1884, to March, 1887; Rev. Charles S. Woodruff, April, 1887, to March, 1890; Rev. J. A. Owen, 1890, still continues (1893).

SUNDAY SCHOOL.

From the beginning of the Sunday-school movement in 1813, there have been found faithful workers in this church, who from year to year have kept up the interest in the school whether preaching services were held or not. The list of those who have been especially prominent in this work is incomplete. Gorline Doremus maintained his interest in the school up to the day of his death. There was a period of depression in 1855, and a material falling off in numbers. The attendance of teachers at that time was from 6 to 12, and of scholars from 40 to 70. The Superintendent was away from home for six months; the former librarian had left, and, owing to the difficulty experienced in warming the building, the school was closed during the winter. In 1858, however, Rev. John Scarlett, writes: "The school was never in a more flourishing condition."

Among those of later years who have been conspicuous for their zeal and earnestness in the Sunday-school work are James Robley, Joseph H. Richards and Stephen A. Tower. James Robley was Superintendent from 1859 to 1866, when Joseph H. Richards succeeded him, and who, for thirteen years, by his faithful, earnest efforts, lifted the school to a high grade. Mr. Richards removed to Elizabeth in 1879, and was succeeded by Chas. I. Reeves (who had been brought into the church during Mr. Richards' service), and who served the school for fourteen years; who in turn was succeeded, in 1893, by Mr. Frank H. Syvelt, the present incumbent.

The present membership of the school is 6 officers, 24 teachers, and 134 scholars in the main school; 3 teachers and 100 scholars in the Bible classes, and 12 teachers and 77 scholars in the primary department; making a total of 356.

ST. LUKE'S PROTESTANT EPISCOPAL CHURCH.

The first church edifice in which the Episcopal Church service was held in this locality was a small frame building 25 by 40 feet, in the rear of a deep lot fronting the turnpike, or what is now Bloomfield Avenue. This was erected by John Wilde, son of James Wilde, the founder of the Methodist Church in the same locality. While the father was a strong believer in the Wesleyan doctrine, John and one or two of his brothers were firm adherents of the Church of England. The locality selected for the first church edifice was in the midst of what was then a manufacturing district. This was in 1846, and there was a large and growing population in that neighborhood. Later, the "new comers," who were mostly settled in the western part of the village, met in this building, and services were held with more or less regularity until May, 1858, when it was decided to organize. On Easter Monday, 1860, St. Luke's Parish was formally constituted by the election of a vestry, and in May following Rev. Henry Marsh was chosen Rector and the Rev. George R. Davis Assistant Minister. The first wardens were Owen Doremus and C. St. John Seymour, and the vestrymen were Dr. R. F. Brower, Richard Naylor, William H. Ashley, H. N. Chittenden and George N. Wright. Mr. St. John Seymour was untiring in his efforts for the church, and to him, more than to any other man, the parish owes its existence to-day. Rev. Henry Marsh served from May 11 to November 5, 1860. Rev. Geo. R. Davis continued in charge of the parish until the autumn of 1862. Services were then held by the Rev. J. D. Moore and others until October 30, 1864, when the Rev. James Chrystal was chosen Rector. The attendance at this time was small, most of the families living at a great distance from the church. The sittings were free, and the expenses were mostly borne by members of the vestry. It was thought the church would succeed better in some other locality, and a site on Fullerton Avenue was thought to be the most desirable, but while the matter was under consideration, Mr. Robert M. Hening, a member of the vestry, offered to give a plot of land on what was afterward known as St. Luke's Place. His offer was accepted, and, in addition, he contributed a large amount toward the erection of a church edifice. Others joined in this undertaking, and in 1865 the corner stone of the new church was laid. It was proposed to build it of stone as the money was contributed, and no contract was made for the labor. This proved to be a serious mistake, for before the building was half completed the cost had exceeded the original estimates for the entire building. The work continued under great embarrassment for a time, and it finally became necessary to mortgage the property in order to complete the building. Further advances were made by individual members of the vestry, and it was finally finished in April, 1870. Rev. Mr. Chrystal resigned as rector in 1867, and was succeeded by Rev. James L. Maxwell, who remained with the church until 1884. During this period the church became much embarrassed, the income being insufficient to meet the large interest account after paying current expenses. The large mortgage, and contingent liability, threatened to bankrupt the church. A settlement was finally effected that scaled down the mortgage and wiped out the contingent liability. Under this settlement the debt was being gradually reduced, when Rev. Frederick B. Carter became rector of the parish in 1884. A few years thereafter the entire debt was paid off, and as the membership of the church increased, the building on St. Luke's Place was found to be totally inadequate to meet the growing demands. At this juncture, Mr. William Fellowes, a parishioner, offered to give the lot on the corner of Fullerton Avenue and Union Street, provided the parish would build there, and complete the edifice free of debt. This being agreed to, and Mr. Fellowes having further contributed most liberally, the corner stone of the present edifice was laid by Bishop Starkey with impressive ceremonies on June 13, 1889, and on Advent Sunday, November 30, 1890, the first service was held therein.

The architect was Mr. R. H. Robertson, of New York, and the design is modernized Gothic in style, and cruciform in plan; 123 feet in length by 84 in extreme breadth. The building contains a nave 82 by 44 feet, two transepts, each 40 feet wide by 20 deep, and a chancel 38 feet deep and 32 wide, including an apsidal vaulted sanctuary 14 feet deep, separated from the choir by an arch. The nave and transepts are nearly 50 feet high from floor to ridge. The church seats 750 persons, and there is an unobstructed view of the chancel, owing to the entire absence of columns—a notable feature. The chancel has stalls for fifty choristers. On its northern side is the organ chamber, containing a fine three-manual instrument by Harrison, having more than 2,000 pipes, and on the southern side is a spacious vestry, which is used also as a place of assembly for the choir just before beginning the processional, and which communicates with the nearest transept by a wide Gothic double door. Both the organ chamber and the vestry are separated from the chancel by passageways opening into the nave, which are utilized as exits for communicants. The robing-room for the choir occupies the full depth of the building beneath the chancel.

The nave is lighted at the west by a cluster of five Gothic windows of equal height, surmounted by a rose window, and the transepts by similar clusters rising in height toward the centre. The choir has two upper windows on the south, and the apse five, all with glass by Booth, the two nearest the choir being designs without figures, and the others figures emblematic of Faith, Hope and Charity; Faith and Hope on each side being represented as women, while Love, in the centre, is represented by a figure of our Lord as the Good Shepherd. The altar and reredos are of commanding design, these and all the other chancel furniture, together with the pews, being of antique oak. The pews have been specially admired for their design and for their comfortableness.

The acoustic properties of the church are remarkably good. There are five entrances. On the north is a church porch, which can be entirely shut off from the body of the building and from other entrances, making it specially convenient for weddings, etc. Another door leads directly into the tower and thence both to the porch and to the nave. The carriage entrance is on the south, and on the southeast and east there are doors for clergy and choir respectively. The building is of reddish brown sandstone from the Belleville quarries, and the tower, when completed, will rise, with its spire, to the height of about 160 feet. The total cost of the property thus far had been about $90,000.

Being entirely free from debt, the church was consecrated on December 20, 1892. The rector had appointed Rev. Alexander Mann, of Orange, as master of ceremonies, who marshalled the clergy and choir into procession. The clergy followed Bishop Starkey, who had his pastoral staff borne before him by his chaplain, the Rev. John Keller, as he walked up the middle aisle repeating, with the clergy, Psalm xxiv. The instrument of donation was then presented by Mr. D. N. Force, the senior warden of the parish. The sentence of consecration was read by the Rev. Frederick B. Carter, the rector of the parish. Before the commencement of Morning Prayer, the bishop made a brief and happy address of congratulation to the congregation, in which he referred to the beautiful gifts of one of the parishioners in particular, as well as to the devotion of the vestry of the church, and he also paid a well deserved tribute to the rector for his faithfulness as a pastor, and for his loyalty as a priest of the diocese to its bishop.

Morning Prayer was said by the Rev. Archdeacon Walker, Dr. Gould, of Philadelphia, Dr. Bishop, Dr. Boggs and Rev. C. S. Abbott. The sermon was delivered by the Rt. Rev. Ethelbert Talbot, D. D., Bishop of Wyoming and Idaho. It was a forcible presentation of the half-forgotten truth that a church to be known by its good works must be a worshipping church; and an earnest exhortation to the congregation present to make good use of the consecrated building. The bishop of the diocese celebrated the Holy Communion, as-

ST. LUKE'S EPISCOPAL CHURCH.

bot and Archdeacon Jenvey. The offerings were received for the Parish House and Sunday school building fund. The music was rendered by the vested choir of between thirty and forty men and boys of St. Luke's, under the direction of Mr. Joseph H. Moore, the organist and choirmaster of the church. The work of the choristers was well done and fully sustained the more than local reputation of Mr. Moore as a reverent, scholarly and efficient church musician.

Among the visiting clergy were the Rev. Messrs. Richard Hayward, Harold Arrowsmith, Frank A. Sanborn, M. M. Fothergill, John S. Miller, F. M. McAllister, of Elizabeth, and Dr Haskins, of Brooklyn.

In 1892 the old church property was sold to Montclair School District No. 8, and with the proceeds, and the promise of subscriptions in addition, a parish building was commenced in 1893 connected by covered cloister with the church. It is expected to be ready on or about Easter, 1894.

The building is intended for the Sunday school, chapel and parish house work. It has a seating capacity of about 400, and is admirably arranged for these purposes. The architect is Mr. Wm. Halsey Wood. The estimated cost of the entire property, with church spire and rectory, will be about $150,000, and when completed it will be free from debt. For convenience of location, commanding site, and admirable arrangements, this property has few equals in the State of New Jersey.

As the parish grew the work of the rector increased, so that for a long time he had most valuable help from Mr. Arthur E. Bostwick in the Sunday school, and as lay reader in church services. Mr. Bayard Whitehorne succeeded Mr. Bostwick in the Sunday school in 1892.

After beginning the parish house it was evident that the work would be greatly augmented, and an opportunity offering, in the fall of 1893, for securing a deacon in orders, whose whole time would be given, it was decided to engage, as rector's assistant, the Rev. Claudius M. Roome.

He entered on his duties at once, and later, on Sunday, February 11, 1894, was solemnly ordained a priest by Bishop Starkey, at morning services.

The members of the vestry at this time, March, 1894, are as follows: Senior Warden, Dexter N. Force; Junior Warden, Frederick W. Gwinn; Vestrymen, Edwin A. Bradley, Joel Jenkins, John T. Weeks, Edward G. Burgess, F. Meriam Wheeler, George I. Wichman, George Batten.

.

THE CHURCH OF THE IMMACULATE CONCEPTION,

(Roman Catholic) is an outgrowth from Belleville. The Rev. John Hogan, pastor of St. Peter's Church, Belleville, visited West Bloomfield, as one of his stations, and about 1856 the edifice was erected. It was located on Washington Street. It continued under the care of the Belleville pastor till 1864. The Rev. Titus Joslyn, the first resident pastor, came to the congregation on February 6th of that year. He was born a Protestant, in Schenectady, N. Y., and was educated in Union College, under the care of his father, Professor Joslyn, of that college. His parents removed to New York in 1843, where he was baptized by Bishop Hughes, June 16, 1845. He entered St. Joseph's Seminary, under the Jesuits, in 1847, was ordained priest in St. Patrick's Cathedral, in New York, March 13, 1852, and labored under the direction of Archbishop Hughes till he came to the parish—West Bloomfield. He remained pastor for over ten years—till September 5, 1874. Under his direction the church was enlarged, in 1856 the tower built, and one-half of the present property purchased. The parish included the Roman Catholic population of Caldwell, Bloomfield and Watesssing.

The Rev. A. M. Steet succeeded Mr. Joslyn as pastor from September 5, 1874, to March 18, 1879. During his pastorate the new rectory, at the corner of Elm and Fulton Streets, was built in 1876.

Rev. Joseph F. Mendl was appointed rector of the parish in April, 1879, by Archbishop Corrigan, who was then Bishop of the diocese of Newark. There were at that time about 900 communicants. In August, 1893, after a thorough canvass of the parish, it was found that there were 1,520—an increase of nearly sixty-seven per cent.

The religious and secular education of the children became a matter of paramount importance with Father Mendl, and in September, 1881, a parochial school was established, with 210 pupils, taught by five Sisters of Charity, from Madison, N. J. This has now an average daily attendance of 250 pupils. The property of Bernard Wallace was purchased for the church the same year.

In 1878 the Church of the Sacred Heart was organized in Bloomfield, it being an outgrowth of the Montclair Church. Caldwell and Verona, which were formerly included in this parish, were subsequently separated, and in 1885 Rev. J. J. Shannessy was appointed the first resident pastor of the new church.

At the time of its organization the church on Washington Street was considered to be centrally located for the population of Montclair and Bloomfield, but after the organization of the

Bloomfield Church it was thought advisable to select a location nearer to the mountain, as the new township was growing rapidly in that direction; and in December, 1891, a large building site was purchased of Theodore Carter on the corner of North Fullerton Avenue and Munn Street, for the sum of $20,000. Additional land was purchased of J. N. Rudgers, in 1892, adjoining the other, for $10,000.

Plans for an imposing church edifice were designed by William Schickel, architect, of New York, and ground was broken in May, 1892. The corner stone was laid October 21, 1893, the ceremonies being conducted by the Right Rev. W. M. Wigger, D.D. The sermon on that occasion was preached by Rev. J. J. Synnott, D.D., a member of the parish, and the first American student who received the degree of D.D. at the Catholic University in Innsbruck, Tyrol, in 1887; he is at present Professor of Theology at Seton Hall College, South Orange, N. J.

The basement of the new church was finished and covered with a temporary roof, and dedicated on Decoration Day, 1893, by Right Rev. W. M. Wigger. The first ser vice in the new place of worship was held on the first Sunday in June, 1893. The basement has a seat ing capacity for 1,000 people. It is built of Belleville brown stone, and cost $26,000.

The style of architect ure of the completed church is to be Roman esque, clear-story, of Belleville brown stone, the tower to be located at the corner of North Ful lerton Avenue and Munn Street. It will have a frontage on North Fuller ton Avenue of 75 feet, and 178 feet in depth. The estimated cost of the building, complete, is $75,000.

Two insurance societies have been established in the parish, one, a branch of the Catholic Benevo lent Legion, "Father Streets's Council," in 1883; another, Branch 426, of the Catholic Knights of America, in November, 1885.

THE CHURCH OF THE IMMACULATE CONCEPTION.

JOSEPH FRANCIS MENDL, rector of the Church of the Immaculate Concep tion, was born in Inns bruck, Tyrol, Austria, March 17, 1843. He was educated in the Gymna sium in Brixen, and spent four years in the study of theology. He was or dained a priest July 25, 1865, and immediately sent on a mission as assist ant curate. At the break ing out of the Austria- Prussian war (Prussia and Italy allied against Aus tria), in 1866, he served as chaplain in the Austrian Army with the commission of Captain, being at the time the youngest priest in the diocese. At the close of the war he returned to the mission, and in 1869 went to the American College,[*] Louvain, Belgium, as prefect, remaining two years, until October, 1871, when he came to this country and was appointed curate of St. Peter's Church, Newark, in October, 1872; he was then sent to St. Paul's Church, Jersey City, as pastor, continuing until 1878. On Christmas, 1878, he came to Montclair, and assumed his present charge. Under his pastorate the church rapidly increased in membership, necessitating, in 1881, the building of a gallery, with an additional seating capacity of 300. There was then a debt on the church of $16,000, which has since been liquidated, and large

[*] Archbishop Riordan, of San Francisco, Archbishop Janssens, of New Orleans, Bishop Spalding, of Peoria, Ill., Bishop Vander Vyver, of Richmond, Va., Bishop Maas, of Covington, Ky., Bishop Brondel, of Helena, Montana, and about 500 priests of this country were graduates of this college.

additional sums raised for the erection of the new church edifice. The amount was raised by him largely among the poorer classes, the total amount exceeding $16,000. He established the parochial school and gave up his own elegant residence on Elm Street for that purpose. He is beloved by his people, respected and honored in the community, and devoted to the interests of his church.

THE FIRST CONGREGATIONAL CHURCH OF CHRIST.

This Church and Society, although of recent origin, having been established long after the founding of the present town of Montclair, has grown to be not only the largest in the township, but, with one exception, the largest church in the State—having a membership of over 700. Its history covers a period of nearly a quarter of a century, all under one pastorate. That its denominational views are in harmony with the sentiments of the community is evinced by its steady growth, the character of its membership, and the far-reaching results of the work accomplished by it. Though one of the youngest churches in this community it is one of the oldest in the State. The motto inscribed on the title page of this work — *Qui transtulit sustinet* — is demonstrated by the past and present history of this denomination.

The preliminary movements which led to the organization of this church are briefly stated in an "Historical Sketch, 1870," published in the "Manual of the First Congregational Church of Christ, Montclair, N. J., 1890," as follows:

"The Great Head of the Church having, as we trust, put into the hearts of many in this region the desire to worship God, and to act, and to come together in accordance with the principles laid down in the New Testament, and with the practice of our New England Fathers, a meeting with reference to this end was held on the 18th of December, A. D. 1869, at the residence of Joseph B. Beadle, at which the following persons were present: Joseph Beadle, Thomas H. Bouden, Samuel Boyd, Samuel D. Crosby, Samuel Holmes, William B. Holmes, David B. Hunt, Charles H. Johnson, Edward S. Pinney, Theodore L. Snyder, Samuel W. Tubbs and Samuel Wilde, Jr. At this meeting after a full interchange of views, it was unanimously resolved: That, be-

FIRST CONGREGATIONAL CHURCH.

lieving that the interests of the cause of Christ in this place demand the organization of a new Church and Society, we do pledge to each other our mutual and hearty support in such an enterprise. A committee on organization was then appointed, consisting of Samuel Holmes, Charles H. Johnson, Samuel Wilde, Jr., Joseph B. Beadle and Edward S. Pinney.

This committee made a report January 17, 1870, recommending a call for a meeting for organization, which was adopted. The following persons were then added to the Committee: Julius H. Pratt, James B. Pearson, and Rev. Daniel S. Rodman.

At a meeting held on the 29th of January, 1870, the Society was organized, and the following persons were elected Trustees: Samuel Holmes, Joseph B. Beadle, Charles H. Johnson, Edward Sweet, Samuel Wilde, Jr., and Julius H. Pratt.

At this meeting Mr. Julius H. Pratt, by request, read a paper entitled "Montclair Prior to the Organization of the Congregational Church," in which he clearly established the "prior claims" of this "new Church and Society." After briefly reviewing the history of the other religious denominations of Montclair, and his own work in connection with them, he says: "As Congregationalists we are not intruders, and we make no apology for being here, for we come only to claim a long neglected inheritance which is ours by indisputable right."

Referring to the little band of Connecticut colonists—30 in number—under the leadership of Rev. Abraham Pierson, who separated from the Church of Branford because of their unwillingness to accept the doctrine of the "half-way covenant," and removed to New Jersey, landing on the west shore of the Passaic, at a place which they named "Neworke"—new work—meaning the "new enterprise," Mr. Pratt says: "I have alluded to the extinct race of Congregationalists who once dominated the greater part of the State of New Jersey, and our time may be profitably employed in a rapid glance at the history of the New England pilgrims who first settled in this region when it was a primitive wilderness."

After a brief review of the events connected with their settlement Mr. Pratt says: "One of the earliest public acts performed by this Puritanic Colony was the formal signing of the document entitled 'Fundamental Agreement,' by 64 heads of families, which document is still preserved among the public records."

The agreement sets forth the desire of the Colonists "to be of one heart and consent through God's blessing, that with one hand they may endeavor the carrying on of *spiritual* concernments, as also of spiritual affairs according to God and a Godly government."

This original Declaration of Independence as to man and dependence on God declares (see "Atkinson's History of Newark":

Deut., i : 13. "1st. That none shall be admitted freemen or free burgesses within our town upon
Exod., xviii : 21. Passaic, in the Province of New Jersey, but such planters as are members of some or
Deut., xvii : 15. other of the Congregational churches.
Jerem., xxx : 21.

"Nor shall any but such be chosen to any magistracy or to carry on any part of said civil judicature, or as deputies or assistants to have power to vote in establishing laws, and making or repealing them, or to any chief military trust of office.

"Nor shall any but such church members have any vote in any such election."

The four Scriptural references in the foregoing are as follows:

"Take you wise men, and understanding, and known among your tribes, and I will make them rulers over you" (Deut., i : 13).

"Moreover thou shalt provide out of all the people, able men, such as fear God, men of truth, hating covetousness; and place such over them to be rulers of thousands, and rulers of hundreds, rulers of fifties, and rulers of tens" (Exodus, xviii : 21).

"Thou shalt in any wise set him King over thee, whom the Lord thy God shall choose: one from among thy brethren shalt thou set King over thee; thou mayest not set a stranger over thee, which is not thy brother" (Deut., xvii : 15).

"And their nobles shall be of themselves and their Governor shall proceed from the midst of them" (Jer., xxx : 21).

"Among the signatures to this Congregational charter are the names of Crane, Pierson, Ward, Harrison, Davis, Bauldwin, Morris, and others whose descendants became a century later, and have ever since continued, the standard bearers and pillars of the Presbyterian Church of New Jersey. No human purpose was ever more clearly defined than that of these early settlers to adhere rigidly to the Congregational faith and order.

"It is a curious question, not fully explained by any historical records. How did it happen that in less than 150 years all the early vows of devotion to Congregational ideas had become broken, and all these churches professing that faith had been swept into the vortex of Presbyterianism, an organization which struck its first roots into the New Jersey soil fifty years after the advent of the Connecticut Colony?"

Mr. Pratt then reviews the history of Presbyterianism, and shows how by degrees Congregationalism became united with and gradually merged into Presbyterianism. Continuing, he says:

"This fatal union which soon embraced all, or nearly all, the churches founded by the Congregationalist settlers in New Jersey proved to be the union of the lion and the lamb, with the lamb inside, which by the succession processes of deglutition, digestion, absorption and assimilation added immensely to the stature and strength of a constitution favored by the accession of a new and rich blood.

"The process of digestion was going on from about 1720 to 1736, when by the 'Adopting Acts,' so called, the present system of Presbyterianism was established on the Western Continent, and the early Congregational Churches of New Jersey thus vanished away.

"What is the lesson taught us by such a distinctive dispensation?

"That the old testament religion is not adapted to modern life—that the new gospel of universal charity must crush all barriers of sect, and exterminate all theological dogmas of human invention.

"The old Puritans had great virtues and great faults. The good in them was transmitted to their posterity, and to-day shines forth in glorious lustre from our Presbyterian churches. Their illiberal and narrow prejudices, which were the fruit of a hard and persecuted life, were swept away by the free breezes of our new World. Now, on the same soil where the old Congregational policy perished, a resuscitated life asserts itself, and with the spirit of 'malice toward none and charity for all,' Congregationalism only seeks the opportunity of joining hands with Christian brethren, of whatever sects, in the great work of regenerating the world."

On the evening of February 19th, 1870, a committee consisting of Rev. Daniel S. Rodman, James B. Pearson, Alexander M. Clerihew, David B. Hunt, and Samuel D. Crosby, was appointed to prepare by-laws and business rules for the society, and on the 29th of March following the basis of Union and By-Laws were adopted.

At a meeting held at the residence of Edward Sweet, April 5, 1870, it was voted that measures be taken toward the organization of a Church, and that the Committee on "By-Laws for the Society" be a Committee on Organization, and to prepare and submit for consideration Articles of Faith and a Covenant.

LIST OF MEMBERS IN THE CHURCH WHEN ORGANIZED.

May 29, 1870, arranged as originally signed, with subsequent additions in chronological order.

Samuel Holmes.   By letter from The Broadway Tabernacle Church, New York City.

Mary G. Holmes.

Jane A. Hemingway.   First Congregational Church, Fair Haven, Conn.

Mary M. McLaughlin.   Presbyterian Church, Montclair, New Jersey.

Lewis S. Benedict,   ″   ″

Harriet J. Benedict,   ″   ″

Sarah Benedict,   ″   ″

Minnie H. Benedict,   ″   ″

John W. Taylor,   ″   ″

Amelia Benedict Taylor,

Samuel Boyd,   Plymouth Church, Brooklyn. N Y.

Sylvia C. Boyd,   ″   ″

Edward S. Pinney,   Presbyterian Church, Montclair, N. J.

Elsie P. Pinney,   ″   ″

Charles E. Baker,   ″   ″

E. Louise Baker,   ″   ″

Thomas H. Bouden.   First Congregational Church, Jersey City, N. J.

Lucy A. Bouden,   ″   ″

Samuel Wilde, Jr.,   Presbyterian Church, Montclair, N. J.

Mary E. Wilde,   ″   ″

William H. Wilson,   First Reformed Church, Hoboken, N. J.

Cynthia Wilson,   ″   ″

Charlotte L. Wilson,   ″   ″

George S. Merriam.   Congregational Church, Yale College, New Haven, Conn.

William B. Holmes.   The Broadway Tabernacle Church, New York City.

Mary H. Holmes.   ″   ″

Nehemiah O. Pillsbury.   Presbyterian Church, Montclair, N. J.

Mary K. Pillsbury,   ″   ″

Adra E. Bradbury,   First Presbyterian Church, Bloomfield, N. J.

Amanda F. Bradbury,   Presbyterian Church, Montclair, N. J.

Israel Crane,   Plymouth Church. Milwaukee. Wis.

Anna B. Crane,   Presbyterian Church, Montclair, N. J.

Anna D. Lloyd,   Elm Place Congregational Church, Brooklyn, N. Y.

Frances J. Platt,   ″   ″

Evelyn S. Platt,   First Congregational Church, Jersey City, N. J.

Charles H. Johnson,   ″   ″

Nettie H. Johnson,   Presbyterian Church, Montclair, N. J.

Joseph B. Beadle,   ″   ″

Laura A. Beadle,   ″   ″

Edward Sweet,   Madison Square Presbyterian Church, New York City.

Carrie W. Sweet,   ″   ″

Anna C. Bull,   ″   ″

Fannie H. Harrison,   Lee Avenue Reformed Church, Brooklyn, N. Y.

Henry Nason,   Presbyterian Church, Montclair, N. J.

Anna G. Nason,   ″   ″

Abbie Y. Smith,   ″   ″

Theodore L. Snyder.   Chestnut Street Presbyterian Church, Louisville, Ky.

Julia L. Snyder,   Presbyterian Church, Montclair, N. J.

Samuel H. Snyder.   ″   ″

Fannie D. Crosby,   ″   ″

Mary N. Crosby,   ″   ″

Jesse H. Lockwood,   Congregational Church, Williams' Bridge, N. Y.

Sarah R. Lockwood,   First Congregational Church, Jersey City, N. J.

Susie G. Shafer,   ″   ″

Samuel W. Tubbs,   Plymouth Church, Brooklyn, N. Y.

Ruth Emma Tubbs,   Sands Street Methodist Episcopal Church, Brooklyn, N. Y.

Alexander M. Clerihew.   First Congregational Church, Jersey City, N. J.

Emily F. Clerihew,   ″   ″

David B. Hunt,   By letter from Presbyterian Church, Montclair, N. J.

Mary A. Hunt,   ″   ″

Mary C. Hunt,   ″   ″

David B. Hunt, Jr.,   ″   ″

Helen E. Terry.   Congregational Church, Northville, L. I., N. Y.

James B. Pearson.   Madison Avenue Presbyterian Church, New York City.

Ellen J. Pearson.   Classon Avenue Presbyterian Church Brooklyn, N. Y.

Charles J. Pearson.

Angeline Horton.   Presbyterian Church, Montclair, N. J.

Margaret A. Hamilton.   Lee Avenue Reformed Church, Brooklyn, N. Y.

John W. Pinkham,   Presbyterian Church, Montclair, N. J.

Cornelia F. Pinkham,   ″   ″

Josiah T. Wilcox,   ″   ″

Helen M. Wilcox,   ″   ″

George W. Leonard,   ″   ″

Mary J. Leonard,   ″   ″

Julius H. Pratt,   ″   ″

Adeline F. Pratt,   ″   ″

Gertrude C. Pratt.   ″   ″

Mary C. Crane,   ″   ″

Abbie F. Crane,   ″   ″

Henrietta G. Chittenden.   Plymouth Church, Brooklyn, N. Y.

Daniel S Rodman,   Second Congregational Church, Stonington, Conn.

Lucy W. Rodman.   ″   ″

Nathan T. Porter.   From Baptist Church, Waterbury, Conn.

Mary C. Porter.   By letter from Second Congregational Church, New London, Conn.

November 6, 1870.

Nettie M. Bradbury,   By letter from Presbyterian Church, Bloomfield, N. J.

Amory H. Bradford   Congregational Church. Charlotte, Mich.

Julia S. Bradford,   Presbyterian Church, Clinton, N. Y.

Francis B. Littlejohn,   The Broadway Tabernacle Church, New York City.

Harry Littlejohn,   ″   ″

Agnes L. Littlejohn,   ″   ″

John Habberton,   Plymouth Church, Brooklyn, N. Y.

Alice L. Habberton,   ″   ″

January 1, 1871.

Dorman T. Warren,   By letter from Presbyterian Church, Montclair, N. J.

Harriet C. Warren,   ″   ″

Henry L. Crane,   ″   ″

Louisa DeLyons,   Second Baptist Church, Savannah, Ga.

Lucy M. Brown,   St. Luke's Church, East Greenwich, R. I.

Mary Jane Adams.   Fifth Avenue Presbyterian Church, New York City.

March 5, 1871.

James Baker.   By profession of faith.

May 7, 1871.

Henry White,   By profession of faith.

Henrietta B. White.   By profession of faith.

Theodore Taylor,   By letter from New England Church, New York City.

Mary R. Taylor,   ″   ″

July 2, 1871.

Charles A. Hopkins.   By letter from Tabernacle Church, Jersey City, N. J.

Sarah L. Hopkins,   ″   ″

Hattie M. Hopkins,   ″   ″

Frederick G Hastings,   Congregational Church, Northampton, Mass.

The following officers were chosen in accordance with the Constitution and By-Laws of the Church: *Deacons*—Samuel Holmes, Joseph B. Beadle, James B. Pearson and David B. Hunt. John W. Taylor was chosen Clerk, and Lewis S. Benedict, Samuel D. Crosby, and Samuel Wilde, Jr., members of the Standing Committee.

A hall was secured on Bloomfield Avenue, near Fullerton Avenue, in the third story of a building since destroyed by fire. This was fitted up as a place of worship, and on the morning of June 5, 1870, the first meeting of the church was held, at which service Rev. Leonard Bacon, D.D., of New Haven, Conn., preached the sermon and administered the rite of Baptism to three children, viz.: Grace Pinney, Lucy Rodgers Bonden, and Edwin Mortimer Harrison. On the afternoon of the same day this church by invitation united with the Presbyterian Church in a union Communion service. Rev. Dr. Bacon and Rev. Dr. Berry presided at the table, and the deacons of each church officiated in the service.

On the 8th of June, 1870, at three and a half o'clock P. M., a council was convened by invitation in the Presbyterian Church to examine the steps taken in the formation of this church, and to consider the propriety of its formal recognition. The following representing their several churches assembled in council:

Orange Valley Church—Rev. George B. Bacon, Pastor; Deacon A. Carter, Delegate. *Second Valley Church*, Orange—Rev. T. Atkinson, Pastor; Mr. A. Baldwin, Delegate. *Belleville Avenue Church*, Newark—Rev. C. B. Hulburt, Pastor; Mr. William D. Russell, Delegate. *Grove Street Church*, East Orange—Mr. R. D. Weeks, Delegate. *First Congregational Church*, Newark—Rev. William B. Brown, Pastor; Mr. J. P. Jube, Delegate; *Plymouth Church*, Brooklyn, N. Y. Mr. T. H. Bird, Delegate. *Church of the Puritans*, Brooklyn, N. Y.—Mr. T. H. Taylor, Delegate. *Broadway Tabernacle Church*, New York City—Rev. Joseph P. Thompson, D.D., Pastor; Deacon W. H. Thompson, Delegate. *First Congregational Church*, Jersey City—Rev. G. B. Willcox, Pastor; Deacon H. D. Holt, Delegate. Also Rev. G. W. Wood, D.D., and Rev. D. B. Coe, D.D.

The Church presented a statement of the steps it had already taken, its Articles of Faith, its Covenant, and the By-Laws of its Ecclesiastical Society, which were unanimously approved. On the evening of the same day, by appropriate services in the Presbyterian Church, this Church received formal recognition, and was welcomed to the Fellowship of the Churches. The exercises of the evening consisted of *Prayer*—by Rev. William B. Brown; *Sermon*—Rev. Joseph P. Thompson, D.D.; *Reading of the Articles of the Church*—Rev. G. B. Willcox (the Church assenting by rising); *Prayer of Recognition*—Rev. Henry M. Storrs, D.D.; *Fellowship of the Congregational Churches*—Rev. George B. Bacon; *Response in behalf of the Church*—Deacon Samuel Holmes; *Fellowship of the Churches in Montclair*—Rev. J. Romeyn Berry, D.D., Benedictine.

The regular weekly Prayer and Conference Meeting commenced on Thursday evening, June 16, 1870.

On June 28th following, the Church and Society extended a unanimous call to the Rev. Amory H. Bradford, of Andover Theological Seminary, to become their Pastor, which was accepted by him; and on the 28th of September, 1870, he was, with appropriate services, ordained to the work of the Gospel Ministry, and installed as pastor of the Church by a council called for this purpose, consisting of Mr. William D. Porter, delegate from Orange Valley Congregational Church; Mr. F. L. B. Mahew, delegate from Second Valley Church of Orange; Mr. Richard A. Thorpe, delegate from Trinity Congregational Church of East Orange; Rev. Allan McLean, Grove Street Church, East Orange; Rev. William B. Brown, First Congregational Church, Newark; Rev. C. B. Hulburt, and Mr. C. C. Collins, Belleville Avenue Church, Newark; Rev. G. B. Willcox and Deacon Winslow Ames, First Congregational Church, Jersey City; Rev. George Pierce and Mr. E. K. Rose, First Congregational Church, Paterson; Rev. S. B. Rossiter, First Congregational Church, Elizabeth; Rev. S. Bourne, First Congregational Church, Harlem, New York; Mr. W. Westerfield, Broadway Tabernacle Church, New York City; Deacon J. C. Barnes, Church of the Pilgrims, Brooklyn, N. Y.; Rev. John H. Brodt, and Mr. William Herres, New England Church, Williamsburgh, N. Y.; Rev. Edward Hawes and Mr. J. M. Edmunds, Central

Church, Philadelphia, Pa.; Rev. A. F. Beard, Plymouth Church, Syracuse, N. Y.; Rev. B. F. Bradford, First Congregational Church of Charlotte, Mich.; Rev. N. J. Burton, D.D., and Rev. M. E. Strieby, D.D.

Rev. Edward Hawes was chosen Moderator, and Rev. S. B. Rossiter, Scribe. The order of exercises at the Ordination Service consisted of *Devotional Services*—by Rev. J. Romeyn Berry, D.D.; *Sermon*—Rev. N. J. Burton, D.D., Hartford, Conn.; *Ordaining Prayer*—Rev. Ray Palmer, D.D., Newark, N. J.; *Charge to the Pastor*—Rev. B. F. Bradford, Charlotte, Mich.; *Right Hand of Fellowship*—Rev. G. B. Willcox, Jersey City, N. J.; *Charge to the People*—Rev. A. F. Beard, Syracuse, N. Y.; *Benediction*—by the Pastor.

The original place of worship selected by the Society was a hall in the third story of a building on Bloomfield Avenue, near Fullerton Street, and before the close of the first year these accommodations were found to be entirely inadequate owing to the rapid growth of the Church, and a permanent place of worship was felt to be an absolute and immediate necessity; and early in the year 1870 a movement was started to raise the requisite funds for the purchase of a site and the erection of a church edifice. Seventy-four persons subscribed $50,000, being an average of over $67 each. All gave liberally according to their means, and some even pledged the widow's mite to carry forward this great undertaking. A large building site was purchased on the corner of Plymouth and Fullerton Street, and the corner stone of the church was laid on the 30th of May, 1872, by the Pastor, Rev. Amory H. Bradford, and an address was delivered by Rev. George B. Bacon, of Orange Valley. Even the Presbyterian Church, ing exercises were held in by Rev. William M. Tay- and the sermon preached City. On the 15th of lor, D.D., of New York was dedicated with appro- October, 1873, the Church original cost of the land priate ceremonies. The the Church was about and the erection of $25,000 where the prop- $75,000. A mortgage of by the trustees provided erty and advances made debt, somewhat reduced for the balance. The tions from time to time, by subsequent subscrip- trustees until January, was carried along by the consent of the congrega-

INTERIOR OF FIRST CONGREGATIONAL CHURCH.
JUNE 8TH, 1890.

1884, when, by a general tion, it was resolved to raise by subscription a sufficient sum to pay off the debt and procure an organ. This movement was made on Sunday, the 15th of February, 1884, under the direction of Mr. Roswell Smith, of New York City. The total amount required—$35,000—was subscribed on that day, payable within a period of three years. The number of persons subscribing, was 111, many of whom were children paying small amounts. The largest sum subscribed was $3,200, the smallest sum being $1.50.

The organ, so long desired by the congregation, was purchased in April, 1882, which, together with the cost of erection, involved an outlay of $6,000, other changes and improvements made in the Church at the time increasing the amount to $10,000.

The growth of the Church has been phenomenal, far exceeding that of most suburban churches. Beginning, as has been shown, with a membership of 84 in 1870, the total number admitted up to January 1, 1893, was 1,002. Of this number at least 50 per cent. was by profession of faith. During the entire period of nearly twenty-three years only one member has been expelled. The loss by death and dismissal—230—leaving the total membership on the 1st of January, 1893, 772.

Soon after the celebration of its Twentieth Anniversary, steps were taken for the enlargement of the church edifice and erection of a chapel which should be suitable for the purposes of the Sunday school. It was decided that the audience room should be enlarged by the addition of transepts, which would make its seating capacity twelve hundred. Under the direction of J. C. Cady & Co., architects, of New York City, work was begun. At the same time Mrs. Samuel Wilde, one of the original members of the church, generously consented to undertake the erection of a Memorial Chapel, which should be devoted to the purposes of the Sunday school. Before that Mrs. Edward Sweet had undertaken the building of one of the transepts, in which she has since placed a beautiful window in memory of her husband. A memorial window of beautiful design was also placed in the north transept by Mrs. Roswell Smith, in memory of her two grandchildren, sons of Mr. George Inness, Jr., and Mrs. Julia G. Inness, members of the church. In about one year the improvements were completed, and the church property as it now stands represents an expenditure of about $175,000. The Memorial Chapel will comfortably seat one thousand people, and is admirably adapted for its purposes.

In 1882 the Pilgrim Mission Chapel was erected on Bloomfield Avenue. It is a beautiful building, perfectly equipped for its work, seating about four hundred people, and valued, including the land, at about $10,000. The land was the gift of Mr. James Beach, of Bloomfield. The Superintendent of the Mission is Mr. Louis Heckman, who was formerly a mechanic in the village, but who on his conversion began an active Christian life, which has been singularly blessed. In 1893 the old Mission building was moved from Washington Street to the northwestern part of the town, and made a basis for work in a district needing Christian influences. So that the work of the church is carried on in the central church building and the two chapels.

Egbert J. Pinney, a child of the church, was organist for about seventeen years, but resigned his position in 1893. The work of the church is carried on in several different directions. It supports a missionary in Chihuahua, Mexico, the Rev. James D. Eaton, and has also been largely instrumental in the erection of the church of which he is pastor. It is deeply interested and constantly bearing a large proportion of the financial burden of the People's Palace work in Jersey City, which is its base of operations in City Missions. Both in the home church and in the Pilgrim Chapel are various organizations Christian Endeavor Societies, classes, etc., by which the work is carried on.

An interesting fact is that the Pastor preached for the church the very first Sunday after its organization; that no other candidate was heard, and he has been with it from that time until the present.

There appeared in the *Christian Union* under date of December 12, 1891, an article entitled "Progressive Methods of Church Work," by Mr. John R. Howard, describing the methods, and giving an excellent summary of the work accomplished by this church during the twenty-one years of its existence up to that period. After a brief description of the then recent improvements, he says :

"This, however, is indicative only of the material prosperity of the First Congregational Church of Montclair, N. J.; and that, in so lovely a town, so near the metropolis, and growing so rapidly as it is, would not be especially noteworthy but for the fact that the church has always been particularly active, aggressive for good both at home and abroad.

"Of course this kind of activity—which shows itself also along the lines of good citizenship and all things valuable in the life of the town, in which the members of the Congregational church are everywhere forward and valued elements—presupposes a gathered society of vigorous-minded, intelligent, cultivated, devoted men and women. The original membership (many yet living and active in the church) comprised an unusually large proportion of such, and Dr. Bradford has been greatly favored by that fact. Yet also, of course, much has depended on the man at the head of it all—the way in which it would hold or lose his people, and the kind of new comers that he would naturally gather about him. He has been tempted many times to go to larger places and ampler salaries—Albany, Boston, New York—and other open fields have again and again solicited him; but he has had the wisdom and the grace to stay where he was, and bring up his own family in his own way. He has grown, and his people with him, in their twenty-one years together. His preaching is eminently practical, simple, emphasizing rather this life's duties than the other life's possibilities; making much of what all Christians believe, and paying little or no attention to the infinite (and valueless) points of difference. While ethical on the one hand and inspiring on the other, it has been largely educational. Within a few years past Dr. Bradford has preached, in course, through the Life of Jesus; First Corinthians; the Epistles of John; Hebrews; and he is now on the Acts. Sunday evening services (largely attended by people outside his own regular congregation) have given courses on Books of the Bible; biographical lectures on Great Heroes of Christianity; notable classes of Literature (fiction, poetry, history, etc.); Marked Movements in religion, philosophy, social interests, labor and capital—in short, a constant application of Christian thought to daily life.

" The question of making Sunday evening services attractive has been solved by hard work on subjects about which people are anxious to hear, and the audiences are nearly always as large as the morning congregation—sometimes larger. This winter, once a month, the people will hear some outsider of note and worth. Sunday evening of last week it was Mrs. Booth-Clibborne, and the thousand dollars raised then and there on her appeal for her work in France shows the responsive temper of the gathering. Mrs. Ballington-Booth, Dr. Charles A. Briggs, and Professor M. R. Vincent are others who are already engaged to come during the winter. Either by exchange or otherwise Dr. Bradford's people hear the best speakers in all departments of Christian life and labor. Not long since, a periodical course of sermons on Christian Evidences embraced such preachers as Professor Tucker, of Andover, Charles S. Robinson, Lyman Abbott, Charles F. Deems, Richard S. Storrs, Dr. Behrends, Ecob, of Albany, and others. Thus Dr. Bradford keeps both his church and himself awake to the best thought of the day; yet care is taken that the thought shall not end in mere entertainment or intellectual self-satisfaction, but issue in works, for God and man. A little volume of Dr. Bradford's discourses, including several on the work of the Holy Spirit, and others on fundamental principles of Christian thinking and doing, was issued a year or so ago, entitled ' Spirit and Life,' which took high rank not only, but finds and helps many readers with its simple and eloquent directness. During this winter he is giving lectures on Congregationalism at Andover.

" There is nothing unique about this Montclair church. It offers no startling innovations or ingenious mechanisms and methods; except that, being neither a city nor a country church, but suburban, it must find a common ground of interest and activity for a very promiscuous gathering of people, both metropolitan and rural. And, as a genuine Christian church, doing excellent Christian work, it is on the right road, because it follows the simple ways of the Master. It teaches the way of *this* life as He did; in study of the Scriptures for moral and spiritual guidance it ' brings forth things both new and old '; and, with a cheerful vigor, ' goes about doing good.'

" Its theology, *Fatherhood*; its polity, *Brotherhood*; revealed and exemplified in Jesus Christ.

" The society was formed in January, 1870, and was in May organized as a church, with eighty-four members, and formally established in the Congregational fellowship by council on the 8th of June. The 28th of the same month Mr. Bradford, then a new graduate from Andover, aged twenty-three, was called, and on the 28th of September installed as the first pastor of the church—and for over twenty-one years he has been their only one. In 1872 their stone building was erected, then far too large for their needs; but now the increased membership (about seven hundred) and the steadily growing congregations have compelled the new enlargement. The need for it is proven by the fact that in the services the church is as well filled as before the extension.

" It is a church of families—a true suburban church. It embraces many professional men, but New York toilers of all kinds are among its attendants, and numerous resident workers, tradesmen, mechanics and townsfolk of Montclair itself, and people from the country near by. It is a capital sample segment of the ' social loaf.'

" It is a church where the young people receive much attention, and well repay it. Most who unite with the church on confession of faith do so by way of the pastor's class, which supplements at that critical time the foregoing work of the Sunday-school and Bible classes. The little catechism and leaflet of suggestions prepared by Dr. Bradford for this class has been published by the Congregational

Publishing Society in Boston, for wider usefulness. The young people are interested in missions, in their Society of Christian Endeavor, and in the work of the church generally.

"It is a missionary church. It has put forth one colony (not as a mission, but an outgrowth) in Upper Montclair. It has in one of the neediest portions of Montclair a mission chapel, which provides a Sunday school, regular preaching services Sunday evenings, and meetings during the week for Christian reformatory and social work. Dr. Bradford's helper, now in charge of it, Mr. Louis Heckman, gladly proclaims himself a rescued one, and is devoting his whole time, tireless energy, and special aptitude to the mission. This includes, by the way, weekly services at the Mountain-side Hospital and at the Penitentiary in Caldwell—from which latter place discharged convicts come in considerable numbers, and stop at the 'Washington Street Mission' to find their friend Heckman and get through him, from Montclair people, some material aid in clothes, money, and sometimes work, as a beginning toward a new and better life. Another similar mission is under way for another part of the town. The Ladies' Missionary Societies (three of them) are in constant activity for the home and foreign fields, and the annual money contributions for missionary purposes are about $10,000. Two of the church members—the Rev. J. D. Eaton and his wife, the latter a daughter of the church—are missionaries in Mexico, and three of the young men of the church are at present preparing for the ministry. Dr. Bradford, about a year ago, delivered an address on 'The Duties of the Suburbs to the Cities,' and this has been circulated in thousands by Dr. Scudder's Jersey City Tabernacle Church, while the Montclair Church, more than any other, has been behind the noble effort of the Tabernacle to reach the neglected portions of its great city. The enthusiasm for such labors of love permeates Bradford's own people, and several of the young ladies of the church have engaged in the New York Rivington Street and other City Mission work. In fact, the ideal aimed at seems to be that of a large central church for the main source of influence and inspiration, with such other focal points of practical altruistic Christian labor as may develop under the demand of need."

Of those who have served as deacons since the organization of the church are Samuel Holmes, Joseph B. Beadle, James B. Pearson, David E. Hunt, Samuel D. Crosby, Alexander M. Cleribew, Franklin W. Dorman, Cornelius A. Marwin, Frederick D. Somers, Joseph Van Vleck, William B. Holmes, Charles H. Johnson.

Those who have served as trustees are Samuel Holmes, Joseph B. Beadle, Samuel Wilde, Charles H. Johnson, Edward Sweet, Julius H. Pratt, Nathan T. Porter, Dorman T. Warren, Henry A. Dike, Joseph Van Vleck, J. Hewey Ames, George H. Mills, Robert M. Boyd, Jasper R. Rand, Ogden Brower.

THE SUNDAY SCHOOL.

The Sunday school was the natural outgrowth of the Church, and was organized, under the most favorable auspices, on the second Sunday of June, 1870, with 72 scholars and 18 teachers. Mr. Charles H. Johnson was chosen its first Superintendent, and continued to discharge the duties of that office with commendable zeal, earnestness and devotion for eighteen years, resigning in December, 1888. He was ably supported by a corps of officers and teachers, fully equipped by previous experience for the work. Mrs. Edward Sweet, a lady of great executive ability, was made Assistant Superintendent. She proved a valuable aid to him in his work, and won the hearts of all by her kindness and affability. After four years of earnest and patient labor, she was compelled to resign the position in consequence of failing health. She was followed by Mrs. Samuel Wilde, who for nearly twenty years has been unremitting in her efforts to increase the efficiency of the school, and has shown by her acts of love and kindness to the children, and her sympathy and encouragement to the teachers, her fidelity and devotion to the Master's cause. Mr. J. H. Bonden, who was elected the first Secretary and Treasurer, continued to discharge the duties of that position in a most admirable and efficient manner for many years. Without a murmur or complaint he has met the increased responsibilities devolving upon him, and in his intercourse with his fellow laborers in the school has displayed that evenness of temper, that tact and wisdom, so essential to harmony and good feeling among officers and teachers. Few suburban schools have been favored by a more efficient, capable and well-trained corps of teachers. Fully appreciating the importance of the work, and their personal responsibility, they have labored with a singleness of purpose to lead those committed to their charge to "a knowledge of the truth as it is in Jesus," and the result of their labors is shown in the large additions to the church by profession of faith.

One important feature in the management of this school has been its ability to hold the scholars as they have advanced to years of maturity, and the able manner in which its adult Bible-class has been conducted. It has had for its leaders learned men of ripe experience and enlarged ideas—men fully consecrated to the work. Among these have been Rev. D. S. Rodman, C. E. Morgan—now a prominent lawyer in Boston, Rev. J. Q. Butterfield—now President of Olivet College, Mr. Roswell Smith, and Mr. J. R. Howard.

The Primary Department—the most difficult of any in the school to manage successfully—has been at different times under the leadership of Mrs. Samuel Boyd, Mrs. Edwin M. Harrison, Miss Annie Bull, Mrs. M. F. Reading, Mrs. C. H. Johnson, Mrs. J. R. Lamsen, and Mrs. Bissell, the present teacher.

The strong love and affection existing between scholars and teachers is shown in the fact that the young men who have gone out from here to enter college have almost invariably, on their return home during vacation, taken their places in the Sunday school. The fact that over $10,000 has been contributed by this school to various benevolent objects during the past twenty-three years is an evidence of the systematic and earnest work which has been done by the officers and teachers. The children have been trained to habits of self-denial and systematic giving of that which was their own, and have been constantly familiarized with special objects of charity and benevolence, and the work connected with such prominent institutions as the Children's Aid Society, the Society for the Prevention of Cruelty to Children, and others of this character. The gifts of the children have been invariably devoted to charitable purposes, and in no case to assist in defraying the expenses of the school.

The musical training of this school is worthy of special notice. This part of the service was for fourteen years conducted by Dr. C. A. Marvin, a highly accomplished teacher and musical composer. Some of his most beautiful compositions were designed especially for the use of this school. It has been observed by visitors who were disposed to be critical that the singing was above the average, and evinced excellent training and culture. The music of the school is now in charge of Mr. John B. Pratt.

In his address given at the 20th anniversary of the school Mr. Johnson alludes in a most touching manner to some of the faithful ones who were with them at the beginning, but who had since joined the heavenly throng above. Among these was Mrs. Julius H. Pratt, "whose memory still rests upon our school like a benediction." He refers to Mr. J. H. Beadle and Mr. Samuel Wilde, who were teachers at the beginning, faithful and steadfast, with the highest and best motives prompting all their efforts, and whose royal gifts of over $5,000 each, made possible this splendid building we now occupy, have joined the innumerable throng above.

Mr. Johnson alludes to the faithful co-operation of Dr. Bradford, the pastor, in the work of the school, in the following terms: "One thing that has cheered and encouraged the hearts of officers and teachers through all these years has been the hearty co-operation of the pastor; he has indeed been the pastor not only of the church, but the school. The sessions have been few indeed, except by reason of illness or absence that he has not been present, to advise, counsel and encourage the teachers in their work."

Referring to Mrs. Wilde, who was about to resign her connection with the school, he says: "The brightness and joy of the present hour is dimmed by the thought that Mrs. Samuel Wilde, who commenced as a teacher in the school at its very first session, and who has held an official position for sixteen years, fourteen of which she was assistant superintendent, now feels it necessary to relinquish the position she has so ably filled all these years."

In December, 1888, Mr. Charles H. Johnson, who had so faithfully discharged the duties of Superintendent since the organization of the school, tendered his resignation, much to the regret of his fellow laborers in the work. The school under his supervision had increased from 72 pupils and 18 teachers to 350 pupils and 45 teachers. More than 200 had been added to the church from the school during his administration, and a few had joined the church triumphant.

He was succeeded by Mr. D. O. Eshbaugh, who filled the position with honor and credit for three years. Referring to his election Mr. Johnson says: "The wisdom of that selection has been manifest from the beginning of his office, and I can bear witness to the fidelity and sound judgment with which he has filled a position to which he brought little previous experience, and I believe I voice the opinion of teachers and scholars in expressing profound and sincere regret that he feels it incumbent upon him to relinquish the office at this time."

Mr. Eshbaugh proved himself a model superintendent, possessing by nature and experience all the requisite qualifications for the office. A man of deep religious convictions, well versed in the Scriptures, sympathetic, kind and affable in disposition; possessing also tact and good judgment, together with a natural love for children. Thus equipped, he entered upon his labors with earnestness, zeal and enthusiasm, receiving the hearty co-operation of officers and teachers, to whom he endeared himself by his uniform kindness and his personal interest in their temporal and spiritual welfare; by the children, to whom he always extended a kindly greeting, he was equally beloved. The three years of his administration were marked by an increase in numbers and interest, and in 1890 forty united with the church by profession of faith, most of whom came from the ranks of the Sabbath-school. The school was never in a more prosperous condition than when he resigned his position in 1891, against the earnest wishes of his associates—his failing health compelling him to relinquish the duties of the office.

Mr. Eshbaugh was succeeded by Mr. Edward F. Meyers, who occupied the position one year. The present officers of the school are: Superintendent, Mr. C. S. Olcott; Assistant Superintendent, Professor John F. Woodhull; Secretary, Mrs. Samuel Wilde; Treasurer, Mr. W. L. Johnson; Librarians, Mr. Walter Lloyd and Mr. W. Skidmore. The present number of teachers is 32, the number of scholars, 210. Number in Young Men's Bible Class, 25. Primary Department: Mrs. A. C. Romer, Superintendent; number of officers, 3; teachers, 14; scholars, 126.

The congregation continued to worship in the hall referred to until 1875. On May 30, 1875, the corner-stone of the new church edifice was laid by the Pastor, Rev. Amory N. Bradford, and an address delivered by Rev. George B. Bacon, of Orange Valley. Evening exercises were held in the Presbyterian Church, at which time the sermon was preached by Rev. William M. Taylor, D.D., of New York. The building was completed in 1875, and on the 15th of October of that year was dedicated with appropriate ceremonies.

REV. AMORY HOWE BRADFORD, D.D.

It was eminently fitting that the First Congregational Church of Christ in re-establishing the form of religious worship introduced in this locality by the Pilgrim Fathers more than two hundred years ago, should choose as their pastor a direct descendant of Governor William Bradford, chief among the "Blessed Company" of the "Mayflower," and one of the chief founders of Congregationalism in this country—himself a descendant of a line of English ancestors who suffered martyrdom because of their adherence to the true faith as delivered to the saints.

One of the first martyrs who perished at the stake in "Bloody Queen Mary's" time was John Bradford, prebend of St. Paul's, and a celebrated preacher. He was born at Manchester, in Lancashire, about 1510; was committed to prison August 16, 1553, where he remained until his death, a period of two years. The numerous letters and other compositions written by him during his imprisonment are remarkable for their able and uncompromising opposition to the dogmatical requisitions of papacy, and for abounding in depth and fervency of plain personal piety and expansive religious feeling.

The early, energetic and persevering opposition of Governor Bradford, of Plymouth, to these dogmas would seem to indicate that he was a worthy descendant of the martyr's immediate family, and that he was so is rendered more probable from the fact that the town of Bradford (meaning Broad-ford), in Yorkshire, Manchester, the birthplace of the martyr, and Austerfield, where Governor Bradford was born, thirty-three years after the martyr's death, are all in the north of England and near each other.

William Bradford, Governor of Plymouth Colony, was born at Austerfield, in Yorkshire, England, in 1588. He went to Holland early in life and joined the Pilgrims, and came to Plymouth in the "Mayflower " 1620, accompanied by his wife, whose maiden name was Dorothy May. This lady never reached Plymouth, but was accidently drowned on the 7th of December, 1620, during the absence of her husband on an examining tour into Massachusetts Bay, and while the " Mayflower" remained in Cape Cod Harbor. She was the first English woman (who died in Plymouth, and the first) whose death is recorded in New England.

Mr. Bradford was chosen Governor in 1621 and was re-elected to that office every year till 1657, except five years—1633, '34, '36, '38, '44. He was one of the most efficient persons in directing and sustaining the new settlement; he " was the very prop and glory of Plymouth Colony during the whole series of changes that passed over it." He married, August 14, 1623, widow Alice Southworth, whose maiden name is supposed to have been Carpenter. He died, May 9, 1657, lamented by all the colonies of New England as a common father to them all. He had by his second wife three children, William, Mercy and Joseph.

REV. AMORY HOWE BRADFORD, D.D., son of Benjamin F. and Mary A. (Howe) Bradford, was born in Granby, Oswego County, N. Y., April 14, 1846. He is eighth in line of descent from Governor William Bradford, probably through Thomas, third son of Governor Bradford by his second wife, Alice Southworth. This Thomas, by his father's will, secured lands in Norwich, Conn., and removed thence after his father's death. He married Anna, daughter of Rev. James Fitch (first minister to Saybrook and Norwich) by the latter's second wife Priscilla, daughter of John Mason, the hero of the Pequot war.

Alexander, the great-great grandfather of the Rev. A. H. Bradford, owned a farm on the eastern border of Connecticut, on the shore of the Pawcatuck River that forms the boundary between Connecticut and Rhode Island, about two miles below the village of Westerly. On that farm the father, the grandfather and the great grandfathers of Dr. Bradford were born, and the old homestead is still in a good state of preservation. Dr. Bradford's mother was Mary A. Howe, daughter of Amory Howe, of Marlborough, Mass., a descendant of Abraham Howe, one of the founders and proprietors of Marlborough in 1660. Dr. Bradford was prepared for college at Penn Yan Academy, was graduated at Hamilton College in 1867; studied at Auburn and graduated at Andover Theological Seminary in 1870. Immediately following his ordination in 1870, he accepted a call from the First Congregational Church of Christ at Montclair, and began his labors in June of that year. In September following he married Miss Julia S. Stevens, daughter of W. R. Stevens, Esq., of Little Falls, N. Y. The eighty-four members of this church who welcomed Mr. Bradford as their pastor, were earnest, liberal-minded, working Christians, made up of different denominations. Mr. Bradford made no inquiry as to the creeds or doctrinal views of the individual members. He determined to "know nothing among them save Jesus and Him crucified." He laid broad the foundation, threw wide open the doors of the church and extended a hearty welcome to Christians of every denomination. He assisted in the organization of the various societies for church work, in all of which he took a personal interest. He met the pastors of other churches in a kind and friendly spirit, and invited them to exchange pulpits. He has grown apace with his own church, which, as the record shows, has had large annual accessions, both by letter and by profession of faith. He has taken an active interest in every public improvement, and in the founding of benevolent and religious societies, one of the most useful and beneficial of which is the Children's Home, designed not only as a permanent home for children of Montclair who have been bereft of their natural protectors, but as a temporary home and resort during the hot summer months for the children of our large cities.

The almost unparalleled growth of the church as a suburban church evinces the character of Dr. Bradford's work, his popularity as a preacher, and his faithfulness as a pastor. Few ministers have ever been more beloved by a people, or have exercised a greater influence in a community. He has frequently supplied the pulpits of the New York and Brooklyn churches during the summer months, and exchanged with the most eminent divines of these cities. During Mr. Beecher's life he often supplied his place in Plymouth Church during the summer vacation; and in a letter commending Mr. Bradford to his European friends, Mr. Beecher wrote that his people were very willing that he should extend his own vacation. Although humorous in form, this showed Mr. Bradford's excellent preaching as a fact.

Dr. Bradford has made several trips abroad, both for study and for recreation. He studied six months at Oxford, and was the first American ever invited to preach a baccalaureate sermon at that institution.

In July, 1891, he was sent as a delegate to represent the Congregationalists of New Jersey in the great International Council of Congregationalists held in London at that time. No American preacher ever received greater honors than was accorded him during his stay. He took a leading part in all the discussions of the Council, and at all times was listened to with rapt attention. He was invited to preach at many of the largest and most prominent churches in England. The religious as well as the secular press of England voiced the sentiments of the people on both sides of the Atlantic in their expressions concerning Dr. Bradford as a man and as a preacher. If, as has been said, a foreign verdict is like a verdict of posterity in its impartiality, some extracts from these foreign journals will be in point. *The Leicester Daily Post*, referring to his sermon preached before the Clarendon Park Congregational Church, said: "The mere fact that this distinguished visitor was one of the few who had been chosen to represent the Congregationalism of the Republic at the International Conference in London, alone speaks volumes to

PARSONAGE OF FIRST CONGREGATIONAL CHURCH.

the eminent rank he had gained among the Independents of America. Had there, however, been the slightest doubt as to his title to the enviable reputation he has gained among the religious preachers and teachers of the New World, it must have been swept away by his discourses yesterday. * * * * Hardly had he passed beyond the opening sentences of his morning sermon than it became clear that he was master in his own field of service—a public teacher of the first rank. In one or two respects Dr. Bradford fills a place in the sphere of pulpit oratory which is distinctively his own. Not only has he strongly marked views on some of the pressing problems of his time, and all the courage of his advanced convictions, but he has at least three of the essentials of success. He has grasp of thought which enables him to grapple with the most difficult subject with no ordinary skill. He has a power of expression which crystallizes his ideas into the most incisive and vigorous phrase. And he has a delivery which, while not of the highest order, is still most effective, sustaining the lively interest of the hearer by, among other things, an occasional sudden transition from a tone that rings through the church to one that is almost inaudible in its mingled softness and depth. After all his paramount title to fame is necessarily not so much his manner as his matter—not so much the words that arouse and 'burn' as the 'thoughts that breathe.' Our American visitor vividly recognizes that he has a mission to fulfil which is higher and broader than the boundaries of any single creed—a Christianity to teach and preach which overleaps even the nobler selfishness of patriotism, and has as its essence that spirit which compelled the famous preacher to be content with nothing less than the 'whole world' as his 'parish."

Another paper referring to "a very remarkable and stirring sermon preached by Dr. Bradford at Mansfield Chapel" says: "He is rich in illustration, cultured in diction, vigorous in thought, and delivered with impassioned yet dignified eloquence. These sermons stamp the preacher as one of the very strongest of our living preachers."

Rev. Joseph Parker, D.D., the "London Beecher," in his criticism of the men who took part in the Council, says of Dr. Bradford : "He is broad in mind, generous in impulse, eloquent in expression— a harmony of the progressive aspects of evangelical truth."

The *Manchester Guardian* says : "Dr. Bradford is a tower of strength to New England Congregationalism. A keen student of Congregational history and polity, his eminence in this department is attested by the fact that he is appointed lecturer for three years at Andover on Congregationalism." (He began the course in 1892 with " English Congregationalism.")

Another writer says : "He is just a trifle theatrical in his style of oratory, but he has to perfection that vigorous gift of driving a point straight home that Mr. Spurgeon's manner illustrates so forcibly. He has a storehouse of anecdote, and has a story to fit every moral that he wants to emphasize. His cultured, refined face will not soon be forgotten by those who had the privilege of listening to him. He is a clear thinker—progressive, reverent, constructive, full of tact, sincerity and spiritual simplicity."

Dr. Bradford's unselfish devotion to his own church and to the Master's cause, and his refusal to entertain the numerous "calls" extended to him by leading churches throughout the country, is thus referred to by a writer in one of the English journals: "His reputation in the United States is not confined to his own body. He is a powerful and impressive preacher, and it is through his own desire, strengthened by the affection of an attached congregation, that he remains in a place so little known as Montclair, and not in one of the large centres of population. Several tempting calls have been made to him to settle in one or another of the large cities of the Union. He frequently, in Mr. Beecher's time, occupied the pulpit in the famous Plymouth Church, Brooklyn. About twenty years ago, not long after he began his ministerial career, he, for the sake of his health, exchanged work for six months with a brother pastor stationed on the Pacific Coast. Here Dr. Bradford was so much liked that every effort was made to induce him to stay, and when he answered that this was impossible, as the East had greater claims upon him than the West, he was entreated to accept a testimonial. He agreed to this provided he could choose the gift. When told he could have anything he liked, his request was that the church in which he had been laboring temporarily should be cleared from all trace of debt. It was a goodly sum that had to be raised, but it was fully subscribed. The act was characteristic of Dr. Bradford."

The utterances of Dr. Bradford, in his discussion of the great questions which are agitating the world, were extensively quoted and freely commented upon by the English press. *The London Independent* of July 10, 1891, said : "Rev. Dr. Bradford, whose course through our principal pulpits partakes somewhat of the nature of a triumphal progress, was last Saturday in Leicester, conducting the anniversary services of Clarendon-Park Chapel. He preached in the morning from the text 'The Kingdom of Heaven is at hand,' and delivered a wonderful oration on the nature and prospect of the Divine Kingdom. He said no phrase ever more exactly defined the ideal to which the Master opened the way than the words 'The realization of righteousness in the life of humanity.' How can wealth and poverty both be filled with the spirit of Christ so that they shall minister one to another? How can the islands and continents be filled with the good news of the Father God and the Saviour Son of God? Silently the Kingdom of Heaven is extending. Its limits are bounded neither by race lines nor continental frontiers. It is a kingdom of spirit in which the individual realizes his privilege in the effacement of himself and in grateful devotion to the service of God in that humanity for which Christ died ; a Kingdom before which the walls separating nations are falling, the selfishness of patriotism is disappearing, and poverty, vice and sectarian rivalry yielding to the magnetism of love."

Referring to the sermon preached by Dr. Bradford, at New Weigh House, London, the *Christian World* said, " Dr. Bradford believes in organism rather than mechanism. He refuses to acknowledge that the men of two centuries ago were more under divine guidance than the men of to day. He holds that where the supremacy of the spirit is recognized, men will not be asked if they accept systems of doctrine written by the dead, but whether they have open minds, living hearts, humble wills, ready to be taught and led by God to-day. He predicts the federation of churches, the cessation of denominational rivalries, and the realization of a universal brotherhood in its fullest expression as what we are moving towards. These are brave words."

During his stay in England, Dr. Bradford visited the village of Austerfield—the birthplace and residence of his American ancestor, Governor William Bradford—which is only two or three miles from Scrooby, where John Bradford became a convert from listening to the preaching of Clyfton, a leading pastor of the Scrooby congregation. He found the church at Austerfield " not in a good state of repair, though its Norman doorway is worthy of a visit." There is an ancient font, probably the one in which Bradford was baptized March 19, 1589.

Dr. Bradford made many friends during his stay in England, but his reputation as a preacher had preceded him. While for many years he confined his labors to his own church in Montclair, his influence was gradually widening and enlarging, and he has been for many years recognized as one of the ablest and most progressive of our American preachers. He received in 1884 his degree of D.D. from Hamilton College, his *alma mater*. He has been a frequent contributor to our best papers and periodicals. In 1888 a volume of his sermons came from the press of Fords, Howard & Hulbert, under the title "Spirit and Life," which has passed through several editions; also "Old Wine in New Bottles." All his writing is marked by profound spiritual insight, moral earnestness and intellectual strength. At the beginning of 1893 he became connected with the *Christian Union*, having charge of the department "The Religious World." He does not leave the pulpit or his magnificent church at Montclair in assuming these new duties.

The Independent, of London, in referring to his connection with the *Christian Union*, says, " The appointment of Dr. Bradford to be collaborateur with Dr. Lyman Abbott is sure to gratify our readers, and may draw the attention of some to the *Christian Union* who do not know how admirable an organ and leader of religious thought that paper is. Dr. Bradford was known to our metropolitan churches before his visit to the International Council made him free of British Congregationalism. On previous visits he had preached in London and had won the best of all tributes to his worth—an interest in his personality, founded on his qualities as a preacher. When he came as a delegate to the Council, invitations to country churches awaited him ; he delivered the address to the students at the sessional anniversary of Lancashire College, and he has become one of the best known American ministers to this country. It is bare truth to say that affection is as marked as admiration in our feeling towards him. Dr. Bradford's position in America is very influential. As a pastor of a suburban church he tells on the life of New York, and his generous popular sympathies have drawn to him the confidence of those among the American churches which are working for the religious future of the nation. He was the correspondent of the New York *Independent* during the sessions of the Council; he has been a frequent contributor to the Boston *Congregationalist* and the New York *Christian Union*. It is not for us to say which of these three excellent papers is best, but believing that friendly sympathy in journalism as in other things is better than rivalry, we are glad of his assumption of the editorial chair. We are equally glad that he is not resigning his pastorate at Montclair, New Jersey. We grudge the withdrawal of such men from the pulpit and the active direction of a church. The strain of a double office is heavy ; but there is no influence which so purifies public men, and fits them for the higher public usefulness, as the consciousness of being sustained by the affection and prayer of a congregation, and the wisdom which comes from intimate association with earnest Christians of many different types of character."

The most recent publication of Dr. Bradford is "The Pilgrims in Old England," being a study of English Congregationalism.

As a citizen Dr. Bradford has taken the lead in most of the reform and educational movements which have been started in Montclair. He assisted in organizing the "Citizens' Committee of One Hundred" for the execution of existing laws and the suppression of public evils. He was one of the organizers of the Reform Club, the object of which was to make a home or place of resort for reformed men, and keep them out of the way of temptation. This was the nucleus of the Young Men's Christian Association. He started the "Outlook Club," a literary organization for the discussion of topics of current interest. He was the father of the Children's Home, one of the most promising and useful benevolent organizations in the State.

Dr. Bradford suggested the American Institute of Christian Philosophy, was its first Secretary, and on the death of the late President was elected to succeed him, and also became editor of its organ, *Christian Thought*; he is also editor of the American edition of the *Review of the Churches*, and is still a member of the Executive Committee. He started the Congregational Club of New York and has been one of its Vice-Presidents since its organization. He was one of the corporate members of the American Board of Foreign Missions. In 1892 Dr. Bradford was chosen to preach the annual sermon of the American Missionary Association, which is one of the great Congregational Missionary Societies.

In September, 1894, Dr. Bradford again went to London in response to an invitation from the officers of Westminster Chapel. This church is situated near Buckingham Gate, on James Street, midway between the Houses of Parliament and Buckingham Palace. The church building is the largest Congregational Building in the world. The church had been without a settled pastor for a long time, and many of the congregation having heard Dr. Bradford on a previous occasion were anxious to hear him again. Dr. Bradford met with a hearty reception and supplied the pulpit for some weeks, and before leaving received a unanimous call from the Church.

On his return home, when it became known that he had received a call from Westminster Chapel, London, his own congregation, as well as the citizens of Montclair of all denominations, were united in their efforts to induce him to remain in his present position.

At the regular meeting of the Congregational Club of New York City, held on Monday evening, October 16, 1893, the following resolution was unanimously adopted:

"*Resolved*, That it is the sense of this Congregational Club of New York and vicinity, that the important work and influence of the Church, which Rev. Dr. Bradford has served so successfully through so many years, and the varied interests of truth with which he is so helpfully and influentially connected, require his continued presence in this country, and make it his duty to decline the flattering call to the pastorate of Westminster Chapel, in London, England."

After a careful consideration of the matter Dr. Bradford declined the call, and decided to remain with the first and only church with which he had ever been connected, and whose interests are interwoven with every fibre of his nature.

Rev. John L. Scudder, referring to his action, says: "We learn with pleasure that Rev. Amory H. Bradford, D.D., of Montclair, has declined the call to Westminster Chapel, London, the largest Congregational Church in that great metropolis. The call was a great compliment to his ability as preacher and a scholar, and demonstrates that he has not only an international reputation, but is the most popular American preacher abroad. We congratulate the Church in Montclair upon the determination of Mr. Bradford to remain in this country, and continue his unique ministry in the State of New Jersey. We believe his usefulness would not be enhanced by a departure for Europe. Though settled in Montclair, his parish extends far beyond the limits of his own State. Through his books, contributions to magazines, public addresses, and editorship of the *Outlook*, his field extends from Sandy Hook to the Golden Gate. He has shown his wisdom in remaining in the United States, where he is universally

Amory H. Bradford.

beloved. America cannot spare him, for he is our best representative of the 'Forward Movement' in this country. The great problems of the race are to be worked out upon this continent where there are no time-honored restrictions, and where changes in practice and in law follow on the heels of public opinion. This nation is to set the fashions for the world, and we want the best men right here on American soil, where their influence will tell the most. London is a great place, but America is greater; and here we trust the good doctor will live and die."

PILGRIM MISSION.

This Mission was organized in 1889, under peculiar circumstances. Neighborhood prayer meetings were being held in various localities by a band of Christian workers. One of these was held on Bloomfield Avenue, in close proximity to a liquor saloon frequented by Louis Heckman, a plain, uneducated workingman. He was induced to attend these meetings, was converted, and soon after began the work of organizing a Mission. Dr. Bradford became interested in his work, and through his aid he was enabled to secure a building on Washington Street, Dr. Bradford becoming personally responsible for the rent. The Methodists and other denominations assisted in furnishing the room suitable for holding meetings. Mr. Heckman made slow progress at first, but after one or two conversions, others came out of curiosity. The meetings at first were held only on Thursday evenings, but as the attendance and interest increased, services were held on Sunday evenings, and it soon became necessary to build on an addition. This was done through individual subscriptions raised by Mr. Heckman. With the increased facilities he opened, in 1891, a Sunday school, beginning with 23 children and 4 teachers. Other Christian workers became interested in the movement, and Mr. James G. Beach, of Bloomfield, presented the Mission with a lot of ground on Bloomfield Avenue, and Mr. Heckman's efforts to raise money to erect a Chapel met with a generous response from liberal and enterprising citizens. Mr. W. W. Egbert donating $1,000 and Mr. Stephen Carey $500; others gave various sums, ranging from $200 down to $5, the sum total amounting to $4,000.

A building was erected 32 x 64 feet, with a seating capacity of 500. All the furniture, consisting of 400 chairs and a fine Brussels carpet, were donated by Mrs. George Innis. A fine organ was presented by the Young People's Society of Christian Endeavor connected with the Congregational Church, and a $100 piano was given by the King's Daughters, a noble band of young ladies worthy of the name they bear.

The Sunday school connected with this Mission is now in a flourishing condition with nearly 200 scholars, 5 officers, and 14 teachers. Mr. Heckman is still filling the position of Superintendent.

Auxiliary societies have been organized, which have done effective work. Among these are the Christian Endeavor Society, the Yoke Fellows Band and the King's Sons. Of the latter society all are young converts of this Mission.

Mr. Heckman, who founded this Mission with the assistance of Dr. Bradford, is a native of Montclair, of humble parentage, and his educational advantages were very limited. Since he began his evangelistic labors, however, he has been a close student, and though still a layman, has done most of the pastoral work connected with the Mission. He has received great assistance in his work from Dr. Bradford, who gave him the use of his library, and became his steadfast friend and supporter in his mission work.

FIRST BAPTIST CHURCH.

With the rapid increase of population there has doubtless been for many years past a sufficient number of Baptists to have organized a church, had the attempt been made. It was not, however, until the autumn of 1885 that systematic efforts were begun in this direction. At that time a few enterprising Baptists met together, and after a free discussion of the matter, decided to have a thorough canvas made of the township for the purpose of ascertaining the number of resident Baptists. Accordingly Rev. Henry Bromley, an aged Baptist of large experience in mission work, a resident of Brooklyn, N. Y., was employed for this purpose. As the result of his efforts he found 58 members of Baptist churches and a number of others who were in sympathy with the movement and gave assurance of their co-operation.

On Nov. 6, 1885, during the progress of these efforts, a neighborhood prayer meeting was held at which there were present thirteen. A second meeting was held Friday evening, November 13, at which there were present 10 young people and 30 adults, Rev. Henry Bromley of Brooklyn, N. Y., and Rev. E. D. Simonds, then pastor of the Bloomfield Baptist Church. It was decided to begin operations at once, and to organize a Sunday school, to be followed by preaching service, and to hold a prayer

FIRST BAPTIST CHURCH.

meeting every Friday evening. Rev. E. D. Simonds agreed to supply the preaching service for a period of three months. The Sunday school was duly organized, Irving Cairns being elected Superintendent and Wm. H. Ketchum, Secretary, and Sunday school and preaching services were held regularly at Montclair Hall until Jan. 6, 1886, when steps were taken to effect a permanent organization by the election of Rev. E. D. Simonds as Chairman, and Irving Cairns as Clerk.

A committee, consisting of Geo. P. Farmer, E. P. Benedict and Irving Cairns, who had previously been appointed to obtain a list of such persons as were willing to unite in the organization of a church, reported that they had secured a list of thirty-eight names by letters from other churches, and five by experience—a total of forty-three,—and recommended the adoption of the following resolution:

" Believing it to be the will of God, as taught in His word, and indicated in His providence, and trusting in His divine guidance, blessing and presence, we, and all whose letters and names have been placed in the hands of the clerk of this meeting, do hereby form ourselves into a regular Baptist Church by the adoption of the New Hampshire Confession of Faith and Church Covenant."

Edwin P. Benedict, First Baptist Church, Hackensack, N. J.
Mrs. Louise M. Benedict, First Baptist Church, Hackensack, N. J.
Alonzo Crawford, First Baptist Church, Hackensack, N. J.
Mrs. Harriet A. Crawford, First Baptist Church, Hackensack, N. J.
Irving Cairns, North Baptist Church, Jersey City.
Mrs. Ella V. Cairns, North Baptist Church, Jersey City.
William Cairns, North Baptist Church, Jersey City.
Mrs. Mary A. Cairns, North Baptist Church, Jersey City.
Thos. V. Carpenter, First Baptist Church, Newark, N. J.
Mrs. M. E. Carpenter, First Baptist Church, Newark, N. J.
Franklin N. Class, Central Baptist Church, N. Y. City.
Mrs. Mary E. Class, Central Baptist Church, N. Y. City.
Mrs. E. Crossman, First Baptist Church, Newark, N. J.
Otis Corbit, Baptist Church of the Epiphany, N. Y. City.
Mrs. Amelia P. Corbit, Baptist Church of the Epiphany, N. Y. City.
G. M. DeWitt, Baptist Church of Port Jervis, N. Y.
Miss Helen M. Dodge, First Baptist Church of N. Y.
Mrs. Minnie Dudgeon, Park Baptist Church, Port Richmond, S. I.
Geo. P. Farmer, First Baptist Church of Bloomfield, N. J.
Mrs. H. E. Farmer, First Baptist Church of Bloomfield, N. J.
Miss Annie E. Farmer, First Baptist Church of Bloomfield, N. J.
Mrs. Mary A. Hoyt, Strong Place Baptist Church, Brooklyn, N. Y.

C. Wesley Jacobus, First Baptist Church, Newark, N. J.
Louis A. Koehler, First Baptist Church, Newark, N. J.
Mrs. Cornelia Koehler, First Baptist Church, Newark, N. J.
William H. Ketchum, North Orange Baptist Church.
Mrs. Louisa P. Kinnan, Schooley's Mountain Baptist Church.
Miss Julia A. Phelps, Baptist Church of the Epiphany, N. Y. City.
Mrs. Mary F. Muir, Park Baptist Church, Port Richmond, S. I.
William A. May, First Baptist Church, Newark, N. J.
W. H. A. Maynard, Herkimer Street Baptist Church, Brooklyn, N. Y.
Chas. S. Salmon, Baptist Church, Schooley's Mountain, N. J.
W. H. Smith, Strong Place Baptist Church, Brooklyn, N. Y.
Mrs. Adelia G. Taylor, First Baptist Church, Bloomfield, N. J.
Amy T. Weaver, First Baptist Church, Bloomfield, N. J.
Theodore C. Van Arsdale, First Baptist Church, Bloomfield, N. J.
Mrs. Louisa C. Van Arsdale, First Baptist Church, Bloomfield, N. J.
Miss May Van Arsdale, First Baptist Church, Bloomfield, N. J.
Miss Jane E. Dodge, by experience
Mrs. Mary M. Taylor, by experience
Mrs. Dora T. Munn, by experience
Miss Sarah A. Hose, by experience
Mrs. Margaret Tyson, by experience.

The report of the Committee was adopted, and the name of the organization decided upon was the "Montclair Baptist Church." The name was changed, August 20, 1890, to "The First Baptist Church, Montclair, N. J."

Geo. P. Farmer was elected Deacon for three years, Thomas V. Carpenter two years, and E. P. Benedict one year. William A. May was elected Church Clerk, and E. P. Benedict, Treasurer.

A Board of Trustees was organized January 22, 1886, consisting of Alonzo Crawford and E. P. Benedict, who were elected for three years; Franklin N. Class and Irving Cairns for two years, and William H. Ketchum for one year. The first covenant meeting of the Church was held March 12, 1886, and the first communion service Sunday, March 14, 1886.

The first letter to the North New Jersey Baptist Association was written under date of June 6, 1886, to the Association in session at Schooley's Mountain, at which time the Church was recognized and admitted a member of the Association.

The first regular installed pastor of the Church was Rev. Geo. F. Warren, formerly of the Fairmount Church, Newark, N. J. His pastorate began on January 18, 1887, and continued for two years. He was succeeded by the Rev. William N. Hubbell, who began his labors June 1, 1890, and was ordained at a council assembled at Montclair, June 16, 1890, on the call of the Montclair Baptist Church, consisting of 89 members, representing 35 churches. The ordination services took place on the evening of June 16, at the Trinity Presbyterian Church of Montclair.

Mr. Hubbell has labored faithfully and systematically to build up the Church, and his labors have been eminently successful. A total of 257 were added to the Church up to January 1, 1894. Of this number 75 were received by baptism and 167 by letter, and 15 on experience. The total number of deaths up to this period were 14. Only 3 names have been dropped from the Church roll. Erasure, 8. Dismissed by letter 38. Present membership, 194.

A number of auxiliary societies have been organized which have accomplished much good in their way. A Woman's Foreign Mission Society, a Woman's Home Mission Circle, a Ladies' Guild, of which Mrs. F. M. Soulé is President; Young People's Society, Wm. H. Farmer, President. A Mission Band organized in 1887, is now known as the Willing Workers.

On June 10, 1890, a series of weekly services in the Swedish tongue was begun under the direction of the Rev. A. F. Bargendahl, of Brooklyn, N. Y. Great good has been accomplished by these efforts, and a class of people have been brought together and instructed in their own tongue that it would have been difficult to reach in any other manner. In April, 1892, this was recognized as the Baptist Swedish Mission of Montclair, and on Tuesday evening of each week services are held in the Swedish tongue by Rev. Olaf Heddeen, of Brooklyn.

On April 6, 1887, plans for church work were adopted, and committees appointed for that purpose. A systematic plan for collections for benevolent purposes was also adopted as follows:

For the Missionary Union, for the Home Mission Society, for Children's Home and Mountain-side Hospital of Montclair, for the Ministers' and Widows' Fund, for the Educational Society, for the New Jersey Baptist State Convention, at stated periods each year.

In May, 1888, a legacy of $200 was received from the estate of Mrs. Amy T. Weaver, which formed the nucleus of a building fund. Additional amounts were received from time to time through the members, and in October, 1889, a lot (80x145 feet) was purchased on Fullerton Avenue, near Bloomfield Avenue. By the latter part of July, 1890, the total sum of $13,026.43 had been subscribed by 135 persons, and soon after plans were adopted for the erection of a chapel, which should include rooms for a ladies' parlor, library, etc. Mr. Irving Cairns, the first and only President of the Board of Trustees, E. P. Benedict, Frank H. Tooker and Geo. P. Farmer, were constituted a Building Committee, and Joseph Ireland, an architect, of New York City, was employed to draft the plans. The building was completed and ready for occupancy, and the first services were held March 1, 1891. The total cost of the present building and grounds is about $25,000; the estimated cost of completing it, according to plans, is $60,000.

REV. WILLIAM N. HUBBELL.

The pastorate of Rev. William N. Hubbell has been successful from the beginning, and under his ministry the Baptist Church has increased in numbers and influence, and has done its share of the work in the community. As an organizer, Mr. Hubbell has displayed great ability, and has shown himself thoroughly qualified for this, his first undertaking in church work.

Mr. Hubbell hails from the great West, although he is of Puritan stock, both on the paternal and maternal sides. He was born in Keokuk, Iowa, June 8, 1862, and is the son of a successful banker. On the paternal side he is descended from Richard Hubbell, who settled at Pequannock, Conn., about 1647. His direct line is through Samuel, son of Richard, and Nathan, Gersham and Abijah. The latter lived at Ballston, N. Y., and was a soldier in the War of the Revolution. He had a son, Hiram, who was the father of Charles Hubbell. The latter married Anna M. Sage, of Rochester, N. Y., a descendant of David Sage, of Middletown, Conn., 1652, through John (1), John (2), Giles and Oren. Deacon Oren Sage, the maternal grandfather of Rev. William N. Hubbell, moved from Ballston Springs to Rochester, where he acquired wealth in the manufacture of boots and shoes. He was a man of great benevolence, and it was partly through his efforts that the University of Rochester was established, he being a large contributor to that institution, of brains and money.

William N. Hubbell is the son of Charles and Anna (Sage) Hubbell. When he was nine years of age, he went with his parents to San Diego, Cal., where he received his preparatory education. He was graduated at the University of Rochester in 1885. He afterward studied law for a time in Minneapolis, Minn., and then took up the study of theology, graduating at Crozer Theological Seminary, Chester, Pa., in 1889. He took a post-graduate course at the same institution, completing his studies in 1890. He was called to the First Baptist Church of Montclair in June of the same year, and was regularly ordained on June 16th following.

Mr. Hubbell's call was made *prior* to June. He was *settled* as pastor on June 1, 1890.

He married, December 31, 1891, Miss Katharine D. Price, daughter of Capt. Joseph D. Price, who served with distinction in the Civil War under Sheridan.

Mr. Hubbell is a close student and a hard worker, and his people are in full sympathy with him and his methods. He is sound in his theological views, and earnest and impressive as a speaker. He is gifted with an excellent voice, and possesses a good knowledge of music, which enables him to conduct the singing when occasion requires. While holding strictly to his own denominational views he is very ready to act with other denominations in the advancement of religious or benevolent work.

THE SUNDAY SCHOOL.

The organization of the Sunday school formed the nucleus of the church organization, and at the

first meeting held No-vember 6, 1885, it was determined to organize a Sunday school with preaching ser-vices following. At this meeting, Irving Cairns was elected Su-perintendent and Wm. H. Ketchum, Secretary. There has been a steady increase in members and inter-est, and the growth of the school will com-pare favorably with those of other denom-inations considering the length of time it has been established. The total of officers and teachers at the present time is, 172; in the Main School, 110; Primary Depart-ment, 40. *Officers.*— Superintendent, Irv-ing Cairns; Secretary, Wm. H. Farmer; Treasurer, Helen M. Dodge; Superintend-ent of Primary De-partment, Mrs H. R. Kimball.

The success of this school from the be-ginning is due to the untiring efforts of Mr. Irving Cairns, the Superintendent. He had a long and suc-cessful experience in this work before com-ing to Montclair, and was fully equipped for the work. He was Superintendent of the Sunday school connected with the North Baptist Church, Jersey City, when he was but nine-teen years of age.

Mr. Cairns is a na-tive of Jersey City, born August 20, 1852. His grandfather came from England about 1830, and assist-ed in the construction of the first railroad built in this country. His mother, a Miss Mary A. Bowering, was also a native of England. Mr. Cairns was educated in the public schools of Jersey City. After this he was employed for a time in a hardware house. About 1870, he and his brother bought out and succeeded to the business of H. T. Gratacap, viz., the manufacture of firemen's equipments, in N. Y. City. They built up a large and successful business. After the death of his brother, Mr. Irving Cairns conducted the business by himself. He and his family placed a beautiful memorial window in the North Baptist Church, Jersey City, in memory of his brother. Mr. Cairns moved to Upper Montclair in 1885, where he resided for a few years, and in 1892 moved to Montclair. He was one of the leaders in the movement to organize a Baptist Church, and was a large contributor to the new church edifice. He was elected

President of the Board of Trustees, and as such had the principal management of the business interests of the church. He had the general supervision of the interior arrangements of the new building. He is a man of warm sympathies and greatly beloved by his associates in the Church and his fellow laborers in the Sunday school. Mr. Cairns married, in 1879, Miss Ella V. Cook, daughter of Elisha Cook, of Jersey City.

THE UNITARIAN SOCIETY.

This Society was organized in October, 1868, and had a total membership of 49, as follows: Mr. and Mrs. Geo. H. Francis and family, 5; Mr. and Mrs. Theodore M. Morgan and family, 5; Mr. and Mrs. C. N. Boyce and family, 6; Mr. and Mrs. J. W. Weidemeyer and family, 5; Mr. and Mrs. A. D. Dickinson and family, 4; Mrs. Joseph Nason and family, 3; Mr. Carl Nason, 1; Mr. and Mrs. F. A. Angell and family, 4; Mr. and Mrs. Broadnax, 2; Mr. and Mrs. Charles Parsons and family, 4; Mr. and Mrs. Charles R. Parsons, 2; Mr. and Mrs. George Parsons, 2; Mr. and Mrs. C. K. Willmer and family, 5; Mrs. George Hawes, 1.

For some two years the pulpit was supplied by clergymen of other Unitarian Societies. Services were held in Watchung Hall, immediately east of the Mansion House, either morning or evening services, Dr. John A. Bellows, Russell Bellows, Dr. John Chadwick, Mr. G. W. Curtis and other Unitarians from time to time leading the service.

The Rev. J. B. Harrison, now of Franklin Falls, N. H., became the pastor in 1870, and continued until 1873, when Watchung Hall was given up. From that time forward Dr. John A. Bellows conducted the religious services of the Society for two years, the services being held in the house of Mrs. Joseph Nason, 121 Gates Avenue. In 1876 Dr. John A. Bellows moved to the State of Maine, and there were no further meetings of the Society.

THE YOUNG MEN'S CHRISTIAN ASSOCIATION.

Early in May, 1891, an entirely local and spontaneous movement for the organization of a Young Men's Christian Association in Montclair took form in the written request of about seventy-five young men, that the ministers of the several churches should call an initial meeting with that end in view. Pursuant to such a call, signed by Rev. A. H. Bradford, D.D., First Congregational Church; Rev. W. F. Junkin, D.D., LL.D., First Presbyterian Church; Rev. W. N. Hubbell, First Baptist Church; Rev. Orville Reed, Trinity Presbyterian Church, and Rev. Joseph A. Owen, First Methodist Episcopal Church, a meeting was held in the chapel of the First Presbyterian Church, Monday evening, May 25, 1891, to consider the matter and, if expedient, begin the work of organizing an association.

Charles H. Johnson, Sr., was elected Chairman, and E. B. Sanford, Secretary. Hon. Elkanah Drake, of Newark, Chairman of the Y. M. C. A. State Executive Committee, and David F. More, State Secretary, spoke in explanation and appreciation of associational work, and in incitement toward a local organization, if the way should appear open. The subject was very freely discussed by Dr. Junkin, Mr. Reed, Rev. F. B. Carter, of St. Luke's P. E. Church, Dr. Bradford, Paul Babcock, C. H. Johnson, Sr., and others. Mr. Babcock in direct opposition, Dr. Junkin and Mr. Carter advising caution, and Dr. Bradford and others strongly encouraging the movement. The result was the appointment of Edward Madison, C. S. Olcott, R. S. Pearce, A. D. French, A. S. Wallace and W. H. Farmer as a committee to name a committee of ten who should thoroughly consider the need and probable field for an association, and report a plan of organization, if organization should seem to be desirable and expedient. These named as a Committee of Ten: A. H. Siegfried, Chairman, E. H. Holmes, Philip Doremus, W. G. Snow, E. B. Sanford, D. F. Merritt, C. I. Reeves, Shepard Rowland, W. H. Ketcham and George Wellwood Murray. This committee gave most careful thought and investigation to the need for and possibilities of the proposed association, and made an exhaustive report to a second public meeting, June 23, when the work of forming a local organization was fully entered upon, and a constitution and by-laws were adopted. About one hundred members gave their names to the association at this meeting.

The first Board of Directors, after some few changes in its formative state, included A. H.

Siegfried, President: A. W. Law, Vice-President; A. D. French, Secretary; Shepard Rowland, Treasurer; C. H. Johnson, Sr., J. A. Sandford, Wm. Wallace, Geo. W. Melick, E. P. Benedict, George Wellwood Murray, Edward Madison, A. S. Wallace, C. S. Olcott, C. W. English and J. G. MacVicar. A Women's Auxiliary Committee of twenty-five was also formed, with Mrs. J. D. Hegeman, Chairman.

During the summer and early autumn of 1891, the membership grew steadily and encouragingly, and plans and methods were formulated. The Association took a three years' lease on the large and time-honored residence, doubly honored as having for several years housed the useful but now declining Reform Club, at 510 Bloomfield Avenue, the Association fitly succeeding to the valuable work of the Club. The building was well equipped by the Association with a reading room, game rooms, social room, gymnasium, reception and office room, etc., and was formally but quietly opened for its new usefulness, November 14. On the Sunday evening following, a mass meeting, in the interest of the new Association, was held in the First Congregational Church—the largest religious meeting ever held in the town—at which strong and inspiring addresses were made by Rev. F. N. Rutan, Rev. W. N. Hubbell, Rev. Orville Reed, Dr. Junkin and Dr. Bradford, and a report was read by the President.

Thenceforward the Association has gone quietly but aggressively about its work of seeking, teaching, entertaining and evangelizing young men through the efforts, largely, of Christian and moral young men. In April, 1892, Thomas K. Cree, Jr., a graduate of the Springfield, Mass., Secretarial Training School, was appointed General Secretary, and took the leadership in direct practical work. The regular paid membership has varied between 388 and 415, and the Association has won its place as a gladly recognized local institution, and as one of the most useful and powerful agents for the general good of the community. The spirit and methods of the Association are well set forth in the following, from *The Christian Union* (now *The Outlook*) of April 29, 1893:

"Few branches of the Y. M. C. A. with which we are acquainted are better organized or doing a more successful work than that of Montclair. This Association does not make the mistake which is so often made of being practically another Church in a community already fully stocked with such institutions. It is rather a complete and capitally equipped club for young men and boys, conducted on Christian principles, furnishing attractive entertainment, physical education, educational classes, literary facilities, and all with so little ostentation of piety, but so much of the genuine article as to be thoroughly popular with great numbers who are seldom found in such places. The religious service, or Young Men's Meeting, has a very much wider range than such meetings usually have. It is held on Sunday afternoons, at an hour when it interferes with no Church service, and, instead of being an evangelistic meeting, is devoted to practical talks by Christian men who are experts in various lines of work, and who are gladly heard because they are recognized as those who have a right to speak on the subjects they have in hand. The evangelistic idea is often overdone or unwisely used. The call to personal consecration reiterated so frequently fails to have any influence, when a different method would lead the young men step by step toward that to which they are some times too swiftly hurried. We have not referred to this Association because is has very much that is peculiar in its methods, but rather because it has a clearer conception of the work which the Y. M. C. A. can best do than most associations with which we are familiar."

The " surface indications " of what can be done by such an association in a comparatively small town are seen in this statistical *résumé* from the annual report of the General Secretary for the year ending October 1, 1893:

" 82 Religious Meetings, aggregate attendance, 3,281 ; 98 Educational Classes, aggregate attendance, 756 ; 4 Practical Talks, aggregate attendance, 155 ; 25 Social Entertainments, aggregate attendance, 3,668 ; 94 Gymnastic Lessons, aggregate attendance, 1,209 ; 13 Committee Meetings, aggregate attendance, 295 ; 125 Daily Visits to Rooms, aggregate attendance, 45,625.

" That is, for a longer or shorter time, under carefully planned and well-directed moral and religious influence and control, the boys and men—young men chiefly—of our community, were taught and entertained, and had free use of cosy Reading Rooms, Game Rooms, and a good Library, in 54,989 distinct instances within one year."

The executive organization at the time of this writing is A. H. Siegfried, President ; A. W. Law, Vice-President ; J. A. Sandford, Secretary ; Wm. Wallace, Treasurer ; Charles H. Johnson, Sr., Edward Madison, A. D. French, George Wellwood Murray, A. S. Wallace, Isaac Denby, Shepard Rowland, J. G. MacVicar, Franklin Ferris, A. S. Badgley, with Thomas K. Cree, Jr., General Secretary.

THE WOMEN'S CHRISTIAN TEMPERANCE UNION.

This Society was organized in the autumn of 1883, its object being the "suppression of intemperance by prayer and earnest personal effort." The first meeting was held on the afternoon of Dec. 6, 1883, in the Chapel of the Congregational Church, about one hundred ladies, representing the Presbyterian, Methodist, Congregational and Episcopal Churches being present. This meeting was in response to an invitation from a committee of ladies from the different churches. Mrs. McLauglin, of Boston, was present and assisted in the organization. One condition of membership was the signing of the total abstinence pledge of the National organization, thereby making this an auxiliary to the W. C. T. U. of New Jersey.

The work of the Society is divided into seven departments, viz., Literature, Juvenile Work, Prison Work, Flower Mission, Parlor Meetings, Helping Hand, and Social Purity.

The work of the first department consists in the distribution of temperance literature.

The work of the second consists in visiting the prisoners of Caldwell Penitentiary once a month on the Sabbath day, and holding religious services ; great good has been accomplished in this department.

A day is set apart in June of each year, known as Flower Mission Day, at which time bouquets of flowers are brought accompanied with appropriate verses of scripture. These flowers are sent to the Salvation Army in New York, to be distributed among the slums.

Parlor meetings are held at the different homes for the purpose of encouraging and promoting the cause of temperance.

The Juvenile Work consists in teaching the children the evil effects of alcohol upon the human body. Two schools, known as the Loyal Temperance Legions, are in successful operation.

The work of the Helping Hand is mainly among the colored women.

The Social Purity department is for the purpose of discussing the best methods of teaching children to lead clean, pure and holy lives.

A cold water drinking fountain for " man and beast," placed by this Society on the principal thoroughfare has had a beneficial effect, and has often led the man to follow the example of the beast, and quench his thirst with nature's beverage rather than by the stimulant prepared by man.

As a method of educating the public on the temperance question, some of the ablest speakers in the country have been secured at different times and have accomplished much good in this direction.

The meetings of the Society are held on the second and fourth Monday of each month, at 3 o'clock in the afternoon, in the parlors of the Y. M. C. A.

Each member pays sixty cents a year, one-half of which is devoted to State and County work, and the balance for the special local work of the Society.

The following persons have served as officers of the Society since its organization : *Presidents*, Mrs. Adia E. Taylor, Mrs. Myra J. Denby, Mrs. H. M. Sandford, Mrs. M. E. Batchelder, Mrs. Arabella DeLong ; *Vice-Presidents* of the first organization, Mrs. L. T. Wolfe, Mrs. A. F. Pratt, Mrs. E. F. Merritt, Mrs. Sarah J. Bird ; those who have served since : Mrs. E. L. Reeves, Mrs. A. S. Wallace, Mrs. Samuel Wilde, Mrs. E. P. Benedict, Mrs. Samuel Crump, Mrs. Sarah McClees, Miss Rebecca Crane, Mrs. R. G. Hutchinson, Mrs. E. Ferris, Mrs. Huntington, Mrs. L. Butler, Mrs. J. Wyman, Mrs. J. M. Burr, Mrs. Ames, Mrs. Romisaville, Mrs. John Anderson, Mrs. Delano, Mrs. E. Ferris ; *Secretaries*, Mrs. M. J. Denby, Mrs. H. H. White, Mrs. E. A. Pulver, Mrs. E. M. White, Miss Irene D. Grover, Mrs. M. L. Penroyer, Mrs. S. L. Reeves ; *Treasurers*, Miss Lizzie Morris, Mrs. H. M. Sandford, Mrs. E. M. Gilbert, Mrs. H. R. Edmonston. Present officers : *President*, Mrs. Arabella DeLong ; *Corresponding Secretary*, Mrs. H. D. Crane ; *Recording Secretary*, Mrs. S. L. Reeves ; *Treasurer*, Mrs. H. R. Edmonston.

THE COLORED POPULATION AND THEIR CHURCHES.

The influx of the colored people in Montclair began about 1870 (the total colored population of the township at that time being 36), and was the result of an effort to solve the servant question. A prominent citizen of Montclair brought from Loudon County, Va., two or three servants on trial. They proved satisfactory, and others, learning that better wages could be obtained at the North, soon followed, and the colored population of Montclair now number about 1,600, most of whom were born in servitude; and, as was the custom, took the names of their masters. All became free under the proclamation of President Lincoln. As a class they are quiet, industrious and well behaved. They retain many of their old time customs, but readily adapt themselves to the new condition of affairs. The larger proportion of them are house servants, yet some have already acquired considerable property. They are a church-going people, and are active in advancing the cause of religion, and have made rapid progress in their Church societies.

UNION BAPTIST CHURCH COLORED.

The preliminary movements that led to the organization of this Church began in July, 1886, in a series of meetings held from house to house, the first one being held at the residence of Lucy Weaver.

These meetings were continued through the year with increasing numbers and interest. The organization was completed and the name of the Union Baptist Church adopted in the early part of 1887, regular meetings having already been held with occasional preaching services at Watchung Hall. The Church records show that:

"At the call of the Union Baptist Church, of Montclair, N. J., a Council convened at its house of worship, Wednesday, January 12, 1887, to consider the propriety of recognizing it as a regular Baptist Church, and also the propriety of ordaining to the work of the ministry, Rev. J. A. Harris, pastor elect. Rev. L. O. Greenville was chosen Moderator, and Rev. Henry B. Waring, Clerk. The Council was composed of the following delegates:

"First Church, Caldwell, Rev. Jabez Marshall and Daniel B. Lewis; First Church, Roselle, Rev. L. O. Grenille and Reuben Smith; Fifth Church, Newark, Rev. Henry B. Waring and Edward Hedden; Roseville Church, Newark, Rev. Albert Stillman; South Church, Newark, Rev. S. E. Verson, P.D.; First Church, Bloomfield, Rev. E. D. Simms."

Services were held at Watchung Hall until 1890, and afterward at Morris Hall. A lot was purchased in 1889 on Bloomfield Avenue, which was sold later at an advance, and another lot purchased on Portland Place, 50 by 126 feet, and a frame building erected thereon, 45 by 110 feet, with a seating capacity of about 500. It is neatly furnished, provided with every convenience, and fitted up with one of the finest organs in this locality. The total cost of the whole property was about $20,000. It contains an audience room, a Sunday-school room, a lecture room, and three small reading rooms.

Rev. J. A. Harris remained until May 1, 1889, and was succeeded by Rev. Mr. Adkins, from North Carolina, who remained about two months. A call was then extended to Rev. Wm. Perry, who began his pastorate July 26, 1889. The total membership was then about 46, and under his pastorate it has since increased to 356. He has baptized nearly 200; the rest were received by letter. When Mr. Perry's pastorate began in 1889, the total amount of real property owned by members of his church and congregation did not exceed $1,000; they now own, according to his statement, about $110,000.

Though the members are mostly persons in moderate circumstances they give liberally of their means, and the amount raised in one year to pay for the services of an evangelist, and for other benevolent purposes, was $800.

Rev. WILLIAM PERRY, the pastor of this Church, was born in Chatham County, N. C., October 22, 1860, three years before the Act of Emancipation. His parents were the property of a Mr. Perry, and, as was the custom, took the name of their master. Soon after the close of the war William was sent to private school, his parents being ambitious to give him an education. In 1879 he attended Wayland Seminary, in Washington, D. C., and during this period became assistant pastor of the Mount Vernon Baptist Church (colored). He remained about two years, and then conducted mission meetings for another year at Garfield City. He labored some time as an evangelist with great success, and subsequently had charge of the Bright Hope Baptist Church, at Princeton, N. J., where, after remaining two years, he came to Montclair. His work among his people here has been marked with great success. He has shown great ability as an organizer, and is earnest and effective as a preacher. He has the faculty of inspiring confidence among his people, and they trust him implicitly, and recognize him as their leader. He is an indefatigable worker, both in and out of the Church, and is seconded in all his efforts by his faithful followers. He has shown himself a good financier, and an able business manager, having conducted all the operations in connection with the purchase of the church property, and the erection and furnishing of the church. He has a comfortable home of his own, acquired by his industry, economy and good management.

THE SUNDAY SCHOOL connected with this Church was organized in May, 1887, with ten scholars and one teacher. The first and second Superintendents were Miss Elliott and Miss Emma Smith. William Grigsby in 1890. The school numbers at the present time 125 scholars, with 16 teachers. The library contains 2,500 volumes.

ST. MARK'S METHODIST EPISCOPAL CHURCH—COLORED.

This Church owes its existence to the efforts of a few individuals— whites— who conceived the idea of organizing a Colored Union Church, that should be supported by representatives of the several denominations. The work began about 1881, by the organization of a Church and Sunday school, the chief promoters of which were, E. A. Snedeker, Rev. J. H. Cooley, D. F. Merritt, and J. W. Snedeker, representing the M. E. Church of Montclair, and Mr. George P. Farmer, of the First Baptist Church of Montclair. The officers of the M. E. Church gave the use of their old building on Bloomfield Avenue, free of rent, in order to start the enterprise. The church was opened in 1881 with a membership of 25 –all colored. This number has gradually increased to about 100. The other denominations interested in the matter recognized the fact that the prevailing system of Methodism enabled that Society to provide pulpit supplies without cost to the new church, and therefore consented to that denominational distinction, under the name of St. Mark's M. E. Church. The colored people were enthusiastic in the work and secured the use of the building, rent free, for five years, from the First M. E. Church in consideration of their putting it in complete repair. They raised quite a sum among themselves, but were largely assisted by the whites. About $1,400 was expended for this purpose, and besides this the colored people raised among themselves, $700 for an organ, and about $300 for carpets. The First M. E. Church gave them the refusal of the property at a valuation of $2,500, agreeing also to donate $500, leaving the amount of $2,000 to be raised by the colored people. A part of this amount has been raised by the colored people, with the prospect of their soon owning the property.

For the first two years, Rev. J. H. Cooley, of the First M. E. Church, was their pastor. Supplies after this were furnished by the Presiding Elder, until about 1888, when Rev. Amos Garther assumed the pastorate of the church, which he still continues.

For the first few years, until 1892, this church was a part of the Newark Conference, and that year, by action of the Colored Conference of New Jersey, it was placed in the Delaware Conference (colored). This church is now in a prosperous condition, and is doing excellent work among the colored people.

The Sunday school was started contemporaneous with the church, by Mr. M. E. Smith, who had the general supervision of both church and school. He continued as Superintendent of the school from 1881 to 1896, and was succeeded by J. W. Snedeker, the present incumbent. There are now 12 teachers—all white—and 150 scholars.

Both in the church and Sunday school the colored people have displayed great liberality, and a commendable zeal in the work, and have evinced their grateful appreciation of the support and sympathy of their white neighbors.

VIEW OF PARK STREET, FROM THE CORNER OF CLAREMONT AVENUE.

Chapter XII.

EDUCATIONAL DEVELOPMENT.

The first School in Newark, 1676.—Act adopted by the General Assembly, 1693, for establishing Schools.—First School Committee, 1697.—First Appropriation by the State Legislature, 1846.—Acts of 1829, 1838, 1846, 1852, 1867, etc.—Schools of Cranetown, West Bloomfield and Montclair.—The First School-house, 1740.—Second School-house, 1812.—Gideon Wheeler, the first Teacher in the "New School-house."—Special School Law for the Township of Bloomfield, 1846.—Teachers, 1846 to 1856.—Trustees, 1831 to 1856.—The "New Departure," and the result.—Increased Facilities.—Establishment of the High School, and its gradual development.—The new School Building, 1892-3.—Efforts of Dr. J. J. H. Love, the first President of the Board, and his Successors, George H. Francis, Thomas Porter, Charles K. Willmer and John R. Howard.—Sketch of Randall Spaulding.—Private Schools.—Washington School.—East End.—Warren Holt's School.—Ashland Hall.—Hillside Seminary for Young Ladies.—Montclair Military Academy.—Free Public Library.

HE early settlers of Newark, though many of them could neither read or write, were men of enterprise, virtue, and more than ordinary intelligence, and they appreciated the importance of having their children properly educated. After purchasing their land, building their habitations, establishing their local government, erecting their church, and constructing their mill, they next gave their attention to the education of their children.

On November 1, 1676, at a town meeting composed of the freeholders of Newark, numbering at that time seventy-five persons, the following action was taken:

"ITEM—The Town's Men have Liberty to see if they can find a competent number of Schollars and accommodations for a School Master in this town."

The "Town's Men"—seven in number—took prompt action to secure a school-master, as appears from the following record, Feb. 7, 1677:

"ITEM—The Town hath consented that the Town's Men should perfect the Bargain with the School Master for this year, upon condition that he will come for this year, and do his faithful, honest and true Endeavor, to teach the Children, or servants of those who have subscribed, the reading and writing of English, and also of Arithmetick if they desire it; as much as they are capable to learn as is he capable to teach them, within the Compass of this year, no wise hindering, but that he may make what bargain he please, with those as have not subscribed. It is voted that the Town's Men have Liberty to complete the Bargain with the School Master, they knowing the Town's Mind."

The first "school master" was John Catlin or Cathling, one of the early settlers from Branford, who also held the office of town attorney and other positions.

The General Assembly of the Province, in October, 1693, enacted the following:

"An Act for Establishing School Masters Within this Province.

"Whereas the cultivating of learning and good Manners tends greatly to the good and benefit of Mankind, which have hitherto been much neglected within this Province. BE IT THEREFORE ENACTED by the Governor, Council and Deputies in General Assembly now met and Assembled, and by the Authority of the same, that the Inhabitants of any Town within this Province, shall and may by Warrant from a Justice of the Peace of that County where they think fit and convenient, meet together and make choice of three more men of the said Town, to make a rate for the salary and maintaining of a School Master within the said Town, for so long a time as they think fit; and the consent and agreement of the Major part of the Inhabitants of the said Town, shall bind and oblige the remaining part of the Inhabitants of said Town to satisfy and pay their shares and proportion of the said Rate; and in case of refusal or non payment, distress to be made upon the Goods and Chattels of said Person or Persons so refusing or not paying, by the constable of said Town, by Virtue of a Warrant from a Justice of the Peace of that County; and the Distress so taken to be sold at a public Vendue, and the overplus, if any be after the payment of the said rate and charges to be returned to the Owner."

This Act was amended in February, 1695, as follows:

"WHEREAS there was an Act made ANNO DOMINE 1693 for the establishing of Schools in each respective Town in this Province, and by experience it is found inconvenient, by reason of the Distance of the Neighborhood, the said Act directing no suitable way whereby all the inhabitants may have the benefit thereof: BE IT THEREFORE ENACTED by the Governor, Council and Representatives, in General Assembly now met and Assembled, and by Authority of the same, that three Men be chosen Yearly and every Year in each respective Town in this Province to appoint and agree with a School Master, and the three Men so chosen shall have power to nominate and appoint the most convenient place or places where the School shall be kept from time to time, that as near as may be the whole Inhabitants may have the benefit thereof."

On the 1st of January, 1697, the town meeting chose a school committee consisting of Theopelus Pierson, Jasper Crane and Thomas Richards, who were authorized "to agree with a School Master to keep School in this Town for the Year according to Act of Assembly."

The first State legislation in behalf of public schools was on Feb. 9, 1816, by which "the Legislature authorized and directed the Treasurer of the State to invest in the public six per cent. stock of the United States in the name of and for the use of this State, the sum of $15,000." Other stocks were added to this in 1817, making an aggregate of $87,076.34.

The first distribution of public funds was by enactment of Feb. 24, 1829, which provided that the Trustees of the School Fund should appropriate annually from the proceeds thereof $20,000 for public schools. This was the first attempt at disbursement. Hitherto it had been all accumulation. The money that had been gathering for thirteen years had reached a level from where it would be safe to distribute, and the Trustees of the fund "are to divide this $20,000 among the fourteen counties in the ratio of State tax paid by the counties." The Chosen Freeholders of the several counties were directed to re-disburse to their several townships in the ratio of the county tax paid by the townships. Townships were required to elect annually school committees of three each, whose duty it was to divide the township into convenient school districts, license teachers for the township, call district meetings of the taxable inhabitants only, and to divide the public money quarterly among the several districts according to the number of children between the ages of four and sixteen years. The district meetings were to determine how many months in the year a school should be kept, and the Trustees were to provide a house or room for the school.

By the Act of February 16, 1831, the Act of 1829 and supplement of 1830 were repealed and a new act substituted. By this Act the sum of $30,000 was annually appropriated from the proceeds of the school fund, to be drawn on or before the first Monday in April. Authority to levy an annual school tax was continued to the townships, and they were empowered to assign all the State money to educate the "indigent poor" if they chose.

The patrons, supporters or proprietors of common schools in the townships were directed to organize their several schools, if not already organized, by the appointment of any number of trustees. The trustees were to report to the Township School Committee their organization; whereupon the Committee was directed to recognize all such schools as being entitled to their proportion of the public money.

The Township School Committees, upon the receipt of the annual reports of the several Boards of Trustees, assigned the public money to each school in the ratio of the number of children taught, as reported to them during the preceding year. If the township had voted all the public money to the use of the poor, then the ratio of distribution was to be as to the number of "poor" children taught in each school.

In March, 1838, there was a new enactment authorizing this $30,000 to be disbursed from the school fund annually, on the usual basis. Township School Committees were again empowered to divide townships into convenient school districts; alter and change them as circumstances may require, and if advisable form them from parts of two or more adjoining townships or counties.

By the law of 1846 the annual sum of $30,000 was continued to be appropriated, but townships were required to raise a sum at least equal to the proportion of the State appropriation, but not to exceed double that sum.

In 1836 the General Government found itself in possession of more money than it wanted, or would be likely to want. By Act of Congress, passed June 23, of that year, it distributed to the several States, as a loan without interest, more than $30,000,000 of this "surplus revenue," as it was called. The sum appropriated to the State of New Jersey was $764,670.44.

A supplement to the Act of 1846, passed March 14, 1857, provided for an annual disbursement of $40,000 of the proceeds of the school fund, and $40,000 from the general treasury, making a sum almost equal to the entire school fund of a third of a century before.

By an Act of 1852, the "Trustees of the School Fund" were authorized to dispose of all that remained of the lands belonging to the State at Paterson, by private or public sale, and invest the proceeds thereof in the school fund.

By an Act of 1867, the formation and re-formation of school districts was taken from the people and placed in the hands of the County Superintendent.

In 1871, an Act was passed, assigning the proceeds from the sales and rentals of "land under water" to the school fund. From this source a large amount is realized annually.

In the same year the Two-mill Tax was enacted. This is an assessment of two mills on every dollar of the assessed value of all taxable property in the State. From this source there was realized in 1875 the sum of $1,237,578.57.

It supersedes the township taxes heretofore required, provided the sum realized by this tax proves to be sufficient to maintain free schools in a given township nine months in the year. "Sectarian Schools" are specially denied any part of the two-mill tax.

SCHOOLS OF CRANETOWN, WEST BLOOMFIELD AND MONTCLAIR.

The first school-house in Cranetown, as near as can be ascertained, was built about 1740. It stood at the junction of the Old Road (now Church Street) and the road leading to Orange, south of what was recently the High School Building. It was a one-story building, built of stone, twenty-six feet long and eighteen feet broad. It faced the east, and the curve in the road was then such that it looked down the street. There was a large fire-place in the southwest corner of the room, and flat desks or tables placed around the sides of the room, far enough from the walls to admit of benches being placed between the desks and the walls. All the seats were slabs, bark side down. At the south end was an oblong platform, two steps in height, which was called "the rostrum." In the centre of this platform was a trap door, opening into the dungeon, where evil doers were sometimes "dropped." The earliest teachers mentioned who occupied the rostrum were Isaac Watts Crane and Hugh Thompson.

Rev. Jedediah Chapman, for many years pastor of the First Church in Orange, came regularly every two weeks, on Saturday, to catechise the children. He was a man of venerable appearance, wore a cocked hat, and always rode on horseback. The children with the master were ranged along the roadside, in single file, and waited with uncovered heads until the minister dismounted and entered the building, when they all followed.

Dr. Grub succeeded Mr. Thompson, and Mr. Tracy, of Scotch-Irish ancestry, followed. He was a severe disciplinarian and held strictly to the proverb "Spare the rod and spoil the child." He made free use of the "weeping willow," and the weeping children failed to move him to compassion. Mr. Smith, Mr. Hinman and Mr. Norton, each in succession taught in this school-house.

The *Second* school-house was built in 1812, on land purchased of Parmenus Dodd, through Israel Crane, at the junction of Old Road and the turnpike, about fifty feet east of the present Presbyterian Church. It was of stone, two stories high, twenty-two by forty feet in size, the second story of which was used for religious services.

Gideon Wheeler was the first teacher in the second school-house. He came from Stepney, Fairfield County, Conn., to New Jersey, about 1809-10. He taught first in Jersey City, afterward at a small village near Parsippany, New Jersey, and came to Cranetown in 1812. He brought with him the following

"RECOMMENDATION:

"HUNTINGTON, FAIRFIELD COUNTY, July 17, 1809.

"This may certify that the bearer, Gideon Wheeler, has made school teaching his business between fifteen and twenty years, and has generally given satisfaction to his employers, and his knowledge of the orthography of the English language, English Grammar, Arithmetic, Mathematics and Astronomy, we conceive, will recommend him to all who wish to have their children acquire useful knowledge under his tuition. His moral character is such as merits the imitation of his pupils if they wish to become useful members in society.

"DEODATE SILLEMAN, JR., Prest."

Mr. Wheeler taught in this school for many years. He was a man of great intellectual force and sound judgment, and considered an excellent teacher for the time. He held the position until declining health compelled his retirement, and his remaining days were spent on his farm. He attracted pupils from Speertown, Verona, the Coit Neighborhood, Tory Corner, and from "between the Mountains." His whole term of service was about eleven years—from 1811 to 1822. He was succeeded by Philander Seymour, a young man from Genoa, N. Y., who had taught for a time "between the mountains," south of Pleasant Valley. He was a man of good education, a popular and successful teacher. He continued teaching from 1822 to 1830, when he removed to Bloomfield. Isaac B. Wheeler, a son of Gideon Wheeler, taught here for a time; also William Hedden and David J. Allen. Warren S. Holt taught school in the same building, and subsequently opened a day and boarding school for young men and young ladies at what is now known as the Mountain House. Amos B. Howland succeeded him March 7, 1836, and was the last teacher in the second school house and the first one in the third.

The second school-house, together with the lot on which it stood, was sold in 1838, to the Society of West Bloomfield Presbyterian Church, for $400, and the third school-house was erected the same year, on land purchased from Ira Campbell, west of, and near the Presbyterian Church This building was sold to the same Church Society, in 1860, for $800. Mr. Howland continued teaching until 1839, and on April 6th, of that year, was succeeded by Miss Harriet Booth, Oct. 3, 1840. Samuel Jones also taught here for a time and was succeeded Nov. 1, 1849, by Edwin C. Fuller, the present tax collector of the township of Montclair. He was assisted by Miss Jane Van Duyne. Miss Phœbe C. Munn was appointed April 25, 1850, and continued during the summer months. She was the last teacher under the old regime of a pay school, the tuition being at that time $2.00 a quarter or $8.00 a year. The Trustees that year abolished the Saturday forenoon school hours, the half holiday having been the immemorable usage. The change met with a strong opposition, the older people claiming that "what was good enough for them was good enough for their children."

Application was made by the township of Bloomfield, in 1849, for a special school law. Resistance was made, but the free school law was enacted in 1849, amended in 1850, and the tuition of all children was henceforth paid by taxation.

Section 1 of the amended Act authorizes the township to "raise by tax at the annual town meeting a sum not to exceed $2,500 in any one year, which money shall not be applied to the building of a school-house or school-houses."

Section 2 provides that "the amount authorized shall not in any one year exceed one-half the amount of taxes assessed the preceding year in said district for all purposes."

Section 3 provides that "the town superintendent together with the township committee shall be and are hereby authorized to unite, divide and alter their school districts, and change the boundaries thereof whenever and as often as they may deem it necessary or expedient for the public benefit." This Act was approved March 6th, 1850.

At the time of the enactment of the law there were seven school districts in the old township. Three of the four in the eastern part of the town were united, and the Bloomfield plan of a Central Grammar and High School and primary schools at a distance from the centre began its growth. The three districts in the western portion of the town remained separate.

The first teacher at the West Bloomfield School under the new law was A. D. Babcock, who received a salary of $300 a year. Edwin C. Fuller returned April, 1852, and was assisted by Miss Phœbe C. Munn; his salary was $340, and hers $200. Miss Phœbe Campbell, appointed Oct. 2, 1852, received $100 salary, and Miss Samantha Wheeler was appointed Sept. 22, 1856, at $125 per annum.

The following named Trustees managed the school affairs of West Bloomfield from 1831 to 1850, at which time the first radical change was made: For the year 1831, Elias Littell, Zenas S. Crane, John Munn, Stephen F. Crane, Caleb Baldwin; 1832, Zenas S. Crane, Matthias Smith, Stephen F. Crane, John Munn, Timothy A. Crane; 1833, Zenas S. Crane, Stephen F. Crane, Nathaniel Crane, Jr., John Munn, Caleb Ward; 1835, Peter Doremus, William Smith, John Munn, Stephen F. Crane; 1836, Stephen F. Crane, Richard Romer, Peter Doremus, William Smith, John Munn; 1838, Elias B. Crane, Zenas S. Crane, Wm. Smith; 1839, John Munn, Jos. H. Baldwin, Elias B. Crane; 1844, William Smith, William S. Morris, Martin S. Moore; 1846, William S. Morris, Calvin S. Baldwin, John D. Taylor, John Munn, Amzi Sandford; 1847, William S. Morris, C. S. Baldwin, John D. Taylor, David Rogers, Nathaniel H. Dodd; 1848, John Post, C. S. Baldwin, A. A. Sanford, Edmund Doremus, John C. Doremus; 1849, C. S. Baldwin, M. W. Smith, John C. Collins, Wm. S. Morris, A. A. Sanford; 1850, A. A. Sanford, John Munn, Chas. Smith, C. S. Baldwin, Anthony D. Ball.

The completion of the Newark and Bloomfield R. R. to West Bloomfield in 1856 was the beginning of a new settlement. It brought to this town active young men with families of children to educate —men who had been accustomed to good schools in the New England States, and who were desirous of having school facilities here equal to those to which they had been accustomed, so that they might avoid the necessity of sending their children elsewhere to be educated. The question of improved school accommodations began to be agitated, and this was brought to a final issue at a meeting held April 2, 1860, Mr. Julius H. Pratt acting as Chairman, and Dr. J. J. H. Love as Secretary. An entire new Board of Trustees was elected, consisting of Peter H. Van Riper, Edgar T. Gould, William Jacobus, Joseph H. Baldwin and John C. DeWitt.

The question of location for a school building next became the all-absorbing topic, and it is a noteworthy fact that the site finally selected was near the same spot where the first school-house was erected more than a century previous. The Trustees called a public meeting on May 10, 1860, recommending the purchase of a lot on the corner of Church Street and Valley Road, both streets being a part of the Old Road, which extended through Bloomfield to Newark, being one of the first laid out in the old "Town of Newark." A large number of the old inhabitants attended the meeting and vigorously opposed the recommendation of the Trustees, resorting to all kinds of quibbles and parliamentary tactics to prevent action. Several meetings followed this, and finally, at a meeting held June 15, 1860, the measure was carried by a vote of 64 to 34, and the Trustees were authorized to purchase the above-mentioned lot, then owned by Grant J. Wheeler, and to erect thereon a school building with accommodations suited to the increased population. On July 10th of that year the Board of Trustees adopted plans and specifications, and on July 30th the contract was awarded to Wm. Sigler, carpenter, and Edgar T. Gould, mason, at a cost of $1,300, the heating apparatus, furniture, etc., making a total cost of $6,021.31. The building was fifty feet in length by thirty-five in breadth, and now forms the north wing of the present grammar school. The south wing was erected in 1869 and the east wing in 1873; the total cost of the completed building, which is now the Grammar School, was $35,000.

Mr. John H. Morrow, appointed December 28, 1860, at a salary of $450, was the first teacher in the original wing of this new edifice. He was assisted, in 1861, by Miss A. M. Munn, and in 1863 by Miss Helen Munn.

Special plans were originated in 1866 for the establishment of a High School adequate to the demands of the best education preparatory to the college or the university. The purpose was to secure the

THE OLD SCHOOL HOUSE, 1856.

services of a principal who should be a graduate from one of the best colleges, and whose character and attainments should secure the best results in education. The High School was to afford facilities "to educate here at home the youth who had been previously sent away to school," and to enable "parents to retain under home influence their children during the period of the formation of character." John W. Taylor, a graduate of Harvard University, became the principal September 1, 1866, and inspired a rapid development of our school system during the four years of his supervision. His tact, ability and enthusiasm in school work, his geniality and his fondness for young life, his instinct for individualizing, and his natural leadership, gave inspiration alike to teachers, students, parents and trustees. Miss Lucy M. Brown was appointed assistant November 23, 1867. Mr. Taylor left during the second year of his administration, and Mr. Jared Hasbrouck filled the position from August 26, 1868, to December 17, at which time Mr. Taylor returned, continuing until 1870, when Mr. John P. Gross, a graduate of Bowdoin College, became the principal. Mr. Gross continued to develop a wide public interest in the School. The increase of pupils rendered a further enlargement necessary in 1873. The first graduating class, composed of thirteen members, was guided through the advanced course by Mr. Gross, and the first diplomas of the Trustees, given in 1874, were made significant of a thorough education. Mr. Gross was assisted in the High School department by Miss Lucy M. Brown and Mr. Edward Thatcher, a graduate of Yale College, and a son of Prof. Thos. A. Thatcher. Miss Abbey M. Munn, at that time a teacher of long experience and distinguished success, was at the head of the Primary Department. Miss Lucy Brown, who for seven years had been an efficient teacher, and was highly esteemed in the community, was called away by death in 1874. Mr. Gross continued for about a year longer, and was succeeded, in the autumn of 1874, by Mr. Randall Spaulding, a graduate of Yale College.

Efficient as the School was at the time, Mr. Spaulding saw that there was room for further improvement in order to meet the growing demands of the community. One of the most important changes made by him was that of requiring the pupils then in school to remain a year longer than the previous time allotted for graduation.

Other improvements have been made from year to year, demonstrating the wisdom, knowledge and ability of the principal. During his administration of nearly twenty years, he has been assisted by a corps of excellent teachers, some of whom were old residents in the community. Among the lady teachers have been Miss Annie Brown, a very successful teacher, who served for six years; Miss F. A. Caldwell, Miss Anna S. Peck, and Miss Mary J. Turner; and of the gentlemen, R. W. Conant, Charles L. Noyes, Edwin B. Goodell, Samuel D. Eaton, Noah C. Rogers, J. Howard Pratt and Arthur E. Bostwick. Miss Eldora Eldredge is worthy of special mention. She has had charge of the grammar department, preparatory to the High School, for nearly eighteen years, and still continues in that position.

The need of increased specialization in the work of the High School led to the employment, in 1886, of Mr. Robert Cornish to take charge of the science department, a man eminently fitted for the work. He continued in this position for six years, and brought the department to a high state of efficiency. The classical department was assigned to Miss Eliza H. Gilbert, who for several years had performed a part of the duties pertaining to it. Her work is characterized by great accuracy and thoroughness. In September, 1892, Mr. J. Steward Gibson succeeded Mr. Cornish in the science department. Miss Turner, who for many years had served most acceptably as preceptress of the High School, was succeeded in 1887 by Miss Margaret A. Emerson, a conscientious and painstaking teacher, who remained three years. Her place was filled by Miss Elsie M. Dwyer, a graduate of Wellesley College, an able and successful teacher of ripe experience.

Other departments have been added—that of modern language and mathematics, in charge of Miss Harriet E. Crouch; Latin and modern history, Miss Mary A. Carter; commercial branches and botany, Mr. William C. Gorman; English and history in charge of the preceptress, Miss Dwyer, assisted by Miss Lucy Evelyn Wight. The unusually long and efficient service of Miss Abbie M. Munn, now in the highest grade of the primary department, and Miss Eldora Eldredge, in the highest grade of the grammar department, renders them worthy of special notice. Miss Eldredge having served eighteen consecutive years, and Miss Munn a much longer period. The names of both these worthy teachers are enshrined in the hearts of hundreds of pupils, many of whom have achieved honor and success in life, and cherish the remembrance of them as among the most delightful associations connected with their *alma mater*.

Since 1874 scarcely a year has passed without material change in the course of study, and new systems and methods have given place to the old ones. Even the early graduates of this school would be surprised at the great changes that have been wrought. The system of manual training was introduced in 1882, and the trustees were authorized to expend the sum of $1,000 to test its practicability. A room was fitted up and fully supplied with the necessary tools and appliances. The manual work the first year in the grammar department consisted in drawing and construction of geometric forms, and in advanced clay modeling; to the second year was assigned a course in joinery; to the third year, wood carving. Girls during this period were instructed in needlework. This department has succeeded beyond the expectations of its promoters, and has been extended from time to time both upward and downward in the grades of the school. The expense of maintaining this department the first year was $726; the second, $600; the third, $583; the fourth, $681; fifth, $695; and the sixth, $687.

The total number of graduates from the High School is 206. Of these, seventy-eight have entered upon a college course leading to a degree. Nine graduates have taken special courses in colleges; seventeen have entered some professional school of law, medicine or teaching. Those who have entered upon a college course are classified as follows: Yale, 19; Wellesley, 11; Smith, 9; Amherst, 7; Princeton, 7; Harvard, 6; Wesleyan, 4; University of New York, 3; Oberlin, 2; Lehigh, 2; University of Minnesota, 1; Williams, 1; Cornell, 1; Evelyn, 1; Columbia, 1; Bryn Mawr, 1; Barnard, 1; Massachusetts School of Technology, 1.

The school census shows the number of children residing within the district between five and eighteen years of age in 1856 as 185. In 1870 there were 150. The next decade, 898. The total number in 1893 was 1,706. The increase from 1856 to 1893 is 1,518; the largest increase in any one year was that of 1871, viz., 150. The smallest increase was in 1872, viz., 6, and the year from 1884 to 1885 showed a decrease of 22.

The total number of scholars enrolled at the present time is 1,300, requiring the employment of 44 teachers, including instructors in special departments. Additions have been made to the old and new buildings during the past fifteen years, in order to meet the increased demands for school facilities. In 1878-9 the west half of the centre primary school was built at a cost of $12,000. In 1884, the east half centre primary, at a cost of $7,118. In 1888 a new school-house was built on Cedar Street, which cost, including the land, $6,895. In 1889-90 a large new brick building was erected on Chestnut Street, which cost, including the land, $15,803.

In 1892 a large plot of land was purchased on the west side of Valley Road, about three hundred yards west of the present grammar school. On this was erected one of the finest and most completely equipped school buildings in the State. The building is 237 feet long and about 84 feet extreme width, covering an area of 15,738 square feet, including porches, etc. The design is of classic style and the exteriors are finished in buff brick and cream white terra cotta. The portion below water level is of dark red brick. All interior carrying partitions and all heating and vent flues are of brick. The floors are laid on Georgia pine joists and on iron beams. All interior walls are furred and a fire stop is at the bottom of each. The building is two stories high and the main flights of stairs are of iron, supported by brick walls, broken by landings and covered with rubber treads. The first floor is arranged with a direct corridor from entrance to entrance, thirteen feet wide, and contains all the wardrobes, being separated for the sexes. They are built on a new plan adapted and used by the architects, Messrs. Loring & Phipps, of Boston, designers of this and many public schools and other public buildings.

Placed at intervals in the first floor corridor are three foot warmers, so arranged that the children can dry their feet and clothes in wet weather. On the south side of this corridor are seven class rooms of different sizes, each having seating capacity of from 54 to 60 pupils or more, according to size, and each room is arranged for the light to come over the left shoulder and back of the pupil. Each class room on this floor, as well as on the second floor, has teachers' closets and book closets, and blackboards of natural slate are on all the wall surfaces not used for other purposes. On the north side of the corridor on the first floor are two recitation rooms, principal's office with fire place, toilets, closets, waiting room and depository. The reference room and connecting library are fitted with delivery desk and book racks for many thousands of volumes. In each corridor two drinking places are furnished for the children's use, made of soapstone set on brackets with nickel self-closing locks.

On the second floor are four class rooms, two recitation rooms, two toilet rooms, and an assembly hall with a seating capacity of 500, with two small ante-rooms and a stage 27 feet wide and 13 feet deep.

On the south side is the chemical laboratory and also conveniences for photographic experiments. Two flights of stairs lead from the second to the third stories, in which is a furnished room for students in drawing, and a large room partly unfinished, 84 feet long by 30 feet wide for gymnasium. The finish of the entire building is of brown ash. All corridors, rooms and staircases are wainscoted in ash to a height of about four feet.

The entire cost, including the land, was $125,000.

From the beginning of the new movement in 1860,—with the exception of his absence during the war—Dr. J. J. H. Love has been continuously a member of the Board of Trustees. To his persistent and indefatigable efforts in the cause of higher education is largely due the present school system, with facilities, equaled by few, and, it is believed, unsurpassed by those of any town of this size in the United States. Dr. Love led and the people followed. Having unbounded confidence in his ability, good judgment and impartial dealings, they gave him their hearty support, and freely voted the

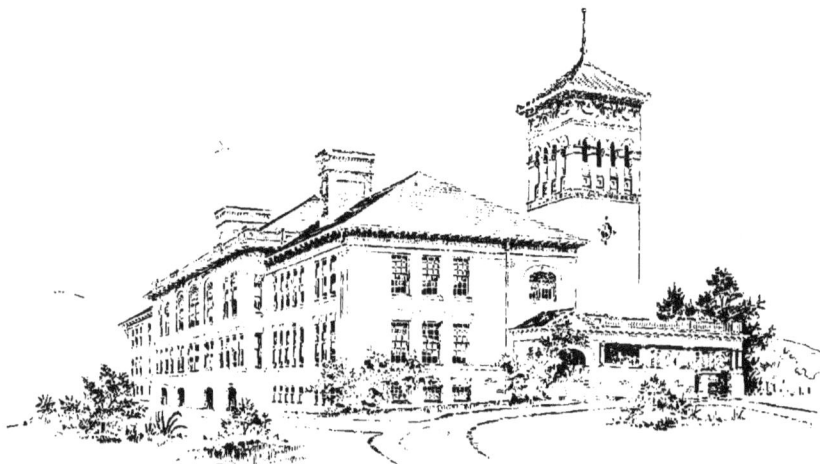

THE NEW HIGH SCHOOL.

appropriations asked for. He served for many years as President of the Board, and then took the position of Clerk, which he has held without intermission up to the present time (1894). His interest in the work has never flagged, and he has given his personal attention to the most minute details. In the erection of the new High School building, he supervised every portion of the work from the foundation to the roof, and, being daily on the spot, nothing escaped his observation.

Mr. George H. Francis succeeded Dr. Love as President, and held the position for some years.

Mr. Thomas Porter, who succeeded Mr. Francis as President of the Board of Trustees, was an enthusiast in the matter of "higher education," and an earnest and zealous worker in the cause. He often visited the school and spoke words of encouragement to teachers and scholars. He lived to see the "new system" firmly established and in successful operation.

Mr. Charles K. Willmer, the successor of Mr. Porter, served sixteen years as a member of the Board, for five of which he was its President. A man of fine executive ability and large business experience, he directed the affairs of the school with consummate ability and tact, and gave great satisfaction to his associates and to the whole community.

Dr. C. H. Marvin rendered faithful and efficient service, as a member of the Board of Trustees, for nine years, and during 1890 and 1891 was President of the Board.

Mr. John R. Howard, the present incumbent, was elected in 1892. His acceptance of the position was gratifying to every one interested in the cause of education. He has a national reputation as a writer and publisher, and since his residence in Montclair, has been active in promoting its moral and intellectual growth, having been prominently identified with the several organizations having this object in view. The erection of the new school building, and the various improvements in connection therewith, have all been accomplished during his administration.

The citizens of Montclair—even those who have no children to reap the benefit—have given their hearty co-operation and have cheerfully borne the burden of increased taxation—knowing that others were benefited thereby—and that every dollar spent in the cause of education would in time enhance the value of their property through the increase of population. Persons living at a distance from Montclair have acquired a residence here for the purpose of giving their children the benefit of its superior educational advantages usually obtainable only at expensive private institutions.

RANDALL SPAULDING.

The present efficiency and high standing of the schools of Montclair is due to the untiring efforts of Mr. Spaulding, covering a period of nearly a quarter of a century. The methods by which this has been accomplished are fully set forth in the history of the schools of this township, and require no repetition in this sketch of his life. While he inherited many of the qualities that conduced to his success, the difficulties which he encountered and overcame in early life were the special means by which this was accomplished. Both his paternal and maternal ancestors were among the early Puritans of New England.

The origin of the name of Spaulding is said to be from *spauld*, meaning shoulder, and *ding*, to strike. The name originated in the Middle Ages, when battles were fought hand to hand. The two-handed sword on the coat of arms justifies this statement. The motto borne on the arms is "*Hinc mihi salus.*" Edward Spaulding, the ancestor, came from England to the Massachusetts Colony and settled in Braintree, where he was made a freeman in 1640. He had a son, *Andrew*, who was the father of Deacon *Isaac*, born in Chelmsford, 1710, who moved to Townsend, Mass. The farm on which he settled is still in the hands of the Spaulding family. He signed a petition for protection against the Indians, December 31, 1740. He had a son, *Benjamin*, born in Townsend, August 14,

RANDALL SPAULDING.

1743, who was "successful in *school teaching*," which occupation was followed by three of his daughters. He was known as "Lieut. Benjamin," and served (probably) in the War of the Revolution. He had a son known as "Capt. *Isaac*," born in Townsend, December 24, 1779. The latter was the father of *Daniel*.

Daniel Spaulding, son of Capt. Isaac, was born in Townsend. He carried on a farm, and was the master of three or four trades, principally that of a cooper. He was a man of considerable ingenuity and skill, and was fairly successful. He married Lucy W. Clement, daughter of John Clement, of Townsend.

RANDALL SPAULDING, son of Daniel and Lucy W. (Clement) Spaulding, was born in Townsend, Middlesex Co., Mass., Feb. 3, 1845. He evidently inherited his fondness for books and his capacity for teaching from his great grandfather. He attended the district school until he was sixteen and then went to the Lawrence Academy, at Groton, where he had an uncle, who was a practicing physician. In order to raise funds to complete his preparatory course he was obliged to resort to mechanical employment, and "*strike from the shoulder*." The last winter he attended the academy he taught the district school in West Groton, and assisted occasionally at teaching in the academy. In all his efforts to acquire an education he was self-supporting, and paid all his own expenses. He entered Yale College in 1866, and was graduated in 1870. He earned some money at college by "coaching" students, but on completing his collegiate course he found himself $1000 in debt. He soon after obtained a position as teacher at Rockville, Conn., where he remained for three years, and not only paid off his old indebtedness but accumulated a sufficient sum to enable him to make a trip to Europe, partly for pleasure, but mainly for the purpose of continuing his studies. He spent seven months at Göttingen, and was a few weeks at Heidelberg and parts of Italy, his course of study being principally history and the German language. On his return in 1874 he accepted an offer to take charge of the school in Montclair. He introduced many new features and raised the grade to meet the demands of the community for a higher system of education. He gradually worked the pupils up to his own standard, and induced them to remain another year in order to attain the requisite proficiency. He received the hearty co-operation of the parents, as well as the trustees, and others interested in the school. He secured the very best teachers that could be found for the various departments, and year by year he continued to advance to a higher standard, the trustees and taxpayers always keeping pace and meeting his own ideas with liberal appropriations, which culminated in 1893 with the finest and best equipped public school building in the State. All this has been accomplished in a quiet way without friction, and with a steady forward movement. No man was ever more beloved by parents, pupils and teachers. He rules by love, yet there is no lack of discipline, and the usual methods of punishment are almost unknown in the several departments of the school. Of the children it may be said.

> "He taught them the goodness of knowledge,
> They taught him the goodness of God."

Many of his pupils who have grown to manhood and achieved success in the various walks of life, look back with pride to their *alma mater*, and remember with gratitude and affection their faithful preceptor.

Mr. Spaulding is one of the foremost educators in the State, and has done much to advance the cause of education in other parts of the country. He has been President of the New Jersey State Council of Education, of the Schoolmasters' Association of New York and vicinity, of the Schoolmasters' Club of New York and vicinity, and was formerly President of the State Teachers' Association of New Jersey.

Mr. Spaulding has added largely to his stock of general information in his travels during his summer vacations. In the summer of 1883 he visited Arizona in company with Dr. H. H. Rusby, partly on behalf of the Smithsonian Institution, and made a large collection of plants indigenous to that locality. Besides obtaining a large variety of those well known to naturalists, he collected some thirty new species, to which no reference has hitherto been made by naturalists. The information thus acquired has been utilized to good advantage in his professional labors. A similar trip was made in 1886 among the Rocky Mountains of Colorado.

As a pastime Mr. Spaulding has done some excellent work as an amateur photographer, and has made a large collection of views of the many places of interest he has visited. In 1888 he visited Great Britain and made a collection of photos for the use of lantern slides in stereopticon exhibitions. He is the author of " First Lessons in Amateur Photography," published in 1885, a work highly appreciated by amateurs in this art. Accounts of his travels abroad have been given at different times through the local papers, and read with a great deal of interest.

In addition to the other societies and organizations referred to, Mr. Spaulding is a member of the First Congregational Church of Montclair, and of the Congregational Club of New York. He has been twice married; first, in 1874, to Miss Florence A. Chapman, who died in 1889, leaving two children, viz., Raymond C. and Edith R.; secondly, to Miss Sarah L. Norris, of Hyde Park, Mass.

THE WASHINGTON SCHOOL HOUSE.

Erected in 1825, for the education of mill children on Sunday, at the west end of the present township, continued to be used for school purposes after the close of the mills and the departure of the mill operatives. The settlement remained, and the population of this neighborhood increased. The schools at the west end of the town were located at too great a distance to enable those at the east

THE WASHINGTON SCHOOL HOUSE.

end to avail themselves of its advantages, and this eventually became a separate school district. Isaac B. Wheeler, son of Gideon Wheeler, taught in this school for a time. A new frame building, capable of accommodating the large increase of children in this locality, was erected, and ample facilities provided.

PRIVATE SCHOOLS.

For more than a quarter of a century before the agitation of " higher education " for free schools began, Bloomfield and West Bloomfield were noted for their private institutions of learning, and some of the most prominent men in the country — divines, physicians, lawyers and statesmen, were prepared for college at one or the other of these well known schools.

From 1810 to 1838 the Bloomfield Academy was considered one of the best preparatory schools in the State of New Jersey. In the origin and maintenance of that academic and theological institution, Israel Crane and other prominent men of West Bloomfield were greatly interested. With such preceptors as Amzi Lewis, Jr., John Ford, Rev. Humphrey M. Perine, Rev. Amzi Armstrong, D.D., and his son, Rev. William J. Armstrong, Albert Pearson, and Dr. Edwin Hall, strong college-bred men, of profound erudition and theological force, this Academy overshadowed the more common education in that part of the town. At the beginning it was financially supported by a Society for the Promotion of Literature, composed of the strong men of the town, and after Dr. Armstrong assumed the financial support by the social and moral aid of the people throughout the Presbyterian parish, Samuel Hanson Cox, and other young men from the Academy, conducted religious services in the second story of the West Bloomfield School-house.

MOUNT PROSPECT INSTITUTE.— This building, now known as the Mountain House, situated on Bloomfield Avenue, near the dividing line between Montclair and Verona, was opened as a boarding-school for boys, about 1838, by Mr. Warren S. Holt. He had previously taught in the public school, where he acquired the reputation of a good teacher, especially in mathematics. His aim was to establish a strictly private school, with a limited number of pupils who, while enjoying the best educational advantages, would at the same time receive a thorough moral and religious training. He had also a separate department for young ladies. His system of education met with the hearty approval of his patrons, but did not prove a financial success, and in 1844 he gave up his school, and became assistant to James H. Randall, at the Bloomfield Academy. He remained with this institution for about two years, when he reopened Mount Prospect Institute, which he conducted successfully for some years. A circular issued by him about this time states that—

"The School is located in West Bloomfield, N. J., fifteen miles distant from New York City, and six from Newark, upon a commanding eminence of 800 feet above the level of the ocean, from which a clear view is obtained of New York, Brooklyn, the Bay, and the surrounding country. This location, for retirement, health, salubrity of atmosphere, and beauty of mountain scenery, is not surpassed by any in the country. It is easy of access, having direct communication with New York four times a day. The object of this institution is to prepare Young Gentlemen for entering college, or a business life, by a thorough and systematic course of instruction. The Principal does not desire a large school, but a select number of pupils, well disciplined, and willing to be guided in the paths of virtue and usefulness. In order to secure and retain desirable members of this School no vicious or unprincipled boy is received, and no one retained in the School whose influence is immoral or in any way injurious to his associates.

MOUNTAIN HOUSE, FORMERLY MOUNT PROSPECT INSTITUTE.

The pupils enjoy the comforts of a home in the family of the Principal, being invited to the parlor, where they associate with other members of the family and those who frequently visit the institution.

"The government of the School is conducted on strictly religious principles, and the pupils are controlled by appeals to their moral feelings, rather than by fear of punishment. The Bible is the standard of morals, and each pupil is required to study it daily; also to attend church with the Principal on the Sabbath."

The school was divided into sessions of five months each, commencing on the first of May and November. The charges for board and tuition in the English branches and Mathematics were from $40 to $45 per quarter; in the Latin and Greek languages, $50—extra for the French, German or Spanish language, $5; Drawing and Painting, each $5; Music, with the use of the Piano, $10.

The circular states that : "Being desirous of securing a proper degree of correspondence in dress, and prevent some of the evils arising from different styles of clothing in the same family, a uniform dress has been adopted for the School." This was as follows: "The coat and pantaloons of very dark blue cloth; the coat single-breasted, to button to the throat, with ten gilt buttons, two upon the collar, placed three inches back—the collar to turn over, with the corners round.

"For summer, the dress suit is dark blue coat and white pantaloons. That for common use should be gray, made of the material known as 'youth's mixt.' For very warm weather, brown linen or drilling."

ASHLAND HALL.—Rev. David A. Frame, who for two years, 1844-5, had been the Principal of Bloomfield Academy, moved his school from that place to his residence in West Bloomfield (now known as "Chelsea Hall," a hotel or boarding-house, on Bloomfield Avenue. Under the name of "Ashland Hall," a "Family Boarding School for Boys," this institution flourished for some fifteen years, attracting wide attention for its many excellent qualities, and drawing patrons from all sections of the country. The pupils were limited to thirty and no day-scholars taken. Its discipline and studies were designed to prepare lads to enter intelligently and unembarrassed upon the duties of any class in college, and to discharge wisely and reputably the prospective duties of a good American citizen. William L. Ward, M.D., now an eminent physician in Newark, was the associate teacher till 1847, when he was followed by Henry B. Munn, Esq., of Silas (1788), now of Washington, D. C., who continued as principal assistant till 1852. Others were associated with and followed him. Hon. Charles M. Davis, afterward County Superintendent of Schools; the late Rev. H. R. Timlow, D.D., and Prof. John Lowry, now of Lenapee College, Tenn., were among the number.

The average number of pupils was about the limit—thirty. They came from the neighboring towns and States, as well as from a distance. Cuba, Texas, New Orleans and Georgia had their representatives. About twenty per cent. became college graduates, and about fifty per cent. entered some one of the learned professions.

Hon. A. M. Bliss and Hon. Edward Morton became members of Congress. Hon. Sam. L. Bigelow, Attorney General of New Jersey. Gen. Schuyler Crosby, of New York, and Judge Arnoux, with his two brothers, were also among the pupils.

The domestic affairs of the school were presided over by Mrs. Frame, wife of the principal, a lady of the most gentle manners, religious life, and of large experience in circles of the most cultivated and refined society.

The presiding genius of the school was its principal, the Rev. David A. Frame. He gave it the characteristics that attracted general attention.

REV. DAVID A. FRAME, was born in Bloomfield, in 1805. His parents, of good Presbyterian stock, came from the North of Ireland, shortly after their marriage, about the time of the disastrous Irish rebellion of 1798, along with many others. They had two sons, William and David. The former became a clerk for Israel Crane, in his store in West Bloomfield. He developed remarkable business ability, and for many years was the senior partner in the leading mercantile house of Bloomfield, and subsequently became Sheriff, filling the office from 1846 to 1849. David became a clerk in the store of Israel Holms, of Belleville, along with the late William H. Brant, of that place. After leaving the store he returned to Bloomfield, and learned the trade of a carpenter. Becoming a member of the Presbyterian Church he decided to obtain a collegiate education and enter the ministry. In 1829 he entered Princeton College, which he left in 1832, with the reputation of a brilliant and eloquent speaker, to commence his theological studies in Auburn Seminary, N. Y. Subsequently he preached in Binghamton, in that State, in Connecticut, and in Morris County, N. J. His close application in the preparation of his sermons, coupled with an intense earnestness in their delivery, at length brought on a partial stroke of paralysis. From its effects he never entirely recovered, but regained sufficient of his old health and strength to enter upon other duties, and to preach occasionally.

In 1841 he took charge of the Bloomfield Academy, succeeding as principal the late William K. McDonald, of Newark, N. J. His administration was very successful, but in 1845, finding himself not in accord with the controlling interests of the Academy, he moved his school to West Bloomfield, locating in a building of his own, purchased some years previously, and which had been fitted up for the purpose. This he named "Ashland Hall," and there continued his school with eminent success, until ill-health caused him to give up the responsibilities of its further care and management. He was much beloved and highly esteemed by his pupils. His government "was decided and uniform, with no excessive indulgence on the one hand or indurating severity on the other." While members of his school, he took the keenest interest in their studies, and when they left he followed them in after-life, with almost parental solicitude.

He died at his residence Sept. 24, 1879. When his death was announced in the papers it was truly said: "Mr. Frame will be remembered by all who ever heard him in the pulpit as a preacher of singular and thrilling eloquence. He was a writer of high excellence, chaste and simple in diction, and a vivid thinker. His impassioned delivery gave his sermons the utmost effect and left an impression not easily lost. In later years increasing deafness shut him off to a great extent from the social intercourse which he loved and which his genial nature, literary culture, commanding memory and conversational powers filled him conspicuously to adorn."

HILLSIDE SEMINARY FOR YOUNG LADIES. What is now known as the "Hillside" or "Montclair House," corner of Orange and Hillside Avenues, was opened for a girls' school about 1855, by Rev. Ebenezer Cheever, formerly pastor of the Second Presbyterian Church of Newark, but then residing in Paterson. There was at that time no house anywhere on the mountain side west of the Hillside House, except the residence of "Squire John Munn," since transformed into the tasteful mansion of Seelye Benedict. Hillside Avenue and Mountain Avenue, as far as Hillside, had first been thrown open, but

was still unworked and untraveled, and the former quite impassable. Henry Nason, whose untiring energy contributed so largely to the upbuilding of Montclair in its early days, began, not long after, the erection of the stone building at the head of Hillside Avenue, taking the stone from the cliffside, in the rear of the premises, and bringing all other needed material over the sod on Montclair Avenue. This afterward became the property of Nahum Sullivan. The mountain side was still in a somewhat wild state, as is indicated by the accompanying illustration. The opossum, weasel or owl were occasionally caught making a raid in the chicken yard of Hillside Seminary, and coveys of quail were not infrequent around the barn or along the fences.

HILLSIDE SEMINARY FOR YOUNG LADIES.

The Rev. Mr. Cheever carried on successfully a girls' school there for about four years. From 1859 to 1872, it was kept as a boarding and day school by Rev. and Mrs. A. R. Wolfe, both of whom had been previously connected for some years with the "Spingler Institute for Young Ladies," on Union Square, New York City. The Hillside Seminary, under their supervision, became one of the most popular and flourishing institutions of the kind in the State. Among the last graduates were a daughter of the Rev. Oliver Crane, D.D., a daughter of Joseph Doremus, a daughter of George G. Draper, and a daughter of Mr. E. C. Fuller, the present Collector of the township. A large number from the families of the early residents of Montclair were graduates, all, for a time, pupils of Hillside Seminary. Among the patrons were found the old time names of Nason, Hening, Graham, Graves, Sullivan, Benedict, Frame, Harris, Baldwin, Crane, Morris, Seymour, Hubbard, Musgrave, Wiedemeyer, Wilcox, Dwight, Holmes, Pratt, Pinney, Clark, Wolfe, Elliott, as well as many of the township of Bloomfield, almost all of whom have now passed away. In its boarding department, Hillside Seminary had a fair and encouraging patronage, not only from the surrounding towns and States, but from the cities of New York and Brooklyn, even including San Francisco, St. Louis, Baltimore, Washington and Tallahassee. It did good work, which its living pupils continue to appreciate, and which will never be lost.

Although it is more than twenty years since Mr. Wolfe and his estimable wife closed the doors of the Seminary, they have continued to reside in Montclair, finding it one of the most delightful spots in New Jersey for suburban residence.

The old house has been converted into a summer hotel, where hundreds of people flock during the summer season to enjoy the cool mountain breezes together with the delightful and picturesque views.

REV. AARON ROBERTS WOLFE, Principal of Hillside Seminary for Young Ladies, was born at Mendham, N. J., Sept. 6, 1821. His grandfather, Aaron Roberts, served with the New Jersey troops in the War of the Revolution, and took part in the battle of Monmouth. The latter was a great-great-grandson of Hugh Roberts, a native of Wales, who was one of the original settlers of Newark in 1666, having previously settled in the New Haven Colony. His name is found among the Branford settlers who signed the "Fundamental Agreement."

Rev. A. R. Wolfe, in his early youth, was a schoolmate of Rev. Theodore L. Cuyler, at Uncle Ezra Fairchild's famous "Hill-Top School," in Mendham. He pursued his preparatory studies at Lansborough, Mass., and was graduated at Williams College in the class of 1844.

REV. AARON ROBERTS WOLFE.

The next eleven years, including his course in the Union Theological Seminary, 1848-54, were spent in teaching and preaching in Florida.

When he left Florida, in the summer of 1855, he put all his effects — library, notes, and things of that sort — on board a sailing vessel at St. Marks, and with a simple grip-sack returned North by way of Nashville and Chicago. On reaching New York he learned that, on the day appointed for sailing, the vessel had been struck by lightning, the mate killed at the foot of the mast, and the vessel laden with turpentine, burned to the water's edge. He looked upon this as a special Providence of God, shaping his life and fixing his home, for it made him a teacher of the young rather than a pastor of a church.

In 1855 he became associated with Rev. Dr. Gorham D. Abbott, in the Spingler Institute for Young Ladies, on Union Square, in New York City. In 1858 he was married to Laura F. Jackson, a teacher in this institution, daughter of Luther Jackson, Esq., of New York. In 1859 he removed to West Bloomfield, and established the Hillside Seminary for Young Ladies, which he conducted with eminent usefulness and success for thirteen years.

Mr. Wolfe is the author of a number of hymns, which were published in "Church Melodies," "Songs for the Sanctuary," and other well-known hymn books.

Mr. Wolfe is still living (1894) near the scene of his early labors, on Hillside Avenue, Montclair. Of his four children — three sons and a daughter — one is preaching in Iowa; another is Professor of Latin in Park College, Missouri.

MONTCLAIR MILITARY ACADEMY.

In the spring of 1887 certain prominent citizens of Montclair—Mr. Thomas Russell, Mr. E. G. Burgess, Mr. E. A. Bradley and others—determined to secure a competent instructor for their sons, so that it would not be necessary to send them to the public school.

After careful consideration they engaged the services of J. G. Mac Vicar, giving him a guarantee of ten pupils, and granting him the privilege of increasing the number if possible.

At this time Mr. Mac Vicar was in his Senior year in Rochester University. He had during his college course taught three years in the public schools in Michigan; the last two years being Superintendent of the Union City schools, where he had seventeen teachers under his direction.

Coming to Montclair directly after his graduation in June, he purchased a small building which he placed on rented land on Clinton Street. The school opened with sixteen pupils, but before the end of the year the number had increased to twenty-four. It then became evident that the school would outgrow its present accommodation.

The gentlemen who first engaged Mr. Mac Vicar offered to assist in the purchase of land and the

MONTCLAIR MILITARY ACADEMY.

erection of a suitable school building. The site on Walden Place, west of Bloomfield Avenue and north of Mountain Avenue, was selected and three and one half acres of land purchased. The building erected here is intended to accommodate 100 boys, and is very complete in all its appointments. Special attention was paid to the question of ventilation, light and heat, and six years of service have proved the perfection of the plans adopted.

A large physical laboratory is a special feature of the building, and great stress is laid on practical instruction in the sciences. Two years later additional land was purchased and a large gymnasium sixty feet square was erected and equipped in a most complete manner. The building is provided with reading and music rooms, lockers, and hot and cold baths in the basement.

From this time the same careful attention was given to the physical development of the pupils that had characterized the mental training. The Harvard system of physical examination and measurements was adopted, and a careful record kept of the physical defects and the development of each pupil. Mr. E. B. De Groot, the physical instructor, devotes his entire time to directing this work among the boys. Classes are organized and each cadet is required to spend one half hour each day in the gymnasium. The work is as thoroughly systematized as any other department in the school.

At about the time the gymnasium was built the school was organized on a military basis. This change was determined upon after a careful inspection of the best private schools in the vicinity of New York, and the results obtained amply justify this change in policy. Erect carriage, promptitude and obedience have been the natural results. The principal is a strong believer in what might be termed

CADETS AT FOOTBALL EXERCISE.

individual instruction. He believes that the peculiarities and natural tendencies of each pupil should be studied by his teachers and his future treatment thus determined. For this reason the classes are all small, seldom exceeding ten. The development of a strong moral character is considered of the same importance as a sound physical and mental training.

For the last three years a boarding department has been conducted in connection with the school, and plans are now being matured for enlargement in this direction. Three acres of land have just been purchased west of the school grounds, and a large building, with accommodation for the principal's family and thirty cadets will soon be erected.

The school has had steady increase in the number of pupils since its first organization, and its future seems assured. It has been the occasion of bringing to Montclair some of its most honored residents.

FREE PUBLIC LIBRARY.

In 1869 the population of Montclair, still called West Bloomfield, numbered about 2,500. A good High School, as already named, had been established on a firm footing, and was prosperous under the management of Mr. John W. Taylor, principal.

But there was no library attached to the school, and there were no books for reference or entertainment to be obtained either by students or their parents. In some measure to supply this need, Mr. and Mrs. Israel Crane, just settled in their cottage home on Fullerton Avenue, resolved to interest as many friends and residents as could be approached in the formation of a subscription library. In this enterprise they were ably assisted by Mr. and Mrs. John W. Taylor. Through the efforts thus made thirty families became subscribers, which number, at that period, represented a goodly portion of the people. Initiatory steps for the organization of a library association were taken in the early part of 1869; the first meeting of the projectors was held at the house of Israel Crane, on the evening of February 23d of that year. There were present, J. W. Taylor, Geo. S. Dwight, F. H. Harris, Samuel Wilde, W. A. Torrey, and Mr. and Mrs. Israel Crane. At this meeting a committee, consisting of Geo. S. Dwight, Israel Crane and J. W. Taylor were appointed to draft a Constitution and By-Laws. This committee reported at a meeting held March 5, 1869, when a permanent organization was effected, and the following officers elected:

President, Geo. S. Dwight; Vice-President, F. H. Harris; Secretary, J. W. Taylor; Treasurer, Israel Crane.

Directors: Samuel Wilde, W. A. Torrey, T. B. Graham, Mrs. Israel Crane, Mrs. J. W. Taylor.

An annual subscription of $3.00 entitled subscribers to membership, and to the use of all books and periodicals.

The nucleus of a library was formed by the purchase of about a hundred books, which were placed in the care of Mr. Getzler, in his drug store on Bloomfield Avenue. The books were read with avidity, and the number of subscribers and of books increased so rapidly that it was thought advisable to remove the library to larger quarters. Accordingly on April 11, 1871, the books were transferred to the Pillsbury Building, on the southeast corner of Fullerton and Bloomfield Avenues. During the winter of 1870-1, a charter was obtained from the Legislature under the name and style of "The Montclair Library Association." This charter provided for the issuance of stock to the amount of fifty thousand dollars, at ten dollars a share.

Through the personal efforts Mr. Israel Crane alone, five thousand of this amount was subscribed, of which $2,700 was paid in. The following persons were elected Directors under this charter, viz.:

Julius H. Pratt, Mrs. Edward Sweet, Mrs. Israel Crane, F. H. Harris, J. R. M. Hening, Rev. J. B. Harrison, Samuel Wilde and W. H. Van Slyke.

The first officers were: President, Dr. J. J. H. Love; Vice-President, Samuel Wilde; Secretary and Treasurer, Israel Crane.

Library Committee appointed by Directors: Mrs. Israel Crane, Rev. D. S. Rodman, Rev. J. R. Berry, D.D.

The duties of the Library Committee were most arduous. The annual subscriptions were only sufficient to cover the running expenses, and it devolved upon this committee to provide funds for the purchase of books. All additions to the library were made either by donations of books, or by means of public entertainments, which last were devised and superintended by Mrs. Israel Crane. Lectures, concerts, tableaux, and the first amateur theatricals ever given in Montclair, were given under her patronage and suggestion during successive winters, always with the cordial assistance of public spirited members of the library association and of the residents at large. These entertainments contributed much to the social enjoyment and growth of Montclair. By these means many hundreds of dollars were raised and in a few years the number of volumes was increased to two thousand. The last important entertainment given for the library was a large Lawn Fête and Supper held, by his generous consent, on the beautiful lawns of Mr. Thomas Russell, in September, 1876, $350 was raised on that occasion. In July, 1871, a lot was leased from Mr. N. O. Pillsbury, free of charge, on the site of the present Baptist Church, and a building erected at a cost of $1,700. The library was well patronized and proved a great boon to the people, despite the curious fact that, upon the addition of Charles Darwin's "Origin of Species" to the catalogue, a small faction arose in opposition, declaring that the library was disseminating dangerous theories, and would harm the young people of the town. On the night of Feb. 28th, 1880, a large amount of property in the vicinity, and the library building, was burned to the ground. The books, however, were saved. There was an insurance of $1,000 on the building and contents.

A room was rented in the Morris Building on Bloomfield Avenue, over the present post office, and the books kept there until April 7th, 1881, when they were transferred to the custody of the trustees of the Public School, with the proviso that, on certain days and hours of each week, the public should have the free use of the library.

In 1884 the Legislature of this State passed "An Act to authorize the establishment of free public libraries in the towns, townships, or any other municipality."

Section 2 requires "That the provisions of this act shall remain inoperative in any town, township or any other municipality in this State, until assented to by a majority of the legal voters thereof, voting on this act at any election at which the question of its adoption shall be submitted to vote by direction of the legislative body of such town or township, etc., either at the time fixed by law for election of the municipal affairs, or at a special election to be held for that purpose," etc.

Section 3 requires, "That if at such an election aforesaid a majority of all the ballots cast shall be 'for a free public library,' it shall become the duty of the legislative body of said town, township, etc., annually thereafter to appropriate and raise by tax in the same manner as other taxes are assessed, levied and collected in said town, township, etc., a sum equal to one-third of a mill on every dollar of assessable property returned by the assessor of said town, township, etc., for the purpose of taxation thereon, which sum, when so appropriated, shall be used for no other purpose than that of a free public library."

Section 4 requires, "That the board of trustees of the free public library shall be immediately formed in any town, township, etc., where a majority of the votes cast shall be 'for a free public library,' consisting of five members, one of whom shall be the chairman of the legislative body of such town, etc., and one the president of the board of education, and three to be appointed by the chairman of the town, township, etc., by and with the consent of the legislative body thereof, to serve for the term of one, two and three years respectively."

Soon after the passage of this act, the citizens of Montclair took action for the establishment of a Free Public Library, in accordance with the provisions of the above named act. *The Montclair Times*, referring to this matter, says:

"After the Ladies' Wednesday Afternoon Club had petitioned the Town Committee to have a vote taken on the subject, the people last year taxed themselves about $1,000, and this year voted for a permanent yearly appropriation at the same rate and for the organization provided by law to administer the affairs.

"The Town Committee appointed, as members of the Board of Trustees, Dr. J. J. H. Love, Dr. Richard C. Newton and Mr. John R. Howard. The chairman of the Town Committee is by law a member *ex-officio* ; and so would be the president of the Board of Education, if the town at large had such a body, but it has only local Boards of the several school districts. The trustees appointed to find suitable quarters finally decided on the second story of Dr. Love's detached two-story brick office building on Church street, next door to the Montclair Club, as the safest and most convenient location for the purpose in the town. Dr. Love, who was president of the Board, thereupon thought it his duty to resign—much to everybody's regret ; and Mr. William E. Marcus was appointed in his place, and elected president of the Board, Dr. Newton being the clerk—that is to say, secretary and treasurer.

"The making of a library in the present day, when the vocation of librarian has become a profession and the art of administering a library has been organized into a science, is a very different thing from the happy-go-lucky way of former years. The thorough classification of books, the admirable advice of card catalogues, the many labor- and time-saving inventions, the accurate records, etc., all need special trained intelligence for the best result. And as the Public Library in this fast-growing town is sure to be a large and important one, the trustees felt that the best beginning would in the end be the cheapest.

"Having secured quarters, which have been put in good order, the Board provided furniture and fixtures of thoroughly solid and workmanlike character—shelving, tables, chairs, card-catalogue case, counter, desk, etc.—and engaged the services of Miss Mary F. Weeks as librarian. Miss Weeks has had years of training and considerable practical experience in the work of a professional librarian, and brought to the work an interest that no stranger in the town would have.

"The old Montclair Library Association, a private corporation, had about 1,500 books, which for some years had been in use as a public library in the Central Public School-house. These books they have placed in charge of the new Public Library and will probably present them out and out. The books were all covered with paper wrappers ; but as that is one of the old customs discarded in the new way, Miss Weeks has for some time been working at the books with the assistance of Miss Agnes Judson, uncovering them, repairing, arranging, entering in the 'accession book,' cataloguing, pasting on the numbers and shelf-labels and classifying them on the shelves. The reception of many books at once entails much of this preparatory labor, which results in convenience and time-saving when the library comes into use. And old books demand more time and care than new ones.

"When these are disposed of, the Trustees intend to go to the people, asking for donations of other books—new or old, but good. No one is to be asked to give a book that no one will want to read ; but many families have many books—duplicates, books out-grown or not needed any more, etc., which will be valuable in a library, and doubtless all who care for the Library at all will be glad to help it in this easy way. Others will take the opportunity of presenting new copies of favorite books or sets, and every book given will bear the name of its donor."

On June 29, 1893, the directors of the Montclair Library Association held a meeting and adopted the following Preamble and Resolution :

Whereas, The people of Montclair have voted for a Free Public Library, thereby doing away with the necessity for our Association, which has for over twenty years occupied this field of usefulness, and

Whereas, We are in full sympathy with the new movement, as it gives assurance of a Library on a sure foundation as to annual maintenance, and being desirous to the full extent of our power to aid the same, therefore be it

Resolved: That the Secretary be instructed to solicit the consent of the Stockholders to the transfer of the Books of this Association to the Trustees of the Free Public Library as a donation or otherwise, as the Directors may determine. And also to make such a disposition of the money in the Treasurer's hands as in their judgment shall most benefit the said Free Public Library.

In response to a circular sent out in accordance with above Resolution, the greater number of Stockholders consented to leave the disposition of the Assets to the Directors, who met on January 19, 1894, and voted to donate the Books to the Free Public Library. They also authorized and directed the Treasurer to pay over to the Free Public Library one thousand dollars as a gift, on condition that the same be used in the purchase of Standard Works on Science, Literature and Art.

CHESTNUT STREET PRIMARY SCHOOL HOUSE was erected in winter of 1890 and 1891. It is a large, roomy, two and one-half story brick building, 35 by 65, containing corridors, cloak rooms, and four class rooms and teachers' rooms. It cost, including land, $18,802.48. Four teachers are occupied in giving instruction in primary studies to an average daily attendance of 138, the enrollment being 174.

CEDAR STREET PRIMARY SCHOOL HOUSE, built in 1889-90. This is a one and one-half story wooden building, with hall, two class rooms and two recitation rooms. It cost, including land, $7,103.32. The enrollment of pupils is 74, and the average daily attendance, 55. All primary ; employ two teachers.

Both of these schools belong to School District No. 8, and are under the same management as the Centre Primary, Grammar and High Schools.

Chapter XIII.

MUNICIPAL AND BUSINESS ORGANIZATIONS, SOCIETIES, CLUBS, Etc.

VILLAGE IMPROVEMENT SOCIETY.—MONTCLAIR FIRE DEPARTMENT.—THE MONTCLAIR WATER COMPANY.—JAMES OWEN, TOWNSHIP ENGINEER.— THE PRESS.— MONTCLAIR TIMES, AUGUSTUS C. STUDER.—MONTCLAIR HERALD, G. C. EARLE AND H. C. WALKER.— UNITED STATES PRINTING COMPANY; JOSEPH E. HINDS.—BANK OF MONTCLAIR.—THE MONTCLAIR SAVINGS BANK.— MASONIC LODGES: BLOOMFIELD LODGE, NO. 40, F. & A. M.; MONTCLAIR LODGE, NO. 144, F. & A. M.—WATCHUNG LODGE, NO. 134, I. O. O. F. GEN. SHERMAN LODGE, NO. 54, A. O. U. W.—OTHER SECRET AND BENEVOLENT SOCIETIES.—THE CITIZENS' COMMITTEE OF ONE HUNDRED. GOOD GOVERNMENT CLUB.—CHILDREN'S HOME. MRS. SAMUEL M. PORTER.—MOUNTAINSIDE HOSPITAL ASSOCIATION.—THE MONTCLAIR EQUESTRIAN CLUB.—MONTCLAIR CLUB.— THE OUTLOOK CLUB.—TARIFF REFORM CLUB.— MONTCLAIR GLEE CLUB.— MONTCLAIR DRAMATIC CLUB.—MONTCLAIR LAWN TENNIS CLUB.

VILLAGE IMPROVEMENT SOCIETY.

THE beautiful shade trees which adorn the streets of Montclair, and which have proved such an attraction to strangers, are the result of a few enterprising individuals who organized what was known as the Village Improvement Society.

The first meeting of this society was held in February, 1878, the object being, as stated, "to promote the planting of trees along the highways."

At an adjourned meeting held on March 27th of that year, the following officers were elected: President, Thomas H. Porter; Vice-Presidents, C. H. Johnson and Philip Doremus; Corresponding Secretary, Randall Spaulding; Clerk, J. E. Hinds; Treasurer, Hiram B. Littell.

The following General Committee was appointed to promote the planting of trees along the several streets on which its members were residents: South Mountain Avenue, Mr. Dike and Mrs. C. Benedict; North Mountain Avenue, Mr. Van Vleck and Mrs. Power; Watchung Avenue, Mrs. Ames and Mrs. A. Littlejohn; Bellevue Avenue, Mrs. Bird and Mr. Clark; Grove Street, Samuel Holmes; North Valley Road, Mr. Wilson and Miss Mead; Chestnut Street, Mr. Burgess and Mrs. Bradley; Claremont Avenue, Mr. E. M. Harrison and Miss A. Hawes; Park Street, C. H. Johnson and Miss Hattie Brown; North Fullerton Avenue, Amzi Sigler and Mrs. Hall; Forest Street, E. Madison and Mrs. Campbell; Old Road, P. Doremus and Rebecca Crane; Willow Street, C. Van Riper and Mrs. D. Hall; Highland Avenue, W. A. Torrey and Miss Parkhurst; Bloomfield Avenue, P. H. Van Riper and Mrs. D. V. Harrison; Clinton Avenue, Frederick Brantigam and Mrs. Robert Hening; Eagle Rock Way, Mrs. L. B. Bull and Mrs. Samuel Crump; Elm Street, Dr. Marvin and Mrs. W. J. Harris; Lexington Avenue, Mr. Hayes and Mrs. Cooper; Lincoln Street, Mr. Tower; Fullerton Avenue, Robert Boyd and Mrs. Wilde; Cedar Avenue, Edward Williams and Miss Weston; Orange Road, south of Eagle Rock Way, Miss Blair and Miss Wilcox; James Street, J. G. Crane and Mrs. Roberts; Central Avenue, William Jacobus and William Sigler; Orange Road, Thomas Russell and Mrs. Carey; Harrison Avenue, Miss Bull and Thomas Porter; Gates Avenue, Mr. Francis and Mrs. Joseph Nason; Union Street, N. T. Porter and Mrs. Pratt; Hillsdale Avenue, Dr. Pinkham and Mrs. Wolfe; Church Street, Dr. J. J. H. Love and Mrs. Joseph Doremus; St. Luke's Place, L. S. Benedict and Mrs. Pinkham; Myrtle Avenue, Mr. Frost and Mrs. F. H. Harrison; Plymouth Street, Mr. Pratt and Mrs. Dr. Clark.

The trees recommended for planting in Montclair, as being best adapted to the soil and climate of this section, were the elm, the Norway maple, the sweet gum, and the tulip trees.

The Executive Committee consisted of Henry A. Dike, Thomas Russell, T. B. Brown, Mrs. L. Ball and Mrs. J. R. Berry.

This Executive Committee was authorized "to employ all laborers, make all contracts, expend all moneys, direct and superintend all the improvements of the association at their discretion."

The Constitution provided that "Every person over fourteen years of age who shall plant and protect a tree, under the direction or approval of the Executive Committee, or pay the sum of one dollar annually, shall be a member of this Association. And every child under fourteen years of age, who shall pay the sum of twenty-five cents, or do an equivalent amount of work annually, under the direction or approval of the Executive Committee, shall be a member of this Association."

The payment of ten dollars constituted a life membership.

Suggestions made by Mr. Julius H. Pratt, who had had large experience in tree planting, were adopted by the Association—among these, the kind of trees to be planted, and certain fixed rules for planting, and for their protection.

MONTCLAIR FIRE DEPARTMENT.

For more than twelve years after the erection of Montclair as a separate township, no provision was made for the protection of its inhabitants against fire. During this period there were occasional fires attended with serious loss of property. Projects were discussed looking to the organization of a fire company, but no definite action was taken.

A fire occurred in the latter part of February, 1880, involving a loss of over $13,000, $7,000 of which was covered by insurance. It began in the Pillsbury building on Fullerton Avenue and was discovered soon after midnight. The Kindergarten School, with all its belongings, and the furniture, together with many of the books belonging to the Library Association, were destroyed. In October of the same year an effort was made to secure a fire department petitioned for by seventeen citizens, but nothing came of it.

The final effort which was made two years later was successful. The details of this, together with a complete history of the Montclair Fire Department, were published in the *Montclair Herald* in 1892-93, from which the following extracts are taken:

"People who resided in Montclair in 1882 remember the big blaze which destroyed the handsome residence of Thorndyke Saunders, causing a damage of $20,000. Many readers will also remember the work they did at the fire trying to save the place from total destruction. But it was in vain. With no water or fire apparatus their efforts were futile. It was after this that Montclairites realized the necessity of some sort of fire department, and the exorbitant insurance rates impressed this need upon them until it was decided to do something toward more adequate protection from the red-tongued fire fiend.

"Through the efforts of Mr. A. B. Howe, Dr. Albert J. Wright and C. M. Schott, Jr., a meeting was held on November 28, 1882, at which Montclair Hook and Ladder Company, No. 1, was organized and the following officers elected: C. M. Schott, Jr., (an ex-member of the Summerville, N. J., Fire Department) Foreman; George T. Westbrook, Assistant Foreman; Dr. Albert J. Wright (exempt member of Owego, N. Y. Fire Department) Secretary; Dr. J. H. Casey, Treasurer. The company was made up of many of the leading members of the township, the following persons being enrolled as members: W. L. Ludlam, W. Lon Doremus, Dr. S. C. G. Watkins, George Inness, Jr., George F. Westbrook, F. A. Brautigam, W. Y. Bogle, J. C. Stevens, J. H. Wheeler, Dr. A. J. Wright, Edward Madison, J. H. Casey, M.D., J. R. Livermore, Hugh Mullen, I. Seymour Crane, James Owen, A. C. Studer, C. M. Schott, Jr., Peter A. Tronson, Wm. L. Doremus, Jesse H. Lockwood, R. M. Hening, E. M. Harrison, Jr., James McDonough, Robert B. Harris, W. A. Riker, Vaughn Darress.

"Subscriptions were made by the residents of the township who desired the protection offered by the company and a truck was purchased. It arrived on April 6, 1883, and was stored in the old engine house of the D. L. & W. Railroad for over a year and remained in service until 1892. On April 24, 1883, articles of incorporation were filed.

"This company, which was the nucleus of the fire department, was unrecognized by the township or township authorities until March 11, 1884, when an appropriation of $500 was voted for at the spring election, to be devoted to the building of a truck house. This building was enlarged in 1892 by the Township Committee and the rooms refitted and refurnished at the expense of the company, a pool table having been presented by George Inness, Jr. The same year a new truck was built for the company at an expense of $1,600 by order of the Township Committee, and fully equipped with all the modern appliances. This committee also provided horses and the company purchased a hanging double harness.

"About this time (1884) the famous Chemical Detail was formed and the apparatus increased by the purchase of a Babcock Chemical Engine by the company. In July of the same year the Township Committee ordered the building of a bell tower, and the purchase of a bell. The tower is sixty-three feet in height, and the bell, weighing 3,410 pounds, bears the following inscription: 'Montclair, N. J., Fire Department. Township Committee, Thomas Russell, President; Stephen W. Carey, Warren S. Taylor, A. Eben Van Gieson, Shepard Rowland.'

"These additions were completed in August, and in September twelve fire districts were established and the custom of ringing the fire bell at 9 o'clock P. M. was inaugurated. Through the efforts of the more progressive spirits among the members of the company, the District Fire Alarm and Messenger Company was formed and commenced operations in February, 1885. The company placed in position and operated twelve public alarm boxes and also fire alarm bells in each subscribing fireman's residence. Want of support caused the failure of this company in August of the same year. During March of that year the department's equipments remained the same except for the addition of a Rumsey pump. The present officers are: President, Franklin P. Zeiger; Vice-President, Walter K. Hunt; Secretary, Raymond S. Pearce; Treasurer, Harold W. Armstrong; Foreman, H. W. Armstrong; Assistant Foreman, John C. Doremus." (1893-4, membership, 320.

FIRE RELIEF ASSOCIATION.— Many years ago the State Legislature passed an act providing that a two per cent. tax should be levied upon all foreign fire insurance companies doing business in this State, this fund being set apart for the benefit of firemen disabled in active service. It is for the purpose of collecting Montclair's share of this money, rendering it available for use here, and distributing it among those for whom it is intended, that the Relief Association has its existence.

When the Hook and Ladder Company constituted the entire Fire Department of the township, they organized and incorporated the Fire Relief Association, September 17, 1883. When hose companies cropped into existence, it became necessary to reorganize, which was done September 4, 1885.

The first officers were: President, Edwin B. Goodell; Vice-President, C. M. Schott, Jr.; Secretary, R. M. Hening. Since this reorganization the government of the Relief Association has been vested in representatives from all the fire companies, now including the Exempt Association. Every member of the Montclair Fire Department is a member of the Association, and, unlike members of benefit companies in general, are obliged to pay no dues whatever, although every one enjoys an equal benefit, and, again unlike the mutual enrichment companies, never fails to collect his benefits.

The sick benefits are distributed by a Board of Visitors composed of representatives of the different companies, and the wolf has been many a time driven from the door of some unfortunate fireman in distress, and unable, by reason of some injury, to work, by the intervention of this fireman's friend and guardian association.

At the annual meeting of the Association held on December 19, 1893, officers for the ensuing year were elected as follows: President, A. J. Varno; Vice-President, Hugh Mullen; Secretary, W. Lou Doremus; Treasurer, John R. Livermore. W. I. Soverel was elected as a visitor for three years. The Board of Visitors is now composed of John N. Haley, Peter A. Tronson and W. I. Soverel. The previous year's financial report showed a very favorable condition of affairs. Balance on hand Dec., 1891, $2,476.60; receipts, 2 per cent. State tax during year, $1,017.65; interest, $102.09; total receipts, $3,596.34; expenditures for relief of injured firemen, $60; general expenses, $89.20, leaving a balance on hand of $3,446.64. Of these funds $2,000 are placed at interest on bond and mortgage on Montclair real estate. The remainder is deposited in savings banks.

The annual meeting is held on the third Monday in December, at the house of Montclair Hook and Ladder Co. No. 1, 647–649 Bloomfield Avenue.

ORGANIZATION OF THE MONTCLAIR FIRE DEPARTMENT.—On March 2, 1885, the Montclair Fire Department was organized by the Township Committee, rules and regulations were adopted, and Charles M. Schott, Jr., was appointed Chief Engineer, with G. A. Westbrook as Assistant Engineer. In November numbered badges were issued to the members of the department. Chief Schott's first annual report was issued in March, 1886, and showed: alarms during year, 23; damage, $18,700; insurance, $16,000.

WATER SUPPLY.—On March 9, 1886, the question of township water supply was defeated at the special election by a majority of 29 out of a vote of 873, and on the morning of that day the bell tower was burned. Chief Schott was reappointed with Assistant Westbrook. In April the bell was taken to the D. L. & W. Depot, and tried there, but with no improvement in the sound, so in July it was placed back in the tower, but one story higher.

In February, 1887, the water supply was again voted upon, and adopted by a majority of 459 out of a vote of 695. In March following the Township Committee appointed Messrs. Owen, Van Gieson and Schott as a sub-committee to revise the rules and regulations of the department.

In June, 1887, the first election for Chief Engineer was held, and Geo. F. Westbrook was chosen, without opposition. He appointed Peter A. Tronson, First Assistant, and Elijah Pearce, Second Assistant. In March, 1888, the first Fire Committee was appointed, consisting of James Owen, Chairman; W. S. Taylor and Chief Westbrook (ex-officio).

At the annual election in June, Geo. F. Westbrook was re-elected Chief Engineer. He appointed Hugh Mullen, First Assistant Engineer, and W. T. Myers, Second Assistant.

On November 17th, the annual parade of the Montclair Fire Department was held, and was followed by the first public trial of the water pressure and drill of all the companies.

In March, 1889, the Township Committee appointed as a Fire Committee: Geo. Inness, Jr., Chairman; W. S. Taylor and Chief Westbrook (ex-officio), and they elected A. J. Wright as Secretary. This committee succeeded in placing the fire bell in charge of the police, and in April they took charge of the fire alarm and the 9 o'clock bell which had, up to that time, been rung by firemen detailed for that purpose.

In June following, Chief Westbrook's report gave: alarms, 15; time on duty, 15½ hours; loss, $4,571; total membership, 117. At the annual election G. A. Westbrook was re-elected. He appointed G. T. Bunten, First Assistant; E. Concannon, Second Assistant, and W. B. Jacobus, Third Assistant.

In March, 1890, the following Fire Committee was appointed: Geo. Inness, Jr., Chairman; W. S. Taylor and Chief Westbrook (ex-officio), and H. L. Yost, Secretary. Chief Westbrook's annual report, in June, 1890, gave the following figures: alarms, 7; membership, 117. At the annual election I. Seymour Crane was chosen as Chief Engineer, and he appointed P. Keller, Jr., First Assistant; W. B. Jacobus, Second Assistant, and J. Jennings, Third Assistant.

In March, 1891, the following were appointed as a Fire Committee: J. B. Pier, Chairman; A. A. Sigler and Chief Crane (ex-officio), and H. L. Yost, Secretary. At the annual election in June following Philip Keller, Jr., was elected Chief. He appointed A. Brooks, Senior Engineer, with John Perrin, Melville Sigler and W. T. Myers, as Assistant Engineers.

In March, 1892, the Fire Committee appointed was: J. B. Pier, Chairman; I. Seymour Crane (ex-Chief), and Chief Keller (ex-officio), with H. L. Yost, Secretary.

At the annual election in June, Philip Keller, Jr., was re-elected Chief Engineer. He appointed

Abraham Brooks, as Senior Engineer, and Wm. T. Myers, John Perrin and Melville Sigler, as Assistant Engineers.

In 1893, the following Fire Committee were appointed: L. Seymour Crane (ex-Chief), Hugh Gallagher, and Chief Keller (ex-officio), with H. L. Yost, as Secretary.

At the annual election in June, Philip Keller, Jr., was again re-elected Chief Engineer, and he appointed Wm. T. Meyers, Senior Engineer, and Jos. Jennings, Theo. Sigler and John H. Banks, District Engineers.

HOSE COMPANY NO. 1 was organized from the detail of HOOK AND LADDER COMPANY NO. 1 ("the Chemical Detail"), March 24, 1887 (names in italics, soon resigned), and the new company was incorporated on December 28 of the same year. The original members were George T. Bunten, Robert B. Harris, Elston M. Harrison, Philip Keller, Jr., *William Oliver*, George H. Hayden, Jesse H. Lockwood, *Frank B. Ritter, Joseph Leist*, W. J. Leddy, Hugh Mullen, James McDonough, William A. Riker, A. G. Spencer, Peter A. Tronson, Wallace W. Wicks. The present membership is twenty-five. At the time of its organization the company elected the following officers:

President, R. B. Harris; Vice-President, J. McDonough; Secretary, F. B. Ritter; Treasurer, J. H. Lockwood; Foreman, Hugh Mullen; Assistant Foreman, P. Keller, Jr. Soon afterward a Silsby carriage was purchased for $850.00, and stored in the truck house. The new company made their headquarters there until 1889, when their present home was completed and turned over to them by the Township Committee, the furnishing, and all the equipments having been procured by the company. At the time of their taking possession a handsome silk flag was presented to the company by a number of ladies.

A hose wagon was subsequently secured, and all the modern appliances provided. The company's home is now one of the best appointed in the town. The hanging harness, and other appliances for "getting out quick," give the place a wide-awake appearance, and the members are fully competent to do the work assigned them.

In 1893 a completely equipped hose wagon was ordered by the Township Committee for the company.

Officers: President, Jas. McDonough; Vice-President, Thos. P. Myers; Secretary, A. F. Smith; Treasurer, Elston M. Harrison; Foreman, E. E. Leach; Assistant Foreman, Fred'k E. Williams.

EXCELSIOR HOSE COMPANY NO. 2.—This company was organized March 24, 1887 (incorporated January 3, 1888), for the protection of the south end of the township. It was originally composed of twenty members, and the service it has always rendered has commended it to the Montclair public and won recognition and praise for it from all sides.

The first officers elected were: President, William H. DeWitt; Vice-President, William F. Haviland; Secretary, F. R. Smith; Treasurer, C. A. Scholtz; Foreman, Abner Bartlett, Jr.; Assistant Foreman, D. W. Ward. The first apparatus secured was a Ramsey four-wheel hose cart purchased soon after organization at a cost of $450, which was paid by subscription of the company and the residents of the South End. The township appropriated $300 with which to build a house for the company, and in this house, built at the corner of Orange Road and Cedar Avenue, the company still has its headquarters, although a number of alterations have materially changed the aspect of the building since that time.

For five years the company continued operations with the hand carriage, and then on June 1, 1892, it was disposed of, and a hose cart and horse purchased from the Newark Fire Department. This apparatus is now in use, and the company is well equipped for active service. It was the first to own a horse, and is the only company which has a man on duty at the hose house at all hours of the day and night. In 1888 the company was presented with a 150 pound fire bell by Carlos A. Scholtz.

The company has on its roll (1893-4) twenty members. Its present officers are: President, William H. Gallagher; Vice-President, William H. Williams; Secretary, Thos. B. Kaveny; Treasurer, William T. Meyers; Foreman, W. W. Meyers; Assistant Foreman, John Van Handlyn. In 1893 a new hose wagon was ordered by the Township Committee for the service of the company.

WASHINGTON HOSE COMPANY No. 3 was organized August 9, 1887, now located at the corner of Bloomfield Avenue and Grove Street. Officers: Foreman, John Perrin; Assistant Foreman, Michael Clarence; President, Edward M. Concannon; Vice President, John M. Jennings; Treasurer, Joseph Jennings. Twenty-three members, including officers.

In October the company received its Silsby two-wheeled jumper. This company was incorporated January 6, 1888. The house was erected and occupied May, 1888.

In 1893 a new house was begun, a hose wagon ordered by the Township Committee, and Mr. Geo. Inness, Jr., presented them with a horse. Present officers (1893-4): President, John Glennon; Vice-President, John M. Smith; Secretary, James A. Durning; Treasurer, John N. Haley; Foreman, Jos. Cavanaugh; Assistant Foreman, Henry Muller. Membership, 25.

CLIFFSIDE HOSE COMPANY No. 4 was organized Feb. 7, 1888, and incorporated Feb. 5, 1889. This is located at Upper Montclair on Bellevue Avenue and railroad crossing, with 15 members. The first officers were: C. H. Huestis, Foreman; Wm. B. Jacobus, Assistant Foreman; President, Irving Cairnes; Vice-President, Frank Lord; Secretary, Frank P. Anderson; Treasurer, August J. Varno.

The company's first apparatus was the old Rumsey pump and hose reel formerly used by the Truck Co. A combination apparatus, consisting of hose wagon with ladders and chemicals, built by Gleason & Bailey, were furnished by the town, and in 1889 the present house was built. Officers: President, Andrew J. Armstrong; Vice-President, Frank Lord; Secretary, John Mancini; Treasurer, L. L. Howe; Foreman, Louis A. Mancini; Assistant Foreman, Walter H. A. Maynard. Present membership, 25.

ASSOCIATION OF EXEMPT FIREMEN OF THE TOWNSHIP OF MONTCLAIR, N. J.—Organized Nov. 24, 1891. Incorporated Dec. 12, 1891. President, John R. Livermore; Vice-President, Wm. L. Doremus; Treasurer, Jesse H. Lockwood; Secretary, F. A. Brantigam; Trustees, P. A. Tronson, C. M. Schott, Jr.; G. F. Westbrook, Wm. Y. Bogle, Geo. Inness, Jr.

The membership is confined exclusively to the exempt members of the Montclair Fire Department.

FIRE ALARM.—An electric fire alarm system was completed in the autumn of 1892, and fifteen boxes placed in convenient localities throughout the township. A map of the township, with the location of hydrants and fire alarm boxes indicated, was compiled by Dr. A. J. Wright, the well known dentist. These, together with full instructions, were printed on heavy white cardboard by the publishers of the *Montclair Herald* at their own expense for free distribution.

In 1893 the system was extended by the addition of 17 boxes, making a total of 32.

ADDENDUM.

This historical sketch covered the time to the fall of 1893, but as many changes in the way of improvement have occurred since that time, it necessitates a brief addition.

The previous account shows that the houses occupied by the companies, the bell and hose tower, the electric fire alarm system, all fire apparatus now in use, and the team used by the truck, are the property of the Montclair Fire Department, while the house furnishings, the horses used by Hose Companies 1, 2 and 3, and the equipments of the members, are company or individual property.

Under the present government, each company is detailed to answer calls from certain boxes, on first, second or third alarms (the Exempts respond to the third); and, in addition, a code of special calls, covering each company, police and ambulance, are in use.

In the spring of 1894, at a special election held for that purpose, it was decided by the voters of Montclair to change the form of government from a township to a town, and in June, 1894, all of the new officials, both elective and appointive, will be in charge.

This will be a most important change to the Montclair Fire Department, in that the Fire Committee will be succeeded by a Board of Fire Commissioners, composed of five members, who are appointed by the Town Council, who will have full charge of all matters affecting the department.

So, gradually, the familiar features of the old style volunteer fireman's organization are disappearing, and it becomes more modern every day; so that this town will soon practically enjoy the services of a model, modern fire department, second to none in the State and the equal of the paid city departments for efficiency, at a very slight cost.

THE MONTCLAIR WATER COMPANY.

THE MONTCLAIR WATER COMPANY was incorporated on the 13th day of January, 1887, under the laws of the State of New Jersey, for the purpose of supplying water to the Township of Montclair, and to other cities, towns and villages of that State.

The consent of the corporate authorities of the Township of Montclair to the organization of the said Company, as required by law, was given on the 13th day of January, 1887.

The incorporators were Whiting G. Snow, Edwin A. Bradley, Jasper R. Rand, and Joseph Van Vleck, of Montclair, N. J.; John R. Bartlett and Henry C. Andrews, of New York, and Albert P. Fisher, of Brooklyn, N. Y.

The capital of this Company is $1,000,000, divided into 10,000 shares, of the par value of $100 each, all of which has been paid into the treasury of the Company in cash.

The directors and officers of the Company are Whiting G. Snow, President; John R. Bartlett, Treasurer; Albert P. Fisher, Secretary; Edwin A. Bradley and Jasper R. Rand.

These gentlemen were the first directors and officers of the Company, and are still serving the Company in those capacities.

A contract with the Township of Montclair, to supply it with water, within nine months from the date of its execution, was made on the 5th day of March, 1887. To comply with this contract, after the necessary surveys and estimates had been made, a contract, to build the works, was made by the Company with Messrs. Tarr & McNamee, contractors, on the 29th day of March, 1887.

After an examination and selection of the location of the well at Watchung, a test well was put down, on the site selected, and an analysis and biological examination of the water was made by Prof. Leeds, of the Stevens Institute of Technology, Hoboken, N. J., and was pronounced to be perfectly pure, wholesome and palatable, and of most unusual excellence and purity. This report was submitted to the Township Committee of Montclair and was approved by them on the 7th day of June, 1887.

The plant was so far completed that water was introduced into the town about December 1, 1887.

The works have been pronounced, by experts familiar with work of that kind, to be first class in every particular, both as to quality of material used in the construction and quality of workmanship.

Mr. Geo. W. Howell, of Morristown, N. J., represented the Company as Engineer during the construction of the works, and Mr. James Owen, of Montclair, N. J., represented the township in the same capacity.

After the completion of the works Mr. Owen was engaged by the Company, as its Engineer and Superintendent, and has been retained in that position ever since.

The supply of water was first obtained from two wells located north of Watchung Avenue and east of Valley Road; one well being 30 feet in diameter and 50 feet deep, with brick walls from the surface to the top of the rock. At the bottom of the 30 feet well are 4 holes, 4 inches in diameter, extending 40 to 50 feet deeper.

There is also one 8 inch well, 30 feet distant from the larger one, 175 feet deep, the water of which flows into the larger one.

The pumps, two in number, were located in the well about 20 feet below the level of the ground, and deep enough to empty the 30 feet well. These pumps are of the Compound Worthington type, each with a capacity of 500,000 gallons per day. They worked against a head of 167 lbs., which is the pressure when the tank on the mountain is full.

The two boilers, of 75 horse power each, on the return flue plan, are located in a brick boiler-house about 25 feet from the well; the steam is carried in a 3-inch pipe to the pumps, with a duplicate pipe of 2 inch, in case of emergency.

The tank on the mountain is built of boiler iron, 40 feet in diameter, and 30 feet high, having a capacity of 300,000 gallons. Its elevation is 680 feet above tide water, and 400 feet above the pumps.

During the year 1890, owing to the increased consumption of water, five 5-inch wells were bored to an average depth of 105 feet. These wells were connected with the large well by means of a syphon arrangement, so that the water flowed automatically into the large well without any extra pumping. The combined delivery of these wells, at their full capacity, amounted to 320,000 gallons of water per day.

In the early part of the year 1893, it was deemed necessary to still further increase the supply of water, and, therefore, a connection was made at Brookdale with the main of the East Jersey Water Company, the company who had built the plant for the supply of the City of Newark with water taken from the Pequannock River, at Pompton, N. J.

A contract was made November 5, 1892, with the West Orange Water Co., to furnish them with water for the purpose of supplying the Township of West Orange, and about May, 1893, connection was made with their mains, and since that time that Company has been supplied continuously from the Montclair plant.

This extra draft, coupled with the increasing demand of the town of Montclair itself, rendered the pumping plant of the Company almost inadequate for the summer consumption of 1893. Therefore, in the fall of 1893, two new pumps were purchased from the Snow Steam Pump Works, of Buffalo, N. Y., with a capacity of 2,500,000 gallons per day.

Two new boilers were also purchased of 180 horse power, and, with a new stack, have been placed in position.

The old pumps have been taken out of the well and placed in a pit specially prepared for them, which gives the plant a total capacity of 3,500,000 gallons per day.

The boiler and pump have also been enlarged.

The following statements will show the increase of the Company's business during the last six years:

MILES OF WATER PIPE LAID.

During and to the year ending Dec. 31, 1888..24 12/100 miles
During the year ending December 31, 1889.. 1 89/100 "
" " " 31, 1890.. 1 72/100 "
" " " 31, 1891.. 4 75/100 "
" " " 31, 1892.. 2 68/100 "
" " " 31, 1893.. 3 80/100 "

Total to January 1, 1894..38 33/100

NUMBER OF FIRE HYDRANTS.

During and to the year ending Dec. 31, 1888......... 223
During the year ending December 31, 1889......... 15
" " " 31, 1890......... 12
" " " 31, 1891......... 10
" " " 31, 1892......... 18
" " " 31, 1893......... 16

Total to January 1, 1894......... 303

NUMBER OF CONSUMERS ADDED.

During and to the year ending Dec. 31, 1888......... 361
During the year ending December 31, 1889......... 193
" " " 31, 1890......... 119
" " " 31, 1891......... 250
" " " 31, 1892......... 181
" " " 31, 1893......... 187

Total to January 1, 1894......... 1341

NUMBER OF TAPS MADE.

During and to the year ending Dec. 31, 1888......... 377
During the year ending December 31, 1889......... 180
" " " 31, 1890......... 160
" " " 31, 1891......... 151
" " " 31, 1892......... 200
" " " 31, 1893......... 102

Total to January 1, 1894.........1170

AVERAGE DAILY CONSUMPTION OF WATER.

During and to the year ending Dec. 31, 1888..133,763 galls.
During the year ending December 31, 1889..155,494 "
" " " 31, 1890..189,480 "
" " " 31, 1891..223,250 "
" " " 31, 1892..318,537 "
" " " 31, 1893..527,564 "

METERS PUT IN.

During and to the year ending Dec. 31, 1888 5
During the year ending December 31, 1889......... 28
" " " 31, 1890......... 24
" " " 31, 1891......... 18
" " " 31, 1892......... 31
" " " 31, 1893......... 40

Total to January 1, 1894......... 146

JAMES OWEN, TOWNSHIP ENGINEER.—As a civil engineer, and as the originator and promoter of the most important improvements in public highways in Essex County during the past twenty-five years, Mr. Owen is without a rival. His connection with the public affairs of Montclair began soon after its erection as a separate township.

Mr. Owen is a native of England, born in London in 1845. The family from which he is descended is of very remote ancestry, the first of these names being the founder of the noble tribe of North Wales and Powys. Mr. Owen was educated at private school and at King's College, London, and served his time at civil engineering with G. K. Radford, now a partner of the eminent engineer and landscape gardener, Vaux, who was formerly associated with Olmstead in laying out Central Park, New York, and Prospect Park, Brooklyn.

Mr. Owen came to this country in 1866, and was first connected with the Indiana Southern Railroad as civil engineer. In 1867 he was associated with Olmstead and Vaux in the laying out of Prospect Park, Brooklyn. In 1868 he was appointed Engineer of the Essex County, N. J., Public Road Board, and has held the position continuously for more than a quarter of a century, and during this period has expended over $2,000,000 on the public highways and other improvements connected therewith. He established the system of radiating avenues from Newark, which is considered the best of any in the United States, and which has since been adopted in many of our large cities and towns throughout the country. He introduced the Telford system of roads, the most durable of any ever adopted, and there has since been constructed over 250 miles of this class of roads in the county. In 1872 he was appointed County Engineer of Essex County, and had charge of the construction of all the bridges. He abolished the old system of wooden bridges, and substituted those of masonry and iron, of which there are now about 1,500 in the country.

Mr. Owen became a resident of Montclair in 1872, and the same year was appointed Township Engineer, and has held it at different periods down to the present time. He served three years on the Township Committee, from 1885 to 1888. It was during this period that the construction of the public water works began, and he has since had charge of that work. He has taken a special interest in the cause of education; was elected a member of the School Board in 1878, and has been re-elected at each succeeding term since. He was chairman of the committee that introduced technical education, this being the first public school in the United States to adopt that system. He was Chairman of the Building Committee on the construction of the new school-house. He served as Health Commissioner of the township for four years. He has read several papers on engineering, and has been a frequent contributor to engineering journals. He has lectured on the construction of roads in different parts of the country before large and appreciative audiences. He attended the World's Fair Congress of Engineers.

He is a member of the following societies and organizations: American Society of Civil Engineers; New Jersey State Sanitary Association; New Jersey State Road Association; and of different local organizations in Montclair.

THE PRESS.

The very first attempt at journalism in Montclair was made in 1866, by two youths named F. A. Wheeler and F. A. Brantigam, in the publication of a small amateur monthly, which they appropriately named *The Pioneer*. The publication was well received, and served its announced purpose of "a devotion to the general observation on passing events" very well for a few months, when its publishers engaged in other and more profitable occupations, and *The Pioneer* passed out of existence.

For several years after that the town-people depended upon the *Sentinel of Freedom*, the weekly edition of the *Daily Advertiser*, of Newark, for their local and general news, and no one ventured the publication of an exclusively local newspaper. It was not until June, 1873, that the proverbial long-felt want was filled by the appearance of *The Montclair Herald*, the publishers of which were Messrs. J. Ogden Clark and Frank D. Sturgis, both of them members of the legal profession. Like the original journal, it appeared monthly, and was filled with interesting accounts of the rapid developments which the town was under going at that time. Houses were going up in all sections; the Montclair and Greenwood Lake Railway had just been opened; work upon the tunnel through the mountain was being carried on day and night, for the extension of the road to Verona and Caldwell; steam rollers were at work upon the macadamizing of Bloomfield Avenue by the County Board, gas lights had just been introduced—in short, Montclair was booming. The *Herald* prospered correspondingly. It was well printed upon tinted paper, and attained a good circulation. But its publishers found the editorial labors devolving upon them so great as to hinder them in their legal pursuits, and the paper literally outgrew itself and died.

For two years following, the local wants were most acceptably recorded in the *Saturday Gazette*, a weekly paper, published by Sylvanus Lyon, of Bloomfield. Equal space was devoted in its columns to the two sister towns of Montclair and Bloomfield, and the tone of the paper was dignified and clean. For more than two years the *Gazette* served its constituency admirably, exerting a wide influence, and fostering a neighborly spirit between the two towns, which but a few years before were one municipality.

In the fall of 1875 W. C. Contant, publisher of the *Arlington Journal*, sustaining serious loss by fire, removed what was left of his plant to Montclair, and began the publication of the *Montclair Journal*. Although the panic had set in, the town was still growing under the impetus it had received in the heighth of its prosperity in "boom times." A weekly newspaper, properly and economically conducted, could exist, though not hold out immediate prospects of great wealth to its editors. The paper established by Mr. Contant, however, started out on the mistaken mission of antagonizing the local government by being "agin it," and attacking public-spirited men, attributing to them selfish motives. It likewise rejoiced in factional fights, and as a natural result the *Journal* soon reached its last number under Mr. Contant's management.

Mr. John Malcolm Campbell was the next to enter the journalistic field of Montclair. He took up the *Journal* where his predecessor left off, and adopted a somewhat similar policy. The number in which the paper gave up the ghost, it was boldly announced that "the *Journal* has now been placed upon a paying basis." But there was evidently a flaw in the basis, for on a cloudy morning in November the publisher and proprietor disappeared, and the plant was seized by the landlord.

Subscribers to Montclair papers had little faith in the staying qualities of the succeeding publication, *The Montclair Times*, which was begun in February, 1877. The present publisher, A. C. Studer, from the neighboring city of Newark, and Charles A. Burr, of Syracuse, N. Y., entered in the work simultaneously, but the latter withdrew in a few weeks and sold out his interests in the *Times* to Mr. Studer. The paper had an uphill struggle for some time, without prospect of political support, for it was neutral in politics for five years, when having passed the "make or break" period the editor followed his personal proclivities and made the *Times* a Republican paper. A department by Rev. Dr. Bradford, under the title of "Chips From My Workshop," was an interesting feature that did much to popularize the paper. In later years also some of the best writers of the town have contributed to its columns, and the paper has taken an advanced position in all matters affecting the welfare and interests of the community. The *Times* has grown in circulation commensurate to the growth of Montclair, and is in the full enjoyment of public confidence. It is still being published by its original publisher, whose record for seventeen successive years of uninterrupted newspaper work has few equals in the State.

The Montclair *Register* was the next journalistic candidate for public favor in Montclair. It was started in 1888 by A. E. C. Minderman, as an independent paper, but subsequently it became the organ of the Democratic party, especially during the Presidential campaign of that year. Its publisher worked faithfully and heroically against great odds for two and a half years before the *Register* met the fate that had been met by so many of its predecessors.

Just as the *Register* was about to expire, William F. Jones started the Montclair *Herald*, also as a weekly paper, but it had scarcely lived six months before its publisher sold out to C. Alexander Cook. He bought the plant of the defunct *Register*, and for a few weeks managed the *Herald* for a stock company of Democrats and Independents. Mr. Cook was succeeded as editor and manager by Dr.

Richard C. Newton, and he in turn by Mr. Martin Synnott. In 1892 the paper was bought by Dr. C. W. Butler, a prolific contributor to its columns, who conducted it for more than a year, with varied success. The *Herald* was then published by G. C. Earle, and edited by H. B. Walker, they having leased the plant from Dr. Butler, who still owns it.

Among the other papers that have come and gone in recent years is the *Altruist*, published monthly by the Altruist Society in the interests of the benevolent work carried on in town under its auspices.

A very bright little amateur weekly was the *Montclair Press*, published from 1889 to '91, by two boys, James and Arthur Owen, sons of Engineer Owen. It gained quite a circulation, and contained many interesting items. The boys set the type themselves and printed the paper upon a small press in their father's barn, doing all the work after school hours. A feature that interested the older people was the department known as "Topics by His Nibs," the contributions for which were from the prolific pen of Engineer Owen. The *Press* grew almost into the sphere of regular journalism, and had gained much popularity when it was discontinued because of the death of the older of the brothers, much to the regret of its many patrons.

The Montclair Journal was published by William F. Jones and Otis McMillan, as a weekly, from 1890 to 1891, and then daily for about a year. It had no connection with the paper of that name that preceded it. There seemed to be no especial requirement for such a paper then and the paper died. Its publication was resumed, however, in March, 1894, and is being published every Thursday by Messrs. Otis McMillan and Arthur Darlington.

AUGUSTUS CHARLES STUDER.

The success of a newspaper is wholly dependent on the man who supplies the brains, and whether, consciously or unconsciously, his individuality is stamped on every page. If his utterances are truthful and honest, whatever his personal views, he will have the confidence of the public.

From the date of the first issue of the *Montclair Times*, by its present editor and proprietor, its course has been straightforward and truthful, and not a word has sullied its pages that any pure-minded man or woman could take exception to.

Augustus C. Studer, editor and proprietor of the *Montclair Times* for the past seventeen years, comes of a race of patriots, and honest, fearless men, loyal to those principles which have governed their country for five hundred years. All save himself were natives of Switzerland, and though he was a native of this country, the first words he ever uttered were in his father's native tongue. His grandfather was a clergyman of the Calvinistic Church, and for forty years officiated in that capacity at Thun, Switzerland. One of his ancestors was engaged in the civil war known as the Sonderbund—severing the bonds—the same state of affairs existing as in our recent civil war—viz., the severing in twain of the republic—his ancestor remaining true and loyal to the government.

Mr. Studer's mother was Elizabeth Oertel, a native of the Grand Duchy of Baden. Her mother took an active part in the movement to establish the independence of Baden, in 1849, by encouraging resistance to the government and on several occasions conveyed important secret dispatches to Frederich Hecker, the patriotic leader.

Mr. Studer's parents came to this country in 1850 and settled in Newark, N. J., where he was born, May 10, 1854, the year of the great cholera epidemic; it was this that led them to return to their native country when he was but four months old; his early environment was therefore amid the scenes of his father's childhood. He attended school at Thun and Geneva, and, while pursuing the usual course of study, acquired a thorough knowledge of German and French. His parents returned to this country in 1864, during the War of the Rebellion, his father being actuated by a desire to assist his adopted country in her efforts to preserve the Union. This he did by enlisting as a private in Company A, Fifteenth Regiment, N. J. Vols., in which he served until the close of the war. An uncle of young Studer—his father's brother—served throughout the war in an Iowa regiment, and rose from the ranks to that of Major of his regiment, and in 1870 was appointed by President Grant consul to Singapore, and was reappointed each successive administration, including that of President Cleveland in 1884.

Young Studer, soon after his return to this country, entered the public schools of Newark, and although he could not speak a word of English, his previous training enabled him to take an advanced position which he maintained until his graduation. His journalistic training began in the composing room of the *Newark Journal*, and he was subsequently assigned to reportorial duties, and initiated into the mysteries of the editor's "sanctum sanctorum." In 1876 he started a jobbing office in Newark, and while thus engaged, he learned of the several abortive attempts of ambitious aspirants for journalistic honors to establish a weekly paper in Montclair. After carefully surveying the field he was convinced that there was an opening in Montclair for a live newspaper. Soon after he began his canvass, however, he discovered that he had a rival in the field, who was not only backed up by the Greenwood Lake Railway, but intended to start a paper in the interests of the company. Mr. Studer withdrew for a time and awaited "developments." These came sooner than he expected, for after publishing two or three numbers, the publisher was glad to sell out at a loss, and in May, 1877, Mr. Studer assumed the management of the *Montclair Times*. The paper at this time was printed in Jersey City, and "filled in," under the "patent process." He soon after bought the plant of the *Montclair Journal*, a defunct paper which had been abandoned by the proprietor, with "all the appurtenances thereof." to the landlord. Thus equipped, Mr. Studer started in as editor, publisher, reporter, compositor, bookkeeper and everything but "devil." Through good management, rigid economy, and the assistance of a few friends, he soon established it on a paying basis. He ran it as an independent journal for about five years, and then raised the republican banner, which he nailed to the mast, determined to follow his own convictions. About a year after he started, his whole plant was destroyed by fire, and as he was only half insured the loss was severely felt. He never lost courage, however, but began

A. C. STUDER.

again with the same earnestness and determination to succeed. Dr. Bradford kindly came to his assistance and started a column entitled "Chips From My Workshop." This gave a new impetus to the paper, not alone because of the public interest in these contributions, but because of the high esteem in which their author was held in this community. The plant was largely increased, the additional facilities enabled him to do all his own press work, and he now has one of the best equipped country offices in the State.

From publishing a partisan paper it was natural for him to drift into politics, and in 1888 he received the appointment of Engrossing Clerk to the lower house of the State Legislature, and two years afterward he ran for Assembly on the republican ticket, and was elected by a plurality of 683. He took a firm stand against the famous coal combine, which came up that year, and the "usual" powers of persuasion failed to win him over. He was re-elected the following year, and was one of the helpless minority which fought so hard against the corrupt ring that controlled the Legislature that year. He was a member of the Committee on Municipal Corporations to whom was referred the famous race track bill that was rushed through the Legislature against the protests of the large delegation of ministers and laymen who met in the Assembly representing every part of the State. He made the minority report of this committee, condemning in the strongest terms possible this infamous bill. His whole course during the two terms was fearless and upright, and every attempt at jobbery was met by a strong and determined opposition on his part. As an evidence of the esteem in which he was held by his party, it may be noted that he was the caucus nominee for Speaker at the beginning of his second term, with no chance, however, for election, as his opponents were largely in the majority. He made an honorable record for himself in one of the most corrupt Legislatures that ever *mis*-represented the State of New Jersey.

He is naturally of a modest and retiring disposition, and while earnestly advocating through the columns of his journal all the great reform movements inaugurated in Montclair, he could not be induced to accept any local office, preferring active service. As a man, however, he is held in the highest esteem in the community, and while true to his principles as a republican, he shares equally the esteem of his opponents.

He has done much to promote public entertainments of a high order, and has for some years represented the various "bureaus" engaged in this work. As local manager of the New York Philharmonic Club he has brought to Montclair a number of musical celebrities.

Mr. Studer was one of the founders of the Montclair Building and Loan Association, in which he has always taken an active part. He is member of St. Alban's Lodge, No. 68, F. & A. M., of Newark, and of several local organizations.

He is domestic in his habits, and prefers the quietude of his own home to public honors or the gaieties of social life. His wife was a Miss Elizabeth M. Ziegler, of Newark, and his family consists of one son and two daughters, to whose mental and physical training he devotes much attention.

THE UNITED STATES PRINTING COMPANY,

HINDS & KETCHAM FACTORY NO. 3.

Since the closing of the Wheeler Mills on Toney's Brook, in 1887, manufacturing industries in this locality have ceased to exist with the exception of Messrs. Crump & Everdell, who had been long established in New York, started their works near the depot of the New York and Greenwood Lake Railway Company in 1875. They purchased grounds and erected suitable two story buildings, covering some 240 x 100 feet, and employed a number of hands, doing a large business in label and color printing, and also in the manufacture of waterproof wall paper.

On the morning of July 4, 1877, the buildings were entirely destroyed by fire, the origin of which was never fully determined, but supposed to have been caused by spontaneous combustion.

As soon as possible a new factory was erected on a much larger and more extensive scale, the size of the buildings being 150 x 240 feet (afterward increased to 150 x 525 feet, the present size), which were fitted up with greatly increased facilities. Mr. Everdell withdrew from the firm at about this time, and Mr. Samuel Crump carried on the business alone very successfully until 1884, when the Crump Label Company was formed, which name was changed to Samuel Crump Label Company in 1888.

This company continued to do an increasing business, employing some 200 hands, until it was purchased in June, 1890, by the Hinds, Ketcham Company, of Brooklyn, N. Y., this being a reorganization of the firm of Hinds, Ketcham & Co., which firm was formed some ten years previous by four employees of the Crump Label Company, who had built up an enormous business, located at Brooklyn, until they were able at this time to purchase the entire business conducted by their former employers. Under this new management the business was somewhat increased until February 1, 1891, when it was purchased by The United States Printing Company, a concern that had been formed with a capital stock of $3,500,000, and included the largest label and color printing manufacturers in the country. The magnitude of this new company can be better realized when we know they at once stripped this Montclair factory of all its machinery pertaining to the printing trade, distributing it in some of their other factories, and immediately purchased an enormous amount of new and improved machinery for the sole purpose of coating paper and card of every description for use in their other factories, which are at present located at Brooklyn, N. Y., Cincinnati, O., and Indianapolis, Ind., where the total product of the Montclair branch is turned into printed labels, show cards, banners, boxes, circus posters, playing cards, and every other form of novelty that can be made from either paper or card, and which are used in every known country on the globe. This Montclair factory, which is known as Hinds & Ketcham Factory No. 3, is one of the largest, if not the largest, and certainly the best equipped works of its kind in the country. The entire building is occupied in the manufacture of its goods, and while the character of the work does not necessitate the employment of as many hands as were formerly kept busy (as there are only some 75 employed now), yet the amount of product is many times greater than it ever was before, as the capacity of the works is at least 30,000 pounds of finished paper and card per day, or about 9,000,000 pounds per year. Over 1,000,000 pounds of imported clay and over 250,000 pounds of powdered glue are used in its production, which is as large a quantity of either of these articles as is used in any one factory in the country.

The paper enters the factory in its crude state from the mills in the East, and is coated in any

UNITED STATES PRINTING COMPANY.

weight and color, calendered, cut into any size sheets, and shipped in strong machine-made cases to the other factories all ready to be put upon the presses for printing. This factory received some time ago an order from one of its Cincinnati factories for a few months' supply of paper, which would take some 65 freight cars to transport to its destination, and over ten cars of lumber for casing of same. The freight paid by the factory to the Erie Railroad, over which all its supplies and product is carried, can be imagined when it is noted that they paid freight on at least 20,000,000 pounds of supplies and completed production in one year.

The factory is well protected against fire as it has a fire brigade of its own, with suitable apparatus, which can be attached to hydrants of its own, and is also supplied with an automatic sprinkler system which would easily flood the building and contents in time of need.

The factory being situated in such a remote portion of the town, is no hindrance to its growth as a residence centre, as probably not over one-fiftieth part of the inhabitants would know of its existence, if it were not for its sonorous whistle, which not only calls its employees to and from their duty, but also blows all fire alarms for the town, as it is connected automatically with the township system.

While the home office of the Company is in Cincinnati, O., all the factories are operated as separate concerns, so that all business of every description for this factory is completed at its own office.

The entire business of the factory, while conducted by home talent, is under the direct supervision of Mr. Joseph E. Hinds, of Brooklyn, the Vice-President and General Eastern Manager of the Company, to whose business sagacity the grand success of this branch of the Company is due.

JOSEPH EDWIN HINDS, Vice-President and General Eastern Manager of the present company, who has been connected with the business for nearly a quarter of a century, is a native of Brooklyn, L. I., born September 18, 1848, of English parentage. He has made his own way in the world since he was eleven years of age. He entered a printing office in New York City when he was fifteen years of age, and five years later found employment with Crump & Co., who were then carrying on the business of colored label printing on Fulton Street. In 1871 he was made superintendent of their New York factory, and when they moved to Montclair, in 1875, he took charge of their new factory and continued in that capacity until December, 1879, when he organized the firm of Hinds, Ketcham & Co.; ten years later they bought out the old firm.

Mr. Hinds was one of the principal promoters of The United States Printing Company and has been its Vice-President from its organization.

During his residence in Montclair Mr. Hinds became interested in the various reform and improvement movements of that period; he was one of the original members of the Village Improvement Society, of which Mr. Thomas Porter was President, and was clerk of the Society during its continuance, and spent much time and labor in promoting its objects. The hundreds of beautiful shade trees which have made this one of the most attractive townships in the State are due to the efforts of this Society, of which Mr. Hinds was one of the most active members. He also assisted in organizing the Montclair Literary and Social Circle, which during its existence afforded delightful entertainment, and did much to improve the intellectual and social condition of the young men of the town. He was its first Vice-President and afterward became President of the Society. He is also a member of Montclair Lodge F. & A. M., and a firm supporter of the objects of the fraternity. He was the original promoter and first Past Regent of Montclair Council, Royal Arcanum, and the first meeting of the Council was held at his house. This has since become one of the most influential Councils in the State.

Mr. Hinds did not remain long enough in Montclair to witness the fruition of all his plans and his hopes, but others have reaped the benefit of his labors, and his zeal and enterprise for the good of the community are not forgotten, and the seed sown by him has borne ample fruit. Mr. Hinds, though located in Brooklyn, still has the supervision of the manufacturing interests of his Company in Montclair.

Mr. Hinds is a man of strong individuality, conscientious and upright in all his business transactions—a firm believer in the brotherhood of man, and his aim in life has been to improve the condition of his fellow-men and to lend a helping hand to the needy and suffering. He married, in 1870, Miss Mary A. Beetham, the issue of which is eight children, seven of whom are living.

BANK OF MONTCLAIR.

With the rapid growth of Montclair it has been a cause of wonder to many of its citizens how they managed for so many years to get along without local banking facilities. It is even more surprising when it is considered that within six months after the Bank of Montclair opened its doors, nearly five hundred depositors had availed themselves of the privilege thus offered.

For more than half a century the people of this locality transacted all their banking business with Newark, Orange and New York City, entailing loss of time, inconvenience, and often considerable expense. It has been a subject of discussion for many years past, and occasional efforts have been made to establish a bank in the township without success. In the autumn of 1888 Mr. Paul Wilcox and Thomas Wilcox Stephens, believing the time was ripe for such an enterprise, determined to make an effort in this direction. Mr. Stephens called upon, and obtained letters of introduction from, Mr.

Benjamin Graham and Mr. E. G. Burgess to Jasper R. Rand and Stephen W. Carey, who gave their hearty co-operation, and arrangements were made for an early meeting. The following gentlemen met by appointment at the office of Mr. Rand, in New York City: Jasper R. Rand, Stephen W. Carey, Paul Wilcox and T. W. Stephens, the present cashier of the Bank of Montclair.

The matter was freely discussed, and it was decided to effect an organization at an early date. Meetings were held from time to time, and other citizens became interested in the movement and pledged their support. Several meetings were held at the house of Mr. Benjamin Graham, who became deeply interested in the enterprise at the outset and was one of the active spirits in securing its success.

It was finally agreed to start with a capital of $50,000, one half the amount to be paid in at once, and the balance when called for by the stockholders. This was done September, 1891. A meeting was held at the house of Mr. Paul Wilcox, on the Valley Road. There were present, Thomas Russell, Stephen W. Carey, Benjamin Graham, A. B. Howe, Philip Doremus, Charles H. Johnson, Sr., Jasper R. Rand, Peter H. Van Riper, Paul Wilcox, Abraham Bussing and T. W. Stephens. After the subscription lists were opened there was no difficulty in obtaining the requisite capital. The citizens of Montclair generally gave it their hearty support, and subscribed liberally to the stock. Outside parties would willingly have taken the whole amount, but it was considered expedient to have as much as possible taken in Montclair.

A meeting for the election of Directors was held at the office of E. B. Goodell, at Montclair, April 2, 1889, and the following named gentlemen were duly elected: Stephen W. Carey, Thomas Russell, Philip Doremus, Charles H. Johnson, Benjamin Graham, William D. Van Vleck, Edwin A. Bradley, Edward G. Burgess, Paul Wilcox, Jasper R. Rand, John R. Livermore, George H. Mills, Andrus B. Howe, Frederick J. Drescher, Daniel O. Eshbaugh, Edwin B. Goodell, W. W. Egbert, Peter H. Van Riper, Abraham Bussing, Edwin A. Bradley, the seventh on the list, declined to serve on account of the pressure of private business, and Mr. Benjamin Strong was elected in his stead. Jasper R. Rand was elected President, Wm. D. Van Vleck, Vice-President, and T. W. Stephens, Cashier.

A BIT OF BLOOMFIELD AVENUE,
Showing the Bank of Montclair.

The bank was formally opened Saturday, June 1, 1889, in what was known as the Van Riper building, on Bloomfield Avenue. Forty-two accounts were opened, and the total amount deposited was $60,000. In January, 1890, at the first annual meeting, seven months after the organization of the bank, the books showed 435 depositors, with a total of $160,000. In January, 1892, there were 1,025 depositors, with a total of $365,000.

The books showed a good surplus each year, but for satisfactory reasons no dividend was declared.

In 1892 a lot was purchased, 60x200 feet, on Bloomfield Avenue, nearly opposite the Presbyterian Church, and plans designed by J. C. Cady & Co., architects, for a bank building. Work was soon after begun and the building completed in the spring of 1893. It is 30x50 feet, three stories high, with basement and cellar. The walls are of brick, with white terra cotta brick front. Rooms above the bank are arranged for offices, one of which is occupied by the Montclair Savings Bank. The new building was opened for business May 13, 1893. The lower part, occupied by the Bank of Montclair, is beautifully fitted up in cherry, with brass trimmings. A separate department is arranged for lady depositors, who number nearly one-third of the entire list.

This has proved thus far one of the most successful banking institutions ever started in this country, sustained largely by private individuals, there being but one manufactory in the township, and the business being confined mainly to general supplies for the residents.

The directors for 1894 are: Stephen W. Carey, Thomas Russell, Philip Doremus, Charles H. Johnson, Benjamin Graham, William D. Van Vleck, Edward G. Burgess, Paul Wilcox, Jasper R. Rand, John R. Livermore, Andrus B. Howe, Frederick J. Drescher, Daniel O. Eshbaugh, Edwin B. Goodell, Peter H. Van Riper, Abraham Bussing, Benjamin Strong, Amzi A. Sigler, J. E. Williams.

THE MONTCLAIR SAVINGS BANK.

The matter of organizing a Savings Bank in Montclair had been discussed by business men for some two or three years before any active steps were taken. According to the minutes of the Bank:

" After informal consultation on the subject of establishing a Savings Bank in Montclair, N. J., the following circular letter was addressed to a number of gentlemen of Montclair and vicinity:

" MONTCLAIR, N. J., September 30, 1892.

" Having carefully considered the advisability of establishing a Savings Bank in Montclair, we have reached the conclusion that the time has come to do so. The success of the two financial institutions now here, which has been much greater in both cases than was anticipated, has been the principal argument in favor of such a step.

" Believing that your assistance upon the Board of Managers of such a bank will be of great advantage to it, you are requested to be present, if you will consent to serve, at the rooms of the Montclair Building and Loan Association, on Friday evening, October 7, at 8 o'clock, to arrange preliminaries, and sign the necessary certificate as a first step toward organization.

" If you are willing to serve and cannot then be present, and will send word to that effect to Mr. Goodell, your name will be inserted in the certificate, and a commissioner will call upon you to take your signature.

" Very truly yours,

"Jasper R. Rand, Philip Doremus, Andrus B. Howe, Edward Madison, Hugh Gallagher, C. Alexander Cook, William H. Ketcham, John R. Livermore, Charles I. Reeves, William Y. Bogle, John S. Carlson, W. Lon Doremus, Edwin B. Goodell.

" In conformity with the request contained in the above letter, the gentlemen addressed met on the evening of October 7, 1892, at the rooms of the Montclair Building and Loan Association, and held an informal meeting.

"At this meeting Mr. Edwin B. Goodell was requested and authorized to proceed to take all the necessary and legal steps required to procure the Certificate of Incorporation for The Montclair Savings Bank, and the Certificate of Authority to open the said Bank for business, and such other matters as might be required."

According to the advertisement duly inserted in the *Montclair Herald*, November 3, 1892, the following named gentlemen composed the corporators of the Bank:

Jasper R. Rand, John R. Livermore, William H. Ketcham, William Y. Bogle, I. Seymour Crane, Philip Doremus, Edward Madison, Andrus B. Howe, John S. Carlson, W. Louis Doremus, C. Alexander Cook, Hugh Gallagher, Edwin B. Goodell, Charles I. Reeves, Charles H. Johnson, Jr., John J. H. Love, David F. Merritt, Charles W. Anderson, Thomas Russell, Amzi A. Sigler, Stephen W. Carey, Thomas W. Stephens, Daniel O. Eshbaugh, J. Edgar Williams, Samuel C. G. Watkins, Cyrus B. Crane.

The first meeting for organization was held January 9, 1893, at the room of the Montclair Building and Loan Association, on Bloomfield Avenue. It was then announced that the necessary Certificate of Incorporation had been filed with the State Banking Department at Trenton, and that the Certificate of Authorization had been duly issued, and that the twenty six gentlemen who had applied for a Savings Bank in Montclair were now duly authorized to organize the bank.

At this meeting By-Laws were adopted, and the following officers were elected:

President, Philip Doremus; Vice-President, Thomas W. Stephens; Secretary and Treasurer, H. D. Crane; Counsel, Edwin B. Goodell.

An Executive Committee consisting of the following named gentlemen in addition to the *ex-officio* members were elected:

William Y. Bogle, David F. Merritt, Andrus B. Howe, John R. Livermore, Edwin B. Goodell.

The bank was duly opened for depositors March 15, 1893. At the close of the first year's business there were 985 accounts opened, and the amount due depositors was $125,229.41.

MASONIC LODGES.

BLOOMFIELD LODGE, No. 40, F. & A. M., was organized in West Bloomfield as early as 1824, and the fact that the furniture of Chatham Lodge—then suspended— was obtained for the new Lodge, indicates that the former had previously existed in this locality. The first communication was held July 24, 1824, in the hotel of Joseph Munn, on the corner of Church Street and Valley Road. A dispensation was obtained from the M∴ W∴ Grand Master, and the Lodge acted under this authority until the regular meeting of the Grand Lodge. The first officers elected were: Simeon Baldwin, W. M.; Daniel D. Beach, S. W.; Joshua Smith, J. W.; Ephraim P. Stiles, Secretary; Zenas S. Crane, Treasurer; Matthias Taylor, S. D.; John Robinson, J. D.; William Frame, M. of C.; and Linus Baldwin, Tyler.

The names of the twenty-seven charter members show that they were mostly residents of this locality: Matthias Smith, D. D. Beach, John Robinson, Joshua Smith, Jonathan Stephens, Linus Baldwin, Benjamin Reynolds, Matthias Taylor, Christopher Garrabrant, William Frame, John Munn, Thomas Speer, Jr., Simeon Baldwin, Zenas S. Crane, L. F. Lewis Mitchell, Joseph Munn, Nathaniel H. Baldwin, John Aikins, Aaron Ballard, Robert Aikins, Peter Doremus, Thomas Ryland, William Young, John Moore, Hugh Boggs, Henry Stanley, Ephraim P. Stiles.

The Lodge was duly chartered by the Grand Lodge and the first regular communication was held September 15, 1824, when the officers named in the dispensation were installed by M∴ W∴ Grand Master, Jeptha B. Munn. Among its members were many names familiar to the old residents of West Bloomfield. The Lodge continued to flourish and increase in membership until the Anti Masonic agitation (fostered and encouraged by politicians) of 1828-32, when hundreds of lodges all over the country surrendered their charters. The charter of Bloomfield Lodge was surrendered about this time, and ceased to exist for twenty eight years. On February 19, 1856, it was resuscitated at Bloomfield, the old warrant being re-issued to them under the name of Bloomfield Lodge No. 40. The new officers were installed by Past Grand Master Jeptha B. Munn, the same individual who, twenty-eight years previous— being then Grand Master of Masons of the State of New Jersey—had installed the original officers. This Lodge is still in a flourishing condition in Bloomfield.

MONTCLAIR LODGE No. 144, F. & A. M., was organized in 1875 and held its first communication under dispensation in Odd Fellows' Hall, October 25 of that year. The charter members were H. W. Force, John P. Turner, A. P. Devoursney, Geo. R. Milligan, Edward E. Wright, Edgar T. Gould, S. D. Chittenden, Peter A. Tronson, Peter Speer, M. W. Smith, Charles Smith, F. H. Harris, Samuel Arbuthnot and Edmund Williams.

At the annual communication of the Grand Lodge in the following January a charter was granted to Montclair Lodge and the Lodge was duly instituted February 10, 1876, by R∴ W∴ Bro. J. C. Fitzgerald, Grand S. W. The officers of the Lodge while under dispensation and during 1876 were H. W. Force, W. M.; John P. Turner, S. W.; A. P. Devoursney, J. W.; E. E. Wright, Treasurer; G. R. Milligan, Secretary; E. T. Gould, S. D.; S. D. Chittenden, J. D.; P. A. Tronson, M. of C.; Peter Speer, Tyler.

Officers, 1877.—H. W. Force, W. M.; J. P. Turner, S. W.; A. P. Devoursney, J. W.; E. E. Wright, Treasurer; W. L. Doremus, Secretary; E. T. Gould, S. D.; T. F. Jacobus, J. D.; P. A. Tronson and R. D. Sargent, M. of C; Peter Speer, Tyler.

Officers, 1878.—H. W. Force, W. M.; P. A. Tronson, S. W.; G. R. Milligan, J. W.; E. E. Wright, Treasurer; W. L. Doremus, Secretary; E. T. Gould, S. D.; T. F. Jacobus, J. D.; J. L. Crone and J. McTaggart, M. of C; Peter Speer, Tyler.

Officers, 1879.—H. W. Force, W. M.; E. D. Hall, S. W.; A. B. Howe, J. W.; E. E. Wright, Treasurer; J. P. Turner, Secretary; E. T. Gould, S. D.; T. F. Jacobus, J. D.; J. McTaggart and Geo. A. Van Gieson, M. of C; Peter Speer, Tyler.

Officers, 1880.—A. B. Howe, W. M.; G. R. Milligan, S. W.; Joseph E. Hinds, J. W.; E. E. Wright, Treasurer; J. P. Turner, Secretary; E. T. Gould, S. D.; George W. Scherf, J. D.; Peter Speer, Tyler.

Officers, 1881.—A. B. Howe, W. M.; G. R. Milligan, S. W.; T. F. Jacobus, J. W.; E. E. Wright, Treasurer; J. P. Turner, Secretary; E. T. Gould, S. D.; George Delong, J. D.; J. McTaggart and Vaughn Darress, M. of C; C. H. Corby, Tyler.

Officers, 1882.—A. B. Howe, W. M.; G. R. Milligan, S. W.; E. T. Gould, J. W.; George Delong, Treasurer; J. P. Turner, Secretary; James H. Casey, S. D.; Vaughn Darress, J. D.; J. McTaggart and John Poole, Jr., M. of C; John G. Treadwell, Tyler.

Officers, 1883.—G. R. Milligan, W. M.; C. W. Sandford, S. W.; W. L. Doremus, J. W.; George Delong, Treasurer; J. P. Turner, Secretary; James H. Casey, S. D.; John Poole, J. D.; T. F. Jacobus and W. R. Courter, M. of C; John G. Treadwell, Chaplain; C. H. Corby, Tyler.

Officers, 1884.—C. W. Sandford, W. M.; W. L. Doremus, S. W.; Vaughn Darress, J. W.; G. R. Milligan, Treasurer; J. P. Turner, Secretary; John Poole, Jr., S. D.; James H. Walsh, J. D.; C. W. English and A. G. Spencer, M. of C; John G. Treadwell, Chaplain; Peter Speer, Tyler.

Officers, 1885.—C. W. Sandford, W. M.; C. W. English, S. W.; A. G. Spencer, J. W.; G. R. Milligan, Treasurer; A. E. Aeby, Secretary; I. N. Rudgers, S. D.; E. E. Leach, J. D.; G. B. Edwards and P. D. Riker, M. of C; John G. Treadwell, Chaplain; T. F. Jacobus, Tyler.

Officers, 1886.—C. W. English, W. M.; A. G. Spencer, S. W.; I. N. Rudgers, J. W.; G. R. Milligan, Treasurer; A. B. Howe, Secretary; C. W. Sandford, S. D.; Elijah Pearce, J. D.; A. C. Hilsinger and P. D. Riker, M. of C; John G. Treadwell, Chaplain; T. F. Jacobus, Tyler.

Officers, 1887.—C. W. English, W. M.; I. N. Rudgers, S. W.; A. C. Hilsinger, J. W.; G. R. Milligan, Treasurer; A. B. Howe, Secretary; Elijah Pearce, S. D.; E. E. Leach, J. D.; W. H. Bartholomew and A. G. Spencer, M. of C; John G. Treadwell, Chaplain; P. D. Riker, Tyler.

Officers, 1888.—A. B. Howe, W. M.; G. R. Milligan, S. W.; A. C. Hilsinger, J. W.; Wm. M. Taylor, Treasurer; F. W. Crane, Secretary; I. N. Rudgers, S. D.; Theodore Sigler, J. D.; T. F. Jacobus and A. G. Spencer, M. of C; John G. Treadwell, Chaplain; P. D. Riker, Tyler.

Officers, 1889.—A. B. Howe, W. M.; G. R. Milligan, S. W.; W. L. Doremus, J. W.; Wm. M. Taylor, Treasurer; F. W. Crane, Secretary; A. S. Badgley, S. D.; Theodore Sigler, J. D.; F. B. Squier and A. G. Spencer, M. of C; John G. Treadwell, Chaplain; P. D. Riker, Tyler.

Officers, 1890.—William M. Taylor, W. M.; Vaughn Darress, S. W.; A. S. Badgley, J. W.; Wm. L. Doremus, Treasurer; F. W. Crane, Secretary; A. B. Howe, S. D.; Theodore Sigler, J. D.; George Delong and Elijah Pearce, M. of C; John G. Treadwell, Chaplain; P. D. Riker, Tyler.

Officers, 1891.—Alfred S. Badgley, W. M.; H. F. Holloway, S. W.; Samuel White, Jr., J. W.; Wm. L. Doremus, Treasurer; Clark Cooper, Secretary; A. B. Howe, S. D.; P. F. Durst, J. D.; G. R. Milligan and Elijah Pearce, M. of C; Joseph T. Farrington, Chaplain; P. D. Riker, Tyler.

Officers, 1892.—Alfred S. Badgley, W. M.; H. F. Holloway, S. W.; Ralph Marden, J. W.; Wm. L. Doremus, Treasurer; Hugo Reid, Secretary; C. W. McKown, S. D.; F. W. Crane, J. D.; Elijah Pearce and I. N. Rudgers, M. of C; Joseph T. Farrington, Chaplain; P. D. Riker, Tyler.

Officers, 1893.—Henry F. Holloway, W. M.; Ralph Marden, S. W.; Hugo Reid, J. W.; Wm. L.

Doremus, Treasurer; C. W. McKown, Secretary; A. B. Howe, S. D.; Elijah Pearce, J. D.; C. W. English and G. R. Milligan, M. of C.; John G. Treadwell, Chaplain; P. D. Riker, Tyler.

Officers, 1894.— Ralph Marden, W. M.; H. F. Holloway, S. W.; Robert F. Green, J. W.; Wm. L. Doremus, Treasurer; C. W. McKown, Secretary; A. B. Howe, S. D.; A. C. Rowland, J. D.; T. R. Taltavall and G. A. Van Gieson, M. of C.; John G. Treadwell, Chaplain; P. D. Riker, Tyler.

Since its institution Montclair Lodge has received forty-five members by affiliation and forty by the conferring of degrees It has lost nineteen by suspension for non-payment of dues, twelve by dimit, and nine by death. The present membership (January 1, 1894) is fifty-nine.

I. O. O. F.

WATCHUNG LODGE, No. 134, I.O.O.F., was instituted at Montclair, May 4, 1869. Its first officers were: Melancthon W. Smith, N. G.; John C. Woodruff, V. G.; Edgar T. Gould, Recording Secretary; Warren S. Taylor, Permanent Secretary; Edward E. Wright, Treasurer.

The following persons have filled the position of N. G. since its organization: John H. Hayden, W. S. Taylor, M. Speer, H. M. Romer, G. R. Milligan, E. T. Gould, W. B. Jacobus, S. A. Gould, S. J. Gould, Theo. T. King, A. E. Munn, E. B. Crane, R. B. Harris, C. F. Dunham, Jno. H. Jacobus, E. D. Hall, M. W. Smith, Geo. T. Bunten, John Murphy, R. B Harris, W. H. Gould, Frank Koegler, Warren S. Taylor, Ed. Crossman, Geo. W. Boxall, David D. Murphy, M. W. Smith, E. M. Harrison, W. H. Stagg, W. H. Dellhagen, Peter Haring, Clark Cooper, J. F. Creamer, E. E. Brooks, Frank McKenna, Thomas J. Courter.

Total number of members since its organization, 174; deaths, 7; present membership, 71.

GEN. SHERMAN LODGE, No. 51, ANCIENT ORDER UNITED WORKMEN.

This Lodge was instituted February 18, 1891, by Past Grand Master Workman J. W. Diefendorf, assisted by E. H. Colyer, P. M. W., Dr. Geo. W. Potter, Medical Examiner and Financier; J. H. Day, of Newark Lodge, No. 31, P. M. W.; C. Schlaeffer, of Elizabeth Lodge, No. 29; James E. Garrabrant, Master Workman, of West End, No. 48, and other visiting brethren. Twenty-six applicants had been examined, and twenty had been approved and returned, which met the requirements of the Constitution to procure a charter. After the obligations had been given, and the exemplification of the secret work, the following named officers were elected and installed for the ensuing term: Past Master Workman, A. C. Studer; Master Workman, I. Newton Rudgers; Foreman, Stephen L. Purdy; Overseer, Amidee Tunison; Recorder, Clark Cooper; Financier, J. D. Keyler; Receiver, Charles W. English; Guide, Isaac A. Dodd; G. W., Henry Wrensch, Sr.; O. W., George Spencer.

Trustees, one year, A. C. Hortsch; two years, T. W. Crane; three years, Carl F. Fentzlaff.

This is said to be the oldest and largest beneficiary order in existence

OTHER SECRET AND BENEVOLENT SOCIETIES.

MENDLETON LODGE, No. 1620.— Meets first Wednesday in each month in Watchung Hall.

CATHOLIC KNIGHTS OF AMERICA, BRANCH 426.— Organized 1886; meets second and fourth Monday of each month at Parochial School.

IRISH NATIONAL LEAGUE.— Organized 1884; meets at time and place designated by President.

CATHOLIC BENEVOLENT LEGION, FATHER STEETS' COUNCIL, No. 83.— Organized 1884; meets first and third Monday of each month in Watchung Hall.

ORDER OF CHOSEN FRIENDS, MORSE COUNCIL, No. 45.— Meets first and third Thursday, in Hayden Building, 548 Bloomfield Avenue.

ANCIENT ORDER OF HIBERNIANS.

KNIGHTS OF HONOR, MONTCLAIR LODGE, No. 2638.—Organized December 23, 1881.

MONTCLAIR COUNCIL, No. 421, ROYAL ARCANUM.—Organized 1879; meets second and fourth Tuesday in each month, in Arcanum Hall, Doremus Building.

CRYSTAL LODGE, No. 244, GOOD TEMPLARS.—Organized 1886; meets every Monday evening in Pillsbury Building.

MONTCLAIR BUILDING AND LOAN ASSOCIATION.—Meets first Monday evening in each month, at 456 Bloomfield Avenue.

PHIL. KEARNEY COUNCIL, No. 35, NATIONAL PROVIDENT UNION.—Meets every second Monday in each month, in Odd Fellows' Hall.

THE CITIZENS' COMMITTEE OF ONE HUNDRED.

This organization was forced into existence by contempt for excise laws and violations of peace and good order on the part of local liquor sellers and their victims. It originated from a suggestion made in the inter-denominational New Year's prayer meeting of 1883. It took preliminary form in a meeting of citizens at the residence of the late Samuel Wilde, January 19, 1883. Its Executive Committee, composed of D. F. Merritt, Samuel Crump, A. B. Howe, H. B. Littell and John J. Carolan, first met January 27, 1883, at the residence of D. F. Merritt, when Mr. Merritt was elected chairman; Mr. Carolan, secretary; Mr. Howe, treasurer; and Mr. Crump and Mr. Littell, auditors.

The agreement which formed the foundation of the general organization bears date of January 19, 1883, and shows the signatures of one hundred and twenty-one men, each of whom subscribed twenty-five dollars " to be used for the creation of a healthy public sentiment in relation to the use and sale of liquor, and to enforce existing laws in Montclair." This agreement, bearing the autographs of the one hundred and twenty-one original members of the general committee, is safely preserved among the documents of the organization.

Montclair has always been an exceptionally temperate, quiet and order-loving town. Many places would have tolerated or ignored the conditions which led to the Citizens' Committee. Indeed, the organization has always been defensive, and, as communities go, its formation was in large part anticipatory and much of its work has been preventive. Yet the report made by the Executive Committee in 1886, discussing the need for the general body at the time of its formation, recites that " a period had been reached when the question had to be determined whether, as in the large cities of the country, the liquor interest should be allowed to dominate, or whether its capacity for evil to the community should be diminished to the lowest possible point." Saloons, licensed and unlicensed, were increasing in number annually, their work of physical death, moral degradation and civic demoralization was assuming cumulatively dangerous proportions and was menacing the highest interests of the entire community.

To meet these conditions, and, as far as possible, neutralize the dangers embodied in them, the Citizens' Committee began active work in the courts to prevent the granting of new licenses to liquor sellers and to secure enforcement of the liquor laws, and it became at once potential in educating and stimulating public opinion. The notable total abstinence meetings conducted in the winter of 1883, by Messrs. Maybee and English, were morally and financially aided by the Committee, and these resulted in a genuine and earnest revival of interest in temperance and abstinence, as well as in the securing of many hundreds of names to the total abstinence pledge.

The Citizens' Committee has never been a so called temperance society. It has been and is non-partisan, and it includes women and men of all shades of opinion as to the general question of the use and abuse of liquor and of its relations to the individual and to the community. These people find a common working platform in the following practical and inclusive declaration of their objectives:

First.—To protect the community, as far as possible, from the evils growing out of the excessive use and the unrestricted sale of intoxicating liquors, by insisting upon a strict observance of the law under license of which the business in intoxicants is carried on.

Second.—To secure the punishment of liquor dealers who violate the law, especially those who make their places resorts for gambling and other vicious practices, who sell liquor to children, and who persist in carrying on this business, directly or indirectly, on Sundays.

Third.—To use every moral and legal effort not only to prevent the opening of new saloons, but to diminish the number of those already in existence.

Along these lines the Citizens' Committee has done an excellent and effective work for eleven years, although, because of hindrances little understood by the public, the things accomplished are not at all what even the workers themselves would like, yet, at this writing, while the population of the town has grown almost three-fold since 1882, the number of liquor sellers has increased but about 20 per cent., the community has been kept and remains exceptionally free from liquor selling evils, such as prevail where no restraint hampers and regulates the traffic.

Early in 1889, the Executive Committee was enlarged from five to twelve members, and subsequently the number was increased to fifteen. D. F. Merritt served as Chairman from the date of organization until October, 1887; Samuel Crump thenceforward until May, 1891; then A. H. Siegfried until October, 1893. The Secretaries have been John J. Carolan, E. P. Benedict, Thomas Hughes, C. S. Olcott and Joseph Hellen. A. B. Howe has served as Treasurer throughout the life of the organization. The current organization is as follows: Charles D. Thompson, Chairman; Wm. Winslow Ames, Secretary; A. B. Howe, Treasurer; John R. Howard, Thomas Russell, Isaac Denby, C. H. Johnson, Jr., E. P. Benedict. A. H. Siegfried, D. F. Merritt, A. A. Sigler, John H. Parsons, C. I. Reeves, R. M. Boyd, Jr., Joseph Hellen.

THE GOOD GOVERNMENT CLUB.

THE adoption of the "Short Law" by a large majority of the citizens of Montclair—alluded to in a previous chapter—was the means of arousing public sentiment in favor of a non-partisan government, which should contain the best elements of each political party, unbiased and uninfluenced by party considerations.

The restriction of the sale of intoxicating liquors, and the prevention of a trolley road from passing through the principal streets of the town, were questions that agitated the public mind and led to the organization of a non-partisan Club having these ends in view.

A meeting for this purpose was held at Henderson Hall on Saturday evening, March 17, 1894.

It was called to order by Rev. A. H. Bradford, D.D., of the First Congregational Church, a staunch republican. After briefly but earnestly stating the object of the meeting—the formation of a non-partisan organization to work for sound morality and clean business administration of the affairs of the town—he nominated as Chairman Rev. F. T. Gates, who has lived in the town a year or so, a Baptist, and a man who, as the business agent of Mr. J. D. Rockafeller, had been in charge of the erection of the great buildings for the new University of Chicago.

Mr. Gates, in his few words on taking the chair, announced himself as a life-long republican, and then gave some admirable reasons for a non-partisan government of any town or city, and the divorce of its business matters from Federal party politics. Mr. Robert M. Boyd, Jr., was elected Secretary, a man independent in national politics, who has always voted the republican ticket in town matters.

For a basis of action, Mr. John R. Howard, independent, offered the following short Constitution, which he described as enough of a skeleton to be invested with flesh and blood and vital organs; a charter specific enough and broad enough for all good purposes:

I.—The name of this Association shall be the "Good Government Club of Montclair, New Jersey."

II.—Its object is stated in its name, and its function shall be to do whatever its members think helpful in gaining that object, especially in the direction of a non-partisan business administration of the affairs of the town.

III. —Its officers shall be a President, a Secretary, and a Treasurer, who, besides doing the ordinary duties of such officers, shall, with an Executive Committee of eight other members of the Club, manage the affairs of the Association under the general direction of the Club.

IV.—The officers and Executive Committee shall be elected annually, at the regular annual meeting to be held on the first Saturday evening of March in each year.

V.—The annual dues shall be one dollar, payable the first year on joining the Club, and thereafter on or before the evening of the annual meeting.

VI.—Any person is eligible to membership who sympathizes with the object of the Club. All applications shall be made to the Secretary of the Club and passed upon by the Executive Committee; all members are entitled to vote who have paid their dues; no member is bound in his individual action by any general action of the Club, but all will be expected to acquiesce in such action and work for the aims of the Club.

With the exception of changing the date of annual meeting from the third to the first Saturday evening of March, in each year, the Constitution was adopted as a provisional charter.

A committee of three, Messrs. J. R. Livermore, democrat, Charles D. Thompson, republican, and J. A. Richards, prohibitionist, were appointed to nominate a committee of five on permanent organization and policy. The nominees were Rev. Dr. Bradford, republican, C. S. Olcott, republican, Paul Wilcox, democrat, J. R. Howard, independent, and A. D. French, republican. Dr. Bradford declined the work, not, he said, because he was not in fullest sympathy with it, but because it would be a physical impossibility for him to attend to its duties. The meeting then by unanimous vote appointed Mr. Charles D. Thompson in Dr. Bradford's place, overbearing Mr. Thompson's earnest protest; and the Committee was duly completed.

This Committee was instructed to confer in advance with the leaders of the several political parties concerning the probable nominees in the respective wards; to ascertain the views of candidates as to their position on the subject of granting liquor licenses and restricting the liquor traffic by ordinance and otherwise; and to report nominations in place of candidates by them deemed objectionable. The Committee were also directed to report at the adjourned meeting, which should be called for Saturday evening, March 24, or earlier, if in their discretion it should be deemed necessary. Further, the Committee were given power to add to their number, and directed to report a plan of permanent organization.

At the adjourned meeting held March 24, a plan of permanent organization was adopted and the following officials elected to serve for the first year:

President, F. T. Gates; Secretary, Starr J. Murphy; Treasurer, Edward F. Myers. Executive Committee: First Ward, G. S. Jefferson and Howard Ayres; Second Ward, Chas. S. Olcott and Paul Wilcox; Third Ward, John R. Howard and Richard P. Francis; Fourth Ward, W. I. Lincoln Adams and Peter Larsen.

CHILDREN'S HOME.

The Children's Home, established in 1881, was the first, and until very recently continued to be the only, institution of a charitable nature in Montclair.

The so-called "fresh air" movement, which had begun its remarkable course about two years previously, under the leadership of the Rev. Willard Parsons, had brought to many people a fuller comprehension of the woes and needs of the little children of the poor than they had hitherto had; and the desirableness of a temporary refuge in the country for delicate and convalescent children had been discussed among them. It remained, however, for the Rev. Dr. A. H. Bradford to evolve from idle wishes and unfruitful sympathy a practical working force and direct it in the proper channel, and he can truthfully be called the founder of the Home.

On the first day of July, 1881, he convened at his house certain women connected with the several churches of Montclair, who were not actively engaged in other philanthropic work, presented the case to them, and asked their concurrence in his plans.

The names of these women who shared with him the first laborious efforts of the undertaking, and who, like himself, are perpetual honorary members of the Board of Managers, are as follows, viz. :

Mrs. Lewis Benedict, Mrs. Edward G. Burgess, Mrs. Sarah J. Churchill, Mrs. Henry A. Dike, Miss M. Elizabeth Habberton, Mrs. John R. Livermore, Mrs. O. P. Meacham, Mrs. Jasper R. Rand, Mrs. Samuel W. Tubbs, Miss Rachel Van Vleck, Mrs. Augustus White.

Acting on the principle that " if 'twere well 'twere done, 'twere well 'twere done quickly," the house owned by Mrs. Dr. Clark, at the corner of Plymouth Street and the Valley Road, was immediately hired, and in nine days, having been, meanwhile, comfortably furnished, provisioned, and provided with a competent matron, and with a financial backing sufficient to insure its continuance, it was thrown open for its first quota of guests assigned it by the Rev. Mr. Parsons. The number received during the ensuing summer reached a total of one hundred and twenty, the greater number remaining two weeks.

The prompt response of the townspeople to personal appeals for help, and the spontaneous sympathy of many, soon made it evident that the scheme was not unwelcome ; not a day passed but some friendly hand left at the Home its gift of food or clothing or flowers :

Each gave in his own way ; the little boy bringing his wagon filled with books and toys ; the butcher sending meat ; the grocer, household supplies ; housekeepers, bread from their own kitchens ; the printer giving his work ; the doctor, his services ; many, their time ; some, comfort and a cheering money ; others, words of God-speed.

During this early time, pressing duties demanded and afterward until more her entire attention, Miss Habberton was well-nigh the mainspring of the undertaking. A teacher by birth and an educator by profession, she possessed the golden key which unlocks the hearts of children, and her tact and ready sympathy did much to cheer the lives of the forlorn little guests, and make them realize the meaning of the sacred name of Home.

Much credit is likewise due to the first matron. Miss Jane Thompson. She was a model housekeeper under discouraging circumstances, and her firm, even rule, together with the sturdy uprightness of her character, could not but influence in the best

OLD BUILDING, CHILDREN'S HOME.

manner those under her sway ; while the Managers felt that they could safely rely upon the wisdom of her judgment. When the coming of autumn made this particular form of charity no longer necessary, the concensus of opinion among those most directly interested was in favor of continuing the Home as a permanent abode, where children would have the benefit of continuous care and instruction.

Consequently, the Children's Home Association was organized in October, 1881, by constituting all persons who had contributed five dollars to the support of the Home members of the Association. At the same time, a constitution was adopted, a Board of Managers chosen, and it was decided to petition the Legislature of New Jersey for articles of incorporation as a permanent institution to whose benefits " children of both sexes under twelve years of age, in needy circumstances or deprived of one or both of their natural protectors, by death or otherwise, might, at the discretion of the Managers, be admitted." The first Board of Managers comprised the following names : Mrs. O. P. Meacham, President ; Mrs. John R. Livermore, Vice-President ; Miss M. E. Habberton, Secretary ; Mrs. Jasper R. Rand, Treasurer ; Mrs. Henry A. Dike, Mrs. Lewis Benedict, Mrs. Mary E. Morrison, Mrs. Shepherd Rowland, Mrs. Samuel W. Tubbs, Mrs. Edward G. Burgess, Miss Rachel Van Vleck, Miss Harriet J. Cooper, Mrs. George W. Lord, Mrs. Samuel Porter, Mrs. George H. Mills, Mrs. James H. Ogilvie, Mrs. E. E. S. Haughwaut, Mrs. D. F. Merritt.

Advisory Board.—Mr. William J. Hutchinson. Mr. Charles I. Reeves, Mr. Samuel Crump, Mr. Wallace W. Egbert, Mr. Dorman T. Warren. Mr. William T. Jones, Mr. George H. Mills; Matron. Miss Jane Thompson.

The certificate of incorporation bears date October 3, 1882. During the same fiscal year the President, Mrs. Meacham, severed her connection with the Home and removed from Montclair. The annual report of that date characterizes her as "one of the most earnest and efficient workers, the memory of whose faithful service and co-operation in all details of the Home work will long be gratefully cherished."

In May of 1883 Mrs. Henry A. Dike was elected to the Presidency—a position which she held four years and until failing health and domestic calamity forced her to abandon the work she loved and for the performance of which she was peculiarly fitted.

To one intimately acquainted with Mrs. Dike no words could do justice to her lovely character; and to one who did not know her, no words could convey an adequate idea of the sweet strength, intellectual poise and rare "common sense" blended in her personality. To the service of the Home she brought ripe culture, a trained judgment and quick insight into people and affairs; while her social influence secured it wide support and her gracious affability disarmed hostile criticism.

NEW BUILDING, CHILDREN'S HOME.

During her administration the financial standing of the Home was sufficiently assured to warrant the purchase of a house and three acres of land on Gates Avenue.

The house was enlarged under the gratuitous supervision of Mr. H. Hudson Holly, and, as far as could be, adapted to the requirements of its new occupants, who, in 1886, took possession of it. In the same year a re-organization of the association was effected whereby its scope was enlarged and all the privileges of Orphan Asylums secured to it, including the adoption and indenturing of children having no other guardian.

In common with every institution depending upon voluntary contributions for support the Home has not escaped periods of depression and discouragement, but at the present time it is prospering in its work and is liberally sustained. The extreme generosity of Mrs. George Inness, Jr., a former manager, has made it possible to erect a new and commodious building skillfully contrived for the special requirements of its family of thirty-five children, particularly for the isolation of the sick.

The substantial structure now in process of erection is half timbered, the lower story being of dressed brownstone, and promises to be an architectural ornament to the town.

As was to be expected in the passage of time, the personnel of the Board of Managers has undergone many changes. Some of the best known and most influential women of Montclair have served upon it for varying periods ; but only two of the original members—Mrs. Shepherd Rowland and Miss Harriet J. Cooper—have remained continuously to the present time. Its first great loss by death was that of Mrs. Samuel Porter—a woman zealous in all good works, but finding here a special field for her love and energy ; a crayon portrait of her bright face adorns the parlor of the Home, recalling sunny memories and commemorating a great misfortune. Mrs. Dike was the next to be called ; and although her active participation in its affairs had terminated some time before, her helpful interest continued to the last. Mrs. Porter's bequest of $1,000 was the first large gift to the Home and was followed by a bequest of $3,000 from Mrs. Dike.* In the year just passed, still another most lovable woman and faithful worker, Mrs. Charles H. Benedict, has obeyed the summons to "Come up higher." Hers was a nature that "made sunshine in a shady place," and no one associated with her will ever forget her unfailing kindliness.

> "The good they planned to do
> Shall stand as if 't were done.
> God finishes the work
> By noble hands begun."

At the present time the Home is under the able management of the following named individuals : President, Mrs. Stephen W. Carey ; Vice-President, Mrs. Decatur M. Sawyer ; Secretary, Mrs. Wilson W. Smith ; Corresponding Secretary, Mrs. Benjamin W. Graham ; Treasurer, Mrs. F. J. Drescher ; Mrs. Shepherd Rowland, Mrs. William H. Power, Mrs. M. F. Reading, Mrs. Thomas Gladding, Mrs. Amory H. Bradford, Miss Harriet J. Cooper, Mrs. Harry Littlejohn, Mrs. J. Soutter Porter, Mrs. Edwin P. Benedict, Mrs. James S. Brown, Mrs. G. D. Finlay, Mrs. William L. Guillaudeu, Mrs. Wallace W. Egbert, Mrs. John Wilts, Mrs. John Weeks, Mrs. William Miller, Mrs. Franklin W. Dorman.

Advisory Board.—Mr. C. D. Anderson, Mr. Paul Babcock, Mr. C. D. Thompson, Mr. Charles Burgess, Mr. George P. Farmer.

The spirit in which the Home was conceived and the high ideal which has ever been kept in view are indicated by the following extracts taken, almost at random, from the published annual reports :

" Without disparaging other forms of Christian endeavor nothing can have more forcible claims upon our attention than the neglected youth of our own vicinity. 'What shall we do with the children ?' is an anxious question equally to the philanthropist and civil economist ; it knocks at the doors of our responsibility with an urgency that will not be denied and must be met by every one who regards the common weal which these boys and girls, soon to be men and women, can do much to promote or impede.

"To the children gathered here the institution is indeed their Home ; and it is the earnest endeavor of its managers to make it represent all that a *model* home should be. Not only have the children been well-cared for, physically, as their healthy and neat appearance at church, and in the public schools plainly testifies, but they have acquired habits of punctuality, industry, self-dependence and mutual forbearance, which are invaluable in any station ; while the lessons inculcated in the principles of Christianity and respect for sacred things cannot fail to be a guide and defence to them in times of doubt and temptation.

"Whenever practicable, a small sum is charged for board, but inability to pay is not allowed to militate against the admission of any child whose needs are pressing. Neither is any one rejected because of unworthy parentage, for, say what we may, many things have been decided for us at birth, and it is not to every one that the qualities which insure success are given. Incompetency and thriftlessness in the parents are disorders to be carefully eradicated from the children by compelling patient continuance in well-doing until diligence and thoroughness become second nature. Strong as are hereditary tendencies they often yield to the stronger agencies of education and environment.

* In 1887 a gift of $1,000 was received from the Misses Charlotte L. and Josephine Wilson, of Orange, in memory of their parents, who lived many years in Montclair.

"The children under our care are gathered from homes desolated by death or intemperance, and while they are chiefly orphans, it must not be forgotten that there is a worse orphanage than that of death, and that children may be orphaned in the saddest sense, though both their parents are living."

The Children's Home is the embodiment of the principle of modifying wrong tendencies and preventing future evil. It seeks earnestly to do its share toward the solution of current social problems; it labors not only to promote a higher intelligence but to instill useful household and hygienic knowledge; to form habits of personal purity, industry and obedience to authority.

MRS. SAMUEL M. PORTER.—At a special meeting of the Board of Managers of the Children's Home, held in memory of Mrs. Samuel M. Porter, on Wednesday, May 21, 1884, the President made the following remarks:

"We are met here to-day to speak a few words of love for our dear friend and co-laborer, Mrs. Porter, and to put on record our sense of our great loss, our sorrow for ourselves, and our deep sympathy for those who were nearest and dearest to her. And when that is done, all that we can do for our dear friend is done, and we must take up our daily life, and and we go on without her, the work of this Home.

"We cannot trust ourselves to say how much she will be missed. The actual labor which she performed here was very great. Time and strength were repeatedly given when most of us would have felt that we were excused from the task. And to this labor was added the most skillful planning and forethought and a most loving influence over all. To know what a power she was in this Home we have only to remember the faces of the children when Mrs. Porter came.

"Shall we ever forget her presence here Sunday afternoons, or cease to hear her cheery, energetic, encouraging tones as she led or directed the children?

"Brightness, cheerlove and untiring helpfulness were her strongest characteristics. 'Sweetness and light' marked every step of her way.

"But our great loss, great as it sinks almost out of sight in comparison with the loss which those of her own household have sustained.

MRS. SAMUEL M. PORTER.

Yet we must believe that God has purposes of love toward them, and that in some way, which we cannot see, He will make even this, which seems to us an irreparable loss, a source of blessing.

"We said that we could do no more for Mrs. Porter. But her influence over us will always remain. We shall keep her in our hearts, and we shall remember forever the love, the unselfishness, the wonderful brightness and cheer, the readiness with which she divined and ministered to every one's need, and the loving outpouring of her life.

"Such a memory can but lead us to strive, each in her own way, to catch the spirit of that life and graft it upon her own."

The following preamble and resolutions were then offered and adopted:

"Whereas, It has seemed right to the Supreme Ruler of the Universe to remove from us by death our sister associate, Mrs. Mary Treadwell Porter, and while we submit to the decree of Him who doth not willingly afflict, it is with hearts chastened by grief over the loss of a dear friend and beloved associate; and

"*Whereas*, We lament her death, not only as a valued member of society and a cherished friend and neighbor, but especially as a co-laborer in the management of the Children's Home, in which she engaged earnestly, assiduously and hopefully, and in every department of which we shall continually miss her guiding and helping hand; be it therefore

"*Resolved*, That we extend our heartfelt sympathy to the family so sadly bereaved, and prayerfully commend them to the loving care of that Friend who is 'a refuge in every trouble, and a very present help in time of need.'

"*Resolved*, That these resolutions be entered upon our records, and a copy of the same transmitted to the family of the deceased."

The Annual Report of the Association for 1884 contains the following in relation to Mrs. Porter's connection with the institution:

"Possessed of dauntless energy of character, unusual executive talent and public spirit, Mrs. Samuel Porter was engaged in many and various enterprises, and her loss will be keenly felt in divers directions and by many people.

HILLSIDE AVENUE.

Warm as were our individual friendships is our personal grief severed, it is in our of an association, in laborers, that we are place. As a manager from the beginning, identical with her fatigue where its prosand her sanguine temspirit lightened and the entire Board.shine she was always every child in the child knew her and was their sympathy Sunday afternoon her smile flashed its instantly understood As a member of the tee, and Chairman of mittee, her labors but what higher her, or anyone, than to every trust.midst of life and its has fallen from her

for her, and deep as over ties so abruptly capacity as members which we were joint to consider her in this of the Home, almost she made its interests own. She knew no perity was concerned, perament and joyous cheered the labors of "In storm and sunat her post. She knew Home, and every loved her. So close with her that, in their singing, her glance or intelligence and was and obeyed by them. Executive Committhe Wardrobe Comhave been incessant; praise can we accord that she was faithful "Suddenly, in the activities, the work hands, and 'with no

slow gradations of decay,' she has passed on through the Beautiful Gate into eternal life; and the rich voice that has so long led the children's hymns of praise has gone to swell a nobler chorus in the wider air of Heaven * * * * *."

The beautiful traits of character that adorned the life of Mrs. Porter were due not only to careful training and early environment, but she inherited from her ancestors—who were among the most notable men in New England—that strong religious sentiment and earnest desire to do good that controlled all her actions and led her continually to seek the happiness of others regardless of herself.

Mrs. Porter was born in New York City, March 23, 1847. Her maiden name was Mary T. Treadwell; she was the daughter of John G. Treadwell.

Mrs. Porter was educated at the Albany Female Academy, and was graduated June 19, 1866. She was married, March 23, 1871, to Samuel M. Porter, youngest brother of Nathan and Thomas Porter (see history of Porter Family) and a member of the firm of Porter Bros. & Co., merchants, of New York City. Mrs. Porter resided in New York for some years after her husband's death, March 19, 1876. Desiring to be near the home of her husband's brothers she removed to Montclair in the spring of 1879, and built the residence No. 20 Harrison Avenue, now occupied by her father and her children. She left two children—Bertha Treadwell and Charles Willson.

MOUNTAIN-SIDE HOSPITAL ASSOCIATION.

The necessity for a public hospital in this locality was brought about by an incident which occurred in the summer of 1890, the particulars of which are given in the Secretary's report of the Association:

"A lady driving through the streets of Montclair one day, during the summer of 1890, saw a little child fall from a third story window to the flagged pavement below. Her sympathies being aroused, she stopped to inquire into the condition of the little one. The child was seriously injured and needed prompt attention. Her heart ached to see him, bleeding and unconscious, placed in a grocery wagon and carried away, and on her way home the question uppermost in her mind was: Why, when there is so much of comfort and plenty in our town, is there not a place provided to which those suffering from accident or sickness, and who are unable to secure proper treatment in their homes, can be carried? The thought began immediately to take shape. Her heart warmed more and more on the subject, until she was compelled to enlist the interest of her friends, which resulted in a meeting called to consider the establishment of a Hospital in Montclair, held at the residence of Mrs. Denby, on Mountain Avenue, June 10, 1890."

There were sixteen persons present, twelve ladies and four gentlemen. Dr. Francis was appointed Chairman, and, after considerable discussion, the Rev. Dr. Bradford offered the following

Resolution: "That in our opinion the time has come when some movement should be made looking toward the establishment of a hospital in our midst."

The resolution was adopted and a committee appointed, to report a plan of organization, etc., which was done, and action taken in accordance therewith. At a subsequent meeting a Board of Governors was appointed, consisting of twelve ladies from Montclair, eight from Bloomfield, four from Glen Ridge, and three from Caldwell. It was decided at this meeting that the Association should be known as the Mountain-side Hospital Association.

The Association was regularly incorporated under and in pursuance of a certain act of the Legislature of the State of New Jersey, entitled "An Act to provide for the incorporation of Associations for the erection and maintenance of Hospitals, Infirmaries, Orphanages, Asylums, and other Charitable Institutions," approved March ninth, A. D. eighteen hundred and seventy-seven, and the several supplements thereto. The following named Governors were appointed to manage its affairs for the first year:

Nannie C. Fellowes, Justine Friend Porter, Jane F. Dodd, Margaret Jane Power, Marie Heyburn Marshall, Mary E. Gilbert White, Mary Chapin Marcus, Harriet H. Duffield, Sarah P. Wyman, Irene E. Huestis, Ida R. Condit, Anna C. Duncan, Grace H. Upson, Martha C. Gallagher, Virginia Bioren Harrison, Sarah J. Bird, Kate B. Dalrymple, Harriet A. Bailey, Eliza Bowden, Caroline D. Crane, Susan C. Stout, Salome G. Howell, Malinda N. Van Vleck, C. Victoria Reynal, Rebecca M. Dodd, Adeline T. Strong and Anna S. Berry.

A cottage situated on Bay Street (the dividing line between Bloomfield and Montclair), was rented, a small addition made to it, and the hospital was formally opened on June 26, 1891. The medical staff consists of Dr. John J. H. Love, Dr. James S. Brown, Dr. Chas. H. Bailey, Dr. Richard P. Francis, Dr. Richard C. Newton, Dr. Edwin M. Ward, Dr. Wm. H. White, Dr. H. B. Whitehorne, Dr. John W. Pinkham. Consulting Physician; Dr. Henry Power, Pathologist.

During the first four months (to October 18, 1891) of its existence thirty-eight patients were treated. From October 18, 1891, to October 1, 1892, 125 new patients were admitted, and from October 1, 1892, to October 1, 1893, 156 new patients were admitted to its wards.

Miss R. G. Reed, a graduate of Bellevue Hospital Training School, was appointed Matron in September, 1891, and still serves in that capacity.

In March, 1891, the Board of Governors purchased a small tract of land near the cottage, which they used for a year and a half, and during the winter of 1892 and 1893 erected thereon a building 46 by 45 feet, four stories high, containing 18 rooms and a woman's ward for 10 beds, a men's ward for 10 beds, a maternity ward containing three beds, and an isolation ward with two beds, all connected by covered corridors eight feet wide. Bath-rooms, nurses' rooms and pantries are provided in addition to the above specified rooms. The total capacity is: Men's ward, 10 beds; women's ward, 10 beds; children's ward, 6 beds; maternity ward, 3 beds; private wards, 5 beds; isolation ward, 2 beds; total, 36 beds.

The total cost for land, building, furniture and permanent improvements to date has been $49,747.19.

In connection with the hospital a training school for nurses has been established, in which nurses are taught how to act in the various emergencies occurring in hospital and private nursing, as well as in the accidents of ordinary life. There is a systematic course of training in cookery for the sick, the serving of food and delicacies in a proper manner, and the feeding of helpless patients or those who resist food. The course of training includes a fixed course of instruction during two years from manuals and text-books, lectures and demonstrations. Eight nurses are now taking this course.

The Board of Lady Governors are all actively interested in the work, giving, through their various committees, much time and attention to the necessary duties. The funds for this work are all donated by residents of the several towns included in the territory from which the hospital draws its inmates.

The following is the list of the Governors, Officers and Advisory Board:

Officers. President, Mrs. Benjamin Strong; Vice-President, Mrs. Amzi Dodd; Recording Secretary, Mrs. Wm. M. White; Corresponding Secretary, Miss Elizabeth P. Freeman; Treasurer, Mrs. W. H. Power; Matron, Miss R. G. Reed.

Board of Governors.—Term expires 1894: Mrs. Amzi Dodd, Miss Kate Dalrymple, Miss M. C. Gallagher, Mrs. Wm. H. Power, Mrs. Benjamin Strong, Mrs. Wm. H. White, Mrs. A. F. Brown, Mrs. Robt. S. Rudd, Mrs. James Gallagher, Mrs. John Van Winkle. Term expires 1895: Mrs. Anthony Bowden, Mrs. D. D. Duncan, Mrs. Wm. Fellowes, Mrs. Chas. F. Harrison, Mrs. Lewis G. Lockward, Mrs. H. R. Norris, Mrs. Joseph Van Vleck, Mrs. Wm. F. Upson, Mrs. Chas. H. Huestis, Miss Euhlie Van Lennep. Term expires 1896: Mrs. Chas. H. Bailey, Mrs. Chas. T. Dodd, Mrs. Geo. S. Porter, Mrs. G. Lee Stout, Mrs. Josiah Decker, Mrs. Silas Stuart, Miss Margaret S. Jarvie, Miss Elizabeth P. Freeman, Mrs. R. C. Newton, Mrs. W. S. S. Hamilton.

Advisory Board.—Mr. Wm. H. Power, Mr. Paul Wilcox, Mr. R. S. Rudd, Mr. Chas. D. Thompson, Mr. Amzi Dodd, Mr. G. Lee Stout, Mr. F. Merriam Wheeler.

In 1894 a suitable lot was purchased on Highland Avenue and Sherwood Street, but it was deemed advisable to defer the matter of building for another year. In the meantime the building known as the Sheridan cottage, situated on a lot adjoining the hospital property, was rented for a year, and a small addition built to increase the accommodations. The formal opening took place on June 26th of that year. Thirty-seven cases were admitted the first year. These were treated by the Surgical and Medical Staff, which consisted of Dr. J. J. H. Love as President, and Drs. Newton, Bailey, Brown, White, Francis, Ward and Whitehorne. Dr. Pinkham was appointed Consulting Physician, and Dr. Henry Power, Pathologist.

The total amount of cash subscriptions and donations the first year amounted to nearly $5,000. In addition to this, numerous articles of clothing, etc., were donated by generous citizens, mostly ladies.

The President's report for the second year showed the actual running expenses to have been $4,362 for 125 patients, four to six nurses, three servants, and occasional extra help. A number of entertainments were given during the year, and the amount of the Building Fund was increased to the sum of $5,700. The new building for the hospital was begun early in the autumn of 1892, and completed in May of the following year. The *Bloomfield Citizen,* of May 27, 1893, contains the following description:

The new Mountain-side Hospital building just completed, and which will be formally opened to-day, is located on the southwest corner of Highland Avenue and Sherwood Street, and faces Highland Avenue looking eastward. The main building is of Colonial type, and was designed by architect John F. Capon, and erected under his supervision. The hospital buildings comprise the main building, a men's ward, a women's ward, and a maternity ward. They are built to surround three sides of a hollow square, and are all connected by a spacious corridor.

The new institution has been erected on the most approved plan for giving room, air and light, and the work has been done in a very substantial manner. The carpenter work was done by Israel Jacobus of Glen Ridge, the mason work by William Doyle of Montclair, the painting by John Jenkins of Bloomfield, and the plumbing by E. D. Ackerman of Bloomfield.

The main building is a four story building. It has a frontage of forty-six feet on Highland Avenue, and a depth of forty-five feet. A large piazza eight feet six inches wide extends the full length of the front of the building. The roof of the piazza is supported by heavy Colonial columns, and the roof is surmounted with an ornamental railing. The building is painted a soft Colonial yellow, with light cream trimming and green shades and shutters.

The interior is finished throughout with natural white pine and walls of hard finish. The flooring is of comb grained yellow pine and varnished. The building is heated by steam, lighted by gas, and the windows so arranged that every room in the building receives sunshine at some portion of the day. The steam piping and the radiators are all beautifully bronzed with a gold tinge.

In the plumbing work all the most approved devices have been used with a view to having the sanitary arrangement of the building as perfect as possible. The basement contains the laundry, coal room, heating apparatus, and the cold room. The latter contains an immense refrigerator, capable of holding a large quantity of ice and in which the meats and vegetables are kept. The floor of the basement is concrete except the laundry, which has a board floor. This room contains a large range and three earthen tubs. The heating apparatus is a Blake and Williams boiler of size No. 4. A dumb waiter starts from the basement and runs to the top floor of the building. On entering the first floor of the building through the large double doors from the piazza the visitor is ushered into a well lighted corridor eight feet wide, full length of the building. The first room on the left of the hall is the reception room thirteen by eighteen feet in dimensions. Directly opposite on the other side of the hall is the dining room. Adjoining the reception room is the dispensary twenty feet in size. Speaking tubes and call bells connect this room with every part of the institution. Following the dispensary is the operating room, eighteen by twenty feet. This room is supplied with two wash basins, hot and cold water and other necessary appliances. Next to the dining room with a butler's pantry intervening is the kitchen eighteen by twenty-six in size. It is equipped with a large double oven range ; an eighty gallon copper boiler, a serving table and a large dresser takes up one side of the room. A ventilating contrivance carries off all the odors arising from cooking. Connected with the kitchen is a refrigerator closet, with pot closet and store room. A stairway four feet six inches wide ascends from the right side of the corridor near the centre of the building to the second floor. At the head of the stairway on the second floor, the first room to the right is the children's ward, thirteen by eighteen. This room is heated and ventilated by the direct indirect system, taking the cold air from the outside of the building under the radiator. Turning to the left is the entrance to the main corridor of the same dimensions as down stairs, with the exception that the front is cut off for the misses' room. Light is admitted to the corridor from the hall at head of stairs, and the rear end. On the left of the corridor are four rooms for private patients, each ten feet six inches by eighteen feet, and on the right next to the lavatories is another room for private patients. The stairs to the third floor go up directly over those from the first floor and the corridor on this floor is the full length of the building with windows front and rear. The third floor contains four large bedrooms, two store rooms and two linen rooms. The fourth floor is used for general storage purposes. Particular attention has been given to the ventilation of the closet.

The corridor connecting the wards with the main building is six feet wide ; it is well lighted and heated. There is a fine concrete cellar under each ward. The wards are each supplied with a bath-room and hot and cold water, and a nurse room is attached to each. There is accommodation for ten patients in both the men's and women's wards ; three in the maternity ward.

The door for the reception of patients is at the rear of the corridor on the first floor. The ambulance can be driven into the square and backed up to this door. The old hospital building will be used as a fever room. It is isolated from the other buildings. Three large cesspools take the drainage from the whole institution.

THE MONTCLAIR EQUESTRIAN CLUB.

This unique and very successful Club was organized in 1876, although it was really started several years earlier in an informal manner by the young people of Montclair, devoted to horse-back riding and other social pastimes.

The first regular meeting was held at the residence of Mr. C. K. Willmer in the spring of 1876, at which time George H. Francis and Frederick Merriam Wheeler were elected President and Secretary, respectively. Among the other gentlemen who constituted its organizers were Carleton W. Nason, Edward W. Sadler, Charles J. Pearson, Charles Francis, C. N. Bovee, Jr., W. Lanman Bull, James R. Thompson, Charles K. Willmer, N. Sullivan, Arthur Foley and Dr. Frank Ely.

Among the lady members, and perhaps one of the most enthusiastic equestriennes, was Miss Florence Willmer (now Mrs. Frederick Merriam Wheeler) and to whose efforts was due the early success and permanent establishment of the Club.

The other lady members were as follows: Miss Bovee, Miss Nannie Thompson (now Mrs. Outerbridge), Miss Alice Thompson, Miss Amy Willmer, Miss Lord (now Mrs. Lloyd), Miss Mamie Clark, Mrs. J. W. Pinkham, Miss Grace Pillsbury, Miss Jennie H. Beach, Mrs. E. W. Sadler, Miss Draper, Miss DeLuze, Miss Hellen Sullivan (now Mrs. Delevan Baldwin, Miss Marion Torry, Miss Chittenden (now Mrs. Wm. E. Pinkham), Miss Power (now Mrs. Arthur Schroeder) and Miss Conradt.

The Club was afterward strengthened by the addition of the following: Alfred E. Beach, P. E. Van Riper, Frank Rogers, Thomas Russell, Dr. J. W. Pinkham, Charles A. Heckscher, Joseph A. Blair, John H. Wilson, Samuel Wilde, A. Ferguson Brown, W. Delavan Baldwin, J. C. Mott, J. M. Wing and others.

During the spring, summer and fall the Club had its regular riding parties at stated intervals, usually holding the meet at the residence of some one of the members, and during the winter months they had exceedingly attractive social evenings every fortnight. There were readings, recitations,

THE "RENDEZ-VOUS."

THE "MEET" AT ROSWELL MANOR.

vocal and instrumental music and dramatic performances—in short, this Club seemed to fill the place, in those days, now occupied by distinct societies, devoted to literature, music or dramatics.

At some of the equestrian meets it was a common thing to see twenty or thirty ladies and gentlemen in the saddle, and as this sport is exceedingly exhilarating the parties were usually very enthusiastic. The regular rides were on Saturday afternoons, but parties were often made up for moonlight nights, or for early morning rides.

At the meets there was always present, at the invitation of the host at whose house the meet was held, a party of friends to see the riders start.

During the second year, the Club inaugurated "hare and hounds" hunting. These paper chases gave considerable zest to the sport, and helped to keep up an active interest in the Club. A description of one of these paper chases taken from the *Montclair Times* of November 17, 1877, will give an excellent idea of the event:

"The Equestrian Club had their second hunt of hare and hounds Saturday afternoon, and from all we can learn the sport was decidedly exciting and enjoyable. The meet was held at the residence of N. Sullivan, Esq. Two prominent members of the Club, a lady and gentleman, represented the hares, and displayed equestrianship of exceptional merit by riding through some very difficult places. They gave their pursuers over an hour's chase across country, but were finally overtaken beyond the mountain near Verona Lake. Dr. Pinkham was Master of the Hounds, and managed his party so well that no accident occurred to mar the pleasure of the day. Miss Rogers was first in at the 'death,' and was awarded a sprig of evergreen to represent the 'brush.' These paper chases have been so successful that the members of the Club will have several more before the season closes. The next social meeting will be held Tuesday evening at the residence of J. R. Thompson, Esq."

The following year the Club imported a pack of beagle hounds and inaugurated "drag" hunting. The beagles, which were purchased in England, were perhaps the first lot of hounds of the kind brought to this country in any large number; being a much smaller dog than the regular fox-hound or harrier, they are slower running and better adapted where there are lady riders in the field.

The Club having become so enthusiastic over cross country riding, it was decided to permanently adopt hunting, and the name of the Club was changed to the Montclair Hunt, and Mr. Edward W. Sadler was made the first Master of Hounds.

The meet on Christmas-day (1878) at Mr. Sadler's extensive place on Grove Street will long be remembered in the history of this Club, as the host had invited the farmers from the country about, and a large number of friends, to see the hunting party start.

The next year the Club decided to procure a draft of regular fox hounds from the kennels of the Queens County Hunt of Long Island, and, in addition, engaged the services of the famous athlete and sportsman, Harry Howard, who continued in their employ until his death some years later. Howard was a typical specimen of a sturdy English huntsman, and his merry voice, as he encouraged his hounds onward, was often heard to the delight of the riders during the different chases. In the year 1879, Mr. Frederick Merriam Wheeler succeeded Mr. Sadler as Master of the Hounds, the kennels being located on the old Baldwin farm, now the site of "Roswell Manor," the present residence of Mr. and Mrs. Geo. Inness, Jr. About this time a number of members from Orange and other parts of the surrounding country joined the Hunt, among whom were Charles A. Heckscher, Henry N. Munn, Edward P. Theband, Frank E. Martin, Douglas Robinson, Jr., the Messrs. Hudnut and Charles H. Lee.

In 1880 the kennels were moved to the vicinity of Tory Corner, about half way between Montclair and Orange, and Mr. Henry N. Munn succeeded Mr. Wheeler as Master of the Hounds. The kennels were newly stocked with a draft of very fine fox-hounds purchased from the sons of Sir Hugh Allen, of Montreal, and the use of live foxes instead of the "drag" was inaugurated. From this time until within a few years ago the Club continued the practice of fox hunting, having changed its name from the Montclair Hunt to the Essex County Hunt.

In 1883 Mr. Charles A. Heckscher became Master of the Hounds, but was succeeded the following year by Mr. Edward P. Theband, who continued to carry on the hunting in a most successful manner until the Club was absorbed by the present Essex County Country Club. During Mr. Theband's time of office (1884 to 1887) the kennels were located in the Verona Valley, where there was plenty of pasture for the hunt horses, and a comfortable club house for the use of the members.

It was a great sight at the opening Meets every autumn to see the pretty little club house decorated with flowers and the Club colors, and presided over by a party of ladies to entertain the company, which latter never numbered less than 500 to 600 invited guests from the Oranges, Montclair, Bloomfield, Short Hills, Morristown, Newark and New York.

General Geo. B. McClellan was also a member of the Club about this time, and was frequently seen at these affairs, and his wife was usually on the reception committee, with Mrs. J. C. Wilmerding, Mrs. F. Merriam Wheeler and other well known ladies from Montclair and Orange. A band of music was always in attendance, and there was generally a high jumping contest of the hunting horses, after which an exhibition of the hounds on a "drag" hunt was given over the surrounding meadows.

Once every few years the Club gave amateur races, at which there was always considerable fun, if not expert sport.

It was in 1887 that the Country Club absorbed the Hunt, but the Montclair riding fraternity, desiring to still keep up the sport of horseback riding, re-organized the Equestrian Club, and during the last few years have been holding their Meets regularly at the residences of the different members—generally on Saturday afternoons during the spring and fall seasons.

The illustration on page 160 gives an excellent view of one of the Meets, which in this case was held at "Roswell Manor." In the party of lady and gentleman riders shown can be recognized the faces of some of the more recent members of the Club, whose names will be found among the list following, viz.:

Mr. E. A. Bradley, Mr. H. S. McClure, Mr. Ogden Brower, Mrs. A. Ferguson Brown, Mr. Seelye Benedict, Mr. Walter Benedict, Mrs. A. E. Bostwick, Miss Bussing, Mr. D. P. Cruikshank, Miss Darwin, Miss Hawes, Miss Campbell, Miss Birdseye, Miss Dening, Miss Conradt, Mr. and Mrs. Geo. Inness, Jr., Mr. F. A. Junkin, Mr. and Mrs. W. E. Marcus, the Messrs. Meyer, Mr. T. W. Porter, Miss Rodman, Mr. and Mrs. J. W. Stewart, Mr. T. W. Stephens, Mr. and Mrs. J. W. Kirlin, Mrs. Bart, Mr. Willis Sawyer, Mr. and Mrs. A. Shroeder, Mr. Tearle, Miss Russell, Miss Eleanor Junkin, Mr. and Mrs. F. Merriam Wheeler, and Mr. and Mrs. J. C. Mott.

MONTCLAIR CLUB.

That the Montclair Club has been a potent factor in the rapid increase in the population of the township since 1887, any one who has observed its workings and noticed its influence on the community will freely admit. Starting with a membership of one hundred and twenty at its first public meeting, it reached about four hundred within five years; and has afforded the means of pleasure and entertainment to more than four times that number annually.

The initiatory movement began in the early part of 1887. Mr. C. L. Topliff and Mr. H. C. Carter conceived the idea of starting a social club on a more general scale than had previously been attempted in Montclair, one which should merit the support of a large class of professional and business men who felt the need of recreation and enjoyment after the worry, care and anxiety incident to life in the great neighboring city. These gentlemen, knowing that several previous attempts had failed, deserve special credit for proceeding in a very thorough, careful and business-like manner, to lay a foundation which should insure ultimate success. They visited the leading clubs in New York, Brooklyn and Jersey City, and communicated with others at a distance—thoroughly informing themselves on all matters connected with club management; they studied carefully the organization-forms of many different clubs; and, finally, taking Lincoln Club of Brooklyn as a general model, prepared a tentative set of By-Laws and had them printed for distribution. They then submitted the matter to Messrs. Jasper R. Rand and William D. Baldwin, who, in turn, interested others; and on June 25, 1887, an invitation was sent out inviting co-operation, signed by W. D. Baldwin, Jasper R. Rand, E. A. Bradley, E. G. Burgess, H. C. Carter, C. L. Topliff, Frederick Engle, E. B. Goodell, S. Benedict, J. H. Wilson and R. G. Park.

The first meeting was held at the house of Mr. Baldwin, and subsequent meetings at the house of Mr. Bradley, and on July 27th, a large number of invitations were issued to attend a general meeting for organizing a club—the paper being signed by the above named gentlemen and others to the number of twenty five in all.

The public meeting was held in Montclair Hall, on August 1, 1887. Mr. W. D. Baldwin opened the meeting; Mr. John R. Howard was elected Chairman, and Mr. H. C. Carter, Secretary. The enrollment showed one hundred and twenty names of those wishing to become members. The By-Laws were discussed and with modifications adopted. The first Board of Directors were nominated and elected—consisting of W. D. Baldwin, Seelye Benedict, E. A. Bradley, E. G. Burgess, H. C. Carter, W. V. Carolin, E. B. Goodell, John R. Howard, Dr. John J. H. Love and Cyrus L. Topliff; and the Directors were instructed to have the Club incorporated, and to make arrangements for temporary quarters, pending the purchase of ground and the erection of a permanent home. The first officers were Jasper R. Rand, President; W. D. Baldwin, Vice-President; H. C. Carter, Secretary, and C. L. Topliff, Treasurer; Mr. Richard G. Park was elected a Director in place of Mr. Carolin, who resigned.

After much searching and investigation of eligible sites it was determined to purchase the property of Dr. John J. H. Love, on Church Street, as being both near to the business centre of the town and yet sufficiently retired. This was done at a cost of $10,000, and the old dwelling-house on the premises was altered for temporary quarters until such time as a club house should be put up, it being then expected that $25,000 would erect, furnish and equip the building. The Board of Directors was instructed to invite plans and estimates from five different architects. To these a sixth was added, later, when the scheme proposed included a music hall in addition to the club house proper. The firm of Lamb & Rich, of New York, were finally selected as the architects, and the praise universally given their completed work proves the wisdom of the selection. The fine bowling alleys in the basement, the convenient arrangement of the offices, retiring rooms, card rooms, billiard and pool rooms, and reading room, on the first floor, the ladies' parlors and dressing rooms and the beautifully proportioned music hall on the second floor; the special dining room, steward's apartments, kitchen, etc., on the third floor, and the artistic harmony and architectural beauty of the whole house, within and without, combine to make it an exceptionally admirable edifice.

Mr. C. L. Topliff, of the Board of Directors, was very active in the matter, and some of the best of the interior arrangements were of his suggestion. The Board passed a special vote of thanks to Mr. Topliff for his "long continued and intelligent efforts in the interest of the Club, and especially in the matter of the new club house, with music hall attached." The original plans contemplated the erection of a building to cost $50,000, but the addition of the music hall to the main building involved an additional outlay of $10,000. A loan on first mortgage was secured from the New York Mutual Life Insurance Co. of $25,000 at 5 per cent., and bonds were issued under a second mortgage to the amount of $35,000 at 6 per cent. Probably the two gentlemen most successful in "placing" bonds and inducing club members and others to join in securing the financial basis for the enterprise, were the President, Mr. Rand, and Mr. Seelye Benedict, of the Board of Directors. This once assured, matters moved vigorously.

The Building Committee consisted of Messrs. John R. Howard, Frederick Engle, Dr. John J. H. Love, and Seelye Benedict. The club house was begun in August, 1888, and completed ready for occupancy in the autumn of 1889. A brilliant opening took place on November 7 of that year, and the "Anniversary Reception" has been an "institution" ever since.

In a circular issued by the Board of Directors, accompanying a set of reduced engravings of the floor plans and some perspective sketches, for the information of the members when the taking of the bonds were in process, is this statement:

"The building of this house, securing by its accommodations a large income, secures also possibilities of artistic, social, dramatic, musical, and various interesting and useful entertainments, which will make life in Montclair a different thing for every gentleman and lady in it. Especial arrangements are included, both in the house and its use, for the accommodation and pleasure of the ladies and families of members. This Club is intended to be instrumental in promoting, and not in disturbing, home happiness; to offer attractions to the feminine as well as to the masculine element in our society, and it is hoped that the earnest interest of Woman may be aroused and her potent influence exerted in its favor."

It was unquestionably a wise move to solicit the feminine interest of the town, for that was the final turning of the scale which made the financial scheme a success, assuring the building of the house. To the credit of the management of the Club it must be said that the promises of the circular have been fulfilled in letter and in spirit. Monday is "Ladies' Day," when the house is thrown open to them from noon to midnight, and in the evening special entertainment is provided and music for dancing in the hall. This is of regular recurrence; while the special occasions of all agreeable kinds that call both men and women together in the hall are constant, and have truly "made life in Montclair a different thing." The Presidents have been Messrs. J. R. Rand, Edward G. Burgess, J. R. Howard and Dr. J. J. H. Love; the Vice-Presidents, Messrs. W. D. Baldwin, J. R. Howard, J. H. Wilson, Dr. J. J. H. Love and J. R. Livermore. After the expiration of Mr. Carter's term as Secretary and Mr. Topliff's as Treasurer, the offices were combined, and have since been filled successively by Messrs. Edwin B. Goodell and Wm. L. Ludlam.

One feature of the Club management is peculiar: "No intoxicating beverages shall be sold or allowed in the club house." This house rule has often been condemned by club men as sure to be the ruin of the Club; but, as a matter of fact, in the minds of the best observers it has been and is the most influential factor in the Club's undeniable success. "Sweethearts and wives" are not afraid to see the men they love go there, and mothers feel safe in having their young men become junior members in a club where they can find rational enjoyment and recreation, without danger. And more than this; the men think what the women feel; there is many a member of the Montclair Club who drinks wine at his own table, and yet is firm in the determination to keep the club house free from the perils of club tippling.

This and other features of the wise and business-like management of its affairs from the first have kept the Montclair Club in a continuous career of agreeable usefulness and financial prosperity. It is without doubt the most important representative institution of the town, and every inhabitant of Montclair will hope for it a long and prosperous life.

THE OUTLOOK CLUB.

The object of this association is to hear the discussion of themes of current and vital interest by prominent thinkers in various fields, and especially to enlarge the views of its members by the wholesome process of hearing " the other side."

The Outlook Club was foreshadowed in a series of fortnightly gatherings for the discussion and reading of pure literature during several winters, from December, 1883, to the spring of 1887, held in the lecture room of the First Congregational Church, Rev. Amory H. Bradford, pastor. The writers and readers were drawn from the town at large, and the general interest made the unpretentious evenings signally successful.

When, in 1887, the Montclair (Social) Club was organized, the efforts of many active workers centred in that, and the literary evenings were discontinued; but two years later, when the Club had passed its infancy, and built a fine club house, it was thought good to revive on a somewhat broader plan the holding of meetings for general culture. Accordingly, the new Outlook Club was organized. A meeting was called in the Congregational Church lecture room, by a printed note of invitation, signed by Rev. Dr. Bradford, Rev. Dr. Junkin, Rev. Dr. Carter, Mr. Paul Wilcox, Mr. John R. Howard and others; and on a raw, sleety, stormy evening, early in December, 1889, about seventy five ladies and gentlemen came together, adopted their brief constitution, and appointed a committee to nominate officers and Executive Committee, and to prepare for a December public meeting.

The first officers elected were: *President*, John R. Howard; *Vice-Presidents*, Rev. F. B. Carter and John R. Livermore; *Secretary*, Wm. H. Peck; *Treasurer*, F. Merriam Wheeler. *Executive Committee*: The foregoing officers, and Rev. A. H. Bradford, D.D., Rev. W. F. Junkin, D.D., Paul Wilcox, Wm. H. Peck. Mr. Paul Wilcox was President for the years 1893-94.

The experiment was a marked success from the very first. The membership was fixed at 200, but the limit has since been raised to 300, and there is always a large waiting list for vacancies at the end of the year. Each member pays annual dues of $4 and receives two tickets for each of the eight meetings. This gives an income of $1,200 a year and insures good attendance at the meetings. The hall of the Montclair Club, where the meetings are held, will seat 500, and is always well filled and sometimes crowded when the Outlook has it. The only expenditures, aside from the rent of the hall, programme and ticket printing and postage, are the compensation and expenses of the speakers. There are eight meetings a year—on the fourth Friday of each month, excepting June, July, August and September, so that the average allowable monthly expense per meeting is $150. This giving out of so large a number of tickets to eight literary entertainments of high grade, at an average cost to the membership of twenty-five cents per ticket, is certainly unusual and evinces the great popularity of this method of educational entertainment. The first public meeting after the organization of the Club was held in Montclair Hall, with an audience of about two hundred. The subject discussed was, "The Sensuous and the Spiritual in Modern Literature." The speakers were Rev. Wm. Hayes Ward, of the *Independent*, Miss Agnes McC. Hallock and Rev. Wm. F. Junkin, D.D.

The range of subjects since discussed has been very wide, including philosophy, science, literature, art, industry, and even politics and religion, although subjects belonging to the two classes last named have had to be handled with delicacy. With observance of all the courtesies of debate, varied and opposing views have been effectively presented with entire freedom; and the educational value of this is highly appreciated, not only by the members but by the community. The speakers are always explicitly informed beforehand that their remarks are expected to be expository rather than disputatious, and the opening speaker furnishes a brief abstract of his positions in advance for the information of those upholding "the other side." Thirty-five minutes are nominally allotted to the first speaker, and, if there be but one opponent, thirty-five minutes to him also. If more than one, twenty minutes each, while the first speaker is allowed ten minutes for rebuttal. These limits, however, are rarely enforced, and considerable latitude is given to the speakers. The character of the work done by this Club is shown in the selection of subjects and speakers—the latter including many of national reputation.

In 1890, *January*, "The Press—Its Powers and Responsibilities." Rev. Chas. H. Eaton, D.D., Joseph Howard, Jr., and Alexander D. Noyes.

February, "'Looking Backward'—Nationalism." Rev. W. D. P. Bliss, John R. Livermore, Clarence W. Butler, M.D., Prof. Daniel de Leon and Charles H. Johnson, Jr.

March, "Prohibition—or What?" E. C. Wheeler, Robert Graham, D. F. Merritt and Starr J. Murphy.

"The Negro Problem" was divided into two parts. The first meeting devoted to that subject was held in *April*. George W. Cable, the novelist, and Rev. J. C. Price, D.D., the famous colored orator, taking part. "The Other Side," was heard in *November*, Thomas Nelson Page, the writer, and Rev. Wm. Junkin, D.D., pastor of the Presbyterian Church of Montclair, formerly of Charleston, S. C., being the speakers.

May, 1890, "Shelley—Poet and Man." Rev. J. H. Ecob, Hamilton W. Mabie. *Readings*, Miss Josephine Rand.

October, "The Economic Theory of Protection." Prof. Van Buren Denslow and Henry George.

December, "The Higher Education of Woman." Mrs. Alice Freeman Palmer, Mrs. Ella Dietz Clymer, Rev. A. J. McVicar, D.D., and President James W. Taylor, of Vassar College.

In 1891, *January*, "The Silver Question." Hon. A. J. Warner, of Ohio, and Prof. J. Laurence Laughlin, of Cornell University.

February, "The American Newspaper." Chas. R. Williams, Paul Wilcox and A. H. Siegfried.

March, "'Looking Forward' (Christian Socialism)." Thomas G. Shearman and Hon. Albion W. Tourjee.

April, "The Theological Outlook." Rev. David Waters, D.D., of Newark, N. J.; Rev. Francis G. Peabody, D.D., of Harvard University; Rev. Charles F. Deems, D.D., of New York; and Rev. Charles H. Hall, D.D., of Brooklyn.

May, "The Impulse Behind Literature." Hamilton W. Mabie, of *The Outlook*, and Robert Nevin, of London, England; *October*, "The Golden Age—Can it be Realized?" Rev. William Lloyd and Starr Hoyt Nichols; *November*, "The Pulpit and Politics." Rev. B. B. Tyler, D.D., and Rev. Charles H. Hall, D.D.; *December*, "Ideal Anarchy," Daniel Greenleaf Thompson, Edwin B. Goodell and John R. Livermore; *January*, 1892, "Economic vs. Political Union among English-Speaking Peoples (The Question of Canada)," Hon. Erastus Wiman and William H. McElroy, of the *New York Tribune*; *February*, "Should Immigration be Restricted?" Prof. Hjalmar Hjorth Boyesen and Hon. A. B. Nettleton, Assistant Secretary of the United States Treasury; *March*, "The New Education,"

Prof. Geo. H. Palmer, Prof. A. C. Perkins, President Geo. A. Gates and Dr. Nicholas Murray Butler; *April*, "Woman's Place in the Labor Field." Moncure D. Conway and Miss Kate Field; *May*, "Did Lord Bacon Write the So-called Shakspeare Plays?" Starr Hoyt Nichols and Roger Foster; *October*, "Relative Value of Arctic and Tropical Exploration," Gen. W. A. Greely and Cyrus C. Adams, of the *New York Sun*; *November*, "The Treatment of Criminals," Professor Charles L. Collin, W. M. F. Round and P. T. Quinn; *December*, "Did Lord Bacon Write the So-called Shakespeare Plays?" Part II., Starr Hoyt Nichols and Hamilton W. Mabie.

The subjects discussed in 1893 were: *January*, "Evolution," Prof. W. B. Scott, followed by a conference of questions and answers; *February*, "Spirit Apparition and a Future Life," Rev. Minot J. Savage, D.D., Prof. James H. Hyslop of Columbia College; *March*, "A Discourse on the Drama," Joseph Jefferson; *April*, "Sunday, and the World's Fair," Rev. Arthur Brooks, Rev. William Lloyd; *May*, "Realism and Idealism," F. Hopkinson Smith; *October*, "The Silver Coinage Question," Hon. R. P. Bland, of Missouri, Hon. M. D. Harter, of Ohio; *November*, "Labor and Law," Rossiter W. Raymond, Ph.D., J. W. Sullivan, of the Federated Union of Labor; *December*, "Business Government for Cities," St. Clair McKelway, Esq., of the *Brooklyn Eagle*, Dr. Lewis G. Janes, President of the Ethical Association of Brooklyn.

The instant success and continuous strength of this admirable institution is a credit to its managers, not only, but to the town, which, with so many other attractions of social, musical, dramatic and general entertainment, has for over four years steadily supported the Outlook Club. It is valued by all who have enjoyed its sessions, and has educated an audience trained to quick appreciation and intelligent taking of a speaker's points, which never fails to impress the experienced talkers who discuss their selected topics.

TARIFF REFORM CLUB.

The nucleus of this small but energetic association must be looked for in a group of men who in 1882-83, chiefly under the inspiration of Col. George A. Miller, met for occasional readings and discussions of questions relating to taxation. In 1884, when the Blaine-Cleveland presidential campaign shook the party loyalty of so many Republicans, these men and others—forty-five altogether—formed the "Independent Republican Organization," having as *President*, J. R. Howard; *Secretary*, J. C. Hewitt; *Executive Committee*, G. A. Miller, E. B. Goodell, S. A. Swenarton, Theo. St. John, E. B. Merritt, F. B. Littlejohn and C. H. Taylor. The organization did earnest work in that campaign, their influence then being in favor of the Democratic national candidate, while for local and congressional matters remaining Republican. The effect of their work as "protesting Republicans" was seen in the reduction of the customary Republican majority in Montclair, on the national ticket, from 198 to 94, in the election in which Mr. Cleveland was first chosen President.

In the campaign of 1888, the same men, with some accession of numbers (seventy-five in all), formed the "Tariff Reform Campaign Club," having the same Executive Committee, enlarged by the addition of Alexander D. Noyes, Dr. C. W. Butler and John R. Livermore, and, as officers: *President*, J. R. Howard; *Vice-President*, E. B. Goodell; *Secretary*, Starr J. Murphy; *Treasurer*, Chas. F. Droste. In that campaign the Club was very active, with circulars, addresses, and a large public meeting. Although Mr. Cleveland was defeated, his "Tariff Message of 1887" to Congress had become a rallying ground for tariff reformers generally, and while the Campaign Club of Montclair had finished the work for which it had been organized, its members were still interested in the cause which had brought them together, and wished for a permanent organization. Soon after the election, therefore, a meeting was called at the headquarters of the Club, and a committee appointed, consisting of Starr J. Murphy and Edwin B. Goodell, to confer with the Reform Club of New York City and neighboring campaign clubs with reference to this, and to consider the feasibility of some form of alliance with the New York Reform Club.

At an adjourned meeting, held Nov. 20, 1888, after winding up the affairs of the old Club, a resolution was adopted to effect a permanent organization to be known as the "Montclair Tariff Reform Club," for the purpose of discussing the principles of natural taxation and also of other subjects of current political interest, notably that of reform in electoral methods and the civil service.

The officers of the new form of the old Club were: *President*, Edwin B. Goodell; *Vice-President*, William A. Houghton; *Treasurer*, Joseph C. Noyes; *Recording Secretary*, Starr J. Murphy; *Corresponding Secretary*, George A. Miller. These were members, *ex-officio*, of the Executive Committee, which included also John R. Livermore, John R. Howard, Theo. St. John, William L. Guillauden, to whom were added in May, 1889, C. W. Butler, C. A. Scholtz, F. A. Angell, A. D. Noyes, and L. A. Wight.

A vigorous educational campaign was begun and every available means used to reach the voters of the District and impart information on matters relating to the tariff. Arrangements were made with the *Montclair Herald*, and this became an important medium of communication with the public. Literature obtained from the New York Reform Club was also freely distributed. Public meetings were held and the subjects discussed by prominent speakers. The result of these and other similar influences was shown at the next ensuing election, in November, 1890, when Thomas Dunn English, representing the cause of tariff reform, was elected to Congress from the Sixth Congressional District, the first time in many years that this district had been represented by other than a Republican.

On February 6, 1891, following the election, a public dinner was held in Montclair at which there were present prominent speakers from abroad, among whom were, Congressman John DeWitt Warner, Charles B. Spahr, Hon. Thomas Dunn English and others. In response to an invitation from the Club a letter was received from Grover Cleveland, in which, after expressing the customary regrets that he could not attend the dinner, he said:

> It gives me great pleasure to note the growth of Democratic sentiments and strength in my native county, and to know that the cause of tariff reform has commended itself to the voters of the Sixth Congressional District. These circumstances furnish exceptional persuasion to an invitation to meet those who by organized effort are pushing on the good work in the county where I was born.
>
> Nothing can excuse the Democratic party if, at this time, it permits the neglect or subordination of the question of tariff reform. In the first place, the principle involved is plainly and unalterably right. This of itself should be sufficient reason for constant activity in its behalf.
>
> Secondly, we have aroused a spirit of inquiry among our countrymen, which it is our duty to satisfy; and finally, there may be added to these considerations, the promise of success held out to the party which honestly perseveres in the propagandism of sound and true political principles.

In 1892 the Club took an active part in the movement for securing a Cleveland delegation from New Jersey, at Chicago, and did good work in the campaign which followed, especially in the circulation of brief tracts, the pamphlet publication "Tariff Reform," and other literature, and in a public meeting. The Club, including a number of excellent and effective speakers, all its public meetings, dinners, etc., have been unquestionable successes. The officers at that time were: *President*, John R. Howard; *Vice-President*, Edwin B. Goodell; *Recording Secretary*, Wm. Whitney Ames; *Corresponding Secretary*, Alex. D. Noyes; *Treasurer*, Theodore St. John; *Executive Committee*, the officers, and Wm. A. Houghton, L. Allyn Wight, Joseph C. Noyes, Geo. A. Miller and Starr J. Murphy. A copy of its address to voters having been sent to Mr. Cleveland, the Club received the following letter from him:

GRAY GABLES, BUZZARD'S BAY, MASS., August 1, 1892.

I have received with great satisfaction your letter of July 25th, giving some account of the Tariff Reform Club formed at Montclair, New Jersey. Although you distinctly stated that you did not look for a reply to your letter I cannot refrain from complimenting the Club and the author of the "Open Letter to Voters," which you inclose. The statement therein contained of the theories and methods of the Republican party and the purposes and objects of the Democratic party, it seems to me, cannot be improved upon. If this is a specimen of the kind of work which will be undertaken by your Club the best results cannot fail to be apparent from its efforts.

Mr. Cleveland's election, and the widespread victory of tariff reform at the polls, in November of that year, gave the occasion for another public dinner in Montclair Club Hall, which, for the time, closed the Club's activity. Having no local aims, and being bound to no political party, the organization follows its own course, sometimes being quiescent for months, sometimes having a series of readings and discussions of matters it is interested in, and taking action whenever it sees an opportunity to advance its principles. Its most recent work was, in 1894, to address the New Jersey Democratic representatives in Congress upon the pending tariff legislation.

The object of the Club as stated in its Constitution is " to promote honest, efficient and economical government, having for its immediate purpose effective agitation in favor of tariff reform as the chief necessity of the time, and also the advancement of a non-partisan civil service, the business administration of public affairs, and the improvement of electoral methods, as essential to a genuine ' government of the people, for the people, and by the people.' It purposes seeking these ends by discussion, by disseminating information, and by all other means which tend directly or indirectly to forward them."

MONTCLAIR GLEE CLUB.

Few of our large cities can boast of a more successful or better managed musical organization than the Montclair Glee Club, and it would be difficult to find in any suburban town of its size so large a number of well trained voices. The projectors of this enterprise had no other end in view than that of mutual improvement and entertainment. It began in 1885 with a double quartette composed of mutual friends who met at one another's houses. Others became interested and the number was finally increased to 36, and it was then decided to form a permanent organization. Prof. E. J. Fitzhugh, the well-known musical conductor and instructor, was engaged as leader. In order to meet the increased expenditure, the Club determined to try the experiment of giving a public concert. All the members volunteered their assistance, and were assigned their several parts as follows :

Sopranos: Mrs. L. L. Ballantine, Miss A. M. Dike, Mrs. L. T. Johnson, Mrs. E. F. Bedell, Mrs. J. B. Hawes, Miss Stella A. Livermore, Miss Emma C. Conradt, Mrs. C. A. Hutchings, Miss Fanny G. Lugar, Miss Laura B. Mills, Mrs. Flora C. Niven, Mrs. Chas. E. Van Vleck.

Contraltos: Mrs. Geo. N. Ashley, Mrs. H. W. Hobbs, Mrs. C. H. Tissington, Miss Kate Conradt, Miss Clara Reading, Mrs. H. K. Hawes, Miss Ella Shafer.

Tenors: James Atkins, C. H. Taylor, Arthur B. Davis, Chas. E. Van Vleck, W. N. Guyer, P. J. Hogan.

Bassos: E. F. Bedell, Dr. John B. Hawes, William Y. Boyle, John Porter, Geo. A. Harkness, H. E. Taylor, Dr. Arthur F. Hawes, C. H. Tissington.

The first concert was held at the Presbyterian Chapel, June 1, 1886. It was conducted by Prof. Fitzhugh, and was in every respect a decided success. Selections were made from well-known composers, and were rendered with skill, delicacy, and good taste and judgment. The audience was a critical one, and showed their appreciation by frequent demonstrations of applause.

Thus encouraged, the Club persevered in their efforts during each year to raise it to a higher plane. Well known artists were secured from abroad, and the citizens of Montclair were treated to a number of first class entertainments, and evinced their willingness to support them by subscribing to a sufficient number of tickets at a price which guaranteed the Club against loss. Two concerts have been held each season, all of which have been successful, and the members have shown a marked improvement in form and execution. Prof. Fitzhugh remained with the Club for two seasons, and was succeeded by Mr. A. D. Woodruff. He proved to be a capable and energetic conductor, and managed the affairs with skill, tact and good judgment. The Club has been in successful operation for about eight years, and has proved itself worthy of the high esteem in which it is held by the people of Montclair. In order to meet the increased expenditures from year to year associate members have been added who are pledged to secure the Club against financial loss. The present membership is 56.

The first officers of the Club were : President, Dr. John Hawes; Vice-President, E. J. Bedell.

Secretary, C. H. Taylor; Treasurer, Wm. S. Boyle; Librarian, C. H. Tissington. Executive Committee: Miss Kate Conradt, Miss Alice M. Dike, Dr. A. F. Hawes, John Porter, Mr. C. H. Taylor.

Present Officers: President, Thomas Russell. First Vice-President, John Porter; Second Vice-President, Chas. H. Baker; Treasurer, John R. Anderson; Secretary, T. E. Lyon.

Those who have served as Presidents of the Club are: Dr. J. B. Hawes, two years; W. V. Carolin, John Porter and Thos. Russell; the latter, elected in 1889, is still in office.

MONTCLAIR DRAMATIC CLUB.

Montclair is composed largely of a class of business men who have been accustomed to theatrical and other amusements, and while there are many other attractions not hitherto enjoyed by them, the lack of this class of entertainment was to many a great deprivation. Mr. and Mrs. Guillauden who had at different times elsewhere conducted amateur theatricals with success, invited a few friends to an entertainment at their own home, and it was then suggested that a public entertainment be given for the benefit of the Children's Home. Others were invited to take part, some of whom had had experience in amateur theatricals. After several rehearsals, an entertainment was given for the above object, on the evening of April 26, 1889, at Montclair Hall. The plays selected for the occasion were "My Lord in Livery" and "I've Written to Browne." The plays were well cast and each one did their part well. A large and appreciative audience greeted them with frequent applause. Unstinted praise was lavished on the participants in this affair, who, thus encouraged, determined to effect a permanent organization; the result was "The Montclair Dramatic Club." Its first officers were: W. L. Guillauden, President; Starr J. Murphy, Vice-President; R. M. Boyd, Secretary; Alexander D. Noyes, Treasurer. The constituent members were:

Miss Minnie Benedict, Mr. A. E. Bostwick, Mrs. A. E. Bostwick, Miss L. R. Bauden, Mr. R. M. Boyd, Jr., Miss Mary Clark, Miss Kate Conradt, Miss M. H. Cunningham, Miss H. B. Cunningham, Mr. C. D. Du Bois, Mrs. C. D. Du Bois, Mrs. D. D. Duncan, Miss Lillian Fenn, Miss Bessie K. Francis, Mr. A. T. Greene, Mr. W. L. Guillauden, Mrs. W. L. Guillauden, Mrs. R. M. Hening, Mrs. Frank Hill, Mr. D. Brainerd Hunt, Jr., Mr. George Inness, Jr., Mr. W. E. Marcus, Mr. Starr J. Murphy, Mrs. Starr J. Murphy, Mr. A. D. Noyes, Miss Josephine F. Rand, Mr. A. F. Reichelt, Mr. A. T. Taylor, Mrs. C. E. Van Vleck, Miss Charlotte Weeks.

The Club has had a very successful experience, and has been free from the petty jealousies that frequently disturb and often disrupt organizations of this character. The annual entertainments given by the Club have been very successful, and delighted audiences have received them with marked favor. The selections have covered a wide range and include farces, farce comedy, high comedy, and melodrama of the lighter sort, and some of the participants have developed decided histrionic talent—notably Miss Josephine Rand (now deceased), daughter of Jasper Rand, Esq., one of the most promising of all those who took part in these entertainments. She was greatly admired for her artistic representations of the characters she assumed and for her many personal qualities. Others have distinguished themselves as amateurs of more than ordinary ability. Among these may be mentioned the names of Mrs. Henry Powers, née Mary Clark, Miss May Marvin, daughter of Dr. Marvin, Miss Stella Bogue, Mrs. D. D. Duncan, Mrs. Du Bois, Mrs. A. F. Bostwick, Miss Benedict, D. B. Hunt, Jr., A. D. Noyes, Starr J. Murphy, Clarence Churchill, Mr. F. T. A. Junkin, Mr. A. F. Bostwick, George Inness, Jr., Mr. A. S. Greene and others.

Besides the projectors of the enterprise under whose able management these entertainments have been conducted, the names of Mr. Alexander D. Noyes, Mr. Starr J. Murphy and Mr. D. B. Hunt, Jr., are worthy of special mention.

The Club has now over a thousand dollars' worth of first-class scenery, costumes, etc., and a complete outfit of everything required for this class of entertainment. The present officers are: Clarence Churchill, President; R. M. Boyd, Jr., Vice-President; Charles Bull, Secretary and Treasurer.

MONTCLAIR LAWN TENNIS CLUB.

This Club started as a local organization in the spring of 1885, with a membership of about one hundred, composed of Montclair people interested in the game. A large plot of ground on Fullerton Avenue, belonging to Mr. Alfred E. Beach, was laid out into courts. Tournaments were held from time to time, and invitations extended to players of national reputation to participate. As an inducement valuable prizes were offered by the Club, and the contests brought together large numbers of people from the surrounding country and from other States, thus indirectly contributing to the prosperity and growth of the township. Several of the members became experts at the game, and challenges were given to and received from other clubs. Among the popular and well-known players who have participated in these games are: Howard A. Taylor, H. W. Sloenm, E. L. Hall, Clarence Hobart, and others. The interest in the Club increased each year and received the hearty support of the community. The tennis grounds being required for building purposes by the Episcopal Church in 1893, the Club was obliged to suspend operations, having no other available grounds. The first President of the organization was Thomas Russell, with Robert M. Boyd, Jr., as Treasurer, and James D. Freeman as Secretary. Mr. Russell was succeeded by John R. Livermore, followed by F. W. Gwinn, Seelye Benedict, and Robert M. Boyd, Jr., the present head of the organization.

UNDER THE WILLOWS,
Beside Llewellyn Road.

Chapter XIV.

THE MEDICAL PROFESSION OF MONTCLAIR.

S has been stated in a previous chapter, that among the inducements held out to emigrants at an early period to settle in New Jersey, were that it was "worthy the name of Paradise," because in addition to its natural advantages it had " no lawyers, *physicians* or parsons."

When the Connecticut colonists settled Newark they brought with them their "parson," but the records do not show that there was any "physician" among them. It is said that the Rev. Abraham Pierson, then pastor, exercised the functions of parson and physician, but Dr. Stephen Wickes in his "History of Medicine in New Jersey" says: "After very diligent search into the history, prior to and after his residence in New Jersey, we have not found a shred of testimony to sustain the claim for him to a medical record."

There were few persons at that period whose knowledge of medicine exceeded that of every intelligent housewife of the present day, and the progress that had been made in the art of medicine up to that time was very small. Pennyroyal, boneset, peppermint, and a few other herbs, were the standard medicines kept in stock by the careful housewife.

Dr. J. Henry Clark, in "The Medical Men of New Jersey in Essex District, from 1666 to 1866" says that William Turner was "the oldest Newark physician, of whom we find any definite record." Reference is made to him in the "Town Record" of 9th of March, 1741, that " the burying ground was sold to Dr. William Turner for the year ensuing."

Dr. James Arents, a Hollander by birth, naturalized in 1716–17, practiced medicine in Newark from that time until 1750.

The inhabitants residing in the vicinity of Cranetown and Bloomfield for more than a hundred years were dependent on Newark physicians. The first one mentioned in this locality was Dr. Joseph Dodd, of Bloomfield, who lived directly opposite the present Glen Ridge station, on Bloomfield Avenue. His practice extended throughout the entire territory, including what is now Bloomfield and Montclair. Dr. Eleazer Ward, father of the present Dr. Edwin M. Ward, of Bloomfield, lived on the Common of that town, and attended some families in the western portion.

Dr. Joseph A. Davis, a pupil of Dr. Joseph Dodd, succeeded him, and was the principal medical man for all West Bloomfield, until the arrival of Dr. J. J. H. Love, in 1855. There was at that period, also, a Dr. Isaac Dodd, of Bloomfield, a large, fine-looking, elderly gentleman, who did considerable medical work in this section, about 1852. A Dr. Janes from New York City settled here, but for some reason his stay was very short. About 1852, Dr. Elias L'Hommedieu, an elderly man from Sussex County, N. J., settled here, but died in the course of a year or two after.

At the time of Dr. Love's arrival in 1855, there was no physician in this immediate locality. Subsequently an old gentleman by the name of Kittridge, settled here, and had a small practice during the absence of Dr. Love in the United States service from 1862 to 1865. Dr. Joseph A. Davis, of Bloomfield, however, attended to most of Dr. Love's patients. The first Homœopathic physician who located here was a Dr. Brower, who died in this vicinity.

Dr. J. A. Pinkham was the first regular practitioner of the old school after Dr. Love. Dr. Clarence Butler, of the new school, came in 1872. Dr. Wm. B. Berry, now of Pasadena, Cal., lived and practiced here, until his health failed, some years before Dr. Brown. Dr. J. S. Brown came next, followed by Dr. Richard P. Francis, Dr. Anna L. Smith, Dr. Richard C. Newton, Dr. Levi W. Case, and Dr. Luther Halsey. Dr. Charles H. Shelton and Dr. Foster are recent additions connected with the new school of practice.

JOHN JAMES HERVEY LOVE, M.D.—According to tradition, John Love, the ancestor of this branch of the Love family, emigrated from the north of Ireland about 1728, and settled at Fagg's Manor, Chester County, Pa. A John Love is mentioned in Savage's " Genealogical Dictionary," as having settled in Boston as early as 1635. Dr. Love's line of descent is from the first John mentioned through *Thomas, James* and *Robert*. Thomas, the great-grandfather of Dr. Love, served in the " Pennsylvania Line " during the War of the Revolution. He was commissioned May 12, 1775, Second Lieutenant of Fourth Battalion, organized in Chester County, Pa. His commission is signed by " John Morton, Speaker of the House," and is filled out, Thomas Love, "*gentleman*," a term in those days of class distinction that referred to the highest class in the social scale. He served as Aid-de-camp to Gen. Samuel Cochrane. Samuel, supposed to be a brother of Thomas, held positions of trust in Chester County, Pa., and during the colonial period served in Capt. Abraham Smith's Company of Col. Irvine's Regiment. Rev. Robert Love, the father of Dr. Love, was settled as a Presbyterian minister at Harmony, Warren County, N. J. He married Anna Thompson Fair, daughter of John Fair, of Warren County, N. J., who was a nephew of Gen. William Maxwell, a distinguished officer of the Revolution.

Dr. J. J. H. Love, son of Rev. Robert and Anna Thompson (Fair) Love, was born in Harmony Township, Warren County, N. J., April 3, 1833. He was prepared for college at a private school in Pennsylvania, was graduated at Lafayette College, Easton, Pa., completing his course of study in the Medical Department of the University of New York. He removed in 1855 to his present locality, which was then an agricultural region and formed a part of Bloomfield. For many years he was the only physician in the neighborhood, and his practice extended north to the Great Notch, south to Orange, and in a westerly direction took in all the Verona Valley. His practice grew with the rapidly increasing population, and he acquired a strong hold on the people, interesting himself in every enterprise and improvement in building up a new town which he foresaw was destined to become an important suburb of the great metropolis. The breaking out of the war checked these movements, and Dr. Love, like many others, felt called upon to sacrifice his personal interests, and sever the ties which bound him to this people, by offering his professional services to the Government, which was then in great need of skilled surgeons and physicians.

He was commissioned Surgeon of the 13th Regiment, N. J. Vols., and was mustered into the U. S. service August 25, 1862. On March 23, 1863, he was assigned duty as Surgeon-in-Chief of the Third Brigade, First Division, Twelfth Corps, Army of the Potomac, which duties he performed in addition to his regimental duties until August 1, 1863, when, under special orders from Corps Headquarters he assumed the position and duties of Surgeon-in-Chief of First Division, Twelfth Army Corps. He continued in this position until January 28, 1864, when he resigned his commission and was honorably discharged from the U. S. service. During the entire period he was engaged in field service.

As a volunteer Surgeon he was sent out by Gov. Olden and assisted in the transportation and care of the wounded after the battle of Williamsburg, Va., May 5, 1862. He was present and on duty at the battles of Antietam, September 17, 1862; Chancellorsville, May 1, 2 and 3, 1863; and Gettysburg, July 1, 2 and 3 of the same year. The Twelfth Army Corps of which he was then Surgeon-in-Chief, First Division was subsequently sent West to re-inforce Sherman's Army ; and was consolidated with the Eleventh, forming the Twentieth Army Corps. Dr. Love was constantly with the army in the field, and assisted in caring for the wounded after the battles of Lookout Mountain and Missionary Ridge, near Chattanooga, Tenn., in December, 1863. Previous to his departure for and his service in the West, while Surgeon-in-Chief of First Division, Twelfth Army Corps, he was a member of General A. S. Williams' staff. He served at different times under Generals Hooker and Slocum. His rapid promotion from the position of regimental surgeon to that of Surgeon-in-Chief of a Division, was not the result of friendly or political influence, but of personal achievement and his skill as a surgeon.

On his retirement from the army he returned to Montclair and resumed the practice of his profession. He was heartily welcomed by his large circle of friends and acquaintance, and his practical knowledge of surgery, acquired by long experience in the army, proved of great advantage to him in the renewal of his practice, as shown by his constantly increasing clientèle and the increased confidence of the community in his skill as a physician.

As a citizen he has been foremost in all public improvements since the establishment of the present township, and in the cause of education he has been pre-eminent. From 1857 to 1862 he was Superintendent of Public Schools of Bloomfield township; and he was one of the first after the erection of the new township of Montclair to advocate the change from the old system of district schools, adapted only to the wants of a country village, to the enlarged facilities and more modern improvements enjoyed by the people of our large cities and towns. To these improvements more than to all others is due the remarkable growth and prosperity of the township, and it is due largely to the indefatigable efforts of Dr. Love that Montclair enjoys the proud distinction of having not only one of the largest and best equipped school buildings in the State of New Jersey, but a well conducted graded system, that affords equal facilities for rich and poor alike, unsurpassed by any suburban town within a radius of forty miles of the great metropolis.

The strong personality of Dr. Love, the wisdom and tact displayed by him on all occasions, were important factors in bringing about these results and in overcoming the opposition which was manifested during the early period of these movements. Dr. Love has been connected with the School Board since 1865, the first six years as its President, and from that period down to the present time as its Secretary. Considering the demands on his time, due to his professional duties, he has done more to promote the cause of education than any other man, and, if measured by the standard of dollars and cents, his contributions to the cause would exceed those of any other citizen to any and all of the improvements that have been made in the township.

He has held many positions of trust and honor, and has assisted in founding several of the societies and associations with which he has been connected. He was President of the Essex District Medical Society in 1873; President of the Orange Mountain Medical Society in 1886. He gave encouragement to the enterprise, and assisted the ladies of Montclair and the adjoining township in founding the Mountain-side Hospital Association, of which he has been President since its organization. He was a member of the Board of Managers of the Rosedale Cemetery Co., at Orange, N. J., and assisted in its reorganization. He has been President of Montclair Gas and Water Co. since 1886; was for three years a member of the Montclair Township Committee; member of the Board of Trustees of the Presbyterian Church. His interest in military affairs began in 1861, when he was made Colonel of the First Regiment, Essex Co. Militia, continuing until he went to the front in 1862, as Surgeon of the Thirteenth Regiment, N. J. Volunteers, with subsequent promotions given in his military record. Since the close of the war he has been active in promoting the cause of the veterans of the war. He assisted in organizing the Society of Veterans of Twelfth Army Corps, and has been its Secretary since 1881. He was one of the organizers of the Society of Veterans of Thirteenth Regiment, N. J. Volunteers, was elected its Treasurer in 1886, and President in 1889. He is also a member of the New York Commandery, Military Order of the Loyal Legion of the United States.

Dr. Love married, in 1860, Miss Frances J. Crane, daughter of Judge Zenas Crane, of Montclair, son of Aaron, who was the son of Job, who is supposed to be a grandson or great-grandson of Azariah, son of Jasper Crane, one of the founders of Newark, N. J. The issue of this marriage is Edith, who married Charles E. Stockder, of Meriden. Conn., Marion (unmarried), and Leslie, now a Sophomore at Princeton, Class of '95.

In person Dr. Love is large, well proportioned, of commanding presence, resolute, determined, full of nerve and energy; cautious until convinced, after careful investigation, of his position, when no amount of pressure can swerve him from the course he has marked out for himself. Generous alike to friend and foe, fearless in the discharge of every known duty, regardless of public opinion or personal considerations, a man of spotless integrity and uprightness of character.

JOHN WARREN PINKHAM, M.D.—RICHARD PINKHAM, the American ancestor of this family, came from England before 1640, with the New Hampshire Colony, and settled in Dover, N. H. He was ordered by a vote of the town in 1648, to "beat the drumme" on Lord's day to call the people to meeting. The spot where he dwelt is said to be the same on which stood the Pinkham garrison, which Richard afterward made his habitation.

Elijah, the grandfather of Dr. Pinkham, removed to Gardiner, Me., in 1800.

The mother of Dr. Pinkham was Fanny Sampson, daughter of Cyrus, a direct descendant of Henry Sampson, of Plymouth, who came over in the *Mayflower* in 1620.

Dr. John W. Pinkham, the subject of this sketch, was born in Gardiner, Me., was prepared for college at the "Friends" Boarding School, in Providence, R. I., and was graduated at Haverford College, Delaware County, Pa., in 1860, and was for some time afterward engaged in teaching school. He was instructor at Haverford College for a year, and was graduated in medicine at Bellevue Hospital Medical College, New York, in 1866. He also attended a course of lectures at Berkshire (Mass.) Medical College, and at the University of Michigan at Ann Arbor. He began practice in New York City in 1866, and one year later removed to Montclair. Dr. Love at that time was the only practising physician in this locality. Dr. Pinkham soon achieved a reputation as a skillful physician, and was not long in obtaining a lucrative practice.

Dr. Pinkham continued in active practice for nearly a quarter of a century, and during that period made many warm friends, who had great confidence in his skill as a physician. A severe illness in 1890 necessitated a change of climate and a temporary abandonment of his practice, much to the regret of his large circle of friends and acquaintances.

Dr. Pinkham has given much attention to the subject of sanitary science, and has made occasional contributions to the various medical journals throughout the country. His contribution to "Wood's Household Practice of Medicine" on the subject of Hygiene, Sewerage and Water Supply, forms one of the most interesting chapters of that work. It was translated into the Spanish language and copied into the Spanish medical journals. He has read papers on this subject before the New Jersey Sanitary Association, and on various medical subjects before the Essex Medical Society and the Orange Mountain Medical Society.

Dr. Pinkham has been too much absorbed in the practice of his profession to take part in the public affairs of the town; he served, however, as township physician for some years. He was the first physician ever appointed to the position, and held it until he retired from active practice in 1890. He was one of the founders of the Mountain-side Hospital, and has been for some time consulting physician. He assisted in organizing the New Jersey Academy of Medicine, and is a member of the Essex District Medical Society, and the Orange Mountain Medical Society. He served one term as President of the County Society. He is a republican in politics, and served one year as President of the Montclair Republican Club.

Dr. Pinkham married Cornelia, daughter of Stephen A. Frost, Esq., of New York City, whose immediate ancestors were settled at Matinecock, L. I.

Stephen A. Frost, above-mentioned, the father of Mrs. Pinkham, removed to Montclair in 1867, where he died in 1892.

John Warren Pincham M.D.

Mrs. Pinkham's mother was Matilda Bowne, daughter of Robert L. Bowne, son of George Bowne, of Flushing, L. I., who was the son of Robert Bowne.

George L. Bowne, referred to above, great-grandfather of Mrs. Pinkham, married Abigail Smith, daughter of Hon. Samuel Smith, of Burlington, N. J., a descendant in the sixth generation of William Smith, of Braham, Yorkshire, England, born A.D. 1570, one of the founders of the Society of Friends. This was a family of great prominence which held lands directly from the Crown.

Hon. Samuel Smith, the great-great-grandfather of Mrs. Pinkham, was Treasurer and Secretary of the Council of New Jersey, under the British Crown, in the period immediately preceding the Revolution. He was the author of a valuable history of the Province of New Jersey.

THE BUTLER AND WILLARD FAMILIES.

CLARENCE WILLARD BUTLER, M.D. Dr. Butler was born in Bellevue, Ohio, May 1, 1848, only son of Rev. Jeremiah Butler, a Congregational minister, who was a graduate of Oberlin College, Ohio, and one of the most thorough theologians of his day. His first pastorate was at Bellevue, Ohio, from whence he moved to Western New York, and was settled for seventeen years at Fairport, Monroe County, N. Y. He was the son of *Stephen*, born in Durham, Conn., March 26, 1776, married Hannah Ward; grandson of *Jeremiah*, born in Durham, Conn., 1746, married Ann Coe, and was descended probably—from Dea. Richard Butler, who came from Braintree, Essex County, England, and settled in Cambridge, Mass, in 1632, and removed thence with Rev. Thomas Hooker's party to Hartford, Conn., where he had sixteen acres in the first division.

The ancestors of the Butler family came from Normandy to England with the Conqueror. Their original name was Fitz Walter, from Walter, one of their ancestors. Theobold Fitz Walter came to Ireland with Henry II., in 1172, and had the office of Chief Butler of Ireland conferred on him, the duty attached to which was to attend on the Kings of England, and present them with the first cup of wine. From the office of Butlership of Ireland they took the name of Butler.

The maiden name of Dr. Butler's mother was Louisa Olive Willard, whose ancestor, Major *Simon Willard*, born in Horsmonden, England, 1605, came to New England in 1634. He was a noted man in the colony; was Commander-in-Chief of the military force in King Philip's War. He had a son, Rev. *Samuel Willard*, born Jan. 31, 1640, pastor of Old South Church, Boston. He had by his first wife eight and by his see and wife fourteen children—twenty-two in all. One of these, a son, Major *John Willard*, born 1673, had a son, Rev. *Samuel Willard*, born at Kingston, Jamaica, 1705, was educated at Boston, Mass., and became the first settled minister in what is now the State of Maine; he married *Abigail Dwight*, a descendant in the same line of President Dwight, of Yale College; they had issue, four children, one of whom, Rev. Joseph Willard, D.D., was President of Harvard College. The eldest son, Rev. *John Willard*, D.D., also married a Dwight, and was the father of Rev. *Joseph Willard*, who married Olive Haven, daughter of John Haven. His leading characteristics were: "conscientiousness, mirthfulness, strong common sense and order." His son, John Haven Willard, born at Lancaster, N. H., Feb. 4, 1795, married Beede Mary Cooper, daughter of Hon. Jesse Cooper, of Canaan, Vt. Their third child was *Louisa Olive Willard*, born Aug. 15, 1821.

Dr. C. W. Butler, the subject of this sketch, was prepared for college by his father, and entered Oberlin, but was compelled to leave during the Freshman course on account of ill health. He decided to enter the medical profession, and was induced by his mother to adopt the "new school" of practice. He began his studies with Dr. C. J. Challie, of Fairport, N. Y., and took his courses of lectures at the Cleveland and the New York Homœopathic Medical College, graduating in 1872. He settled the same year in Montclair and was the first in this locality to introduce the new school of practice. He had neither friends nor influence, and found the people of this locality wedded to the "old school" and strongly opposed to any new experiments. The outlook was anything but promising, and would have deterred many young men from attempting any innovation contrary to long established customs, but

Dr. Butler had come to stay, and determined to "fight it out on this line," even if it should take the best years of his life to accomplish the desired results. He had been a close student and was fully convinced that the new school of practice—and *no other*—was the correct one, and to this he has firmly adhered from the first. Inscribed on his escutcheon was the motto of the Willard family, " *Gaudet patentia dures* "—patience in overcoming difficulties—; he waited, and persevered; his progress was slow at first, but "nothing succeeds like success," and he was successful in his treatment in many cases where old methods had failed. His clientèle increased from year to year, and includes many of the oldest and wealthiest families in the township. He confines himself strictly to the practice of medicine, leaving that of surgery to others. His professional opponents are among his warmest personal friends. During his long and successful practice, Dr. Butler has acquired more than a local reputation. He is not only called into consultation with his professional brethren in different parts of New Jersey, but in New York and Brooklyn, and is recognized as one of the most skillful and best informed practitioners of homœopathy in this State. He is a member of the American Institute of Homœopathy, the International Hahnemannian Association, of which he was President in 1891 ; of the New Jersey State Medical Society, of which he was President in 1888 ; was Vice-President of the International Homœopathic Congress, which held one of its five yearly meetings at Atlantic City, N. J., in 1890.

Although one of the busiest men in the township, Dr. Butler has found time to devote to public affairs. As a staunch democrat he has fought with the minority for twenty years, and has witnessed the steady growth of his party both in strength and in numbers, frequent accessions having been made from the ranks of his opponents. For sixteen years he has been Chairman of the Democratic Committee and the recognized leader of the party in Montclair, and through his able management the party has reduced the majority of its opponents and occasionally scored a victory. The party was without an "organ" in Montclair until 1892. In 1890, a stock company was organized which started the *Montclair Herald*, run in the interest of the democracy. It was not a political or financial success, and, in 1892, Dr. Butler purchased the stock, and made it a thorough democratic paper. Within a year it doubled its circulation, and is now recognized as one of the best party journals in the State.

Dr. Butler inherits the prominent traits of both his paternal and maternal ancestors. He is aggressive without being offensive. Obstacles to success in any undertaking must be removed—by direct assault if necessary, if not by slow approaches, but nothing can swerve him from a course he has once marked out for himself.

In October, 1877, Dr. Butler married Mary E., oldest daughter of H. H. and Eunice Wilcox, of Adrian, Michigan.

Though not a "society man," Dr. Butler is prominent in all social affairs. He was one of the original members of the Montclair Club, and served three years as a member of the Board of Control. He is a member of the Watchung Lodge, F. & A. M., and though heartily endorsing the principles of Freemasonry, is able to devote but little time to that special object.

JAMES SPENCER BROWN, M.D.—Dr. Brown may be classed among the "Waterbury Colony" of Montclair, having been born in Waterbury, Conn., March 23, 1863, and is a direct descendant of one of the early settlers and most prominent residents of that town. His American ancestor, Francis Brown, was one of the company who came to New Haven in advance of the colony and spent the winter of 1637-8 in a hut on the corner of what is now Church and George Streets. He signed the Colony Constitution in 1639. He married Mary Edwards, in England, and, among other children, had a son *Samuel*, who married Mercy Tuttle in 1679; *Francis*, one of their children, born in 1679, married Hannah Alling; of this marriage there was a son *Stephen*, born August 10, 1713, who married Mabel Bradley ; they had a son *Stephen*, born January 15, 1750, who settled in Windsor, Conn., where he married Eunice Loomis. Of the issue of this marriage there was a son *James*, born in Windsor, December 2, 1776. James became a resident of Waterbury, Conn., in 1802, and found employment with Lieut. Ard Williams, a manufacturer of fire-arms. In early life he connected himself with a military company, and finally became colonel of the regiment. He was an original partner in the third rolling mill erected in Waterbury in 1830, afterward known as the Brown-Elton Company, and continued a member of that firm until his death. He was a member of the First Congregational Church, and was made deacon in 1848, and during the remainder of his life was known as "Deacon Brown." He was also a prominent member of the Masonic Fraternity. It is said of him, that he "was remarkable for his truth and industry, and sobriety"; a most exemplary man, faithful in all the relations of life. He married Lavinia Welton, of Windsor. Among other children, they had a son Augustus, born August 20, 1841, who married Sophia, daughter of Jacob De Groff, of Poughkeepsie, a descendant of one of the old Holland families of New York State.

James Spencer Brown, the subject of this sketch, was the son of Augustus and Sophia (De Groff) Brown. He was early left a fatherless orphan, and at about eight years of age he removed with his mother and sister to Brooklyn, N.Y. He received a thorough education at the Polytechnic Institute, and after two years' experience in a business house he determined to study medicine, having a natural taste in that direction. He entered the College of Physicians and Surgeons, graduating in 1884, and soon after went to Europe, continuing his medical studies at the University of Heidelberg and Guy's Hospital of London. Being fully equipped for the duties of his profession he returned to his native land in 1885. His mother at this time had been five years a resident of Montclair, and through the advice of his professional brethren he was induced to locate there. Although the youngest in his profession his skill as a surgeon and physician soon became known, and he has enjoyed a continued increasing and lucrative practice. He has performed many important operations in surgery, and was the first one of the local surgeons to perform an abdominal section, and was also the first to operate for appendicitis. He performed successfully the operation of symphyscotomy, the first of the kind in this State, and the twenty-ninth in the United States. He is highly esteemed by his professional brethren:

J. S. BROWN, M.D.

is Secretary of the Orange Mountain Medical Society, a member of the Essex Medical Society, and has been for six years township physician.

He married, December 9, 1887, Helen B., daughter of Thomas Russell, Esq., one of the most prominent and best known citizens of Montclair, and a representative of one of the old Scottish families. It is of great antiquity, its ancestors having accompanied Edward III. to the siege of Berwick and to the battle of Hallydon Hill in 1333. The Russell, or, as it was formerly written, Rozel, from whom this family descends, then settled in Scotland, and was denominated Russell, of that ilk. The motto, "Promptus," inscribed on the arms, has always been a prominent characteristic of this family.

CHARLES HENRY SHELTON, M.D.—Daniel Shelton, the founder of the Shelton family in this country, came from Yorkshire, England, in 1686, and settled in Stratford, Conn. He resided in Stratford until about 1707, when he settled at Long Hill, in Huntington, where he died in 1728.

Charles S. Shelton, the father of Charles Henry, was a native of Huntington, and a lineal descendant of Daniel, the ancestor. He became a missionary physician, stationed at Madura, East Indies. He married Miss Henrietta Hyde, a descendant of the famous Annie Hyde of England, through William Hyde, the American ancestor, one of the original proprietors of Norwich, Conn.

Dr. Charles Henry Shelton was born at Jaffna-Patam (Jaffna-Patam was a small island on the north-west coast of the large island, Ceylon), on the Island of Ceylon, May 14, 1854, his father having been a temporary resident at that place. His father returned to this country in May, 1856, and settled in Davenport, Iowa; from thence he moved to Springfield, Ill., in 1859, and at the breaking out of the war became surgeon of the First Engineer Corps of the West. Charles H., the son, began his studies at the public school of Springfield, and in 1869 came East with his parents (they having settled in Jersey City, N. J.), and was prepared for college at Hasbrouck Institute, Jersey City. He entered Yale and was graduated in the class of 1877. He studied medicine with his father (who had become a convert to the school of homœopathy in 1867), and was graduated at the New York Homœopathic Medical College in 1880. His father having died in 1879 he began practice in Jersey City while still a student, and continued his father's practice for four years. He removed to Montclair in the autumn of 1883, and soon secured a good clientèle. He located (was for a few months on Clinton Avenue) on Fullerton Avenue and later removed to Grove Street. His practice has steadily increased and he has made many converts to the new school of practice. For the first few years he was active in the Congregational Church and Sabbath-school, but of late years the duties connected with his profession have absorbed his whole time. He is a member, and was formerly Vice-President of the New Jersey State Homœopathic Society; he is also a member of the New York Homœopathic Alumni Association, the New York Club for Medico-Scientific Investigation, and other medical societies. He was one of the organizing members of the Montclair Club. He married, in 1882, Miss Henriette Adèle Huggins, a granddaughter of Henry Wood, Esq., at one time a prominent merchant of Jersey City. Issue, four children: Henry Wood, Nettie May, Willis Huggins, and Charles Keith (deceased).

RICHARD COLE NEWTON, M.D.—Dr. Newton was born in Roxbury, Mass., July 23, 1851. He removed with his parents to South Orange, N. J. in 1857. He was prepared for college by Rev. Frederick A. Adams, and was graduated from Harvard in 1874, and from the College of Physicians and Surgeons, New York City, in 1877, and spent eighteen months as an interne in the Charity Hospital, New York. He entered the U. S. Army in 1880 as Assistant Surgeon; was post-surgeon at Fort Stanton, New Mexico, for two years; at Fort Cummings, New Mexico, one year; at Fort Sill, Indian Territory, one year, and four years at Fort Elliott, Texas. While at the latter place he was promoted to the rank of Captain. He came East in the fall of 1887, and was stationed at David's Island, New York harbor. The following year he came to Montclair, where he has since continued. He resigned his commission in the Army in May, 1889. He is a member of the County Medical Society; State Medical Society; Orange Mountain Medical Society; the Society for the Relief of Medical Men of New Jersey; the Society of the Military Surgeons of New Jersey, and various other societies and clubs.

RICHARD P. FRANCIS, M.D.—Dr. Francis was born in New York City, March 8, 1861; removed with his parents to Montclair in 1868; was graduated at the High School in 1877; continued his studies at a private school in New York for two years; was graduated at Harvard in 1883, and took his medical course at Harvard Medical School. He spent eighteen months in Boston City Hospital and returned to his home in Montclair in 1888. He was for two years associated with Dr. Pinkham, and, on the retirement of the latter, became his successor in practice. He was one of the founders of the Montclair Hospital, and has been Secretary of the Medical Staff since its organization. He was one of the original members of the Montclair Protective Association. He is a member of Montclair Club, and is Health Inspector of the township.

LEVI W. CASE, M.D.—Born in Frenchtown, Hunterdon Co., N. J., January 28, 1850. He received his preparatory course at Hightstown, N. J., and was graduated at Lafayette College in the class of '74. He taught school at the High Street, Newark, Academy one year, and was two years a teacher in the celebrated Charlier Institute of New York. He prosecuted his medical studies during a portion of the time; entered the College of Physicians and Surgeons, graduating in 1880, and in the spring of that year began practice in Chester, Morris Co., N. J., where he remained for nine years, until 1889, when he removed to Montclair. He is a member of the County Medical Society; Morris County Medical Society, and the Microscopical Society. He is examining physician for the Ancient Order of United Workmen, also for the Knights of Honor.

HERBERT WEST FOSTER.—Born in Putnam, Conn. Prepared for college at the Putnam High School, but did not enter. Was graduated at the New York Homœopathic Medical College, in the spring of 1891; served on the house staff at Ward's Island Hospital, Department of Public Charities and Corrections, from May, 1891, to May, 1892; was then Resident Physician of the Hahnemann Hospital, New York, from May, 1892, to May, 1893, when he began practice in Montclair, with the endorsement of some of the most eminent physicians of the "new school."

The following is a brief outline of his ancestry: Timothy Foster, of Walpole, Mass., bought land and settled in Dudley in 1748. The following is on the gravestone of his youngest son, Joseph, who lived at Windham, Conn.: "He enlisted in the Army of the Revolution at 13 years of age and was one of 13 brothers who together with their father, served in the war in the aggregate over 60 years." Timothy Foster's eldest son, Ebenezer, had a son, Peleg, who was the doctor's great-grandfather.

On his mother's side, Moses Wild settled in western Massachusetts in 1638. He married, and, after several generations, Miriam Wild married Earl Westgate, of Portsmouth, R. I., who was the doctor's great-grandfather.

Among other other family names are West, Davis, Harris, Shepardson, Colton and Fuller.

L. W. HALSEY, M.D.—Born in Binghamton, N. Y., entered Oberlin College in 1879; was graduated at the College of Physicians in 1883, serving a portion of the time in the hospital; began practice in his native town in 1883, succeeding his maternal grandfather, who for fifty years was a resident physician in that place. In 1892 he sold his practice and came to Montclair.

His paternal grandfather was a prominent lawyer of Binghamton, was twenty years Surrogate of Suffolk County, N. Y., and was for two years State Senator, fifteen years Presiding Judge, and one term Surveyor-General of the State.

HISTORY OF THE CRANE FAMILY.

The family of Crane is quite ancient and honorable. Ralph Drake accompanied Sir Francis Drake to America in 1577, and Robert Crane was of the first company that came to Massachusetts Bay in 1630, Sir Robert Crane was of Essex County, England, in 1630; and Sir Richard, in 1643, was of Wood Rising, Norfolk, England.

FIRST GENERATION.

JASPER CRANE (1) and Alice, his wife, came from London in 1637 or '38, to the New Haven Colony. He was one of the original settlers of the New Haven Colony and signed the first and "Fundamental Agreement," June 4, 1639, at a general meeting of all the free planters at New Haven, at the barn of Mr. Newman. Tradition says that he had the stewardship and oversight of the property of the Rev. John Davenport. Jasper Crane, Sr., was one of those at New Haven who attempted the settlement of the lands on the Delaware and was repulsed by the Dutch natives, Swedes and Fins.

He was a surveyor and trader, and with Mr. Myles laid out much of the town plot at New Haven, and located grants, settled division lines and disputed titles. He was a selectman, and one of the civil managers of the new settlement (New Haven). In March, 1641, he had a grant of 100 acres in the east meadow. In 1643 he was in the list of estates at New Haven at £480. In 1644 he was freed from "watching and trayning" because of his weakness. In 1644-5 he had a second grant of 16 acres of upland in East Haven, where he built his house in which Jasper, Jr., was born. Soon after this, not being satisfied with his location as a merchant, he sold his place in 1652 and purchased in Totoket (afterward called Branford), and removed thence with his family, where he, with Mr. William Swayne and some 20 others from Southampton, L. I., with Rev. Abraham Pierson as their leader, founded the new town of Branford. Jasper Crane, Esq., and Mr. William Swayne were the first deputies to the "General Court of Electors" from Branford, May, 1653, and four years after, in May, 1658, he was chosen magistrate of the New Haven Colony, which he held until 1663. On the union of the two Colonies he was chosen an assistant (Senator) to the General Court at Hartford. He was Justice of the County Court at New Haven in 1664-5, one of the magistrates convened at Hartford by the Governor in 1665, and one of the assistants and magistrates of Connecticut in 1665 6-7, and magistrate in the New Haven Colony in 1658.

Jasper Crane did not remove with the first company that went to settle (Milford first called) Newark, N. J., though he was one of the 23 persons who signed the first contract in 1665. On January 20, 1667, a new church covenant was formed for those who left Branford, and Mr. Crane headed the list of signers and church members under the new organization, with others, who signed the agreement in 1665, and after disposing by deed of his property at Branford in 1667-8 he joined his associates at Newark.

He, with Robert Treat (afterward Governor of Conn.), were the first magistrates in Newark. In 1668-9 they represented Newark in the General Court the same year, and were again chosen deputies in 1669-70.

In 1675 he was deputy and magistrate at Newark. He was one of the purchasers of the Kingsland farm, a large tract of land located at what is now Bellville. He was ranked with the strong minded men of Connecticut and New Jersey, lived to an advanced age, and died in 1681. His sons, John and Deliverance, had seats in the first meeting house in Newark. Children: John Crane; Hannah, who married Thomas Huntington, one of the signers of the "Branford Agreement"; Deliverance, or Delivered, born July 12, 1642, died without issue; Azariah, born 1647, died November 5, 1730, aged 83 years; he married Mary, daughter of Robert Treat, Governor of Connecticut.

When Mr. Treat left New Jersey for Connecticut he "betrusted his property at Newark to his son, Deacon Azariah Crane, who lived in the stone house at Newark, and was a man of integrity and standing."

"Deacon" Azariah had issue: Nathaniel, Azariah, Jr., John, Robert, Mary Baldwin and Jane Bull.

Jasper, Jr., born at East Haven, April 2, 1657, removed with his father to Newark. He purchased the estate of Robert Lyman in Newark in 1682, after Mr. Lyman returned to New England. Jasper died March 18, 1712, aged 61 years.

SECOND GENERATION.

"DEACON" AZARIAH CRANE, third child of Jasper (1) and Alice Crane, was born, 1647, probably at Branford, then a part of the New Haven Colony. He died, Nov. 5, 1730, aged 83. He was one of the signers of the "Fundamental Agreement," a deacon in the First Church of Newark, and held many offices of trust in the "Towne." He left his "silver bole" to be used by "the church in Newark forever." He married Mary, daughter of Robert Treat, one of the original settlers of Newark, and afterward Governor of the Connecticut Colony. "In the overturn of the government by the Dutch," in 1673, he "was betrusted with the concerns of his honorable father-in-law, Mr. Robert Treat." In 1715, he is spoken of by himself as having been "settled" for many years at the mountain. He had two sons, Nathaniel and Azariah, both born or lived in Cranetown "by the spring." (This, according to the statement of Joseph Dorennus, was what is now known as the Frost property on the north-east corner of Myrtle Avenue and Orange Road.) He had also John, Robert, Mary Baldwin and Jane Bull.

THIRD GENERATION.

Nathaniel and Azariah Crane, Jr., sons of "Deacon" Azariah and Mary (Treat) Crane, founders of the Crane family of Cranetown.

NATHANIEL CRANE AND HIS DESCENDANTS.

NATHANIEL (1), eldest son of "Deacon" Azariah and Mary (Treat) Crane, was born in the town of Newark, and was one of the founders of Cranetown. He married and had issue, William, Noah and Nathaniel (2).

FOURTH GENERATION.—LINE OF NATHANIEL.

WILLIAM (1) CRANE, eldest son of Nathaniel (1) (Deacon Azariah, Jasper) was born in Cranetown. During the war of the Revolution, he was Lieutenant in Spencer's Regiment, Continental Army; Captain, ditto, March, 1777. He married and had issue: Matthias, James, Isaac, Jonathan, Jonas, William (2), Zadoc, Oliver.

NOAH CRANE, second son of Nathaniel (1), (Deacon Azariah, Jasper) was born in Cranetown, May 1, 1719. He married Mary   and had issue: Samuel, born Oct. 29, 1746; Esther, born Feb. 12, 1749; Joseph, born Feb. 1, 1751, died November, 1832, married Hannah, daughter of Daniel Lamson; Elizabeth, born April 13, 1753; Caleb, born Jan. 17, 1762, died Sept. 17, 1768; "Major" Nathaniel (2), born Oct. 29, 1757; Mehitable, born June 17, 1764, married Gen. William Gould of Caldwell, an officer of the Revolution; Mary, born 1766, died Sept. 9, 1768; Nehemiah, born July 1, 1771, died Sept. 27, 1777.

FIFTH GENERATION.—LINE OF NATHANIEL.

MATTHIAS CRANE, eldest son of *William* (1) Nathaniel, Deacon Azariah, Jasper), was born in Cranetown. He married Elizabeth, daughter of Job Crane, and had issue: Israel.

OLIVER CRANE, youngest son of *William* (Nathaniel, Deacon Azariah, Jasper), was born in Cranetown. He married Susannah Baldwin, a descendant in the fifth generation of John Baldwin, Sr., one of the original settlers of Newark. They had issue: *Stephen Fordham*, Lydia Sarah, Amos, Zophar, Nathaniel M., Isaac W., and Rachel, who married Amos Baldwin.

SAMUEL CRANE, eldest son of *Noah* (Nathaniel, Deacon Azariah, Jasper) and Mary Crane, was born at Cranetown, October 9, 1746.

Dr. Wickes, in his "History of the Oranges," makes several quotations from Jemima Cundict's diary of Revolutionary events. One of these contains the following in reference to Samuel Crane.

"September y' 12, 1777, on Friday there Was an alarm, our Militia was Called. The Regulars Came over into elesabeth town Where they had a Brush With a Small Party of our People; then marched Quietly up to Newark & took all the Cattle they Could, there was five of the militia [of] Newark, they killed Samuel Crane & took Zadock and Allen heady and Samuel freeman Prisoners, one out of five run and escapt." * * *

Samuel Crane married   and had issue: Caleb, Zenas, Cyrus, and Nathaniel (3).

NATHANIEL, known as "Major" Nathaniel Crane, fifth child of *Noah* (Nathaniel, Deacon Azariah, Jasper) and Mary Crane, was born at Cranetown, February 15, 1762. He married Hannah, daughter of William Crane (son of Nathaniel), and died without issue. He served with the New Jersey Militia in the War of the Revolution, in Capt. Marsh's Troop of Light Horse. He was a man highly respected in the community, and was for many years a leader of the choir in the First Presbyterian Church of Orange, and was tendered the thanks of that parish for his valuable services on several occasions at their annual meeting. He gave to the Presbyterian Church of Bloomfield their bell, and in his last will he gave the most of his estate—about $10,000—to the use of the Bloomfield Church, with the proviso, that when a Presbyterian Church should be organized in West Bloomfield, the income of the property was to go to the new church.

SIXTH GENERATION.—LINE OF NATHANIEL.

ISRAEL CRANE, only son of Matthias (1) (William, Nathaniel (1), Deacon Azariah, Jasper) was born in Cranetown, March 15, 1774. He inherited from his ancestors those sterling qualities which made him a "man among men." He was known as "King" Crane, and well deserved the name for he was a born ruler and leader of men; he was the Vanderbilt of his time, and had he lived at a later period would have been a "railroad king." In early life he entered Princeton College, intending to study for the ministry, but was compelled to give up his studies in consequence of failing health. He then entered upon an active business career in which he met with almost unprecedented success in every undertaking. He was a prince among country merchants, and did the most extensive business of any man or firm for miles around. He opened and developed an immense brown-stone quarry in Newark, one of the largest in this part of the country, employing at times from three to four hundred men. He projected the Newark and Pompton Turnpike which opened a large extent of country, thereby enhancing the value of farm property, and affording the farmers better facilities for transporting their produce to market. Associated with him in this enterprise were New York capitalists. He was president of the company and subsequently acquired their interests, and became sole owner of the property. He was one of the first to utilize the immense water power of the Passaic Falls, near Paterson, and erected there the second cotton mill. He controlled the water power on Tony's Brook, and erected the first cotton mills on the stream, which he afterward sold to the Wildes. In the management of his extensive business interests he displayed wonderful sagacity, and great executive ability. At the same time he gave encouragement to and promoted every new enterprise that gave promise of success. He did more to develop this region of country than any man before or since. He was honorable and upright in all his dealings, and a man of large-hearted liberality. In an historical sketch of the Bloomfield Presbyterian Church, prepared by Rev. Stephen Dodd, in 1854, reference is made to "Israel Crane, who was early chosen a ruling

ISRAEL CRANE.

Elder, and still retains the office, and who bore a prominent part in the erection of the house, and to whose prudent and enlightened counsels, and acknowledged ability and enterprise, the church and parish will ever feel their indebtedness, and who, in a green old age, is permitted to rejoice in your prosperity."

Mr. Crane at that time was one of the two only remaining members out of fifty-nine from the First Church in Orange, and twenty-three from the First Church in Newark, who, in the month of June, 1798, withdrew from the above named churches and organized the church at Bloomfield. When, in 1837, it was proposed to start a church in the "Upper Village," or West Bloomfield, he entered heartily into the work, and gave liberally toward the new enterprise, his own children becoming faithful and consistent members of the First Presbyterian Church of West Bloomfield.

Mr. Crane married Fanny, daughter of Dr. Matthias Pierson, of Orange, the first resident physician at the Newark Mountains, a great-grandson of Thomas Pierson, one of the Associates from Branford, of the New Haven Colony, who settled in Newark in 1666. It is said he was a near kinsman, and probably a brother of Rev. Abraham Pierson, who came with the colony as its minister.

The issue of Israel and Fanny (Pierson) Crane was Mary Stockton, died young ; Matthias, Eliza wife of Captain Ephraim Beach, the civil engineer, who laid out the Morris Canal about 1828—Abigail, wife of Dr. Isaac Dodd ; Mary and James.

STEPHEN FORDHAM CRANE, eldest son of Oliver (William, Nathaniel (I.), Deacon Azariah, Jasper), and Susannah (Baldwin) Crane, was born in Cranetown 1762. He married Matilda Howell Smith, daughter of Peter Smith, who was Washington's private secretary in the winter of 1779-80, and was proposed by Washington for membership in the American Union Lodge, F. & A. M., where he was "duly initiated, passed and raised to the sublime degree of Master Mason," General (Bro.) Washington assisting in the ceremony. His name appears on the list of members of American Union Lodge at an "Entered Apprentices' Lodge," held at Morristown, N. J., December 27, 1779, for the celebration of the Festival

HOMESTEAD OF ISRAEL CRANE, ON GLEN RIDGE AVENUE.

of St. John the Evangelist. Among those present on that occasion were Bros. Washington, Arnold (Benedict), Samuel Holden Parsons, Van Rensselaer, and other distinguished officers of the Continental Army.

After the war Peter Smith was a magistrate, and later County Clerk of Sussex County.

Stephen Fordham Crane had issue : Emeline H., Susan P., Oliver, Sarah U., Stephen Smith and Crane.

<h3>SEVENTH GENERATION—LINE OF NATHANIEL (I).</h3>

REV. OLIVER CRANE, D.D., LL.D., clergyman, Oriental scholar, and poet, son of Stephen Fordham (Oliver, William, Nathaniel, Deacon Azariah, Jasper) and Matilda Howell (Smith) Crane, was born in West Bloomfield, now Montclair, N. J., July 12, 1822.

His early education began in his native town with Gideon Wheeler as his instructor, in the school-house afterward used by the First Presbyterian Church. By dint of energy and perseverance he prepared for college and entered Yale University as Sophomore, and graduated thence with honors in the class of 1845, and from Union Theological Seminary in 1848. He was ordained in April of the same year, and soon after appointed a missionary of the American Board of Commissioners of Foreign Missions to Turkey. He acquired the Turkish language and did efficient service during the next five years at Broosa, Aleppo, Aintab and Trebizond. He returned to America the following year and became pastor of the Presbyterian Church in Huron, N. Y., and, in 1857, of that in Waverly, N. Y. Being reappointed missionary in the spring of 1860, he went back to Turkey and was assigned to Adrianople, but, in 1863, circumstances necessitated his return to his native land. The next year he was elected Professor of Biblical and Oriental Literature in Rutgers Female College, New York City, but

declined, to accept a call from the Presbyterian Church of Carbondale, Pa., where he was installed as pastor. In the spring of 1870 he resigned, and the following year settled in Morristown, N.J., where he devoted himself largely to literary work, among other things aiding Gen. Henry B. Carrington this college classmate in the preparation of "The Battles of the Revolution," which has become a standard work. Previously, in 1865 66, he had been appointed by his presbytery to prepare a manual for the use of its churches, and in 1869 he had been elected moderator of the large Synod of New York and New Jersey. In 1880 he was chosen Secretary of his college class, in which capacity he prepared an exhaustive biographical record of every member, a book which was a pioneer in this line of publication. In 1888 he published a hexametrical line-by-line version of Virgil's Æneid, the result of much critical labor, which was favorably received. In 1889 he issued a small volume of poems under the title of "Minto and other Poems." In 1856 he was elected a corporate member

REV. OLIVER CRANE, D.D.

of the American Oriental Society, of which he is now one of the senior members. He is a member of several historical societies, and for four years past has been, by appointment of the Governor, a member of the Board of Examiners of the Scientific College of New Jersey. The degree of A.M., was conferred upon him by his *Alma Mater;* M.D., by the Eclectic Medical College of New York City, in 1866; D.D., by the University of Wooster, O., in 1880, and LL.D., by the Westminster College, Fulton, Mo., in 1888, the last being mainly in recognition of the scholarship evinced in his version of Virgil's Æneid. His life has been an active one, including, as it does, extensive traveling in Turkey, Europe, Egypt and Palestine, assiduous investigating and versatile writing. He now resides in Boston in comparative retirement, still occupying his time in literary pursuits.

Dr. Oliver Crane married, September 5, 1848, Marion D. Turnbull, and had by her five children: Louina M., died young; Elizabeth M. (wife of Rev. John S. Gardner); Caroline H. (wife of Edward C. Lyon, Esq.); Oliver T. (married Gertrude N. Boyd); and Louina Mary (wife of Harry C. Crane). Mrs. Crane July 23, 1890. Dr. Crane married, September 1, 1891, Sibylla A. Bailey, of Boston, Mass., where they both now reside. Dr. Crane did much in starting improvements in Montclair, laying out and making, mainly at his own expense, Clermont Avenue from Valley Road to Forest Street, and also Forest Street from Clermont Avenue to Walnut Street, and so opened up for settlement that part of the town. He was one of the corporate members of the First Presbyterian Church in the town, and took an active part in all its interests.

Vol. V., No. 4 of the "Magazine of Poetry" contains a sketch and a few selections of the poems of Mr. Crane. The genius of the poet and the beauty of expression is shown in the two stanzes of one entitled:

THE GLEANER.

"Where has thou gleaned to-day?"—Ruth xi., 19.

O gleaner, who homeward as if in retreat
  Art wearily plodding thy way,
Thou hast patiently wrought in the dust and the heat
But why bringest thou with thee no bundle of wheat?
  Oh, where hast thou gleaned to-day?

"I have gleaned in the field where the Master assigned,
  And have stayed where He bade me stay;
Where the owner and reapers alike were kind,
And permitted me many a sheaf to find,
  I have gleaned as a reaper to-day."

MATTHIAS (2) CRANE, son of Israel (Matthias, William, Nathaniel (1), Deacon Azariah, Jasper) and Fanny (Pierson) Crane was born at Cranetown, May 2, 1802. He married Susan, daughter of Jeptha Baldwin (born 1776), son of Benjamin (Benjamin, Joseph, John Baldwin, Sr., one of the original settlers, who signed the "Fundamental Agreement"). Matthias Crane was a farmer, and resided at the homestead on Bloomfield Avenue. He had issue, Edward Bishop, Israel, Catharine Baldwin, Mary Clarissa, Abba F., Francis, and Henry Lindsley, unmarried, and resides at the homestead on Bloomfield Avenue, Montclair.

Catharine Baldwin was married to Robert M. Boyd of Montclair. Mary C. married Samuel Friedly, and resides in Richmond, Va. Abba F. married Mr. Dodd, and resides at Bloomfield.

EDWARD BISHOP CRANE, eldest child of Matthias (2) (Israel, Matthias (1), William, Nathaniel (1), "Deacon" Azariah, Jasper) and Susan (Baldwin) Crane, was born in West Bloomfield, now Montclair. He married Ellen F., daughter of Samuel Baldwin, of Bloomfield. They had issue: Frank W., Nellie F., married Dr. Soper (now of Upper Montclair), Samuel B., and Edna G.

Frank W. Crane, eldest son of Edward B. Crane, is a civil engineer by profession, and has held many positions of trust in this line, and has been connected with prominent railroad interests. He married Mary Tolfree, of Orange, and has one child, Harold T.

ISRAEL (2) CRANE, second son of Matthias (2) (Israel, Matthias (1), William, Nathaniel (1), Deacon Azariah, Jasper) and Susan (Baldwin) Crane, was born at West Bloomfield, N. J., August 23, 1835, in the homestead on the south-west corner of Bloomfield Avenue and Willow Street. He was prepared for college at Ashland Hall, then under the direction and ownership of Rev. David A. Frame, and was graduated from Princeton College in 1854. He studied law for a time in the office of Judge Amzi Dodd, in Newark, N. J.

As early as 1868 he foresaw the possibilities of Montclair, and began making improvements of various kinds. He was always in full sympathy with every progressive movement which might benefit the town. His own property he divided into building lots, laid out streets, planted trees, etc. The opening of Union and East Plymouth Streets, from Fullerton Avenue east, was largely due to his enterprise.

He was one of the first to build houses for renting, and has erected a number of handsome cottages costing in the aggregate $100,000, including his own homestead, No. 16 East Plymouth Street.

He has shown commendable zeal and energy in the cause of education, having been one of the chief promoters of the first, and until recently the only, public library in Montclair. He was one of the original members of the First Congregational Church and also of the Montclair Club. He married Anna L. Barnes, niece of A. S. Barnes, deceased, the well known book publisher, and also a niece of Julius H. Pratt's wife, deceased. He has one child, Percy Waldron, who is a member of the Class of '95, of Yale University.

HENRY L. CRANE, youngest son of Matthias and Susan (Baldwin) Crane, was born at the homestead of his father, in Montclair. Has been for the past seven years engaged in the coal business. He married Ella F., daughter of Truman B. Brown, of Brooklyn; issue, one son, Leroy L.

THIRD GENERATION.

AZARIAH CRANE, JR., AND HIS DESCENDANTS.

AZARIAH (2) CRANE, son of Deacon Azariah Crane, was born in the town of Newark, and was one of the founders of that part of Newark which afterward became "Cranetown." Azariah (2) married Rebecca, and had issue: Azariah (3), Job, Gamaliel, Ezekiel, Josiah, Moses, Stephen. In 1733, he grants three acres at the " mountain plantation " to his well-blood son-in-law, *Zachariah Baldwin*. In 1753 Azariah, Jr., conveys to his son, Azariah (3), a tract of land south of what is now Union Street, extending to the top of the mountain, and bounded by the property of Nathaniel Crane.

FOURTH GENERATION.—LINE OF AZARIAH (2).

JOB CRANE, son of Azariah, Jr. (Deacon Azariah, Jasper), married ———— and had issue: Aaron.

STEPHEN CRANE, youngest son of Azariah, Jr., who was the son of Deacon Azariah, son of Jasper Crane, was born in Cranetown, and married Rhoda ————. He was in communion with the Mountain Society previous to 1756. Among those who entered into covenant with the Montclair Society during the pastorate of Rev. Jedediah Chapman, was " Rhoda, wife of Stephen Crane." In the description of the boundaries of Newark it says, " thence along the line of Caldwell township to a point in the First Mountain called Stephen Crane's notch."

At a convention of the committees of the several counties held at New Brunswick in response to the appeal of the " Freeholders and Inhabitants of the County of Essex, Province of New Jersey, to take action in regard to the late acts of Parliament, etc." 72 gentlemen took part in the deliberations. " Stephen Crane of Essex was in the chair." At this meeting Stephen Crane was appointed one of the delegates to the General Continental Congress held in the city of Philadelphia, September, 1774.

In the absence of any proof to the contrary it is presumed that Stephen, son of Azariah (2) is the one referred to.

In the records of those who served in the the War of the Revolution is found the name of Stephen Crane, who served with the First Regiment, " New Jersey Line." Continental Army. He also served with the New Jersey Militia in Captain Squire's Company, Second Regiment, Essex Co.

The children of Stephen Crane and his wife Rhoda were: Martha, baptized 1757; Lois, baptized 1760; JEREMIAH, born April 2, 1770; Sarah, born 1776; Stephen Bradford, born 1779. The church records show another child of Stephen, " name unknown."

FIFTH GENERATION.— LINE OF AZARIAH (2).

AARON CRANE, born in Cranetown, son of Job (Azariah, Jr., Deacon Azariah, Jasper), married ———— and had issue: Thomas Jeptha, Timothy, Elias B., Zenas Squire.

SIXTH GENERATION.—LINE OF AZARIAH (2).

ZENAS SQUIRE CRANE, son of Aaron (Job, Azariah, Jr., Deacon Azariah, Jasper), was born in Crane-town, October 20, 1793, on the homestead situated on the Valley Road, near the junction of Church Street, subsequently purchased by Grant J. Wheeler, and now occupied by the latter's son.

"Squire" Crane, as he was known, began life as a clerk in the store of Job Dodd, in Bloomfield. When but eighteen years of age he was elected a constable for Bloomfield township. A year later, on the breaking out of the war of 1812, he responded to his country's call, and, though a mere youth, shouldered his flint-lock musket, and enlisted in a New Jersey regiment, doing service at Sandy Hook, and in the southern part of the State, defending the coast against the invading forces. On his return he entered the militia service, and on May 15, 1821, was made lieutenant, and subsequently captain, of the First Company, Second Battalion, of the Fifth Regiment, acting as such for more than eleven years. In 1826 he was appointed a Justice of the Peace by the Legislature, which office he held with great credit for fifty-four consecutive years. His rulings during all this time were never reversed by those of a higher court, and the decisions rendered by him were at all times sound and logical. He received an appointment as Commissioner of Deeds a year later, and in 1837 he was appointed a Lay Judge of Essex County, in which capacity he served until 1853, when he was also appointed a Master of Chancery. When the building of the present court house was proposed, Judge Crane was one of the members of the Building Committee.

There was, perhaps, not another man in Essex County who was so well informed as to the general transactions in real estate, since Judge Crane was a surveyor and surveyed the lands and prepared the deeds for nearly every transaction made in this vicinity for fifty years. He was also one of the corporate members of the Presbyterian Church, and served as a Trustee for more than twenty years. Among the archives of the public schools is a book wherein Mr. Crane has recorded the organization of the present school on May 17, 1831, to which he subscribes himself as President of the Board of Trustees, of which he was a member for many years. Few men in this vicinity ever led such a life of public usefulness. He was for a long period the President of the Rosendale Cement Co. of Jersey City; and at one time he owned all the lands bounded by a line running from the corner of Valley Road to a point at the top of the mountain, near the lands of Mr. Pillsbury, and from thence to the Old Road, then known as the Pompton Turnpike, the lands being bounded on the east and west by Valley Road and the Caldwell Township line.

At the Presidential election in 1880, Judge Crane and "Uncle" Nathaniel R. Dodd marched to the polls early in the morning, the former bearing aloft an American flag. Quite a number of voters had preceded them, but all waited until the two old veterans had deposited their ballots. The Judge was a loyal adherent to his country, a staunch supporter of the old Whig party, and subsequently an uncompromising Republican.

He was married to Miss Maria Searing, September 24, 1821, in the old Bloomfield Hotel, the service being performed by the Rev. Dr. Judd, who was at that time the pastor of the Presbyterian Church of that place. Six children were the issue of this marriage, viz.: Sarah A., wife of Thomas Jessup, who lived and died at Newburgh, N. Y., Angelena, wife of Hon. Stephen K. Williams, now living at Newark, Wayne County, N. Y., Mary Elizabeth, wife of Mr. John Andrus, now living at Hackensack, Bergen County, N. J., Theodore T., now living at Yonkers, N. Y., and Frances J., wife of Dr. J. J. H. Love, of Montclair.

JEREMIAH, son of Stephen (Azariah (2), Deacon Azariah, Jasper) and Rhoda Crane, born April 2, 1770. The homestead of Jeremiah stood on the foundation of what is now the cottage of the Thomas Porter property, near the corner of Harrison Avenue and Union Street. His farm extended from what is now Harrison Avenue to the top of the mountain. He was a man of considerable note in his day. He married Elizabeth Corby, born June 22, 1774, and had eleven children, viz.: Purthana, Hannah, William, Julia, Rhoda, Israel, Lina, Ira, Mary, Eliza Ann, Martha.

IRA, son of Jeremiah (Stephen, Azariah (2), Deacon Azariah, Jasper) and Elizabeth (Corby) Crane, was born in the homestead of his father and succeeded to the estate. He was a man of considerable prominence, and was an officer in the Presbyterian Church at Bloomfield; he served on the Town Committee, and held other offices of trust and responsibility.

He purchased the property on South Fullerton Avenue, and built the house (since altered and remodeled) now owned by Dr. Butler.

He carried on the shoe business during most of his life. He married Margaret Norwood, and had issue: *Jarvis G.*, Angeline, Israel.

JARVIS, son of Ira and Margaret (Norwood) Crane, was born in the old homestead on Harrison Avenue and Union Street, Feb. 7, 1831.

He was a carpenter and builder, and erected some of the best houses, in his day, in Montclair, among which Dr. Love's and Samuel Wilde's, on Fullerton Avenue, Julius Pratt's on Elm Street, William Terry's, George S. Dwight's, J. C. Hart's, Joseph Van Vleck's, Robert M. Boyd's and many others. He afterward engaged in the hardware business, which he carried on successfully for many years. He bought the lot adjoining that of his father on Fullerton Avenue, and built the house now occupied by his son, Dr. Frank S. Crane. He moved to Boonton, N. J., about 1854, and resided there some five years. He then married Henrietta Smith, and had three children, viz.: Ira Seymour, Frank S. and Alice B.

IRA SEYMOUR, eldest son of Jarvis and Henrietta (Smith) Crane, was born in Boonton, N. J., Dec. 29, 1855. Four years after his birth he was taken by his parents to West Bloomfield (now Montclair) the old home of his father. He enjoyed the best educational advantages then to be had in the township, and graduated from the High School in 1873. He learned the carpenter trade with his father and worked at it for eight years. In 1881 his father bought out the hardware business of William S. Morris, and took his son, Ira Seymour, into partnership with him under the firm name of J. G. Crane & Son. It continued under that name until 1888, when the father retired, and Ira Seymour has since carried on the business alone. He is one of the most public-spirited and progressive men of the present generation, as well as one of the most popular. He helped to organize the Fire Department, and was elected Assistant Foreman of the company, and in 1890 was made Chief of the Fire Department. Under his able management the department has increased in efficiency and strength, and is one of the best conducted fire departments connected with any suburban town in the State. In 1891 he became a member of the Town Committee, and was made the first township Treasurer, after the creation of that office, and has given great satisfaction to the taxpayers by the able manner in which he has discharged the duties of his office. He is connected with numerous other business enterprises, in all of which he has shown the same business capacity and enterprise. He is a director in the Montclair Building and Loan Association—one of the strongest of its kind in the State. He is a stockholder in the Montclair Bank, and a director in The Montclair Savings Bank.

In religious matters he has evinced the same energy, earnestness and devotion that have characterized all his business affairs. He is a deacon in the First Presbyterian Church, and a member of the Board of Trustees.

Mr. Crane married, in 1882, Caroline A., daughter of Joseph Doremus and Caroline (Mead) Doremus. (For line of descent see Doremus Family.) His wife deceased Oct. 14, 1892, leaving two children, Ira Seymour, Jr., and Henrietta Mead.

Mr. Crane bought a plot on Church Street, opposite the Presbyterian Church, comprising a part of the Matthias Smith estate.

DR. FRANK SMITH CRANE, second child of Jarvis G. and Henrietta (Smith) Crane, was born at the homestead, adjoining his present residence, July 4, 1861. He was educated at the public school of Montclair, receiving all the advantages of the "higher education," and was graduated at the New York College of Dentistry in 1885. He began practice at once in his native town, and although others long established preceded him, his clientèle gradually increased and he has now all he can attend to. The friends of his early youth showed their confidence in him as a man, and in his professional skill by extending him their

J. Seymour Crane

patronage. He enjoys an excellent reputation among his professional brethren as a skillful practitioner. He is a member of the New Jersey State Dental Society, of the Central Dental Society of Northern New Jersey, and of the Alumni Association of the New York College of Dentistry. He is also a member of Montclair Lodge F. & A. M., Orange Lodge of Elks, and of the Montclair Athletic Club. He married, December, 1886, Sarah L. Crolious, daughter of George C. and Catharine (Lownds) Crolious, of Brooklyn. His children are: Frank Leroy, born October, 1889; Harriet Stevens, born October, 1890, and Dudley Winthrop, born January, 1891.

THE BALDWIN FAMILY.

BALDWIN is an old name, and quite common as early as the conquest of England, and is found on the roll of the Battle Abbey. Baldwins, Earls of Flanders, were contemporary with Alfred the Great. Baldwin 2d married Elstruth, daughter of Alfred; Baldwin the 5th, married the daughter of Robert of France, whose daughter Matilda married William the Conqueor. In 1198 Robert Fitz Baldwin had large estates in Bucks County, England. Richard Baldwin, of Bucks County, England, was the ancestor of most of the American families of this name. The name is often spelled in the early records, Baldwyn.

JOHN BALDWIN (1) came probably from Bucks County, England, and was one of the original settlers of Milford, Conn. He joined the church March 16, 1648. He married Marie Brewen, daughter of John Brewen, of Pequot (New London), and in his will, 1681, names children: *John*, Josiah, Nathaniel, Joseph, George, Obadiah, Richard, Abigail, Sarah, Hannah and Eliza Peck.

JOHN (2) BALDWIN, SR., son of John (1), was born in Milford, Conn., March 16, 1648. He married, Oct. 30, 1663, Hannah, daughter of Obadiah Brewen (or Bruen), a niece of his stepmother. He married, secondly, before 1686, Ruth Botsford, of Milford, and in his will, 1702, names children: Sarah, Hannah, Eliza and *John* by his first wife, and Samuel, Daniel, Joseph, Timothy, Elanthan, Nathaniel and Jonathan.

He was one of the original settlers of Newark, and together with his nephew, John, Jr., signed the "Fundamental Agreement." He was a man of some prominence in the community and held various public offices. He was a "Sealer of Leather" in 1676; "Fence Viewer" in 1695; one of the "Town's Men," 1697-98; Surveyor of Highways, 1681-86, etc. In the first drawing for "Home Lotts," John, Sr., drew lot 54. "At Town Meeting 12th Decem'r 1670 it was Agreed that the Land that is Left unlaid out shall be Laid out to them to whom it falls By Lott; and the first Lott fell to John Baldwin Sen'r to have His whole Second Division of Upland and One Acre for his staying on the place the first Summer."

JOHN BALDWIN (3), son of John (2) and Hannah (Bruen) Baldwin, was born in Newark about 1670. His children were: Josiah, David, John (4) and Obadiah.

JOHN (4) BALDWIN, son of John (3), was born in Newark, N. J. His will, 1758, names four daughters: Dorcas or Dorcas, Joanna, and Mary Elizabeth. According to the genealogical tree of Mr. Samuel H. Congar, he had also *Joseph*. He owned a large farm on the Orange Road, and probably erected the house where his children and grandchildren were born.

JOSEPH, son of John (4), was born in the homestead of his father, on Orange Road; he purchased several tracts of land on and near the mountain. A quit-claim deed from Henry Jacobus to Joseph Baldwin, dated 1783, described the property as "lying over the mountain, lately belonging to Vincent Pierce, being on the west side of said mountain; the whole of the said tract undivided, contains three thousand and six hundred acres, and commonly known as the Ashfield tract, the said right having been sold by the commissioners for the county of Essex to William Baldwin in 1779." A deed by Mary Ashfield, dated 1784, conveys one hundred acres to Joseph Baldwin, Jr., on Newark Mountain, known as the Ashfield Tract. A deed, dated Dec. 27, 1792, from Joseph Crane, of Cranetown, conveys to Joseph Baldwin, fifty-four acres, being a part of the farm which the said Joseph Crane bought of Cornelia Hetfield.

The date of Joseph Baldwin's birth is not shown. During the war of the Revolution he served in Capt. Squere's Company, Second Regiment, Essex. He married Esther, a daughter of Noah Crane, and a sister of Deacon Joseph Crane, sometimes called "Captain," whose homestead is shown among the old landmarks. The issue of this marriage was; Mary, who "entered into covenant with the Mountain Society," March 26, 1774 The issue of this marriage was Mary, "who entered into covenant with the Mountain Society;" she married Linus Dodd; John J., Joanna (married David Riker); Elizabeth, Esther (married John Wardell); Joseph, Naomi (married Noah Baldwin); Caleb, Zenas, Hannah.

The property of Joseph was divided among his children, some of whom acquired additional acres, holding farms adjoining, along the line of Orange Road, extending north to Tony's Brook, near the present D. L. & W. R. R. That portion lying along the Orange Road subsequently became known as the "Baldwin Neighborhood."

JOHN J. BALDWIN, son of Joseph and Esther (Crane) Baldwin was born in Cranetown in 1771, at the homestead of his father on Orange Road. The house now owned by William H. Sears, 259 Orange Road, stands on the original foundation of the house where Joseph was born. He was a noted character in his day, and one of the most prominent men in this part of the town of Newark. He served with the New Jersey troops in the war of 1812, probably as an officer, as he was always called, during the later years of his life, Capt. Baldwin. He represented his district in the legislature, was an uncompromising whig in politics, a man of great influence in the community, of strong common sense, and, while not gifted as a speaker, he was forcible in argument, and kept himself informed on the chief topics of the day. Like his father, and all his immediate ancestors, he was a thrifty and successful farmer, and considered well-to-do in the community. He married, August 13, 1779, Lydia, daughter of David Dodd, of Bloomfield, and after her decease married her sister Sarah. He had issue Reuben D., born 1806, Joseph H., born 1808, Sarah D., born 1811—married Anthony D. Ball; and Abby E., born 1815, Joseph H. BALDWIN, second child of John J. and Lydia (Dodd) Bald-

JOSEPH H. BALDWIN.

win, was born January 12, 1808, in the house which stood on the corner of Orange Road and Elm Street, on the property now owned by W. Irving Adams. He attended the district school then kept by Gideon Wheeler, and acquired a good knowledge of the rudimentary branches. He inherited considerable property from his father, and kept his farm under thorough cultivation. He had a large apple orchard well stocked with the finest fruit, and had a comfortable income from the sale of his cider. He occasionally took part in public affairs and was for some time Surveyor of Highways. He was one of the early members of the Bloomfield Church, and assisted in organizing the First Presbyterian Church of West Bloomfield, of which he was long a trustee. He was an exemplary Christian, and always prompt in his attendance at Divine service both on the Sabbath and week days. Considering his means he was generous in his support of public and private charities. Honest and straightforward in all his own business affairs, he had implicit confidence in others, and was loth to believe evil of any one. For this reason people seldom took advantage of him, and in all his business transactions his word was as good as his bond. He was of a kind and genial disposition and beloved and respected by his neighbors. He married Lydia A. Munn, a descendant of the Munns, who settled in Newark about 1750. He had issue: Lydia D., Mary F. and Phebe L.; the latter married William J. Harris (brother of Col. Fred. H. Harris, of Montclair), and now resides in West Virginia. The two first mentioned reside at the homestead, on Orange Road, corner of Elm Street.

THE DOREMUS FAMILY.

LINE OF DESCENT FROM CORNELIUS DOREMUS, 1690.

CORNELIUS DOREMUS, the ancestor of the Doremus family, came from Holland about 1690, and settled at or near Acquackanonck (now Passaic), New Jersey. The name of his wife is not known. His children were Johannes, born at Middleburg, Holland, about 1687; Thomas, born at Acquackanonck, about 1690; Cornelius, born about 1692; Hendrick, born 1695, and Joris, born about 1697.

THOMAS DOREMUS, son of Cornelius, born at Acquackanonck, New Jersey, about 1690, resided at Wesel, N. J., married, Oct. 4, 1712, Anneke Abrahamse Ackerman, born at Hackensack, N. J. He had six children: Cornelius, born April 4, 1715; Godliue, of Jacksonville, N. J., baptized Nov. 14, 1720; Abraham, of Cedar Grove, N. J., born about 1722; Peter, of Cedar Grove, born about 1725; Johannes, born about 1726; Anneke, baptized May 5, 1756.

CORNELIUS DOREMUS, son of Thomas and Anneke Abrahamse (Ackerman) Doremus, born April 4, 1715, lived at Doremustown, N. J. He married, about 1738, Antje Young, and had ten children, viz.: Hendricus, of Wesel, N. J., baptized March 3, 1739 (married Sept. 25, 1760, Margaret Van Winkle), Thomas, born April, 1741, great-great-grandfather of Professor Ogden Doremus, of New York; Peter, of Slaterdam, N. J., baptized June 8, 1744; Maritje, baptized May 17, 1746 (married Bartholomew Dodd, of Beavertown); Johannes, of Doremustown, born about 1749, died 1821, hotel keeper; Jannetji, baptized 1754; Susanna, born 1756; Aletta, born about 1758.

PETER DOREMUS.

PETER DOREMUS, born probably at Doremustown, lived at Beavertown, N. J., baptized June 8, 1744, married, 1776, Polly (Mary) Dev. He had issue: Jacob, Richard, Cornelius, Peter and two daughters, one of whom married Henry Berry, the other married —— Speer.

PETER DOREMUS, son of Peter and Polly (Dey) Doremus, was born near Beavertown, N. J., Feb. 17, 1787. He moved to Cranetown about 1807, where he had the second largest store in Bloomfield township, there being but two stores in Cranetown at that time. His place of business was at the present location of his son, Philip Doremus. He did a thriving business for many years. In politics he was an old line Whig. He was a man of uprightness and honesty and highly respected in the community.

He married, Oct. 3, 1810, Rhoda, daughter of Deacon Joseph Crane (son of Noah, who was the son of Nathaniel, son of Azariah (2) of the original settlers of Cranetown). They had issue: Joseph, born Sept. 12, 1814; Thomas Lamson, born July 31, 1816; Owen, Edmund, Hannah Maria (born Oct. 25, 1823, and married William Corwin), Philip, Marcus, born Nov. 15, 1827; Emma Harrison, born June 22, 1831 (married Louis E. Meeker, moved to Portland, Oregon).

JOSEPH DOREMUS, oldest son of Peter and Rhoda (Crane) Doremus, was born in Cranetown, Sept. 12, 1814, in the old Doremus homestead, which stood on the spot now occupied by his brother Philip, as a residence, on Bloomfield Avenue, at the junction of Glen Ridge Avenue. His education began at the early age of three years, when he was sent to a private school kept by Rebecca Horton, in her own house. He afterward attended the school kept by Gideon Wheeler, David D. Allen and others, in the schoolhouse which stood on the site of the First Presbyterian Church. After leaving school he entered his

JOSEPH DOREMUS.

father's store and remained with him until 1846. He was earnestly solicited by his father to continue, but had no fondness for that line of business. He accepted a position as bookkeeper for James Crane, son of Israel Crane, and was afterward for several years engaged in a morocco establishment in Newark as clerk and manager. At the same time he was associated with his brother in the business of glass staining for church purposes. etc.; his brother had the reputation of producing the best goods in the country. In 1859, Mr. Doremus was elected the first Register of Essex County, and held the position until 1864. From 1864 to 1889, he had the sole charge of the official searching department. He has since been engaged in the same line of business on his own account, and has probably a better knowledge of the old land titles of Essex County than any other person. He was Clerk of Bloomfield township for thirteen years, from 1846 to 1859, and has been Commissioner of Appeals for Montclair for nineteen years. He is a Masonic veteran of nearly forty years' standing, and is one of the oldest surviving members of the Bloomfield Lodge, which in former times met in West Bloomfield. Although well advanced in years his mental faculties are clear and he is still strong and vigorous for a man of his age. He is one of the very few connecting links of the Revolutionary period, having known and conversed with several of the old veterans. He is a walking encyclopedia of the events connected with the beginning of the present century, and all the old landmarks are as familiar to him as "household words." He married, in 1836, Caroline, daughter of Jacob K. Mead, of Bloomfield, and had issue: three daughters, Martha M., Mary Kline and Caroline, deceased, who was the wife of I. Seymour Crane.

THOMAS LAMSON, second son of Peter Doremus, about the year 1838, moved to Louisiana, where he engaged in business. He was a man of strict integrity and uprightness. In 1852 he came North and married at New Haven, Conn., and one year after his return died, Nov., 1853, of yellow fever at Centerville, La.

OWEN DOREMUS, third child of Peter and Rhoda (Crane) Doremus, was born in Cranetown, May 15, 1819. His love of art was developed at an early age, and he sought every means in his power to gratify it. He studied portrait painting with Caleb Ward, of Bloomfield, and followed that for a time, but afterward became associated with a Mr. Chapman in New Rochelle, N. Y., in the glass staining business. He excelled in this line and produced some of the finest work in the country, which compared favorably with that of the best Italian and French artists. His work adorns many of the leading Protestant and Catholic Churches throughout the country, and was much sought after by leading architects. He dissolved his connection with Mr. Chapman and carried on business for a time in Orange, and later in Montclair. His residence was on the corner of Bloomfield Avenue and Bay Street, and he had a place fitted up in the rear of his house as a studio and workshop. He was thoroughly devoted to his art and had achieved a national reputation as an artist in this line.

EDMUND DOREMUS, fourth child of Peter and Rhoda (Crane) Doremus, was born in Cranetown, Sept. 20, 1821. Died April 5, 1887. He attended the school kept by Warren Holt at what is now known as the Mountain House. He was studious and attentive as a scholar, and displayed great aptitude for mechanics. He learned the trade of millwright in which he greatly excelled. He went to Whiteport, New York, to superintend the erection of machinery for the Newark and Rosendale Lime and Cement Company, and became their business manager. He was later a stockholder in the company and managed its important works at Whiteport to the entire satisfaction of his associates for thirty-five years. He was succeeded by his son Fred. He was active in the public affairs of Ulster County, and devoted much time and energy to the cause of education. He was prominently identified with the Episcopal Church in an active member. He married, in 1843, Caroline, daughter of Isaac A. Harrison, of West Orange, N. J., a descendant of Sargent Richard Harrison, one of the original settlers of Newark. He had seven children, most of whom settled in Kingston, N. Y., and that locality. His son, W. Louis Doremus, came to Montclair in 1877, and has since been associated with Philip Doremus, his father-in-law.

PHILIP DOREMUS.

PHILIP DOREMUS, sixth child of Peter and Rhoda (Crane) Doremus, was born in the old homestead which stood near his present residence on Bloomfield Avenue, Oct. 29, 1825. He was ambitious to acquire a good education and was sent to the boarding school of Warren S. Holt. He decided to adopt his father's occupation, but realized the necessity of a more thorough knowledge of the details of the business than could be acquired in a country town, and in 1844 he went to New York City and engaged first with a retail and afterward with a wholesale and retail grocery firm, spending altogether about seven years with both firms. He returned to his native town in 1848 and assumed charge of his father's business. He continued it as a general country store for a number of years in the same location.

In 1853 he built a two-story frame building on the original site. As the population increased and railroad facilities brought the residents within easy access of the city, he found it necessary to change his stock of goods to suit the wants of the new community, and he gradually "weeded out" his stock of general merchandise and limited his trade to groceries and crockery, of the finest class of goods, especially adapted to the wants of the wealthy classes who for many years past have been his largest patrons. In

1890 he erected the building he now occupies, which is one of the finest and most attractive buildings for business purposes in this part of the country. As a merchant he has met with deserved success, and has kept pace with the growth of the township.

He is a man of advanced and liberal ideas, and was for many years associated with Dr. Love and others in the School Board, and always took an advanced position for the cause of "higher education." He was for six years a member of the County Board of Freeholders, and a part of the time was Chairman of the committee that had charge of the county penitentiary. He also served for several years as a member of the Town Committee. He was one of the founders and is still a director of the Montclair Bank. He was also one of the founders of the Montclair Savings Bank and was elected its first President, still holding that position.

Probably no man in Montclair has been more prominently identified with the cause of religion than Philip Doremus. Self-sacrificing, earnest, conscientious, he has taken a leading position in every movement tending to the advancement of religion and the improvement of the moral and social condition of the community. His religious experience began early in life as a member of the Seventh Presbyterian Church, corner of Broome and Sheriff Streets, New York. When he finally decided to settle in West Bloomfield, the home of his youth, he brought with him his letter to the First Presbyterian Church, in which he subsequently served as an elder for about thirty years, and was for fifteen years Superintendent of the Sabbath school. Mr. Doremus has always been an earnest advocate of church extension. He assisted in the early movements to found a church at Upper Montclair, and, in 1886, believing that circumstances favored the organization of a new church, he with others withdrew from the First Presbyterian Church and organized the Trinity Presbyterian Church, which has since more than doubled its membership. Mr. Doremus was elected one of the two first elders of the new organization, and still holds that position.

During a European tour which he made in 1883 his letters to the *Montclair Times* showed him to be a writer of no mean ability and a keen observer of men and things. His description of the places he visited were read with great interest by the patrons of that paper. Mr. Doremus combines all the qualities of the Christian gentleman, quiet and unostentatious in his manner, strong in his convictions of right, yet tender, affectionate and kind to all. While in no way lacking the courage of his convictions, he would sacrifice his own interests rather than wound the feelings of another.

Mr. Doremus was married, Nov. 20, 1851, to Hester Ann Yarrington, daughter of B. C. Yarrington, in old St. Bartholomew's Church, by Rev. B. M. Yarrington, cousin of Mrs. Doremus, who has since officiated at the marriage of each of their daughters. The children are: Mary Yarrington, married to Dr. S. C. G. Watkins; Caroline S., married to W. Low Doremus; Annette C., married to E. B. Goodell, a practicing lawyer in Montclair; Adah N., married to Joseph B. Renwich, of Montclair.

THE HARRISON FAMILY.

RICHARD HARRISON, SR., and RICHARD, JR., came from West Kirby, in Cheshire, Eng., in 1644, and were among the early settlers of the New Haven Colony. They removed to Branford, then a part of the New Haven Colony, where Richard, Sr., died in October, 1653; his daughter Mary married Thomas Pierson, one of the original settlers of Newark, and Elizabeth married John Morris.

SECOND GENERATION.

SARGENT RICHARD HARRISON was one of the original Branford settlers of Newark, and his name is attached to the "Fundamental Agreement." In the drawing of their "Lotts," with their "Number and Places," Sargent Harrison drew No. 34. At a "Town Meeting held October 31, 1674, Sargeant Harrison," with others, was "chosen a Committee to consider of such things as may tend for the Good of the Town; also they have Liberty to debate of such things with any they shall see Occasion so to do, without calling a Town Meeting."

At a "Town Meeting, Dec. 11, 1674, Serg't Harrison," with others was "chosen to go down to

Elizabeth Town to treat with the Governor upon the particulars written, and if they can agree without, not to deliver that writing; but in Case he will not hear them then they are to present this Writing to him, and leave it with him."

As a military officer Sargent Richard Harrison held in the new colony the rank of *Ensign*. He also served as one of the "Town's Men." His children were Samuel, Benjamin, born 1655, John, Joseph, born 1658, Daniel, and Mary—all, probably, born in Branford.

THIRD GENERATION.

Daniel Harrison, son of Sargent Richard, was born in Branford in 1661. Came with his father to Newark. The only mention made of him in connection with the town was in 1705, as "Fence Viewer." He died December 10, 1738. As his father acquired property in the outlying districts he was probably one of the early settlers of that part of Newark now known as Orange. In his will he names children: Daniel, *Moses*, Abigail Farrand, Lydia Baldwin, and his grandson Jonathan, son of Jonathan.

FOURTH GENERATION.

Moses Harrison, son of Daniel, was born, probably, in Orange, in 1709; he died February 18, 1763. In his will he names *Jonas*, Anna, Damaris, Abigail and Sarah. He names Jonas, his son, and Jabez, as executors.

FIFTH GENERATION.

Jonas Harrison, son of Moses, was born, probably, in Orange. His will names children, Aaron, Daniel, *Moses*, Jabez, and four daughters.

SIXTH GENERATION.

Moses Harrison, son of Jonas, was born in Orange about 1758. He was possessed of a vivid imagination, a retentive memory, and an inexhaustible supply of anecdotes and stories of his eventful life, with which he entertained his hearers on every occasion. He was a frequent visitor at Paulus Hook—now Jersey City—and as soon as his presence was noised abroad large crowds would gather to listen to his narration of revolutionary and other tales, which were told with such minuteness and earnestness, and with a depth of pathos and humor, that his hearers were taken in imagination to the very spot. He had served with the New Jersey troops in the war of the Revolution, and his vivid description of these scenes were listened to by his hearers with the deepest interest. He drew a pension from the government up to the time of his death. In 1802 he removed to what was then known as Speertown, now Upper Montclair, and purchased about sixty acres of land, being a part of the Egbert farm, extending from Midland Avenue to the top of the mountain. He lived to a ripe old age and raised a large family of children, of whom all except one have long since passed away. His wife was Sarah Vincent, a descendant of an old French Huguenot family, which emigrated to America after the Revocation of the Edict of Nantes. Her parents settled in the Wyoming Valley, prior to the War of the Revolution, and, at the time of the Indian massacre, she, then a little girl, was captured by the Indians, and afterward exchanged. The issue of the marriage of Moses Harrison with Sarah Vincent was Jared E., Jane, Phebe, Rebecca, Maria, Eliza, Emma, John, Bethuel and Flavel. Of these *Jared E.* is the only surviving one.

Jared E. Harrison, son of Moses and Sarah (Vincent) Harrison, was born in Orange, March 20, 1803, and was brought by his parents to the Speertown neighborhood while an infant. When he grew to manhood he improved the farm and added many acres to it, and had one of the finest apple orchards in the township, and was known as one of the most thrifty and prosperous farmers. He was a man of considerable influence in the community and has held many positions of honor and trust. Before Montclair became a separate township he served on the Bloomfield Township Committee and also as Road Master. He was one of the original directors of the Newark and Bloomfield Railroad Company, and was instrumental in opening the first railroad communication between West Bloomfield and New York City, which changed the whole of this part of the country from an agricultural to a prosperous suburban township. He was a member of the First Presbyterian Church of Bloomfield, and helped to organize the new church in West Bloomfield, contributing liberally to the erection of the church edifice. He served on the Board of Trustees and was a faithful attendant until prevented by declining health, the result of advancing years. He is still living (1894). He married Catharine, daughter of Peter Egbert, a descendant of one of the old Holland families who were among the original settlers of Speertown. Five children were the issue of this marriage, two of whom died in infancy. Of those living, are Edwin M., Daniel Vincent and Nathan.

Edwin M. Harrison, eldest child of Jared E. and Catharine (Egbert) Harrison, was born at the homestead on Valley Road. He attended the old public school, and completed his education at the school of Warren Holt. He went to New York City in 1840 and began as clerk with Benjamin Taylor in the grocery business, where he remained five years. In 1848 he started in the commission business on his own account, and later became associated with his brother Daniel Vincent. and subsequently with his brother Nathan, with whom he is still connected.

He resided in Williamsburg—now Brooklyn, E. D.—for a number of years. In 1866 he returned to the home of his childhood, and purchased fifty acres of the Egbert property adjoining that of his father. In 1870 he purchased a plot on the corner of Claremont and Mountain Avenues, where he erected a substantial and attractive villa. He has been active in promoting the several improvements in the township, and served for a time as Road Commissioner. He married Mary Frances Hamilton, daughter of Silas N. Hamilton, a direct descendant of Andrew Hamilton, Governor of East and West Jersey from 1692 to 1697, and of West Jersey from 1699 till the surrender to the Crown in 1702. John Hamilton, a son of Andrew, was Governor of East and West Jersey united, 1736 to 1738, and of the State as separate from New York, 1746 to 1747.

The issue of the marriage of Edwin M. Harrison with Mary Frances Hamilton is Florence M., Carrie V., Kate Erwin, Edwin Mortimer and Harold.

JARED E. HARRISON.

Daniel Vincent Harrison, second child of Jared E. and Catharine (Egbert) Harrison, was born at the homestead on Valley Road, March 30, 1828. He attended public school, and afterward the Warren Holt Academy.

He was associated for some years with his brother Edwin M., in the commission business, and in 1848 started in business on his own account. He resided in Jersey City for some years, and in 1860 returned to Montclair. He invested largely in real estate on a part of which he realized a handsome profit. He built a handsome residence on Bloomfield Avenue, near Mountain Avenue, where he has since resided.

He married Frances P., daughter of John Munn (see history of Munn family). Their children are: Edwin M., Jr., Josephine, Elizabeth D. (deceased), Jared E., Kittie (deceased), Augustus Smith and Benjamin Vincent.

Nathan Harrison, youngest son of Jared E. and Catharine (Egbert) Harrison, was born at the homestead on Valley Road (within the present township of Montclair) May 24, 1834. He attended Warren Holt's school and the old private school on Montclair Avenue, known as Ashland Hall. He

began his business life as a clerk in a New York commission house, and later became associated with his brother Edwin M. in the commission business, which still continues. He married, first, Cornelia L'Hommedieu, daughter of Elias L'Hommedieu, of Orange County, N. Y., a descendant of an old Huguenot family. He married, second, Katharine M., daughter of Jacob F. Mayer. Issue: Frederic M., Sarah Vincent, Marion Virginia, Paul and Edna.

THE MUNN FAMILY.

The Munns were originally among the early settlers of Connecticut. Joseph, Benjamin and Samuel, three brothers, came from Connecticut about 1750, and settled in Newark.

Capt. Joseph Munn, of West Bloomfield, was a son of Isaac, born 1749—son of Joseph, born 1721. He came to West Bloomfield and purchased from Simeon Crane, July 7, 1801, the property on the corner of Church Street and Valley Road, where he built the first tavern. The second building, which is still standing on the same property, was built after the turnpike—now Bloomfield Avenue—was cut through. This was one of the most noted taverns of the day, and Capt. Joseph Munn, the proprietor, was one of the most popular and well-known hotel men in this part of the country. Members of the Masonic fraternity for miles around made this hotel their headquarters, and Bloomfield Lodge was organized there, and held its regular communications for many years, until the political excitement growing out of the Morgan affair compelled this with many other lodges to surrender their charters. Captain Munn was a genial host, and a man of great influence and prominent in all the military organizations. His brother Jeptha was Grand Master of Masons of the State of New Jersey.

Capt. Munn carried on a large hat manufacturing business in connection with Nathaniel Baldwin, the first postmaster of West Bloomfield.

Henry B. Munn, for some time a teacher at Ashland Hall, was born in the old Stephen Van Courtland house (since burned) that stood just south of the mouth of Second River, Essex County, Newark, N. J.; was prepared for college under Rev. David A. Frame, late of Ashland Hall, Montclair; graduated at College of N. J., at Princeton, 1847; associate teacher at Ashland Hall, 1847-1852; student in law office of late Col. A. C. M. Pennington, 1852-1854; in spring of 1854, to Wisconsin with L. G. Farwell, ex-Governor of Wisconsin, and settled first at Madison, Wis., and then to Portage City; was admitted to the bar in 1855, and in partnership with D. P. Williams opened a land office in connection with law office for practice before the local and United States land office; was elected Mayor of the city in 1858, and to the State Legislature in 1859. Subsequently elected and served till after the close of the late war as Superintendent of City Schools. In 1859 he attended Government land sales at Osage, Fort Dodge and Sioux City. Subsequently became interested in unimproved lands in Western Iowa and Missouri.

From 1866 to 1872 associated with W. C. Dodge as Attorney and Solicitor of Patents. After dissolution of partnership he spent a year in the West, and in 1873 formed partnership with ex-Governor L. G. Farwell, for transaction of real estate and banking business at Grant City, Mo., and also with Chas. F. Stansbury, as Attorney and Solicitor of Patents at Washington.

With the exception of a few special cases his law practice has been what is termed by the profession, chamber practice. He was admitted to bar of Supreme Court of D. C., 1872; United States Supreme Court of D. C., 1888; member of National Bar Association, 1893.

Since the death of his partners he has been practically out of business. Has resided in Washington since 1866, with the exception of three years in Grant City, Mo.

In 1881 he married Cornelia L. Farwell, daughter of ex-Governor L. G. Farwell. Issue: Henry Farwell, Helen Cornelia, Marguerite Campbell and Henry Tinslow.

WHEELER FAMILY,

OF CONCORD, MASS.; STRATFORD, CONN., AND WEST BLOOMFIELD, N. J.

LINE OF GIDEON WHEELER.

THOMAS WHEELER, of Concord, Mass., came to Fairfield in 1644, with Rev. John Jones and his company. He was one of the proprietors of Fairfield township, and was a prominent citizen. His eldest son was named Thomas.

SERGT. JOHN WHEELER, son of Thomas (1) and Ann Wheeler, came with his father's family from Concord to Fairfield, apparently in 1644, being then quite young. He owned a large part of Grover's Hill, at Black Rock, where he resided, and in 1681 paid tax on 1,004 acres of land, he being the third from the highest in the town of Fairfield.

William A. Wheeler, Vice-Presi-
had a son John (2).
John, Sr., and Elizabeth (——)
married Abigal Burr, March 22.
children. He married, secondly,
whom he had six children, the
CAPTAIN JABEZ WHEELER, son
(Porter) Wheeler, was born Feb-
of a company in Col. Whitney's
War of the Revolution. He had,
GIDEON WHEELER, son of
Stratford, Conn., 1764, and was
taught school in Connecticut for
moved to Jersey City, where he
Persippany. He began teaching
achieved quite a reputation as a
matician, and in 1819 prepared
the original manuscript of which
granddaughter in Bloomfield.
by Governor Williamson in 1818,
also a surveyor and conveyancer.
spent on his farm on the Orange

He was the ancestor of Hon.
dent of the United States. He
LIEUT. JOHN (2), son of Sergt.
Wheeler was born in 1664; he
1692, by whom he had seven
Lydia Porter, of Windsor, by
fourth of whom was Jabez.
of Lieut. John (2) and Lydia
ruary 25, 1721. He was Captain
Connecticut Regiment in the
among other children, Gideon.
Jabez Wheeler, was born in
educated in Weston, Conn. He
about thirty years, and then re-
taught for a time, and later in
in Cranetown about 1811, and
teacher. He was a noted mathe-
an almanac, which was published,
is now in the possession of his
He was appointed magistrate
1820, 1822 and 1828. The
latter years of his life were
Road, near its intersection with

GRANT J. WHEELER.

Fullerton Avenue. He had, among other children, Isaac B. and Grant Johnson Wheeler. Isaac B. Wheeler taught school for a number of years in Bloomfield and West Bloomfield.

GRANT J. WHEELER, son of Gideon Wheeler, was born at Weston, near New Haven, Conn., January 1, 1807, and came with his father to West Bloomfield in 1811, and attended the school of which his father was teacher. He learned the tailor's trade, and subsequently carried on an extensive business at Pecktown, near East Orange. He was subsequently connected with the Rosendale Cement Company. In 1843 he removed to Haverstraw, N. Y., where he built and managed a lime kiln. Later he started in the lime business in Newark with Reuben D. Baldwin.

In 1850 he exchanged his residence on Spring Street, Newark, for the farm known as the Elias B. Crane property on Orange Road, West Bloomfield, on which he made many improvements. About 1855 he opened, through his property, a section of Mountain Avenue, and a few years later Hillside Avenue, and a part of Orange Road extension, thus preparing for, and inviting, the improvements subsequently made.

In 1853 he was chosen to represent this district in the Legislature. He was a strong advocate of the then proposed Newark and Bloomfield Railroad, and secured large subscriptions to the stock. While

in the Legislature he introduced an amendment to the charter of the road and secured its passage, and by his activity and firmness largely aided in conferring, at that early date, the benefit of railway communication.

On coming to West Bloomfield Mr. Wheeler engaged in the manufacture of straw air-dried boards, leasing for a time the mill formerly occupied by the Wildes, and at the expiration of the lease, in company with James C. Beach, purchased the property. At this mill he made the first steam-dried strawboards ever made in the United States. [See account under the head of " Industries on Tony's Brook."]

In 1866 Mr. Wheeler was elected a Chosen Freeholder from Bloomfield (then including Montclair), and after the erection of Montclair Township, in 1868, was re-elected to represent it in the Board for ten consecutive years. He also served on the Town Committee for some years.

He was a warm friend of the public school, was elected Trustee in 1851, and re-elected at the expiration of his term. He owned the property on Church Street where the school-house now stands, and offered to give it for a public park provided the township of Montclair would buy the remainder from other parties. They did not accept his proposition, and it was afterward bought by the township for school purposes. He was a member of the Presbyterian Church and a generous contributor to its support, and was for eleven years a Trustee of the Society. He died in 1883.

He married, October 8, 1829, Mary W. Mingis, of Bloomfield, daughter of John Mingis. He had four children, viz.: Sergeant John M., killed at Fredericksburg, Va., while serving with the 26th New Jersey Volunteers; Charlotte D., who died in 1857; Francis A., born June 19, 1844, died in 1889 at Dayton, N. J.; Julius Hawley.

JULIUS HAWLEY WHEELER, youngest son of Grant J. and Mary W. (Mingis) Wheeler, was born at Newark, N. J., June 19, 1847. He was but three years of age when his parents moved to West Bloomfield; he received his education under the old district school system. After leaving school he engaged in the coal business with William Sharp, at Bloomfield, and was afterward for a time in the plumbing business. He entered his father's employ in 1875, and four years later he and his brother bought out their father's interest and continued the business under the name of Francis A. Wheeler & Co. After the removal of the manufactory to Waverly, N. J., a stock company was organized under the name of The Wheeler Manufacturing Company, of which Julius H. became President and still holds that position.

Mr. Wheeler was one of the charter members of the Montclair Fire Company, and served seven years as a fireman. He married, in 1890, Alice H. Harrison, of Ohio, a descendant of the Harrison family, of Orange.

THE HARRIS FAMILY.

COLONEL FREDERICK HALSEY HARRIS, eldest son of William H. and Phebe H. (Baldwin) Harris, was born in Newark, N. J., March 7, 1830. His immediate ancestor was Moses Harris, of Morrisania, N. Y., a descendant—probably— of Robert Harris, who came from Gloucestershire, England, before 1642, and settled in Roxbury, Mass. Descendants of this family moved first to Springfield, Mass., thence to Westchester County, N. Y. Rev. William Harris, of White Plains, N. Y., referring to Robert, the grandson of the ancestor, says : " I do not remember to have heard my father say anything of the Harris family, except that his grandfather, Robert Harris, was a very active, well built man, not large in stature, but in his old age, hale and enterprising."

The name of Harris is of Welsh origin, and means "The son of Harry." Harry being a nickname for Henry. The latter, as a christian name, is given by Webster as of " Old High German origin, meaning the head or chief of a house."

William H., the father of Colonel F. H. Harris, married Phebe H. Baldwin, daughter of Robert, the son of Zadock Baldwin, who served in the New Jersey Militia in the War of the Revolution. Her mother was Mary Gould, daughter of General William Gould, a soldier of the Revolution. General

Gould's wife was the sister of Major Nathaniel Crane, son of Noah, son of Nathaniel, son of Azariah 2d, son of Azariah 1st, who purchased, previous to 1680, the large tract of land subsequently known as Cranetown or West Bloomfield. William H. Harris was born in New York City, and removed with his father, Moses, to Newark, about 1804, when he was a few weeks old. He was an architect and builder, and carried on business for some years. About 1842 he purchased a quarry at Little Falls, N. J. He furnished the stone for the construction of Trinity Church, New York, and from this and his Newark quarries he supplied the stone for St. George's Church, and public buildings in New York, also for Boston and other places. He sold out his quarry in 1853, and bought one hundred acres in West Bloomfield (now Montclair) formerly known as Cranetown, it being a part of the original purchase of Azariah Crane and was the property left by the will of Major Nathaniel Crane to be sold and the proceeds invested in trust for the support of the ministers of the First Presbyterian Church in West Bloomfield. William H. Harris bought this property on account of his wife's early attachment to it, her grandmother, the sister of Major Crane, having been born at the homestead, which formed a part of it. The boundaries began about 200 yards east of the Orange Road and extended to the top of the mountain. Mr. Harris laid out the property and cut the streets and avenues, which were run through it. He occupied the positions of Chosen Freeholder, U. S. Government Assessor, Director of the Newark and Bloomfield Railroad, in which he took an active part, especially the negotiation between the Morris and Essex Railroad Company and the Newark and Bloomfield Railroad Company, which resulted in the building of the latter road, and Trustee of the church for several years. He died in June, 1887, leaving issue: Frederick Halsey, William J., Mary C., Fanny C. and Robert B.

Col. Frederick H. Harris, the subject of this sketch, received a thorough preparatory education at private and boarding schools, intended to enter Princeton College and pursue his studies as a physician, but owing to his father's ill health was compelled to abandon his studies and assist him in the extensive quarry business in which he was then engaged. After his father had sold the Little Falls quarry he continued in the employ of the company who had purchased it, having charge of their extensive works in New Jersey. He moved to Montclair in 1858, and continued in that business until 1858. He had a strong desire for professional life and began that year the study of law, and was admitted to the bar in 1862. Shortly after this he commenced raising a company for the war, which formed a part of the Thirteenth Regiment, N. J. Vols., Company E, of which he was made Captain.

Just before he left for the war he was presented with a sword by the citizens of Montclair, the speech being made by Julius H. Pratt, Esq. It has inscribed on it the following legend: " Presented to Captain Fred. H. Harris by his friends, Montclair, N. J., August 21, 1862"; was worn by him during the whole three years of service, and it now adorns the wall of his residence and is highly prized as a memento of his service.

This is one of the most noted regiments of the war, and with the exception of the battle of Antietam, when he was on the sick list, Col. Harris was with his regiment in every engagement in which it participated. It was attached to the First Division, Twelfth Army Corps. He took part in the battle of Chancellorsville, May 1, 2 and 3, 1863, Gettysburg, July 1, 2 and 3, 1863, and in the autumn following his regiment, as a part of the Twelfth Army Corps, was sent west to join the Army of the Cumberland, and participated in the several engagements of Sherman's campaign, including his famous "march to the sea" (from Atlanta to Savannah) and his campaign through the Carolinas, with the Twentieth Corps, which was made up by a consolidation of the Eleventh and Twelfth Corps. He was commissioned Major, August 16, 1864, and on the 12th of October following was placed in command of the regiment as senior officer, owing to the illness of the Lieutenant-Colonel, the Colonel having been placed in command of the Brigade.

At the battle of Bentonville, fought March 9, 1865, "his regiment held the key to the situation," and he distinguished himself by his coolness, and the splendid manner in which he handled his men, under the most trying circumstances. John Y. Foster, in his "History of New Jersey Troops in the War," gives a minute description of the part taken by the Thirteenth in this battle. Referring to the fact that the Fourteenth Corps was being forced back by the rebels and retreating in great confusion, he says: " At this juncture Major Harris was directed by the brigade commander to deploy and place the regiment on the other or right side of the ravine, using his judgment as to the best position, as rapidly as possible, and once in position to construct such defences as could be quickly made." The order was promptly obeyed, the line being formed on the edge of the ravine as nearly on a prolongation of the brigade line as the nature of the ground would admit; and the men at once commenced to construct a defence of rails and other such materials as were at hand. Soon after this the enemy appeared in three lines of battle, emerging from a belt of woods into a cleared field a short distance to the left of the Thirteenth, on the opposite side of the ravine. The position of the Thirteenth up to this time was not observed by the advancing rebels. Major Harris waited until they were within 150 yards of his position before he gave the order to fire. At the same time the artillery from the rear opened on them with their batteries, and the enemy was driven back in confusion, and made no attempt to renew the attack at that point. As shown by subsequent events this was the decisive point in the battle, and was due to the coolness and gallantry of Major Harris. Foster in his account says: " The action in this, the last battle of the war, was, throughout, of the most gallant character. Had the regiment failed to hold its position, either through incapacity on the part of its officers, or want of steadiness among the men; had the line giving way under pressure of the stragglers from the front and fallen in with the ebbing tide, the battle must inevitably have been lost and the final victory over Johnston's army delayed, perhaps, for weeks." The regiment was highly complimented by corps, division and brigade commanders. Col. Hawley, commanding the brigade, said: " You are entitled to the thanks of this whole army, for you have saved it." In reply to Lieut.-Col. Harris, who asked for orders, he said: " I have no orders to give, for I know you will hold your position without." General Williams, commanding the division, remarked at the time in reference to the action of Lieut.-Col. Harris: " He ought to be brevetted a Brigadier-General for that."

Major Harris had been promoted Lieutenant-Colonel previous to the battle, but his commission had not reached him. On the 26th of March following he was regularly mustered in as Lieutenant-Colonel, and continued in that capacity until mustered out of service. He was twice brevetted, once for gallant and meritorious service in Georgia and the Carolinas, and again for his gallantry at the battle of Bentonville.

At the close of the war, in 1865, Colonel Harris returned to Newark and began the practice of law, and in the spring of 1866 he was called to the Secretaryship of the American Insurance Company, of Newark, which position he held for seventeen years, until 1883, and was that year elected President as the successor of Mr. Stephen G. Gould (a son of General Gould), deceased.

The annual income of the company when he became connected with it in 1866 was about $120,000, its total assets about $170,000, and its net surplus about $140,000, and the stock was selling at par. In 1893 the income was about $700,000, the total assets about $2,340,000, the net surplus about $1,170,000, and the stock was selling in the market at 200 per cent. It is one of the oldest, and much the largest, fire insurance companies in the State of New Jersey.

For many years after the war, when the struggle was going on between the old and new regime, Col. Harris was among the boldest and most determined of the old residents in promoting the various public improvements rendered necessary by the increasing population, composed largely of men of wealth and refinement from our large cities. He stood side by side with Mr. Pratt, Dr. Love and others in their efforts to improve the public school system (of which he was at one time a trustee), which has since become one of the marked features of Montclair. He was for many years the recognized leader of the republican party of this township; and while he invariably declined to accept political honors, he was one of the most earnest workers for the success of his party.

He has long been identified with the Presbyterian Church, and, as President of the Board of Trustees and Clerk of Session, he rendered important service in the management of its temporal and spiritual affairs.

He assisted in organizing the Veteran Association of the Thirteenth Regiment of Veterans in

1886 and became its first President, in which position he continued until 1889, during which time the Gettysburg monument was built and in the success of which he took an active part and a deep interest. He is a member and was for some years commander of Phil Kearney Post No. 1, G. A. R. He is also a member of the Society of the Sons of the American Revolution, and of Montclair Lodge No. 144, F. and A. M., of which he was a charter member; he is also a director of the Montclair Library Association, and one of the managers of Rosedale Cemetery. And it was at his suggestion and by his efforts the cemetery was enlarged in the direction of and for the accommodation of the people of Montclair; is a member of the Society of the Army of the Potomac, Society of the Army of the Cumberland, of the Board of Trade, City of Newark, and of the New England Society of Orange. By his energy and force of character he has been prominent and influential in the various enterprises with which he has been connected, and has often been promoted to leading positions.

The homestead of Colonel Harris, near the corner of the Orange Road and Myrtle Avenue, occupies a portion of the original 100 acres purchased by his father in 1853. He enlarged one of the old buildings on the place and made numerous improvements which give it an attractive and picturesque appearance. Among the numerous relics which adorn the interior is an old-fashioned upright clock of antiquated appearance, formerly the property of Major Nathaniel Crane, the woodwork of which was made from one of the apple trees which grew on the place.

Col. Harris married, in 1865, Elizabeth J. Torrey, daughter of Charles Torrey, of Bethany, Wayne County, Pennsylvania, and a granddaughter of Major Jason Torrey, one of the pioneers of that county, who came originally from Connecticut. Five children are the issue of this marriage, viz.: Ellen, who married Charles M. Dutcher, of Brooklyn; Elizabeth, Jane Howell, and Frederick Halsey (deceased in 1879) and Anna Marion.

THE PRATT FAMILY.

LINE OF DESCENT OF JULIUS HOWARD PRATT, OF MONTCLAIR, FROM LIEUT. WILLIAM PRATT, OF SAYBROOK, CONN., 1645.

The name of Pratt derives its origin from a locality, and is from the Latin Pratum, a meadow. The name appears in the roll of the Battle Abbey, A.D., 1066, as one who accompanied William the Conqueror and participated in the battle of Hastings. William de Pratellis accompanied Richard Cœur de Lion to the Holy Land, and on a certain occasion saved the King from capture by the Turks by personating the King and permitting himself to be taken instead, for which service he was knighted and highly honored.

LIEUT. WILLIAM PRATT, the American ancestor of this branch of the Pratt family, came from Hertfordshire, Eng., and as his lineage is easily traced back into the 14th century, it is highly probable that he is descended from William de Pratellis. He emigrated to New England and settled in Cambridge, Mass., previous to 1632, and moved thence to Hartford, Conn., in 1636. He was one of the band who went from Hartford on the expedition against the Pequods in 1637, which resulted in the extermination of this tribe. In 1645 he settled in Saybrook, Conn., in that part now known as Essex. He represented the town of Saybrook in the General Assembly twenty-three times from 1666 to 1678, and by order of the General Court, October, 1661, he was "established Lieutenant to ye Band at Sea-Brook." He was a warm friend of the Indian Chief Uncas, and one of the executors of his will, and received from the latter large grants of land.

Julius Howard Pratt's line of descent from Lieut. William Pratt, is through "Ensign" *John Pratt*, eldest son of the latter, born February 20, 1644; *John Pratt, Jr.*, born September 5, 1671; *Azariah Pratt*, born 1710; "Deacon" *Phineas Pratt*, born June 27, 1717, who had a son *Julius*, the father of Julius H. Deacon Phineas Pratt, the grandfather of Julius H., was a soldier in the War of the Revolution, and assisted Bushnell in the construction of the famous torpedo boat known as the American "Turtle," which became such a terror to the British fleet in New York Harbor. Phineas Pratt

Julius A. Ball

volunteered the hazardous attempt to blow up one of the British men-of-war lying in the East River. He selected a cloudy night and ran within a few feet of the ship, when, owing to the sudden appearance of the moon through a rift in the clouds, he was discovered and hailed by the watch on deck. He immediately descended, and came up about half a mile distant; he was chased and fired at by the British, but effected his escape. He was highly commended by the Commander-in-Chief and released from further active service. Julius Pratt, the father of Julius H., was the pioneer in the ivory manufacturing business of this country, which he established in Meriden, Conn., in 1812, and laid the foundation for the immense wealth and prosperity of that town. He married Lydia De Wolfe, of Westbrook, Conn., a descendant of one of the early settlers of Lyme. They had issue, Harriet Melinda, born April 24, 1818; *Julius Howard* and William McLane.

JULIUS HOWARD PRATT, second child and eldest son of Julius and Lydia (De Wolfe) Pratt, was born in Meriden, Conn., August 1, 1821. He was graduated from Yale College (which was founded in the native town of his ancestor, Lieut. William Pratt), in 1842, and soon after engaged in the ivory goods manufacture, established by his father in 1818. He was connected with the selling department in New York City for eighteen years, during which period the sales for the firm averaged nearly half a million dollars' worth of ivory combs per annum, while their market extended all over North and South America. The product of table cutlery (mostly ivory handled) and of piano keys amounted to a still larger sum. The delicacy and perfection of the process employed was illustrated in the World's Fair at London, in 1851, by the exhibition of a single sheet of purest ivory fifty-six feet long and fourteen inches wide, which had been sawed by automatic machinery from the section of an elephant's tusk about five inches in diameter.

In 1857, Mr. Pratt removed with his family to West Bloomfield, which at his suggestion was changed to the present name of Montclair. In a paper entitled " Montclair Prior to the Organization of the Congregational Church," which he read before the Congregational Church of Montclair (of which he was one of the founders, and President of the Board of Trustees for seventeen years), in June, 1870, says: " Thirty-three years ago with my family I moved from a Connecticut home to this promised land. We brought with us our Lares and Penates, not forgetting our flowering shrubs and grafts from the lucious fruit trees which had endeared to us the place of our earlier years, that we might perpetuate for our children the sweet perfume, the delicious flavors and the dear associations of the old New England home. The territory now occupied by Montclair was wholly agricultural land, poorly cultivated and largely covered with decaying apple trees. A few farm houses scattered here and there enlivened the landscape with their white walls and green blinds, and gave shelter to, perhaps, one thousand inhabitants throughout the entire area of the present township of Montclair. In that year (1857) the steam locomotive for the first time labored up the steep grade by which our elevated site must be reached, bringing in its train sometimes two or three, seldom more than twenty passengers. The old stages which plied between here and Newark continued their mission for a few years later, because the railroad itself was not a formidable competitor in its rate of speed, and perhaps because the stages having to all appearance survived since the time of Noah's Ark continued to possess a charmed life."

From the period of his advent to Montclair (1857), for more than a quarter of a century Mr. Pratt was a leader in nearly every public enterprise connected with Montclair, and to his efforts probably more than to any other individual is due the present growth and prosperity of the township. He was always in advance of the times, and in his progressiveness sometimes appeared aggressive, but he foresaw what others were slow to grasp, and he could ill-brook the restraint of those who sought to handicap him in efforts for improvements. He never shrank from the controversies which the prejudices of the slow native population occasioned. The laying out of new roads, the revolution of the public school system, and the founding of a progressive church were movements in which he took a prominent part. His most important achievement, however, was the building of the New York and Greenwood Lake Railway, in order to provide competition with the Morris and Essex Railroad Company. This enterprise he carried through at a cost of about $4,000,000 in the face of bitter opposition, but with the result of saving to the town of Orange, Bloomfield and Montclair more than $200,000 per annum in the cost of their traffic and transportation. His experience was like that of many other pioneers whose private interests are made subordinate to their public spirit. Having sacrificed the earnings of a successful business career in this effort for the public good, and having accomplished his work as a local reformer, he has since led a quiet life, finding satisfaction in witnessing the happiness of thousands of new comers around the foot hills of Orange Mountain, who unconsciously enjoy the fruit of his former labors. In 1888, Mr. Pratt once more displayed his progressive character by proposing a new water supply for the city of Newark and vicinity by a gravity system connecting with the Pequannock River, distant about twenty-five miles. The plan was adopted, and his property and water rights along the river which controlled the supply were bought by the East Jersey Water Company, which secured the contract from the Newark authorities. By this transaction and other successful enterprises, Mr. Pratt, in a measure, retrieved his fortunes and is financially comfortable in his declining years.

The only enterprise of a public nature which he has promoted in later years has been the organizing of the Arlington Cemetery in the township of Kearny, which is recognized as one of the most beautiful and best managed rural cemeteries in New Jersey, and of which he has been continuously the chief officer. The picturesque and attractive features of this cemetery illustrate how the sombre abode of the dead can be transformed into a garden of beauty, and the old traditional ministry of sadness can become a cheerful occupation.

His occasional contributions to the press have been received with marked favor by the public. His style is graceful yet vigorous and forcible, and often poetical. His journey to and life in California in 1849, with its thrilling adventures and hairbreadth escapes, was graphically described by him in a sketch published in the *Century Magazine* for April, 1891.

In 1843, Mr. Pratt married Miss Adeline F. Barnes, daughter of Eli Barnes, of New Haven, Conn., and sister of Alfred S. Barnes, of Brooklyn. She died in March, 1886, greatly lamented by the community whose social and moral life she had in a great measure influenced and directed.

The Montclair Times of April 3, 1886, in referring to the death of this noble woman, said:

"No woman ever lived in this village who has exerted a wider or more beneficent influence. In our social and religious life she has been one of the most conspicuous figures. And yet no person was ever more averse to publicity. She was prominent not so much because of her exceptional gifts as her exceptional goodness. The reputation for sociability and good feeling which has distinguished Montclair was almost created by this beautiful and indefatigable woman. Very seldom does a person in no position of prominence, with no special advantage not possessed by others, win so large a place in so many hearts. And yet the causes are not hard to find.

"She was absolutely unselfish; she lived to do good and make others happy; she was the friend of the poor and the friendless; she sought no recognition for what she did. Gifted with great physical strength, she was able to do what others equally willing could not attempt. Without neglecting her own home, she had a mysterious way of bearing the griefs and sharing the anxieties of almost all the homes in the village, while it was small enough for one person to know all. Her sympathy was magnetic because it was so genuine. Wherever there was sickness or suffering she was sure to be found. 'She went about doing good.' If she had wealth it was not used for herself but for others. If she had not money to give, she gave strength and love just the same.

"She was one of the original members of the Congregational Church, and she worked for its welfare with tireless zeal. Yet she was no sectarian. She was simply a Christian. She was almost passionately evangelistic. Her religion was her life. She wanted every one to enjoy her faith. For years she was President of the Ladies' Aid Society, and her influence was felt in all the departments of the church's activity. Before the organization of the Congregational Church she worked with the same spirit in the Presbyterian Church. She was greatly interested in missions, and the only one of her children living who could not be with her during her last hours, was her daughter, Mrs. Eaton, who is a missionary in Mexico. When the Woman's Christian Temperance Union was organized, she threw into it her intense and eager enthusiasm. It was the last public work in which she had a part. Nothing which concerned human welfare and happiness was foreign to her. She may be said to have given her life to this community. In her home, in society, in the Sunday School, in the Church, in all beneficent work, she was constantly interested. During her sickness her flowers were divided and sent to others who were sick; and her constant prayer was for those whom she desired to see more heartily consecrated. 'Her thread of life was strung with beads of love and thought.'

"* * * Her life was beautiful and beneficent; her death painless and peaceful; her memory is a benediction and an inspiration. She belonged to the whole community, and the whole community is sad at its loss."

Eight children were the issue of this marriage, two dying in infancy and six others now living, viz.:

HARRIET AMELIA, the wife of Henry F. Torrey, Montclair. Died September 15, 1893.

GERTRUDE CLIFFORD, who married Rev. James D. Eaton, both now in the service of the American Board of Foreign Missions in Chihuahua, Mexico.

WILLIAM A., Superintendent of Mines in Mexico.

ADELA, the wife of Charles H. Johnson, Jr., in Montclair.

THE PRATT HOMESTEAD BUILT IN 1856, NOW NO. 55 ELM STREET.

JULIUS HOWARD, Proprietor and Manager of an Educational Institution in Milwaukee, Wis., and John Barnes, now residing in Montclair.

He bought a farm in 1856 and built his first residence on Elm Street, which he caused to be widened from a narrow farm road to its present width, and along which he planted the elms which suggested the name of the street, and which for twenty-five years have been an ornamental feature of the town. At that time his house was the only one occupying the area between Fullerton Avenue and the Bloomfield line in one direction, and Bloomfield Avenue and Orange Road in the other direction. A view of the house is shown in the accompanying illustration.

During his public career in Montclair Mr. Pratt has made enemies, but at the same time he has made many warm friends. A man of great decision of character, and one who has the courage of his convictions, no amount of argument or opposition could swerve him from a line he had marked out for himself. His pertinacity and strong determination of character are hereditary traits and have marked his course through life. He has given liberally of his means in aid of public and private charities, and always extended a helping hand and a word of encouragement to those who were fighting life's battle's amid adverse circumstances.

THE CHITTENDEN FAMILY.

LINE OF DESCENT OF HENRY A. CHITTENDEN FROM WILLIAM THE ANCESTOR.

WILLIAM CHITTENDEN, the American ancestor of this family, came from the parish of Canbrook, in Kent, near London, England, in 1639, and settled at Guilford, Conn., which was then a part of the New Haven Colony. He was one of the six persons selected to purchase lands in Guilford, and was the chief military man in the plantation, bearing the title of " Lieutenant." He had been a soldier in the English Army in the Netherlands, where he held the title of " Major." He was a chief magistrate

H. A. CHITTENDEN.

in the colony and a deputy to the General Court until his death. He was a man of great executive ability and common sense, and did much to advance and protect the interests of the little band of colonists who had left their native lands in order to enjoy the free exercise of their relig- ions principles. The old homestead in Guilford which he occupied is still in the hands of his de- scendants and is known as " Mapleside." The name of Chittenden is said to be derived from the British and Welsh, from the words chy [house], tane [lower], din or dun [hill], meaning the " lower house under the hill." The line of descent of Henry A. Chittenden is through Thomas, one of the ten children of William; thence through Josiah, born in Woodbury, Conn., in 1677, " Deacon " Simeon (1), born in Guil- ford, 1714; Simeon (2), a soldier of the Revolution. who enlisted with the Guilford troops in the " Lexington Alarm." He was the father of Abel. ABEL CHITTENDEN, son of Simeon (2), was born in Guilford in 1779. He was a man of prominence in the community, of great force and energy of char- acter, and possessed strong religious convictions. Married Ann Hart Bald- win, daughter of Timothy Baldwin and Olive Norton. He resided on the lot occupied by William the ancestor. His children were: Henry Baldwin, Olive Norton, Sarah Dudley, Anna Hart, *Simeon Baldwin* —of whom hereafter.—and Henry Abel.

SIMEON BALDWIN, fifth child of Abel and Anna Hart (Baldwin) Chittenden was born at the homestead in Guilford, Conn., in March, 1814. He was for many years the head of the well-known New York dry goods firm of S. B. Chittenden & Co., was a well-known philanthropist, one of the most prominent as well as one of the most popular men in Brooklyn. He represented his Congressional District in Congress from 1874 to 1881, and was one of the most influential members during that term. He was also Vice-President of the New York Chamber of Commerce for a number of years. He died in 1889. The library building which he gave to Yale College is a beautiful and enduring monument to his memory.

HENRY ABEL CHITTENDEN, youngest child of Abel and Anna Hart (Baldwin) Chittenden, was born at the homestead of his ancestors in Guilford, Conn., in April, 1816. He was educated at Guilford and began his business career at a very early age in New Haven, Conn., and afterward went to Hartford, where for many years he was a prosperous and leading merchant. He was one of the early advocates of temperance, and took a prominent part in what was known as the "Washingtonian" movement. He subsequently removed to New York City, and was for many years associated with his brother Simeon B. in the wholesale dry goods business, and later carried on business on his own account. He was for many years a resident of Brooklyn, and was one of the founders of Plymouth Church. He introduced Rev. Henry Ward Beecher at the Broadway Tabernacle to the first eastern congregation where he distinguished himself, and was instrumental in the calling of Mr. Beecher to Plymouth Church. Mr. Chittenden was one of the pioneers in the great abolition movement, and a prominent actor in the "underground railroad" system which conveyed numbers of fugitive slaves to places of safety, he assisting by generous contributions of money and by personal efforts. He individually maintained a church at Washington in the cause of "free speech" for a period of six years about this time. Plain, outspoken and fearless, he carried on the crusade which finally resulted in the nomination of Abraham Lincoln as the standard bearer of the Republican party. He is a man of strong religious convictions, a thorough Bible student and possesses a wonderfully retentive memory, being able to quote offhand from almost any portion of the Scriptures. As a public speaker he is earnest and and impressive and on his favorite subject, "The Second Advent," he is eloquent. He is very orthodox in his religious views and is firm and unyielding in his convictions of truth as expounded by the Bible. In 1845 he wrote a pamphlet entitled, "A Reply to the Charge of Heresy," wherein he maintained that there is no future life for mortals out of Christ. This pamphlet has had an enormous circulation, and is still published in Boston.

Mr. Chittenden is the oldest surviving settler of that interesting coterie of New York business men who began the settlement of West Bloomfield—later Montclair—as a place of suburban residence nearly forty years ago. He came about 1856 and purchased a large tract of land on the corner of what is now known as Grove Street and Glen Ridge Avenue. He built the "old homestead," improved his spacious grounds, and there amid pleasant surrounding of trees, flowers and shrubbery has since continued to reside. He married, in 1844, Miss Henrietta Gano, of Ohio, a descendant of Francis Gerneaux, one of the French Huguenot refugees who came to America in 1686 and settled in New Rochelle, N. Y. Her great-grandfather, Rev. John Gano, was the son of Daniel, and grandson of Stephen, and great-grandson of Francis, the ancestor who Americanized and changed his own name for simplicity to that of Gano. He was born in 1727, was a noted Baptist preacher, who organized the first Baptist Church in New York City, and was ordained as its pastor in 1762. He early espoused the cause of the colonists in their struggle to shake off the British yoke, and became chaplain in Washington's army, and remained with his beloved commander, whose friend and spiritual adviser he was, until the close of the war. He was known as the "Fighting Parson"—was a man of great personal courage, and always found at the front encouraging the soldiers with his genial presence and cheerful words. He removed to Kentucky and died at Frankfort in 1804. His son, Major-General John Stites Gano was a distinguished officer in the war of 1812, and the principal founder and proprietor of Covington, Ky. He died in 1822. His son, Major Daniel Gano, the father of Mrs. Chittenden, was the first white child born in the region known as the city of Cincinnati, in 1794. He was a gentleman of the old school, noted for his kindness of heart, great learning and courtly manners. He was a liberal patron of the fine arts, something of a poet, and counted among his most intimate friends Henry Clay, General Winfield Scott, Governor Clinton, General Harrison and the Marquis de Lafayette. His beautiful home "Acacia" was the mecca and rendezvous for all the distinguished people of that time. He did much to build up his native city, and was beloved by all who knew him. His daughter, Mrs. Henry A. Chittenden, still living, inherits many of his amiable qualities, and is greatly beloved by her large circle of friends and acquaintances. The issue of the marriage of Henry A. Chittenden with Henrietta Gano is eight children—two deceased, Henrietta, aged three years, and Belle, aged thirteen. Those now living are Henry A., Jr., the editor; Anna C. Duncan, wife of the eminent lawyer, D. D. Duncan, formerly of St. Louis, but now of New York City, Daniel Gano, Charles Baldwin, Elizabeth L., wife of Dr. W. E. Pinkham, of New York, and William Lawrence.

Daniel Gano's latest namesake and descendant is Gano Westervelt Chittenden, born November 9, 1890, the son of Henry A. Chittenden, Jr., for many years in the editorial service of Mr. James Gordon Bennett on the *New York Herald* and the *Telegram*, his mother being Alice Westervelt, of Paterson, N. J., a well-known magazine and newspaper writer.

William Lawrence Chittenden, known as the "Poet Ranchman," youngest child of Henry A. and Henrietta (Gano) Chittenden, was born in Montclair, N. J., March, 1862. He is named from William the ancestor and from his maternal grandmother, who belonged to the distinguished Lawrence family. William L., or "Larry," as he is familiarly known, enjoyed all the advantages of the higher education for which Montclair is famous. As a lad he was popular with his schoolmates, full of fun, and fond of practical jokes; he was "irrepressible," it is said, and became the "scapegoat" of the village, preferring to bear the sins of others rather than "peach" on his companions. Fond of athletic sports, bathing, fishing, etc., he gave more attention to these than to his books. Later in life he saw his mistake and made up for lost time in hard study and reading. His early athletic training served him a good purpose in later years, for he became famous as a rider, swimmer and diver, and distinguished himself by his boldness and daring in the summer of 1891, at Spring Lake Beach, N. J., by rescuing two New York young ladies from drowning in the surf at the great risk of his own life. Referring to his business career and his genius as a poet, the Gal- veston *News* says of him: "When very young Larry went into the wholesale dry- goods business with his father and uncle, and few poets have a better appreciation than he of what there is in a fine piece of dry-goods—after it has been properly made up. He also has done much repor- torial and literary work for the New York papers. In 1887 he went into the cattle business with his uncle Mr. S. B. Chittenden and settled in Jones County, Texas, where as a bachelor he now resides. The solitary life on the ranch, listening to the songs of the birds and the music of the night winds, developed Larry's poetic in- stincts, and his spirit rose in song. He has wrought his life into his lines, and our readers may well be proud of his success. His 'Ranch Verses,' as Larry terms them, assumed tangible form and were published in a volume issued by G. P. Putnam's Sons, of New York. The first edition was soon ex- hausted, and the second edi-

tion, more elaborate than the first and beautifully illustrated, has lately been issued. The critics of this country and Europe were unstinted in their praise of the work, and Larry finds himself on the high road to fame in this his first attempt to reach the public. In Western parlance, 'honors are easy' with him and he bears them modestly." The Boston *Home Journal* says of the volume: "It is full of true poetic genius and is a very welcome contribution to our best American poetical literature." The London *Saturday Review* says: "Ranch Verses are tuneful, manly in sentiment, and musical in flow. They have a right cheerful tone and are full of spirit and vivacity. The joy of existence and the sense of perfect sympathy for free and tameless nature animates Mr. Chittenden's lyrics." "Sure to become a favorite," says the Glasgow (Scotland) *Herald*. *Public Opinion* says: "Will win from readers old and young unstinted praise and warm eulogy. The bold intellect of the author, tempered by culture and refinement, has produced a volume that must bring him fame." "Ranch Verses," says the *Review of Reviews*, "are worthy of a place beside those of Riley, Harte, Field and Miller." Not an adverse

S. Parkhurst

criticism of the work has yet appeared, and a volume could be compiled of the many pleasant things said by his reviewers. In the words of the St. Louis *Republic:* "We repeat that 'variety is the soul of it all and the spice of life pervades it.'" The Montclair *Times,* believing that in this case a "prophet hath honor in his own country" and among his own kindred, emphasizes the sentiments expressed by others, and says, " All honor to our Poet Ranchman."

THE PARKHURST FAMILY AND COLLATERAL BRANCHES.

Four families of this name, bearing arms, are mentioned by Burke as early as the fifteenth century; two were of London, one was of County Norfolk, one of County Surrey. One of this name was Lord Mayor of London in 1635. Another, Rev. John Parkhurst, was Chaplain to Queen Elizabeth —so stated in Alice Strickland's "Queens of England." The London family bore *Arms.* Argent a cross ermines between four bucks trippant ppr. *Crest.* –Out of a pallisado coronet or, a buck's head erased argent attired of the first.

GEORGE PARKHURST, the American ancestor, was of Watertown, Mass., as early as 1643. He married Susanna, widow of John Simpson, and removed to Boston about 1655. He had a son George (2) by his first wife, born in England in 1618.

GEORGE (2) PARKHURST, son of George first by his first wife, was born in 1618 in England and came over with his father. He remained in Watertown. He married, and had, among other children, John.

JOHN (1) PARKHURST, son of George (2) married and had a child, John (2).

JOHN (2) PARKHURST, son of John (1), was born in Watertown. He married and had children, Isaac and Jonas, who removed to Milford about 1735.

JONAS PARKHURST, son of John (2) was born in Watertown, married Abigail Morse, and removed to Milford, Mass. They had a son, Ephraim.

EPHRAIM PARKHURST, son of Jonas and Abigail (Morse) Parkhurst, was born in Milford, Mass., Dec. 27, 1743. He married Jemima Mayward, and had a son Nathan.

NATHAN PARKHURST, son of Ephraim and Jemima (Mayward) Parkhurst, was born in Milford, June 20, 1770. He dwelt mostly on the " Island," so called, and for many years owned a mill seat just below Charles River Bridge; he was a clothier and miller by trade and did an extensive business. He married Ruth, daughter of Deacon Nathaniel and Elizabeth (Nelson) Rawson, born October 25, 1770.

DEACON NATHANIEL RAWSON, born July 9, 1745, was the son of Thomas, who was the son of Wilson, who was the son of Grindal Rawson. "The faithful and learned pastor of the Church of Christ in Mendon, who died February 6, 1715. This Grindal Rawson was the author of a work entitled 'Confessions of Faith,' written in the Indian and English tongues. He was the friend and classmate of Cotton Mather. By an order passed by the General Court of Massachusetts, July 31, 1692, he, with others, was desired to accompany the General and Forces in the expedition against Canada, to carry on the worshiping of God in that expedition." Grindal was the son of William, who was the son of Edward Rawson, the progenitor of all bearing the name of Rawson in the United States. He was born in Gillingham, Dorsetshire, England, April 15, 1615. He was married in England to Rachel Perne, daughter of Thomas Perne, and grand-daughter of John Hooker, whose wife was a Grindal, sister of Edmund Grindal, Archbishop of Canterbury in the reign of Queen Elizabeth. Edward Rawson came to Newbury, in the Colony of Massachusetts Bay, as early as 1637. He was a grantee of that town, chosen Publick Notary and Register, 1638, and was annually re-elected until chosen Secretary of the Colony.

The issue of the marriage of Nathan Parkhurst with Ruth Rawson was Evelina, born 1797; Ziba, born 1799; Stephen Rawson, of whom hereafter; Parmenus Parsus, born 1802, and Waldo, born 1807.

STEPHEN RAWSON PARKHURST, third child and second son of Nathan and Ruth (Rawson) Park-hurst, was born at Milford, Mass., March 19, 1802. He enjoyed the usual advantages of a common school education, with a brief term at the academy. It was his father's wish that he study civil engineering, but for this he had neither taste nor inclination. His fondness for mechanics was shown in early life, but it was not until the necessity arose that he developed the wonderful inventive genius that afterward placed him in the front rank of American inventors. He was but nineteen years of age when his father died, and, being thrown on his own resources, he began the battle of life with nothing save his own indomitable will, pluck, energy and perseverance. He first took to himself a wife and then obtained a situation in the carding department of a woolen mill, where he not only mastered the details, but saw the necessity for and the advantages to be gained by improved machinery. His first invention, although a very important one, he neglected to patent, and thereby failed to reap the benefits of it. His services, however, became valuable to his employer, and by the time he reached his majority he had accumulated a capital of $2,000, with which he started in business for himself. He was successful from the beginning, and was constantly engaged in making improvements in cotton and woolen machinery.

His elder brother succeeded to the father's business in Milford. Stephen next assumed it, who, after carrying it on for a short time, and making still further improvements, met with a great disaster in the destruction of the building by fire. After many hard struggles he decided to remove to New York City, where he soon after constructed machinery for the manufacture of his several inventions, and organized a company for the purpose of operating the business known as the Atlas Manufacturing Company. This was subsequently transferred to Newark, where the business is still continued in that name.

As an inventor Mr. Parkhurst did more to revolutionize the manufacture of wool and cotton than any man since the days of Amos Whittemore and Eli Whitney. His first invention was known as the Burring Machine, for which he obtained Letters Patent May 1, 1845. The object of this invention was to remove the burrs, and other foreign substances, from wool before carding, thereby preventing damage to the card clothing, and effecting great saving in labor and material, and to free cotton from seeds and other substances injurious to the staple, thereby materially enhancing its value.

When used in combination with a carding machine, as it generally is, the burr cylinder is placed next the feed rollers, draws the unburred wool from between them on to plain surface, between narrow, toothed, or serrated steel rings, placed upon a light, hollow, rigid, metallic cylinder, called a burr cylinder; the plain surface being somewhat less in diameter than the serrated rings, allows the material to be drawn below the periphery of the steel rings on to the plain surface, and leaves the burrs on top to be knocked off by a revolving guard over the burr cylinder into a trash receptacle in front. The wool being thus freed from burrs, is stripped from the burr cylinder in the rear by a rapidly revolving card-clothed cylinder of the carding machine, and passes on through the machine in the ordinary process of carding. Previous to this invention various attempts had been made, especially on burring wool, to devise some means whereby the burrs could be removed without injury to the fibre and the wool rendered more serviceable for high grade manufacturing purposes, but with only partial success. At the time of the introduction of these machines into use, the old methods of picking the burrs from the wool by hand, or cutting them out with common sheep shears, was generally resorted to. But this process was slow, tedious, expensive, and unreliable, and wool, which was very burry—especially foreign wools of this description—was only used to a very limited extent in this country, in consequence of the great difficulty and expense incurred in removing the burrs.

Besides inventing numerous other machines of a similar character, Mr. Parkhurst made many improvements in his burring machine. He was subjected to a long and expensive litigation in defending his patents, and Judge Nelson of the U. S. Circuit Court, in giving his decision in 1865, remarked that "this invention was very meritorious."

He invented his Double Burring Machine in 1862. His steel ring cylinders and feed rollers as applied to carding machines are still regarded as the best in the market, and his machinery for cleaning wool is considered far superior to any machine for this purpose in this country or in Europe.

His Steel Cylinder Cotton Gin, patented long before the war, was of inestimable value to the planters of the South. One planter wrote: "The cotton that I ginned on them last year sold for one and a half cents more than my saw-gin cotton." This was especially adapted to the long and short staple cotton, without injury to the fibre. It received the First Medal and Diploma at the Fair of the American Institute in 1869.

Mr. Parkhurst had a large sale for his Cotton Gin at the South before the war. He lost heavily, however, at the breaking out of the war, and after that confined his attention principally to the manufacture of other machinery. He removed to Montclair, or what was then West Bloomfield, about 1857. He purchased the Mountain House property, where he resided for a number of years until his death in April, 1887.

He was a man of unimpeachable integrity, uprightness of character, generous to a fault, and greatly beloved by his associates and employees—to any and all of whom he was ever ready to lend a helping hand.

Mr. Parkhurst married Thankful Legge, daughter of David Legge, of Mendon, Mass., who served as Sergeant in the War of the Revolution, and was with Washington at Valley Forge. He was a descendant of John Legge, of Salem, 1631, who came in the fleet with Winthrop and lived at Marblehead. Members of this family were noted for their personal prowess and courage; several of them took part in the Colonial as well as the French and Indian Wars; their descendants were largely represented in the War of the Rebellion. David Legge was the son of William, who was probably the son of John Legge, of Mendon, who married Hannah Nelson, daughter of Gersham and Abigail (Winthrop) Nelson born at Rowley, 1714.

The issue of Mr. Parkhurst's marriage with Thankful Legge was Sylvester, born 1822, died 1824; Elizabeth, who married Warren Holt; Emily Ruth and Henry C. The latter was a bright, promising young man who inherited much of his father's inventive genius. Referring to his untimely death, the *Milford Journal* says: "Among the lost by the late explosion of the steamer *Princess* on the Mississippi River, was Henry C. Parkhurst, only son of Stephen R. Parkhurst, of New York, formerly of this town. By this sad casualty a father and mother and two sisters, with a large circle of relatives, have been bereaved of a most dutiful and affectionate son, brother and friend. In his business relations, which were very extensive, he had the confidence and esteem of all with whom he was in any way connected. He leaves behind him the record of a short life well spent, and the cheering consolation to his friends that his record was on high. He was a prominent man, and was acting as traveling agent of the establishment when he lost his life. His education was received at the Mountain House School, kept by Mr. Warren Holt, then one of the most popular educational institutions in the State. It was this fact that led his parents subsequently to settle in this locality and to purchase the building.

Mr. Warren Holt (long known as one of the most successful teachers in West Bloomfield), who married the second child of Stephen R. Parkhurst, erected on the crest of the mountain, near Bloomfield Avenue, one of the beautiful villas in that locality. The site on which this house rests affords the most extended view of any other in the township. Looking toward the east there is an uninterrupted view of the whole country from the mouth of the Hudson River to the terminus of the Palisades. Looking west there is a beautiful view of the township of Verona in the valley, with the Second Mountain and the township of Caldwell in the distance; looking north, the beautiful Passaic Valley, with its numerous towns and villages, easily discerned on a clear day.

THE BOYD FAMILY.

LINE OF DESCENT OF ROBERT M. BOYD.

It is stated in "Burke's Landed Gentry," that "This family is of very considerable antiquity, having a common ancestor with the Boyds, Earls of Kilmarnock, the last of whom bearing the title suffered on Tower Hill in 1745 for his devotion to the ill-fated race of Stewart. The first recorded ancestor, Simon, brother of Walter, High Steward of Scotland, witnessed the foundation charter of the monastery of Paisley in 1160, and is therein designed 'frater Walteri filii dapiferi.'" He was father of Robert, called *Boyt* or *Boyd*, from his complexion, the Celtic word Boidh signifying fair, and from him derived the various families of the name. The lands of Kilmarnock were granted by Robert the Bruce to his gallant adherent, Sir Robert Boyd, who had been among the first associates of the prince in his arduous attempt to restore the liberties of Scotland. Sir Robert was father of three sons: Sir Thomas, his heir; Alan, who commanded the Scottish archers at the siege of Perth, in 1339, where he was slain. The eldest son, Sir Thomas Boyd, was taken prisoner, together with King David II. at the battle of Durham in 1346.

JAMES BOYD, one of the four brothers who migrated to America, was of Kilmarnock stock, originating in Ayreshire, Scotland; transferred to County Down, in the North of Ireland. This James, the third brother, sailed from Belfast, Ireland, August 9, 1756, with his wife and children. His eldest son, *Samuel*, visited America four years earlier than his father, and returned to Ireland, whence he came back as a permanent settler in 1756, and thereafter resided in Little Britain Parish, Conn., until his death, May 27, 1801, in his sixty-seventh year. He served in the French and Canadian War, and furnished a substitute in the Revolution. His son *James*, who settled in Winsted, Conn., forged the chain that was stretched across the Hudson from Fort Washington to the Jersey shore during the Revolution, to prevent the British ships from passing up the river. He had a son, *Samuel*.

SAMUEL (1) BOYD, born June 24, 1802, was engaged as a trader and manufacturer in Winsted till 1833. He was prominent in military and other affairs in his native town and was Captain of a militia company. He went to New Orleans in 1836 in company with four friends, all of whom died during the great yellow fever epidemic of the following year. He was the first taken and after his recovery nursed his friends. He was a member of the Howard Benevolent Association and did a noble work in nursing the sick during the prevalence of that terrible scourge. He made many friends and was successful in all his business operations. He invested largely in real estate and owned a beautiful residence in Lafayette, then a suburb above, now a portion of the city of New Orleans. He was popular with the masses and served as a member of the Board of Aldermen. He returned to New York City in 1850, and engaged in the commission hardware business. He was appointed Appraiser in the New York Custom House in 1860, and held that position until his death in 1885. He was for some years a resident of Brooklyn; was one of the founders and a prominent member of Plymouth Church during the early part of Beecher's pastorate and was instrumental in calling him to the church. He removed to West Bloomfield about 1856, and later built a house on Fullerton Avenue, on the site now occupied by the Wilde Memorial Chapel, where he resided until his death. The house was removed to Grove Street and is at present occupied by Dr. Shelton. He was one of the founders of the First Congregational Church in Montclair, and was instrumental in calling Dr. A. A. Bradford as its pastor. He was a man of genial nature, sympathetic, and of large-hearted liberality. He was a friend of the poor and unfortunate, and delighted in doing good and helping others. He married, September 20, 1825, Sylvia Coe (still living, 1893), daughter of Jonathan and Charlotte (Spencer) Coe, a descendant of Robert Coe, who came from England in 1634 and settled in Connecticut.

They had issue, *James M.*, deceased; *Marianne* (married Henry B. Keen); *Sarah Jane*, married Thomas Howe Bird (see sketch); *Robert Munro*, of whom hereafter; *Alice Isabel*, born in New Orleans, La., married Rev. Nelson Millard—issue, Ernest Boyd and Ethel Florence.

ROBERT MUNRO BOYD, fourth child of Samuel and Sylvia (Coe) Boyd, was born in Winsted, Conn. His education was received at the public school and academy in his native town. He came to New York about 1852 and engaged as clerk in the wholesale dry-goods business, and in 1868 he became a partner in a large importing house, of which he has since become the senior partner, the business having been successfully conducted for more than a quarter of a century. His success is due in a great measure to the confidential relations established between himself and his employees. They are treated like men, and made to feel that the interests of employer and employee are mutual. His aim in life has been to apply the golden rule in all his relations with his fellow men. Modest and unassuming, yet a man of great energy, force and determination of character.

A portion of his early life was spent in New Orleans and later in Brooklyn. He removed to Montclair in 1856, and has not only witnessed but has aided materially in its growth from a little village of a few hundred inhabitants to a suburban township of over 10,000. He has invested extensively in real estate both in Montclair and Upper Montclair, which he has greatly improved. He has been

Robert M. Boyd

especially interested in the laying out and improvement of streets, and was for some years a member of the township Road Commissioners. He has also served several years as trustee of the First Congregational Church. In 1869 he built his present house, 51 Fullerton Avenue, where he has since resided. He married Kate B., daughter of Matthias Crane, grand-daughter of Israel Crane, and sixth in descent from Nathaniel Crane, one of the original settlers of Cranetown. Issue: Robert M., Jr., Susie Belle, and Bertha Louise.

ROBERT M. BOYD, JR., son of Robert M. and Katharine (Crane) Boyd, was born in Montclair, May 5, 1863. He began his education in the primary department of the Montclair public school, passing through the various grades, graduated with honor, and took the valedictory. Entered Yale in 1880; took a Latin prize in the Freshman Class and the mathematical prize in the Sophomore. He was appointed to speak at the Commencement and took the Cobden Club medal for excellence in political economy. He entered Columbia Law School in 1884, graduating in 1886 with the degree of LL.B., and took the degree of M.A. from Columbia School of Political Science. He began practice in the office of Davies, Cole and Rapallo, New York, the same year. He spent one year with the Title Guarantee and Trust Company, and later opened an office on his own account at 32 Liberty Street. On January 1, 1889, he formed the present co-partnership of Murphy, Lloyd & Boyd, and has already acquired a corporation litigative and real estate practice. He is an indefatigable worker, and his college athletic training enables him to attend to his increasing responsibilities. Courteous, and even generous to his opponents, yet he leaves no stone unturned to win his case by honorable means. During his college life he took an active part in athletic games, and in these he has been a leader in Montclair. Whether at play or work, he obeys the Scriptural injunction, "Whatsoever thy hand findeth to do, do with thy might." He has been Secretary, Treasurer, and President of the Tennis Club; Secretary, Vice-President, and President of the Dramatic Club, and Governor of the Athletic Club. He is equally earnest in religious affairs and is assistant deacon in the First Congregational Church.

HENRY NASON.

Mr. NASON was among the first of the "new comers" to Montclair. He was a native of Augusta, Me., born June 11, 1818. He came to New York City at an early age and began business as clerk with one of the largest firms in the city, without compensation. At the age of twenty-one he started in business for himself at Farmington, Me. He purchased grain from the farmers direct, shipped by teams to Hallowell, and thence to New York by water. He was the first to engage in the grain business in that locality. Later he returned to New York City and engaged in the wholesale flour and grain business, on the corner of Water and Broad Streets, becoming, with his brother-in-law, Captain Collins, one of the leading firms in this line. He was for some time a resident of Brooklyn, and was one of the founders of Pilgrim Church (Dr. Storrs).

He resided for two years in New York City, and in 1859 removed to Montclair, where he purchased a large tract of land on the mountain slope. He built the large stone mansion which faces Hillside Avenue, using the trap rock from the cliff directly in the rear. He was the pioneer on the mountain slope, and erected altogether fourteen houses. He opened at his expense Hillside Avenue and Mountain Avenue from the Turnpike to the Haskill property, afterward continued to Llewellyn Park. He also opened Gates Avenue, giving it his wife's maiden name. He was enthusiastic, public-spirited, a man of intense energy and an earnest worker in the cause of temperance. His personal influence brought to Montclair many of its best citizens. He was a trustee in the Presbyterian Church, and became one of the founders of the Congregational Church. He subsequently removed to Virginia and bought a plantation six miles from Orange Court House, which soon became a settlement, with a post office, and later, when a railroad was cut through, he encouraged the enterprise, and in recognition of his aid, the company, after his death, named the place Nason. He at once established a colored Sabbath School, which became very large, and in which every member of his family, old enough, was a teacher.

The children were taught to sing the Bradbury hymns, and as soon as they were able to read he presented them with Bibles. Sixty Bibles were thus given away, and a flourishing church was finally established on the plantation.

On a business trip to Montclair, September 6, 1876, he died very suddenly immediately after his arrival. He was buried in Rosedale Cemetery, Orange.

Mr. Nason was twice married, first to Sarah Wingate, of Maine, by whom he had three children--two sons and a daughter. He married, secondly, Anna Gates, a native of Massachusetts, but educated and married in New York City, by whom he had eight children. Henry, the eldest, married Emelie Woodruff, and resided for many years in Montclair, now of Redlands, Cal. Joseph Wingate, the second son, died in service of the Union Army during the Civil War (for record see Montclair in the Rebellion). The third child, Sarah, married Geo. Innes, Jr., who died suddenly in Virginia; two, Theodore and Charles, died in infancy. The others were Horatio, Arthur, Frederick, Isabel, Malcolm and Anna; the latter married Hamilton Guthrie, and resides in Colorado; Isabel resides with her mother at San Diego, Cal.; the other sons referred to are engaged in business in California.

R. M. HENING.

ROBERT McCLAY HENING was one of the pioneers of the new settlement, and was present and took a prominent part in the discussion which gave the new township its present name. He was a native of Steubenville, O., born in 1812, his father, James Gordon Hening, a native of Virginia, having removed thence, in the early part of the present century, R. M. Hening received a collegiate education in Virginia. He subsequently established an extensive mercantile business in Alexandria, Mo., which he carried on for some five or six years. About 1845 he removed to St. Louis, Mo., where he joined the old-established house of James E. Woodruff, the firm afterwards being changed to Hening & Woodruff, with branches at New Orleans and New York. He was one of the most prominent merchants in St. Louis and was for some time President of the Chamber of Commerce, and was held in high esteem by the members of that body. The death of his partner in 1856 necessitated his removal to New York the same year. The members of the St. Louis Chamber of Commerce adopted a series of resolutions expressive of their esteem of him as a merchant, and of their personal regard as a man; and presented him with an elegant silver service, consisting of salver, coffee urn, etc., on which was inscribed the following: "Presented to R. M. Hening, late President of the Chamber of Commerce by the Merchants and Marine of said city, as a testimonial of their regard and esteem."

R. M. HENING.

Mr. Hening carried on the business successfully under different firm names until after the close of the war, when he retired from the firm, and devoted himself to other financial enterprises, principally in New Jersey. In 1860 he purchased a large tract of land on Mountain Avenue, in Montclair, where he built a handsome residence. He was especially interested in public affairs; was a member of the Board of Chosen Freeholders of the county; was twice a candidate for the Legislature, and in both cases was honored by receiving votes from the opposite party. He was essentially a gentleman, kind, courteous and polite; and a man of great liberality. He took a prominent part in the erection of the new township, and was very active in pushing forward the new railroad enterprise. Soon after coming to the town he united with the First Presbyterian Church, but subsequently withdrew and united with

St. Luke's Episcopal Church, which was then in rather a weak condition. He bought a fine piece of property which he presented to the Church, and also made a liberal donation for the erection of the church edifice. He died in January, 1875.

Soon after the death of Mr. Hening a special meeting of the Vestry of St. Luke's Church was held and the following preamble and resolution was adopted:

WHEREAS, The Vestry of St. Luke's Church having heard of the death of our late esteemed associate, Mr. Robert M. Hening; therefore, be it

Resolved, That in the death of Mr. Hening the Church and community have occasion to mourn the loss of one whose genial presence, uprightness and integrity of character, wise counsels, unaffected kindness of heart, and thoughtful and unselfish solicitude for the comfort and welfare of others endeared him to all who enjoyed the privilege of his acquaintance.

For several years a most earnest and efficient member of this Vestry, feeling a deep interest in the welfare and prosperity of the Church, not alone evidenced by words but by munificent liberality, freely giving of his means in the erection of our beautiful church building, and in sustaining the ministrations of the Gospel, the Vestry cannot let this occasion pass without bearing record to their uninterrupted confidence and affectionate regard during the long and pleasant official and personal intercourse they have enjoyed with their departed and lamented friend. They will ever cherish his memory in affectionate remembrance, and as a testimony of respect will attend his funeral in a body.

Resolved, That these proceedings be placed upon the minutes of the Vestry and the Secretary be requested to forward a copy to the afflicted family, with the assurance of our sincere and earnest sympathy in the great bereavement they have sustained.

ALFRED TAYLOR, Secretary Vestry.

MONTCLAIR, January 20, 1875.

Mr. Hening was twice married; first to Elizabeth Plummer Hyde, second to Sarah Mills Carrington. He had issue by his first wife, Julia E., who married Albert Pearce. Elizabeth A. (who married Thomas B. Graham), Robert McClay, and James Woodruff. He had three children by his second wife.

Robert McClay Hening, third child of Robert McClay and Elizabeth Plummer (Hyde) Hening, was born in St. Louis, Mo., June 7, 1847. He came East with his parents in 1856, and was educated at the Brooklyn Polytechnic Institute. He was engaged for a time in his father's office, and subsequently represented the gold department of Edward Sweet & Co. in the Exchange, remaining until gold reached par, and was afterward in the office of that firm. Later he started in business for himself, dealing specially in government bonds and miscellaneous securities, and had charge of the department of government bonds for the house of Edward Sweet & Co. Subsequently he bought a seat in the Consolidated Stock Exchange, dealing in stocks, petroleum, etc., continuing until 1891. He has since been engaged in the real estate business in Montclair.

GEORGE GARDINER DRAPER.

MR. DRAPER was born at Brookfield, N. H., October 7, 1843. *James*, the American ancestor of the Drapers, was the son of Thomas Draper, of the Priory of Heptonstall, Vicarage of Halifax, Yorkshire County, England, born at Heptonstall 1618, died at Roxbury, Mass., July, 1694. He married Miriam, daughter of Gideon Stansfield and Grace Eastwood, of Wadsworth, Yorkshire. He emigrated to New England previous to 1676, being at Charlestown that year. He subsequently settled at Roxbury, Mass., where three of his children were born, and moved thence to Dedham, where he resided for some years, and finally returned to Roxbury.

The descent of George G. Draper from James, the ancestor, is through *James* (2), *James* (3), *Joshua*, and *Asa*, who was his father. The latter married Ruth Whittemore, daughter of *Thomas*, and a direct descendant of Thomas Whittemore, one of the earliest settlers of Charlestown, Mass., about 1638-9. The farm of Thomas, the ancestor, was bounded east by Chelsea and south by Mystic River. This remained in possession of the Whittemore family until 1845, and the homestead remained intact until 1866, when it was destroyed by fire. This family traces its origin from John, Lord of Whytemore. Earlier than the year 1300 is the first recorded name, that of John, Lord of Whytemore, having his domicile at Whytemore, on the north side of the parish of Bobbington, in the manor of Claverly, in Shropshire. At the present time the same locality bears the name of Whittemore. The Anglo-

etymology of the word Whytemere, is *white meadow*, or *lake*, and the first John, Lord of Whytemere, derived the name of the family from the place where they originally resided.

George G. Draper, son of Asa and Ruth (Whittemore) Draper, was educated in his native town, and removed to New York City about 1836, where he obtained a position as clerk in the once prominent firm of L. & V. Kirby. His large acquaintance with Vermont and New Hampshire business men,

WILLOW BROOK HOMESTEAD.

together with his peculiar abilities as a salesman, gained for him a recognized position in the trade, and soon enabled him to begin business on his own account. About the year 1840 he formed the house of Welling, Root & Draper, and subsequently was a member of the firms of Draper, Aldrich & Frink, Draper, Aldrich & Co., Draper, Knox & Ingersoll, and Draper, Knox & Co., importers and commission merchants. In these several connections he was uniformly successful until, in the financial cyclone of

Samuel Wilde

1857, the last-named firm succumbed. During the remaining years of his life he was comparatively inactive in business, although busily and conscientiously occupied in an honorable closing up of his old affairs. He was one of the most popular and energetic of New York merchants, and in point of ability and reputation ranked with such men as Simeon B. Draper, his esteemed cousin, and other prominent men of that period. While taking no prominent part in politics, he was among the first to join the ranks of the republican party, and was loyal in his support of the government during the war. He encouraged enlistments of young men and in some cases even supported their families during their absence. He sent quantities of food, provisions, fruit, wine and clothing to army hospitals for the benefit of sick and disabled soldiers. Although his means were limited during the latter years of his life, he never failed to respond to the calls of charity and benevolence. Any case of suffering or want that appealed to him found a quick and ready response. Deserving young men found in him a faithful friend and wise counselor.

Mr. Draper spent many years in Brooklyn, where he was well known in social circles and highly esteemed. He was a regular attendant at Plymouth Church. After closing up his business affairs in New York, he sold his Brooklyn property and purchased what was known as the Willow Brook Farm in Montclair, consisting of about 66 acres situated on Washington Avenue, near the Orange Road, and running to the Bloomfield line. The property was formerly owned by Jason Crane; the house, built in 1764, is still in an excellent state of preservation, and is one of the most picturesque of the old landmarks of Montclair. (See view.)

Mr. Draper was one of the parties who were instrumental in naming the present township. Being a native of Claremont, N. H., he suggested that name, but as it was found that there were several other places of this name, it was reversed and called *Montclair*.

Though not a member of any church, he exemplified in his daily walk the teaching of the Bible, and endeavored to live up to the "Golden Rule." He married, December 5, 1846, Miss Annie C. Ballard, of New York. Issue : Georgia Annie, Charles Ballard, Rebecca Ballard, Ruth Clara, and Frank Ballard.

SAMUEL WILDE.

Samuel Wilde was born in Dorchester, Mass., October 5, 1831, and died in Montclair, N. J., March 8, 1890. He was a descendant of John Wilde, who came from England in 1688, and settled in South Braintree, Mass. John Wilde married in 1690, Sarah Hayden, granddaughter of Richard Thayer, who was made a freeman in 1640, and became a resident of Braintree, Mass., in 1641. She was a descendant of William Hayden, who came over in the "Mary and John," in 1630, and settled in Dorchester, Mass. The children of John and Sarah Hayden Wilde, were John, Samuel, William and Sarah. The Samuel referred to had, among other children, a son Joseph (grandfather of Samuel Wilde, the subject of this sketch), who was a Lieutenant in the Continental Army, in the War of the Revolution, his commission being signed by John Hancock (see *fac simile* of commission on opposite page, together with the arms of the Wilde family and collateral branches) who was an officer in the War of the Revolution. His son Samuel (who was father of the subject of this sketch) was born in Dorchester, Mass., in 1800, and removed to New York City in 1829, where he engaged for a time in the hardware and looking-glass trade. Later he engaged in the coffee and spice business, under the firm name of Withington & Wilde, his partner being the pioneer in this country of the process of roasting coffee by machinery for the grocers' trade. He resided for some years in New York, and subsequently removed to Williamsburgh, now Brooklyn, Eastern district. He became quite prominent in the abolition movement in the days when men were persecuted for daring to express their opinions or utter a word against the institution of slavery. He was a warm friend of the colored race, and often assisted in their escape from bondage, by the "underground railroad," and at one time harbored at his own store a fugitive slave. He built a church for the colored people on South Third Street, Williamsburg, which was attended by the white as well as the colored people, he being elected a deacon of the church. He married Sarah, daughter of Robert Jones of Chester, England, by whom he had four sons and seven daughters.

SAMUEL WILDE, the second son, the subject of this sketch, removed with his parents in early childhood to New York, and later to Williamsburgh, where he received the best educational advantages, and studied for a time with his uncle, Rev. John Wilde. In 1848, he entered his father's counting-room, and some years later became a partner in the house under the firm name of Samuel Wilde & Sons, consisting of himself and his brother Joseph. After the death of the father it became Samuel Wilde's Sons. Another change took place after the death of his brother Joseph, in 1878, Samuel Wilde succeeding him as the head of the firm, continuing in this capacity for twelve years, and during this period, under his able management the business largely increased and became one of the leading houses in this line in the country, and attained a reputation for the purity of its goods and honesty in its dealings, second to no other house. The business was continued at the same location where it was first established in 1814. Mr. Wilde conducted his business on Christian principles and applied the "golden rule" to all his business transactions; and it is said that he never sold a bill of goods that he would not willingly take back, and return the money if a customer was dissatisfied. "Honesty" was not a matter of "policy" with him, but a well-grounded principle. He was not only lenient, but liberal towards his unfortunate debtors, preferring to suffer loss rather than cause suffering to another. Mr. Wilde was a director in the Chatham Bank, the Meriden Cutlery Company, and other institutions.

Like his father, he early espoused the cause of the weak and down-trodden, and became an ardent abolitionist at a time when it required courage of the highest order to be identified with the abolition party. He was an earnest worker with his father in the colored church and Sunday School of Williamsburgh. He married, in 1853, Mary E., daughter of Joshua Lunt, of West Falmouth, Maine, a descendant of Henry Lunt, who came from England on the ship "Mary and John," in 1634, and settled first in Ipswich, and afterwards in Newbury, Mass.

Mr. Wilde removed with his family to Montclair in 1860, and purchased a house partly finished on Eagle Rock Way, now Llewellyn Road. He completed and finished the house, and greatly improved and beautified the grounds. Three years later he sold the property and purchased a plot on Union Street, on which he erected a fine house and laid out the grounds in a tasteful manner. This he subsequently sold and the property is now owned by Mr. Russell. He had great faith in the future of Montclair as a suburban town and continued to invest in real estate. About 1864 he bought a plot on what was then High Street—now Fullerton Avenue. On that he commenced the erection in 1870 of one of the finest residences in the town, built of brown stone, in the most substantial manner, requiring three years to complete. He planned all the interior arrangements, the especial feature of which was his library—extending from the second floor to the peak of the Gothic roof, 27 feet in height, closely resembling the interior of a beautiful Gothic church. The decorations and furnishings were all made to harmonize with the general design. Mounted on a loft in the same style of church architecture he erected an organ, and arranged everything in a manner suitable for the entertainment of his numerous friends. His extensive library covers the entire space of two sides of the room, and is well stocked with the best works of standard authors.

Mr. Wilde was a strong advocate of the present school system, which has done so much for the advancement of Montclair. He was one of the Trustees, and established a system of prizes known as the "Wilde Prizes" to encourage greater proficiency in the scholars in the various branches of study.

He was a member of the Town Committee in 1871, and advocated the adoption of numerous public improvements. He represented the Assembly District in the State Legislature in 1872-73, and made for himself an honorable record.

When he first removed to Montclair Mr. Wilde united with the First Presbyterian Church, but withdrew with others in 1870 and became one of the founders of the First Congregational Church of Christ. He was one of its first Trustees, and continued in office for about eighteen years, and its first Treasurer—was a member of the Building Committee, and during the whole period of his life in Montclair, up to the day of his death, was one of the most faithful workers in the church and Sabbath School, having taught a class until his failing health compelled him to relinquish those duties, and almost the last act of his life was to provide a most delightful and attractive stereopticon entertainment for the children of the Sabbath School.

The "Words of Remembrance" uttered by his Pastor, Rev. Dr. Bradford, voiced the sentiments of all who knew him. He says:

"It is a great thing to have lived as many years as our friend in the midst of suffering and pain, and to have kept his faith; to have been associated in the affairs of business so long, and to have preserved a spotless reputation; to have engaged in politics and never to have had a suspicion of dishonor attached to his name; to have lived all these years and be able to say at the last: 'I have fought a good fight, I have kept the faith, I have finished my course.' And so it is that we are gathered here in celebration of victory. We mingle our tears with those who weep, but we feel that the causes of sorrow are fewer than the reasons for rejoicing.

"It is fitting that we should recount to one another some of those traits of character and of life which have made the name of our friend a dear and honored name among us.

"Of his beautiful fidelity in his home we may not speak, and yet there is no need, so evident was it and so constant. We might speak of his honorable reputation in business circles where never a shadow of suspicion crossed the minds of any concerning his integrity and manliness. We might speak of his brief career in politics, where he was always known as a man absolutely incorruptible, one whose very look was a reproof to any who should dare approach him with the suggestion of a bribe. * * * In a thousand quiet ways he was always helping those who were oppressed.

"He was public-spirited. For the last twenty-five years no good work has been started in this community which has not had his active and hearty sympathy. In the library of this house meetings have been held for many of the most prominent movements for the improvement of the town, and no man among us was more earnest than he in advocacy of wise plans for advancing the public interest.

"He was the constant friend of our educational institutions, not only here but in the country at large. Only a few months ago the President of one of our Western colleges came East in an emergency, and met a quick response from the generosity of Mr. Wilde. Many other institutions both North and South have been liberally aided by him. For many years Mr. and Mrs. Wilde have given the prizes in our public schools, and it is peculiarly fitting that the school sessions should have been adjourned this afternoon in memory of their friend.

"From the organization of the church until his strength had failed, so that it was impossible for him to continue the work, he and his wife provided the flowers for the Sunday services, and for the anniversary occasions of both church and Sunday School. Often I have found him and his wife at work with the flowers on Sunday morning, when a large part of the congregation were enjoying their rest."

Dr. Bradford alluded to the building which he planned, and to other work he did, familiar to those who knew him in his daily walk. Mr. Wilde was long an invalid, but his choice and well-stocked library afforded him ample opportunity to gratify his literary taste. He was a collector of old and rare books and prints; and a bound volume of Shakespeare, made up of a collection of rare old prints, some of them over a hundred years old, was a work on which he spent much time and showed excellent judgment. Astronomy was a favorite study of his, and he erected an observatory in the rear of his house, where he placed a telescope of great power, said to have been the largest at the time of any in the State, and by means of which he made many important observations. He also made experiments in photography which afforded him an interesting pastime, and his work compared favorably with the best amateurs.

Mr. Wilde was a man of fine personal appearance; in his manner he was modest and unassuming; and while a member of the Legislature he requested those who addressed him not to use the prefix of "Honorable," as was the custom; he disliked anything that had even the appearance of vain glory or egotism.

He was naturally retiring and shrunk from observation. He gave liberally to objects of charity and benevolence, but only the recipients were aware of the extent of his gifts, as he invariably followed the rule: "Let not thy right hand know what the left hand doeth."

CHARLES KNIGHT WILLMER.

Although an Englishman by birth, Mr. Willmer has been a resident of this country for half a century, and has become as thoroughly identified with its institutions as though to the manor born. His ancestors for several generations were hard working people, who "earned their bread by the sweat of their brow," and have made their influence felt for good wherever their lot has been cast.

Mr. Willmer was born in Liverpool, Eng., October 6, 1826. His father was a prosperous news agent in Liverpool, who had built up a large and extensive business, and was thoroughly familiar with all the periodical literature of the day. Charles K., the son, was sent to school at the Mechanics' Institute in Liverpool, where he acquired a sufficient knowledge of the rudimentary branches to fit him for an active business life. At the age of fourteen he entered his father's employ, and after serving an apprenticeship of four years, having reached the age of eighteen, he came to this country and established business for himself (although representing his father) as an importer and dealer in foreign periodicals. He commenced business in 1844, and carried it on by himself for the first year; he then associated with him Mr. L. M. Rogers, his brother-in-law, and together they built up an extensive trade in foreign periodicals. Mr. Rogers, the partner of Mr. Willmer, returned to England in 1858 to assume the charge of the foreign office, and the entire management of the business in this country was left to Mr. Willmer. In 1868 the firm became an integral part of The American News Company, under the name of "The Willmer & Rogers News Company," which in February, 1879, was changed to the "International News Company," still holding the same relations to The American News Company, the former having charge of all imported periodicals; also of German periodicals published in this country. In 1879, when the name was changed, Mr. Willmer was elected to the Secretaryship of The American News Company, and has since continued in that position. This is the largest News Company in the world, and one of the largest business corporations in this country, controlling, as it does, the sale of newspapers and periodicals in almost every town and village throughout the United States.

Mr. Willmer resided for a number of years in Brooklyn. In April, 1863, he removed to Montclair and purchased from Sidney B. Day about thirteen acres of ground on the Orange Road, lying between the farms of Zenas Baldwin and Gideon Wheeler, and extending thence toward the mountain about 1,100 feet to Harrison Avenue, known as the Stiles homestead property. A part of the homestead, which is still standing, is said to be upward of one hundred years old. It was enlarged, and additions made to it in 1862 by Sidney B. Day, who purchased it from the Stiles estate. The present dining room and library form a part of the original homestead. A narrow road formerly ran along the line of Mr. Willmer's property in a westerly direction to the mountain, which was made use of to cart wood from the mountain. This was closed in 1865, when Mr. Henry Nason, in connection with Mr. Willmer, opened what is now known as Gates Avenue.

In making Montclair his residence, Mr. Willmer appreciated the importance of improved educational facilities, and gave freely of his time and money to further this end. He was in hearty accord with Dr. Love and others in their efforts to change the old district school system to the present system which is far in advance of most suburban towns. He was made a Trustee in 1873, and for a period of eighteen years he labored faithfully and earnestly to promote the educational interests of Montclair. For nine years— 1883-1891—he was President of the Board, and in that position exercised a potent influence in advancing the cause. His views were always in harmony with the majority of his colleagues, and when he retired, in 1891, he was the oldest member of the Board, except Dr. Love. He earned the gratitude of his fellow citizens by his faithful and persistent efforts in carrying forward the system of higher education.

Charles K. Wilmer.

Being a Democrat in politics he has always worked with the minority, but at the same time has worked hopefully and has lived to see his party firmly established with brighter prospects for the future. During the war he gave substantial evidence of his patriotism by his generous contributions in aid of enlistments, and of the many benevolent undertakings in aid of the Union soldiers. As a public-spirited man he is held in high esteem by his fellow citizens.

Mr. Willmer married, in 1852, Harriette Wheeler, daughter of Dr. John Wheeler, of New York City, an oculist of repute, born in Birmingham, England. Eight children are the issue of this marriage, only three of whom are now living, viz.: *Edward C.*, deceased; *Florence*, who married Frederick M. Wheeler, now living in Montclair; *Alfred L.*, deceased; *Philip*, deceased; *Amy*, married Charles K. Rogers, the son of her father's former partner; *Ethel*, deceased; *Charles*, deceased, and *Jennie*.

THE ADAMS FAMILY.

LINE OF DESCENT FROM HENRY ADAMS, OF BRAINTREE, MASS., 1630.

The earliest record of the English branch of the Adams family is that of John Ap Adam, who was summoned to parliament as Baron of the Realm, 1296 to 1307. It is said that Ap Adam (i) " came out of the Marches of Wales." " Marches " refers to borders, particularly the confines of England on the borders of Scotland or Wales; the Lords of the Marches were noblemen, who in the early days inhabited and secured the Marches of Wales and Scotland, ruling as if they were petty kings with their private laws. In the upper part of a Gothic window on the south-east side of Tidenham Church, near Chepstow, England, the name of John Ap Adam, 1310, and " *Lems*, argent on a cross gules, five mullets or," of Lord Ap Adam are still to be found (1895), beautifully executed in stained glass of great thickness, and in perfect preservation. Inscribed on the arms is the motto, *sub cruce salus*.

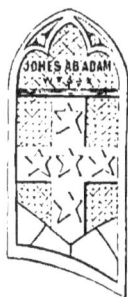

Lord John Ap Adam married Elizabeth, daughter and heiress of John, Lord Gourney, of Beviston and Tidenham, County of Gloucester. In the eighth generation Sir John Ap Adam changed the name to " Adams."

Henry Adams, of Braintree, Mass., 16th in line of descent from Lord John Ap Adam, emigrated to New England in 1630, in the ship " Fortune," and in February, 1641, was granted 40 acres of land by Boston, of which Braintree was a part. He brought with him eight sons, and was the great-grandfather of John Adams, second President of the United States, who erected a granite column to his memory in the churchyard at Braintree, with the following inscription :

" In memory of Henry Adams, who took his flight from the dragon of persecution in Devonshire, England, and alighted with eight sons near Mount Wollaston. One of the sons returned to England, and, after taking time to explore the country, four removed to Medford and the neighbouring towns, two to Chelmsford. One only, Joseph, who lies here at his left hand, remained here. He was an original proprietor in the township of Braintree, 1639."

The descendants of Henry Adams, of Braintree, have filled the highest positions in the various departments of the Government, and many of the most noted clergymen, authors, and other professional men, trace their line of descent from this branch of the Adams family. Samuel Adams, the patriot; Hannah Adams, the first authoress of this country; Adams, the inventor of the steam press; Adams, the founder of Adams Express Co., are all descendants of Henry of Braintree.

WASHINGTON IRVING ADAMS, who has been for twenty-five years a resident of Montclair, and has been identified with the various public and private enterprises connected with the history of the township is, from the best evidence that can be obtained, a descendant of Henry Adams of Braintree. John Adams, second President of the United States, in passing to and from Washington and his home in Braintree, Mass., stopped frequently at the house of Jesse Adams, at White Plains, N. Y., and always addressed him as *cousin*.

Jesse Adams married Mary Sycard, daughter of Jonathan Sycard (now Secor), and Sarah Flandreau, descendants of the French Protestant Huguenot families of Sycard and Flandreau, who fled from Rochelle, France, in 1684, and settled in New Rochelle, Westchester Co., New York.

Mr. Adams has in his possession the large iron-bound chest in which Ambroise Sycard and his wife, Jennie Serrot, packed their little all, on the night of their embarkment from Rochelle, France.

Washington Irving Adams was born in New York City, March 25, 1832. His father was Barnabas Scureman Adams, who married Elizabeth Carhart, June 12, 1831, born February 7, 1803, daughter of *Hackaliah* Carhart, born at Rye, N. Y., Jan. 30, 1755, and married April 2d, 1785, Margaret Anderson, daughter of Isaac Anderson, of Rye.

Hackaliah Carhart was the son of *Thomas* (2), born about 1718, and Elizabeth (Purdy) Carhart,

"IRVING ROEL," RESIDENCE OF W. IRVING ADAMS, LLEWELLYN ROAD.

granddaughter of Hackaliah Brown, of Rye, who was the son of Thomas Brown, of Rye, Sussex Co., England.

The family of Brown, of Rye, Westchester Co., N. Y., was descended from the Browns of Beachworth, in the County of Kent, England, founded by Sir Anthony Brown, who was created Knight of the Bath, at the coronation of Richard II.

His son, Sir Stephen Brown, was Lord Mayor of London in 1439.

Sir Thomas Brown, living in the time of Henry V., was the father of Sir Thomas Brown, treasurer of the household of Henry VI., from 1444 to 1460.

Thomas Brown, Esq., of Rye, Sussex Co., England, emigrated to Concord, Mass., in 1632.

His sons were Thomas, and Hackaliah, of Westchester Co., N. Y.

The name of Rye, Westchester Co., New York, was given in honor of the Brown family, of Rye, Sussex Co., England.

The first American ancestor of the Carhart family was Thomas Carhart, born in Cornwall, England, about 1650. He arrived in New York, August 25, 1683, holding the appointment of Private Secretary to Col. Thomas Dongan, English Colonial Governor of the Colonies at that date.

Thomas Carhart married, in 1691, Mary Lord, daughter of Robert Lord, of Cambridge, and Rebecca Phillips, of Boston, Mass., and granddaughter of Major Wm. Phillips, Major Commandant of the military forces of the Province of Maine in 1665.

The name of Carhart is apparently of Saxon and Danish origin, from:

> *Car,* Anglo-Saxon, a rock, or *caer,* a town or city.
>
> *Hearte,* Anglo-Saxon, and *Herte,* Old Saxon, from which is derived the word, heart.
>
> *Heart,* Anglo-Saxon, and *Hert,* Danish, from which is derived the word *hart,* a stag.

Arms of 1420.   *Shield,* ar. two bars sa. in chief, a demi Griffin, issuant of the last.

> *Crest,* a demi man, naked, ar. a wreath about his head, sa. in right hand an oaken branch, vt. Acorns, or.

Crest of 16th Cent.   *Crest,* a stag, ermined, attired.   *Edmondston's Heraldry.*

These arms were achieved and granted in the reign of Richard II., or soon after.

The issue of Barnabas Seureman and Elizabeth (Carhart) Adams, was Washington Irving, Elizabeth Armenia, Margaret Emily, Mary Louise and Elma Maria. Washington Irving, the eldest, was educated at the public schools of New York. He entered the service of the Scovill Manufacturing Company in 1858, and rapidly rose, through successive grades of responsibilities, until he was appointed in 1878 agent of the company, with entire charge of the business in New York. In the same year he was elected director of the company. In 1875 he became president of S. Peck & Co., manufacturers of photographic apparatus in New Haven, Conn., who had previously come under the control of the Scovill Manufacturing Company. In 1889, when the Scovill & Adams Company succeeded to the photographic department of the Scovill Manufacturing Company, Mr. Adams was made president and treasurer of the new corporation. Under his able management the business of the company has grown, until the Scovill and Adams Company has become the largest and most influential manufacturing firm of photographic apparatus in the world. During the 1876 centennial in Philadelphia, Mr. Adams was identified with Dr. Edward L. Wilson, of that city, and others, as first vice-president of the Centennial Photographic Company. He was for many years chairman of the executive committee of the National Photographic Association of America. When only twenty-one years of age he was elected school trustee in the Ninth Ward, New York City, but since then has persistently refused to accept any proffered public office under the Municipal or State government. He was for many years a vestryman of St. Luke's Episcopal Church. Since young manhood he has been prominently identified with the Masonic fraternity, having served twenty-one years as secretary of Lafayette Lodge, No. 64, of New York City, and two years as master. On February 9, 1893, he was presented by the lodge with an elegant past master's jewel, set with diamonds, in recognition of his long and faithful service. In Capitular Masonry he was advanced and exalted in Corinthian Chapter to R.A.M. In the Chivalric Order, he was created and dubbed a knight templar in Morton Commandery, No. 4, all of New York City. He is also a member of the Society of Colonial Wars, by virtue of descent from three ancestors entitling him to membership.

Mr. Adams removed with his family to Montclair in 1868, and purchased property on Llewellyn Road, then known as Park Avenue, which was within the original boundaries of Llewellyn Park. The homestead connected with the property was of the then prevailing style of architecture of unpretentious country homes. He utilized as far as possible the buildings, together with their surroundings, adding to and enlarging the homestead with interior and exterior modern improvements. The landscape features were also improved by the addition of shade and ornamental trees, until the place presented a decided and most picturesque appearance, forming one of the most attractive and delightful homes in the township. The accompanying illustrations give a better idea of the picturesqueness of the place than could any written description. Mr. Adams subsequently purchased considerable unimproved real estate, and with characteristic enterprise has erected several attractive dwellings.

Mr. Adams married Marion Lydia, daughter of Hon. George Briggs, of New York City; issue, Briggs Booth, born September 5, 1861, died December 24, 1873; Charlotte Elizabeth, born November 24, 1862, died February 24, 1864; W. I. Lincoln and Mary Wilson.

WASHINGTON IRVING LINCOLN ADAMS, third child of Washington Irving and Marion Lydia (Briggs) Adams, was born in New York City, February 22, 1865. He was educated at the Montclair High School, graduating in 1883. In the same year he became associated with his father in business in New York. Naturally of a literary turn of mind, he early assumed editorial charge of *The Photographic Times*, an illustrated weekly magazine, and the leading organ of photography in this country. He is a writer of ability, and is the author of a number of books on photographic subjects. He is also editor of "The

RESIDENCE OF W. I. LINCOLN ADAMS, ORANGE ROAD.

American Annual of Photography," an illustrated record of photographic progress, which has attained a yearly circulation exceeding twenty thousand copies. He has artistically photographed all the picturesque and historical portions of Montclair and its surroundings, and in 1889 made a most attractive collection of his photographs, and published them in photogravure, entitled " Montclair : a Series of Photogravures from Nature." It was of these photographs that Mr. George Inness, Sr., said : "They are very charming, and should prove extremely useful in the development of the landscape art of our country." Some of these photographs are reproduced in this work, and Mr. Adams has assisted the author also in other important ways, including the contribution of some valuable historical material which he had collected. Mr. Adams is a charter member of THE OUTLOOK and MONTCLAIR CLUBS, and an active member of The Congregational Club of New York and Vicinity, and of The Quill Club. He is a member, also, of the American Institute

W. Innis Adams

and of the Society of Amateur Photographers of New York, and an honorary member of at least half a dozen other photographic and scientific associations. He is also a member of the Executive Committee of the Good Government Club, recently organized. Mr. Adams recently built the handsome Colonial residence on Orange Road, where he now resides. He married, November 21, 1889, Miss Daisy Grace Wilson, daughter of the late James Wilson, Esq., of Georgetown, Ohio, a descendant of James Wilson, of Pennsylvania, one of the signers of the Declaration of Independence, whose ancestry dates back to the time of Edward I. The children of W. I. Lincoln and Daisy (Wilson) Adams are Wilson Irving, born August 9, 1890, Marian Elizabeth, born November 12, 1891, and Briggs Kilburn, born May 6, 1893.

MARY WILSON ADAMS, youngest child of Washington Irving and Marion Lydia (Briggs) Adams, was born in Montclair, N. J., July 8, 1869, married October 31, 1892, William Palmer Brigden, of Norwich, Conn. Their child, George Irving, was born November 8, 1893.

VIEW FROM "IRVING ROCK."

Chapter XV.

THE FAMILIES OF BRAUTIGAM, SWEET, HOLMES, PORTER, VAN VLECK, JOHNSON, NOYES, BENEDICT, SULLIVAN, BALDWIN (W. D.), CAREY, RUSSELL, RAND, WILSON, UNDERHILL, MILLER, BURGESS, BRADLEY, FARMER, ESHBACGH, HOWARD, GRAHAM, WHEELER (F. MERRIAM).

AMONG the last of the old New York settlers who began the development of the present township, some thirty years ago, is J. CASTOR BRAUTIGAM. Mr. Brautigam has outlived most of his contemporaries, and old "Father Time" has dealt kindly with him, he having passed the allotted time of "three score and ten" years. He has witnessed the little village of a few hundred inhabitants grow to a flourishing township of over ten thousand.

The great-grandfather of Mr. Brautigam came from Germany, in 1755, and settled in Philadelphia. His ancestors were prominent in the Reformation, and one of them, a Catholic Bishop, after a careful study of a Lutheran catechism, renounced his faith, with all that it implied, and became an ardent "reformer."

J. C. Brautigam was born in Northumberland, Pa., April 29, 1821. When he was but six years of age, his father died, and he was placed in charge of his grandparents in Philadelphia. He attended the best private school, and mastered all the ordinary branches of education by the time he had reached the age of twelve. He then entered the employ of Edward C. Biddle, one of the largest publishers in the country. A strong friendship was formed between employer and employed, which continued uninterrupted for a period of sixty years, until 1893, when his old employer died

J. C. BRAUTIGAM.

at an advanced age. Mr. Brautigam remained in his employ for eleven years, and in 1844 he went to Chicago, and there established what was then the second book concern in Northern Illinois. The population of Chicago was then smaller than Montclair is at the present time. In 1847 he sold out to his partner, and removed to New York City, where he became a member of the firm of White, Sheffield & Company, one of the largest paper houses in the country. He continued this connection until 1869, when he bought out his partners and organized the firm of Brautigam & Watson. About 1876 he sold out to his partner and retired from business.

Mr. Brautigam's first visit to this part of the country was by stage from Newark. He was favorably impressed with its healthfulness and beauty, and in 1864 he purchased twenty acres at the south end

Edward Sweet.

of the town. He opened what is now Cedar Avenue, and gave it the name on account of the large number of cedars in that locality. He also opened High Street, south of Cedar Avenue, some 1,500 feet through his property. He was a member of the first Township Committee after the erection of Montclair as a separate township, and was Chairman in 1875–6. He was also a member of the first Board of Road Commissioners, continuing for two years. Although a Republican he is non-partisan in politics and received alternately the nomination of the republicans and democrats and was the first town officer elected on the democratic ticket.

Mr. Brantigam, in 1872, bought a large plot on Mountain Avenue, where he erected an elegant residence which he sold some six years ago to Dexter N. Force, of the firm of H. B. Claflin & Company. He built a number of houses in the town at different periods.

Mr. Brantigam is the oldest living member of St. Luke's Episcopal Church. He became a member when services were held in the little frame building on Pine Street, near the D. L. & W. R. R. depot. He was for many years one of its most active supporters; he served as Warden and Treasurer for a number of years.

Mr. Brantigam married, in 1845, Miss Mary J. Nicholls, a native of England. Eight children were born to them, four of whom are still living. His only daughter, Josephine, was married to Samuel J. Holmes. His son, Frederick A., is a resident of Montclair; James C., another son, resides in Orange, and John D., a third, resides in Philadelphia.

EDWARD SWEET.

The name of Sweet is variously spelled, Sweet, Swete, Swett and Swaite. According to Burke, the Swete, or Swett, family, bearing arms, gules two chevrons between as many mullets in chief and a rose in base argent seeded or. *Crest*: On the top of a tower, issuing ppr. an eagle, with wings endorsed or, in the beak an oak branch vert; was formerly of Trayne, in Edward VI.'s time, and subsequently of Oxton, in the County of Devonshire, which furnished many colonists to New England.

Of this number, *James Sweet*, called son of Isaac, was brought by his mother, Mary Sweet, a widow, from England, and settled in Salem, Mass., about 1631.

EDWARD SWEET, the subject of this sketch, was born at Ipswich, Mass., October 23, 1815. He was a son of Captain Aaron Sweet, of the same town, who was a descendant (probably) of James, the emigrant. He was graduated in Yale College in 1844, and took a theological course at New Haven Theological Seminary. After spending a year or more in travel, he, in 1849, accepted a call from the Haydenville (Mass.) Congregational Church. He entered with zeal and earnestness upon this, his first field of labor, which gave great promise of success. His people were pleased with his preaching, and became warmly attached to him personally. Much to his sorrow, and to the regret of his congregation, he was compelled, in consequence of his failing health, to relinquish his charge.

At the suggestion of his brother, who was a member of the Boston banking house of Brewster, Sweet & Co., he removed to New York, where he soon after established himself in the same line of business, which he carried on successfully for some years in his own name, and at a later period formed a co-partnership with his brother-in-law, Mr. W. L. Bull, under the firm name of Edward Sweet & Co. This firm dealt largely in government securities, and was noted for its loyal support of the Government during the critical period of the war, when dangers at home and abroad seriously imperilled its credit. Mr. Sweet was a staunch Republican before the war, and never entertained a doubt of the final issue of events, or of the ability of the Government to meet its obligations. He was a man of unimpeachable integrity and uprightness of character, and was much respected in the business community. In the Stock Exchange, of which he was long a member, he was held in high esteem, and his word was considered as good as his bond.

During his residence in New York he was an active member of the Madison Square Presbyterian Church, then under the pastorate of Rev. Dr. Adams.

Mr. Sweet married, in 1863, Miss Caroline W. Bull, daughter of Frederick Bull, of New York, and a grand-daughter of Jirah Bull, of Milford, Conn. The ancestor of this branch of the Bull family was Henry Bull, of Roxbury, Mass., who came in the "James" from London, in 1635, and removed thence to Boston. He was one of the Boston majority of heretics (Society of Friends) who went to Rhode Island with Mrs. Hutchinson, and was one of the purchasers in 1638, being the eighteenth name of the signers of the compact or covenant for civil government in that year. He became Governor of the Colony and held many positions of trust. He had a son Jirah, who kept a garrison hotel at Narragansett during Philip's war. This Jirah had also, among other children, a son Jirah, and the name appears to have been continued through successive generations.

Governor Henry Bull, the ancestor, is said to have been a brother of Thomas, who was in command at Saybrook, when Governor Andros attempted to gain the place for his master, the Duke of York. When the clerk of Andros insisted upon reading the patent, Captain Bull commanded him in a loud voice to forbear, and then read the protest. Governor Andros, pleased with his bold and soldier-like appearance, said, "What's your name?" He replied, "My name is Bull, sir." "Bull," said the Governor, "It's a pity that your horns are not tipped with silver." This family was conspicuous during the colonial period, and during the period of the Revolution, and were prominently represented in civil and military capacities in Rhode Island and Connecticut.

The mother of Mrs. Sweet (née Bull), whose maiden name was Lanman, was a daughter of Abby (Trumbull) daughter of David, the son of Governor Jonathan Trumbull, the famous war governor of the Revolution, known as "Brother Jonathan." He was the son of Joseph, of Suffield, Conn., son of John, of Roxbury, Mass., who was the son of John Trumbull, the emigrant settler of Roxbury in 1636.

Two years after his marriage with Miss Bull, Mr. Edward Sweet removed to Montclair and purchased a large plot of ground, where the present homestead property is now located. The main street leading to his property—Gates Avenue—was subsequently laid out by Mr. Nason, who named it after his wife. Mr. Sweet erected on this plot a large and commodious house, and the laying out of the grounds and other improvements which he made from time to time afforded him rest and recreation from the cares of business. Here he entertained his numerous friends, who always found a hearty welcome and were loth to leave his hospitable board. He was one of the founders of the Congregational Church of Christ, and gave liberally, not only to the erection of the original church edifice, but to the several improvements which have since been made. Few men who have lived in Montclair since its erection as a township have ever been held in higher esteem. His failing health during the latter years of his life prevented him from taking any active part in its affairs. He was known as a whole-souled, generous man, of a genial nature and kindly disposition, who delighted in doing good and contributing to the happiness of his fellow-men. He was of a retiring nature and avoided all appearance of ostentation, but those who enjoyed the "inner circle" of his acquaintance found in him a warm and steadfast friend. He was the soul of honor and uprightness. He was a gentleman—not formal and precise, but dignified and genuine. His own fireside was the pleasantest spot on earth, and its influence attended him in all the affairs of life.

THE HOLMES FAMILY AND COLLATERAL BRANCHES.

SAMUEL HOLMES, or "Deacon Holmes," as he is well known, traces his descent through three well-known families of Connecticut, many of the descendants of whom have achieved distinction in the various walks of life in which their tastes or inclinations led them.

The family of Holme or Holmes has been established in the County of York, Eng., since the period of the Norman conquest. The first mentioned of this name is John Holme, of Paull-Holme, whose grandson Olenor Holme was comptroller to the Empress Maud, and received the honor of Knighthood from that Princess.

FRANCIS HOLME, the American ancestor, emigrated from England as early as 1648, and settled in Stamford, Conn. His son John, born in England, came with him and settled at Greenwich, Conn., and was one of twenty-four proprietors who afterwards settled at Bedford, Westchester County, N. Y.

THOMAS FITCH, Esq;

Captain-General, and Governor in Chief, in and over His Majesty's *English* Colony of Connecticut, in *New-England*, in America.

To _Samuel Bull Junr_ .... Greeting.

BY Virtue of the Power and Authority to me given, in and by the Royal Charter .... and .... of the said Colony, under the Great Seal of England. I do by these .... special Trust and Confidence in your Loyalty, Courage and good Conduct, constitute .... N. Y. .... to be .... of the .... Company, in a Regiment of Foot, raised within this Colony, to be employed for the defence of His ...... Dominions in North-America, and particularly of the Possession ...... Connecticut there, in .... mander in Chief shall judge most conducive to the King's .... to proceed there .... of the said Commander in Chief ; of which Regiment .... S .... You are therefore carefully and diligently to discharge the Duty of a .... during, and exercising said Company, to train, both inferior Officers and Soldiers, in the Service aforesaid, to keep them in good Order and Discipline ; hereby commanding them to obey you, as their .... Officer ; and yourself to observe and follow such Orders and Instructions, as you shall from Time to Time receive from Me, or the Command in Chief of the said Colony, for the Time being, or other your superior Officers, according to the Rules and Discipline of War, pursuant to the Trust reposed in you.

GIVEN under my Hand and the public Seal of the ..... Colony, at .... the .... Day of .... in the .... Year of the Reign of His Majesty King GEORGE the Third, Annoque Domini 176.

His Honor's Command;

George Wyllys Secrety

Tho' Fitch

JONATHAN TRUMBULL, Esquire,

General and Commander in Chief in and over the STATE of CONNECTICUT in AMERICA.

To _Samuel Judge_ ( ) Gent. GREETING.

YOU being by the General Assembly of this State accepted to be _Captain of the_ _Company in Stratford in the 27th Regiment in this State_

reposing special Trust and Confidence in your Fidelity, Courage and good Conduct, I DO by Virtue of the Laws of this State, me thereunto enabling, appoint and impower you to take the said _Company_ into your Care and Charge, at their _Captain_ carefully and diligently to discharge that Office and Trust, exercising your inferior Officers and Soldiers in the Use of their Arms, according to the Rules and Discipline of War, ordained and established by the Laws of this State, keeping them in good Order and Government, and commanding them to obey you as their _Captain_ and you are to observe all such Orders and Directions as from Time to Time you shall receive, either from me, or from other your superior Officer, pursuant to the Trust hereby reposed in you.

GIVEN under my Hand, and the Public Seal of this State, at _Hartford_ the 31st Day of _January_ A. D. 1783.

By His Excellency's Command,

George Wyllys Secretary

Jon Trumbull

Stephen, son of John, had a son *Benjamin*, who served in Capt. Clark's company, 14th Regiment, Connecticut Militia. *Israel*, son of Benjamin, married *Sarah Judd*, and moved to Waterbury, Conn. The issue of this marriage was *Samuel Judd* (father of Dea. Samuel Holmes), of whom hereafter; *Reuben*, of whom hereafter; *Israel*, of whom hereafter; *Ruth*, of whom hereafter; and *Miles*.

SAMUEL JUDD, the eldest son of Israel and Sarah (Judd) Holmes (father of Dea. Samuel Holmes), was born in Waterbury, Conn., October 28, 1794. He moved to Southington, Conn., in 1825, where he remained until 1834, when he returned to his native town and became identified with its manufacturing interests. He was a prominent stockholder in the Waterbury Brass Company and for sixteen years was the faithful overseer of one branch of its business. He was very methodical, careful and pains-taking in all his business as well as other affairs. In the affairs of the church with which he was long connected he evinced many of the traits of his Puritan ancestors. A deep thinker, yet reserved in the expression of his views; cautious in all his dealings, yet upright and straightforward—a man of the strictest integrity, measuring himself by the orthodox standard, and expecting the same treatment from others in return. He married May 2, 1822, Lucina, daughter of Hezekiah Todd, of Cheshire, Conn.; he died May 1, 1867. He had issue, *Israel*, of whom hereafter; *Sarah*, born July 6, 1829, married Rev. Jesse W. Hough (she died in Santa Barbara, Cal., April 5, 1877); *William B.* and *Hannah*, who died young; and *William B.* again, of whom hereafter.

Reuben, second son of Israel and Sarah (Judd) Holmes, was born February 11, 1798, graduated with Honor at the West Point Military Academy, was valedictorian of his class, and afterwards distinguished himself as an Indian fighter in the West. During the Black Hawk War, and while still holding his commission as Captain in the U. S. service he was elected Colonel of a regiment of Illinois volunteers, and became their leader in that war. He died of cholera in 1833 at Jefferson Barracks, near St. Louis, Mo. A part of the inscription on the monument which marks his last resting place is as follows: * * * * "and there awaits the last review"; * * * * "erected by his companions in arms."

Israel (2), third son of Israel and Sarah (Judd) Holmes, was born December 19, 1800. He was one of the chief founders of the great brass manufacturing industry of this country; he made trips to England in 1829, and again in 1831-34, to procure skilled workman for the various branches of the business.

Ruth Wood, fourth child of Israel and Sarah (Judd) Holmes, was born April 26, 1799. She married Preserve W. Carter, and was the mother of President Franklin Carter, of Williams College.

Miles, fourth son and youngest child of Israel and Sarah (Judd) Holmes, was born March 20, 1802, at Waterbury, Conn. He resided in the South and in the State of Wisconsin most of his life. He died in Waterbury, Conn., August 23, 1865.

Sarah Judd, the wife of Israel Holmes (1), was a direct descendant of Thomas Judd, who came from England in 1633 and settled in Cambridge, Mass.; removed to Hartford, Conn., 1636, and to Farmington, Conn., about 1644. In the churchyard at Waterbury, Conn., is a headstone containing the following inscription : " Here [lies] the body of THOMAS JUDD, ESQ., the first Justice, Deacon, and Captain in Waterbury, who died January ye 4, A.D. 1747, aged 79."

Thomas, above referred to, was a son of the first Thomas, the emigrant proprietor. He had a son *John*, who also had a son *John*. The latter had a son *Samuel*, known as *Captain Samuel*. He was the great grandfather of Deacon Samuel Holmes. He held a commission as First Lieutenant in the Colony under the reign of King George III. (see *fac simile* of commission on opposite page), and on March 15, 1762, was commissioned by Gov. Thomas Fitch, of Connecticut, to raise a " Company of Foote." The commission states : " I do hereby authorize and empower you by beat of drum or otherwise to assist your Captain in raising by inlistment a company of able bodied, effective volunteers within the colony of about ninety-five men, including officers for the ensuing campaign, etc."

He served in different capacities during the War of the Revolution, and on the 24th of January, 1783, was commissioned Captain by Governor Trumbull (see *fac simile* of commission on opposite page). After the close of the war he opened a tavern at Waterbury, which he kept for fifty years; it became a noted resort for passengers on the stage route between New Haven and Albany. He was a noted character in his day. He married *Bede*, daughter of Isaac Hopkins, and on her way home after the marriage ceremony she rode behind him on a " pillion " (a cushion attached to the rear of the saddle).

This *Bede Hopkins* was a descendant of *John* Hopkins, who came from England with his wife Jane to Cambridge, Mass., in 1634; moved to Hartford in 1635. His son Stephen, born 1634, married Dorcas Bronson; they had a son *John*, who was one of the youngest of the original proprietors of Waterbury. He became " Leftenant " in 1716, and several times represented his town at the General Court. He held many offices of trust and honor. When the new meeting house came to be seated in 1729, he was one of the revered dignitaries who were voted into the first pew at the west end of the pulpit. He had a son, *Ebenzer*, who was the father of Isaac Hopkins referred to above. Some of the most distinguished divines and educators in the country descended from this branch of the Hopkins family, among whom was Mark Hopkins, for many years President of Williams College.

Israel, eldest child of Samuel J. and Lucina (Todd) Holmes, was born at Waterbury, Conn., August 10, 1823. He is connected with several of the manufacturing companies of Waterbury; also with a banking institution. He resided in Liverpool, Eng., from 1859 to 1871.

DEACON SAMUEL HOLMES, second son of Samuel J. and Lucina (Todd) Holmes, was born at Waterbury, Conn., November 30, 1824. He attended public school until he was eleven years of age, when he began working in a button factory with his father, and from that time until he reached the age of fifteen he worked in the factory during the summer and attended school in the winter at the Waterbury Academy and at a boarding school. At the age of sixteen he entered the general store of J. M. L. & W. H. Scovill, as clerk until 1845, he having then attained his majority. The company that year opened a salesroom for their goods in New York City, and he became their assistant manager. In 1850 a joint stock company was formed under the name of The Scovill Manufacturing Company, in which he was a stockholder and director, and soon after assumed the management of the New York business. The business increased in volume from year to year aided by his skillful direction, and the stock increased in value yielding large dividends. He was prosperous and happy and fortune smiled upon him during those years, in which he was also stockholder in various other companies, which yielded satisfactory returns. In 1873 he severed his connection with The Scovill Manufacturing Company and entered into a new co-partnership in the manufacturing line and dealing in metals, which promised well, but owing to circumstances beyond his control, proved a most disastrous venture, and came near causing his financial ruin. His creditors as well as his numerous friends, who had unbounded confidence in his integrity stood by him nobly in his trouble, and he was thus enabled to ride over his difficulties, but he was compelled for many years to carry a heavy financial burden. In 1876 he was appointed to the treasurership of the Bridgeport Brass Company and also to the management of the New York business. It was not in a very flourishing condition at the time, and a change for the better was soon apparent. The business showed a large annual increase, and largely through the judicious and economical management of Deacon Holmes the stockholders received constantly increasing dividends. At the beginning of his administration Deacon Holmes purchased quite a block of stock on credit, the dividends on which, together with the subsequent sale of his stock, enabled him to liquidate a considerable portion of his old indebtedness. His connection with the company ceased in 1890, the majority of stock having been previously purchased by a syndicate, which assumed the direction of the company.

In 1867, before his misfortunes, Deacon Holmes purchased several tracts of land, in all about 100 acres, in Montclair, lying near Watchung Avenue, and on the mountain slope. Through the assistance of his numerous friends he was enabled to carry this throughout the period of his business misfortunes, which resulted to the benefit of his creditors, and on his retirement from business in 1890 he began to develop and place it on the market, it having in the interim appreciated in value. He laid out streets and avenues, and divided the property into building plots, several of which have been sold at a large advance over the original cost. He continued Highland Avenue through his mountain tract; Edgewood Avenue and Holmes Place, both laid out and named by him, intersecting the former and connecting with

Saml Holmes

Mountain Avenue. The homestead property, corner of Watchung Avenue and Grove Street, comprises about 17 acres, adjoining and near to which he has some 42 acres, which is being laid out and developed for market. The improvement of his property, from which he has derived a corresponding benefit, has also largely enhanced the value of the surrounding property, and opened up a new and exceedingly attractive part of the township of Montclair.

For nearly half a century Deacon Holmes has been actively engaged in religious, benevolent and educational affairs, to which he has not only devoted the best years of his life, but has given liberally of his means, when not embarrassed by business difficulties. He is the oldest member in office, by several years, of the Executive Committee of the American Missionary Association, having began his connection with that body in 1864. He has been a corporate member of the American Board of Foreign Missions since 1870, and was for many years Treasurer of the American College Society, and since its union with the Educational Society in 1872, under the name of "The American College and Education Society," he has continued his interest in and membership of the new organization and as its first Vice-President.

He was a member and one of the Secretaries of the first National Congregational Council held at Boston in 1865, and of subsequent Councils held at Oberlin in 1871, and at Worcester, Mass., in 1889; and also a member of the International Congregational Council held in London in 1891, where he represented the American Missionary Association as its delegate.

He endowed the Professorship of Hebrew in Yale College in 1868; and, for the benefit and encouragement of the young men of Waterbury and vicinity, to assist them in acquiring a collegiate education he established five scholarships in the academic and scientific departments of Yale, all of which, together with the Hebrew Professorship, were named in his honor.

Soon after his removal to New York City in 1846, Deacon Holmes identified himself with the Broadway Tabernacle Church, and was for many years and until his removal to Montclair a Deacon and Trustee of the Society and Superintendent of the Sunday School. He was also largely engaged in Sunday School mission work. He was one of the founders of the Congregational Church of Montclair in 1870, was one of its first Deacons, and is the only one who has held the office consecutively since its organization. Immediately after the formation of the Society he suggested the name of Mr. Bradford, who was soon after called by the church and became its first pastor.

With a single exception Deacon Holmes has had a successful business career, and whatever mistakes he has made have been due to his natural kindness of heart and over-confidence in his fellow men. In his endeavor to follow closely the golden rule he expected too much from others. He came out of his difficulties, however, with a reputation untarnished. Neither his ability, his judgment, nor his unswerving integrity were ever questioned.

His love for his fellow men is unbounded, and he makes no distinction of race or color. His life has exemplified his firm belief in the Fatherhood of God and the Brotherhood of Man.

> " He hath an eye for pity, and hand
> Open as the day for melting 'charity.' "

So to do good, and to better the condition of his fellow men has been the aim of his life, and he has been identified with almost every benevolent undertaking in the church and out of it since he came to Montclair.

He married, June 3, 1856, Mary H. Goodale, born November 12, 1829, daughter of Deacon David and Millicent Warren Goodale, of Marlboro', Mass., a descendant of John Goodale, who settled in Salem about 1696 and removed thence to Marlboro', Mass. Issue, *Ellen Warren*, born November 18, 1857, married June 17, 1881, Rev. Frank A. Beckwith, who died in San Francisco, December 12, 1885; *Samuel Judd*, born October 18, 1859, married S. Josephine Brautigam March 18, 1886; *Arthur*, born July 5, 1861, died August 5, 1861; *Mary Goodale*, born December 1, 1862; *David Goodale*, born October 18, 1865, married to E. Annie Bate, April 7, 1886; *George Day*, born June 15, 1867, graduated at Yale College, 1890.

WILLIAM BUSKIRK HOLMES, youngest son of Samuel and Lucina (Todd) Holmes, was born at Southington, Conn. (his father having removed thence from Waterbury), July 31, 1831. His father returned to Waterbury, where William continued to reside from early childhood. He was educated at private school and the Waterbury Academy. After leaving school he was employed by the Benedict & Burnham Co., of Waterbury, from 1843 to 1850. He then came to New York, and was in the employ of the Scovill Manufacturing Co. for fifteen years. In January, 1865, he started in the business of photographic supplies, in which he is still engaged. He moved to Montclair in 1856, and became the pioneer of the "Waterbury Colony." He induced his brother and many others to purchase property and settle there, and thereby assisted materially in the early development of the township. He was at one time a large owner in real estate, and sold to Mr. Carey the plot of ground on Orange Road occupied by the latter. He was a liberal entertainer, and among his distinguished visitors was Horace Greeley. He named some of the prominent streets in the township, among which was Plymouth Street, on the corner of which the Congregational Church edifice now stands. He was one of the founders of the Society, and has served several years as a Deacon of the Church. He was instrumental in locating the church edifice on its present site.

Mr. Holmes married Mary H. Bull, daughter of Frederick Bull, who was for a long time an elder of Dr. Adams' church, of Milford, Conn. Her grandmother was a direct descendant of Governor Trumbull, of Connecticut, known as "Brother Jonathan." Mr. Holmes has four children, viz.: William T., Edward H., Caroline S., and Henry L.

THE PORTER FAMILY.

The Porters were among the early comers of what was known as the "Waterbury Colony," representing the same element—although with far advanced ideas—of the Connecticut colonists who, two hundred years previous, planted the standard of civil and religious liberty in Eastern New Jersey, and became the parent stock of what is now comprised in Essex County, New Jersey, and it is a noteworthy fact that the homestead lot of the Porters is a part of the original grant to Deacon Azariah Crane, who married the daughter of Governor Robert Treat, of Connecticut, both of whom were leaders in the establishment of Newark, or New Worke, as the new enterprise was then called.

The name of Porter is among the early surnames mentioned in English history, and no less than thirty-six of this name are mentioned by Burke as having been granted arms by their ruling sovereigns. Among the earliest mentioned is that of Endymion Porter, Groom of the Bedchamber to Charles I., a celebrated courtier of the period, who descended from Robert Porter, brother of Sir William Porter, Knight, living temp Henry V. The motto borne on the shield of the famous knights representing this family—Vigilantia et Virtute—has been a characteristic of the descendants through subsequent generations.

DANIEL PORTER, the founder of the Connecticut branch of this family, was early in the colony, previous to 1644. He was licensed to "practice physic and chirurgery" in 1654 by the General Court. In 1661-2 it was ordered that his yearly salary should be paid out of the public treasury, while his fee-table was established by law. He was required to attend upon the sick in Hartford, Windsor, Wethersfield and Middletown. He was more particularly a bonesetter, as is shown by the following record:

"For the encouragement of Daniel Porter in attending the service of the country in setting bones, etc., the court do hereby augment his sallery from six pounds a year to twelve pounds per annum, and to advise him to instruct some meet person to his art."

Daniel (1) had a son Daniel (2) born February 2, 1652, who followed his father's calling as a "bonesetter." The latter had a son Daniel (3) born March 5, 1699, who married Hannah, daughter of John Hopkins, a descendant—probably—of William Hopkins, of Roxbury, Mass., who married Hannah Goffe, a daughter of Goffe the regicide. The latter was a descendant of Stephen Hopkins, who came over in the Mayflower in 1621. Daniel (3) had a son Timothy (1) born June 19, 1735, who was also a

N. T. Porter

physician. He had a son Daniel (4) born September 23, 1768, who was the father of Timothy (2) born January 30, 1792. This Timothy married Polly Ann Todd, daughter of a Mr. Todd, a descendant of Christopher, one of the earliest settlers of the New Haven Colony, and owner of the land now known as the "campus" of Yale College.

NATHAN T. PORTER, son of Timothy, was born at Waterbury, Conn., December 10, 1828, and received his education at the schools in that place and at the academy at Easton, Conn. Close attention to his studies, aided by his quick intellect and retentive memory, enabled him rapidly to master whatever he undertook.

It was the practical subjects that especially attracted him, and about his home he took the lead in every enterprise.

His later career was the logical development of these tendencies. The small manufacturing town

RESIDENCE OF N. T. PORTER, GATES AVENUE.

of those days afforded too small a field for his ambition, and in 1854 he went to New York, entering the employ of A. W. Welton, a dry-goods commission merchant in Liberty Street. After he and his brother Thomas had been in the employ of this house about a year, they were admitted to the firm, which then became A. W. Welton & Porters, a high compliment to those who had been so short a time in the business. A further evidence of Mr. Welton's confidence was that he allowed his name and personal responsibility to remain after he had ceased to participate in the profits of the business. The firm name was later changed to Porter Bros., and finally to Porter Bros. and Company. From the beginning until he retired from active business Nathan was the leading member of the firm and brought the house successfully through such trying periods as the panic of '73. It was also mainly due to his fine business ability that the small business whose management he undertook in 1855 grew to its later magnitude. He combined in an unusual degree the ability to direct the more important matters and at the same time keep thoroughly acquainted with all the details of the business. Prominent among his business characteristics were, energy, care and promptness. It has been well said of him that he could transact more business in an hour than most men could in a day. In 1881, poor health compelled him to retire from his more active duties in the business. During his long and honorable business career he was identified with many enterprises to which he gave close personal attention. His connection with the National Shoe and Leather Bank, of New York City, first as Director and afterward as Vice-President, brought him into prominence as a financier. He was very influential in its affairs and was held in the highest esteem by his associates on account of his courtesy and strong personality, as well as his ability and good judgment. For many years he was President of the Cheshire Manufacturing Company and Cheshire Brass Company, of West Cheshire, Conn.; Director in the Patent Button Company, of Waterbury, Conn. (all of which were successful under his management), and served in several other companies in an official capacity. On October 16, 1862, Mr. Porter married, at New London, Conn., Miss Mary C. Comstock, a sister of Mrs. Thomas Porter.

Mr. Porter resided in New York and Brooklyn during the earlier years of his business life. In June, 1868, he removed to Montclair, having purchased, in conjunction with his brother, a large tract of land situated on Union Street, Gates Avenue, Harrison Avenue and Clinton Avenue, which had formerly been a part of the old Crane farm. Mr. Porter and his family lived in the Union Street house until the erection of the house on the corner of Gates and Clinton Avenues in 1891. In the quiet of this suburban village he found a much needed rest and recreation, where he could for the time being lay aside the cares of business and enjoy the advantages of country life. He took pleasure in superintending the work on his place, and prided himself on his garden, to which he devoted many of his leisure hours while at home, a diversion which helped materially to relieve the strain resulting from a too close application to business. He showed the keenest interest in public affairs of the township. He was for three years a Commissioner of Roads, and for two years a member of the Township Committee. While holding these offices he devoted much time to them, and conscientiously performed their duties. The demands on his time, however, were too great, and after his last year on the Township Committee he declined to be a candidate for re-election.

His father was a Baptist, and in his youth Nathan became a member of that church, but he was too liberal in his religious views to be bound by any merely denominational distinctions, and became one of the original members of the First Congregational Church, in which he always took the greatest interest. As Trustee and Treasurer of this Church he rendered valuable assistance. By his personal efforts and liberal contributions he aided materially in paying off the Church debt, as well as in the enlargement of the building and other improvements. He gave liberally to other benevolent objects, but always without ostentation. He continued to take an active interest in all these matters till his failing health necessitated an entire change. Since his retirement from active business he has spent his time partly in Montclair and partly at his old home in Waterbury, among the scenes of his youth.

Mr. Porter has never been fond of society in its formal sense, though he was always known as a most companionable and sociable man. He was popular among his large circle of friends and acquaintances, and his presence was always welcome. His keen sense of humor made him an appreciative listener, and his vein of wit made him an entertaining talker. On all occasions he was a thorough gentleman. One of Mr. Porter's most prominent traits was his fondness for his home, and there was nothing he enjoyed more than being with his family. With his children he was like one of themselves, entering into all that interested them. He was an ideal husband and father.

The issue of his marriage to Miss Comstock was three children. James Soutter, born at Jersey City, New Jersey, October 22, 1865; Nathan T., Jr., born at Brooklyn, December 5, 1867, and Hiland, born at Montclair, December 10, 1871.

James Soutter Porter was educated at Montclair public school, and entered the employ of Porter Bros. & Co.; married Miss Grace Jewett Shively, daughter of Andrew J. Shively, at Brooklyn, N. Y., on April 28, 1892.

Thomas Poole

Nathan T. Porter, Jr., prepared for college at the Montclair High School and entered Yale in 1886, graduating in 1890. After graduation he entered the employ of Porter Bros. & Co., and became a member of the firm January, 1892. He married at Troy, N. Y., February 24, 1892, Miss Caroline Chester Knickerbacker, daughter of Thos. A. Knickerbacker, a descendant of the old Dutch family whose head, Johann Van Berger Knickerbacker, settled at Albany in 1652.

Hiland Porter received his education at the public schools in Montclair, and is now in the employ of Porter Bros. & Co.

THOMAS PORTER, third son of Deacon Timothy and Polly Ann (Todd) Porter, was born in Waterbury, Conn., Feb. 7, 1831. He was educated in the common schools and academy of Waterbury, and the Staples Academy in Easton. While attending school in the winter he worked on his father's farm and brickyard in the summer.

In the autumn of 1854, he went to New York City in the employ of Arad W. Welton, who in a

RESIDENCE OF THOMAS PORTER, UNION STREET.

little store in Liberty Street was selling the goods of the Cheshire Manufacturing Company. He had scarcely mastered the details of the business when, through the defection of other and older employees, a large share of the responsibility devolved upon him, and he called to his assistance N. T. Porter, who was still living in Waterbury. Under the management of the two young men, the business received a large and rapid development, being conducted under the name of A. W. Welton & Porters. After a few years Mr. Welton retired and another brother, Samuel M. Porter, entered the partnership. The firm of Porter Brothers was then assumed, which later, on the admission of some employees as partners, was extended to Porter Brothers and Company. The affairs of the firm were so successfully and efficiently managed, that it soon acquired a high reputation, and has continued in uninterrupted prosperity to the present time. The firm removed to Chambers Street, thence to 113 and 115 Broadway and finally to 78 and 79 Worth Street.

Thomas Porter was for many years a director in the National Shoe and Leather Bank. He was known and recognized as one of the leading merchants of New York, and during the period of the War was a staunch supporter of the Government. While many New York merchants doubted and shaped their course accordingly, his faith in the ability of the Government to maintain itself in its entirety never for a moment wavered. He belonged to that class of New York merchants who were honest from principle and not from policy, and who believed in applying the golden rule to every day transactions of life.

Owing to the death of one of the three brothers and the failure in health of another, the cares of the extensive business of Porter Brothers & Company, rested mainly upon Mr. Thomas Porter as the leading and most experienced member of the firm, and he was practically the responsible head for the last ten years of his life. At the time of his death he was President of the Cheshire Manufacturing Company, the Cheshire Brass Company, of Barnard, Son & Company, the Patent Button Company and the Vulcanite Manufacturing Company.

As a business man Mr. Porter was prudent, courageous and energetic, and possessed a high sense of mercantile honor. Unswerving integrity, and a determination to fulfill at any cost every honorable obligation, were the ruling principles of his business career.

Mr. Porter resided for a number of years in Brooklyn, where he was prominent in social circles and an active member of the Washington Avenue Baptist Church. The climate of Brooklyn seemed ill adapted to the health of his family and he was persuaded by Mr. Samuel Holmes to try the climate of Montclair. In 1868 he purchased, in connection with his brother Nathan, thirty acres, situated on what is now Union Street and Harrison Avenue, which was originally part of the Jeremiah Crane farm. He moved his family out and occupied for two or three summers the small house which rests on the foundation of the original homestead of Jeremiah Crane. The health of his family improved to such an extent that he finally decided to settle permanently in Montclair. He fixed up the homestead property which he continued to occupy until 1886, when he built the beautiful home on the crest of the hill which he occupied up to the time of his death. The following from the *Montclair Times* of Nov. 16, 1890, refers to his usefulness as a citizen of Montclair, also to his sudden death:

"Not since the sudden death of Henry A. Dyke has the community been so shocked as at the announcement yesterday of the death of Thomas Porter. He had been at business the day before, and during the evening conversed with his family and with friends who had called concerning business and social matters. He never seemed in better health than when he retired Thursday night. On Friday morning about five o'clock he was taken suddenly ill and in a few minutes passed away.

"Mr. Porter has been a prominent figure in social and business circles both in Montclair and New York. For a long time he has been head of the great firm of Porter Bros. & Co. In our local affairs he has occupied many positions of eminence and usefulness. For a number of terms he was President of the Board of Trustees of our public schools and always used his influence for the maintenance of the high standards which have distinguished the schools. His addresses at the commencements many remember as impressive and appropriate. When the Village Improvement Society was organized, and while it lasted, he was its President. He always took a lively interest in public affairs. Socially he was a most delightful and genial man. His beautiful home has been opened on many occasions, and all who knew him well were glad to be numbered among his friends. He was a member of the Baptist Church in Orange, and was greatly interested in whatever concerned the progress of religion in the community and the world. Montclair owes much to him, and while in the last few years he has not been personally as conspicuous in the life of the community as before, it has been only because other duties compelled him to give his attention elsewhere.

"An honored citizen, an earnest Christian, a business man whose reputation was unstained, he was one who apparently could ill be spared by the community, his family or his church. The sympathies of a host of friends are with those who have been so suddenly called to part with one who was as dear to them as life itself."

Mr. Porter was a member of the Washington Memorial Association, being one of a company of gentlemen who purchased the site of Washington's Headquarters at Morristown, and erected the memorial at that place.

He was President of the Village Improvement Society of Montclair, and was for twelve years Chairman of its Board of Education. In this latter capacity, by his successful efforts in stimulating a public interest in education, by his able addresses on anniversary occasions, and by his prudent manage-

J. VanVleck

ment of the affairs of the office, he did much to establish a school which has fitted scores of young men for college.

When about fourteen years of age he united with the Waterbury Baptist Church and was an active member and Sunday School Superintendent until his removal to New York. In New York he was a prominent member of the Madison Avenue Baptist Church, and on his removal to Montclair united first with the Bloomfield Baptist Church and continued his membership there until Dr. Edward Judson, son of Adoniram Judson, the famous missionary, accepted a call to the Orange Baptist Church, when he took his letter to that church. He became a warm friend of Dr. Judson and a great admirer of his preaching. The intimacy that existed between them enabled Dr. Judson to form a just opinion of the personal characteristics of Mr. Porter, which he gave expression to after the latter's death as follows:

"I have just returned from the funeral of Mr. Thomas Porter, of Montclair, a warm personal friend of mine, and an honored member of the Orange Church. * * * * He was sixty years old, having just entered the autumn of life—that period when, having outlived the fever and friction of youth, we come into smooth adaptation of our environments, and we inherit the wealth of varied and numerous relationships. Mr. Porter was a man of peculiar social grace. His commanding and almost regal carriage, his features strong and rugged, yet mobile and transparent, revealing every movement of the noble spirit behind them, his unvarying courtesy, his quiet unselfishness, his considerate treatment, especially to those who occupied humbler social positions, marked him as a gentleman of the old school. His benignant presence will be peculiarly missed in the social circles which he frequented. But besides this he was a man of strong principle. His moral intuitions were acute. His whole nature revolted against whatever was crooked or unclean. He was fearless in avowing his convictions. And yet he was neither morose nor ascetic. He was always kindly in his construction of the conduct and motives of others. The opinions he held as a Christian and as a Baptist were definite and pronounced. Without prodigality he was large-hearted and benevolent. I found in him a firm helper in my Orange field, and his friendliness has followed me through all my experience in lower New York."

The characteristics of Mr. Porter were clearly hereditary. It will be observed that his ancestors in a direct line for four successive generations were physicians, and in early life he was strongly inclined to follow that profession, but was dissuaded from doing so by his parents. He seemed to possess remarkable gifts in this direction, and would no doubt have made his mark had he been permitted to follow his own inclinations. He frequently assisted the afflicted when physicians or surgeons were not available.

Mr. Porter married, in 1863, Miss Annie Comstock, daughter of M. M. Comstock, a direct descendant of *William*, the ancestor who owned land in Wethersfield in 1641, and settled in New London in 1649.

The line of descent is through *John* (1), *John* (2), *Peter* (1), *Peter* (2), *Peter* (3). The first Peter, who was the great grandfather of Mrs. Porter, was Captain of a Company of Lattimer's Regiment in the War of the Revolution, and was stationed at Fort Trumbull when New London was burned.

The issue of the marriage of Thomas Porter and Annie Comstock was Thomas W., Howard and Roland. Only the eldest, Thomas W., is now living, and is at present the head of the firm of Porter Bros. & Co. He married, June 12, 1894, Miss Lillian Mary Ward, youngest daughter of the late General Rodney C. Ward, of Brooklyn.

JOSEPH VAN VLECK.

Two families of the name of Van Vleck are mentioned in the colonial records of New York. In the *New Netherlands Register*, page 100, it is stated that "Van Vleck (Tielman) may justly be regarded as the founder of Bergen (N. J.). He came originally from Bremen, studied under a notary in Amsterdam, came to this country about 1658, and was admitted to practice the same year. He was made the first Schout and President of the Court at Bergen, September 5, 1661. After the capture of the country by the English he returned to New York and resided there in 1671."

Isaac Van Vleck, probably a brother of Tielman, settled at or near Albany. He married, 1st, Cornelia Beckman; 2d, March 5, 1680, Catalyntje de Lanoy. He was a dealer in beaver skins in 1674 and '76, as stated in Stoothoof Papers. He made an affidavit June 11, 1690, relating to the troubles under the administration of Governor Lester. He had several children.

Joseph Van Vleck, the subject of this sketch, is a descendant of Isaac Van Vleck. His mother before her marriage was Ann, daughter of Joseph Hasbrouck, a Captain in the War of the Revolution, a descendant of Abraham Hasbrouck or Has Brouck, who removed from Calais into the Palatinate in Germany about the middle of the seventeenth century, belonging to the body of French Protestants whom religious persecution forced from their native land. From Germany the family went to England in 1675, and emigrated the same year to New Netherlands (New York), and was of the patentees of New Paltz (Ulster County, N. Y.) in 1676. Two of his sons, Jan and Abraham, with ten others, all Huguenots, obtained a patent of 40,000 acres on the west shore of the Hudson River, September 29, 1677, and settled there. Many of his descendants were conspicuous in the early history of New York State, and especially in the War of the Revolution. Joseph, of New Paltz (probably the great-great-grandfather of the present Joseph), was the grandson of Abraham (2). He was a prominent man and filled several public offices. He married Elsie Schoonmaker, daughter of Captain Joakim Schoonmaker, a native of Hamburg, Germany, who was one of the first settlers of America, having come over in the employ of the Dutch West India Company while the country was under Dutch government and control.

Joseph Van Vleck, son of Peter and Ann (Hasbrouck) Van Vleck, was born in Marbletown, Ulster County, N. Y., November 19, 1830. He attended the Kingston Academy until he was fourteen years of age, and began his business career as clerk in a country store. He came to New York City in 1849, and was engaged in a wholesale boot and shoe house. In 1860 he entered the house of Phelps, Dodge & Co.,—the largest house in their line of business in the United States—and in 1879 was admitted as a partner. He resided for a number of years in Brooklyn. He spent the summers of 1868-69-70 in Montclair, and was so favorably impressed with it as a summer resort that he determined to make it his permanent residence. In July, 1868, he purchased the property fronting on Upper Mountain Avenue, containing about four acres, and subsequently bought about eight acres additional. He was mainly instrumental in opening the street from Mountain Avenue to Valley Road, which his neighbors named Van Vleck Street. At the time of his purchase there were only three other houses on the avenue. He made many improvements and built five additional houses, thus adding materially to the taxable property in the township. His interest in the public affairs of Montclair led to his election in 1874 as Commissioner of Public Roads. Little comparatively had been done at that time in the way of improvements, and the streets and avenues were not much in advance of ordinary country roads. He saw the necessity of a radical change, and two years later, when he was elected a member of the Township Committee, he earnestly advocated the McAdam system of roads. He wrote a paper on this subject, which was published in the county papers, and afterward in pamphlet form. The taxpayers were slow at first in adopting any changes that would materially increase their taxes, but later they were convinced that every dollar expended in street improvements added to the value of their property, and Mr. Van Vleck's suggestions were finally adopted. As a member of the Township Committee he favored liberal appropriations for public improvements, and the impetus given to the movement at that time—from 1876 to 1879—during his administration led to greater efforts in this direction by subsequent administrations, which were ratified by the taxpayers. He improved the system of public accounts and brought order out of confusion.

In all his efforts Mr. Van Vleck has been influenced by the one desire to make Montclair a model suburban town, and to this end he has contributed liberally of his own means, and has cheerfully borne his share of the increased expenditures.

He was for a time connected with the M. E. Church, but in 1874 united with the First Congregational Church, in which he has since been one of its most active and earnest members. He was the Treasurer of the Society for about ten years, and for a number of years has served, and still serves, as

Deacon of the Church and Trustee of the Society. He has been identified with and is a liberal contributor to the various benevolent organizations originating with this church and society.

Mr. Van Vleck married, in 1852, Miss Amanda Niles, daughter of William Niles, a descendant of *John*, born 1603, who came to America in the "Speedwell" in 1634, settled in Braintree, Mass., in 1639, and was one of the grantees of Dorchester lands, from which place he removed to Braintree. The name was originally spelled Niel, but at the close of the seventeenth century the present orthography was adopted. The issue of the marriage of Mr. Van Vleck with Miss Niles was ten children, six of whom are deceased; three are married.

CHARLES HENRY JOHNSON.

One of the founders of the First Congregational Church of Christ, and for seventeen years the Superintendent of the Sunday-school connected with this church, was born in Ithaca, Tompkins County, N. Y., May 10, 1833. He is a descendant of Sir William Johnson, who settled in the Mohawk Valley, in 1735, and was conspicuous for his great influence with the warriors of the Six Nations, he having been appointed Colonel of all the tribes by Governor Clinton. For his services while in command of the expedition, which resulted in the defeat of the French under Dieskau, at the head of Lake George, he received the title of Baronet, and a gift of £5,000 from Parliament. He died July 24, 1774.

Colonel Arthur S. Johnson, the father of Charles H., the subject of this sketch, served with distinction in the War of 1812, and afterward became one of the most prominent lawyers in Central New York. He was District Attorney of Tompkins County at the age of 21, and was Surrogate and Judge for many years. He was highly esteemed for his great legal ability as well as for his many personal qualities. He married Charlotte Roxana Shattuck.

Charles Henry Johnson, fifth child of Nathan and Charlotte Roxana (Shattuck) Johnson, was educated at the high school of Tompkins County, N. Y. Having decided to adopt a mercantile career he removed to New York City, in 1854, where he found employment in a large wholesale grocery house. He remained with this house about three years, and during that period the knowledge he acquired from study and observation laid the foundation of his subsequent successful business career. In 1857 he organized the firm of Pinney & Johnson, commission merchants. The firm for many years was one of the most prominent in this line, and its business operations have extended to nearly every quarter of the globe. For many years it had extensive connections with South America, Germany, England, China and the West Indies. Mr. Pinney, of the firm, died in 1876, and the business was carried on by Mr. Johnson until his retirement in 1893. He is a man of unflinching integrity and uprightness of character, and is a fitting example of the Christian merchant, whose religious principles are exemplified in his every-day life—a "living epistle, known and read of all men." To the people of Montclair he is

CHARLES H. JOHNSON.

known as the Christian gentleman, whose whole aim in life has been to make the world better. His work as a Sunday-school Superintendent was begun at the Tabernacle Church in Jersey City, in 1863, at which place he removed soon after his marriage with a lady of that place. He succeeded A. S. Hatch, the banker, as Superintendent of the school connected with that church. He was then a young man of 30, full of vigor and enthusiasm, and earnest in his devotion to the Master's cause. Under his administration the school grew in numbers and influence and became the second largest in the State of New Jersey, numbering 625, including teachers and scholars, at the close of his six years' labors. He was equally active in the affairs of the church in which he served both as deacon and trustee, and was also President of the Young Men's Christian Association. He removed to Montclair in 1869, where, finding no Church of his faith and denomination, he identified himself with the Presbyterian Church, but on learning that there were a number of residents in Montclair who held to the doctrines which he had been taught from his childhood up, he united with them in founding the new church, and soon began the work of organizing a Sabbath-school. The history of this school is a history of his work, which began under the brightest auspices in June, 1870, with 72 scholars and 18 teachers, and through the storms of winter and the heat of summer he, for seventeen consecutive years, was invariably at his post unless prevented by sickness. Both teachers and scholars, whatever their position in life, always received a kindly welcome, and he took a personal interest in each one, watching over them with tender and parental care as the shepherd watches over his sheep, never for a moment losing sight of even one stray lamb. He was their advisor, counselor and benefactor. How many, through his influence and efforts, have been gathered into the fold of Christ, and their names enrolled in the Lamb's Book of Life, only the councils of eternity will reveal. The little ones of tender years grew up under his fostering care, and became co-workers with him. It required great wisdom and tact to harmonize all the varied elements, to prevent discord, and preserve peace at all times. These characteristics he possessed in a marked degree, which were not only hereditary, but combined with Christian graces and a kindly genial nature, enabled him to control and direct the affairs of the school, which grew and prospered under his management. He inspired the teachers with his own enthusiasm and love of the work.

In the church he has been equally conspicuous as a worker, counselor, friend and brother to rich and poor alike. As a deacon he has fulfilled all the required conditions—"grave, holding the mystery of the faith in a pure conscience, being found blameless," and "purchased to himself a good degree, and great boldness in the faith which is in Christ Jesus." As a trustee he has managed the business affairs with fidelity and economy, as one who must give an account of his stewardship. His love, fidelity and devotion to his pastor has been exhibited to a marked degree, and through every difficulty and trial he has "stayed his hands" and encouraged him in his work. He has given liberally and even bountifully in aid of every benevolent and religious undertaking connected with his own church as well as assisting others "not of the household of faith" in their work and labor of love.

Mr. Johnson has been for a number of years a member of the Chamber of Commerce, Consolidated Exchange, Mercantile Exchange, and of the New York Board of Trade and Transportation. He was one of the founders and is still a director of the Bank of Montclair. He has been for twenty-three years a trustee of the church, a member of the American Home Missionary Society, American Congregational Union, and of the Congregational Club, New York.

Mr. Johnson married, in 1858, Miss Henrietta Holdane, daughter of G. W. Holdane, Esq., of Jersey City.

CHARLES HALDANE JOHNSON, son of Charles H. and Henrietta (Holdane) Johnson, was born in Jersey City, N. J., May 12, 1859. He was prepared for college at public school and at Hasbrouck Institute; entered Columbia College in 1876-7, and was graduated at Cornell University in 1880, and at Columbia Law School in 1882; admitted to the Bar of New York the same year. Believing that the West offered a more promising field for ultimate success than any place nearer home, he went to Colorado, where he became associated with District-Attorney McLivesay, whose jurisdiction covered six counties. Mr. Johnson engaged in the trial of many important cases and achieved marked success as a prosecuting attorney. After a year's experience he returned East and began practice in New York City. His experience in the West proved of valuable assistance to him, although he subsequently entered upon an entirely different line of practice. His success in the metropolis has been principally in the management of cases outside of court. He is well read in the law, thorough and careful in his legal investigations, and discusses legal questions with clearness of illustration and strength of argument. He has had charge of large interests, necessitating occasional trips to the West and to Europe, which have been attended with satisfactory results to his clients. He has been a resident of Montclair for many years, and since his return has taken a great interest in the political affairs of his County and State. He is an able and forcible speaker, and in every campaign since he resumed his residence in New Jersey his services have been in demand. He canvassed his State in 1884 under the direction of the State Republican Committee. Upon the retirement of Dr. Love, who for many years has been President of the Republican Club of Montclair, Mr. Johnson was elected to succeed him, and the Club has continued to prosper under his administration. He is a good organizer and an indefatigable worker. He managed with much ability the campaign of 1892, and with marked success that of 1893. He is a member of the Montclair Club and other organizations, and was for a time Assistant Superintendent of the First Congregational Sunday School. He has been for several years one of the trustees of the Montclair Public School, a director of the Montclair Savings Bank, and one of the Executive Committee of the Citizens' Committee of One Hundred, organized for the enforcement of law and order.

Mr. Johnson inherits many of the personal traits of both parents. He is a man of great force and moral earnestness ; genial, exceedingly affable, yet firm in his convictions of right ; conscientious, upright, and a man of strict probity and honor, personally popular with all his friends and associates. He married Adela, daughter of Julius H. Pratt, Esq. His children are Holdane Kennet, Allen, and Elizabeth.

CHARLES H. NOYES.

CHARLES H. NOYES was one of the early settlers of Montclair when it became a place of suburban residence. He descended from an old Puritan family which emigrated from England to Newbury, Mass., in the 17th century, and is still largely represented in Newburyport and vicinity. Mr. Noyes came to New York City early in life, and was for many years at the head of the well-known dry-goods and commission house of Noyes, Smith & Co., and was widely known in business circles of New York, New England and the West. In 1862 he purchased property in Montclair and was identified with the early development of the township. He removed to Brooklyn in 1866, and six years later returned to Montclair, where he again purchased property and decided to make it his permanent home. He died here in 1881. He married Miss Jane R. Dana, daughter of Alexander H. Dana, well known as a lawyer and writer on philosophical subjects, who spent most of his life in Brooklyn and died in Montclair in 1887. The family of C. H. Noyes comprised Charles S., a practicing lawyer in New York City ; Alexander D., William B., a practicing physician in New York ; Jennie D. and Henry R.

CHARLES S. NOYES, first son of Charles H. Noyes, was born in Brooklyn, N. Y., graduated from the high school of Montclair, from Amherst College in 1880, and from the Columbia Law School in 1882. In 1892 he was married to Ella E. Shafer, daughter of I. Calvin Shafer, of Montclair. They had one child, Alexander G., now deceased.

ALEXANDER D. NOYES, second son of Charles H. Noyes, was born in Montclair in 1862, prepared for college at the high school of Montclair, was graduated at Amherst College in 1883, taking third rank in his class. He chose journalism as a profession and became identified with the *New York Tribune* in 1883; subsequently financial editor and editorial writer on the *New York Commercial Advertiser* and *New York Evening Post*, which latter position he still occupies, writing also for numerous other periodicals. He is identified with social circles in Montclair, is a member of the Montclair Club, Dramatic Club, and Tariff Reform Club. He is a leader in the latter, and did effective service in behalf of tariff reform as a public speaker during the last Presidential campaign.

WILLIAM B. NOYES, third son of Charles H. Noyes, was born in Montclair, graduated from the high school of Montclair, from Amherst College in 1888, and from the New York College of Physicians and Surgeons in 1890; studied subsequently at Seney Hospital, Brooklyn, and at Berlin and Vienna.

THE BENEDICT FAMILY.

The name Benedict is derived from the Latin, *benedictus*—blessed, well spoken of. The first to illustrate the name was St. Benedict, an Italian, most illustrious in early history, who, about 520 A. D., established the order of the Benedictines, so famous all over Europe.

The Abbé de Benedictis, the distinguished secretary of Cardinal Mazarin, made himself famous by the ceremonies instigated by himself in honor of the Queen of France.

In England, in the year 640, the name was made famous by a noted Saxon, who introduced vast improvements in architecture. He was afterward canonized.

In Denmark, the prodigies of bravery performed by Benedict, brother of Canute the Fourth, covered the name with honor.

Tradition says that the Benedict family is of Silesian origin, bearing the titles of Count of the Banat and Baron of the Holy Roman Empire, the last German Count Von Benedict having passed first to France and then to England in the time of Edward the Sixth.

The American genealogy of the Benedict family begins with the pioneers of Christian civilization in the settlement of the new continent.

Among those who went into voluntary exile, rather than endure the oppression of the Stuarts in the State and Lands of the Church, was the first American progenitor, Thomas Benedict, of Nottingham-shire. He landed in Massachusetts, then a settlement seventeen years old. He was one of the few American forefathers who sought to introduce civilization and Christianity into this then savage country. He settled finally on Long Island, and there was charged with the powers of government. In the language of the old records, "he was empowered to act in point of government and was invested with magistratical power on the Island." He was the arbitrator of differences, civilized and savage, the pacifier of the offended Indian chief. It is said that when Uncas, the celebrated Sachem of the Mohegans, complained to the United Colonies in New England, because the Mohansick Sachem of Long Island had killed some of his (Uncas') men, the matter was referred for adjustment to the famous "Captain Mason and Thomas Benedict." He was a member of the first legislative body to convene in America and afterward was a member of the Colonial Legislature. He was foremost in the organization and sending out of colonists to plant new settlements, intrusted with these functions by the voice of the people, whose entire confidence he commanded. All sorts of offices in Church and State clustered around him, forced upon him by popular choice.

He is identified with the founding of the first Presbyterian Church in America, at Hempstead, Long Island, where the tablet is still in preservation that records the event.

His sons were prominent in the early Indian wars, while his descendants have fought in the battles of every war, from the direful King Philip's War to the multitudinous battles of the greatest civil war in history. His son JOHN held many public offices of state.

JOHN, the second, served as representative, and was a public-spirited citizen.

CALEB, the son of John, the second, moved from Long Island and settled in Connecticut at New Canaan.

CALEB, son of Caleb, held many important offices of Church and State. His two brothers, Lieut. Ezra and Capt. Benjamin Benedict, rendered important service during the War of the Revolution, and the latter, it is said, was on duty at Tappan during the trial and execution of Major John André, the British spy, during the latter part of September and 1st of October, 1780.

EZRA, son of Caleb (2), lived in New Canaan, was a Colonel of militia and prominent as a military man. He married Hannah, daughter of Moses and Betsey (Seymour) Comstock, a direct descendant of Christopher Comstock, who came from England about 1652, and settled at Fairfield about 1654. He brought with him his family coat-of-arms engraved upon a silver tankard, which descended to Major Samuel Comstock, before the latter's death. He gave the pitcher for preservation to the church in Wilton to be used as a part of the articles for communion service, supposing it would be retained by the church just as he left it. The tankard was sent to New York, however, and wrought into a more comely fashion of the day and the design of the grantor thereby defeated.

It is a noteworthy fact that the first Comstock who settled in England—a German baron—fled from Germany in the sixteenth century because of his participation in the *Von Benedict* treason.

THE BENEDICT HOMESTEAD.

LEWIS ST. JOHN BENEDICT, son of Ezra, was born in New Canaan, Conn., Oct. 24, 1811, and was in direct line of descent from Thomas Benedict—the father of all. He graduated from Yale College in 1834, and married Harriet, daughter of Czar Jones, son of Ebenezer, *Ebenezer, Ebenezer, Jacob, Isaac and William*, who was the first Deputy Governor of Connecticut and a son-in-law of Governor Eaton, who was the first Governor of Connecticut, and who held the position for twenty consecutive years. E. Czar Jones, referred to above was a member of the Connecticut Legislature in 1837-38.

Lewis St. John Benedict, after his graduation, began the study of medicine, which he relinquished for flattering business opportunities. He became a member of the well-known firm of Benedict, Hall & Company, prominent during the War of the Rebellion as large manufacturers of boots and shoes, being awarded enormous contracts by the United States Government for the supply of the Federal forces, in army and navy.

In 1850 Mr. Benedict moved to Brooklyn, residing on Columbia Heights for thirteen years. He was one of the pioneer members of Plymouth Church during the early pastorate of Rev. Henry Ward Beecher, and for a number of years acted as one of the Trustees of that historic church. In 1863 he retired from business and moved to Montclair where he purchased twelve acres of land on a part of which is now located the Benedict residence, corner Mountain and Bloomfield Avenues. He was one of the original members of the First Congregational Church. He was regarded as a public spirited citizen, was identified with the progress of the town, a man of genial temperament and personal popularity; he commanded universal respect. He died Oct. 23, 1884.

His immediate family are: Harriet Benedict Beecher, wife of Col. Henry Barton Beecher, son of the

SEELYE BENEDICT.

Rev. Henry Ward lia, wife of John Ward cipal of Montclair vember 28, 1880; An member of the insur- & Benedict, 145 Court and Montague Edward Lewis Bene- eral Manager of Bank fornia; Seelye Bene- after) Sarah Benedict, diet, Emily Keeler Kirkham, wife of saic, N. J.; Walter St. ber of the insurance Benedict, 145 Broad- and Montague Streets, Seelye Benedict, and Harriet (Jones) Brooklyn, and gradu- inary, East Hampton, 1867. and at Yale Col- 1871. During the he was engaged in the ness in San Francisco, sale lumber business at after which he asso- others as General

Beecher; Mary Ame- Taylor, formerly Prin- High School, died No- drew Czar Benedict, ance firm of Benedict Broadway and corner Streets, Brooklyn, diet. Cashier and Gen- of Pleasanton, Cali- diet (of whom here- Martha Hartt Bene- Benedict; Caroline George A. Milne, Pas- John Benedict, mem- firm of Benedict & way and corner Court Brooklyn. son of Lewis St. John Benedict, was born in ated at Williston Sem- Mass., in the class of lege in the class of years 1872 and 1873 manufacturing busi- Cal., and in the whole- Albany and Oswego, ciated himself with Agents for the State

of New York of the North-Western Mutual Life Insurance Company of Milwaukee. Conceiving greater possibilities in the general business of fire insurance he founded the old and well-known insurance firm of Beecher and Benedict, later Benedict & Benedict, of New York and Brooklyn. He is a leader of social circles of Montclair, where he now resides, and is one of its most energetic and enterprising citizens.

He was active in organizing the Montclair Club, and, with one exception, raised a larger amount toward the building fund than any other individual. Liberal, free-hearted, generous to a fault, he has done much to promote other public enterprises, and advance the interests of the township.

Rabun Sullivan

NAHUM SULLIVAN.

As a resident of the Mountain Side, then sparsely settled, Mr. Sullivan was well known to the people of Montclair twenty years ago. He formed one of the little colony of New York merchants who began the settlement of the mountain region, and opened up that part of the township which has since become one of the most attractive portions of Essex County. His father, Arthur Bull Sullivan, was born in Waterford, Ireland, in 1761. He was descended from one of the oldest families in Ireland, of whom Burke says:

"This family deduces its descent from Oliol ollum, King of Munster, in Ireland, who is said to have reigned in the second century of the Christian era, and whose lineage the Hibernian chronicles trace from Heber Fionn, one of the sons of Milesius."

This family bore *Arms*. Per fesse, the base per pale, in chief or, a dexter hand couped at the wrist, grasping a sword erect gules the blade entwined with a serpent ppr. between two lions rampant respecting each other, of the second, the dexter base vert, charged with a buck trippant or; on the sinister base, per pale argent and sable a boar passant counterchanged. *Crest.* On a ducal coronet or, a robin, in the beak a sprig of laurel ppr. *Motto.* Lamh foisdin-each an uachtar; that is, What we gain by conquest we secure by clemency.

Arthur Bull Sullivan came to this country when he was nine years of age. He espoused the cause of the patriots at the breaking out of the War of the Revolution, and enlisted in Captain Gearhart's company, Second Regiment, Hunterdon, N. J., also State troops.

He married Margaret Dunn, of New Brunswick, N. J., and had issue: Thomas, *Nahum*, Jeremiah, and Margaret.

Nahum Sullivan, second son of Arthur Bull and Margaret (Dunn) Sullivan, was born in New Brunswick, N. J., September 11, 1817. He was educated in his native town, and came to New York when he was sixteen years of age, and entered the house of Thomas Hunt & Co., of which Wilson G. Hunt was a junior partner. Several changes took place in the firm from 1838 to 1843, and in the latter year it became Wilson G. Hunt & Co., Mr. Hunt having taken as partners Mr. Sullivan and two others. Other changes took place in the firm during the next few years, and in 1860 Mr. Hunt retired as a general partner, and became a special partner with his successors, Messrs. Sullivan, Randolph & Budd. In 1867 the name of the firm was changed to Sullivan, Budd & Co., two others being admitted as members—Arthur T. Sullivan and Theodore F. Vail. On the death of Mr. Budd the firm became N. Sullivan & Co., and in 1878 to Sullivan, Vail & Co., consisting of Arthur T. Sullivan, Theodore F. Vail and Howard Randolph as general partners, and Wilson G. Hunt and Nahum Sullivan as special partners.

Mr. Sullivan's life was one of constant activity, and while he had accumulated a fortune he was never known to require others to do that which he could not do himself. He was a merchant of the old school; honesty with him was a matter of principle, not of policy. The firm of which he was a member was one of the best known and most substantial of any in New York. His partner, Wilson G. Hunt, was one of the founders of the Atlantic Telegraph Company. Mr. Sullivan continued in active business until January 1, 1878.

In 1870 Mr. Sullivan removed with his family to Montclair, purchasing the homestead of Mr. Nason, on Mountain Avenue, which he immediately improved and beautified, converting it into one of the first residences in the vicinity. He endeared himself to his neighbors, and was beloved and respected by the entire community, rich and poor alike, for his generous and manly qualities, which characterized all his transactions, either public or private. While he was ever foremost as one of the merchants of this country, he never sought political or public honors, having neither time nor inclination to fill the offices of public trust which he was often urged to accept. As a citizen he was a staunch republican, and an ardent supporter of the party and its principles. At the time of his death he was Vice-President of the Broadway Savings Bank, and at various times he was director in the Lorillard Insurance Company, and in the Central National Bank.

Mr. Sullivan married, in 1844, Miss Sarah Martin Runyan, daughter of Mordecai Runyan, a descendant of Richard Runyon or Rognion, one of a colony of French Huguenots who settled in New Jersey during the latter part of the last century. Richard, the ancestor, was born in 1719; he married Jane Van Court (born August 13, 1727) and had issue seven children, the third of whom, *Elias*, born June 7, 1749, married, January 9, 1771, Deborah Clark. It is probably through Elias that Mordecai, the father of Mrs. Sullivan, is descended.

The death of Mrs. Sullivan, which occurred November 30, 1881, was a shock from which her husband never recovered. She was a sweet, loving, gentle woman, greatly beloved by her friends and neighbors, and sadly missed by the whole community. Her husband felt the loss deeply. His vigorous mind and body were unimpaired, but it is thought, to a greater or less extent, his prostration was due more to that blow than to any bodily illness with which he might have been afflicted.

He was a Christian gentleman, and a man of generous impulses. He died September 1, 1884, leaving but one child, Helen Runyan, the wife of W. D. Baldwin.

WILLIAM DELAVAN BALDWIN.

There were two distinct branches of the Baldwin family in this country, not immediately connected. The Baldwins who were among the early settlers of this locality were all descendants of the Connecticut branch, while W. D. Baldwin, who for so many years occupied the Sullivan homestead in Montclair, is a descendant, probably, of John Baldwin, one of the early settlers of Dedham, Mass.

Baldwin is one of the oldest names mentioned in English history. It is said there was in England a Baldwin as early as A.D. 672. The Baldwins, Earls of Flanders, were contemporary with Alfred the Great, whose son Baldwin (2d) married the daughter of Robert, of France, whose daughter, Matilda, married William the Conqueror. Baldwin, Archbishop of Canterbury, with a train of 200 horse and 300 foot, his banner inscribed with the name of Thomas O'Becket, went on a crusade with Richard Cœur de Lion in 1120. The name is said to be derived from the words *Bald*, quick or speedy, and *win*, an old word signifying victor or conqueror—the true signification being "The speedy conqueror or victor." In 1198 Robert Fitz Baldwin is mentioned as holding lands in Bucks County, England. Sir John Baldwin, of Bucks, was Chief Justice in 1536. The English branch of the Baldwins bore *Arms*, argent, a saltire sable. *Crest :* On a mount vert a cockatrice argent wattled, combed and beaked or, ducally gorged and lined of the last.

The mother of W. D. Baldwin was Sarah Jane Munson, daughter of Oscar D. Munson, of Vermont, a descendant of Richard Munson, of New Hampshire, one of the petitioners, in the winter of 1689-90, for Massachusetts jurisdiction. The mother of Sarah Jane Munson was Sarah Latin Bennett, daughter of Aaron Bennett, of New Brunswick.

W. D. Baldwin, the subject of this sketch, was born in Auburn, N. Y., Sept. 5, 1856. He was educated at the High School of his native city, and began his business career as a boy in the office of the Osborn Mowing Machine Co. He was a young man of quick perceptions, honest, industrious, obliging and courteous, and soon won the confidence of his employers. Soon after reaching his majority he was sent abroad as manager of the company's European business, which he managed successfully for five years, evincing great tact and business sagacity. It was during his residence abroad that he met Miss Helen R. Sullivan, daughter of Nahum Sullivan, with whom he returned to this country and was married at the home of the bride in Montclair, Oct. 19, 1881. After his marriage he spent another year in Europe, returning to Montclair in 1882; at the same time he resigned his connection with the Osborn Mowing Machine Company, and soon after became connected with the Otis Elevator Company as its treasurer. As a resident of Montclair he was one of the most prominent as well as one of the most popular of its citizens, ready at all times to promote its social as well as its religious affairs. He was active in politics, and during the Presidential campaign of 1884 was made President of the Blaine Republican Club. He was one of the governors of the Essex County Club, and an active participant in

W D Baldwin

all its affairs. He was one of the founders of the Montclair Club, the first meeting of which was held at his house, and while he continued a resident of Montclair was one of its most active and earnest supporters. He was a vestryman in St. Luke's Episcopal Church, and used his best endeavors to advance the cause of religion and build up the church. During his seven years' residence in Montclair his influence was felt throughout the entire community, and when circumstances necessitated his removal to Yonkers, N. Y., in 1888, to assume the management of the Otis Elevator Works, his departure was greatly regretted by a large circle of friends and acquaintances.

As a citizen Mr. Baldwin has always been active in promoting the interests of his fellow-citizens with reference to public enterprises and internal improvements, to all of which he contributed liberally.

In business dealings he is uniformly courteous, but quick to apprehend and prompt and efficient to act. In the midst of public duties and business cares he has never forgotten or neglected the arts which contribute to the amenities of life, and tend to elevate its dignity and enlarge its enjoyment.

Mr. Baldwin has already become prominent in the community where he now resides, and evinces the same readiness to serve his fellow-citizens in whatever way he can be most useful. He is a Director and Vice-President of the First National Bank of Yonkers, and is Junior Warden of St Paul's Episcopal Church.

His domestic relations have always been of the happiest and his home life is a model of peace and comfort. "Given to hospitality," he delights to welcome his numerous friends, and leaves no stone unturned to contribute to their happiness and enjoyment—in all of which his loving and devoted wife, who inherited from her mother those noble qualities which characterize true womanhood—heartily unites with him in all his efforts. Six children have been born to them, five of whom are still living, viz.: Martin Sullivan, born July 18, 1883; Delavan, born Aug. 9, 1886; Helen, born Dec. 25, 1887, all at Montclair; Louise, born July 14, 1889, at East Hampton, L. I., during a temporary residence there; Elsie, born at Yonkers March 28, 1891, deceased Feb. 14, 1892; Runyon, born at Yonkers Aug. 28, 1892.

STEPHEN W. CAREY.

Most men of the present day who seek, or evince a readiness to accept, public office, are influenced to a greater or less extent by selfish motives.

It is a rare and exceptional case to find a man whose time is wholly absorbed during business hours with matters requiring the closest concentration of thought and intense application to details, to dismiss from his mind at the close of the day everything connected with his business affairs, and on returning home to seek the needed rest and recreation, to enter a new field of operations requiring the same attention, careful consideration and sound judgment; rendering such service to his fellow-citizens without compensation or hope of reward. Such is the public record of Stephen W. Carey in Montclair. Some of the most important changes and public improvements in the township have taken place since he became a resident. To what extent he is entitled to credit for these is shown in the following sketch, which, with the exception of the mere outline, is gleaned from records and other sources outside of his own immediate circle.

The family of Carey is one of the most ancient and honorable mentioned in English history. According to Burke the family of Cary or Carey derives its surname from the manor of Carey or Kari, as it is called in the Doomsday Book, lying in the parish of St. Giles in the Heath, near Launceston. In the year 1198, Adam de Karry was Lord of Castle Karry in the County of Somerset. Sir Robert Cary, a descendant in the sixth generation of Adam de Karry, vanquished the presumptuous Arragonois, for which King Henry V. restored unto him a good part of his father's lands, which for his loyalty to King Richard II. he had been deprived of by King Henry IV., and authorized him to bear the arms of the Knight of Arragon, for, according to the laws of heraldry, whosoever fairly in the field conquers his adversary, may justify the bearing of his arms. Various descendants in this line were raised to the peerage. George Cary, Esq., was Recorder of Londonderry and M.P., in 1613. He had a grant of Red

Castle (an Irish estate in the barony of Innishowen, County Donegal) from Sir Arthur Chichester, Baron of Belfast, who was Lord High Treasurer of Ireland in 1618.

It is from the Irish branch of the Carey family that the subject of this sketch descends. His father, David Thomas Carey, was a native of Dublin, Ireland, and at the age of fourteen years was sent by his parents to this country to attend school, but chiefly to escape the conscription laws in force during the wars of 1812 and 1814.

Through the duplicity of the Captain of the ship in whose care he was placed (with several hundred pounds sterling to defray the necessary expenses for a time) the money was misappropriated and the youth left a stranger in a strange land, communication with his home being very meagre during those years. He was thus forced to make his own way from an early age.

Shortly after reaching this country he enlisted on the American privateer "Yankee," and was wounded while in her service as a powder boy.

Landing in a New England seaport village, where he received kind and friendly treatment, he naturally made that his home to which he returned from time to time, in the intervals of the voyages in

"A GLIMPSE OF BROOKLAWN."

which he was engaged. At the age of twenty-four he became the Captain of a merchant ship and so continued until his death at the age of forty years.

It was at a little seaport town on the Island of Martha's Vineyard that he met and married his wife, Mary Chase West, daughter of Peter West, a direct descendant of Sir Francis West (second son of Lord Delaware). Several branches of the West family did active service both under the King's command in the French and Indian War, and at the storming of Quebec, and on the plains of Abraham, and later in the Revolutionary War, aiding the colonies to gain their independence, and again in serving the United States in the war with Great Britain.

Captain Carey died at Alexandria, Va., in 1838. His devoted wife did not long survive him. Their death left three orphan children under fourteen years of age.

Stephen W. Carey, the only son, was thus left (not unlike his father) at the age of twelve to make his own way in the world. His guardian was the senior member of a shipping firm in South Street, New York. Into this house he entered at the age of thirteen years and, with but a rudimentary education obtained in the New England schools, commenced his business career.

With this house he has been uninterruptedly connected for a period of more than forty-nine

years. In March, 1854, at the age of twenty two, he founded the present freight brokerage firm of Carey, Yale & Lambert. For several years he has been one of the members of the Committee of Five on Foreign Commerce and Revenue Laws of the Chamber of Commerce of the State of New York. For upward of thirty-nine years he has been a member of the New York Produce Exchange, and for nine years of which was one of its Board of Trustees. He has also been a Director in many of the Marine Insurance Companies of the port of New York.

In the spring of 1871 he became a resident of Montclair, from which time to the present he has been closely identified with its growth and progress. He purchased the property known as Brooklawn, lying along the Orange Road, in 1874, on which he spent several thousand dollars in improvements. Every natural feature of the old place was utilized to enhance its beauty. The little brook that ran along the front of it was enclosed with a rustic fence, and rustic arches and bridges span it at intervals, while near the main entrance the brook forms a beautiful waterfall, and the view from this point, looking up through the arches and overhanging boughs of the trees, is one of the most pleasing and picturesque of the many that are to be found in this delightful suburban township.

The house, which is of brown stone, Gothic style of architecture, is partially hidden by the trees. There is no attempt at display either in the house or the surroundings; art has been employed only to further enhance the beauties of nature.

The extensive improvements made by Mr. Carey on his own place attracted the attention of his fellow citizens, and his aid and co-operation was sought in the furtherance of public improvements. At their earnest solicitation he became a member of the Township Committee, continuing in office for six consecutive years; was Chairman of its Finance Committee, serving as Treasurer for the township at the time of its funding the bonded indebtedness incurred by the obligation to the New York, Oswego and Midland Railway Company. By pledging their individual credit, he, together with other members of the Committee, saved to the township many thousands of dollars, and placed the indebtedness on a sound financial basis. Such unselfish devotion to the public interest, at great personal risk and sacrifice, merits the lasting gratitude of his fellow citizens. Mr. Carey is foremost in every enterprise tending to the further advancement of the township interests. He is at present a member of the Committee of Seven appointed for the purpose of considering the matter of a more extended form of government for the township. He was one of the founders of the Bank of Montclair, was Chairman of the Subscription Committee, and is still a director. He is also a director of the Montclair Savings Bank and of the Montclair Gas and Water Company.

While not an active participant in the various religious and benevolent enterprises of Montclair, he has been a liberal contributor, and no one ever appealed to him in vain for assistance. He was a large contributor to the Washington—now known as the Pilgrim—Mission, and has rendered financial aid to several of the churches from time to time, regardless of sect or denomination. No man in the whole community is more respected or holds a warmer place in the hearts of the people.

Mr. Carey married, in 1863, Miss Sarah S. B. Yale, daughter of Dr. Leroy M. Yale, and the issue of this marriage is Stephen W. Carey, Jr.

Mrs. Carey has been no less active than her husband in the benevolent organizations that have engrossed the attention of her sex, and has done much to promote the work of the Children's Home Association, of which she is now the honored President.

THOMAS RUSSELL.

The people of Montclair who have witnessed its rapid growth during the past twenty years, and the remarkable changes and improvements that have taken place, are perhaps not aware that, with the exception of the actual cost of time and labor expended, this has been accomplished without cost to the taxpayers. The men who have directed its affairs have given their time, labor and business experience without any compensation whatever. Among those who are especially deserving of mention for their unselfish devotion to the public interests is Thomas Russell, an old and leading merchant of New York City, but for the past twenty years a resident of this township.

With the exception of the mere outline, the facts contained in the following sketch were compiled from the public records and from published statements without the knowledge or assistance of Mr. Russell, who, it is well known, is averse to having any mention made of either his public or private acts, but it is due to the public and to the friends of Mr. Russell that "honor to whom honor is due" should be given.

Thomas Russell was born in Glasgow, Scotland, in 1529. After receiving a liberal education, he entered the house of John Clark, Jr., & Co., proprietors of "Mile-End Spool Cotton," in 1845, being then sixteen years of age. Of his early business career, it may be said that he was faithful, industrious, honest and capable. He mastered the details of the business and in due time was promoted to a leading position in the office, which he held up to the time of his departure for this country. In 1856 he was sent by his firm to New York City to assume the entire charge of this branch of their business. He has had the management of their affairs for nearly forty years, during which time the business has steadily increased. and the goods of the firm have attained a wide reputation.

Mr. Russell is one of the oldest merchants in New York City. Most of the firms who were in business when he commenced have long since passed out of existence. He is one of the few who passed through the several financial crises and maintained his credit unimpaired.

Mr. Russell was for many years a resident of New York City, but he was induced in 1874 to visit Montclair, and soon after decided to make that his permanent residence. He purchased the Samuel

THOMAS RUSSELL.

Wilde homestead, a quiet, picturesque spot hidden among the trees, located on Union Street and Orange Road. He made many alterations and changes in the general appearance, greatly improving the entire surroundings. He soon became interested in the various public improvements which were being made, and was finally induced to accept an appointment on the Township Committee. In this position he earned the lasting gratitude of his fellow citizens by the efforts of himself and his associates to reduce the bonded indebtedness of the township, and during a most critical period pledging his own private credit to meet the defaulted bonds until permanent arrangements could be effected.

It was during his term of office that some of the greatest changes were wrought in the affairs of the township, and which laid the foundation of its subsequent growth. At the beginning of his administration the streets were poorly lighted, there being only sixty-five lamps in the whole township. Before the close of his term there were over two hundred lamps and provision made for their proper care. The contract for the introduction of water was made by Mr. Russell and his associates, and an impetus was given to public improvements during this period, the results of which were far reaching. Property owners cheerfully submitted to the increased taxation, knowing that the appropriations for the various objects were wisely and judiciously expended.

From his early childhood Mr. Russell has been an earnest worker in the cause of religion. During his residence in New York City he was an elder in the Associate Reformed Church, and was also Superintendent of the Sabbath school. Soon after his removal to Montclair in 1874 he united with the First Presbyterian Church, and has since labored earnestly not only to advance the cause of religion in his own church, but in the whole community. He was elected Superintendent of the Sunday school in 1876 and continued to hold the position for sixteen years, being heartily supported in all his efforts by the officers and teachers of the school. The little children who first greeted him as their superintendent grew up under his fostering care, many of whom united with the church and finally became teachers in the school. Others have joined the happy throng of the church triumphant to greet him with songs of praise when he shall be called to his reward above.

THE RAND AND WHIPPLE FAMILIES.

JASPER RAYMOND RAND.—The earliest record of the Rand family is that of the Vicar of Norton, 1578, Prebendary of Durham (England), 1606, of Gateshead, County Durham, and of London, having *Arms*, Or, a lion rampant, charged with three chevrons. *Crest:* Out of a coronet a boar's head in pale.

ROBERT RAND, the American ancestor, born in England 1599, married Alice, daughter of Nicholas Sharpe, born 1601. He came with his wife to New England, and settled in Charlestown, Mass., in 1624. He had a son, Robert, who lived in Lynn, who had a son, Zachariah. Daniel, the son of Zachariah, was born in 1700; married Mary, daughter of Major John Keyes, in Marlboro, Jan. 8, 1720. They settled in Shrewsbury, Mass., and he was one of the founders of that town and of the church. Their second child was *Solomon*, born March 13, 1723, who married Deborah, daughter of Jabez Dodge, Sept. 15, 1741. Jasper, eighth child of Solomon and Deborah (Dodge) Rand, born March 10, 1760, married Rachel, daughter of Joseph Knowlton, April 30, 1783. Jasper Raymond, son of Solomon, when but eighteen years old, was a private in the War of the Revolution, a member of "Capt. Ebenezer Ingall's Company, Col. Job Cushing's Regt. of Militia belonging to the State of the Massachusetts Bay in the Continental Sarvis." His brother Daniel became a colonel. His brother Ezekiel was a sergeant in the battle of Bunker Hill, and his younger brother Artemus afterward died in the service of his country. Jasper Raymond (father of the subject of this sketch), eighth child of Jasper and Rachel (Knowlton) Rand, was born in Shrewsbury, Mass., June 6, 1801, and settled in Westfield, Mass. He was one of the founders of the Westfield Bank, and twice represented his town in the State Legislature, and was a man of weight and influence in town affairs. He married Lucy, daughter of Joshua Whipple, who was the son of Joshua, a descendant—probably—of "Elder" John Whipple, born about 1605, who received a grant of land in Ipswich Hamlet (now Hamilton) in 1638. The latter was a man of great prominence, and held the chief offices in the town, and served on some of its most important committees. He had a son, John, who was also a prominent "Captain of a troop to march for Marlboro against the enemy." Matthew, his son, known as "Major Matthew," was the father of William, who was the father of William, signer of the Declaration of Independence and Brigadier General at the capture of Burgoyne. The *Boston Transcript* of 1851 refers to the death of Capt. John Whipple, aged 84, as "the son of Capt. Job Whipple, of the American army, who was wounded in the battle of Bennington, fighting in the regiment of his uncle, Col. William Whipple, one of the signers of the Declaration of Independence."

JASPER RAYMOND, the subject of this sketch, son of Jasper Raymond and Lucy (Whipple) Rand, was born in Westfield, Mass., October 17, 1837. His education was obtained in the common school and academy of his native town and of Fairfax, Vt. At an early age he entered the office of his father, who was then engaged in the manufacture of whips at a time when Westfield made whips for all the world.

He continued until 1865, when his father having retired, he and his brother succeeded to the business and continued it until 1870, when they sold it out and removed to New York. Mr. Rand was associated with another brother, Albert Tyler, for a time in the manufacture of the celebrated Laflin and Rand powder. In 1872 his brother, Addison C., began the manufacture of the Rand Rock Drills, and other mining machinery, and Jasper Rand became associated with him later; they subsequently organized the Rand Drill Company, which for nearly a quarter of a century has been one of the leading firms of the country in this line of business. Addison C. Rand above referred to is President of the Company.

RESIDENCE OF J. R. RAND, HAWTHORN PLACE.

Mr. Rand became a resident of Montclair in 1873 and has since been recognized as one of its most energetic and enterprising citizens. He purchased a plot of ground on one of the most beautiful and elevated sites in the township, and erected thereon a large and commodious residence of the then prevailing style of architecture. With a frontage on Hawthorn Place, the land slopes gently to the eastward, and along the line of Gates Avenue. The beautiful shade trees, the spacious lawn, and the great variety of plants and flowers, add much to its natural beauty, the location being unsurpassed for health and for its picturesque surroundings.

Mr. Rand entered heartily into the numerous plans of those who sought to make Montclair a model suburban township, which should be second to none in the vicinity of the great metropolis. Although his extensive business interests required every moment of his time during business hours, he yielded to the wishes of his fellow citizens of Montclair, and served for three years as a member of the Town Committee and two years as a member of the County Board of Freeholders. The records of these departments show the extensive improvements made and the increase in realty value during those periods. Mr. Rand was one of the organizers of the Bank of Montclair and became its first President, and still holds that position. He has devoted much time and attention to the management of its affairs, and the business has increased to such an extent as to justify the erection of a large and commodious building for the accommodation of its patrons. Mr. Rand was one of the founders of the Montclair Club, and rendered material assistance in raising the requisite amount for the splendid building which it now occupies, one of the largest and best equipped club houses of any town outside of New York City. He became its first President in 1887, continuing in office until 1890; and during this period its membership was largely increased as well as its social attractions and financial prosperity.

Great credit is due to Mr. Rand for his zeal and activity in this as well as in other public enterprises that have added to the social, business and educational features of Montclair.

As a member of the Board of Trustees of the First Congregational Society, he has rendered important service, and its financial affairs have been ably managed.

Mr. Rand married, in 1860, Annie, the daughter of Peter Valentine, who, in 1815, married Mary, a daughter of John Osborn, of Hempstead, N. Y., and Elizabeth Wannamaker, his wife. Her father died during her infancy. John Osborn, her maternal grandfather, was descended from Richard Osborn, who came in the ship "Speedwell" from England to Hingham, Mass., in 1635. Two years later he engaged in the Pequot war, for which service he was afterward awarded a grant of 80 acres of land.

The first ancestor of the Wannamakers in this country was Pieter Wannamaker (or Van der Maker), born in Darmstadt, in the lower Palatinate. He was one of the Palatines who, upon the revocation of the Edict of Nantes, fled from Catholic oppression and settled upon the west bank of the Hudson River in 1710. With him came Conrad Frederick; and their children—Hendrick Wannamaker and Elizabeth Frederick—became the parents of Elizabeth Wannamaker, who married, John Osborn in 1782.

Richard Osborn (the father of John Osborn), born 1717, married Christine, a daughter of Jacobus De Baen, who was the oldest son of Joost De Baen, who emigrated from Holland in 1683, and in the following year became schoolmaster and town clerk of New Utrecht. He was a large property owner in that place and also in New Rochelle and Bergen County, N. J. He afterward removed to Kinderkamack, N. J., and the records of the Hackensack church show that he was an elder, a church-master, and generous in its financial support.

The name Valentine is one of the oldest on record and had its birthplace in Italy in the second century.

The issue of the marriage of Mr. Rand with Miss Valentine was three daughters and two sons:

1st. Florence Osgood.
2d. Albert Holland—died in infancy.
3d. Josephine Freeman.
4th. Annie Grace, died February, 1889.

Jasper Raymond, at the present time a student at Cornell University.

Josephine, who married Elfrie Drew Ingall, of Ottawa, Canada, in April, 1892, died in December of the same year. She was an accomplished and rarely gifted woman, whose apparently untimely end brought lasting sorrow into many households besides her own.

JOHN HOWARD WILSON.

JOHN HOWARD WILSON.—On the paternal side Mr. Wilson is descended from an old New England family of this name. His father, John Overing Wilson, was the son of Robert Gardner Wilson, son of Dr. John Wilson, of Hopkinton, Mass., who married the daughter of John Overing, of Boston, Mass. Robert Gardner Wilson, the paternal grandfather of John H., married Rebecca Conant, daughter of Levi Conant, son of William, William, Lot, John, Lot, son of Roger, the ancestor. The name is derived from the Celtic Conan, formerly of Wales and Cornwall, and subsequently of Brittany.

Roger Conant, the emigrant and ancestor of most of those bearing the name in America, was baptized at All Saints Church, in the parish of East Budleigh, Devonshire, England, April 9, 1592. He was the youngest of eight children of Richard and Agnes (Clarke) Conant, "who were esteemed for their exemplary piety." He emigrated to New England in 1623, and settled first in Plymouth, but left there on account of "an ecclesiastical diversity of views," and in 1624-25, he was chosen by the Dorchester Company to manage and govern their affairs at Cape Ann, Mass., being recommended as "a pious, sober and pru-dent gentleman." Although he is not universally recog-nized as the first Gov-ernor of Massachu-setts, Roger Conant is fairly entitled to that honor, for the colony of which he was the head made the first permanent settlement in the Massachusetts territory, and was the germ from which the Massachusetts Bay Colony sprung. His influence for purposes of colonization was very great, and but for him the colony would have been abandoned. John Overing Wilson married, in 1843, Mary, daughter of Jesse Morse, at Natick, Mass. On the maternal side Mr. Wilson is descended from the old New England family of Coolidge, many mem-bers of which were earnest and steadfast patriots and followers of the fortunes of the colonies in the Revo-lutionary days. The

J. H. WILSON.

name of Mr. Wilson's ancestor, John Coolidge, appears on the Lexington Alarm Roll of Col. Peirce's regiment, which marched to the Concord and Lexington battle-fields, April 19, 1775. The same ancestor afterward saw eight months' service as a member of Bremer's Massachusetts regiment, enlisting immediately after the Concord fight.

The hereditary traits of John H. Wilson were exemplified in his school-boy days as well as in his subsequent professional career. He was born in Natick, Mass., and entered Yale in 1864, graduat-ing in '68. He studied law for a time with his uncle, Joseph Warren Wilson, in Norwalk, Conn., and removed thence to Flushing, New York, in 1869, where he soon after made the acquaintance of Henry A. Bogert, Esq. From a student in the law office of Mr. Bogert he became permanently associated with him in his practice, having charge of the department of Court practice, embracing commercial, real estate, etc. The defeat which many times followed his undertakings at the beginning, determined his ulti-mate success, for his defeat in any enterprise, instead of discouraging, aroused all the dormant energies of his nature, and tenaciously he fought his way through difficulties and overcame obstacles.

Mr. Wilson after leaving Flushing resided for three years in Brooklyn, and moved thence to New York City. In 1877 he married Carolyn Ives, daughter of William H. Dawson, Esq., of New Haven, Conn., and decided to make Montclair his permanent home. He bought a plot of land on Park Street, one of the most beautiful and romantic spots in the outskirts of the town, which formerly belonged to Lucy Stone, being a part of the old Noah Crane property. The old forest trees were left standing, and through the deep ravine that skirts the homestead plot flows the same rippling brook where the Lenni Lenappe stopped to quench their thirst on their journey to the sea. The Swiss cottage, half hidden by the trees, has often attracted the eye of the artist and formed a valuable acquisition to his portfolio.

For the first few years Mr. Wilson enjoyed the quietude of his country home and mingled but little in public affairs. During the presidential campaign of 1880, however, he entered actively into politics. The defeat of Blaine, the republican candidate for President in 1884, only made him the more determined in his efforts to win, and in the campaign of 1888 he took the stump and made a vigorous canvass for Harrison, the standard bearer of the republican party, with gratifying results. The following spring he accepted the nomination and was elected a member of the Township Committee, of which he was made Chairman, has since been annually re-elected to the same position and has deservedly received the approbation of his fellow citizens for the excellent work he has done. His time, his talents, and his energies have been unstintingly devoted to public improvements of every character, in all of which he has had the hearty support of his colleagues. During his administration the appropriations for the improvement of streets and roads have doubled in amount, and have been judiciously expended. The successful establishment of the present sewerage system is largely due to his efforts. His professional services were freely given to secure the best results. He participated in the negotiations with the repre-sentatives of Orange and Bloomfield for an outlet through these places. It required considerable diplomacy and shrewdness to accomplish the desired results. He vigorously worked for a union with Orange in the construction of an outlet to tidewater, which resulting in the enlarging of their system so as to take in Bloomfield and Montclair. Next to the introduction of water this is by far the greatest public improve-ment ever made in Montclair, and the most beneficial to property owners.

Mr. Wilson was the first to urge upon his fellow citizens the necessity for a change in the form of local government, by exposing the weakness and difficulties connected with the old township system, and afterward by procuring the appointment of a committee to consider the necessity for a change, and to report upon the best form of government to adopt. The results of these efforts has been the adoption by the voters of Montclair of the present town government. By this act his administration was fully endorsed and the people of the new town, under a new and more perfect form of government, have entered upon what, it is believed, will prove an era of renewed prosperity. For these good results no one is entitled to more credit than Mr. Wilson.

Mr. Wilson has been equally active in promoting all the interests of the town. He is a member of the Congregational Church, and has been connected with the Sunday school. He is a member of the Montclair Club, was a member of the Board of Directors for three years, Vice-President for two years, and has now been re-elected for a second term of three years as a director. He was one of the original members of the Outlook Club, which has always received his earnest and hearty support. He was an alternate delegate to the Republican National Convention of 1892, at Minneapolis, Minn., which nominated Harrison for the Presidency. He is Vice-President of the Town Republican Club and Chair-man of that branch of the County Republican Committee located in Montclair.

From Yale University he has received the degrees of Bachelor of Arts and Master of Arts. He is a member of the Phi Beta Kappa Society, and of several college fraternities connected with Yale. Whether in politics, professional or social life, Mr. Wilson has always preserved a spotless escutcheon and maintained a high character.

THE UNDERHILL FAMILY.

LINE OF DESCENT OF WILLIAM WILSON UNDERHILL, FROM CAPTAIN JOHN UNDERHILL, 1630.

Capt. John Underhill, the progenitor of the family from which William Wilson Underhill is a descendant, was one of the most famous of the early New England settlers. He was a noted Indian fighter, and is said to have slain 150 Indians on Long Island, besides being one of the commanders of the expedition which exterminated the tribe of Pequods in Connecticut. He was the son of John Edward Underhill, of Huningham, England, a near relative of Edward Underhill, who was distinguished by the title of "Hot Gospeller," and who exchanged the life of a country gentleman for that of a soldier and courtier.

During the reign of Elizabeth, when the prosperity of the family was at its height, the Underhills acquired property in almost every parish within six miles of Eatington. They became connected by marriage also with many of the best families of the County

W. W. UNDERHILL.

of Warwick, and attained the honors of Knighthood. Among the first mentioned of the name is that of William Underhill, of Wolverhampton, County Stafford, who "lyved in the yere of our Lord 1423." The family bore Arms, argent a chevron gules between three trefoils slipped vert. Crest, a hind lodged or on a mount vert. Capt. John Underhill, the American ancestor, born in 1597, early imbibed an ardent love of liberty. He was strongly solicited to go with Governor Carver, Elder William Brewster, and other worthies to the settlement of Plymouth. He came over with Winthrop "as captain of any militia force that might be employed or instituted," as he had served under the great Dutch Prince in the War of the Netherlands in 1630. He disciplined the Boston militia, and was one of the first deputies from Boston to the General Court. He was one of the founders and the first Captain of the Ancient and Honorable Artillery Company of Boston. In 1637 his great friend, Sir Harry Vane, sent him as commander of the colony troops to Saybrook, Conn. The same year he was "disfranchised and eventually banished from the jurisdiction of Massachusetts, his ideas of religious toleration being more liberal than those around him." He was a representative from Stamford, Conn., to the General Court in 1633.

In 1644 he moved to Long Island and became a resident of Flushing. In 1655 he was made by Governor Nicoll high sheriff of North Riding on Long Island. He died at an advanced age, July 21, 1672, and was buried on his estate in the Underhill burying-ground at Matinecock, formerly Kenilworth or Kilingworth, Queens County, Long Island. The seal of Capt. John Underhill, attached to his name as a witness in a conveyance from the Indian proprietors of Matinecock, Long Island, to Matthew Prior, dated Kilingworth, 22d of June, 1664, are "argent three trefoils slipped vert." He had a son, John, of Matinecock, who became a member of the Society of Friends, and was the ancestor of the Long Island branch of the family.

Nathaniel, son of John, born in 1663, removed to Westchester, N. Y., in 1685, and bought lands of John Turner. The children of Nathaniel were Thomas, Nathaniel, Jr., Benjamin, Abraham, John,

Mary, and William Barton. A son of Nathaniel, Jr., was Abraham, who had a son Isaac, born June 21, 1726, at whose house in Yorktown Major André stopped for breakfast on the morning of the day of his capture at Tarrytown. A son of Isaac was Joshua, father of Ira B. Underhill, who married a Miss Abigail King, of Philadelphia.

WILLIAM WILSON UNDERHILL, the subject of this sketch, son of Ira B. and Abigail (King) Underhill, was born in New York City, September 13, 1839. He was educated at several schools, at Burlington College and the University of Pennsylvania. After his father's death he went to New York and engaged for a time in the commission business. At the beginning of 1862 he went abroad and made an extended tour. In December, 1862, he entered the office of the United States Fire Insurance Company, New York City, as Assistant Secretary. He was made Secretary in 1866, and President in 1882, having succeeded his uncle to that position, who had filled it for twenty-five years. The same office has been presided over by an Underhill since 1849.

While eschewing politics in the ordinary sense of the term, Mr. Underhill has given time and thought to the leading issues of the day.

Brought up in the simple faith of the Society of Friends, suburban life had more attractions for him than the city, and after visiting Montclair he was favorably impressed with its many attractive features, and in 1883 he purchased the property on the corner of Harrison Avenue and Llewellyn Road, a part of the Riker Estate, formerly the homestead farm of Frederick Vincent.

When called upon by his fellow citizens to serve in a public capacity, he consented to serve as a member of the Township Committee, and during the two years he occupied that position he favored the most advanced ideas of progress and reform.

He is also a member of the Essex County Microscopic Society, the Montclair Club, and the Insurance Club of New York; also President of the New York Inland Underwriters' Association, and Secretary and Treasurer of the Tariff Association of New York. Having no associates there of his own faith, he is an attendant at St. Luke's Episcopal Church.

Mr. Underhill married Miss Emily H. Griffen, daughter of John L. Griffen, Esq., of New York City, a descendant of the Griffens of Westchester County, N. Y. They have issue seven children, viz.: Louise Griffen, Wilson, John Griffen, Mabel King, Arthur, Clarence King, and Ernest.

THE MILLER AND DEMAREST FAMILIES.

COLONEL GEORGE ALFRED MILLER.— Colonel George A. Miller was born in New York City, August 30, 1853. He is probably descended from John Miller, who settled on Long Island about 1649, from Lynn, Mass., and who married a daughter of Rev. Abram Pierson, whose son was the first President of Yale College. Colonel Miller's father was *Levi*, his grandfather *Joseph* (both born in Somers, Westchester County, N. Y.), son of *Samuel*, born in Harrison, Westchester County, N. Y., November 14, 1757; removed thence to Somers, after the War. He did service in the War of the Revolution, as shown by the following statement copied from the records of the War Department at Washington:

" Near the end of 1775 he volunteered for 12 months as a Ranger, under Capt. Micejah Townsend & Col. Hammond, and was on duty as guard to the Committee of Public Safety, executed their orders in arresting and dispersing Tories, prevented their congregating to concert measures or to furnish supplies of forage or provisions. When the British war vessels sailed up the Hudson River—the Rose & Phenix—he, with his company was ordered to guard along the shore to prevent their landing. After this he went to the 'Big Lot' near Mamaroneck where Tories were organizing, killed Capt. Wm. Lounds.bury, on whom was found a British commission to enlist men, and captured all but two of his men. He was employed on entrenchments at Horns Neck on York Island when N. Y. City was evacuated (Sept. 15, 1776) and retreated with the army to White Plains and was on Holton Hill or near it when the battle (Oct. 28, 1776) took place at White Plains.

" In 1777 or 8 (probably 1778) he enlisted for one year as 'minute man' under Capt. Wm.

Moger—afterward insane—& Col. Thomas, and while at North Castle was attacked by a large body of horse with a sharp engagement in which his father was killed and he retreated.

"Near Round Hill (a portion probably of Greenwich) Conn. he with his company attacked the advanced guard of a body of British horse, killed Capt. Theall besides wounding a number of others. After this, during 1780, 1781 and 1782, he continued to serve in the militia under Capt. John Thomas and Capt. St. John in the command of Col. Thomas, and Under St. James Miller, on alarm, and as the emergency required, which were short tours of which he could not give the details, but he claimed it aggregated from 6 to 12 months of actual duty."

The mother of Colonel Miller was Marianne Adeline Demarest (Miller) a descendant of David des Marest, a French Huguenot, who emigrated to this country in 1663, and on his arrival joined the Huguenot Colony on Staten Island. He brought with him his wife, his two sons, Jean and David, with their wives and children, and Samuel, an unmarried son. He removed in 1665 to New Harlem, and in 1677 disposed of his property there and bought from the Tappan Indians a large tract of land lying between the Hackensack and Hudson rivers, which included the present township of Hackensack. This David des Marest was a native of Beauchamp, a little village of Picardy, in France, near the city of Amiens. The family of des Marest was very numerous in that part of France and highly respectable. One Samuel des Marest, a Professor of Theology, and his two sons, Daniel and Henri, prepared what has been pronounced the finest edition of the French Bible that has ever been published.

Colonel Miller's line of descent from the ancestor is through Jean, son of David, born 1645, Petrus, born 1709, Jacobus, born 1735, Jacobus, born 1767, and James, born 1791, who was the father of Marianne Adeline, wife of Levi Miller and mother of Colonel Miller. Colonel Miller was educated in New

COL. GEO. A. MILLER.

York City, and was graduated at Columbia Law School in 1873. He was admitted to the bar in 1874, shortly before which he had entered the office of Scudder & Carter, with which, and the succeeding firm of Carter & Ledyard, he has ever since been connected. These firms have, both of them, at all times, had charge of litigations involving large interests, and the name of Mr. James C. Carter, who is the senior member of the firm, is of national reputation. The department of work which has engaged a large part of Mr. Miller's attention has had relation to pleading and procedure, in which he has had large experience. He is Professor of Law in the Metropolis Law School, where he lectures on practice and pleading at common law and under the Code. He is also a member of the New York Bar Association and of the New York Reform Club.

Yours very truly
E. G. Burgher.

Colonel Miller has also achieved distinction as an officer of the National Guard, S. N. Y. He began his military career in 1873 as a member of the famous Twenty-second Regiment, having joined Company A that year. He was an enthusiast in military affairs, and in time became thoroughly proficient in military tactics, remaining only one year as private, being promoted corporal in 1874, sergeant in 1876, second lieutenant in 1881, and in six weeks following was elected captain, passing from a non-commissioned officer to the highest company rank of a commissioned officer within a period of less than two months. In 1886 he became Major, and in 1888 Lieutenant-Colonel of the Regiment. He was an efficient officer, a thorough disciplinarian, and withal popular with the rank and file. Colonel Miller rendered important military service in connection with this Regiment, having been a participant in many of the exciting events in which the Twenty-second Regiment was conspicuous, notably the railroad riots of 1877. In 1889, at the unanimous request of the officers of the Twelfth Regiment, he was transferred thence, and served as its Lieutenant-Colonel with distinction until 1892, when he resigned, after an active service of nearly twenty years in the National Guard.

Colonel Miller became a resident of Montclair in 1873, and has been more or less identified with public matters, especially with politics, in which he has always been on the side of reform without regard to party affiliations. He was one of the founders of the Tariff Reform Club, and has been active in promoting its objects. He was also one of the founders of the Montclair Club.

He married, in October, 1878, Julia E. Wainwright. He has two children, viz.: George A., Jr., and Gertrude.

EDWARD GYRE BURGESS.

The name of Burges or Burgess, as appears from ancient documents, was formerly De Burges, afterward Burches, and subsequently Burgess. From the French derivation of the name it is probable that the English ancestor came from Normandy with the Conqueror, and was among those to whom lands were apportioned for military service rendered. Eleven persons of this name are mentioned by Burke as having received Coat-of-Arms in recognition of distinguished service. Those borne by Charles Montoliere Burges, of Beaufort County, Sussex, were: *Arms*—Per fesse argent and ermine a fesse azure fretty or, a bordure of the third bezantee, on a canton gules a bend of the first, charged with a baton of Knight Marshall ppr. *Crest*—A camel's head ppr. erased gules.

The American ancestor of the New York branch of this family was Edward E. Burgess, who came from England to this country about 1760, and settled in Watervliet, now Bethlehem, in Albany County.

Edward G., Sr., the father of Edward G., was a successful merchant in Albany for a number of years. He removed to Jersey City in 1840, and was one of the originators of the system of floating grain elevators which has revolutionized the grain business in the country, and enabled those engaged in the grain trade to handle millions of bushels in the same time that thousands were handled under the old system. He with others owned the first grain floating elevator and established the new system as early as 1848, in face of great opposition. He is on the roll of honor of the Produce Exchange, having volunteered his services during the riot of 1863.

An uncle of Mr. Burgess, Sr., Leonard Burgess, was for many years a prominent manufacturing jeweler in Albany. Another uncle, Daniel Hewson, a prominent resident of Auburn, was a warm friend and neighbor of William H. Seward.

The mother of E. G. Burgess was Mary Tanner Wands, daughter of James Wands, and granddaughter of John Wands, of the township of New Scotland, formerly Bethlehem, Albany County, New York, who came from Glasgow, Scotland, about 1750. He and his brother "Ebenezer" are the only persons of that name who ever settled in this country. In the history of New Scotland, it is stated that "from 1750 to 1775 there was a large emigration of a sturdy, industrious class from Scotland, Ireland, England, etc., possessing an intelligence which inspired them with courage to promote the well being of each other, and by their influence to give to the reformed religion an example worthy of Christianity."

Among the names prominently mentioned in this connection is that of John Wands. He was a thrifty Scotchman and an industrious farmer. At the outbreak of the French and Indian War, he shouldered his "flint lock" and fought the wily savages—the allies of the French—with that courage and determination which distinguished the hardy Scotch pioneer. A powder horn artistically inscribed with designs of Fort Stanwix and other fortifications—now in the possession of E. G. Burgess, his great-grandson—is evidently a record of his achievements. He was stationed for a time in a stone church in the village of Schoharie which was then used as a fortification; this old church is still standing. During the War of the Revolution he was known as "Ensign John Wands"; he was ensign of First Regiment Albany Militia, commanded by Colonel Henry Quackenbush. In the war of 1812, the family was represented by Peter, Joseph and James W. Wands, who volunteered their services.

John Wands was evidently a prominent member of the Masonic Fraternity, and one of the organizers of the lodge in his locality. The history of New Scotland states that as early as 1794 a Mason's lodge was in existence at New Scotland. Among the few names of the members given are John Wands, Gloud Wands, James Wands and eight others. It is further stated that "James Wands 2nd, was a teacher previous to 1794." James B. Wands was Supervisor of the town in 1832, and again in 1837. Another account states that "Dr. Wands, from New Scotland, practiced in the township of Guelderland about eight years and then removed to Cohoes." Thomas D. Wands, the granduncle of Mr. Burgess, was Supervisor of his district in Albany for many years. He was a stove manufacturer and was a near neighbor and friend of Thurlow Weed. The families of Wands and Burgess were both prominent in Albany County, and held many offices of trust both before and after the Revolution. William E. Burgess, a cousin of Edward G., is specially mentioned in the annals of the town for the part he took in the Mexican War. Another cousin, Ebenezer E. Wands, now occupies the old homestead of the great-grandfather, and had six boys in the Civil War, James M., James E., Robert J., Thomas, Alexander H. and Oliver.

EDWARD G. BURGESS, son of Edward G. and Mary T. (Wands) Burgess, was born in Albany, N. Y., but removed with his parents in early childhood to Jersey City. He was educated at the public schools of that city and subsequently entered the service of the Grain Elevating Company, of which his father was the leading spirit, being President of the Company at the time of his death in 1872. He was made President of the Company in 1873, and conducted its affairs successfully until 1884. He then became associated with Annan & Co., and in 1891 the firm was changed to the International Grain Elevating Company, Mr. Burgess becoming its President.

He is one of the Board of Managers of the New York Produce Exchange, elected to serve from May, 1892, to May, 1894; he is also one of the Managers of the New York Produce Exchange Building and Loan Association.

Mr. Burgess' connection with the affairs of Montclair extends over a period of more than twenty years, during which time it has grown from a small suburban village to a township of nearly twelve thousand inhabitants. As a public spirited citizen he has done his share to promote public improvements and physical and educational development. He first purchased a house on Chestnut Street, where he resided for about ten years. In 1883 he bought the property on the mountain slope fronting Mountain Avenue, near Gates Avenue. On this he erected a large and substantial brick villa of the English Gothic style of architecture. Its broad verandas and spacious rooms give to it an oriental appearance and an air of comfort and restfulness, while its picturesque surroundings, with its beautiful shade trees, spacious lawn and magnificent view, all combine to make it a model home and delightful retreat. In improving and beautifying his own home, Mr. Burgess has not been unmindful of the interests of his neighbors and fellow citizens, and has done what he could to improve their condition and promote their happiness. He was one of the founders of the McVickar Military Institute, which has already attained high rank as a private educational institution for boys, fitting them for the practical duties of life; also preparing them for college. Mr. Burgess was also one of the founders of the Montclair Club and of the Montclair Athletic Club. He assisted in organizing the Montclair Bank, which has done so much for the business

E. A. Bradley

interests of the township and is still one of its Directors. He is also a Trustee of St. Luke's Church. He is a member of the Society of the Sons of the Revolution by virtue of his descent from John Wands. He married Elizabeth M. Atkins, daughter of Chas. H. Atkins, of Jersey City. Three children are the issue of his marriage, viz.: Charles E., Edward G., Jr., and Herbert R.

The Atkin, family referred to is one of great antiquity and prominence in the history of England and Ireland. Burke, in his "Landed Gentry," says: "Sir Jonathan Atkins, Knight of Givendale, County York, Governor of Guernsey, born in 1603, died 1702, aged ninety-three years, leaving by his first wife, Mary 2nd, daughter of Sir William Howard, of Haworth Castle, Cumberland, and sister of Sir Charles Howard, 1st Earl of Carlisle, three sons. One of these settled in Ireland about 1640, and founded that branch of the family. The others remained in England."

EDWIN A. BRADLEY.

Mr. Bradley was born in Rumney, Grafton County, N. H., February 14, 1840, son of Moses, who was born at Rumney, 1810, and grandson of Eben, who was born at Plaistow, N. H., 1772.

The American ancestor of the New Hampshire branch of the Bradley family was Daniel, of Haverhill, Mass., who came in the "Elizabeth" from London, Eng., in 1635. He was killed by the Indians August 13, 1689.

Abraham, son of Joseph, a descendant of Daniel, was the immediate ancestor of the New Hampshire Bradleys. Several of the Bradley family were killed by the Indians March 15, 1697, when Mrs. Dustin was made prisoner.

Through his grandmother Mr. Bradley is descended from Richard Hall, who settled in Bradford, Mass., about 1670. He had a son, Joseph, born in Bradford, 1680, who was the father of Joseph, born in Bradford, 1707, married Deborah Abbott, daughter of Thomas Abbott, of Andover, Mass. The last Joseph probably removed to Chester, N. H., and had among other children Jonathan, born in Chester, N. H., December 19, 1745, who married, June 20, 1776, Desire Butterfield, born in Chester, N. H., February 23, 1750. Their daughter, Sarah Hall, born in Concord, N. H., November 22, 1767, married Eben Bradley, grandfather of Edwin A.

The mother of Edwin A. Bradley was Marenda Chapman, daughter of Mark H. Chapman, a descendant of the Sanbornton, N. H., branch of the Chapmans. Mark H. was born in Boxford, Mass. Mark H. Chapman was the second husband of Sarah Greenough, the mother of Marenda Chapman, a descendant of William Greenough, who emigrated from the West of England in 1650 and settled in Boston, Mass.

Edwin A. Bradley, the subject of this sketch, was educated at Newbury, Vt., and Northfield, N. H., and afterward entered his father's employ, who at that time was engaged in mercantile business at Haverhill, Mass. E. A. Bradley soon after he reached his majority bought out his father's business, and in 1867, in company with Mr. George C. Currier, removed to New York City, where they started in the manufacture of building materials under the firm name of Bradley & Currier, changing the firm in 1885 to The Bradley and Currier Company, Limited. Beginning with a small trade their shipments now extend to almost every part of the globe. Mr. Bradley has kept apace with the times and often anticipated the changes and improvements in this direction. His company employs upward of 600 men. His is probably the largest house in this line of business East of the Mississippi. He has managed the business successfully for over a quarter of a century.

Mr. Bradley was attracted by the beauties of Montclair as early as 1877, and soon after purchased a plot of ground on the corner of Mountain Avenue and Van Vleck Street, being a part of the original "Crane" property. He erected on this a large and commodious house, which he occupied for some years. After the death of Mr. Dike he bought the property owned by that gentleman, situated on Mountain Avenue on the slope of the mountain, embracing one of the finest and most extended views within fifty miles of the metropolis.

While taking no active part in politics, Mr. Bradley has shown himself to be one of the most public-spirited citizens in the township, and has co-operated with his fellow citizens in the various public improvements that have been made. He has long been a vestryman of St. Luke's Episcopal Church.

Mr. Bradley married into an old distinguished Huguenot family. His wife, Mariana, was the daughter of James C. Gulick, of New York City, whose ancestor came from Holland after the revocation of the edict of Nantes, and settled first on Long Island and afterward removed to Middlesex County, N. J. James, the grandfather of James C. Gulick, served with the New Jersey troops in the War of the Revolution. Other members of the family also served as officers and privates of the New Jersey troops. A brother of James Gulick was killed at the battle of Monmouth.

On the maternal side James C. Gulick is descended from Thomas Galbraith, who came from Scotland and settled in Somerstown, Westchester County, N. Y., and afterward changed his name to Calbraith. The family of Galbraith is one of the remotest antiquity. Its name is derived from the Celtic, being formerly called "Clann a Bhreatanuich," and originally belonged to the Lennox. It was in the Parish of Baldernoch, County Stirling, that the Galbraiths of Baldernoch (anciently Baldrunich, or Druidstown), Chiefs of the name, had their place of residence. There is a charter from Maldruin, Earl of Lennox, to Maurice Galbraith, in the reign of Alexander II., conveying to him the lands of Gartonbenach; and in the year 1238 the same barony was granted to Arthur Galbraith. The family sprang from the Galbraiths of Gigha, who descended from the Galbraiths of Baldernoch, having fled with Lord James Stuart, youngest son of Murdach, Duke of Albany, from the Lennox, after burning Dumbarton in the reign of James I. The Galbraiths were called "Children of the Briton" and were once reckoned a great name in Scotland.

The children of Edwin A. Bradley and Mariana (Gulick) Bradley, are Edwin A., Jr. (deceased), George Gulick, Herbert Chapman, Ethel, Harold Hall and Mariana.

GEORGE PENRICE FARMER.

The name of Farmer is from the Saxon Fearme or Froome, which signifies food or provisions. The Farmers were of Saxon origin, and in the reign of Edward IV., of England, were seated in Northamptonshire. Only one family of that name is mentioned as having emigrated to this country during the colonial period.

George P. Farmer, one of the founders of the First Baptist Church of Montclair, and its Senior Deacon, is a native of England, where he was born May 8, 1836; he came with his parents to this country when but three years of age. More than thirty years of his life was spent in Philadelphia, where his parents settled. He received his education in the public schools of that city, after which he obtained a position in the commission house of E. C. Pratt, and in 1865 became a partner in the house under the firm name of E. C. Pratt, Bro. & Co., afterward Pratt & Farmer. The business was carried on successfully for a number of years in Philadelphia, and in 1870 removed to New York City, where the firm had conducted a branch for a number of years, and which now became the headquarters for the firm. Mr. Farmer resided in Brooklyn for about six years. He visited Montclair during the Centennial year, and was so well pleased that he decided to make that his future home. Four years later, in 1880, he bought the Baldwin farm, fronting on the Orange Road, containing about fourteen acres. This was one of the famous apple farms of West Bloomfield, and the remains of the old cider mill which for more than a hundred years had ground the products of the orchard into the choicest cider, and often distilled into "applejack," was a conspicuous feature of the place when it passed into the possession of Mr. Farmer. Not a trace of the "early industry" is now left. A beautiful lawn with handsome shade trees now covers the spot, and the transformation is so complete that those "who knew it in former days would know it no more." The only relic of the former industry left standing is a few choice Canfield and Harrison apple trees, which still bear their fruit in season, and add to the many attractive features of the place. Mr. Farmer utilized the old homestead foundation and some of the framework of the homestead, but no part of it would now be recognized in the beautiful modern villa that attracts the passer-by, nestled behind the beautiful shade trees and weeping willows which were planted by him. The rushing brook, which in the spring time swept everything before it, destroying the roads and the neighbors' fences, now meanders along under the roadway and through the homestead lot, restricted in its course by the art of man, but ever flowing onward.

> "Man may come and man may go,
> But I go on forever."

The old Orange Road, with its un-sightly crooks and curves, its rough and uneven road-bed,

bordered with stones and broken-down tiful avenue, winding passing the beautiful either side, with their ing to the very edge, other objectionable the view. These im- a great extent to the aided by some of his bors. He has recently provements by cutting his own place, one of son Avenue.

taken a leading part in this community, a and decided views in but charitable to those While a resident of Deacon in the Broad of that city, and on lyn, N. Y., united Avenue Baptist came to Montclair in was no Baptist Church field. He attended Church in Montclair finally took his letter tist Church, where he several years, waiting time when a sufficient

and half-decayed trees fences, is now a beau- its serpentine course, villas fronting it on spacious lawns reach- with no fences or features obstructing provements are due to efforts of Mr. Farmer, enterprising neigh- made still further im- wide avenues through which is named Madi-

Mr. Farmer has in the Baptist Society man of pronounced matters of religion, who differ with him. Philadelphia he was a Street Baptist Church his removal to Brook- with the Washington Church. When he 1876 he found there nearer than Bloom- the Presbyterian for a short time, but to the Bloomfield Bap- labored earnestly for and watching for the number could be

GEORGE T. FARMER.

gathered together to organize a church nearer home. A movement was finally begun in the summer of 1885, and the first meeting of the present organization was held in his house, and afterward in Montclair Hall, where the Baptist Society in Montclair worshiped for several years. He was elected the first and the Senior Deacon, and on the expiration of his term of office was re-elected. He has been unceasing in his efforts to build up the Church and extend its influence, and when in the autumn of 1889 it was decided to erect a house of worship, he was made a member of the building committee.

Mr. Farmer has been conspicuous in the affairs of the town and was one of the earnest advocates of a "higher education" against a strong and determined opposition of a class of taxpayers who were unwilling to meet the additional expenditure required. He has never advocated any measure that he has not been willing to share his pro rata of the expense even where he himself was the least benefited.   He served two years as a member of the Road Commissioners and two years on the Town Committee and in both positions he was an earnest advocate of progress. It was during his time of office, 1883-84, that some of the most radical changes were made. The streets had been laid with the common gravel which soon washed away and left the streets in a most deplorable condition. Mr. Farmer obtained permission to macademize a single block as an experiment. This met with strong opposition at first and Mr. Farmer was roundly abused, but several miles of streets have since been treated in the same manner, and the citizens of Montclair are under great obligations to Mr. Farmer for this, one of the greatest improvements ever made in the township. In laying sidewalks he practiced the greatest economy with the most satisfactory results, having used only about one-third of the amount appropriated during his term of office as Chairman of the Sidewalk Committee, and over 50,000 feet of sidewalk was laid in two years. The subject of lighting the streets also received his special attention. Several of the most thickly populated streets were in total darkness, in many cases the lamps having been removed. He, as Chairman of this Committee, had new lamp posts erected and lamps better distributed and lighted. Mr. Farmer served as one of the Town Committeemen during the greatest crisis through which Montclair ever passed, viz.: that of funding the debt of Montclair Township amounting to $100,000, which by a decision of the United States Supreme Court became immediately payable, and for which all property, public and private, was held liable. Mr. Farmer was one of the three—the others being Mr. Stephen W. Carey and Thomas Russell—to whom the entire matter of this judgment debt and its settlement was referred, resulting in its satisfactory liquidation within a period of eight months, greatly to the advantage of the town and placing its credit upon a sound financial basis.

In his management of the affairs of the township Mr. Farmer's ideas have often been in advance of his associates and fellow citizens, and his acts have often caused bitter opposition to him personally, but subsequent events have demonstrated the wisdom of his course. Although decided in his convictions of right, he is a man of unswerving integrity, conscientious, upright, and no one can question the honesty or purity of his motives, however much they may criticise his acts. He is recognized by friends and foes alike as a man of progressive ideas, and one who has the welfare of the whole community at heart.

DANIEL OSCAR ESHBAUGH (or ESCHBACH).

The ancestor of Mr. Eshbaugh was John Eschbach, who was born December 15, 1747, and emigrated from Germany in early life and settled in Northampton County —now Lehigh County— Penn. His maternal ancestor was Jacob Follmer, who came from Germany and settled in Berks Co., Penn., in 1737. George Jacob, a son of the latter, was a commissioned officer in the Revolutionary War, serving his country faithfully for nearly five years. He also served four terms as representative in the Legislature of Pennsylvania. In 1802 he was elected to the State Senate and died in 1804 before his term expired. His son, Colonel Daniel Follmer, who was the grandfather of D. O. Eshbaugh, took part in the war of 1812, and was for many years Colonel and Brigade Inspector of Militia. The family of Mr. Eshbaugh on both the paternal and maternal sides, presents an unbroken record of honest industry and thrift, virtuous citizenship and pure Christian lives. Rev. E. R. Eschbach, D.D., of Frederick, Md., is a first cousin of the subject of this sketch.

Daniel C. Eshbaugh, third son of John A. and Mary (Follmer) Eshbaugh, was born in Northumberland County, Penn., May 24, 1850. When he was six months of age his parents removed to Niagara County, N. Y., and nine years later to Tama County, Iowa. That part of the country was considered at the time the "Far West," and was very sparsely settled. The Eshbaughs in attempting to open up a farm on the unbroken prairie endured many of the hardships and trials that befell the early pioneers. The two eldest sons, imbued with the same spirit that distinguished their ancestors, left the farm at the breaking out of the Civil War, entered the Union army, and rendered faithful service to their country. The eldest, William, served four years in the Second Iowa Cavalry, and the other, Frank, three years in the Sixth Iowa Cavalry. Daniel being then but eleven years of age remained at home to assist his father on the farm. For several years he was a great dependence to his parents. Though loyal and obedient,

D.O. Eshbaugh

and willing to serve them until he should have attained his majority, he was ambitious to obtain an education. This could only be done by partly purchasing his time of his father, and working his way through college. The outlook under such circumstances would have discouraged most young men, but he determined to make the attempt, and his proposition to his father was accepted. With only a small sum which he had earned by his own efforts, he, at the age of eighteen, entered the Academy connected with Iowa College at Grinnell. In order to earn his way he did almost every kind of work. During vacations he helped run a threshing machine, and worked in the harvest field. During term time he dug cellars, made garden, husked corn, built fence, lathed houses, and for a time acted as janitor of one of the college buildings. He taught several terms of country school, and after term was able to make up his work and catch his class again. In 1870 he entered college, and as he advanced in his studies was able to devote more of his time in teaching, and less to hard labor. By these means he worked his way through college, graduating in 1874, with health much impaired, and an indebtedness of about three hundred dollars. He took high rank in his class and graduated with honor. In 1875 he began the business of negotiating loans on Iowa real estate. In 1876 he formed a copartnership with General L. A. Grant (who was Assistant Secretary of War under President Harrison) under the name of the New England Loan and Trust Company. He prospered in business, but after five years of severe labor and mental strain his health failed, and he was compelled for a time to retire. In 1882, in connection with others, he purchased General Grant's interest in the business, and the Company was incorporated under the laws of the State of Iowa, retaining the same name. He was elected its Treasurer, and in 1890 was made President. The Eastern office of the Company since its organization in 1880 has been in New York City. A large and successful business has been done. The capital of the company has been increased at various times from $50,000 to $750,000. Connections of the highest character have been formed in the United States and abroad, the business annually increasing with the most gratifying results to the stockholders as well as to its numerous patrons.

In 1886, Mr. Eshbaugh was transferred from the Des Moines office of the company to the New York office. Preferring a suburban residence to the turmoil and rush incident to a life in the city, he decided to locate in Montclair, where, in his quiet and unobtrusive way, he soon made his influence felt. Uniting immediately with the First Congregational Church he became interested in the various objects and work connected with it, more especially in the Sabbath school, where he was recognized as a devoted and earnest teacher. On the retirement of Mr. Johnson from the Superintendency, Mr. Eshbaugh was the unanimous choice of the teachers for that position. His work in this connection is fully set forth in the history of the Church and Sunday school, which forms a separate chapter of this work. His efforts have by no means been limited to the Church and its connections. When it was proposed to organize a bank in Montclair in order to meet the wants of a growing population, he helped the project as he could. He was elected one of the Directors, and the history of this institution, with its almost unprecedented success, shows the wisdom of the stockholders in their choice of the men to direct its affairs. He assisted in organizing the Savings Bank and was one of its first Managers, but owing to a pressure of other duties was obliged to sever his active connection with it. He was a charter member of the Montclair Club and has taken an active interest in its affairs. He is also a member of the Advisory Board of The Children's Home.

In other matters connected with the township, Mr. Eshbaugh has shown himself an enterprising citizen who has the best welfare of the people at heart. His life has been devoted to the good of his fellow men, and his early struggles taught him to sympathize with those whose environments are of a similar character. His sterling honesty and integrity, his indomitable will and perseverance, and his deep religious nature are the distinguishing characteristics to which his success as a business man, and the high esteem in which he is held by those who know him, are mainly due. He is recognized as an able financier, and a conservative, thorough-going business man. He has done much to promote the cause of education, and has always taken a deep interest in his *alma mater*. He was the second alumnus of Iowa College to be elected Trustee, a position which he still holds. He has been active in various benevolent and religious societies, is a member of the Congregational Club of New York, The American Institute of Christian Philosophy, and other religious and social organizations.

Mr. Eshbaugh married, July 16, 1874, Miss Catharine G. Otis, daughter of John M. and S. Georgiana (Eaton) Otis. Mrs. Eshbaugh graduated from the same college two years previous to her husband. She is a descendant of the best New England stock and is one of the finest types of American womanhood. Culture and refinement are united in her with the practical qualities of the efficient wife and mother. Her father's mother was the daughter of Zebular Marcy, who was an inmate of Forty Fort—located in the Wyoming Valley—at the time of its capture by the Tories and Indians. Marcy was Captain of a company of militia and by some means became a special object of hatred to the Tories and they determined to kill him. After the surrender a number of Tories and Indians entered the Fort and inquired of his wife—a woman of great physical strength and courage—for her husband, and she boldly informed them of his escape. Their threats to "kill and quarter them" had no effect on her. While holding a brass pan of corn bread which she had just taken from the fire, an Indian approached and attempted to take it from her. The savage reckoned without his host, for she held it with a firm grip determined not to part with it, and only yielded when he attempted to draw his scalping knife. This interesting relic is now in the possession of Mrs. Eshbaugh's father, Mr. Otis. The Captain Marcy referred to was in the same line of descent as General Randolph B. Marcy, Governor W. L. Marcy and other distinguished members of that family.

Mrs. Eshbaugh, through her father, is a descendant of Col. John Otis, of Barnstable, Cape Cod, who represented that town in the General Court for twenty years. He commanded the county militia, was Chief Justice of the Court of Common Pleas, was the first Judge of Probate of Barnstable County, and Counselor from 1706 until his death, September 26, 1727. He was the father of Judge James Otis, who did more than any other man to sow the seeds of the American Revolution, and was the most eloquent speaker and earnest patriot of his time.

The mother of Mrs. Eshbaugh, whose maiden name was Eaton, was the daughter of Eben and Sarah (Spofford) Eaton. Eben was born September 9, 1789, and died July 13, 1883. His father fought at the battle of Bunker Hill, and his grandfather in the French War. The gun carried by the father is still in possession of a member of the family. Eben was forty three years deacon of the Hollis Evangelical (now Plymouth) Church of Framingham, Mass., "using the office well, purchasing to himself a good degree of, and great boldness in, the faith which is in Christ Jesus." He was a descendant of Jonas Eaton, who came from England and settled first in Watertown, then at Lynn, and finally at Roxbury about 1640. The line of descent is through John, born September 10, 1645; Jonas, born May 18, 1680; Benjamin, born May 6, 1727; and Ebenezer, father of Eben, born May 12, 1750. Hon. Lilley Eaton, the historian of Reading; Gen. Joseph H. Eaton, U. S. A.; Col. Elkanah C. Eaton, of Plainfield, Conn.; and Cyrus Eaton, the Annalist of Warren, Maine, were all descendants of Jonas, of Roxbury.

The children of Mr. and Mrs. Eshbaugh are Catharine Clare, born 1875; Mary Genevieve, born 1877; William Hardy, born 1879; Margaret, born 1883; Helen, born 1885; Daniel Otis, born 1889.

JOHN RAYMOND HOWARD.

John Raymond Howard, the subject of this sketch came to Montclair with his family in October, 1881, from Brooklyn, N. Y.

His father, John Tasker Howard, was a prominent citizen of Brooklyn from 1826, when he settled there, until his death in 1888. He had come with his father, Joseph Howard, from Salem, Mass.; their earliest ancestor in this country being Abraham Howard, an Englishman from London, who, with his son Joseph, a physician, settled in Marblehead in 1720, and afterward went to Salem.

The firm of J. Howard & Son were long known as successful shipping and commission merchants in New York, and Mr. J. T. Howard, the son, developed into an intelligent and far-seeing man of affairs. He was actively connected with the beginnings of many important enterprises: The first steamship line to New Orleans, the first passenger-steamer (and subsequent line) to California, explorations of the Isthmus and the Panama Railroad, the American Telegraph Company, the Republican Party (whose first Presidential campaign was largely conducted from Mr. Howard's office, owing to his then intimate business association with Colonel Frémont, the nominee, and many other undertakings that required prophetic faith, in their inception. In Brooklyn, Mr. Howard was a promoter of the best things; an original member of the Hamilton Literary Association and of the Hamilton Club that grew out of it, a member of the Brooklyn Club and the Long Island Historical Society, and for many years a director and first vice-president of the Philharmonic Society; one of the founders of the Third Presbyterian Church, of the Church of the Pilgrims, and finally of Plymouth Church, in all the early years of which he was a foremost worker, and with whose pastor, Henry Ward Beecher, he at once formed a firm and close friendship, never broken or marred during forty years.

The mother of John R. Howard was also of a family well known and esteemed in Brooklyn, that of

Eliakim Raymond, town from New York bered as the founder Church, and as a various public institu- his children, John H. president and organ- Collegiate and Poly- after that also first izer of Vassar College; was a clergyman and in Central New York, English Language and Brooklyn Polytechnic, of the Boston School T. Raymond became Howard –a woman of usual breadth and and generous culture, family, too, came from Richard Raymond, an when he became a free- setts Colony, in 1634, the first jury impan- became in 1655 one of Norwalk, Conn, the father of Eliakim, weary seven years of the Revolu- Coast Guard, and took part in the mond, a first cousin of Eliakim, him moved to the Western Re-

who moved to that in 1822, a man remem- of the First Baptist trustee and director in tions of his time. Of Raymond was first izer of the Brooklyn technic Institute, and president and organ- Robert R. Raymond eloquent "Free-Soiler" later Professor of Literature in the and finally Principal of Oratory; and Susan the wife of John T. noble character, un- quickness of intellect, The Raymond Salem, Mass., where Englishman, settled man of the Massachu- He was a member of eled in that town, and the early settlers of Nathaniel Raymond, served through the tionary War as a Sergeant in the Battle of Long Island. Mary Ray- married Charles Sherman, with serve (the "Connecticut Fire

Lands") in Ohio, and there became the mother of John and William Tecumseh Sherman.

John R. Howard was born in Brooklyn, N. Y., on May 25, 1837. In 1853 he was sent to the University of Rochester (N. Y.), where his uncle, John H. Raymond, was Professor of the English Language and Belles Letters. He was graduated there as A.B. in 1857, receiving the degree of A.M. in 1860. In the fall of 1857 he became teacher in the Morristown (N. J.) Academy. In February, 1858, he went to California for a six months' ramble, returning to take, in September of that year, position as Instructor in English grammar, composition and elocution in the Brooklyn Polytechnic. In the fall of 1859 he went to Europe for a year of travel, and returned thither again in the winter of 1861 to study mine engineering at the School of Mines in Freiberg, Saxony, after a few months in the mining regions of Cornwall, England.

In April the war of the Rebellion broke out, and in June, like many other young American students abroad, Howard broke up his studies and came home, with the idea of enlisting in one of the new volunteer regiments. Colonel John C. Frémont, about that time appointed Major General, and put in command of the "Western Department," had seen much of young Howard in California, and had had some experience of him during a critical armed seizure of the Mariposa mines by a rival company, and he offered the would-be private a captain's commission, and the position of secretary and aide. Captain Howard, under commission from President Lincoln in the special staff corps of Additional Aides-de-camp, served with Frémont during the arduous and tumultuous organizing months in Missouri. During this time he had the satisfaction of preparing, under instructions of the General commanding the Department, the first two deeds of manumission freeing slaves of Missouri rebels, under Frémont's famous Proclamation. The Proclamation was shortly after countermanded by the President; but the two slaves had become free men—the first beneficent fruit of "the war power, in Emancipation." Howard further served with Frémont in the "Mountain Department" in Western Virginia, and in the exciting chase after Stonewall Jackson in the Shenandoah Valley. Later, when Frémont was unjustly "shelved" by the War Department, Captain Howard was ordered to Washington, where he was assigned to duty as a member of Courts Martial during several months, and then sent as Division Judge Advocate to General Gustavus A. DeRussy, commanding the heavy artillery division in the forts south of the Potomac. After a year of this interesting and necessary, but not inspiriting duty, in charge of four brigade-courts for trying enlisted men, and one division court for trying officers, having vainly sought more active field-work, Captain Howard resigned February 1, 1865, and returned to New York.

There, a year and more of engagement in a mining engineer's office, and nearly two years of editorial newspaper work, brought him to an opportunity of helping found the firm of J. B. Ford & Co., established in December, 1867, with the chief intent of publishing Henry Ward Beecher's "Life of Jesus the Christ." How the house prospered, started "Plymouth Pulpit" and "The Christian Union," became known as the "Beecher Publishing House," issued works by Horace Greeley, William Cullen Bryant, Harriet Beecher Stowe, and other notables, went down under the weight of the Beecher trouble and the general depression of trade, reorganized in 1878 as Fords, Howard & Hulbert, and continues to this day, is matter well known to those who take interest in such things. From the foundation of the house in 1867 to the present time, Mr. Howard has been steadily engaged in its labors, almost without vacations, except three brief trips to Europe, in 1871, 1873, and 1886, two of these being on business.

In Montclair, Mr. Howard, having come from Plymouth Church in Brooklyn, with his family became identified with the Montclair Congregational Church. After a brief residence in the town, he built a home on Mountain Avenue, where he has since lived. Although engaged in an exacting business, he has interested himself in many things conducive to the good of Montclair. For eight or nine years he conducted an adult Bible class in the Congregational Church, and was chairman of the Executive Committee of a literary association there, that held fortnightly public meetings during several years. He was among the organizers of the Montclair Club, and has for years been on its Board of Directors, having been also vice-president and president. When the Outlook Club, for monthly public discussions, was begun, he was made its president, and worked in that place for three years, retaining his place on the Executive Committee after resigning the presidency. He has been for years on the Public School Board, during recent years as its president; president of the Tariff Reform Club; member of the executive committee of the Citizens' Committee of One Hundred (Law and Order Society); one of the trustees of the Free Public Library begun in 1893; and generally, like most busy men, has found time to take part and lot with his neighbors in whatever seemed to be for the common benefit.

Mr. Howard has a family of nine children—a daughter and eight sons. His wife, Susan Merriam, is a daughter of the late George Merriam, of Springfield, Mass., of the publishing firm that made Webster's Dictionary a national force; and a sister of Mr. George S. Merriam, who formerly lived in Montclair, and who will long be remembered here as an accomplished and delightful man. Mrs. Howard's maternal grandfather was the Rev. John Fiske, who was minister for sixty years in New Braintree, Mass.;

his ancestor, John Fiske, having been on that same first jury impaneled in Salem, with Richard Raymond, about two hundred and fifty years ago. Mrs. Howard's great grandfather, Col. James Mellen, was an aide on the staff of General Washington during the Revolutionary War.

THE GRAHAM FAMILY.

LINE OF DESCENT OF BENJAMIN GRAHAM—FROM THE ENGLISH ANCESTOR.

All the Grahams of America were originally of English descent, and the family is one of great antiquity. In Burke's "Landed Gentry," it is stated that: "In the year 435 Graeme was made Governor of Scotland and guardian to the young King Eugene II. He broke down and leveled with the ground the famous wall of Antonius, extending across the island from east to west, from Abercorn to Dumbarton, which is called from him to this day 'Graeme's Dyke.' From him descended William de Graham, who flourished in the reign of King David I. He obtained from that monarch a grant of the lands of Abercorn and Dalkeith, and witnessed the charter to the monks of Holyrood House in 1128. Directly descended from him was Sir William Graham, of Kincardine, styled in the charters 'Wilhelmus Dominus de Graeme de Kincardine.' He was commissioner to treat with the English, 11 December, 1406; had a safe-conduct to England, 15 May, 1412, and another from thence to Scotland about the release of James I., 16 April, 1413."

BENJAMIN GRAHAM, for some years a resident of Montclair, was born in England in 1849, of Scotch ancestry, being a collateral descendant of the house of Graham of Claverhouse. His father was a merchant in London and his immediate ancestors were prominent landed proprietors. His mother was Eliza Helen Chapman, and her mother, who was a Langford, was a descendant of the Langfords of Shropshire, England. Burke says: "From authentic records it appears that this family were seated in the County of Wilts at an early period. In the Roll of Edward III. we find, 'Le Sire de Langford port d'argent et gules pales de vj en chef d'azure une leopard passant d'or.' Several manors and estates formerly their property in that country still bear the name appended, viz., Stephen Langford, Little Langford, etc. Edward Langford, a descendant of this family, in 1745 joined the forces raised by the English insurgents in support of Charles Edward, and was at the battle of Preston Pans. After the ruin of the Stuart cause he was compelled to seek safety in flight, and retired to Penzance in Cornwall."

Benjamin Graham, a descendant of these two families mentioned, was educated at private school and had a mercantile experience of a few years in England. He came to this country soon after reaching his majority, and engaged in the export business, continuing until 1879, when he entered the banking house of Jesup, Paton & Co.; he remained as the confidential clerk of this firm until 1884, when Morris K. Jesup retired, and under the new firm of John Paton & Co., Mr. Graham became a partner. The business was continued under this name until 1892, when Mr. Paton retired, and the firm was reorganized as Cuyler, Morgan & Co., Mr. Graham becoming second partner, Mr. Cuyler, the head of the firm, being a nephew of Morris K. Jesup, with Morris K. Jesup and John Paton as specials. This is now one of the leading banking houses in the city. Mr. Graham is also interested in various other business and railroad enterprises. He is Vice-President of the Rochester Railway Co., of Rochester, N. Y., a Director of the Rochester and Irondequoit Railway Co., Director of the Keokuk and Western Railway Co., Vice-President of the Western Securities Co. of Fort Worth, Texas, and other corporations.

Mr. Graham has been conspicuous in the social affairs of Montclair. He assisted in organizing the Montclair Club, and was subsequently appointed to serve an unexpired term of one of the directors, and at the expiration was elected to the full term of three years. He was one of the original members of the Outlook Club, also of the Athletic Club. He was one of the projectors of the Montclair Bank, and several of the preliminary meetings were held at his residence. Being a banker of long experience his advice and counsel were of great advantage to his associates. He subscribed liberally to the stock, was made one of the Directors of the Bank, and has been Chairman of the Executive Committee since its organization. Its unprecedented success as a suburban bank is due in no small measure to the wise management of its directors.

Mr. Graham and his family are connected with the Congregational Society.

Mr. Graham married, in 1879, Mary R., daughter of J. D. Stout, one of the old and highly esteemed merchants of New York City, who established, in 1848, in connection with his brother, the wholesale grocery house of J. S. & J. D. Stout. They did a large shipping business with the South, up to the beginning of the Civil War, at which time the firm went into the shipping commission business, under the title of J. D. Stout & Co. About June, 1880, Mr. Stout retired from business and was succeeded by his two sons. He died in 1891. He was a charter member of the Mercantile Exchange, and an earnest and enthusiastic republican. Mr. Stout was a direct descendant of Richard Stout, the first of the name in America, born in Nottinghamshire, England, in 1648, married Penelope Van Princess, and lived in Monmouth County, N. J. J. D. Stout's line of descent was through Jonathan, third son of above, who married Miss Bullen, and moved to Hopewell, Hunterdon County. David, fifth son of Jonathan, born 1706, married Elizabeth Larrison, and had nine children. Their third son, James, married Catharine Stout, daughter of John Stout. They had three sons and four daughters. Charles, the third son, married Aelsa Saxton, daughter of Jared Saxton. James D. Stout, the father of Mrs. Graham, was their youngest son. James Stout, the great grandfather of Mrs. Graham, served with honor in the War of the Revolution, both in the "New Jersey Line," Continental Army and with the State Militia. He was Lieutenant in Captain Maxwell's Company, Second Regiment, Hunterdon, and afterward Captain in Third Regiment of Hunterdon. Captain Joseph Stout (probably brother of Captain James) was wounded Sept. 15, 1777. The record of this family is remarkable, no less than twenty-six of this name having served with the New Jersey troops in the Continental Army during the war. Mr. and Mrs. Graham have three sons: Geoffrey, Ralph and Benj., Jr. Ralph died in 1885.

FREDERICK MERRIAM WHEELER.

The Wheeler family were found in various shires among the Landed Gentry, Knighthood, Members of Parliament and Baronets in the seventeenth century, and one was a Governor of the Leeward Islands. Members of the family were closely connected with King Charles I.

Sir William Wheeler, Knight, Member of Parliament for Queensborough, was created a baronet August 11, 1660. He was married to a lady of the Royal Household, of whom, in Melville's Memoirs and Carte's History of England, the following circumstance is related :

"King Charles I., at the beginning of his troubles, delivered to Lady Wheeler a casket, which she was to take care of, and return to His Majesty on the delivery of a ring. The evening before the king was beheaded, the ring was sent to Lady Wheeler, and the casket delivered to the messenger."

Wheeler, of Martin Hussingtree, in Worcestershire, Eng., was created a baronet in the reign of Charles II., 1660. The family bore Arms—three leopard faces. Crest—out of a ducal coronet a double-headed eagle displayed. Motto—" Facie tenus."

Frederick Merriam Wheeler, the subject of this sketch, is a direct descendant of this branch of the Wheeler family. His great grandfather, Allen Wheeler, resided at Hartlebury, in Worcestershire, Eng. His great-uncle, William Wheeler, possessed the manor and estate of Waresly, near Hartlebury, which had been in this family for many generations; he resided at "Winterfold House," near Kidderminster. A part of the Winterfold estate belonged to this branch of the Wheeler family since the reign of Henry IV., 1399.

Mr. Wheeler's grandmother, on his father's side, was Mary Ann Corbet, a direct descendant of Sir Peter Corbet, of Caus Castle, in Shropshire, a noble Norman who came over with William the Conqueror, 1066. Her mother, Mary, was the daughter of John Yate, of the Marsh House, near Wenlock, a most ancient and respectable family. Samuel Yate, her cousin, was a man of unbounded hospitality and benevolence. He was High Sheriff for the County of Montgomery, and possessed large estates in the counties of Salop, Hereford, Montgomery, Stafford and Somerset.

The Corbet family exemplified the teachings of their ancestors in perpetuating the motto borne on their Arms, viz.: "Deus pascil corvis" (God feeds the ravens).

FREDERICK MERRIAM WHEELER, of the above described lineage was born in Brooklyn, N. Y., August 6, 1849. His father, John Wheeler, a native of England, married Martha Jane, eldest daughter of Francis W. Merriam, of Brooklyn, a direct descendant of Joseph Merriam, born in England about 1605, and came to America in the ship "Castle" 1638, and settled in Concord, Mass. His grandson, John Merriam, of Concord, married Mary Wheeler.

F. M. WHEELER.

Frederick Merriam Wheeler was graduated at Summit Academy, N. J., and subsequently attended the Polytechnic Institute of Brooklyn. He studied mechanical engineering four years under Henry J. Davison of New York City—one of the most noted mechanical engineers in this country. He afterward took up hydraulic and marine engineering as a specialty, and since 1869 has been associated with The Blake and Knowles Steam Pump Works, and The Geo. F. Blake Manufacturing Company. He has been for some years a Director and Secretary of the latter company.

He is the inventor of the Wheeler Patent Surface Condenser, which is largely in use throughout this country and abroad, and universally recognized as the standard surface condenser in modern engine practice. It has been adopted by the U. S. Navy, and used for testing and laboratory work in nearly all the mechanical institutes and schools of technology throughout the country. Mr. Wheeler is also the patentee of a number of pumping machines, and other inventions in this line. In 1890 he organized the Wheeler Condenser and Engineering Co., of which he is a Director and Vice-President. The extensive works of this company are located at Carteret, N. J. Mr. Wheeler is also a Director and Secretary of the Ludlow Valve Manufacturing Co. He is one of the charter members of the American Society of Mechanical Engineers, and the Society of Naval Architects and Marine Engineers. He is also a member of the American Society of Naval Engineers and the Engineers' Club. He served as a member of the Advisory Council of the Engineering Congress at the Columbian Exhibition.

After leaving Brooklyn, his native city, Mr. Wheeler resided for some time at Staten Island. He married, in 1876, Florence, eldest daughter of Charles K. Willmer of Montclair, and after a short residence in New York City decided to make Montclair his home.

In 1893 he purchased for a residence the old Nason place on Gates Avenue, now known as Braebank, which he has greatly improved and beautified.

Both Mr. Wheeler and his wife have been prominent in social circles in Montclair for many years. Mr. Wheeler was the founder of the Montclair Equestrian Club, which subsequently became the Montclair and Essex County Hunt, and now the Essex County Country Club. He has been one of the Governors of the Country Club since its organization. He was one of the founders of the Outlook Club, and one of the early members of the Montclair Club, and at one time on its Board of Directors.

While assisting in the various public improvements from time to time, the subject which has interested Mr. Wheeler most is that of a public park for Montclair, which he has been agitating for years, offering to contribute liberally toward the enterprise. Others, however, to whom he applied failed to sufficiently appreciate its importance to unite with him in his landable efforts in this direction. In other public matters he has always been heartily enthusiastic. Mr. Wheeler has no particular taste for politics, but has always worked in the interests of good government. In church matters he has served on the vestry of St. Luke's Parish for many years, and was a member of the Building Committee of the new church edifice.

The issue of the marriage of Mr. Wheeler with Miss Willmer is Beatrice Molineux, Knight Willmer, Cottrell Corbett and Gladys Willmer.

Chapter XVI.

PAUL WILCOX.

THE Wilcox family of Tennessee, from whom the above named is descended, undoubtedly had a common origin with those of the same name in New England. Burke's "Landed Gentry" states that "the English branch, settled at County Essex and County Middlesex, bore *Arms*: Argent a lion rampant between three crescents sable ; a chief vair. *Crest* : Out of a mural coronet or, a demi lion rampant, sable collared vair." The ancestor of the Tennessee branch came from England in the early part of the last century. John, the great-grandfather of Paul Wilcox, married the daughter of "Squire Boone," brother of the famous Daniel Boone. Dr. George Boone Wilcox, son of John, was a noted physician, who practiced for forty years in Boone County, Mo. Dr. John Wilcox, his son, the father of Paul, was one of the most prominent physicians and surgeons in Missouri, and afterward in Indiana. Owing to his Southern sympathies in the early part of the war, he was driven from his native State and settled in Indiana, where he made many warm friends and acquired a large practice. He was considered the best surgical expert in the Middle Western States. Among his most intimate friends and associates were: President Harrison, Vice-President Hendricks, United States Senator Joseph E. McDonald and other distinguished Western men. He married a Margaret H. Griffin, of Culpepper Court House, Va., a descendant of an old and well-known family of Virginia. Her grandfather on her father's side was a Zachariah Griffin, who served with the Continental Army throughout the Revolutionary War.

Paul Wilcox, son of Dr. John and Margaret H. (Griffin) Wilcox, was born in Boone County, Mo., Oct. 3, 1858. He was prepared for and graduated at De Paw College, Indiana, with the highest honors, being chosen valedictorian. He afterward studied in Berlin and Leipsic, Germany, and was graduated at Columbia College Law School in 1884. He read law in the office of Mitchell & Mitchell (one of whom is the present District Attorney) New York City, and was admitted to the Bar in 1885. He began practice on his own account in 1886, continuing for four years, until 1890, when he formed the present copartnership of Wilcox & Barkley. Although one of the younger members of the Bar of New York, his success as a corporation lawyer has been marked. In many of his most important causes he has been arrayed against some of the oldest and ablest lawyers in the city. He spares neither time nor labor in his legal investigations. He discusses legal questions with a clearness of illustration, a strength of argument, a fullness and variety of learning rarely equaled by one of his age and experience. He represents many of the largest corporations in the city. Among these may be mentioned the American Press Association, the largest newspaper corporation in the world, comprising ten thousand newspapers and having its various sub-companies in fifteen different States. He is also a Director in this Association.

He secured the adoption of favorable laws for American corporations in Canada and argued successfully important cases in England connected with the Thorne Type-Setting Machine Company.

Paul Wilcox.

Mr. Wilcox has been but a few years a resident of Montclair, but during this period he has exerted an important influence in the community. He purchased in 1888 the Bayles homestead on Upper Montclair Avenue, which is one of the most beautiful sites in the township, affording as it does one of the most extended views to be had from any point on the mountain. The main house, as it stood originally, is of brown stone, of the early English style of architecture. To this Mr. Wilcox has added a large extension, which is in rough cast, or cement, to correspond somewhat with the original design. The interior of dining room, 27 by 60 feet, is made to correspond with the exterior, but is far more elaborate. It is of

J. N. WILCOX.

the early English style, finished in antique oak, with high wainscot in square panels and heavy beam ceiling.

Mr. Wilcox has taken a leading part in the social affairs which are among the most attractive features of this beautiful suburban township. He was one of the organizers and most active promoters of the Outlook Club; has been a member of the committee since its organization and was elected its President in 1895. He is Vice-President of the Montclair Club, and has been equally active in advancing its interests. Probably the most important service he has rendered to the people of Montclair was the conspicuous part he took, and the material aid given by him in the organization of the Montclair Bank. The first meeting of its projectors was held at his New York office in Temple Court, where the preliminary steps were taken to insure its success. For his active efforts in its establishment, as well as those of his associates, the citizens of Montclair are indebted for one of the best and most successfully managed banking institutions to be found in any suburban village or township in this part of the country. Mr. Wilcox was a subscriber to the original stock and has been a director since its organization.

Mr. Wilcox married, in 1884, Miss Mary Maul, daughter of William G. Maul, of Omaha, Nebraska, whose ancestors were among the early settlers of New Jersey. Uriah Maul, her great-grandfather, served throughout the War of the Revolution, in Capt. Bloomfield's Company, Third Battalion, First Establishment; Capt. Mott's Company, Third Battalion, Second Establishment; Third Regiment; also, First Regiment.

Mrs. Wilcox has been equally prominent with her husband as a leader in social affairs, and has taken an active part in the musical and literary life of Montclair. She is a woman of rare intellectual and musical gifts. She is a member of the Sorosis, before which she has often sung, and an active participant in its deliberations. Before coming East she sang in the Presbyterian Church at Omaha.

The issue of the marriage of Mr. Wilcox with Miss Maul is Harold, born 1885, and Gladys, born 1890.

EDWIN BURPEE GOODELL.

EDWIN BURPEE GOODELL, is eighth in descent from Robert Goodell, the ancestor, one of the early settlers of Massachusetts Bay. Titus Goodell, a native of New Hampshire, the great-grandfather of Edwin B., was a soldier in the War of the Revolution, and was killed at the battle of Stillwater.

Edwin B. Goodell was born at Rockville, Conn., May 7, 1854, was prepared for college at the High School, he and his brother being the first to enter college from this school. He was graduated at Yale in 1877, and taught in the public school at Montclair from 1877 to 1879. He returned to Yale in the autumn of '79, and was graduated at the Law School, with the degree of LL.B., in 1880. He was awarded by the Yale Faculty the Deforest Prize Medal, for the best written and delivered English oration, in 1877, and the John A. Porter Prize of $250, for the best essay on an assigned subject, in 1890. After leaving the Law School he returned to Montclair and taught for another year until 1881, and was admitted to the Bar of Connecticut in 1880, that of New York in 1882, and of New Jersey in 1883. With a branch office in New York City, his practice is principally in New Jersey, his main office being located at Montclair, which has been practically his residence since 1877. Mr. Goodell was one of the original promoters and most active members of the Tariff Reform Club. He was a member of the original committee appointed to organize the Montclair Club, one of the Board of Governors, and succeeded Mr. Topliff as Secretary and Treasurer. He was one of the original Trustees of the Trinity Presbyterian Church, and is still connected with it in that capacity, and was for two or three years Secretary of the Sabbath school. He married Annette C., daughter of Philip Doremus; issue four children, three sons and one daughter.

STARR JOCELYN MURPHY.

The above names represent three distinct families who became united by marriage. Mr. Murphy, who represents the present generation of his family, was born at Avon, Conn., June 17, 1860; son of Rev. *Elijah Douglass* Murphy, D.D., of New York City, born at Potsdam, St. Lawrence County, N. Y., grandson of *James*, of Williamstown, Mass., and great-grandson of *James*, who was born in Ireland and emigrated to this country in the latter part of the last century. James, the son of the ancestor, served in the War of 1812.

Mr. Murphy's mother was the daughter of Rev. Simeon Smith Jocelyn, of New Haven, Conn., born 1799, son of *Simeon*, of North Guilford, Conn., born Oct. 22, 1746, son of *Nathaniel, Jr.*, born Dec. 19, 1724, son of Nathaniel (1), born about 1699.

Rev. Simeon Smith Jocelyn, referred to above, married Harriette Starr, daughter of Daniel Starr, a Revolutionary soldier who served as a fifer in Capt. Return Jonathan Muggs' Company (Fourth Connecticut) enlisted April, 1775, served under Gen. Wooster, marched to the Northern Department, Gen. Schulyer's, and took part in the operations along Lakes George and Champlain, assisted in the reduction of St. Johns in October, and was afterward stationed at Montreal. This Daniel Starr was the son of *Joseph, Jr.*, son of *Joseph*, who was the son of *Comfort*, son of Dr. *Thomas*, who was the son of Dr. *Comfort Starr*, the emigrant, who settled in Cambridge, Mass., in 1634.

S. J. Murphy, the subject of this sketch, was prepared for college at Adelphi Academy, Brooklyn, N. Y., graduated at Amherst College with the degree of A.B., in 1881, and at Columbia College Law School, in 1883, with the degree of LL.B., and the additional degree of LL.B. *cum laude*, and was admitted to the bar of the State of New York in May of that year. While attending the Law School he also studied in the office of Bangs & Stetson, and immediately after admission to the bar entered the office of Carter & Hornblower. From 1886 to 1889 he practiced independently, and in the latter year organized the firm of Murphy, Lloyd & Boyd.

As a resident of Montclair, Mr. Murphy is comparatively a newcomer, having settled here in 1887. He has taken an active interest in public and political affairs, though outside of party lines. He was one of the founders of the Tariff Reform Club, and in the last Presidential campaign advocated its principles from the platform. He is the Secretary of the local Good Government Club. He was a charter member of the Montclair Club, and served for three years on the Board of Directors. He was also much interested in the Dramatic Club, and has frequently appeared upon its stage, generally in comedy rôles.

Mr. Murphy was induced to settle in Montclair mainly because of his marriage, in 1887, to Miss Julia Brush Doubleday, daughter of John Mason Doubleday, Esq., one of the oldest and most respected citizens of Montclair, who was an important factor in the early development of the township. He was a direct descendant of the famous Capt. John Mason, who led the expedition against the Pequots, which resulted in their extermination. He was also a descendant of Jonathan Edwards, James Pierrepont, John Ogden, and, through the marriage of his male and female ancestors, his line of descent comes through the Stoddards of Boston, Gov. Bradford, of the Mayflower, Rev. Thomas Hooker, the founder of Hartford, Conn., and other well-known New England families. The line of descent from the Doubledays is through *Elisha*, who settled in Yarmouth, Mass., in 1676, thence through *Elisha, Elisha, Ammi* and *John Tilden*, who was the father of John Mason Doubleday.

The issue of the marriage of Mr. Murphy to Julia Brush Doubleday is three children.

GEORGE WELWOOD MURRAY.

GEORGE WELWOOD MURRAY was born in Edinburgh, Scotland, March 8, 1856, the son of Welwood and Lily (Gourlay) Murray. He came to this country an infant and settled in New York City, where he attended public and private schools, and was graduated at Columbia College Law School in 1876. He also studied law with Edgar Ketcham and with Sanford & Robinson, later Robinson & Scribner. He was admitted to the Bar of New York in March, 1877, and at the beginning of the same year became associated with Anderson & Young, now Anderson, Howland & Murray—at first having charge of their real estate law department—and has since continued his connection with this firm, later as a partner, his specialty being corporation law.

During his residence in New York Mr. Murray was connected with the Judson Memorial Church as a Deacon and a Trustee. He removed to Montclair in the spring of 1894, and purchased a plot of ground on Mountain Avenue on the side of the mountain, a part of the old Joseph Baldwin farm, and has there erected a dwelling. Although retaining his membership and interest in the Memorial Church in New York, he has largely identified himself with the Baptist Church and Sunday School of Montclair. He is a member of the Montclair and the Outlook Clubs, a Director of the Young Men's Christian Association, and a member of the New York Bar Association. He married, in 1878, Caroline, daughter of William and Sarah (Sylvester) Church. He has one child, Lily Sylvester Murray.

THE DENTAL PROFESSION.

Dentistry as a profession was comparatively unknown to the early settlers of Cranetown and West Bloomfield, and the country doctor, whose practice extended over half the county, was expected to be fully equipped for all "dental operations." His "equipment" consisted of two or three pairs of forceps, or turn-keys, and in the operation it was often a question of *strength* and endurance between the doctor and his patient, the latter being compelled to endure the pain until the strength of the doctor was exhausted, or something "gave way," frequently a part of the tooth or jaw, and it became necessary to resort to heroic treatment. Under this, however, "endurance ceased to be a virtue," and the patient himself resorted to *extreme measures*. When the doctor succeeded in extracting the molar he had nothing to replace it with, and after a few operations the patient was left to regret the lack of development in the dental art.

Such was the condition of affairs a quarter of a century ago. Later one or two dentists came and settled here for a time, but met with indifferent success, and soon retired. Three members of the profession have, within the past few years, established a successful practice, viz.: Dr. S. C. G. Watkins, Dr. A. J. Wright and Dr. Frederick S. Crane.

SAMUEL CHARLES GOLDSMITH WATKINS, D.D.S.

The failure of his predecessors did not deter Dr. S. C. G. Watkins from locating in Montclair as a professional dentist. He made a casual survey of the field, and satisfied himself that there was a good opening for a skillful practitioner, and his success was assured from the beginning, his clientèle at the present time far exceeding that of most suburban dentists.

Dr. Watkins began the study of his profession early in life with a natural aptitude for it, being possessed of considerable mechanical ingenuity as well. He owes his success, perhaps, as much to heredity as to his early training. His paternal ancestors, who were first of Wales, then of England, and finally were the founders of the Irish branch, left their impress on every age. This family represents in the female line the ancient and distinguished house of Vaughan, of Golden Grove, which derived from Hugh Vaughan, Esq., of Kidwelly, gentleman usher to King Henry VII., 1497. One branch of this family bore *Arms:* Or on a chevron gules, three horse-shoes of the field; on a chief of the second three fleur-de-lis of the first. *Crest:* A lion rampant gules holding in his dexter paw a fleur-de-lis or. *Motto:* "Virtuti avorum." Descendants of the English branch of the Watkins family accompanied Cromwell to Ireland, and for military services rendered were assigned lands in County Monahan. One branch removed thence to County Kings, where the great-grandfather of Dr. Watkins was born, whose son, Samuel Watkins, emigrated from Ireland in 1819, to accept a government position. He had endorsements and recommendations from the Earl of Ross to the Duke of Richmond, who was stationed at Quebec at that time. Soon after his arrival he received a grant of the largest tract of land ever given to one man, on condition of his settling at Little York (now Toronto), Ontario. He thus became the founder of the Canadian branch of the Watkins family.

A family legend dating from the time of Cromwell (1649-50) states that during a vigorous fight between the Protestants and Catholics—the former being victorous—a Catholic priest was sheltered and secreted by one of the family—a female—in this line of Watkins descent. On the day following the Catholics routed the Protestants and drove them over the banks of the river Ban. The plucky woman referred to drew near to the priest whom she had saved and, extending her hand in token of salutation, immediately grasped the hand of the priest, dragging him into the river, and both perished together.

Samuel Watkins, above referred to, distinguished himself in the suppression of what is known as the McKenzie Rebellion of 1835, and for his services was rewarded with a colonelcy in the Canadian forces. His son, Charles W., father of the subject of this sketch, took a prominent part in resisting the Fenian raid into Canada in 1866. He married Harriet, daughter of George Beckwith, of Yorkshire, England, a grandson of Lord George Beckwith, a Colonel in the British Army. This very ancient family bore

originally the name of Malbie, or Malbysse, being lineally descended from the marriage *temp* Henry III., of Hercules de Malbie, grandson of Sir Simion de Malbie, Lord of Cawton, in Craven, with Beckwith, one of the daughters of Sir William Bruce, Lord of Uglebarby, derived from Sir Robert Brus, Lord of Skilton Castle, in Cleveland, a noble Norman knight, ancestor of the Bruces of Scotland.

Dr. Samuel C. G. Watkins, son of Dr. Charles W. and Harriet (Beckwith) Watkins, was born at Ashgrove, Halton County, Ontario, March 27, 1853.

His early life was spent on his father's farms, and his knowledge of the rudimentary branches was obtained at the county school. At the age of fourteen he removed with his parents to Detroit, Mich., and two years later he went to Boston and studied with a well-known dentist; he obtained a fair start in life, but met with an almost irreparable loss, by being burned out in the great Boston fire of 1872. He lost everything except his pluck and perseverance. He began life anew, spending all his spare time in attending lectures at the Boston Dental College, from which he graduated with honor in 1875.

He came to Montclair in 1876, where he soon acquired an extensive practice among the best class of residents.

He has made numerous contributions to dental literature, notably upon the treatment of children's teeth, and the use of amalgam in filling. He is the inventor of amalgam instruments which bear his name, a dental record book, a machine for making tapering screws and the Watkins toothbrush; also a sectional head-rest for dental chairs, which bear his name. He has received many honors from his professional associates; in 1886 he was unanimously elected President of the Alumni Association of the Boston Dental College. The same year he was elected President of the Central Dental Association of Northern New Jersey, of which he was one of the founders in 1880, and has been Chairman of the Executive Committee for the past eight years. In 1889 he was made President of the New Jersey State Dental Society, and has also been a member of the Executive Committee for a number of years. He is a member of the First District Dental Society of New York, and of the Odontological Society of New York, and in 1879 became a member of the American Dental Association. In 1891 he was made Second Vice-President of this society, and was re-elected in 1892-93. He is a member of the Clinic Committee of the World's Columbian Dental Congress, also Chairman of the State Committee of New Jersey, and it was in his office that the first steps toward the Columbian Congress were taken, and presided at the first meeting held at the Hoffman House in New York, in April, 1890. He now occupies the chair of Lecturer on Operative Dentistry in the New York Dental School of the University of the State of New York.

Wholly absorbed in the duties of his profession, Dr. Watkins has had but little time to devote to local affairs. He took an active interest, however, in the organization of the fire department; was a charter member of Hook and Ladder Company No. 1, and is now on the list of exempt firemen, having rendered nine years in this capacity. He was one of the charter members of the Montclair Club, also an early member of the Athletic Club. He is a Director of the Montclair Savings Bank, and member of the Board of Trustees of the Trinity Presbyterian Church.

He built for himself, in 1879, a residence on Fullerton Avenue, which was destroyed by fire in 1885. He rebuilt soon after on the same location. His office is in the lower story of his residence, a part of which is adorned with a large collection of curios, of which he is exceedingly fond.

Dr. Watkins married, first, Miss Margaret A. Thompson, of Boston, deceased, and secondly Miss Mary Yarrington Doremus, daughter of Philip Doremus of Montclair. The issue of this last marriage is three children, viz.: Philip Doremus, Anne Yarrington, Lawrence Beckwith.

DR. ALBERT J. WRIGHT.

Dr. Wright has carried on the practice of his profession in Montclair for the past twelve years, and has achieved deserved success as a skillful practitioner. His experience as a dentist covers a period of nearly a quarter of a century. He was born at Fort Edward, N. Y., March 16, 1848. Twelve years later he moved to Brooklyn with his parents and received a thorough education at the public schools of that city. He began the study of medicine at the New York Homœopathic Medical College in 1867, and entered the New York College of Dentistry in 1869, graduating in 1876. He practiced for some years in Brooklyn and then in Owego, Tioga County, N. Y., where he became well and favorably known as a dentist, and as an enterprising and public-spirited citizen. He was a prominent member of the fire department of that town and was active in promoting other public enterprises. He came to Montclair in 1882, and although an entire stranger in the community, he soon acquired a fair practice, and his clientèle has increased annually.

He was formerly an active member and is still a contributing member of the Brooklyn Dental Society, of the Sixth District Dental Society of New York, a delegate to the New York State Dental Society; was later a member of the New Jersey State Dental Society.

Dr. Wright was among the first to advocate the organization of a fire department for Montclair, and from the beginning up to the present time has been unremitting in his efforts to improve its efficiency and increase its numbers and strength. His previous experience as a fireman and his willingness to assist in the various duties pertaining to the organization, has won for him the admiration of his associates and of his fellow citizens generally. He had done much to improve the various departments, and the excellent system of fire alarms and signals is largely due to his efforts.

ART AND ARTISTS.

"Like attracts like." The artist, ever absorbed in the beauties of nature, selects for his permanent abode the place offering the greatest variety of natural attractions—the hills, the woodland, the vale, the rippling brook, the old thatched cottage, with its quaint well-sweep together with animal life in all its varieties. That some of the most prominent artists in America should find the brightest realization of their dreams along the slope of the Watchung Mountain, which combines all these attractions, is not surprising. Probably no other place of its size in the country has drawn together so many well-known artists. First came Harry Fenn, whose illustrations of " Picturesque America," Europe and the East, are familiar as household words; next came George Inness, who is without a peer as a landscape artist in this country. His son, George Inness, Jr., followed in his father's footsteps, but found objects of greater interest in animal life than in the portrayal of inanimate nature. Hartley, the sculptor, was also attracted by the natural beauties of Montclair, and Earle, the character artist, has discovered the quaint and the queer, even in his surroundings.

HARRY FENN.

Residents of Montclair, who are familiar with the works of Harry Fenn, the artist, have little idea to what extent the beauties of this locality have entered into his numerous illustrations.

From his beautiful home on the mountain side, where he has lived for more than twenty years, he has

"Viewed the landscape o'er and o'er,"

and every tree and shrub, every nook and corner of the mountain, every rivulet, every old cottage or barn, every old well-sweep, or vine-covered stone wall, are familiar to him, and have at times served to embellish the pages of his numerous works of art. The following brief sketch of his life, taken from the *American Bookmaker* of September, 1889, will be of interest to his numerous friends and admirers:

"Harry Fenn was born in 1840 at Richmond, Surrey, England. He displayed his tendency toward art at a very early age, and when not six years old used to spend his half holidays with a toy paint box out of doors. One of his earliest memories dates back to a day in Richmond Park, when he sat almost buried in the high ferns trying to sketch a mighty oak. While struggling with the intricacies of branch and foliage he was disturbed by a lady and gentleman who alighted from a carriage to investigate the occupation of the tiny artist. They expressed themselves as much interested in the embryo landscape, and inquired the little boy's name. The incident had almost faded from the child's mind, when one day a parcel was delivered at his home; and what was his surprise and joy to find a real artist's water color box, with silver mounted brushes; and enclosed was a card inscribed with the pleasant words: 'For Harry Fenn, with the best wishes of the Rev. John Selwyn, Bishop of New Zealand.'

"Mr. Fenn learned the art of wood engraving in the school of the Brothers Dalziel. In the meantime he painted and sold water colors.

"When about nineteen he took his little box of sovereigns, and spread the contents in a row on his father's desk. He then surprised that gentleman by a request that he should make the row just as long again, in order that the aspiring artist could go to see Niagara, promising to return in six months.

"For six years he stayed in America and then went to Italy for a short term of study. Before sailing Harry Fenn gave away his gravers, informing his fellow workers that he intended thereafter to use only brush and pencil, but

HARRY FENN.

they scoffed at his ambi-
he would come home in a
mind
trated his first book,
soon followed by the 'Bal-
These works marked an
making, and opened the
of to-day
an extended tour in the
gather material for 'Pict-
owing to the enterprise of
successful. This journey
rapid out-door sketching,
versant with the charac-
About this time he joined
who started the 'American
New York.' After a great
ceeded in filling one room
mens of that branch of art,
to Europe to make sketches
and several years later,
made a long sojourn in the
uresque Palestine.' Sinai
months the two artists'
arduous work lay in cross-
the Convent of Mount
ing mountains. * * * *
tion, accuracy of drawing,
acterize Mr. Fenn's work
to art he has been as con-
he has been persevering
"Rarely indeed can an
many years of successful
a store of general culture
overlook the fact that art,
requires that the soil in
kept mellow and well irri-
other talents than the

tion, and assured him that
very different frame of
"On returning he illus-
Whittier's 'Snow Bound,'
Lads of New England'
era in the history of book
way for the great successes
"In 1870 Mr. Fenn made
United States in order to
uresque America,' which,
the Appletons, proved so
was a great education in
and made the artist con-
teristics of our territory,
a small band of pioneers,
Water Color Society of
deal of labor they suc-
with presentable speci-
"In 1871 Mr. Fenn went
for 'Picturesque Europe,'
with J. D. Woodward, he
Orient, working on 'Pict-
and Egypt.' For fourteen
lived in tents. Their most
ing the desert of Arabia to
Sinai, and in the surround-
"Great fertility of inven-
and delicacy of finish char-
"In dedicating his life
scientious and manly as
and industrious,
artist point back to so
work coupled with so rich
"Artists are very apt to
Like many other things,
which it grows should be
gated by the cultivation of
merely imitative.

"In this respect Mr. Fenn's career may well serve as a model for students who would reach the same result."

From *Our American Illustrators*, MR. F. HOPKINSON SMITH:

* * * * "And last, but not least, this delightful little thing of Harry Fenn's — Oh, you fellows can criticise the precise, exact work of an exact man, but I tell you, that but for Harry Fenn this present school of American illustrators would not exist. We live in a peculiar age, and in a mercenary one. Art for art's sake is all very well over on the other side, and now and then, some American, more liberal than another of his money-loving and money-making friends does a big, generous thing, as you can see for yourself any time you walk into the Metropolitan Museum, but for all that art for the sake of the dollar is more prevalent.

"Harry Fenn's illustrations of 'Picturesque America' entitle him to be called the nestor of his guild, not only for the delicacy, truth and refinement of his drawings, but also because of the enormous financial success attending its publication—the first illustrated publication on so large a scale ever attempted—paving the way for the illustrated magazine or paper of to-day simply because it showed the publishers the commercial value of pictures inserted in pages of printed type.

"'Picturesque America' paid, and paid enormously, and soon there was not enough artists to go round among the other publishers. * * * *

"If Fenn had made a dead failure of that book instead of a success—a brilliant success for the time in which it was issued—some of the distinguished illustrators of to-day would probably have been measuring tape at Macy's. They certainly would not have gone into illustrative art."

LAWRENCE C. EARLE.

As a man, Mr. Earle is little known to the people of Montclair. As an artist, however, his name is as familiar as "household words." His recent achievements at the World's Fair have brought him into special prominence, and while he has through this means made a wide circle of acquaintance, his reputation was already made.

Mr. Earle is a native of New York City, born Nov. 11, 1845, and educated at the public school. Although he early developed a taste for art he gave little attention to it until after completing his regular studies. His father removed in 1857 to Grand Rapids, Mich., and engaged in the manufacturing business, and Lawrence remained with him as assistant for three years. Excessively fond of out-door sports, he frequently painted birds and other game secured on his hunting expeditions. He went to Chicago in 1869, and studied at the Academy of Design under Sherlaw. In 1872 he went abroad and studied under Barth and other masters. He returned to Chicago where he remained until 1881, and then went to Florence and Rome, and studied under Simmonetti in water colors. He returned to Chicago, and in 1889 came East, following the line he had marked out for himself, viz., character studies in water colors. In 1893 he executed two large paintings in water colors for the Columbian Exhibition, 33 by 18 feet long, to be placed in the Liberal Arts Building, entitled, "Glass Blowing Industry" and "The Potter Industry." Among his best works are "The Old Taxidermist," "The Book Worm," "The Village Postmaster," "Solitude," "Easter Moon," "The Game Keeper's Children," "The Board of Education," "The Disputed Account," "An Old Salt," "The Mischief Makers," "The Old Flute Player," "The Mud Turtle Club," "The Ball Nine," etc.

Church, the famous painter, says of him: "Earle is an artist from head to foot. He is one of the best water color painters we have, and I know of no one who is a finer, technically, here or abroad. His 'Flute Player,' which was in the Water Color Exhibition at the Academy two years ago, was simply superb from that standpoint, and thoroughly artistic otherwise. He is very versatile, understands thoroughly the use of all mediums, paints a good portrait, splendid in dogs or birds, and is a first-class landscape artist. I think water color is his forte, and some of his old men, perhaps, show him at his best."

JONATHAN SCOTT HARTLEY.

JONATHAN SCOTT HARTLEY, National Academician, Member of the Society of American Artists, of the Architectural League, Players' Club, etc., etc. It is said that "a prophet hath no honor in his own country," but this proverb does not apply to the people of Montclair, who feel highly honored in claiming as fellow-citizens men who have attained the highest rank in their profession; and the personal achievements of these men, although not identified with the home of their adoption, forms an interesting chapter in its history.

Jonathan Scott Hartley, in the front rank of modern sculptors, was born of English parentage, in Albany, New York, September 22, 1845. Gifted with a strong tendency toward art, it only needed the slightest encouragement and even a casual opportunity to determine the life-work of the future sculptor. This was found while yet in his teens by employment in a monumental yard at the capital of the State of New York, a city, by the way, which has contributed to the guild of American art many of its most eminent stars. In such an atmosphere it was very natural for young Hartley to drift to the then Mecca of our national sculpture—the studio of Erastus D. Palmer. And as to the significance of the fact,

it should be recalled that American sculpture was then little more than an expression. As a matter of fact, sculpture seems to have been the last of the arts to be cultivated on American soil. But since the advent of Palmer, Hiram Powers, H. K. Browne, Crawford, Story and Greenough, a rapid movement has taken place in this Western world that promises astonishing results in the near future. Connected with this advance in plastic art no one has been more prominent, more prolific in creation and workmanship, more tireless and devoted in founding and organizing clubs and societies of broad scope and enduring purpose than Hartley himself. For instance, it was in his somewhat cramped dingy studio, at 596 Broadway, New York, was organized the Salmagundi Club amid a group of roystering Bohemians, eventually to become a unique institution in the clubland of the world, at whose door many worthy men knock in vain for admission to membership at this writing. Moreover, when speaking of this branch of his useful career to painters, sculptors and architects alike, it is well to remember that in his services to the Art Students' League, in his capacity as a lecturer and teacher of the theory and technique of his profession, and later as the author of the work "Anatomy in Art," now a standard authority in art schools and in many institutions of learning, he has a standing quite apart from the rank and file of sculptors. Had it not been for the versatile quality exemplified in what has been said, Hartley would easily have been at the top of his profession on other grounds. Whenever called upon to compete in ideal work, he has been more than ordinarily successful, and there came a recognition of that class of art-worthy which has been the keynote of his studio life *Conscience*. If an artist be not sincere, if he indulge in passing off counterfeit work, if he give way to a dash fad, he is building his house of sand. In the wonderful museum of models which literally stack his twin studios in West 55th Street, can here be studied what has been achieved during a period of marvelous industry, the very point which is here adduced, and the writer of this can say, after having been a familiar visitor in the chief studios in Europe and America, that no such like collection either in variety of composition, in mere original conception, in widely differing portraiture of man, woman or child, in bold and striking departure from the conventional, can be found anywhere on the earth. These may seem startling words; they are nevertheless true.

Among Hartley's principal works in the Ideal are:

"The Whirlwind," "King R?oe's Daughter," "Psyche," "The Bath," "Satan Vanquished," and other creations.

Reference has been made elsewhere to some of the more conspicuous of his achievements, among which not already spoken of, may be named the Eight Reliefs on the interior of the Saratoga monument, illustrative of the surrender of Burgoyne; the Daguerre monument in the National Museum at Washington, the memorials to John P. Howard placed in the University of Vermont at Burlington, the memorial to Algernon Sydney Sullivan in the Metropolitan Museum, New York, the monument to John Ryle, founder of the silk industries at Paterson, New Jersey.

If taking from this list several of his public or what might be termed artistic works, we may note as perhaps the earlier, the statue of Miles Morgan, one of the Pilgrim Fathers, now standing in Springfield, Mass., a commission from H. T. Morgan of New York. It is a robust figure eight feet high, and well-known to New Englanders. But it was the figure of the "Whirlwind" which has been the most universally admired, showing as it did not only a profound knowledge of anatomy but a subtle and poetic conception of lines, beauty of form and handling of drapery to-day unmatched by the work of any sculptor on this side of the Atlantic. Another of Hartley's works which woke up the sluggards of American sculpture was "The Defeat of Satan," which gave him the gold medal of the American Art Association as far back as 1887. Yet while this interesting phase of an artist's life may claim public attention, portraiture itself is a most difficult branch of the sculptor's art, and vastly different from the task that confronts the painter with pigments, easel and canvas. This can be appreciated by any one who will take the trouble to watch the method of a conscientious modeler of the human head, intent on likeness, expression, intellect and character. Mr. Hartley's busts in this respect are the marvel of the profession and the admiration of the critic and connoisseur. Not to speak of the John Gilbert which stands alone, his A. H. Wyant, Cyrus W. Field, Dion Boucicault, John Drew and Susan B. Anthony, he has a distinct gift in the treatment of children, as shown in the cabinet bust of his own boy, Inness. Hartley likewise has been fortunate in having been thrown in contact with strong men. For instance, among his sitters and friends of whom he has made characteristic busts unsurpassed in our time, have been Edwin Booth, Noah Davis, George Inness, his father-in-law; Lawrence Barrett, Ashley W. Cole, T. W. Wood, President of the Academy of Design; Felix Morris, John Drew, Dion Boucicault, Jno. T. Raymond, the actors; Ada Rehan, Thomas Moran the painter; J. H. Dolph, Judge Van Voorst, W. C. Church, founder of the "Army and Navy Journal;" John D. Crimmins, Julien T. Davies, Cyrus W. Field, and many other notables of the present day.

However, Mr. Hartley's most important work is the statue of John Ericsson, on the water front at the battery. This commission given by the State of New York is the only official recognition made to a sculptor by the municipality. It was unveiled on April 26, 1893, with imposing ceremonies, the parting of the flags of the United States and Sweden being saluted by twenty-one guns from the U. S. Monitor Miantonomah, which Ericsson himself had designed. This national event was further dignified by the passing of the allied squadron up the Hudson River in a Naval parade unexampled in modern times.

The domestic side of Hartley's life is as interesting as that which is in the public view. Married to a beautiful and gifted woman, who has inherited her father's genius and sympathy for color, and who dispenses a gracious hospitality, surrounded by a group of lovely children, living in an ideal home within earshot of two celebrated artists (father in-law and brother in-law), George Inness and George Inness, Jr., it would seem indeed, that this fortunate sculptor has little to long for which belongs to mortals.

GEORGE INNESS.

"Let us believe in art not as something to gratify curiosity or suit commercial ends, but as something to be loved and cherished, because it is the handmaid of the spiritual life of the age."

That George Inness, acknowledged to be the greatest landscape painter in America, should select Montclair as a permanent place of residence, evinces an appreciation on his part of its great healthfulness and beauty, and affords cause for congratulation to its citizens, and more especially those who have labored so earnestly to develop its many attractive features.

To what extent the remarkable gifts possessed by Mr. Inness are due to the law of heredity, can only be conjectured, his environments having contributed little or nothing to their development.

The family of Inness is one of the oldest in Scotland, and is derived from the place of that name. The earliest reference to the surname is that of Sir James Inness, of Scotland, who was knighted in 1441, he being 15th in descent from one Barowald in the time of King Malcom, of Scotland.

George Inness, the subject of this sketch, was born in Newburgh, New York, May 1, 1825. He removed with his parents to Newark, New Jersey, when quite young, and very early in life developed a taste for art, which at first was discouraged by his father, who preferred that he should follow a mercantile life; but finding that the son had no inclination in that direction he was afforded such opportunities for acquiring a knowledge of the rudiments of drawing and oil painting as were most easily obtainable at the time. At the age of sixteen he went to New York to study engraving, but ill health obliged him to return home, where he continued to sketch and paint. When twenty years of age he spent a month in the studio of Regis Gignoux in New York City, which was all the regular instruction he ever had, and after this period he "groped his way by the dim light of nature," being wholly self-taught. He began landscape painting in New York City, and subsequently made two visits to Europe and lived in Florence and Rome for some time. For several years after his return he made his home near Boston, where some of his best pictures were painted. In 1862 he went to reside at Eaglewood, near Perth Amboy, New Jersey, and a few years later removed to New York City. He was elected a National Academician in 1868. From 1871 to 1875 he again resided in Italy. He again removed to Montclair in 1884, and purchased the place known as The Pines. In this beautiful, secluded spot, away from the noise and

turmoil of the city, he has produced some of his finest works. Here he has enjoyed the opportunity of studying nature, and nature is the self-evident of God. It has been truly said of him that "he is in the world and yet not of the world." Except when wandering through the fields and over the hills and mountains drinking in the beauties of nature, his whole time is spent in his studio.

Few persons in Montclair have enjoyed his intimate acquaintance, so wholly absorbed is he in his art. His devoted wife, however, who relieves him of all the cares of life and attends to all his business affairs, has made his home beautiful and attractive, and extends a hearty welcome to his friends and admirers. It is a fact not generally known that Mr. Inness spends some hours every night in his favorite literary pursuits, which to him are a pastime and a means of recreation. If the results of these are ever brought to light, much of the inner man and the secret of success of this remarkable man will become known. Appletons' Cyclopedia of American Biography says of him: "The art life of Inness is marked by two distinct styles, the first indicating careful finish and conscientious regard for details, the second style, formed with the expanding grasp of the principles of art, shows a richer appreciation of the truths of nature, is broad and vigorous, paying higher regard to masses than to detail. * * * No painter has represented the aspects of na- ture in the American climate with deeper feeling, a finer esti- mate of light and color, or a better com- mand of technical re- sources. He has been more influenced by the French school of landscape than any other American artist, yet his style is distinct and original. He is an absorbed reader of Swedenborg, and many of his paintings have a spiritual or alle- gorical significance." Among his best pict- ures are "The Sign of Promise," "Peace and Plenty," "Going Out of the Woods," "A Vision of Faith," "A Shadow of Death," "The Apocalyptic Vision of the New Jerusalem and River of Life," "A Passing Storm," "Summer Sunshine and Shad- ow," "Summer Afternoon," "Twilight," "Light Triumphant," "Pine Grove," "Barbarina Villa," "Joy After the Storm," "View near Rome," "Washing Day near Perugia," "The Mountain Stream," "Autumn," "Italian Landscape," "Passing Clouds," "The Afterglow," "The Morning Sun," and "Delaware Water Gap." His "American Sunset" was selected as a representative work of American art for the Paris Exposition of 1867. In 1878 he exhibited at the Paris Exhibition, "St. Peter's, Rome, from the Tiber," and "View near Medfield, Mass.," and in the National Academy, "An Old Roadway, Long Island." In 1882 he exhibited at the Academy Exhibition in New York City, "Under the Greenwood,"; in 1883 "A Summer Morning"; in 1885 "A Sunset," and "A Day in June"; in 1886 "In the Woods," "Sun- set on the Sea Shore," and "Durham Meadows."

The *Photographic Times* of April 7, 1893, says of him:

"At the age of sixty-eight George Inness is the most prolific and eminent landscape painter of his time. This is the almost unanimous verdict of artists, critics, connoisseurs and collectors alike. During an active and unceasing art

LANDSCAPE BY GEORGE INNESS.

career covering over half a century in many climes and countries he has painted thousands of canvases now found in public and private galleries in all quarters of the world. And yet, strange as it may seem, there cannot be found in this vast number of works two pictures duplicating precisely the same method, although all, it is safe to say, bear the individual impress of the genius of George Inness; and, singular enough, although hundreds of artists of high rank have tried, none have succeeded in producing an imitation so close that the deception would not be apparent on a brief examination. Thus there may be quoted as illustrating this fact a solid bit of wisdom uttered by Mr. Inness himself in his usually terse and comprehensive speech. He says

"'The master should exercise his control over the pupil by restraining the latter's tendency to imitation, and by leading him to the perception of those principles through which facts are represented according to their relative significance.'

"Again, as this painter has achieved great fame for clear and brilliant epigrams not only on art, but on many intellectual themes, it is well to recall these words:

"'What few painters have to learn is to keep the shop closed in the presence of nature—to see and not think we see. When we do this our eyes are lighted from within, and the face of nature is transformed, and we teach the world to see reality in a new light—such is the mission of art.'

"These words of the painter may give some idea to the layman why Mr. Inness has reached the pinnacle on which he now stands, and like a truly great man he is constantly reaching out *for higher* flights. He is never satisfied. He is always after the Beyond. He feels that there is a mystery in landscape always on the verge of revelation to his brain, but always just eluding his eager grasp. It is not too much to assert that Mr. Inness has been the greatest experimenter in modern art, whether in this country or in Europe, and he has never conducted his work with any view to pecuniary gain—although in his later years it has come in a rich abundance. It has been, moreover, a mistake to suppose that he confined his painting strictly to the delineation of landscape. In fact, he has exhibited a versatility unexampled in a career covering so many years. No branch of painting has he left untouched; portraiture, figure subjects, marines, quiet pastorals, or what not. Mr. Inness, likewise, is a poet, not only in the ordinary phraseology in metre, but as between idealism or literalism in art he is the high priest of the former. In a critical notice of the painter published some years ago, and even before, perhaps, he had reached his present lofty place in the profession, the present writer said: 'He has never borne the trade-mark of a Master. To one, certain of his qualities may suggest Corot; to another, his atmospheric effects may recall Turner; a third may see Constable in his cloud-swept skies, or hint at Ruysdael; while others may consider the strongest external influence derived from Rousseau.'

"None but a man of positive individuality can enter so boldly into a spiritual conflict over the problems of art and nature. The vehement yet subtle nature of George Inness has all to do with his pre-eminence to-day. A slave of no fleeting fad in art, like that fathered by Holman Hunt, or another springing up like a threatened flood the confines of which he was yet able to put a precise value on—impressions on the one hand and pre-Raphelitism on the other. When it is considered that Mr. Inness is wholly self-educated; that in his early youth he was physically infirm; that during his whole life he has been without any art master save his own dominating self, the length and breadth of his genius will be the better appreciated. Furthermore, he is a many-sided man, deeply interested in doctrinal and economic questions, an alert, brilliant and earnest declaimer and conversationalist; a wonderful graphic and correct writer and speaker of the English language—and, added to all these accomplishments, he is the possessor of a quaint humor, an absolute independence of all pecuniary bondage, and a profound contempt for the shame and shoddies of the period in which we live."

GEORGE INNESS, Jr.

GEORGE INNESS, JR., third child of George and Elizabeth (Hart) Inness, was born in Paris, France, January 5, 1854, and received most of his education abroad. He inherited from his father that love of art and wonderful gift as an artist that has distinguished his honored sire. From 1870 to '74 he was a pupil of his father in Rome, and of Bonnat in Paris in 1875. After his return to this country he resided in Boston, Mass., till 1878, then occupied a studio with his father in New York City, and devoted himself to animal painting, beginning to exhibit at the National Academy in 1877. He removed to Montclair, New Jersey, in 1879, and the same year married Julia, daughter of Roswell and Annie (Ellsworth) Smith, and since 1880 has occupied the beautiful residence known as Roswell Manor. Among his works are "The Ford" and "Patience," exhibited in 1877; "At the Brook" and the "Pride of the Dairy" sent to the Academy in 1878; "Pasture at Watchung," "Monarch of the Herd," "Returning to Work" (1886); and "After the Combat" and "A Mild Day" (1887). He was elected associate of the National Academy in 1893. It now remains to indicate briefly the high position which the Junior Inness has achieved in the still rising art of this era and which promises to be as secure and lasting as that of his distinguished father, although following, perhaps, somewhat different lines. It is, moreover, fortunate, when he had just passed his thirty-fifth year, and after having been engaged in the

Geo James Jr

front rank of artists for over twenty years, that he has now reached that point in his career as a painter, where as gold medalist of the American Art Association and by various forms of academic and critical recognition, he stands thoroughly equipped to compete in the great art movement of this present year for the highest honors of either hemisphere. He would have been a dullard, indeed, if, as a son of George Inness, and having breathed with keen appetite the atmosphere of art from his cradle, he had not made more than an ordinary mark in his profession as a painter. His chief gift is a paramount feeling for color—an intellectual endowment that no kind of artifice can compass. In his individual instance it is highly probable that this, the highest attribute of the painter, was inherited from his father, and it is frequently asked alike, by artist and layman, what do you mean by color or by a colorist in art? By a study of the masters down to our own time, indeed from Correggio to those painters familiar to the American public, such artists as George Inness the elder, A. P. Ryder, A. H. Wyant, John La Forge, Wm. M. Chase, T. W. Dewing, Horatio Walker, Dwight W. Taylor, the tangible, pictorial expression of color in its highest form may be found in the work of that man who can best combine colors to produce tone. This the Junior Inness does to a degree that is a marvel to his professional brothers, and which led to his election as an Associate of the National Academy of Design by a vote almost unprecedented in that body. In 1883 his theme which brought the flattering recognition was a large canvas called "News from the Boy." In the peculiar style of farm scene and country life which distinguishes his work, the story told is that of an old woman reading a letter from her son to the father in the farm yard, where with the natural accessories of chickens, cattle, and so on, is set forth with a skillful handling of light and shade.

Although Mr. Inness has not been a prolific painter in his manhood, for many cares not appertaining to his profession have made many inroads on his working hours, he has produced works of which no artist, whatever his eminence, need be ashamed. His canvas, "Bathing Horses in the Surf" a scene taken from the historic beach at Newport—won him the gold medal at the competition of the American Art Association some eight years ago. Another work in the same vein was the "Training of the Surf Horse," bought by the late J. G. Holland, and, as may be imagined, is full of action, with all of the fascinating interest of a sunset sky subduing the waters on the sand. Not to point out particularly this artist's thorough education as a pupil of Bonnat, as a close student in the art capitals of Europe, subsequently as a popular illustrator on the *Century Magazine*, and notably of Schwatka's famous book, "Schwatka's Search," it is proper to say that he is a many-sided artist, has dipped into almost every branch of painting, and has a thorough poetic feeling constantly expressed in embellishing his luxurious home with the best examples of original work in sculpture, bric-à-brac, and the handiwork of his fellow co-laborers. Moreover, there is no artist in this country upon whom a more brilliant future is dawning than George Inness, Jr.

ROSWELL SMITH.

FOUNDER OF THE CENTURY MAGAZINE.

DURING his comparatively brief residence in Montclair, Roswell Smith became better known to its citizens, and exerted a greater influence for good than many who have been identified with the place from its earliest settlement as a suburban township.

As a writer and publisher his fame is world-wide, but his personal characteristics, which made him one of the most lovable of men, and the good he accomplished in the world are known only to his most intimate friends, or those who were the recipients of his kindness.

Roswell Smith was born in Lebanon, Conn., March 30, 1829. His early environment conduced to the development of personal traits inherited from his Puritan ancestors. Lebanon was the home of the Turnbulls, and other distinguished men famous in American history.

The father of Mr. Smith was a man of strong integrity; his mother quietly faithful to every virtue of her sphere. They gave to their son a thorough religious training, and a good common school education. At the age of fourteen years he left his father's farm, and went to New York City, acquiring his first knowledge of the publishing business in which he was destined to become famous in the house of Paine & Burgess. After three years he returned to Providence, and entering Brown University, followed the English and Scientific course. He then began the study of law with Thomas C. Perkins, one of the ablest men of the times, at the Hartford bar, and during this period lived with his uncle, Roswell C. Smith. He there made the acquaintance of Governor Ellsworth, and through him obtained a position with the latter's brother, Henry L. Ellsworth, the first Commissioner of U. S. Patents, who at the time had a land and law office at Lafayette, Ind. Mr. Smith became associated with him in the practice of law, and was a member of his household, and married Annie, his daughter, the young girl whose hand sent that first famous electro-telegraphic message between Baltimore and Washington, across the inventor Morse's wire, "What hath God Wrought?"

His law practice was not very remunerative, and the failing health of himself and wife led him to seek a milder climate, and he spent some time upon a ranch in San Antonio, Texas. He subsequently returned to Lafayette and resumed business there for a time.

In 1870, after traveling abroad for a time in company with Dr. J. G. Holland, Mr. Smith settled in New York City, gave up the profession of law, and with Dr. Holland and the firm of Charles Scribner & Co., founded *Scribner's Monthly*, now the *Century Magazine*. While he had the counsel and assistance of all the members of the firm, the controlling interest in the stock was held by Dr. Holland and Roswell Smith, the latter assuming the business management. He had unlimited faith in the enterprise, which others deemed a hazardous venture, and threw himself into it with energy and enthusiasm. Its success was assured from the beginning, and in 1873, at his suggestion, the company began the publication of *St. Nicholas*, a children's magazine, with Mrs. Mary Mapes Dodge as editor. He bought up other children's periodicals, and merged them into this one. It was a bold and rather risky venture, which few men would have had the courage to undertake in view of the great commercial depression which then existed. The results, however, justified the policy pursued, *St. Nicholas* rapidly attaining a larger circulation than had been reached by any of its predecessors in the same field. In 1881 Mr. Smith and some of his younger associates purchased the interest of Dr. Holland and the Scribners in these magazines—the sale being coupled with the condition that the name of the company and of its principal magazine should be changed. His most intimate friends were of the opinion that no periodical could undergo such a radical alteration without serious financial difficulties. The result again justified his business foresight. The circulation largely increased, averaging over 200,000 copies per month—a considerable number being sold in England. The idea that an American magazine could gain a large circulation in England originated with Mr. Smith, and he personally arranged the sale of both the company's magazines in that country. Under his presidency the Century Company gradually extended in the line of book publication. Among these were "Laudes Domini," a series of hymn and tune books, by the Rev. Charles S. Robinson, which had an immense sale. The work which for years to come will be the crowning achievement of Mr. Smith is the "Century Dictionary." This work was designed in 1882, when Mr. Smith made the proposition to adapt the "Imperial Dictionary" to American demands. He supported the undertaking with his usual foresight and liberality. When the plans of the editors matured and reached far beyond the original limits, he did not lose faith, and no similar undertaking was ever attempted in this country where so much money was expended before a profit could be realized, or success in any way assured. Doubts were soon dispelled; the first edition had been expected to last a year, but it was soon evident that it would be exhausted in six months, and a second and larger edition was at once begun, which was followed by a third.

"He established from the first," says his biographer, "an identity of spirit, a unity of interest between the editorial and counting room upon the broad and sure foundation of a common aim pointing toward the highest ideals, whether of commerce, ethics, or art.

"The authorized 'Life of Lincoln' was made available to the great mass of the people largely through the liberality and determination of Mr. Roswell Smith. When George Kennan was gathering in

Roswell Smith

long and painful journeys the materials for his great work on the Siberian Exile System, his most frequent and most sympathetic correspondent, outside of his own family, was the busy President of the Century Co.

"It is chiefly, however, as a man of business genius that Roswell Smith will be remembered by those who knew him best. Goodness is more enduring than greatness; love is longer-lived than admiration; and Roswell Smith will be remembered by all who knew him, because they loved even more than they admired him.

"The spirit of trust and confidence which Mr. Roswell Smith manifested toward those who coöperated with him, and in his generous desire that they should share in the prosperity which his genius made possible, aroused an enthusiasm which a more worldly and selfish method of dealing never could have created. * * * The world is better and happier because Roswell Smith lived in it.

"'Diligent in business, fervent in spirit, serving the Lord,' was the precept that hung printed in gold, just above his office desk. But his practice was yet better; he rarely led in mirth, full of cheer as he was, but may be all the more for that he was a very happy man, and it was one of the richest sources of his daily happiness to be not diligent simply, but chivalrous in business.

"His faith was as simple and unquestioning as that of Faraday; his appeal to divine guidance in every matter of importance was as natural and habitual as that of Gordon."

Following is the very true inscription engraved on Roswell Smith's tomb:

ROSWELL SMITH, BORN MARCH 30, 1829, DIED APRIL 19, 1892.

A MAN OF GOD IN FAITH AND LIFE, PURE IN MOTIVE, FIRM IN PRINCIPLE, JUST WITHOUT RIGOR AND GENEROUS WITHOUT WEAKNESS, IN ENTERPRISE LARGE AND UNSELFISH, ORIGINAL IN CONCEPTION AND BOLD IN PERFORMANCE, IN CITIZEN LIFE BROADMINDED AND DILIGENT, IN HIS FRIENDSHIPS BROTHERLY AND STEADFAST, IN HIS LOVE PROFOUND, HE DESIRED BREADTH OF LIFE RATHER THAN LENGTH OF DAYS, AND BEFORE HIS YEARS HAD GROWN HEAVY SANK UNDER THE BURDEN OF HIS PEERAGE.

Hon. HENRY L. ELLSWORTH, previously mentioned as the father of Annie (Ellsworth) Smith, wife of Roswell Smith, was the son of Hon. Oliver Ellsworth, and twin brother of Governor William W. Ellsworth, of Connecticut. The "Records of Windsor" contain the following reference to Oliver Ellsworth:

"In memory of Oliver Ellsworth, LL.D., an assistant in the Council, and a Judge of the Supreme Court of the State of Connecticut. A member of the Convention which formed, and of the State Convention which adopted the Constitution of the United States, one of the Envoys Extraordinary and Minister Plenepotentiary, who made the Convention of 1800 between the United States and the French Republic."

Oliver Ellsworth, born April 29, 1745, was the son of *William*, born April 12, 1702, married Mary Oliver, of Boston; he was the son of *Thomas*, born September 2, 1665, son of *Josias*, or Josiah, born 1629; son of the ancestor *John*, who was of Boston, 1646. The "Records of Windsor" contain the following in regard to Josiah:

"Sargeant Josiah Ellsworth, æ 60 years, he dyed August, ye 20 day Anno 1689."

Mrs. JULIA (SMITH) INNESS, the only surviving child of Roswell and Annie (Ellsworth) Smith, was born in Lafayette, Ind. She married, in 1879, George Inness, Jr., an artist of great repute, a son of the celebrated landscape artist. She moved to Montclair in 1880, where her father had erected and presented to her and her husband the beautiful residence fronting on Walnut Crescent, known as Roswell Manor. It is of the colonial style of architecture, and is provided with every modern convenience and luxury that can be found in a suburban home. It occupies an elevated position, overlooking the country for miles around, affording one of the most delightful and picturesque views to be found anywhere in the township. Mrs. Inness, who is a recognized leader in Montclair society, is also foremost in works of charity and benevolence. She is deeply interested in the work of the Children's Home, and a generous contributor to its support, giving at the same time her personal attention to the numerous details connected with the institution. She has also been a frequent and generous contributor to the First Congregational Church, and the beautiful memorial window which adorns the north transept of the church was contributed by her in memory of her children. She founded the Montclair Chapter of the Society of the Daughters of the Revolution, and the numerous applications for membership indicate the deep interest awakened in its objects. Mrs. Inness inherits from her parents those noble traits of character that distinguished them throughout their long and useful lives, and to contribute to the happiness of others is her chief aim in life. She is greatly beloved and respected in the community from the highest even to the lowest.

ADDISON HOWARD SIEGFRIED.

Of those classed as "new comers" in Montclair there is probably no man better known or more highly respected in the community than Mr. A. H. Siegfried, the subject of this sketch. He has been among the foremost in all the great reform movements inaugurated here within the past few years. The command, "Whatsoever thy hand findeth to do, do it with thy might," has been exemplified in every act of his life, resulting in the success of every undertaking with which he has been connected, both here and elsewhere. The rapid growth and increased interest in the Young Men's Christian Association are due largely to his efforts. His success in life is explained, in part at least, by his heredity. The name "Siegfried" is in itself an inspiration, partly because of its meaning and partly because it runs back through the history and mythology of centuries to "Siegfried, King of the Danes," and to "Prince Siegfried," whose name's-day, September 23, is marked in both German and English chronology, while Wagner has immortalized a heroic bearer of the name in the greatest of his works.

On the paternal side Mr. Siegfried traces his line back to the beginning of the eighteenth century, in the person of Jacob Siegfried, a native of Germany, known to have been a resident of Northampton County, Pa., prior to 1730. Mr. A. H. Siegfried blends German, Welsh and Massachusetts Yankee blood. His grandfather, the Rev. George Siegfried, married Sarah Wilgus, a Welsh woman, in 1794. Their youngest son, the Rev. Benjamin Young Siegfried, is a native of Berks County, Pa. He learned the printer's trade in Philadelphia, educated himself in theology there while working at his trade, began his work in the Christian ministry before he was twenty-one, removed to Ohio in 1837, where he has ever since been unceasingly active and greatly useful as a clergyman of the Baptist Church—active as such, even yet, at seventy-seven years of age, in and about Zanesville, Ohio.

Mr. Siegfried's mother was Sarah E. Muzzy, descendant of Robert Muzzy, one of the first settlers of Ipswich, Mass., 1634, and daughter of Thomas N. and Lorinda B. Muzzy, who were among the early pioneers from Massachusetts to the Ohio wilderness. Benjamin, a grandson of the ancestor, was in the expedition against the Indians in 1707, where he was taken prisoner and remained in captivity in Canada until 1710. Several of this name were residents of Cambridge, Mass.

A. H. Siegfried, son of Rev. B. Y. and Sarah E. (Muzzy) Siegfried, was born near Zanesville, Ohio, April 25, 1842, and spent his boyhood there and in Cambridge, in the adjoining county eastward. His father was, besides being a clergyman, an editor and a practical printer, and conducted the *Christian Register*, Zanesville, in the early fifties. Young Siegfried was put to setting type and "printer's devil" work generally in his eighth year, when he had to stand on a chair to reach his cases of type. It was there he first evinced, or perhaps acquired, that exactness, method and reliability which form such an admirable basis of character, and which in his case were developed at an unusually early age. It is indicative of his remarkable self-reliance at that age, that in his boyhood he made his first trip to New York City quite alone, and at his own expense, where he spent two or three days at one of the principal hotels, seeing the attractions of the town. He has since admitted that Barnum's Museum was at that time Gotham's chief glory.

Later, he spent four and a half years in the academic and collegiate departments of Marietta College, Ohio, where he maintained himself as an organist, choir director and conductor of musical conventions. He also conducted on his own account several successful courses of popular lyceum lectures. Among the most notable of these was a series extending from Cincinnati to Pittsburg, by

A. H. Siegfried

Frederick Douglas, in the principal towns of Southern Ohio and Western Virginia. Directly after the war, race prejudice, of course, ran high, and it required skill, tact, coolness and judgment to steer between the Scylla and Charybdis of political factions. The lectures were a triumphant success, however, reflecting credit upon the distinguished speaker and his youthful manager.

The Weekly Journalist, Boston, outlining Mr. Siegfried's newspaper career, says that for twenty-four years he has been engaged in newspaper work, either as a publisher or advertising manager. From 1869 till the middle of 1882 his connection was with the *Courier-Journal*, *Commercial*, and the long since dead *Ledger*, in Louisville, and the *Pioneer Press* of St. Paul. In 1882 he came to New York as eastern business manager of the Chicago *Daily News*, which position he resigned in September, 1893, to become general business manager of the *Ladies' Home Journal*, Philadelphia, the most largely circulated monthly magazine in the world. The sound integrity and high principle of the ideas and methods of the Chicago *Record* and *Daily News* and the *Ladies' Home Journal* are well adapted to him and he to them. Mr. Siegfried has always been known as a one-rate, definite and open-method newspaper man—positive, decisive, square-cut, and with a high sense of business honor. He believes that newspaper circulation should be measured as accurately as dry goods or land, and that advertising has, and always should have, a definite and relatively inflexible basis of value and sale. As an evidence that this is not mere theory with him, it is a fact that he once squarely declined an order which ran up into five figures, because the advertiser wished to "cut" it by twenty cents, simply that he might be able to say that he had "cut" the published rates of *The Chicago Daily News*. Afterward Mr. Siegfried secured the order at his own price, the 20 cents included. Nothing more quickly irritates him than assault upon right newspaper methods. But while unconquerably resolute where a sense of duty is concerned, those who come oftenest in contact with him know best the warm geniality of his nature and disposition, and his frank readiness to aid those who ask the benefit of his influence or advice. His sound judgment and good common sense, taken in connection with his wide knowledge of men and affairs, have brought him much into demand for counsel and information by young men generally. It not infrequently happens that he is consulted by representatives of newspapers as to facts which concern their own publications. The confidence he thus unconsciously invites from his contemporaries and competitors indicates not only the extensiveness of his information and soundness of advice given, but reveals the broad sympathies of his nature, as well as its entire freedom from petty and narrow prejudices.

Mr. Siegfried, from boyhood, has been ready in speech, and in youth was prominent in debating and literary societies—which is not strange, as he comes from a line of preachers and public speakers. In 1890 he was selected to deliver the annual address before the National Editorial Association at St. Paul, where his "Criticism of the Counting Room" attracted large attention and shook a good many "dry bones." He is in frequent demand as a platform speaker on practical questions of moral and social reform, Young Men's Christian Association work, and so on, but he never appears before an audience, large or small, without careful preparation, and unless he feels that he really has something to say that ought to be said.

Among others of his popular lectures are two interesting ones on several of his canoeing trips—a sport in which he is yet much interested. He began extended cruises in the early seventies, and in 1879 went to the source of the Mississippi. His paddle and sail have carried him many thousands of miles and over nearly all the noted American waters. He, with W. L. Alden and N. H. Bishop, are the remainder of the earliest devotees of this sport, and his lectures and writing did much in its infancy to arouse interest in and love for it.

After establishing himself in business in the East, Mr. Siegfried lived for a time in Brooklyn, but being desirous of getting away from the noise and tumult of the city he visited several suburban towns, contiguous to New York, and finally decided on Montclair, which came nearer to his ideas of comfort, beauty and healthfulness than any place he had seen, and in 1884 he removed thence with his family. His object was rest and recreation, but he could not be idle, neither could he "hide his light under a bushel," and without any special effort on his part his influence was soon felt in the community, and his services were in constant demand by his neighbors. Nature had been lavish with him in her musical as well as other gifts. With a fine tenor voice and the ability to direct others, he naturally became a precentor and director and held leading positions in this line in the Congregational and other churches. He was also capable of conducting the instrumental as well as the vocal services, and in the absence of the organist could always be relied on as a substitute, having served professionally as organist in leading churches of Marietta, Louisville, St. Paul, etc. For the benefit of the people of Montclair he introduced a series of musical entertainments for which he secured the services of a number of leading artists, much to the delight of those who found it inconvenient to visit the metropolis at night in order to enjoy this privilege. His greatest work, however, has been in connection with the Young Men's Christian Association and the Citizens' Committee of One Hundred. From the nucleus of the Young Men's Reform Club he aided in founding the Association, and bent all his energies to make it a success. He was its first president. The young men of Montclair rallied round him and gave him their hearty support, and this is now one of the strongest and best managed associations of the kind in the State.

Mr. Siegfried, until his recent removal to Philadelphia, was a member of the Congregational Club of New York and Vicinity; of the Montclair Club; of the New Jersey State Executive Committee Young Men's Christian Association, and Chairman of its Sub-committee on the Public Press; Vice-President and member of the Executive Committee of the Outlook Club, Montclair; President of the Quill Club, New York; Chairman of the Montclair Citizens' Committee of One Hundred, the law and order league as related to liquor selling, and was connected with many other organizations. In February, 1894, he was unanimously elected President of the Young Men's Christian Association State Convention of New Jersey.

Personally and socially Mr. Siegfried may be described as a man of fine tastes, a good listener, an entertaining conversationalist, and an indefatigable worker in anything he undertakes. He not only makes friends but keeps them. He is frank almost to bluntness, but is sincere in his opinions, possessing, withal, a warm and liberal generosity of feeling- that "touch of nature that makes the whole world kin."

Mr. Siegfried married, in 1868, in Marietta, Ohio, Miss Mary E., daughter of Dr. A. B. and Mrs. M. A. Heterick. The issue of this marriage is three children. His eldest daughter, Miss Mary Holton Siegfried, has already taken a high position in the musical world. She was graduated with distinguished honor from the Metropolitan College of Music, New York. She holds a Fellowship degree in the American College of Musicians—the body which sets the standard of professional ability and scholarship for the entire country—has successfully held the position of organist of the First Congregational Church, Montclair, has played both as church and concert organist in leading churches and music halls in New York, Brooklyn, etc., and is regarded by her older fellows in music as one of the most brilliant and promising among the younger eastern organists, pianists and teachers.

TWO HEROES OF THE WAR.

The incidents referred to in the following biographical sketches of Abram P. Haring and Harry Little-john read like a romance, and unless supported by documentary evidence, would appear incredible. The failure of these men to receive proper recognition is due to their extreme modesty in failing to press their claims at the proper time, and the compiler of this work claims the honor of making the discovery and furnishing to the world the record of two heroes which has hitherto remained buried in oblivion. If ever the records of the War Department are carefully searched it will be found that some of the greatest heroes, who composed the "rank and file" of the Army, remain unrecognized, while the self-constituted ones, who were promoted through personal influence, have inscribed their *own* names and achievements on the pages of history.

ABRAM PYE HARING.

VOLUME XLI., page 136, of the "Rebellion Records" contains the following paragraph:

"Haring. Lieut. Abram P., 132d Regiment, N. Y. Vols. Had not eleven men of the 132d under Lieutenant Haring in the blockhouse at Batchelor's Creek, N. C., withstood a rebel army for over one hour, Newberne would have been captured by the rebels."

"Honors of the Empire State in the War of the Rebellion," by Thomas S. Townsend, pages 348-9, contains the following:

"Had not eleven men of the regiment under Lieut. Abram P. Haring kept back the rebel army until the rest of the regiment came up, Newberne would have been captured."

The above is the only record of one of the most remarkable and gallant achievements of the War of the Rebellion. Had it occurred under any European government the hero would have been decorated with the highest honors in the gift of his sovereign. The only recognition ever received by Mr. Haring is the simple bronze medal, presented by the Secretary of War, inscribed "The Congress to Abram P. Haring, late 1st Lieut. Co. G., 132d Regt. New York Vol. Infty."

The facts obtained from Mr. Haring, who is as modest as he is brave, are as follows:

In the winter of 1861, the Confederate army, owing to the efficiency of the blockade, which cut off their sources of supply, were greatly in need of the munitions of war, and learning that a large amount of ammunition, stores, etc., had been sent by our government to Newberne, N. C., determined on the capture of the place. A large force of infantry, cavalry and artillery, composing a part of Pickett's division, was sent on the night of February 1, 1864, to make the attack. It was a dark, rainy [at 2 A.M.] night, and objects could only be distinguished at a short distance. To reach their place of destination the rebel troops were obliged to cross a bridge which spans Batchelor's Creek on the road to Newberne. Lieutenant Haring, who was then engaged in outpost picket duty, was

A. P. HARING.

left with a detachment of *eleven* men as a reserve, and to guard this bridge. His regiment was some four miles distant, and his nearest supports over a mile distant. He had a line of earthworks which were intended only to guard against a small attacking force. Mr. Haring was never caught "napping;" his first intimation of the approach of the enemy was a few shots and the tramp of men on the opposite side of the bridge. He at once gave orders in rapid succession as though in command of a large force. "One to six fire, seven to eleven fire!" and so on. The enemy, believing that a large body of troops were in their front, were cautious in their movements, and after firing several volleys brought up their artillery to cover the attack of the infantry, and under the continuous fire of the artillery, three separate attempts were made to cross the bridge, and each time repulsed by the small force in front. Lieutenant Haring, in the meantime, while keeping up the firing by a portion of his men, ran along up and down the river bank with the remainder, shouting and yelling like demons to the *imaginary* reinforcements to "hurry up," at the same time giving orders in quick succession to "fall back one! forward two! fire!" etc. This ruse was kept up and the enemy held in check for two hours, until reinforcements arrived which consisted of detachments of 150 men. In the meantime the ammunition of this little band of Spartans had given out, but they "held the fort" until assistance came. With this small additional force the enemy was held in check until 9 o'clock the next morning. In the meantime while a feint of attack was kept up in front a large force of Confederates crossed the stream some distance above, and flanked the small force defending the bridge. The men, finding themselves surrounded, attempted to force their way through the rebel ranks. About half the number succeeded; the rest were captured. Lieutenant Haring, with half a dozen men, made a rush and broke through, and about a quarter of a mile distant found a brigade of Federals drawn up in line of battle. He was immediately ordered to fall into line on the extreme left. Being familiar with the topography of the country he informed the officer in command that the position was indefensible, and that they would certainly be flanked, and so it proved. The Confederates extended their line of battle for a long distance in front, keeping up an occasional firing. In the meantime a large flanking force which had been sent out began an attack in the rear of the Federals' column, and before they were aware of it they found themselves completely surrounded. Lieutenant Haring, being on the extreme left, made a break with his men, without waiting for orders, and struck out for the swamp, and succeeded in making his way to his regiment. He immediately reported to his colonel the condition of affairs, and told him that unless he moved his command at once they would be surrounded by the enemy. Lieutenant Haring was immediately ordered to take command of the Monitor train, the front car of which was covered with corrugated iron, and provided with swiveled howitzers.

Before reaching Newberne Lieutenant Haring discovered the enemy's cavalry approaching on a parallel line toward Newberne. He immediately halted the train and opened fire with his howitzers, but when the enemy came up with his artillery he was compelled to move, having several men killed in as many minutes. On reaching a bridge just outside of Newberne, he was ordered to take his command and remain at the bridge. In the first engagement at the bridge several of the enemy were killed, the fire of Lieutenant Haring's men being directed by the sound, while that of the Confederates was at random, it being impossible to discern any object in the darkness.

Mr. Haring has been a resident of Montclair since 1876. He purchased, in 1880, the Beatty farm, on Valley Road, and remodeled the homestead, and resided there until 1891. In 1893 he moved into the large new house which he erected at 66 Park street. The house was designed by E. R. North, architect, and is the style known as colonial renaissance.

Mr. Haring comes of the old Holland stock, one branch of which settled at Tappan about 1650, and the other—from which he is descended—on Manhattan Island. His mother was a Miss Van Ostrand, a descendant of one of the old Rockland County, N. Y., families. He was born in New York City November 15, 1840. He attended public school in New York until he was fifteen years of age, and then entered a fancy goods house. He afterward obtained a position with Otis & Co., wholesale millinery and fancy goods, remaining until the spring of 1862, the second year of the war. Without consulting any of his friends he walked from his place of business one day to a recruiting office, and enlisted. This was in August, 1862. He was immediately assigned to Company C, 132d Regiment, N. Y. Volunteers, commanded by Colonel P. J. Claassen, which was attached to the Second Empire Brigade, Eighteenth Army Corps. He was soon after promoted to Sergeant Major on the non-commissioned staff, and in January, 1863, was made Second Lieutenant, and in March following was promoted First Lieutenant of Company G. He was soon after sent with his regiment to Newberne, N. C., where he was engaged most of the time on outpost picket duty, a position attended with constant danger and very little glory. It was while engaged in this service that he had the memorable encounter with Pickett's division in February, 1864. At the battle of Southwest Creek, N. C., in the spring of 1865, he was wounded by a ball passing through his cheek, fired by a sharpshooter. After the first day the wound was left undressed for four days, which prolonged his sufferings, and he was rendered unfit for service for several weeks. He was honorably discharged in May 1865, by reason of wound, as First Lieutenant. Had his case been properly presented to the War Department he should have retired with rank of Major, and the brevet of Lieutenant-Colonel, to which he was justly entitled. His own modesty and the neglect of his friends prevented his receiving these honors until the time for granting them had expired.

At the close of the war he returned to his old position in New York where he remained for two years, when he engaged in the business of manufacturing stationer under the firm name of Stewart, Warren & Co.

He is a member of the Military Order of the Loyal Legion, U. S., also of the Medal of Honor Legion, U. S.

He married, in 1866, Miss Emma Hollett, of Cornwall, N. Y., a daughter of Amos M. Hollett.

HARRY LITTLEJOHN.

HARRY LITTLEJOHN, who has resided on Watchung Avenue, Montclair, since 1870, has earned his right to citizenship as well as a place on the "Roll of Honor" for services rendered his adopted country in her hour of need. He is of Scotch parentage, and received an early education in Leslie, Fifeshire, Scotland; afterward he attended the School of Arts in Edinburgh. His uncle, Dr. H. D. Littlejohn, is a noted physician of that city. He came to this country in 1858, and engaged in mercantile business for two years, and in March, 1860, he went to Cuba and engaged in the manufacture of chemicals for purifying sugar. He returned to New York in March, 1861, and soon after enlisted in Company D., First Regiment, Oregon Rifles, a company belonging to one of those embryo regiments whose full organization was never completed, the whole regiment being composed of this one company, most of the members having enlisted with the understanding that they were to be Second Lieutenants and First Sergeants. The company was sent to the front at Williamsport, Md., a small town on the Potomac River, where, with a company raised in that town, and another raised in Martinsburg, Va., they did outpost duty on the Upper Potomac. Mr. Littlejohn was made Corporal immediately after his enlistment, was quickly promoted to First Sergeant, and, on the company's arrival at Williamsport, was unanimously elected Second Lieutenant.

In December, 1861, while his company was doing picket duty at Dam No. 5, on the Upper Potomac, Lieutenant Littlejohn, like many others at that particular time, was eager for a brush with the enemy. The company at this time was guarding several miles of the Potomac, and especially the Baltimore and Ohio canal, by which supplies were forwarded to Washington. (The several dams are made to supply the canal with water.) His wishes were gratified sooner than he anticipated, for on Saturday, December 7, while visiting the picket at Little Georgetown, he saw a large force coming out of the woods in the direction of the dam. (This proved to be a force of 600 infantry and a battery of artillery under the command of "Stonewall" Jackson, who was sent to destroy the dam.) Riding quickly back to the headquarters of his company at Four Locks, Lieutenant Littlejohn informed Captain Robinson of the enemy's approach, who immediately called out the reserve, and marched to the dam, a mile below. While he, with his small force, was marching toward the dam on the Maryland side, the rebels were pursuing a parallel course on the Virginia side. Lieutenant Littlejohn's men opened fire on the rebels, which was immediately returned, and a running fire kept up until they reached the dam at night. The Confederates took advantage of the darkness to cut away the dam, placing relays of men to work with axes and shovels. In order to deceive the enemy and convey the impression that he had a large force, Lieutenant Littlejohn scattered his few men about on the opposite bank and again opened fire, driving the rebels from their work and forcing them to seek shelter.

Early the following morning the rebels opened fire with their artillery and musketry. In the meantime Lieutenant Littlejohn, with his small force of fifteen men, had taken shelter behind the parapet of the dam, and kept up a continuous fire, which prevented the rebels from working their guns. A number of percussion shells were fired by the rebels against the rocks in the rear of the little Spartan band, which exploded without any serious damage. This unequal contest was kept up for nearly three hours, until reinforcements arrived, and the rebels were driven back and compelled to abandon the attempt.

Another attempt was made by the rebels on Dec. 17 following to destroy this dam, but they were again repulsed with severe loss.

In February, 1862, by order of the Adjutant-General, the company was consolidated with the Third Maryland Volunteers. The letter of the company, "D," was then changed to "C," thus becoming the Color Company. The regiment was then assigned to General Bank's command, and on August 9, 1862, for the first time, as a regiment, engaged the enemy at the battle of Cedar Mountain.

After Bank's retreat under General Pope, the regiment was assigned to Third Brigade (General Green), First Division (General Williams), Twelfth Army Corps (General Slocum), until April, 1864, and

RESIDENCE OF H. LITTLEJOHN, WATCHUNG AVENUE.

was then assigned to the Ninth Army Corps, under General Burnside, and took part in the several engagements under General Grant, including the battles of the Wilderness and the Petersburg Campaign.

Lieutenant Littlejohn was promoted Captain September 1, 1862. He was wounded by the explosion of a shell in front of Petersburg, Va., June 17, 1864, and on his return to duty he was made Assistant Inspector-General on the Brigade Staff. He was honorably discharged under General Orders Circular No. 75, A.G.D., Sept. 22, 1864—on Oct. 7, 1864.

He participated in the following engagements: 1. Dam No. 5, Dec. 7 and 18, 1860; 2. Boliver

Heights, Va., May 30, 1862; 3, Cedar Mountain, Va., Aug. 9, 1862; 4, Beverly Ford, Va., Aug. 24, 1862; 5, Chancellorsville, Va., May 1,2,3, 1863; 6, Raccoon Ford, Va., Sept. 17, 1863; 7, Wilderness, Va., May 6, 1864; 8, Spottsylvania C. H., Va., May 10, 11, 12, 1864; 9, Shady Grove, Va., June 1, 1864; 10, Cold Harbor, June 2, 1864; 11, Before Petersburg, Va., June 17, 1864; 12, Hicks Station, Va., Weldon and P. R. R., Aug. 19, 1864; 13, Do., do., Aug. 21, 1864; 14, Poplar Grove Church, Sept. 30, 1864.

Soon after his return from the war he became connected with the Eagleton Manufacturing Company, and later with the publishing house of F. J. Huntington & Co., and March, 1870, he engaged with the Scovill Manufacturing Company. Later he assisted in forming the Scovill & Adams Company, of which he was elected Secretary, a position he still holds.

He removed to Montclair October, 1870, locating on Watchung Avenue, having purchased the old Zeek homestead, which he remodeled and made of it a beautiful and attractive residence, as shown in the accompanying illustration.

October 3, 1889, Captain Littlejohn married Charlotte Louise, daughter of the late William H. Wilson, who for many years was a prominent citizen of Montclair.

CHURCH STREET.

Chapter XVII.

ARCHITECTURAL FEATURES OF MONTCLAIR HOMES.

HE stranger visiting Montclair is attracted by the large number of beautiful villas and cottages of a style of architecture entirely unlike that seen in most suburban towns and villages. There is a variety and yet a harmony in style and proportion which indicates the progressive character of the people.

About the beginning of the present century architecture became a lost art on the other side of the Atlantic, and it was not in fact until toward the close of the sixties that any real healthy regulation took place. Ease, comfort and convenience was sought without regard to architectural proportions or adaptation to the topography of the country. Those who have watched the progress of rural architecture for some years past have noticed a marked advance in architectural design and proportion. The change began with the English Gothic, followed by the Italian, the Grecian, the French villa, with Mansard roof and tower, and lastly the so-called "Queen Anne." In nearly all suburban towns throughout this country these are the prevailing styles in architecture, and it is a notable fact that, in many cases, the owner has tried to outdo his neighbor in originality and variety of design, thereby violating every rule in architecture and in topographical features of location, which would indicate that the proprietor himself was either his own architect, or sought to impress his individuality on the style of architecture.

> "* * * * You shall see a man
> Who never drew a line or struck an arc,
> Direct an architect and spoil his work,
> Because, forsooth, he likes a tasteful house !
> He likes a muffin, but he does not go
> Into his kitchen to instruct his cook ;
> Nay, that were insult. He admires fine clothes,
> But trusts his tailor ! Only in those arts
> Which issue from creative potencies
> Does his conceit engage him ?"—HOLLAND'S KATRINA.

There is a class of old domestic work which is to be found everywhere throughout the more early settled States, such as the old manor houses along the valley of the James River in Virginia, on the banks of the Hudson, and a few of the older cities of Boston, New York, and Philadelphia, which is unique in style, attractive in appearance, and combines many of the most important elements conducive to convenience and comfort. To utilize this style of architecture, and combine it with all the modern improvements, creating a new and distinctive type of American villa—known as American Domestic—was the work of a young architect—Frank E. Wallis—an assistant of Richard M. Hunt, and now a permanent resident of Montclair.

A number of the most beautiful houses in Montclair have been designed by him, and many others of the same character, from designs published by him, and modified to suit the taste of the architect and the convenience of the owner.

It is this distinctive feature of Montclair, added to its extreme healthfulness, that has induced so many strangers after a short residence during the summer season to become permanent settlers. The homes described and illustrated in this work have been selected with a view of illustrating the various styles of architecture, the topography of the country, and the taste displayed by the owners in utilizing the natural beauty of the surroundings.

FRANK E. WALLIS.

As an architect, Mr. Wallis has become well and favorably known to the people of Montclair, having designed some of the most beautiful houses in the township. He is recognized as one of the pioneers, if not the chief promoter, of the prevailing style of architecture known as the colonial.

Mr. Wallis's maternal grandmother was Mary Cary Dunham; his mother's father was Nicholas John Meating, of the British Navy. The Careys and Dunhams, from whom she descended, were prominent Royalists in New York at the beginning of the War of the Revolution, and were obliged to flee to New Brunswick. On account of their loyalty to the British Government they were awarded a large grant of land in what is now St. George, N. B., and which still remains in the hands of their descendants.

Frank E. Wallis was born in Eastport, Me., June 14, 1864. He removed with his parents to Boston at the age of ten years, and was there educated at the public schools. As a boy he was excessively fond of drawing, and spent most of his time at this, to the neglect of his other studies. Both his father and grandfather were amateurs in water and oil colors, although neither followed it as a profession. It remained for the younger Wallis to develop the gifts which became his under the natural law of heredity. He completed the routine of the elementary branches of education at the age of fifteen, and entered the office of Edward C. Cabot, at that time the oldest as well as the leading architect in Boston. Under this distinguished tutor he spent nine years of faithful study, and, while in his daily task he followed the style of his preceptor, he was continually working out new and original ideas of his own, which in later years he put into practice. He subsequently spent two years in the office of Peabody & Stearns, after which he went abroad, traveling through France, Italy and Spain, closely observing the various styles of mediæval architecture, of which he made numerous sketches. His pursuit of knowledge was attended with many of the difficulties which beset Americans traveling in foreign countries, and he was once arrested as a German spy, but succeeded in establishing his innocence.

After his return home he traveled south for a time in the interest of an architectural paper, visiting Virginia and South Carolina, where he made a study of the old colonial houses, of which he gave a minute account in the paper he represented, and his literary contributions were illustrated with numerous sketches. It was through this means principally that the public was educated up to the present prevailing style of colonial architecture, which has to a large extent superseded the French villas and English gothic. Mr. Wallis subsequently extended his trip further south and added a number of interesting sketches to his collection. As the final result of his experience he published a work entitled, "Old Colonial Architecture and Furniture," which has been generally adopted by the profession. The entire edition of three hundred copies, at $20 per copy, met with a ready sale. Mr. Wallis presented the Massachusetts Historical Society with twenty elaborate drawings of houses and churches in New England. He is a frequent contributor to architectural and other journals on subjects of interest to the profession.

In the autumn of 1888 he entered the office of the famous architect, Richard M. Hunt, and has been associated with him in the construction of some of the finest buildings in the country. Mr. Wallis made all the working drawings for the Administration Building at the World's Fair in Chicago, and had entire charge of the work. He received a diploma from World's Fair Commissioners for drawings.

Mr. Wallis removed to Montclair in October, 1888, and soon after built himself a home. He married, Oct. 15, 1888, Miss Grace L. Parker, daughter of Charles F. Parker, of Boston, a descendant of the famous Capt. John Parker, who led the minute men at the battle of Lexington.

WILLIAM FELLOWES.

THE design shown in the accompanying engraving of Mr. Fellowes' house, on the corner of Fullerton Avenue and Union Street, is by far the most imposing and attractive residence in Montclair. The style of architecture is known as the French château. It is of red sand stone ashler, brown-stone trimming and tile roof. It covers a space of 60 by 60 feet, three stories high, and commands a fine view of the surrounding country. Houses similar in style are found in the suburbs of large cities, but this is the only one of the kind in Montclair.

Mr. Fellowes was attracted by the beautiful surroundings of Montclair, and decided on making this his future home.

William Fellowes, although a native of Louisville, Ky., born June 8, 1836, is a descendant of *William* Fellows, of Ipswich, Mass., 1643, born in England 1609. The original spelling of the name is Fellowes: the family is a very ancient one, now seated at Ramsey Abbey and Haverland Hall, County Suffolk, England, *Isaac*, the youngest son of William, the ancestor, born in England 1635, was a voter in the town of Ipswich, and "possessed of rights of commonage, and, with the title of 'Corporal,' had a seat appointed him in the meeting-house." He married Joanna Bourne, and had, with other issue: *Jona-than*, born Sept. 28, 1689; *Jonathan* (2d), his son, was born at Ipswich 1707; he had a son, *Cornelius*, born 1738, father of *Jonathan*, born 1770; the latter had a son, *William*, who was the father of the subject of this sketch. He married *Caroline Davis*, daughter of Charles Davis, of Roxbury, Mass., born 1772, who was fifth in descent from *William*, an original settler of Roxbury, Mass., 1635, through *Ebenezer*, Colonel *Aaron*, and Captain *Aaron*, born 1735, father of above-mentioned Charles. Colonel Aaron Davis was captain of Roxbury Militia, 1775; later, colonel of Massachusetts Militia; member of Massachusetts Provincial Congress, 1774-7; member of Massachusetts General Court, 1775-6. Captain Aaron Davis served with the Minute Men at the battle of Bunker Hill. William Fellowes, eldest son of William and Caroline

(Davis) Fellowes, removed with his parents to New York City in 1847. He was prepared for college at private school—at Churchill's Military Academy, Sing Sing, and at Swinburne's Academy, White Plains, N. Y. He entered Columbia College, but left at the end of his sophomore year, and in 1858 went to New Orleans and worked as a clerk for his uncle's firm—Fellowes & Co., cotton factors. At the breaking out of the war, in 1861, he joined the Confederate army as a member of the Louisiana Washington Artillery. He took part in the first battle of Bull Run, July 21, 1861; second Bull Run, August 27, 1862; Antietam, or Sharpsburg, Sept. 16 and 17, 1862; first and second battles of Fredericksburgh; he was captured at the latter engagement, sent to Washington, subsequently paroled, and went to his father's home in New York sick with pneumonia. As soon as he was sufficiently recovered he went abroad, and while in Paris obtained, through Mr. Mason, a special exchange, with permission from the Confederate Government to enter the Confederate Navy. He remained in Liverpool until the spring of 1864, hoping to be assigned to one of the rams then in course of construction. Failing in this, he ran the blockade in the steamer "Old Dominion," and entered Wilmington, N. C., July 3. He rejoined his old command and was present at the surrender at Appomattox, April 9, 1865. He returned to his father's home in New York, and from there went to Texas, and on his return to New Orleans, in 1868, entered the employ of Bradish Johnson, where he remained for two years. In 1874 he married Miss Ann Carter Eustace, of Shrevesport, La., a descendant of an old and well-known Virginia family. Her grandmother was Ann Carter, daughter of Catharine Tayloe and Landen, of Sabin Hall, a direct descendant of John Carter, known as "King Carter," who was a member of the House of Burgesses, England, in 1649, and in 1654 was a member of the Virginia House of Burgesses from Lancaster County, and commander-in-chief of the forces sent against the Rappahannock Indians. The father of General Carter built Christ Church, the first church erected in Lancaster County, Va.

Mr. Fellowes went with his wife to England in 1877, and soon after his return, in 1879, visited Montclair, where, after a residence of four years, he made another trip abroad in 1884, with his wife and daughter, Harriet Davis; leaving them at Stuttgart, Germany, he returned to Montclair in October, 1885, and soon after purchased two lots on the corner of Fullerton Avenue and Union Street. One of these he reserved for himself, and the other he presented to St. Luke's Episcopal Church. The plans for his home were drawn by F. B. Kimball, the well-known architect of New York, and the work was begun in April, 1888, and the exterior completed one year later.

RESIDENCE OF FREDERICK J. DRESCHER.

It would be difficult to find a more beautiful location near the centre of Montclair for a suburban residence than that of Mr. Drescher's home on the corner of Park Street and Claremont Avenue. The view selected as shown in the accompanying illustration is from the southeast looking up Claremont Avenue, with the mountains in the distance as a body guard. The style of architecture is a combination of the Queen Anne and French château. The underpinning and first story is of rough faced brown stone. The framework above is sheathed and painted light cream or ivory color, giving a strong contrast to the stone work. The interior arrangements are complete and all the space utilized to the best advantage for convenience and comfort. Hardwood trimmings are used in all the rooms on the first floor. On the south side is the library and dining room, communicating by sliding doors. The library has a paneled wainscot of walnut, and the doors and window trimmings are of the same material. The fire-places in both rooms are of glazed tiling, with elegant hardwood mantels, mirrors, etc. The dining room is finished in antique oak, with furniture to correspond. There is a centre window of stained glass, which sheds a soft light over the whole, giving a pleasing effect. The hall is trimmed in oak, including the staircase, which is lighted at the landing by a large stained glass window of elegant design, representing a pastoral scene. A large antique clock of elaborate design stands in the rear of the hall, near a large open fire-place. (A smoking room and toilet room opening out of the hall complete the arrangements on this floor.) The parlor, on the north side, shows a beautiful blending of colors, the walls and ceilings being in ivory and gold, and the trimmings and furniture all harmonize both in color and finish. The whole interior arrangement evinces excellent taste and good judgment.

Mr. Drescher, to whom Montclair is indebted for some of its finest dwellings and other improvements, was born in Philadelphia, near the Schuylkill River, October 12, 1839. His parents were Germans. He removed with them when quite young to New York City, where he attended the public school and afterward took a commercial course in Goldsmith and Renwick's Business College. Like most boys he tried first one place and then another, and finally, having arrived at a suitable age, leased a stand in Washington Market and started in the provision business. He was successful in this and subsequently ran two stores on Eighth Avenue, both of which yielded a fair income. He sold these to good advantage and formed a partnership with John K. Lasher, wholesale produce merchant in the same business. This he afterward sold out, and for some time carried on an extensive business on Washington Street. About 1872 he disposed of his New York business and in the meantime his father having erected a large building in Hoboken, he decided to go into the business of fancy groceries, both wholesale and retail. From the beginning of his business career he made it a point to buy and sell strictly for cash. He watched the market closely and bought only the finest grade of goods in large quantities, all of which underwent his personal inspection. His methods of doing business prevented the possibility of failure, and success has attended all his efforts.

Desiring to enjoy the fruits of his labors he sought a country home. He was favorably impressed with Montclair, and in 1885 he bought a place on Claremont Avenue, near Valley Road, where he resided for six years, and in the meantime bought other property, built and sold, realizing a fair profit on his investments. He began the erection of his present home in 1889, which is acknowledged to be one of the finest residences in Montclair. Through his investments and improvements he has added over

RESIDENCE OF FREDERICK J. DRESCHER.

$150,000 to the taxable property of the township. While taking no part in the public affairs of the township, he has been in hearty accord with everything tending to its social advancement. He was one of the early members of the Montclair Club, and when it was determined to enlarge its field of usefulness, and erect a building suitable for the purpose, he zealously supported the movement, and subscribed liberally to the stock. He is a stockholder and director in the Montclair Bank, a member of Montclair Lodge, F. & A. M., of Pentalpha Chapter, No. 11, R. A. M., of Hoboken, to all of which he has given his generous aid as circumstances required. He was an officer of the Ninth Regiment National Guard, State of New Jersey, and also formed Company F of the same regiment. Honest and upright in all his dealings, a man of unimpeachable integrity, honored and respected in business and social circles, he well deserves the success he has achieved.

He was married in 1865 to Miss Eleanor Eliza Compton, daughter of William H. Compton, a descendant of an old Jersey family. Her great grandfather, Job Compton, was Lieutenant in a Monmouth County, N. J., Regiment, which rendered important service in the War of the Revolution.

THE "FARLEY HOUSES" ON THE MOUNTAIN SLOPE.

THE "Farley Houses," as they are now designated, have become a prominent feature of the south-western slope of the mountain—a region of country recently developed by Mr. James J. Farley, who, though but a few years a resident of Montclair, has, with commendable zeal, energy and enterprise, added to the natural beauty of this locality by the erection of a class of houses, unique in style, tasteful in design and elaborate in finish both exterior and interior. The six houses already completed by Mr. Farley have drawn to this neighborhood a class of residents who will doubtless prove of great benefit to

RESIDENCE OF JAMES J. FARLEY.

the community. The architectural design of these villas may be classed under the general head of "American Domestic," although in many respects they have a striking resemblance to the French château. The plans are by Montrose W. Morris, a prominent architect of Brooklyn. While the exterior is both pleasing and attractive, these houses are designed with especial reference to the carrying out of the ideas of Mr. Farley as to interior arrangements. On this he has bestowed much time and thought, his object being to combine convenience and utility, with all that artistic skill can suggest. These interiors are fitted up in hardwood, mostly oak, of the best workmanship, and the decorations and coloring are made to harmonize with the general appearance.

The one at present occupied by Mr. Farley is similar in its exterior appearance to the others. The house is 48 feet front with a round tower breaking through the roof; the whole of the exterior is shingled. The house contains three rooms front, the dining room being octagonal in form and finished in antique oak. It has a foyer hall with brick colonial mantel. A peculiar feature of the parlor in this house is that of a window built in the chimney outside, opening over and forming part of a mantel of antique oak. The window lights are of cathedral glass, arranged in a variety of colors, and when the rays of the setting sun shine through these a most beautiful effect is produced in the parlor and foyer.

These villas overlook a wide and extended range of country, and, on a clear day, Brooklyn Heights, the Bridge and New York Bay can be clearly discerned.

Mr. Farley, to whom the people of Montclair are indebted for these and other substantial improvements, is a native of New York City, born May 11, 1859. He is but two or three generations removed from his English ancestors who spelled the name Farleigh. He is a unique character and has a fondness for the unique, a giant in stature, six feet four in height and well proportioned. Conscious of his individual *greatness* he resolved with Ingersoll Lockwood, General Woodward, and others, to bring together in one harmonious whole the *greatest* men of the present age, and so, in 1880, they founded the famous Order of Titans. Beginning with half-a-dozen members in New York City it now extends from Maine to California, with a membership over two hundred, not one of whom is less than six feet two in height. On the list of members are found the names of Hon. Chester A. Arthur, General Winfield Scott Hancock, "Long John Wentworth," Lieut.-Governor William Dorsheimer, Dr. Chas. A. Doremus, Colonel Alfred Wagstaff, the author, Frank Vincent, Jr., Hon. Chas. W. Fuller, and others. W. J. Pierce is one of the highest members with six feet five and a half inches. R. W. Dayton, C. G. Dinsmore and Howard Mitchell are six feet four. Colonel Wagstaff, James A. Farley, W. L. Hammersley, R. A. C. Smith and Ingersoll Lockwood are over six feet four. Every man is able to touch a banner eight feet above the ground without rising on his tiptoes.

The Titans, according to the theory of their organization, are the descendants of the old demigods who were employed by Jupiter to hold up the heavens so that the skies might not fall on Mount Olympus. These modern Titans have three meetings a year. On the 1st of March the members are reminded that " We are nearing the day on which it is our custom to celebrate with becoming solemnity, united with dignified mirth, the awakening of Mother Earth." On this occasion an invocation is delivered by the High Priest in Latin, calling on Mother Earth to hear her sons as they lift up their voices to her, and to wake up from her sleep and bring the happiness of flowers and fruit and good health to all the earth.

In June the Titans make a visit to the ocean to salute Father Neptune. In the autumn, about Thanksgiving time, they are again called together to put Mother Earth to sleep. This is the last of the Olympian banquets of the year, and the members are notified that the event is to be celebrated with " collation, potation, fumation, cantation, conversation, oration, narration, cachinnation, and jollification." The crest of the Order is Titan supporting the heavens; their motto: Usque Ad Superos, and their flower the violet.

In selecting a residence on the mountain slope in Montclair, Mr. Farley made a wise choice, and in perfect harmony with the rules governing the Order of Titans.

Mr. Farley is not limited in his knowledge to Grecian mythology, but passed through the usual course of public instruction in the schools of New York, completing his business course at the Packard Institute, and after many years spent in the employ of the D., L. & W. R.R. Co., rose to a high position of trust.

He married, in 1887, (?) Jennie Morgan Osborne, daughter of Alexander Osborn, who came from the vicinity of Osborne Castle, England.

CHRISTOPHER ANDREW HINCK.

ALTHOUGH Mr. Hinck is among the more recent settlers of Montclair, the extensive improvements he has made in the township, and the large amount expended by him in opening and improving streets and avenues are matters of record, and entitle him to recognition in a history of Montclair.

Mr. Hinck was born in Kebding Bruch, Province of Hanover (now a part of Prussia), November 1, 1831. He came of a good and respectable family, his father being of that class of well-to-do intelligent farmers who compose the bone and sinew of the German Empire. His maternal grandfather, Hein Fick, was a man of more than ordinary intelligence, and of great influence in the community, and at the time of the French invasion in 1810, was elected Mayor of a large district, and clothed with ample authority to protect the interests of his fellow citizens.

Mr. Hinck was educated under a system which has long been compulsory, requiring parents to send their children to school from the age of eight to fourteen years, and at the present time a failure to do so involves a penalty of imprisonment to the delinquent. Under such a system, which in his day existed in a more modified form, Mr. Hinck acquired an education sufficient to fit him for a mercantile career. He afterward spent five years in a mercantile house, and then concluded to try his fortune in the New World. He left home and landed in New York City in 1851, a total stranger. His frank, open manner and pleasing address, made a favorable impression on those with whom he was brought in contact, and he soon made friends that "clung closer than a brother." Among those who took a kindly interest in his welfare, and who offered to assist him, was Wilson G. Hunt. He made the acquaintance of other prominent merchants, who invited him to their homes and honored him with their confidence. He obtained employment in a wholesale woolen house, where, by his strict attention to business, his industry and moral uprightness of character, he won the confidence of his employers. He served a year in one house, and two years in another, and during this period he acquired a thorough knowledge of the business, and laid the foundation for his subsequent successful business career. In July, 1854, having by careful economy saved something from his yearly income, together with a few hundred dollars received from his mother, he started in business for himself under the firm name of Hinck, Harms & Co. He separated from them in 1859, and organized the firm of Hinck & Pupke, which later became Hinck Bros. He continued in active business for more than a quarter of a century, and passed through several financial crises in which some of the oldest business houses in the country were compelled to suspend; but through all these and the frequent fluctuations of prices incident to the war, he maintained his credit unimpared, and met all his obligations promptly. He made it a principle of his life never to purchase in excess of his ability to pay promptly in cash when due. With abundant opportunities for speculation during the war by risking his capital, and with the chances of acquiring wealth rapidly, he preferred the "slow and sure" course, and was satisfied with fair profits and quick sales, and when the rapid depreciation in prices took place at the close of the war, he found himself in a condition to dispose of his stock without impairing his capital. From the beginning of his business career he sought to establish confidence between himself and his customers by fair dealings, and would never permit any misrepresentations in regard to the quality of goods for the purpose of making a sale. His conscientious regard for the truth forbade him to take any advantage whatever of those who trusted in his judgment and in his integrity. Honesty as a principle and not as a mere matter of policy was rooted and grounded in his nature, and instilled into his mind through the early teachings of his parents, who believed that character was more to a man than riches, or worldly honors. His uniform kindness and courtesy toward all with whom he came in contact had much to do with his success in life. He believed that every friend made added that much to his capital, and every enemy made impaired it to the same extent.

After accumulating a moderate fortune Mr. Hinck retired from business in 1883, with a spotless escutcheon, conscious that he had wronged no man and that his gains had been honestly acquired. He was then able to carry out a long cherished plan of a visit to the fatherland, and to mingle again amid the scenes of his childhood. He visited various parts of Europe and spent some three years with his family at Hanover, which, during his absence, had been merged from an independent kingdom into the great German Empire. This enforced idleness however, began to wear on him after the long and busy life which he had led, and he determined to seek some occupation which should again call forth his dormant energies and give activity to his mind and body. Soon after his return to the land of his adoption he visited Montclair and was attracted by its beauty and the healthfulness of its location. He finally purchased what was known as the "Sadler Place," comprising the homestead and fourteen acres, nearly adjoining the home of Inness the artist, know as "The Pines." He enlarged and improved the homestead, which he changed from the simple farm house to the beautiful modern villa. The grounds were laid out in lawns and shade and fruit trees of the finest variety were added, and the whole place made to blossom like the rose, presenting a most beautiful and picturesque appearance. He subsequently purchased three acres additional which he added to the homestead property.

He became impressed with the great social, educational and other advantages of Montclair—of its healthfulness and other attractive features, and, with characteristic energy, and faith in its future greatness, determined to do his share toward its further development. He purchased a tract of land north of Oxford and east of Grove Street, and another tract of land lying west of Grove Street, north of Greenwood Lake Railroad. Between Montclair Avenue and Grove Street, and running from Walnut to Chestnut Streets, he opened a new street to which he gave the name of "Christopher"—that being his christian name—thus perpetuating the name of its projector; this he graded so as to form a perfect drainage, curbed and macadamized it, all at his own expense. He also made the same improvements at Chestnut Street, from Grove Street to Montclair Avenue. About 600 feet north of Chestnut Street, from Grove to Forest Street, he cut an avenue in 1892, which he named Columbia Avenue, in commemoration of the quadrennial event of that year. He has erected fifteen houses on Christopher Street, one on Walnut Street—a double brick building, and a beautiful villa on the corner of Grove and Chestnut Streets, and has prepared plans for further improvements in this direction. While benefiting himself by this large expenditure of money, he has proved a public benefactor to the township, by the enhanced value of other property arising therefrom, and has thus added materially to the wealth of Montclair.

In 1857, when fortune had smiled upon him, Mr. Hinck began to feel the necessity of a helpmeet, and his thought naturally turned toward the fatherland which he resolved to visit, and, amid the scenes of his childhood, he found the woman of his choice, in Johanna Maria Fliedner, whom he married after a brief courtship, and returned with her to the land of his adoption. She proved a valuable helpmeet and wise counselor, and his success in life is due largely to her aid and co-operation in all his plans, thus verifying the proverb, "Whoso findeth a wife findeth a good thing, and obtaineth favor of the Lord." Ten children have been born to them, eight of whom are still living; these are Maria, Henry John, Georgine (deceased), George Frederick, Edward Louis, Louisa, Ernest Christopher, Edmund (deceased), Alfred John and Otto Helmuth,—the latter named from Count Von Moltke and Bismarck. A friend of the family communicated the fact to count Von Moltke, he sent his photograph to his namesake on the back of which was subscribed: "With the best wishes for Otto Helmuth," signed, Field Marshal Count Von Moltke.

THOMAS S. GLADDING.

Thomas S. Gladding graduated at Brown University in 1875. He taught the sciences at Suffield (Conn.) Institute and Worcester (Mass.) Academy for three years. He came to New York City in 1878 and formed a copartnership with Mr. C. M. Stillwell, under the firm name of Stillwell & Gladding, analytical chemists, and official chemists to the New York Produce Exchange. Mr. Gladding is a member of the American Chemical Society and the English Society of Public Analysts. He became a resident of Montclair in 1887, and purchased the Hening property on Mountain Avenue. He is an active member and a trustee of the Baptist Church; also a member of the Montclair Club.

Chapter XVIII.

UPPER MONTCLAIR.

THE beautiful region of country known as Upper Montclair has for its northern boundary the township of Acquackanonck in Passaic County; Watchung Avenue is the boundary line between it and Montclair; the township of Bloomfield lies on the east and that of Verona on the west. The Greenwood Lake R.R. passes in a northerly direction through the centre of the village, having three stations within the present boundaries of Upper Montclair, viz.: Watchung, Upper Montclair and Montclair Heights. The surface of the country is high, almost unbroken upland, with a gradual slope from the mountain toward the east, thus affording perfect drainage, and freedom from all malarious influences. It has two flourishing churches—the Christian Union, Congregational, and St. James, Episcopal - a beautiful cemetery, known as Mount Hebron Cemetery, lying on the outskirts of the township, a large brick school-house, a public hall, some half-dozen stores, an engine house, with a good fire engine, provided with all the modern fire apparatus. Some of the finest residences in the township are located in this neighborhood, notably those of Mr. C. H. Huestis and Dr. Morgan W. Ayres. Most of the houses are of the style known as American Domestic; there are a few, however, of the English Gothic, which present a beautiful and picturesque appearance.

All of this part of the township was originally known as Speertown (so called from the Speers, who owned large tracts of land in this neighborhood) and extended from the Fordham Crane house (Washington's headquarters) in Montclair to the line of Acquackanonck township.

When the Hollanders, who gained influence at the Indian trading place of Acquackanonck on the Passaic River, made the purchase of the Acquackanonck tract in 1679 and 1684, they laid their farms in parallel strips along the northern Newark border back to the mountain, and were thus brought in immediate contact with the Puritan settlers. Many of the old familiar names connected with Acquackanonck township are found among the early records of this part of Montclair township. Among these are the Speers, Egberts, Van Giesons, Seiglers, Pauluses, Posts, Garrabrantses, Van Rikers, Vreelands, Van Wagoners, Sips, Stymets, Van Winkles, Garitses, and Peterses.

COPY OF AN OLD DEED.

This Indenture, Made the fourteenth day of Desembre in the fourteenth year of the Reign of our Sovereign Lord George the third by the Grace of God of Great Britain, France and Ireland King Defender of the Faith &c. and in the Year of our Lord One Thousand Seven Hundred and Seventy four BETWEEN Robert Drummond of Acquackanonck in the County of Essex and Eastern Division of the Province of New Jersey Merchant, of the first part, and John Spear of Newark Bounds in the County and Province aforesaid, Yeoman of the second part WITNESSETH that the said Robert Drummond for and in Consideration of the sum of Seventy pounds Current money of the Province of New York to him in hand paid by the said John Spear at or before the Ensealing hereof the Receipt whereof he doth hereby Acknowledge and himself therewith fully satisfied Contented and paid and therefrom doth Exonorate Acquit and Discharge the said John Spear his Heirs Executors and Administrators for ever by these presents Hath Given Granted Bargained Sold Aliened Released Enfeoffed Conveyed and Confirmed and by these presents doth Give Grant Bargained Sell Alien Release Enfeoff Convey and Confirm unto the said John Spear his heirs and assigns forever All that Certain Tract or Parcel of Land Situate Lying and being within the bounds of a large Tract sold by Peter Sommans on the East side of Peckmans River in the County of Essex aforesaid BEGINNING at a Rock Oak Tree being the South East Corner of the aforesaid Tract and from thence running first North Easterly along the Bounds thereof Twenty one Chains and forty Links more or less to the Division Line between the Lots No. 1 and No. 2, thence North Sixty three Degrees West as the Division Line

reas Sixteen Chains and Ninety Eight Links or so far as to compleat Thirty Acres, thence South Twenty Seven Degrees West twenty Chains and ninety five Links and from thence to the beginning Containing Thirty Acres as aforesaid Bounded South Easterly by Land now in the possession of the said John Spear North by Lot number two West by Land of Paulus and Petrus Paulesse and South by land now possessed by Nicholas Garrabrantse Together with all Woods under-woods Hunting fowling Privileges Hereditaments and Appurtenances whatsoever to the same belonging or in any manner of ways appertaining also all the Estate Right Title Interest Property Claim and Demand whatsoever Either in Law or in Equity of him the said Robert Drummond in or to the above said Granted and Bargained Premises or to any part thereof TO HAVE AND TO HOLD the above said Granted and Bargained Premises with the Appurtenances unto the said John Spear his heirs and assigns to the only Proper use benefit and behoof of him the said John Spear his heirs and assigns for ever and he the said Robert Drummond for himself and his heirs doth Covenant and Agree to and with the said John Spear his heirs and assigns that before and at the time of the Sealing hereof he the said Robert Drummond is the true and Lawful owner of the above Granted and Bargained premises and is Lawfully seized and possessed of the same in his own proper Right as a good sure Perfect and Absolute Estate of Inheritance in Fee Simple and hath in himself good right full Power and Lawful Authority to Grant Bargain Sell Convey and Confirm the same unto the said John Spear his heirs and assigns in manner as aforesaid ALSO that the said John Spear his heirs and assigns shall and may for ever hereafter Lawfully Peaceably and Quietly have hold and Occupy Possess and Enjoy the same free and Clearly Acquitted and Discharged of and from all other and former Gifts Grants Bargains Sales Leases Mortgages Wills Entails Jointures Dowries and all other Incumbrances whatsoever (Excepting and Reserving all and every Such Particular Rights and Privileges as were Mentioned in a Certain Instrument or Article of Agreement from under the hands and seals of Ganet Van Ryker, Cornelus Doremus, Peter Stymets, Paulus Paulesse, Feunis Spear, Hartman Vreeland, Michael Vreeland, Hendrick Garritse, Abraham Garritse, Hessel Peterse, Adrian Post, Peter Peterse, Jacobus Post, Hendrick Post, Adrian Post Junr., Arie sop, Adrian Post, Ganet Van Waggoner, Elias Vreeland, and Jan Tomisee, Bearing date the 2d. day of April Anno. Dom. 1745) and the said Robert Drummond for himself and his heirs doth further Covenant and Agree to and with the said John Spear his heirs and assigns that the above said Granted and Bargained Premises in the Quiet and Peaceable Possession of the said John spear against all and every Person and Persons whatsoever Lawfully claiming or to claim the same or any part thereof he the said Robert Drummond shall and will Warrant and forever Defend IN WITNESS WHEREOF the first party to these presents hath hereunto set his hand and Seal the day and Year first above written.

SEALED AND DELIVERED   }
IN THE PRESENCE OF   }   ROBT. DRUMMOND.   [Seal]

The words   the said   in the four- }
teenth (14th) line was Interlined }
before the delivery of these Presents. }

TEUNIS VAN RIPER.
SAML. HEPNER.

The main road which connected the settlement of Speertown with that of Cranetown was laid out in 1765, and is described as "Beginning at a road leading from 2d river to the mountain near Garrit Speer's field." It followed the same line of the present Valley Road, passing through the lands of Peter De Garmo, Rineer Van Gieson, Gideon Van Winkle, John Egbert, Noah Crane and William Crane, the southern terminus being at William Crane's house, later known as "Washington's headquarters"; this road was for many years and until long after the Revolution known as the "Speertown road." This was no doubt the road so frequently used by the American Army during the War of the Revolution. It connected with or intersected the "road from Newark to Horseneck," as described in the original boundaries of Caldwell Township, 1768, as follows: "thence on a straight line to the top of the First Mountain, to where a certain road laid out along the line of lands of Stephen Crane, deceased, intersects the top of said mountain."

Watchung Avenue, known in early times as "Oak-tree lane," began at what is now Valley Road and ran to Egbert's house, under the mountain. It was cut through to its present eastern terminus within the past few years.

What is now Bellevue Avenue was an old road that ran from the Speertown Road to Stone House Plains, and was known as the "Stone House Plains road."

The construction of the Greenwood Lake Railroad through this part of the country, with a few capitalists, began operations as early as 1870. They purchased farm lands, which they divided into villa plots, and began making improvements. The panic of 1873, however, caused a temporary suspension, and there was no activity in the real estate market for the next two or three years. About 1876 a few families from Montclair, Brooklyn, and other places, moved into the neighborhood and began making improvements. There were at that time but few streets, the principal ones being Valley Road, Watchung and Bloomfield Avenues, Mount Hebron Road, Montclair Avenue, Park and Grove Streets. Since then there has been opened and graded upward of twenty miles of streets, and there are now over two hundred dwellings, which, with the improvements, represent a valuation of between $1,000,000 and $2,000,000.

Among the enterprising capitalists who became interested in the development of Upper Montclair was Mr. T. G. Sellew, of New York, who was favorably impressed with the beauty and healthfulness of the locality during a temporary residence. He first purchased about fifty acres, and later made an additional purchase of seventy acres. He laid out and macadamize streets through his property, built a number of fine houses, and made other improvements. As a resident he has done probably more than any other man to develop the property of this vicinity.

RELIGIOUS INTERESTS OF UPPER MONTCLAIR

The Holland population which occupied that portion of the present township known as Speer-town, in the early part of the last century, had their religious associations with the Acquackanonk and Second River. Their ecclesiastical annals of Second River, where a Dutch church was erected in 1727, will reference, in the recognition of these by a later period. As the northern end of the town, from the farms of William Crane was placed to these ministries and their ministrations of Second River a long distance and little west of the river. Ira's Vincent, James Hegeman, John Low and Thomas Cadmus, from among the Dutch population of ...

[text largely illegible]

...to the Mount Hebron District, and the result was the gathering to the Mount Hebron District.

Since its organization, worshipers have been ... Cornelius Erie A. Osborne, James Post, John Taylor, James Kent, James ... Armstrong, James Crane, Warren H. S. Johnson, Bacon, M. Low, Philip Doremus, Edgar T. Garret, Gary E. Van Gieson, John Crane, Henry B. Low.

The of this number was drawn from the Presbyterian members of Bloomfield and Montclair. The Montclair enrolled the field thirty-eight communicants in 1870 and had five new communicants ...

In 1870, Mr. James Garret ...gift of a large sum ... to the erection of Mr. Van Gieson, superintendent, ... in the premises ... with the dedication of the hymns as the Young Men's Christian Association, of ... aided ... and societies, largely supported by Mr. H. B. Low, was also active ... Mr. Van Gieson got this house, expressed a wish to meet the charge of the board and aid the orphans ... other hands, and Mr. Low's acceptance in the name of the Presbyterian Church of Montclair.

In 1873, Mr. Littell conveyed the lot of land now occupied by the St. James Episcopal Church to J. Romeyn Berry, Daniel V. Harrison and Philip Doremus, in trust, with the following conditions: "And should there be organized hereafter at any time before the expiration of ten years from the date of this instrument a church, a religious society, formed and constituted according to the rules and customs of the church known as the Presbyterian Church in the United States of America, having a connection with the Presbytery of that church, duly incorporated," *i.e.*, then the Trustees were authorized to convey said lot to such new Presbyterian Church.

CHRISTIAN UNION CONGREGATIONAL CHURCH.

BETWEEN 1873 and 1878, a number of families had moved into this locality from Montclair, Brooklyn, and other places. These families, representing different denominations, feeling the need of a place of worship where all could unite, started a movement in 1878, looking to the erection of a church edifice, it being understood by them that an organization was to be effected which should be non-sectarian. Entertainments of various kinds were held for the purpose of raising funds, the most popular and successful of these being the harvest home festivals, in which Mrs. Thomas H. Bird was the leading spirit. The people of Montclair, young and old, of all denominations, and those of the surrounding neighborhood, entered heartily into the work, and these festivals proved a source of delightful entertainment to the residents as well as the summer visitors during the summer and autumn, and the total amount realized from this source was about $1,500. In addition to this sum nearly $4,000 was subscribed by parties interested in the movement. A building plot, in a desirable location, was secured from Mr. H. B. Littell, who for many years had been the Superintendent of the Presbyterian Mission School in this neighborhood, and who consented to donate the property for

CHRISTIAN UNION CONGREGATIONAL CHURCH.

the purpose of erecting a church edifice. The terms of conveyance, however, were not clearly understood between Mr. Littell and the several parties engaged in the new movement, and complications arose at a later period which led to the abandonment of the enterprise by what had become known as the Christian Union Congregational Church.

When a sufficient sum had been raised to warrant the undertaking, the building was commenced and the corner stone laid October 22, 1878.

When the church edifice was completed and ready for dedication, the projectors of the new movement learned for the first time that it had been erected on a lot previously conveyed to other parties pledged to the interests of the Presbyterian Church.

After careful consideration it was deemed advisable to abandon the first undertaking and begin anew. A Sunday-school was started in the little village school-house which was carried on successfully by Mr. F. W. Dorman. Rev. George A. Gates accepted an invitation to preach for them and preaching services were held in the school-room on Sunday afternoons for a year and a half. He was a man eminently fitted for the work of building up a new church, and consented to accept only a moderate compensation until such time as a permanent organization could be effected, and a suitable place of worship provided.

The same means were employed to raise funds as had previously been adopted, Mr. Gates entering heartily into the work. A lot was finally purchased and a neat frame building erected, less pretentious then the first, but large enough to meet the wants of the community. Mr. Gates by a unanimous vote of the church was invited to become its pastor. A council was called April 13, 1882, at which Rev. A. H. Bradford, D.D., of the First Congregational Church of Montclair, presided, and Mr. Gates was regularly installed as pastor. The charge to the pastor was delivered by Rev. Dr. Brown, and the right hand of fellowship given by Rev. Dr. Bradford. The charge to the people was delivered by Rev. Lyman Abbott, D.D.

At the beginning of the service Mr. Dorman, Chairman of the Board of Trustees, gave a brief statement of the financial affairs of the Society, and reported a balance still remaining unpaid of $1,500. Before the close of the service this amount was pledged and the church was dedicated free of debt.

Mr. Gates continued his labors until 1887, and under his ministrations the church grew in numbers and influence and became noted for its benevolent contributions. The Sunday-school also grew and prospered under the leadership of Mr. Dorman.

In the winter of 1887 Mr. Gates was invited to the Presidency of Iowa College. He hesitated long before giving his final answer, and had he consulted his own feelings in the matter, he would have remained with the little church in Upper Montclair to which he had become so strongly attached. After a careful consideration of the matter, however, he was convinced that the presidency of a growing college in the far West opened to him a wider field of usefulness. It was a severe loss to the church, but subsequent events showed the wisdom of his choice.

The following biographical sketch of Mr. Gates appeared in *The Cyclone*, and was published in the *Junior Annual* by the students of the Junior Class of Iowa College, 1889:

JANUARY 21, 1851, is a date of considerable interest to Iowa College students, for it was on this day that their president first opened his eyes upon this world in the little village of Topsham, Vermont. Here he spent his first few years as any ordinary child might have done, varying the monotony of life by occasional tumbles into the river and narrow escapes from a watery grave.

When five years old his parents removed to East St. Johnsbury, where he attended common school. At an early age he showed special aptitude as a student. Play days were spent among the hills, woods and trout-streams. A passionate love for such scenes and sports was acquired which takes him to similar ones always for summer vacations.

When seven years old he lost his father, and with two other children was left to the care of his widowed mother. Then he learned what it was to work and to do without many of the things dear to every boy's heart. From the experience of these years he knows how to give aid and sympathy to the many Western students who, in like circumstances, are now striving under his guidance to obtain an education.

When sixteen he taught his first district school. He had nine pupils, received fifty cents a day, "boarded round," built the fires in the school-house and swept it. He prepared for college at St. Johnsbury Academy, during the summer vacations working on a farm at munificent salaries, receiving for one summer $5.00 a month, which he now thinks was more than he was worth at that work. In 1869 he entered Dartmouth College, from which he graduated in 1873, ranking high in a class of ninety, although every winter term was lost by teaching. The first two years after graduation were spent as principal of the Academy at Morristown, Vt. After this it was his intention to study law, but he was persuaded by a friend to spend a time at Amherst Theological Seminary. During a summer vacation he accompanied the family of Samuel Johnson, one of the merchant princes of Boston, to their summer residence at Nahant, as tutor and companion to his two boys. Mr. Gates had made his plans to go to Europe this year, but was finally prevailed upon by Mr. Johnson to remain and prepare his son for college. So successful was he that in eight months his pupil was ready to enter the freshman class. The remaining four months were spent by the Johnson family in Europe, Mr. Gates traveling with them. When the others returned to America in the fall of 1873, he turned his steps to the University of Göttingen, where he spent seven months listening to the lectures of Lotze, the leading philosopher of the century. The two months of Easter vacation he traveled in Italy, then spent the summer semester in the University of Bonn. During the summer he studied the French language and customs at Paris, and in the fall went to Switzerland, where he sought out the humble lecture room of Godet, the Professor of Theology, and author of many of the best New Testament commentaries, with whom he spent several weeks of delightful companionship. President Gates says that he owes more to Lotze and Godet than to any others of the great men with whom he studied. Afterward he was at the Universities of Zurich and Leipsic for a short time, and then, in January, 1880, he turned his face homeward. His plans of entering the legal profession were now changed, and he went to Andover to complete his theological course After graduation he preached for two months for the church at Littleton, New Hampshire.

His next work was at Upper Montclair, New Jersey. The story of it is like a bit of romance. It was a little community about twelve miles from New York to which business men from the city were beginning to turn to find quiet homes.

A Sunday-school had been organized before President Gates went there. For a year and a half he met the people in the school-house Sunday afternoons and preached to them at a salary of $600. The work grew and the people became interested. As a result of his labor a council was called April 13, 1882, which received the church into fellowship, ordained Mr. Gates, installed him as pastor, and dedicated, free of debt, a new house of worship costing $10,000. Although it was a new church, his salary was raised to $1,200, then to $1,500, and again to $1,800, and the church was, moreover, the banner church in the United States for benevolent contributions in proportion to its membership.

Once, in December, 1882, Mr. Gates left his pastoral work for a short trip to Syracuse, New York. There, December 14, he was married to Miss Isabelle A. Smith.

During the fall of 1887 the trustees of Iowa College were searching the country for the man whom they should call to undertake the duties of President.

At the National Congregational Council in Chicago, one of the trustees asked Dr. Ward, of *The Independent*, "Who is the man foreordained to be President of Iowa College?" Reflecting over night, he replied, "George A. Gates, of Upper Montclair, New Jersey." Further investigation convinced the trustees that Dr. Ward was right, and on Washington's birthday, 1887, the official vote was taken and the following commencement President Gates was inaugurated.

He entered into the college work with the whole-hearted earnestness which characterized his former labors. Iowa College has prospered as never before. He has bought, by special contributions for that purpose, a beautiful residence one block from the college campus, which will become the college's permanent "President House," when it is fully paid for. Here President Gates is at home with his mother, wife and two children. Here he has his office, and is always accessible to the students, and ready to help and advise them as they need.

His Sundays are generally spent with the Congregational Churches of the State in the endeavor to bring more closely together the college and its natural constituency. From the influences thus spread many students have come to Iowa College.

The church was without any settled pastor for the next three years. A call was extended to Rev. William O. Weeden in November, 1890, and in May of the following year he was installed as pastor. He was faithful in his efforts and endeavored to continue the work so successfully carried forward by his predecessor, but his usefulness was impaired through failing health, and in April of the present year he was compelled to relinquish his charge.

REV. WILLIAM O. WEEDEN.

Rev. William O. Weeden was born at Providence, R. I., April 4, 1855. His preparatory course was at the high schools of that city. He was graduated at Amherst College in 1877, and studied at Andover Theological Seminary. He traveled two years abroad, making a tour of Palestine, and other places in the East in company with Rev. Henry M. Field, Dr. Lyon and others. On his return he took a post graduate course at Andover and afterward was for six months assistant pastor of the De Witt Memorial Church, New York City. In the autumn of 1884 he received a call from the First Congregational Church of Beatrice, Nebraska, where he was ordained and installed as pastor. A severe illness, which impaired his constitution, necessitated his resignation, and he again went abroad, traveling in Japan, where he visited missions and studied missionary fields. On his return he was called to the First Congregational Church at Springfield, Vt., one of the largest in the State, remaining there about two-and-a-half years. He then accepted a call to the Bushwick Avenue Church of Brooklyn, but found the climate of that city induced throat trouble, thus necessitating another change. In November, 1890, he received a call from the Christian Union Congregational Church of this place, and in May of the following year was installed as its pastor, continuing until April, 1894.

ST. JAMES EPISCOPAL CHURCH.

AMONG the residents of Upper Montclair there has been for many years individual members of the Episcopal Church; these for a time united with the members of other religious denominations in their worship, and it was not until 1885 that any concerted effort was made to establish a distinct organization.

In February, 1880, the stone building was completed by the contributions of the residents of Upper Montclair, with the expectation that it was to be used as a Christian Union Church. Some disagreement having arisen, and the title to the land having passed to the Trustees of the Montclair Presbyterian Church, the building was, on February 22, 1880, dedicated as a Chapel of that Church. A Congregational Society having been formed, held services there for a few months, but subsequently made other arrangements, and as there were not sufficient members to sustain a distinctive Presbyterian Church, the building remained closed for some time.

In 1885 the advisability of obtaining possession of the Chapel, and holding in it the services of the Episcopal Church, was discussed by a few families in the neighborhood. It was at first attempted to establish a mission in connection with St. Luke's Church, but for various reasons this plan was abandoned for the time.

During the summer of 1887 the project was again started, and subscriptions and pledges were obtained for the support of the mission. The bishop of the diocese and the rector of St. Luke's Church of Montclair gave consent to the formation of a new mission, and the property referred to passed into the hands of the new organization. The church building was newly furnished and properly arranged for church services. The Rev. P. McD. Bleecker was placed in temporary charge by the Bishop, and the first services were held on the morning of the fourth Sunday in Advent. At a meeting of persons interested in the work of the mission, called for the purpose of completing the organization, Mr. W. H. Howell was elected Warden and Mr. Wilbur Huntington, Secretary; Mr. W. H. Parsons, Treasurer; A. J. Varno, W. H. Littell, and other names subsequently added.

ST. JAMES EPISCOPAL CHURCH.

On December 12, 1888, Bishop Starkey gave his canonical consent to the formation of St. James Parish. At the parish meeting to take steps for incorporation, the following gentlemen were elected officers: William H. Power and Wilbur Huntington, Wardens; Auguste J. Varno, W. H. Parsons, John Mancini, William H. Littell, F. B. Littlejohn, G. L. Prentis, Charles Richards and J. H. Schoonmaker, Vestrymen.

At a meeting of the Vestry, held January 29, 1889, the Rev. Richard Hayward, of the diocese of Chicago, was unanimously called to be Rector of this Parish.

Improvements in the church edifice have been made from time to time, and in 1892 important modifications were made in the interior of the church. All plaster was removed, the ceiling was raised and ceiled in wood, and the walls were covered with rough terra cotta tiles. The interior is beautifully furnished, the woodwork being of antique oak, highly polished. The altar was designed by Tiffany & Co., of New York; the lectern designed by Lamb & Rich, architects, of New York; the font and reredos are all gifts to the church as memorials or thanksgivings. It may be truly said that there are few country churches more artistic in design and treatment, or more reverent and churchly in expression.

The church is supported solely by voluntary contributions. All seats are free. It has a seating capacity of about 150; the present membership is about 80.

MOUNT HEBRON CEMETERY.

" There is no Death ! What seems so is transition ,
This life of mortal breath
Is but a suburb of the life elysian
Whose portal we call death."—LONGFELLOW.

THIS cemetery is located in the northwest corner of Montclair Township, at Montclair Heights, on the east side of the mountain, about three minutes' walk from the station on the Greenwood Lake R.R. It contains about twenty acres, occupying an elevated position, affording a very extended view from almost every point of the compass. On a clear day, Brooklyn Heights, the Bridge and a part of Greenwood Cemetery can easily be seen—as well as the banks of the Hudson, the Palisades, from the southernmost point at Weehawken, extending north to its termination above Closter. The projectors of this enterprise designed it not simply for local use, but parties from Jersey City, Paterson, Newark and Little Falls, are owners of plots on which they have expended large sums of money. The cemetery is beautifully laid out with macadamized roads, is provided with a lodge for the keeper, a receiving vault, and other improvements are constantly being made. A number of costly monuments have been erected, and everything has been done to make the place attractive and beautiful, and a fit resting-place for departed loved ones.

The Mount Hebron Association was organized in February, 1863, for the purpose of procuring land to be held in trust for cemetery purposes. The following persons were elected Trustees to serve for one, two and three years: Peter G. Speer, Star Parsons, Rymer Speer, M. S. Crane, W. R. Jacobus, Thomas C. Van Reypen, Aaron Sigler, Stephen Ennis, and Rymer S. Speer. Peter Speer was elected President and held the position up to the time of his death. He was succeeded by Rymer Speer, who held the position from 1865 to 1875; Arzy E. Van Gieson, 1875 to 1884; Rev. J. C. Cruikshank, 1884 to the present time. The present officers are: *President*, Rev. J. C. Cruikshank, Little Falls; *Secretary and Treasurer*, Thomas C. Van Reypen, Montclair Heights; *Trustees*, Henry V. Praget, Jersey City; William Beattie, Little Falls; Henry Smith, Little Falls; George Fisher, Brookdale; W. Sigler, Montclair; A. T. Van Gieson, Upper Montclair, and J. D. Mockridge, Montclair; Thomas Cowley, Keeper and Superintendent.

SCHOOLS.

PRIOR to the Revolution, the people of this locality had little use for schools, the country was sparsely settled, and the Hollanders, who inhabited the neighborhood, were content to cultivate their farms and leave the matter of "book larnin" to those who had leisure to devote to it. They listened once a week to the good old Dutch dominie, who in- structed them in the "shorter catechism." Some of them, who had acquired a knowledge of the elementary branches in the old country doubt- less taught their children to read and write.

There was probably no public building erected for school purposes previ- ous to 1816, for, as has been stated, when Enos A. Osborne opened a Sunday school in this neighbor- hood in 1816, he held it first in a barn, and after- ward in private houses. The first school-house was probably erected about 1827, and stood on the corner of Bellevue Ave-

NEW SCHOOL BUILDING.

nue and Valley Road or what was formerly known as the Stone House Plains Road. The little frame building which now stands in the centre of the village was erected about 1849, on the spot where the old school-house stood. The land was given by James Van Gieson for school purposes, and the deed

Morgan W. Ayres.

stipulated that when the land should no longer be required for this purpose, it was then to revert to his heirs.

When the influx of the "city people" began early in the seventies, the need of better accommodations was felt; it was not, however, until within the past ten years that anything was done toward the erection of a new school building.

In 1884, a lot was purchased of Joseph Lux on Bellevue, near Wellwood Avenue, on which was erected a large brick school-house, the total cost, including the land, being $8,848.83. A corps of efficient teachers was provided, and an excellent school established. This was known as the Tenth School District. There was a gradual increase in the population, and before the beginning of the second decade, it was found that additional room would be required. In the summer of 1893 this building was torn down, and a new one erected of brick on the same site, a part of the old foundation being utilized. The total cost of the new building, with the improved heating apparatus, was $22,293.51. The interior arrangements are all in accordance with the latest improvements for the comfort, health and convenience of the children.

The average attendance of children at the present time is 125. The principal of the school receives a salary of $1,250. He has five assistants whose aggregate pay is $3,050 per annum. The total annual expenses are about $5,000.

MORGAN WILLCOX AYRES, M. D.

DANIEL AYRES, the grandfather of Dr. Morgan W. Ayres, was for more than a quarter of a century a prominent merchant of New York City, and for nearly forty years a leading member of the old John St. M. E. Church (still standing). His diary—recently discovered—contains interesting facts connected with his own life; also of the Ayres and Smith families: "Born at Haverstraw, May 18, 1790; educated at College School of Ref. Dutch Church; graduated May 12, 1802, with diploma much too good, I think, for my small attainments, but it was kind. Entered iron store of Blackwells & McFarlan; indentured for six years; remained there thirty-one years." After completing his apprenticeship in 1808, he says: "Agreed with Blackwells & McFarlan for three years at a salary of $300 till twenty-one years of age, when I received $500, in 1816 increased to $1,000." "In 1812 war declared against England; had to perform military duty; was made Sergeant; Hugh Maxwell, our Captain (Hugh Maxwell was the distinguished lawyer, politician, collector of customs, etc., whose daughter married Gen. Phil. Kearney); outpost for service, Harlem Heights. My employers furnish a substitute, and my military services close. At the close of the war was presented by my employers with $100 as a 'peace present.' In 1817 salary increased to $1,500 for five years. Purchased a plot 137 Elizabeth Street for $750, and built a brick house upon it for $2,400. Placed my father and mother there, where they ended their days; mother died 1843, father (Thomas) in 1844. In 1820 purchased a house and lot at 94 John Street for $3,250."

In 1830 Daniel Ayres organized the firm of McFarlans & Ayres. They had large money interests in New Jersey, and were also largely interested in the Morris Canal Company. Through the latter they became involved and suspended payment in 1832, with assets amounting to $30,000, liabilities, $300,000. Their creditors gave them an extension, and in two years the entire amount was paid with interest.

In 1835 he organized the firm of Boorman, Johnston, Ayres & Co. His diary states that "in 1844 my partners permitted me to invest my earnings at once, and I find myself worth $87,000." He soon after retired from business.

Referring to family matters he says: "My paternal grandfather, Daniel Ayres, married Sarah Smith, at Smith's Clove, back of New Cornwall, Orange Co., N. Y. The place received its name from her grandfather. He sent his son to England to take letters patent for the tract upon the death of his father, but it was found the son had taken it out in his own name. In my library is an ancient pocket bible, with the name of Thomas Smith, 1714. My father said it was the pocket bible of his (Thomas

Smith's) father in England, and that there was a tradition that there was valuable property in the Vale of Aylesbury, in which the family claimed an interest.

"The children of Daniel Ayres and Sarah Smith (Strockem) were Thomas (my father) and Kamp Ayres. After the death of her second husband, James Strockem, my grandmother married Daniel Devoe, in 1775. My grandfather Devoe married for his second wife, Sarah Turrell. He was a Captain in the War of 1812, and afterwards a Member of Congress.

"My father, Thomas Ayres, was born at Smith's Clove, September 24, 1754. My mother, Mary Devoe, born at New Rochelle, December 30, 1758. She said that her mother, Hester Devoe, was French, and could scarcely speak English."

Daniel Ayres (son of Thomas) from whose diary the foregoing was taken, married Anna Morgan, of New York City. He had three sons, and two daughters: Daniel, Gabriel Disosway, Joseph Blackwell, Mary Anne and Eliza.

Daniel Ayres, son of Daniel and Anna Morgan Ayres, was born at Jamaica, L. I., October 6, 1822, was educated at Daniel H. Chase's School at Middletown, Conn. Entered Wesleyan University at Middletown in 1841; leaving there he entered Princeton in his junior year, to obtain better scientific instruction under Professor Joseph Henry, and graduated with degree. Took full course in the Medical Department of the University of the City of New York in 1844, and soon after settled in Brooklyn, N. Y. He was one of the founders of the Long Island College Hospital, and was a prime mover in the establishment of the Brooklyn City Hospital. The Wesleyan University at Middletown gave him degree of LL.D. in 1856.

During the war, he served in the New York Corps of Surgeons, participating in the results of many of the principal engagements. Owing to an intense desire to embody his views in physiology and pathology in a series of lectures, he gave up his general practice in 1880, and devoted himself to the arrangement of his large store of notes, bringing out his thoughts in a manner calculated to render clear many hitherto obscure problems. His teachings were wonderfully lucid, practical, and stripped of the mystery surrounding the older physiological dogmas. He held for a number of years the chair of Emeritus Professor of Clinical Surgery.

His peculiar methods of teaching gave him a pre-eminence attained by few, and there can be no question but that his influence upon medical science will continue to be felt for years. Shortly before his death, in 1892, he gave to the cause of education more than half a million of dollars, considering it but a small contribution toward so grand a cause.

He married, October 6, 1848, Charlotte Augusta Russell, daughter of Daniel and Mary (Willcox) Russell, of Portland (opposite Middletown, and formerly known as Chatham), Conn. This branch of the Russell family was descended from William Russell, born in England, 1612, came to America in 1639, and settled in the New Haven Colony. His only son, Noadiah, born at New Haven, 1650, was graduated at Harvard College in 1681, and was settled as pastor of the First Congregational Church at Middletown in 1687. He was one of the twelve ministers who founded Yale College at Saybrook in 1700, and was one of the framers of the famous "Saybrook Platform." He married Mary, daughter of Giles Hamlin, one of the original settlers of Middletown. He had issue nine children, viz.: William, Noadiah, Giles, Mary, John, Esther, Daniel, Mehitable and Hannah. William, his eldest son, succeeded him as pastor of the First Congregational Church at Middletown, June 1, 1715. Dr. Trumbull says of Rev. Noadiah Russell: "He was a gentleman of great respectability for knowledge, experience, moderation, and for pacific measures on all occasions."

Dr. Morgan Willcox Ayres, son of Dr. Daniel and Charlotte Augusta (Russell) Ayres, was born in Brooklyn, N. Y., Sept. 7, 1851. He attended the public schools of that city and was afterward sent to Professor Chase's school at Middletown, one of the best known educational institutions in New England. His father and two uncles—all physicians—were educated at the same school. He was graduated at the College of Physicians and Surgeons in New York City, in 1875. During a portion of the time while at college he was Assistant at St. Peter's Hospital, Brooklyn—of which his father was then consulting surgeon—and continued there after his graduation, his whole term of service there covering a period of three years.

In 1876 he settled at that part of Montclair Heights bordering on the township of Acquackanonck, and his practice extended over a large portion of that township, as well as Upper Montclair, and for some years he was the only physician in that locality. His practice has grown with the increase in population, and covers an extent of territory almost as large as the whole of Montclair proper. While educated in the old school of physicians, he is wedded to no theory, but is a man of advanced ideas and adopts whatever he finds best in either the old or new school of practice, according to circumstances. His methods have proved successful and he enjoys the unlimited confidence of his large clientèle.

Notwithstanding the fact that his time is almost wholly absorbed by his professional engagements, he has consented on several occasions to fill public positions, and has heartily co-operated in every move-ment tending to advance the interests of the township. He served three years as a member of the Township Committee, at a time when some of the most important improvements were made. He is an earnest advocate of the "higher education" for which Montclair is famous, and has exerted his influence to furnish the best facilities in his own school district. He has served three years as a member of the Board of Trustees of the Tenth School District known as Mt. Hebron District, at Upper Montclair, and it was during his administration that the present large and commodious school-house was begun and completed; at the last municipal election, the first one under the "Short" law, he was elected a mem-ber of the Board of Education to serve for three years.

Dr. Ayres resided for some years at Montclair Heights. In 1891 he moved to the corner of Bellevue Avenue and Park Street in Upper Montclair, where he resided until 1894. The year previous he purchased a plot on the corner of Lorraine Avenue and Park Street, where he erected a handsome house to which he removed in the spring of 1894.

Dr. Ayres married Sarah Ella, daughter of Rev. Charles A. Roe, who was the son of Austin, of Connecticut, and of Butler, N. Y., son of Daniel, one of the first settlers of Butler, Wayne County, N. Y., son of Daniel, of Long Island, who served in the Revolutionary War, who served as Captain of Second Company Col. Clinton's Regiment, New York, son of John, of Long Island, son of Nathaniel, born in Long Island, 1679, son of John, born in Ireland, 1628, died at Port Jefferson, L. I., 1711. Rev. E. P. Roe, the author, is a descendant in the same line through Nathaniel, son of John, the ancestor.

Issue of the marriage of Dr. Ayres with Miss Sarah Ella Roe: Harry Morgan, Daniel Roe, and Russell Romeyn.

DR. OLIVER SOPER.

Dr. Oliver Soper, is of New England and Holland Dutch ancestry. His great-great-grandfather was Samuel Soper, who married Esther Littlefield, in 1731; they lived at West Bridgewater, Mass.; ten children were born to them—six boys and four girls. Oliver, son of Samuel, born 1740, married Ruth Staples, of Bridgewater, in 1763, and removed to Taunton about that time. They had one son, Oliver, and five daughters. This Oliver, the second, married Rebecca Paul, and remained at Taunton. They had seven children, one of whom was Benjamin, born July 19, 1809, is the father of Dr. Soper, and is still living, aged 85 years. Benjamin married Mary, daughter of Peter Abraham Kip, born 1789, a descendant of Hendrick Hendrickson Kip, who removed from New Amsterdam to Hackensack before 1690. His grandson, Peter, owned a large tract of land at Pollifly, now Hasbrouck Heights. Another grandson, Henry, bought a tract of land which included a large portion of what is now Rutherford. The Kip family went from France to Holland in 1652.

Hendrick Kip, the father of Hendrick Hendrickson Kip, was born in 1576. He was a member of the old established trading company which organized in 1588 for the purpose of discovering a north-east passage to the Indies around the coast of Asia. Failing in this, they employed Hendrick Hudson, in 1609, who sailed in one of their ships and discovered the Hudson River in September of that year.

Peter Abraham Kip, the maternal grandfather of Dr. Soper, married Maria Stuyvesant, a lineal descendant of Peter Stuyvesant, the first Dutch Governor of New Amsterdam.

Dr. Oliver Soper, son of Benjamin and Mary (Kip) Soper, was born in Bergen County, N. J., December 29, 1843. He attended school in his native town and afterward at Taunton, Mass. He began the study of medicine with Dr. Robert S. Newton, of New York City, in 1873, and was graduated at the Eclectic Medical College of New York (of which Dr. Newton was President), in March, 1877. He began practice at Lodi, in Bergen County, N. J., where he carried on the drug business at the same time. He served as physician to the Board of Health for nearly two years, and was examining physician for the Metropolitan Life Insurance Company for three years. He removed to Upper Montclair in 1892, and has had a successful and increasing practice.

He married, first, Emma Garrabrant, deceased, by whom he had three children; he married, secondly, Nellie F., daughter of Edward B. and Ellen (Baldwin) Crane, a grandson of Israel Crane, one of the most famous men of his time in East New Jersey.

THOMAS HOWE BIRD.

THOMAS H. BIRD was known to the people of Upper Montclair as one of the founders of the new settlement, which within the space of a few years was transformed from the broad pasture lands, orchards, meadows and uplands, into a beautiful suburban village, with its well graded streets, its attractive homes, and other evidences of progress and enterprise. Like the little colony of Puritans who landed on the banks of the Passaic River to establish a " New Worke " [Newark], Mr. Bird, after years of successful labor in other fields, came to what is now known as Upper Montclair to begin a "*new work*." The record of the growth and progress of the new settlement shows his foot-prints in every direction. Like his Divine Master he " went about doing good," and the very atmosphere was fragrant with his presence.

> " His life was gentle ; and the elements so mixed in him, that
> Nature might stand up and say to all the world. This was a man."

Mr. Bird was of Puritan stock with all the objectionable features eliminated. He was born in Boston in April, 1831. He was educated at board-ing school at Framingham, Mass.; came to New York City at the age of nine-teen, and entered the house of H. B. Claflin & Co., where he remain-ed for a short time. Later he started in the white goods busi-ness under the firm name of Thomas H. Bird & Co. He after-ward sold out this business, and about 1860 enter-ed Wall Street as banker and stock broker, and was for thirty-four years a member of the Stock Exchange. As a business man Mr. Bird was universally es-teemed for his in-tegrity and incor-ruptible honor. The good work of his life, however,

RESIDENCE OF MRS. THOMAS H. BIRD, UPPER MONTCLAIR.

was in connection with Bethel Mission, Brooklyn, of which he was one of the founders in 1852, and for many years its superintendent. It was at his suggestion that in 1866 this Mission was offered to Plymouth for adoption, it having been for a number of years previous sustained by teachers from

Yours Truly, Thos. H. Bird.

Plymouth Church Sabbath School. At a memorial service held in Plymouth Church soon after the death of Mr. Bird, many of his old friends and associates gave expression to their sentiments regarding their deceased brother and his life work. Mr. Robert S. Bussing said : " It was my privilege to become acquainted with Mr. and Mrs. Thomas H. Bird nearly fifty years ago, soon after they were married, meeting them for the first time as teachers in the old Bethel Mission Sunday School, then on Main Street, near the Catharine Ferry, and I soon learned to love Mr. Bird as a very dear friend. Among the pleasant recollections of my past life, especially those that relate to active Sunday-school work in the old Bethel, will always be my association with Mr. Bird and his devoted Christian wife, both so very faithful to the welfare of the Mission."

Rev. Lyman Abbott said : " His life was framed in with prayer. It was his custom before he went to his business in the morning, the last thing, to kneel down in his room alone for a word with God, as one before he goes to his business stops for a moment to kiss his wife, and it was his custom when he came back from business to go back to that room and kneel down again and have a word of prayer with God, as though starting out in the day, he said ' I have come for my orders,' and as though going back at night he said, ' Here is my report.' What he said in that chamber, alone with his God, no one, I suppose, save himself and his God, knows. But he was one who carried the spirit of God with him, and who lived in the spirit of the Lord Jesus Christ, and whoever knew him, whoever knew his wife, whoever knew his home, needs no assurance that if happiness and usefulness are the tests and measures of success, his life was a successful one."

Mr. George F. Bell, another fellow laborer with Mr. Bird, said of him : " He was willing to serve but never wanted to be foremost. When I was ordered by Plymouth Church to go to the Mayflower and take care of that mission, and the only man that could be chosen for the superintendency of the Bethel was Mr. Bird, his being chosen I do believe was the cause of his leaving Plymouth Church and going out to New Jersey to live."

Mr. F. P. Blair said of him : " I think I never knew a man whose religion seemed to be more natural than Mr. Bird's. It was not put on ; it had not the appearance of being put on ; it was just the same apparently on Monday as it was on Sunday, and just the same all the week. * * * I think he was one of the most lovable and genuine men I ever knew."

Mr. Bird was for many years a deacon in Plymouth Church, and although exceedingly modest and retiring, was recognized as one of its leading spirits. He came to Montclair in 1873, and was for several years associated with Dr. Bradford in the work connected with the First Congregational Church. The *Montclair Times* said of him :

" Coming to Montclair with his devoted wife, he resumed the same line of work in which he had been engaged in the city, and for several years assisted in the conduct of the neighborhood meeting which has since merged into the Washington Street Mission (now known as the Pilgrim Mission). Mr. Bird was a retiring, unassuming man, but those who knew him could not fail to recognize the lofty ideal toward which he was constantly moving, and the devotion of his life to all things manly and noble. In all the relations which he sustained, in his beautiful home, in his business, in the three churches of which he was an honored member, in his work among the poor and the outcast who had nothing to give in return, in his walk among those who were fortunate enough to be his friends he was ever unassuming, earnest, loyal and helpful. There has never lived in our community a man who has left behind him a more spotless or a more honorable name."

Mr. Bird moved to Upper Montclair in 1881, where he made for himself a pretty and rural home. There is no attempt at display either in architecture or the surroundings. Everything has an air of simplicity and comfort, strictly in accordance with his own taste. The Gothic cottage partly hidden by the trees indicates the character of the man. In the world his light shown brightly through deeds of devoted charity and love, while he himself always remained in the background. The home is picturesque and pleasing to the eye, affording a fine study for an artist. Some of his happiest hours were spent in this delightful retreat, and here when the autumn leaves were falling, and nature was about to wrap herself in her winter garments, his spirit took its flight and he passed from earth to that blissful abode, a " house not made with hands, eternal in the heavens."

As soon as he decided to make Upper Montclair his home, he began laying his plans with others for the organization of a church, which should include Christians of every denomination, with a platform on which all could unite. The "Harvest Home" entertainments of which he and his wife were the leading spirits, formed the nucleus for a fund for the erection of a church building. Besides the large amount contributed by himself, he raised several thousand dollars among his business and other friends, and when the building was finally completed, and through a misunderstanding it passed into the hands of another denomination, he went cheerfully to work without a murmur or complaint to raise funds for the erection of another building, which should become the property of a united band of Christian laborers, and at the completion of the building he went heartily into the work of building up and uniting Christians of every denomination under the one banner. This was the beginning of an enterprise which within ten years changed a little hamlet of some twenty unpretentious houses to a large and flourishing village of over two hundred houses—some of them costing many thousand dollars each—two churches, besides several public buildings. The action taken by the Trustees of the church he helped to organize express the sentiments of the whole community.

The Trustees of the Christian Union Congregational Society request the clerk to enter upon their records the following minute on the death of Thomas H. Bird:

"Mr. Bird died at his home at Upper Montclair, on Wednesday, the 18th day of November, 1891, in the 61st year of his life and in office as President of the Board of Trustees of the Society.

"His associates have no words in which they can properly express the loss which has come to the Church and Society.

"For over ten years he has been a Trustee and President of the Board, and during all that time it is hardly beyond bounds to say that he has given to the Church and Society a full half of his strength and thought, and this when business and personal demands on him in other directions were pressing and intense. In its days of weakness as well as those of its greatest strength, his liberal hand and his wise judgment have been, under the Providence of the God he served, an unfailing reliance. In the vicissitudes through which it has passed, his wisdom, prudence and firmness, have been of an estimable value. A faithful, true, courteous, forbearing, lovable associate, he combined the attributes of a true, christian gentleman. To the many expressions of love and appreciation which his death has brought from those connected with him in his other fields of life and work, we add this our sincere tribute, that our records may bear some witness of the beautiful, useful life of him who has gone before us."

F. W. DORMAN.
A. B. HUNT, JR.
H. LITTLEJOHN.
C. W. ANDERSON.
                              Trustees.

UPPER MONTCLAIR, NEW JERSEY, November 25, 1891.

Mrs. Sarah J. Bird, née Boyd, the faithful and devoted wife of Mr. Bird, worked side by side with him for nearly forty years. She first met him in Mr. Beecher's church, both having united with that church at the same time, being then strangers to each other. She began the work of her life at Bethel Mission, Brooklyn, at the age of sixteen. Volumes might be written of the work of the noble, self-sacrificing woman among the poor and outcasts of the great "City of Churches." Hundreds have been rescued by her from lives of shame and degradation, and gathered into the fold of Christ. Said one who has known her for many years : "The influence for good of Mrs. Bird over the Bethel people, in all the years gone by, particularly over the older girls and mothers of the children, will never be fully realized ; but I know scores upon scores will enthusiastically respond, at the mention of her name, 'God bless Mrs. Thomas H. Bird for her kindness to me.'"

Although it is more than twenty years since Mrs. Bird left Brooklyn, she has never for a moment laid aside her work at this mission, but every Friday she leaves her home in Upper Montclair to meet her class at the Bethel Mission.

Her work at Montclair and Upper Montclair in connection with her husband is familiar to the people of these localities. In addition to this, she started a few years ago a Wednesday afternoon class for women among the slums of New York City, which she carried on successfully for a long time, but was obliged to discontinue it in consequence of the imperative demands on her time elsewhere.

Shortly after her husband's death, Mrs. Bird opened a Sunday mission for men at 209 Madison Street, now moved to 105 Bowery, New York, where hundreds of hungry men are fed every Sunday, and at the same time the seeds of gospel truth are sown which often finds a lodgment in hearts prepared through these acts of kindness in relieving their temporal wants. It not infrequently happens that young men of education and refinement, who have seen better days, find their way into this mission, and their steps are turned homeward and upward to a better life. While Mrs. Bird receives occasional aid from other sources, the mission is mainly supported through her private resources.

DEACON DAVID BRAINERD HUNT.

DEACON HUNT is a native of Attleboro, Mass., where he was born April 7, 1811. He is a descendant of Enoch Hunt, one of the early settlers of Weymouth, Mass. His father, Richard, was deacon of the Congregational Church of Attleboro for sixty years, and was interested in the founding of Amherst College, where his eldest son, the brother of David B., was educated. David B., the subject of this sketch, had only limited educational advantages—a few months of each year to the district school, and six months at the Academy. He began his business career at the age of eighteen in a Brooklyn, N. Y., dry goods store, and after clerking for some years he engaged in business for himself, but failing health compelled him to give up for a time, and he subsequently acted for others in the same line of business. In 1865 he removed to Montclair, where he resided for many years, and was one of the founders of the First Congregational Church. In 1881 he removed to Upper Montclair, which was then a mere hamlet. He was one of the leaders in the religious movement which led to the organization of the Christian Union Congregational Church in 1882, and since then has been one of its main supports. He has held the office of deacon since its organization.

Mr. Hunt married, in 1841, Mary A. Gaylord, daughter of Martin Gaylord, of Lebanon Springs, N. Y. Two children are the issue of this marriage, viz.: D. B. Hunt, Jr., and Mary Charlotte, who married John H. Parsons, Esq.

CHARLES HENRY HUESTIS.

JAMES EUSTIS, or Huestis, the ancestor of Charles H., was one of two brothers who settled in Fairfield, Conn., about 1660, and removed thence to East Chester about 1663.

Benjamin, the grandfather of Charles H., born in 1765, served in the War of the Revolution.

CHARLES HENRY HUESTIS, son of William and Diantha D. (Horton) Huestis, was born in Yonkers, N. Y., March 28, 1838. He was prepared for college but prevented by circumstances from entering. In 1855 he entered the banking house of Henry Mendell, then located at 176 Broadway, where he remained until the breaking out of the Civil War, joined Company A, Seventy-first Regiment, and took part in the first battle of Bull Run.

Company A, to which Mr. Huestis was attached, lost heavily during the engagement, its commander, Captain Hart, being among the severely wounded. Mr. Huestis was subsequently attached to the Quartermaster's Department, under the command of Captain A. W. Putnam, U. S. A., and continued under his successors, General J. J. Dana and General C. H. Tompkins, until the close of the war. Under the authority of his commander, General Tompkins, he raised a band for the Quartermaster's Department, and purchased all the instruments. This band was specially honored by Secretary Stanton after the fall of Richmond, who sent for it, and when the public announcement of the fact was made by President Lincoln, the latter requested this band to play "Dixie," the favorite tune of the Confederates.

After the close of the war Mr. Huestis went to Richmond with a party of capitalists, who bought the charter of the old Bank of Virginia, which was reorganized under the name of the National Bank of Virginia. He remained as an officer of this bank for about eighteen months, returning to New York in 1866, where he engaged in the stock and brokerage business, first under the firm name of Haskell

& Huestis, afterward Huestis & Webb, and later succeeded to the business of Wood & Davis, under the firm name of Wood, Huestis & Co., that being the present firm. He is a member of the New York Stock Exchange; also of the "Old Guard," which had its origin with the "Light Guard," the original Company A of the Seventy-first Regiment, of which Mr. Huestis is a veteran.

Mr. Huestis married Miss Irene E. Mendell, daughter of Henry Mendell, Esq., his old employer, who was a descendant of one of the old Massachusetts families.

In 1886 Mr. Huestis, while suffering from malaria, concluded to try the climate of Upper Montclair, and after remaining a few months he recovered his health, and concluded to make this his permanent home. He purchased thirteen acres, which comprised a part of the old Speer estate, and, with others, opened an avenue in front of his property, which they named Lorraine Avenue. He erected a beautiful villa, which is one of the attractive features of Upper Montclair. It is 66 by 40 feet; two and a-half stories high, the first story being of ruble granite, and frame work above; it has a round tower on the south west corner, and a broad piazza extending thence along the entire front. The location is one of the finest in the township.

The End

www.ingramcontent.com/pod-product-compliance
Lightning Source LLC
Chambersburg PA
CBHW030857270326
41929CB00008B/464